Flamenco on the
Global Stage

FLAMENCO ON THE GLOBAL STAGE

Historical, Critical and Theoretical Perspectives

Edited by K. Meira Goldberg,
Ninotchka Devorah Bennahum *and*
Michelle Heffner Hayes

McFarland & Company, Inc., Publishers
Jefferson, North Carolina

LIBRARY OF CONGRESS CATALOGUING-IN-PUBLICATION DATA

Flamenco on the global stage : historical, critical and theoretical perspectives / edited by K. Meira Goldberg, Ninotchka Devorah Bennahum and Michelle Heffner Hayes.
      p.   cm.
Includes bibliographical references and index.

ISBN 978-0-7864-9470-5 (softcover : acid free paper) ∞
ISBN 978-1-4766-2102-9 (ebook)

1. Flamenco.   2. Flamenco—Social aspects.
I. Goldberg, K. Meira.   II. Bennahum, Ninotchka.
III. Hayes, Michelle Heffner.

GV1796.F55F62 2015   793.3'19468—dc23   2015032660

BRITISH LIBRARY CATALOGUING DATA ARE AVAILABLE

© 2015 K. Meira Goldberg, Ninotchka Devorah Bennahum and Michelle Heffner Hayes. All rights reserved

No part of this book may be reproduced or transmitted in any form or by any means, electronic or mechanical, including photocopying or recording, or by any information storage and retrieval system, without permission in writing from the publisher.

Front cover: costume design for Triana by Néstor de la Torre, 1929 (collection of Ninotchka Devorah Bennahum, gift of Carlota Mercé de Pavloff)

Printed in the United States of America

*McFarland & Company, Inc., Publishers
Box 611, Jefferson, North Carolina 28640
www.mcfarlandpub.com*

For our mothers, and our daughters…

Table of Contents

Acknowledgments	0
Introduction	1

Part I—Mapping Spanish Dance on the International Stage

Three Centuries of Flamenco: Some Brief Historical Notes (MARTA CARRASCO BENÍTEZ)	23
Ancient Dancers of Cádiz, *Puellae Gaditane* and Creations of Myth (KATHY MILAZZO)	33
Hopeful Futures and Nostalgic Pasts: Explorations into Kathak and Flamenco Dance Collaborations (MIRIAM PHILLIPS)	42
From the *Járaca* to the *Sarabande* (ANA YEPES)	56
Spanish Dance in Europe: From the Late Eighteenth Century to Its Consolidation on the European Stage (ROCÍO PLAZA ORELLANA)	71
Fandangos and Bailes: Dancing and Dance Events in Early California (ANTHONY SHAY)	81
Hispanomania in Nineteenth Century Dance Theory and Choreography (CLAUDIA JESCHKE *with* ROBERT ATWOOD)	95
Some Notes Toward a Historiography of the Mid-Nineteenth Century *Bailable Español* (KIKO MORA)	103
Antecedents of Carmen in the History of Spanish Dance (GERHARD STEINGRESS)	117

Part II—Becoming Flamenco: Gitano Embodiment and Modernist Subjectivity

Jaleo de Jerez and *Tumulte Noir*: Primitivist Modernism and Cakewalk in Flamenco, 1902–1917 (K. MEIRA GOLDBERG)	124

The First Academy of Flamenco Dance: Frasquillo and the "Broken Dance" of the Gitanos (CLARA CHINOY)	143
The Critical Reception of *Le Tricorne* (JOAN ACOCELLA)	157
Purity and Commercialization: The View from Two Working Artists, Pericón de Cádiz and Chato de la Isla (JOHN C. MOORE)	166
Carmen Amaya, 1947: The (Gypsy) Beloved of America Reconquers Europe (MONTSE MADRIDEJOS)	178
Flamenco: The Real Stories (BROOK ZERN)	187
Spanish Artists in Love and War, 1913–1945: Meditations on Female Embodiment and Populist Imagination (NINOTCHKA DEVORAH BENNAHUM)	193

Part III—Disobedient Bodies: Flamenco in the "New" World

Normative Aesthetics and Cultural Constructions in Flamenco Dance: Female and Gitano Bodies as Legitimizers of Tradition (CRISTINA CRUCES-ROLDÁN)	210
Las Tocaoras: Women Guitarists and Their Struggle for Inclusion on the Flamenco Stage (LOREN CHUSE)	225
Dancing the Ideal Masculinity (RYAN ROCKMORE)	234
Flamenco in *La flor de mi secreto*: Re-Appropriation and Subversion in a Film by Pedro Almódovar (NANCY G. HELLER)	244
Flamenco Fusion: Cross-Cultural Coalitions and the Art of Raising Consciousness (JORGE PÉREZ)	252
Y Para Rematar: Contemplations on a Movement in Transition (NIURCA MÁRQUEZ)	260
Blancenieves, Flamenco and National Identity (WILLIAM WASHABAUGH)	271
Choreographing Contemporaneity: Cultural Legacy and Experimental Imperative (MICHELLE HEFFNER HAYES)	280
Glossary	293
Bibliography	299
About the Contributors	319
Index	323

Acknowledgments

The creation of this volume grew out of love: love of flamenco, love of history, love of feminist discourse. It is our greatest hope that this book, like the many artists within its pages, will move around the world and be read by citizen-artist-scholars who believe that dancing is history.

Every book requires the labor of many hands. First and foremost, the coeditors would like to thank the authors of the texts in this volume for sharing their peerless research and precious time. We are honored that they have entrusted us with their work, and humbled by their faith and enthusiasm for this project. We wouldn't have been able to integrate the many voices in this volume without the assistance of our copy editor, Mary Brooks, editing assistant Lauren Vallicella and indexer Emily Zinn, associate director, Interdisciplinary Humanities Center, University of California, Santa Barbara.

K. Meira Goldberg spent many hours in the thoughtful translation of the Spanish articles into English. Her deep knowledge of flamenco and extraordinary command of the Spanish language made this valuable scholarship accessible to a whole new readership. We look forward to a transatlantic discourse.

The editors would like to thank also the Dean's Office of the College of Liberal Arts and Sciences at the University of Kansas, which provided vital research funds to make this book possible. Associate dean and director of the School of the Arts Henry Bial gave priceless advice and continuous support during the long process of completing this volume. Special thanks goes out to Eddie Peralta, digital imaging specialist, University of California, Santa Barbara. Paula Courtney, director of digital media services at the University of Kansas, made the many moving parts fit together as a whole.

K. Meira Goldberg takes great pleasure in thanking co-editors Michelle Heffner Hayes and Ninotchka Devorah Bennahum for their brilliance, sagacity, and stubborn perseverance in making this book a reality. Awam Amkpa, Pennee Bender, Alice Bloch, Lynn Brooks, Clara Chinoy, Cristina Cruces-Roldán, Thomas DeFrantz, Brenda Dixon Gottschild, Susannah Driver-Barstow, Frank Flynn, Hanaah Frechette, Ariana Markoe, Kiko Mora, Carlota Santana, Larry Stern, Leslie Roybal, Cara De Silva, Juan Vergillos, and Estela Zatania all generously proffered astute readings, valuable references, and wise counsel. Many thanks also to Barbara Cohen Stratyner, Curator of Exhibitions at the New York Public Library for the Performing Arts, Tanisha Jones, Director of the Archive of the Recorded Moving Image at the New York Public Library for the Performing Arts, and Tatiana Weinbaum, Lorca Massine, and Theodor Massine, for supporting my research on Macarrona. I am grateful for the consideration of all my FIT colleagues, but most especially to the infinitely patient Interlibrary Loan crew, headed by Paul LaJoie. To my beloved elders, Izzie, Barbara, Lois, Malcolm and Carol, to my love, Arthur, and to our brilliant and beautiful daughters, Ruby and Amelia: you know … this book is for you.

Ninotchka Devorah Bennahum would like to extend her deepest thanks to her co-editors, Michelle Heffner Hayes and K. Meira Goldberg, without whose visionary feminist flamencology none of these stories would have made it to the page. Further, I thank my colleagues in the Department of Theater & Dance at the University of California, Santa Barbara, whose art and scholarship provide daily inspiration and guidance. I'd also like to thank Eva Encinias-Sandoval, Joaquín and Marisol Encinias for their consummate artistry and vision, esteemed colleague Paul Scolieri and Jacob's Pillow archivist Norton Owen. They have given flamenco a place to grow as art and intellectual discourse in New Mexico. Last, I'd like to thank Carlos Siverio and our beautiful daughter, Mariana Lucia, who brings infinite light and giggles.

Michelle Heffner Hayes would like to thank Ninotchka Devorah Bennahum and K. Meira Goldberg for their passionate collaboration on this project, as well as Elba Hevia y Vaca and the staff of the Philadelphia Flamenco Festival for the opportunity to think deeply, write and talk about some of the ideas in this book, photographer Liliam Dominguez for her trove of flamenco images and the memories they represent, Sherrie Tucker and Tami Albin for their friendship and theoretical insights, and the faculty and staff in the Department of Dance at the University of Kansas, especially Patricia Baudino, Cecil, proofreader, and associate chair Jerel Hilding for allowing me to close my door and write while you "held down the front lines." For their loving support and infinite patience, Hayes wishes to thank her husband, Will Katz, and their daughter, Ruby Katz.

Introduction

> Carmen Amaya is the sound of hail on the windowpane, the cry of the swallow, a thin, black cigar between the lips of a pensive woman, a thunderstorm of applause. When she and her family come to town, they consume the ugly, the torpid, and the dull the way a swarm of insects consumes the leaves on the trees. Not since Serge Diaghilev's Ballets Russes have we been able to experience this kind of lovers' tryst in a theater.
> —Jean Cocteau[1]

> Preciosa throws away her tambourine and runs.
> The wind giant pursues her with a hot sword.
> —Federico García Lorca[2]

The body of history and the body as history—this volume emerged out of a question: *Why have scholars been deaf to the language of the body as a central text in flamenco history?* The word *flamenco* evokes the body of an imagined woman—a *bailaora*. She is a *Gitana*, Spain's exotic Other. She is wrapped in a heavily embroidered shawl, emblem of wealth and empire, with a red rose in her dark hair. Her corset-defying bends, lascivious hips, and sinuous arms and hands seduce the viewer, only to reject this invading gaze with a stamp of defiance. *Orlando*-like, she is present throughout the centuries, transmogrifying, yet hewing to her essentially sensuous and rebellious nature. In one avatar, she is quintessentially *fin-de-siècle*, Pre-Raphaelite. In another, she is dancing Giselle's other half. She appears in the literary Orientalist and vanguardist mind to be part human, part panther, part mythic abstraction, caught on the wings of history running backward into the future.[3]

From sixteenth-century literature, inquisitional documents, travel diaries, and intimate accounts, through twenty-first century staged political actions disseminated online by Flo6x8, the Spanish dancer seems always to burn with desire for subjectivity and authenticity. Forged in the vast stretch of time during which the Spanish Empire rose and fell, the indigenous Americas were populated by descendants of Europe and Africa, and capitalism and democracy were born, flamenco reveals to audiences their own deeply held beliefs. The flamenco body is a kinetic site of ideological resistance, its embodied articulation carries the cruel burden of marginalization and nomadism.

Flamenco music and dance circulate on the global stage through social encounters and theatrical performance, commercial concerts, feature-length and documentary films, critical reviews, scholarly histories, theoretical analyses, biographies, websites, online videos, and public political action. As it always has, flamenco lives on the streets and stages of Spain, especially southern Spain—Andalusia—in a circuit of festivals, *tablaos* (flamenco clubs), classes that draw students from all over the world, and communal celebrations. Established flamenco communities as far flung as Berlin, Philadelphia, Cape Town, and Tokyo celebrate, teach, perform, and innovate. Ubiquitous, yet still ephemeral—instantiations that leave few traces—representations of flamenco galvanize the conflicted but enduring stereotypes that have resonated throughout its history. These moments give rise to new tensions surrounding each context.

Yet, despite the proliferation of global flamenco activity, flamenco scholarship (flamenco as seen through a historical and critical lens) remains difficult to encounter, particularly outside of Spain. Once found, non–Hispanophone flamenco scholarship reads as fragmented in its theoretical framework and divergent in its narrative. Accounts of flamenco depend a great deal on oral histories, personal memories, the status of books in print, and the atmospheric conditions of archives. As a result, certain aspects of flamenco's history are documented in detail, while others are cast in shadow. Although *aficionados* (lovers of flamenco) and scholars have been writing about flamenco since its commercial emergence in the mid-nineteenth century, their frequently self-published works rarely achieve the wide audience commanded by the performances they chronicle. Relatively few books and academic journal articles on flamenco exist in English; and those that are available mainly focus on the guitar and song components. While these works provide important information, the dancing flamenco body frequently evades critical analysis. These discussions fall prey to a host of unexamined assumptions that underpin the reception of dancing bodies from specific cultural or disciplinary contexts.[4]

In the past few decades, an abundance of work has been presented at specialized academic conferences or in online magazines and blogs, but most of this work is published in Spain and is inaccessible to readers who lack fluency in Spanish. Foreign scholars often share the results of their painstaking work through interpersonal relationships, by sharing dissertations, attending conference presentations, or making "boots on the ground" research trips to archives and bookstores in Spain, and visits to the personal collections of aficionados outside of Spain. As a result, flamenco scholarship often travels within a relatively small circle of acquaintances, with the connections formed through the labor of discovery. Without outlets for the publication and distribution of this scholarship, substantive discussions about flamenco history and culture stall in the absence of wider, informed critical discussion.

The concept for this book emerged in a conversation between the coeditors at the joint meeting of the Society for Dance History Scholars and the Congress on Research in Dance in November 2012 at the University of New Mexico, home to the only university flamenco dance program in the United States. We were encouraged by the number of flamenco scholars who had traveled to Albuquerque to participate in the conference and the level of integrity of new dance studies research. We lamented, however, the lack of publication opportunities for the dissemination of this and other exciting research taking place internationally. As instructors of flamenco and flamenco history at the university level, we were dismayed by the lack of resources available to students curious about the history and culture of flamenco. We dreamed of a book—articulated within a multidisciplinary, historically rigorous, theoretically rich framework—that would privilege the dancing body.

This book brings together powerful voices in the international dialogues that comprise flamenco scholarship, illuminates some of the "dark corners" in the narrative, and complicates some of the stereotypes that continue to pervade our work. This curated collage of work by no means represents all the scholarly activity on flamenco occurring across the globe; it suggests an extensive, but not exhaustive, inquiry. We have translated representative works by some of Spain's most important flamenco historians, critics, and cultural theorists, and created a link between the widely divergent methodologies, political agendas, and frames of reference of those who feel passionately about flamenco. In the process, we have discovered many ties that bind us. Established flamenco scholars from beyond Spain's borders contribute to the composition, and new voices suggest productive avenues for exploration. Thankfully, the account is necessarily incomplete. It is our hope that this publication will generate future publications by authors within and outside this book, and that the tremendous energy and time invested by the authors in these pages will propel our shared dialogue forward.

Histories of Flamenco

All of the essayists in this book reference a canonical body of texts. In looking to imagine flamenco's past, we turn to written sources: theoretical treatises, tourist accounts, official documents, and literature. And yet, in imagining the past, should we not imagine, as exists today, a teeming universe of dance beyond the pale of sanctioned practices written into official accounts? How, reading what has been written about Spanish dance of the past, may we imagine what has *not* been written? As Claudia Jeschke, with Robert Atwood, writes in "Hispanomania in Nineteenth Century Theory and Choreography,"

> It is a truism of dance historiography that theory does not explain practice. Similarly, practice does not necessarily exemplify theory. Both constitute knowledge practices and cultures relatively independent of one another, each working in a different context.... Spanish dances became symptoms for Otherness ... they stand as synonyms (or metaphors) for sensuality, desire ... [they] subvert the aesthetic dichotomies and moral stereotypes as they appear in the dance theories. Spanish dances ... design dance identities in the gaps between ethnography, artistic demands and strategies of embodiment.

And so, we reference the iconography of visual culture, ranging from the tapestry cartoons of renowned Spanish painter Francisco de Goya, who immortalized the Gypsy costumes, national dances, and pastoral pleasures of Spain's *majos* (the urban bohemian youth), to cigar box images and sheet music.[5] We consider changing fashions in dress and in costume.[6] We listen, critically, to contemporary reconstructions of the music of past eras and compare them to the flamenco music of today, wondering whether and how they may differ from their original models. And we look to the dancing body as archive, deeply grooved with dance practices passed from generation to generation, as we essay intertextual and paratextual readings of the dance of the distant past.

Important written records of the popular Andalusian dances that led to flamenco, beginning perhaps with Martial's account of the provocative dances of the *puellae gaditanae* (maids of Cádiz) from the first century BCE and continuing Spanish moralist Juan de Mariana's descriptions of the zarabanda in his *Tratado contra los juegos públicos* (Treatise against Public Celebrations, 1583). Each focuses on the lasciviousness and amorality of these dances, an essential component in the lens through which flamenco was viewed even into the twentieth century.[7]

Poet and dramatist Francisco de Quevedo's *Carta de Escarramán a la Méndez* (c. 1610) describes the life of the *Jaque*, or bandit, and voices the veiled resistance to the rigid constraints of social hierarchy embedded in forms, like the *jácara*, that lead to flamenco. Miguel de Cervantes's *La gitanilla* (1613) describes the main character's dancing as "rich with *villancicos, coplas, seguidillas* and *zarabandas*" ... all song and dance forms leading directly to flamenco.[8] Cervantes's most famous character, *El ingenioso hidalgo Don Quixote de la Mancha* (1605, 1615), whose "ingeniousness" ties Quixote to the *agudeza*, or "sharp-wittedness" of the Jaque, already took up the sympathetic depiction of the common folk, and parodic critique of Crown and Church.

Later in the seventeenth century, Madame d' Aulnoy (Marie Catherine le Jumel de Barneville) wrote *Mémoires de la tour d'Espagne, 1679–1681* (Paris, 1690) and *Rélation du voyage d'Espagne (Paris,* 1691) that, "although eventually proven to be fictitious memoirs, based on both earlier travel literature and her fertile imagination," nonetheless record and propagate Spanish dance and "whining" Gitano song as they existed in the late seventeenth-century imaginary.[9]

In accounts of his 1764–1765 trip to Spain, Pierre-Agustín Caron de Beaumarchais, author of *The Barber of Seville* (1773) and *The Marriage of Figaro* (1777), described a fandango, descended from the scandalous sixteenth-century zarabanda—a shared ancestor of classical Spanish dance (the *escuela bolera*) and flamenco. Giacomo Casanova, who visited Spain in 1767, wrote, "nothing more lascivious could be seen," echoing Beaumarchais' description of the fandango as "lascivious" and "obscene."[10] And British travel writer Henry Swinburne, who visited Spain between 1775 and 1776, likewise described the fandango as a dance that "exceeds in wantonness all the dances I ever beheld."[11]

In contrast to these voyeuristic characterizations of Spanish dance, Jerónimo de Alba y Diéguez, writing under the pseudonym "El Bachiller Revoltoso" (The Rebellious Student), provides a markedly different perspective on the eighteenth-century dance and music that would evolve into flamenco. His diary of life between 1740 and 1750 in Seville's Gitano neighborhood of Triana describes performers, dances, audiences, and performance sites, and gives an account from within the community of the genocidal *gran redada* or "General Imprisonment" of Gitanos of 1749.[12] José Cadalso's 1789 *Cartas marruecas*, in the description of a fiesta organized near Cádiz by a Gitano named Tío Gregorio, provides, as Marta Carrasco explains, definitive confirmation of "the existence of a unique and different kind of popular music in Andalusia."[13]

In the nineteenth century, during which flamenco was consolidated as a performance genre, important texts on Spanish music and dance, and flamenco, were proliferated. Well-known travellers' accounts, such as Washington Irving's 1832 *Tales of the Alhambra*, or Alexandre Dumas's 1854 *De Paris à Cádiz*, represent dozens, if not hundreds, of accounts published by lesser-known authors. As Rocío Plaza Orellana explains, during the Napoleonic invasions of 1808–1814, "Spain became one of the most important theaters of war of the era. Contingents of soldiers from diverse nations, fighting for and against Napoleon, faced each other on Spanish soil," and from "foot soldiers" to "officers," many went on to publish travel accounts.[14]

Many of these accounts became immortal. Prosper Merimée traveled in Spain in 1830, and on October 1, 1845, he published his novella *Carmen* in the *Revue des Deux Mondes*, which Henri Meilhac and Ludovic Halévy adapted in 1875 into an opera that has become one of the most iconic performances of "Spanishness." George Borrow's 1841 *The Zincali, or, an account of the Gypsies of Spain with an original collection of their songs and poetry, and a copious dictionary of their language*, recounts five years spent among the Gitanos in the 1830s. Théophile Gautier wrote seminal accounts of Spanish dance on the French ballet stage in the 1830s, and in 1840 he published an account of the Spanish tour he had taken that year. Baron Charles Davillier brought illustrator Gustave Doré with him on his 1862 visit to Spain, which resulted in many widely circulated images (some of which are reproduced in this book). Painter John Singer Sargent toured Spain in 1879, producing his well-known *El Jaleo* in 1882.[15] In October 1882, French composer Emmanuel Chabrier described a performance in a *café cantante* in Seville, noting the rhythms of the *palmas* (flamenco hand-clapping) for use in the 1883 Paris premiere of his *España*.[16]

Many of the renowned dancers discussed in this volume set out *por los mares*— across the seas—during the nineteenth century. Others, such as Amparo Álvarez, "La Campanera" (1828–1895), never left Spain, yet through Doré's engraving of her (see Figure 1 in Maria Carrasco Benítez's essay) and through her pupils, such as maestro José Otero Aranda, achieved fame.[17] Dolores Serral, Mariano Camprubí, Francisco Font, and Manuela Dubinon brought Spanish dance to the Paris Opéra in 1834, setting the stage for Fanny Elssler's wildly successful *Cachucha* of 1836, which she brought to New York's Park Theater in 1840.[18] Lola Montez and Pepita Soto traveled all the way to California. Marie Guy-Stephan partnered Marius Petipa on a tour of Spain and was "baptized" as Andalusian in the 1846 "Asamblea General" (General Assembly) described by Estébanez Calderón. Rosita Mauri (1850–1923), the daughter of a Spanish ballet maestro, was a star at the Paris Opéra when the illustrious Juana Vargas, "La Macarrona" (1870–1947), known in the cafés cantantes of Seville, Málaga, and Madrid, made her international debut at the Éxposition Universelle of 1889.[19]

Parallel to flamenco's emergence as a performance genre, the first serious documentation of flamenco, or "flamencology," emerged. Serafín Estébanez Calderón, "El Solitario," published his *Escenas andaluzas* in 1846, documenting flamenco's native Andalusian-Gitano ethos. He noted artists such as singers "El Planeta" and "El Fillo," whose lineage, through Tomás El Nitri and Antonio Chacón, reaches into the present. Antonio Machado y Álvarez, "Demófilo" (1848–1893), published his pivotal *Colección de cantes flamencos* (1881), providing an exhaustive catalog of flamenco verse literature. An early folklorist Demófilo recognized that in order to fully understand flamenco's dimension of resistance, it should be considered from a multidisciplinary perspective.[20]

Demófilo, like many of his contemporaries, was inspired by Enlightenment scholar Johann Gottfried von Herder's "momentous collection of international folksong texts." For Herder, these songs embodied the *Volkgeist* ("the soul of a people").[21] Scholars such as Demófilo mined Spanish history and folk culture for clues about their identity as a nation. Thus, *zarzuela* (light opera) composer Francisco Asenjo Barbieri (1823–1894) transcribed and published the *Cancionero del Palacio*, a compilation of fifteenth- and sixteenth-century court music, in 1890. Philologist Hugo Schuchardt (1842–1927), Demófilo's colleague and collaborator, wrote *Die Cantes flamencos* in 1881.[22] Musicologist Felipe Pedrell (1841–1922) published his *Cancionero musical popular español*, a four-volume compilation of popular Spanish songs, in 1922. Prolific musicologist and theater historian Emilio Cotarelo y Mori (1857–1936) published a bibliography of the controversies surrounding the morality and legality of Spanish theater in 1904, and a collection of sixteenth- to eighteenth-century *entremeses, loas, bailes, jácaras* and *mojigangas* (short theatrical works that could include dance) in 1911.[23] Julián Ribera y Tarragó (1858–1934), Spanish medievalist, Arabist, and musicologist, published his *La música árabe y su influencia en la española* (Arabic music and its influence on Spanish music) in 1927. The work of Ribera's followers (and detractors) led, in 1948, to the publication by Hebraicist and linguist Samuel Miklos Stern of twenty *xarchas* (in medieval Islamic Spain, short verses in the vernacular), which scholars now believe had a profound impact on European music, including flamenco.[24]

In addition to literary studies, dance manuals, dating from the seventeenth century, are an important resource for flamenco scholars. They include Juan de Esquivel Navarro's 1642 *Discursos sobre el arte del danzado* (translated and annotated by Lynn Matluck Brooks in her 2003 *The Art of Dancing in Seventeenth-Century Spain: Juan de Esquivel Navarro and His World*)[25]; Pablo Minguet è Irol's 1737 *Arte de danzar a la Francesca*; Antonio Cairón's 1820 *Compendio de las reglas del baile*; and José Otero Aranda's 1912 *Tratado de bailes de sociedad, regionales españoles, especialmente andaluces, con su historia y modo de ejecutarlos*. Legal documents, performance contracts, and royal proclamations all provide rich sources of documentation about flamenco's history (and we refer readers to Lynn Matluck Brooks' 1988 *The Dances of the Processions of Seville in Seville's Golden Age*).[26] Also, there is a long line of important critics whose interpretations of Spanish dance and flamenco add to our knowledge. They include Théophile Gautier, Eugenio Noel, André Levinson, John Martin, Walter Terry, Anna Kisselgoff, Valerie Gladstone, Joan Acocella, Ángel Alvarez Caballero, Félix Grande, and Alistair Macaulay.

The search for an authentic national spirit led composer Manuel de Falla and his much younger friend, poet Federico García Lorca, to organize the 1922 *Concurso de Cante Jondo* in their native Granada, allowing only nonprofessional flamencos to participate. In 1933, Lorca published his famous essay on the mysterious and magical spirit of flamenco: *duende*.[27] And Fernando el de Triana's 1935 *Arte y artistas flamencos*, with photographs and biographies of the most important flamenco artists of the nineteenth century, is a landmark and a seminal resource.

In 1936, with support from Nazi Germany and Fascist Italy, Francisco Franco's forces attacked Spain's democratically elected government, sparking a Civil War that ended in Republican Spain's defeat in 1939. The ensuing decades of Franco's dictatorship (1939–1975) tightly bound flamenco's development in the mid-twentieth century to Franco's desire to rebuild the economy by promoting Spain as a tourist destination. In 1954, Hispavox records released the first of a series of flamenco anthologies, which gave international play to the notion of flamenco as a complex musical form of expression, artistry, and technical difficulty.[28]

In 1963, flamenco singer Antonio Mairena and poet Ricardo Molina published *Mundo y formas del cante flamenco*, asserting flamenco as an essentially Gitano form born of the pain of social injustice and marginalization, a legacy hidden in the bosom of family and only brought to light by Gitano artists.[29] Molina and Mairena echoed and elaborated on the view of flamenco Modernists such as Lorca, who said, "the truth of the *cante jondo* resides in ten or twelve Gypsy families living between Seville and Cádiz"—long-standing family networks and trade routes along the Guadalquivir River basin, the Royal Road linking Cádiz and neighboring agricultural communities like Jerez de la Frontera with urban centers like Seville.[30] Molina and Mairena's influential book, appearing during the 1960s incongruities of civil rights struggles in the United States, democratic Europe's desire for economic recovery after World War II, and Spain's continuing Fascist regime, inspired Americans such as Donn Pohren to emigrate to Spain and set up outposts for flamenco tourism in small Andalusian towns like Moron de la Frontera. Pohren published one of the earliest and still influential books on flamenco in English, *The Art of Flamenco*, in 1962.[31] His work captures the complexity of a historical moment when the rhetoric of conserving and protecting tradition shared the same ideological structure as the propaganda for a dictatorial regime.[32]

With the Spanish Constitution of 1978 came a huge upwelling of cultural improvisation, economic expansion, and opening up to the rest of the world. In Madrid of the 1970s and 1980s, "New Flamenco" as a genre of World Music exploded, incorporating musical ideas from around the world, nontraditional instruments like flute, violin, and the Afro-Latin *cajón* (box), and artists from other genres, such as Brazilian percussionist Rubem Dantas and jazz guitarist Carlos Benavent. One of the most influential flamenco guitarists of the twentieth century, Francisco Gustavo Sánchez Gómes, "Paco de Lucía" (1947–2014), released *Fuente y Caudal* in 1973 and, with illustrious singer José Monje Cruz, "Camarón de la Isla" (1950–1992), *La leyenda del tiempo* in 1979.

Flamenco scholarship likewise saw a renaissance. In 1976, Luis Lavaur's *Teoría romántica del cante flamenco* countered Molina and Mairena's essentialist approach by considering flamenco as a response to Romanticism.[33] Scholars combed archives (the Cátedra de Flamencología y Estudios Folclóricos Andaluces had been inaugurated in Jerez de la Frontera in 1958), producing seminal advances in flamenco historiography.[34] Breeching the wall between archival research and oral history, scholars such as José Luis Ortiz Nuevo employed oral history to preserve and make accessible flamenco's genealogical record, publishing *Pepe el de la Matrona. Recuerdos un cantaor sevillano* and *Mil y una historias de Pericón de Cádiz* in 1975 (translated by John C. Moore in 2012).[35] Ortiz Nuevo made another monumental contribution to opening flamenco to the world by organizing in 1980 the first Bienal de Flamenco in Seville. José Blas Vega detailed the evolution from dance academies to performance venues in his 1987 *Los cafés cantantes de Sevilla* and a year later, with Manuel Ríos Ruiz, published an encyclopedia that is still authoritative, the *Diccionario enciclopédico ilustrado del flamenco y maestros del flamenco*. In 1990, Ortiz Nuevo published a compilation of articles on flamenco in the nineteenth-century Seville press, *¿Se sabe algo? viaje al conocimiento del arte flamenco según los testimonios de la prensa sevillana del XIX. desde comienzos del siglo hasta el año en que murió Silverio Franconetti (1812–1889)*.

In 1993, the Centro Andaluz de Documentación de Flamenco opened in Jerez. Javier Suárez Pájares, Joán M. Carreira, Enrique C. Ablanedo, and Lynn Garafola co-edited an edition of the Society of Dance History Scholars Studies in Dance History, *The Origins of the Bolero School*. Ortiz Nuevo embarked on study of the hybridization of flamenco with nineteenth-century Cuban performance forms, publishing with Faustino Nuñez *La Rabia del Placer: El nacimiento cubano del tango y sus desembarco en España (1823–1923)* (1999), and culminating in 2012 in a three-volume compilation of notices of Andalusian performance in the nineteenth-century Cuban press, *Tremendo asombro*.

Theoretical approaches to flamenco study have also blossomed. Gerhard Steingress applied sociological analysis to flamenco in his 1993 *Sociología del cante flamenco*. Anthropologist William Washabaugh published *Flamenco: Passion, Politics and Popular Culture* in 1996, and in 1998 anthropologist Cristina Cruces-Roldán published *Flamenco y trabajo: un análisis antropológico de las relaciones entre el flamenco y las experiencias cotidianas del pueblo andaluz*. In 2000, Ninotchka Bennahum published *Antonia Mercé "La Argentina": Flamenco and the Spanish Avant-Garde*, the first feminist dance history of Spanish modernism. Cruces-Roldán released her two-volume *Más allá de la música: antropología y flamenco* in 2002–2003, followed by her appointment as the inaugural director for the first multi-disciplinary doctoral program in flamenco studies at the University of Seville in 2004. Michelle Heffner Hayes' *Flamenco: Conflicting Histories of the Dance* analyzed gender, race, class and sexuality in representations of flamenco. In an attempt to reconfigure methodologically how flamenco is theorized, Bennahum published a second feminist historiography *Carmen, A Gypsy Geography* in 2013. Today, there are a number of excellent online resources for flamenco researchers, including Alberto Rodríguez's *Flamenco de papel*, David Pérez Merinero's *Papeles flamencos*, *De flamenco*, edited by Estela Zatania since 2001, and Faustino Nuñez's *El afinador de noticias*.

Universities outside Spain have begun to nurture flamenco scholarship. The most

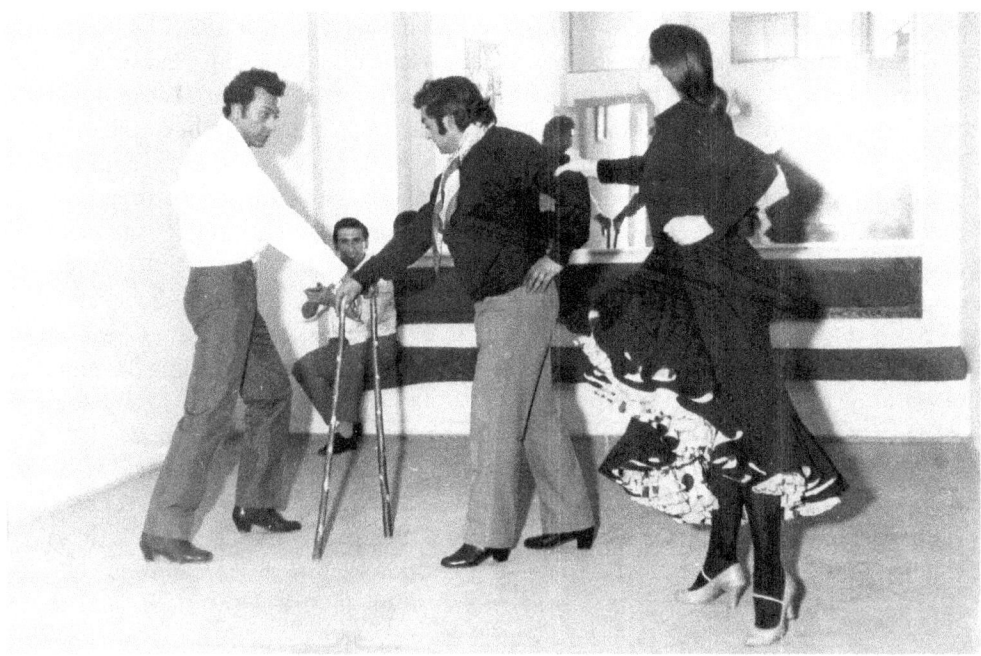

Figure 1: Los Bolecos—Rafael García Rodríguez ("El Negro"), Antonio Montoya Flores ("El Farruco") and Matilde Coral, 1969. The singer is Barrilito, seated, and the photograph was taken during rehearsals for a performance at the Hotel Lux de Sevilla (collection of Rocío García Corrales).

venerable program of study is located at the University of New Mexico, under the direction of Eva Encinias-Sandoval. Other colleges and universities with dance studies programs important to flamenco include the University of Kansas, the University of California, Santa Barbara, and the University of California, San Diego, Sarah Lawrence College, Fashion Institute of Technology, State University of New York–Brockport, Franklin and Marshall College, and the University of Maryland. And exciting research has been produced recently at the campuses of the University of California in Riverside and Los Angeles, the University of Roehampton in London, Arizona State University, and Jacksonville University.

Some Editorial Considerations

It is perhaps not surprising that, to edit discussions of flamenco in a book for publication and therefore homogenize its presentation, contradicting issues and tensions emerged within the scholarly dialogue, especially for a book that attempts to complicate flamenco's most easily consumed stereotypes. Some of these are editorial style issues, but even these seemingly insignificant decisions can challenge the preferences of individual authors and readers. Spanish or other non–English words are italicized in the first usage in each essay and then appear in normal, or roman, font. Short definitions are provided parenthetically or in the body of the paragraph, and key terms are defined in the glossary. The word "flamenco" is not capitalized. The names of dance forms appear in lowercase unless they also refer to the specific title of a dance, such as when a *farruca* is also the title of a dance, *Farruca*. Citations appear as notes, and a full bibliography of works appears at the end of this book. To aid the reader, the coeditors have added to the original endnotes of each author, sometimes providing cross-references between the essays when an idea in one essay refers to a discussion in another.

Beyond stylistic issues, there are some decisions made by the coeditors that tap into complex (and heated) arguments that surround flamenco. Among the most significant of these decisions is the capitalization of the Spanish word "Gitano" in reference to the Roma in Spain (capitalization was left alone when the term was part of an exact quote). Editorial decisions involving the usage of the words "Gypsy" vs. "gypsy" and "Gitano" vs. "gitano" evoke the polemics about relationships between art and the ethnic, national, and regional identities inside flamenco that we hope this book addresses. We are only too aware of how much complexity underscores the entwined history of the fictional Gypsy and flamenco, within and outside of Spain.[36] While this polemic has been exacerbated by the global financial crisis, making access to tourist dollars and audience share ever more important in an economy rent by 25 percent unemployment and a crumbling social safety net, its roots extend back centuries. Spain has, since at least the eighteenth century, been seen as a land of bandits and Gypsies, considered "Moorish" or "African" rather than European.[37] Much of this negative stereotyping—to reference the theories of Roger Bartra, this "cage"—emanates from the colonizing ambitions of European and American powers.[38]

There is general agreement that the Gitanos of Spain have been a persecuted and marginalized group as long as they have resided in the country. As José María Olmo Gutierrez points out in his *Historia antropológica del racismo en España*, persecution and legal discrimination against the Spanish Gypsies began with the Catholic monarchs' proclamation of 1494, and only ended with the Spanish Constitution of 1978.[39] The first bands of Spanish Roma or Caló entered Spain from France around 1425 and were granted permission by Alfonso V of Aragon to wander as penitents for three months.[40] They called themselves "Egyptians," the origin of the English word "Gypsy" and of the Spanish word "Gitano." Trading on their dark looks, Oriental mystique, and their own negative or ambivalent image, they claimed to have been exiled from their homeland as punishment for having betrayed Christ. They were followed by successive waves of immigrants who it appears wandered first in India, then in Persia, then in Byzantium, and then in Europe, and many who stayed and adapted the peripatetic lifestyle of their fathers and grandmothers to life in Spain. They filled a niche on the lowest rungs of society as itinerant traders and smugglers, fortune-tellers and practitioners of folk medicine, and street performers.[41]

Few people contest that Gitano performance and performers contributed to the development of flamenco. As Cristina Cruces-Roldán says in her essay in this volume, "flamenco is an alloy of medieval ecclesiastic music, the Spanish songbook and the regional folklore of the Iberian Peninsula, and the legacy of Gitano performance. Even the dances and music of enslaved Africans disseminated by cultural exchange with America lent various movements and sounds to the musical system of flamenco."[42] But the significance and veracity of the image of the Gitano within flamenco's emergence as a music and dance genre evokes bitter controversy and is hotly debated.

The Napoleonic campaigns of 1807 to 1814, as James Parakilas eloquently analyses in "How Spain Got a Soul," had "begun with the abdication of the Spanish royal family and [were] fought against a leaderless people."[43] The rise in the European imaginary of the figure of the Spanish guerrilla, the outlaw, and the Gitano, led to the erasure of representations of Spain as a political power, as represented by the grandee, the conquistador, and the ruling class.[44] The "radical demotion, or marginalization, or exoticization that turned the nation whose rulers had once called themselves 'the Catholic monarchs' into a place that was barely part of Europe" is, understandably, highly objectionable from the Spanish perspective.[45] The development of flamenco out of this Orientalist and suggestive imagery of bandits and Gitanos cannot be separated from the "condition, common to musicians in many parts of the world today, of being able to produce a marketable art only by exoticizing oneself and one's culture."[46]

In the early decades of the twentieth century, as discussed in Michelle Heffner Hayes' essay in this volume, members of the Generation of '98 sought to combat the stereotypical image of "Andalucized" Spain as nothing but flamenco and bullfighting. In his *Señoritos, chulos, fenómenos, gitanos y flamencos* (1916), Eugenio Noel lampooned the excesses of Andalusian culture, decrying "*Clichés, ya estereotipados, ideas muy bien hechas han divulgado la Andalucía pintoresca*" ("Stereotyped clichés, worn out ideas, have disseminated the picturesque image of Andalusia").[47] And even though, far from Noel's *antiflamenquismo*, the efforts of artists and intellectuals such as Antonio Machado y Álvarez ("Demófilo"), Manuel de Falla, and Federico García Lorca to modernize and dignify flamenco, as with the organizing of the Festival of Cante Jondo of 1922 and Federico García Lorca's 1933 essay "Juego y teoría del duende," take a different tack, their work can be seen as a response to the colonizing gaze of the foreign audience.[48]

These issues have not lost their potency, as Enrique Baltanás describes:

The Andalusian nationalist discourse of today, which is not exclusive to any particular political party, attempts to appropriate flamenco with the intention of turning it into an "identity marker," a Product of Cultural Interest (Bien de Interés Cultural, or BIC), as a patrimony regulated by the Public Administration, a sort of "denomination of origin" label that would prevent it from having the product confused with other types of "false," "impure," or "denaturalized" flamenco.[49]

With Franco's lengthy dictatorship, combined with the continued economic disparity between Spain and other Western nations, this self-stereotyping propagated as Spain and flamenco became an increasingly popular attraction for tourists from more prosperous nations. Once again, as with the Abraham Lincoln Brigades portrayed by Hemingway, and especially with the 1941 advent of Carmen Amaya on the U.S. stage, Spain was imagined as flamenco: partisan, outlaw—Gitano.[50]

As Walter Starkie said in 1935, and as Joan Acocella addresses in this volume, Gypsies are the "national minstrels" of Spain.[51] Like the blackface minstrels who brought performance of the United States to the world, flamenco dance, even as it incorporated representational elements of exoticized "put-on Spain," still, as Gerhard Steingress says, "carried inside itself the germ of an unconscious rebellion against the system within which it had been born."[52] As in the United States, the "national dances" held in their heart an infinitely tragic emptiness, an alienation from their own form, a disavowal of their own reflection. It is not an overstatement to say that flamenco's development in the twentieth century, the story of the complex relationships between this plurality of myths and ethnic and national identities, is implicit in the seemingly simple decision of whether to capitalize the word "Gitano."

In our view, the strategies of auto-exoticization and exploiting one's own negative or ambivalent image, like the fictitious image of the Gitano, lie at the heart of the formation of flamenco in the context of nineteenth-century Romanticism. Flamenco as an art form evolved in part because of the tension and friction between Gypsy and non–Gypsy worlds. As K. Meira Goldberg writes in her 1995 doctoral dissertation, "Border Trespasses: Gypsy Mask and Carmen Amaya's Flamenco Dance,"

> Even though there is endless debate over whether the Andalusian or the Gitano is, in the eyes of a particular audience, the "authentic" source of flamenco forms, this competition has been fruitful, because it has led to a process of mutual reflection. It is a kind of house of mirrors, with Spanish versions of the Gypsy and Gypsy versions of the Spanish, each reflecting not each other, but what lies between them: the changing forms of flamenco performance.[53]

As Foucault might have said, even as the form of what signifies "flamenco" flows and develops and crosses back and forth from camp to camp, "the two forces are not superimposed, do not lose their specific nature, or do not finally become confused"—each side "constitutes for the other a kind of permanent limit, a point of possible reversal."[54] The role of the audience—especially the foreign audience—in shaping flamenco has been to catalyze the crystallization of this alloy by always desiring to reach the deepest point in its own reflection—the mysterious and ultimately unknowable heart of the imagined Gitano.

It is important to distinguish *gitanismo*—the fashion for what Gerhard Steingress calls the "pretend Gypsy," and what Parakilas calls "put-on Spain,"—from the living traditions and practices of flamenco and of flamencos.[55] We aim with this volume to present the nuanced and strongly argued analyses of important flamenco scholars, all grounded in deep experience, current methodologies, and sophisticated theoretical constructs. But we also appreciate the cultural differences reflected in the capitalization or not of ethnic and national identifiers. In Spain, *gitano* is not capitalized. Neither is *español* or *andaluz*. To many flamenco scholars in Spain, battling the ghetto-izing stereotypes that obligate them to contend with the gravitational pull of the Gypsy image as they seek to write a fuller and more nuanced historiography of the form, the incessant discussion of Gitanos in flamenco, and the distinctions made between Gitanos and non–Gitanos is racist—as racist as it would be to distinguish between African American, Japanese, and Seville flamencos. Among progressive Spaniards, as in other European countries, it can be considered offensive to discuss issues of "race" and national identity. We recognize and respect this difference.

But across what Paul Gilroy calls the Black Atlantic, with its toxic legacy of slavery and institutionalized racism, a plethora of important scholarship has emerged. English-language scholars such as Cornel West, Henry Louis Gates, Robert Farris Thompson, Brenda Dixon Gottschild, and Manthia Diawara, French-language theorists such as Frantz Fanon, Pierre Bourdieu, Michel Foucault, Amié Césaire, and Serge Gruzinski, and Spanish-language writers such as Antonio García de León Griego, Roger Bartra and Ricardo Pérez Montfort all seek to articulate the processes of cultural production, identity formation, and resistance.

The word "flamenco" carries the history of these disturbing social and political tensions. George Borrow described the early usage of the term (which means "Flemish" in Spanish) in his 1843 book, *The Zincali*:

> Gitanos, or Egyptians, is the name by which Gypsies have been most generally known in Spain ... but various other names are applied to them; for example, New Castilians, Germans, and Flemings; the first of which titles probably originated after the name of Gitáno had begun to be considered a term of reproach and infamy. They may have thus designated themselves from an unwillingness to utter, when speaking of themselves, the detested expression "Gitáno," a word which seldom escapes their mouths.[56]

In other words, the term "Gitano," by which Spanish Roma refer to themselves today, was not used in this manner in 1843—even before the advent of flamenco as a named form of performance.[57] And, the representational imagery of the Gitano is implicit in flamenco's very name.

As the word "black" was adopted in the 1970s by African-American theorists and activists and "queer" was adopted in the 1990s by the gay rights movement, and despite the fact that the term "Gypsy" has been contextualized as racist in many circles, the word *gitano* has been embraced by flamencos of Roma descent. Following Clara Chinoy and John C. Moore, we as editors have decided upon the term "Gitano/a" in this volume. Even though in Spanish the word is never capitalized, we have chosen to capitalize the term so that it is used as the name of a people, the same way we might use Pashtun or Italian. We recognize that even as the "pretend Gitana" was represented on stages around the globe, real Gitanos were generally despised and never set foot on stage until the advent of the *cafés cantantes* in the 1860s and 1870s. We recognize that the image of the Gitano in flamenco is a fiction, an essentialist and, yes, racist, stereotype that has been divisive and destructive. It has limited and circumscribed the careers of many important artists, from Antonio Chacón to Carmen Amaya, and continues to appear as a referent for contemporary artists like Belén Maya and Israel Galván. But we believe that the only way to begin to dismantle this set of limiting stereotypes is to deconstruct, examine, and analyze them for what they really are.[58]

Organization of This Book

The first section of this book, "Mapping Spanish Dance on the International Stage," provides the setting for the emergence of what we have come to recognize as flamenco. Marta Carrasco Benítez offers an overview of historical and cultural influences that have shaped the art form in "Three Centuries of Flamenco: Some Brief Historical Notes." She begins with the *corridos gitanos* (Gitano ballads) described in Cervantes' *La Gitanilla*, the early seventeenth-century documentation of the Andalusian dances performed by Gitanos and that became flamenco. She then traces the historical timeline through the eighteenth-century accounts of the performances in Triana in Seville's noble houses, the cruel treatment of Gitanos during the gran redada of 1749, the contested origins of the word "flamenco," and flamenco's professionalization boom in 1920s. She covers the antiflamenquismo of the Generation of '98 to the Concurso of 1922, the technical evolution of flamenco dance out of escuela bolera, and she ends with contemporary figures such as Israel Galván, whose experimentations opened a new era in flamenco choreography.

In "Ancient Dancers of Cádiz, *Puellae Gaditanae* and Creations of Myth," Kathy Milazzo dismantles the persistent association between the ancient Roman dancers and flamenco performers. She describes how these images were invoked by the texts of the Church in the early seventeenth century and then recreated in the imagination of Romantic authors during the nineteenth century. Her analysis reveals the lack of historical evidence to establish this connection, despite the persuasiveness of the myth.

Miriam Phillips traces the interstices of two culturally distinct, yet formally similar, traditions in "Hopeful Futures and Nostalgic Pasts: Explorations into Kathak and Flamenco Dance Collaborations." She deconstructs the historical narratives in kathak and flamenco, outlining their purported intersections and divergences. Phillips explores the productive space of collaborations between artists in both forms, particularly from the late twentieth century to the present, and examines questions of fusion, hybridity, and diachronous or synchronous alignments.

"From the *Jácara* to the *Sarabande*," by Ana Yepes, charts the evolution of the seventeenth-century jácara through three extant choreographies. Jácara, as a form, refers to a musical genre and dance, a brief poetic composition, a ballad that forms part of a theatrical performance, and also to the outlaw character featured in those performances. Because jácara is associated with the zarabanda of seventeenth-century Spain, it may be that the rhythm of the jácara, with arms carried overhead and the use of castanets as in Spanish dance today, arrived in France to the song of zarabanda and became the French sarabande, with circling arms and gliding movements. Certain formal elements of jácara and zarabanda, such as the use of the hemiola and circular motions of arms and wrists, suggest they feed into the forms that in the nineteenth century became flamenco.

Rocío Plaza Orellana focuses on the role of Spanish dance in the development of the Romantic ballet. The ballet d'action of Noverre and his contemporaries began to include national dances as *divertissements*; they were a lively and colorful antidote to the tired neoclassicism of the eighteenth century. Plaza Orellana discusses the role of Spanish dance in breaking down barriers between *danse noble, demi-caractère*, or *comique* during the 1820s, as character dances hybridized with ballet. These dances were performed by the great ballerinas of the day, undermining the old hierarchy of roles, and responding to great social transformations of the rise of capitalism and the growth of a new audience—the bourgeoisie.

Anthony Shay's "Fandangos and Bailes: Dancing and Dance Events in Early California" sheds light on the presence of Spanish dance in what is now California during the Spanish colonial period of 1769 to 1821 and the Mexican colonial period of 1821 to 1848. Shay culls from descriptions of social gatherings and histories of the time, illuminating the role of dance in shaping constructions of gender, race, and class, and articulating the hierarchies within Spanish-American society.

The public enthusiasm for Spanish dances filled European ballrooms and theatres during the 1800s. Claudia Jeschke, with Robert Atwood, explores the development of the escuela bolera and other Spanish dances in "Hispanomania in Nineteenth Century Dance Theory and Choreography." Using two ballets by Henri Justamant as case studies, they trace how the choreography of these forms supported and reflected their use as a symbol for "Otherness" in theatrical presentations of the late nineteenth century in Europe.

While European ballet employed Spanish dances as divertissments, within Spain, escuela bolera and folk dances achieved the fully autonomous role of what would be called the *bailable*, which literally means "danceable." In "Some Notes Toward a Historiography of the Mid-Nineteenth Century *Bailable Español*," Kiko Mora follows the evolution of Spanish dances within Spain and their export to Europe and the United States. Set in the context of profound political and social changes in Spain, the bailable revealed the tensions of class and race that fed conflicting perceptions of Spanish national identity.

Gerhard Steingress's "Antecedents of Carmen in the History of Spanish Dance" theorizes the development of the iconic figure of Carmen from Prosper Mérimée to Antonio Gades. He maps the appearance of Spanish dance on the stages of the European ballet, from the emergence of the escuela bolera and flamenco within Spain to the professionalism of the flamenco ballet in the twentieth century. Through Spanish dance and flamenco, Gades revealed himself to be the heir of a complex cultural history, and in Steingress' words, "a synthesis of the best of Andalusia and Spanish culture."

The second section of this book, "Becoming Flamenco: Gitano Embodiment and Modernist Subjectivity," charts the emergence of flamenco during the late nineteenth century through the mid-twentieth century. In "*Jaleo de Jerez* and *Tumulte Noir*: Primitivist Modernism and Cakewalk in Flamenco, 1902–1917," K. Meira Goldberg unravels the process by which signifiers of race, gender, and Empire came to endow the flamenco body with a particularly Spanish "blackness," one that simultaneously recognizes and elides connections to Africa and African American cultures in representations of Gitano identity. Tracing the danced and written dialogue between the artists of the avant-garde in Spain and abroad, Goldberg connects the performances of Gitano artists like La Macarrona to other innovations by dancers, musicians, and visual artists exploring art forms of the African diaspora on the global stage. She unmasks the Africanist elements in the development of *tangos*, *garrotín* and *farruca*, following the footprints of the cakewalk's arrival in Spain.

Clara Chinoy describes the differentiation and academicization of flamenco dance styling in "The First Academy of Flamenco Dance: Frasquillo and the 'Broken Dance' of the Gitanos." Through a biographical account of the life and career of Francisco León Fernández, "Frasquillo" (1898–1940), she traces the development of flamenco dance as a technique and repertory through informal and professional performances, and, eventually, lessons in the dance academies. Frasquillo's importance exceeded the span of his relatively short life. His influential pedagogy, including the Gitano repertory within the institution of the dance school, speaks to the progressive absorption of the Gitano style into the flamenco academy.

In "The Critical Reception of *Le Tricorne*," Joan Acocella analyzes the complex responses from audiences and critics to the performances of the Ballets Russes in England and France contrasted to those from Spain. While most European audiences focused on the elements of modernism and primitivism in the work, Spanish critics emphasized the ballet's depictions of Spanish culture and national identity. The challenges posed by modernist experimentation in *Tricorne* intersected with arguments about cultural appropriation and Spain's place within an international hierarchy of power.

John C. Moore's "Purity and Commercialization: The View from Two Working Artists, Pericón de Cádiz and Chato de la Isla" confronts some of the most contentious arguments in flamenco history, the concepts of purity and the corrupting influences of commercialism, and fleshes out the lived experiences of flamenco artists who depended on professional performance to make a living. Accounts of the artists' lives reveal the economic constraints that influenced the development of *ópera flamenca* and flamenco in the tablaos. Moore uses excerpts from interviews with the singers to give depth to the tensions between their individual artistic preferences and the demands of professionalism, and offers a nuanced perspective on a continually changing flamenco repertory.

In "Carmen Amaya, 1947: The (Gypsy) Beloved of America Reconquers Europe," Montse Madridejos follows Amaya's triumphant and significant return to Spain after eleven years of post–Civil War exile and international stardom. Using press accounts and critical reviews, Madridejos reconstructs the path of Amaya and her company as they toured Spain with *Embrujo Español*. Beguiled by her wealth and celebrity, yet perturbed by the choreographic evidence of her Gypsy identity, which would become iconic and transformative, Madridejos documents the anxiety and pleasure that Amaya's performances produced in her audiences.

Brook Zern's "Flamenco: The Real Stories" mirrors the contentious conversations between flamencologists about the art form's history and culture. Structured as a conversation between a Purist and a Progressive, Zern captures the themes of flamenco's contested origins, its proponents, cultural identity, historical evidence, fusion, drunkenness, and spontaneity in a "flamenco farce."

Ninotchka Devorah Bennahum's "Spanish Artists in Love and War, 1913–1945: Meditations on Female Embodiment and Populist Imagination" considers the complex relationship between Spanish modernity and flamenco. Focusing on issues of feminist embodiment and populism, Bennahum deepens our collective understanding of two consummate Spanish artists: the inventor of modern Spanish dance-theater, Antonia

Mercé, "La Argentina" (1888–1936) and Encarnación López Júlvez, "La Argentinita" (1895–1945), a singer and dancer whose populist theatrical and musical collaborations with García Lorca extended from 1920 until the assassination of Lorca at the start of the Spanish Civil War. Each of these artists added to an evolving global discourse surrounding Spanish Modernism; each yielded a deepened understanding of twentieth-century history and civic identity. Neither La Argentina, who died several days before General Franco crossed from Morocco into Spain, signaling the start of the bloody Spanish Civil War, nor García Lorca, who was martyred days before Franco's attack, would have to live through a fascist dictatorship. La Argentinita, a strong resistor to fascism's censorship, essentially lived in exile in the Americas.

In the third section of this book, "Disobedient Bodies: Flamenco in the 'New' World," scholars examine the social construction of flamenco spectacle as simultaneously enacting and resisting the discursive practices of gender, race, class, and nationhood. Cristina Cruces-Roldán's "Normative Aesthetics and Cultural Constructions in Flamenco Dance: Female and Gitano Bodies as Legitimizers of Tradition" sets the stage for considering the ways in which the concepts of tradition, authenticity, masculinity, femininity, and Gitano and non–Gitano were defined and redefined from the eighteenth century to the present. Bodily techniques, the division of labor, the hierarchy of forms, and the organization of social spaces reified a sexual dimorphism and racialized categories of majority (Spanish) and minority (Gitano). These divisions reflect a hierarchy of power and influence that presented as a priori the "natural" categories of gender and race. Roldán describes the process by which the standardized codes for dancing become "hypersexualized" and the Gitano flamenco aesthetic "hyperracialized." That which is standardized, however, may also be disrupted, and Roldán explores the spaces where dancers employ anti-hegemonic actions in response to these codes, particularly in recent decades.

In "*Las Tocaoras*: Women Guitarists and Their Struggle for Inclusion on the Flamenco Stage," Loren Chuse gives visibility to recent generations of female guitarists. She traces the presence of *tocaoras* from the nineteenth century through their disappearance during the twentieth century and their re-emergence in the twenty-first century. Chuse describes the issues that contribute to their marginalization and, through interviews with contemporary female guitarists, suggests how these tocaoras continue to negotiate the complex barriers that exclude them from the world of flamenco guitar.

The relationship between societal codes of masculinity in Spain during the Franco era and the "aesthetic idea of the *bailaor*" forms the foundation of Ryan Rockmore's "Dancing the Ideal Masculinity." Rockmore situates his analysis in a reading of Spanish national identity following the Civil War until 1975, the year of Franco's death. He describes the discourses that shape masculinity, the Church and the State during the twentieth century, and how the masculine role constructs and is informed by specific codes and attitudes.

Nancy G. Heller's "Flamenco in *La flor de mi secreto*: Re-Appropriation and Subversion in a Film by Pedro Almódovar" reads the subtextual messages conveyed by a *nuevo flamenco* (new flamenco) duet between Joaquín Cortés and Manuela Vargas. The dance scene simultaneously propels the character development in the film, advances the story, comments upon the history and status of flamenco dance in the 1990s, and speaks to the social political climate of Spain following Franco's regime. Through a close analysis of scenic elements, Heller identifies how the different sensory components of choreography, camera angles, and sound express an aesthetic of hope.

Jorge Pérez theorizes the transgressive capacity of world music artists such as Chambao and Ojos de Brujo in "Flamenco Fusion: Cross-Cultural Coalitions and the Art of Raising Consciousness." He anchors his analysis in the "celebratory" and "anxious" narratives of flamencology concerning the concepts of purity and authenticity. Locating these artists within a trajectory of hybridity and commercialization in the history of flamenco, Pérez engages the ways in which flamenco both resists and reifies notions of resistance.

A new generation of flamenco artists access the central tenets of tradition by transcending convention in Niurca Márquez's "Y Para Rematar: Contemplations on a Movement in Transition." Writing from her position as a choreographer and dancer, in dialogue with artists like Juan Carlos Lérida, La Niña NINJA, and José Luis Rodríguez, among others, Márquez analyzes experimental, multidisciplinary works that treat flamenco as a movement language and a contemporary form of expression. These staged works break from the traditional boundaries of *palos* (song forms) and performance conventions "in an overt attempt to interrogate and widen the critical performative discourse surrounding the festival and art-making of flamenco in Spain and abroad."

In "*Blancanieves*, Flamenco and National Identity," William Washabaugh shares his "excitements and arguments" through a formal analysis of Pablo Berger's 2012 *Blancanieves*, a Spanish rendition of Snow White. Although the film ostensibly uses the German fairy tale as its storyline, Washabaugh investigates the movie's hidden narrative of Spain's relationship to the figure of Carmen. He positions the character of Blancanieves from the film in a critical dialogue with other historical and filmic Carmens, commenting "on the disturbing political uses to which the Carmen-image has been put for over a hundred years."

Michelle Heffner Hayes' "Choreographing Contemporaneity: Cultural Legacy and Experimental Imperative" takes as its starting point the curious oppositional binary of tradition and innovation. Through a reading of moments in flamenco history marked by ideological conflict, she relocates experimentalism within the unstable dialogic process through which flamenco tradition continually reinvents itself. Hayes frames flamenco "tradition" as a construct of productive tensions that impel change. She conducts a theoretical analysis of different "contemporary interventions" in flamenco choreography that rigorously engage with history even as they disrupt, displace, and discomfit outmoded essentialisms, successfully relocating flamenco at the center of contemporary interrogations about art and its place in the social fabric, and in the global marketplace.

New Paradigms for Consideration

Dominant narratives about flamenco coalesce around key themes in the literature and practice: exotic femininity, Spanish national identity, "blackness," antiflamenquismo, gitanismo, and political protest among them. It is important not to exclude the performance of flamenco from its discussion in any context, because flamenco as an art form does not sit passively in the gaze of those who document it. Many of the authors of the essays in this book are flamenco dancers or guitarists, and the perspective of the authors is frequently informed by multiple layers of awareness influenced by different positionings within the spectacle. As flamenco artist K. Meira Goldberg says in her essay, dancers, for example, "proclaim their presence as free, autonomous, and powerfully subjective beings ... [they] are not simply objects of gaze: they see, and they represent."[59]

It is both despite and because of the nostalgic pull of flamenco's passionate stereotypes and the corresponding push by practitioners and scholars to advance or disrupt aspects of these representations that linger, lurk, and reappear at different instances that flamenco scholarship fails, in a productive way, to fall into narrative coherence with an unbroken timeline of unassailable "facts." Certainly, we as scholars welcome the intellectual rigor of academic inquiry, which adds voices and information to the critical discussion, but we recognize that there is a danger in the desire for establishing a "flamenco canon." Indeed, it is insistence on a single authority that has resulted in the exclusion of varying perspectives and the perpetuation of persuasive myths. The dissenting voices of flamenco's histories have value in representing the multiplicity of people and experiences they document.

Many of the essays in this book address the plurality of voices between theory and practice, between practice codified as genre in the academy and all of the vernacular practices that operate outside that framework. Fields of signification press upon one another and, to borrow and paraphrase upon Joan Acocella's beautiful turn of phrase, "deliquesce into the cultural miasma." How may we usefully extrapolate from the archive of the dancing body, proposing readings of textual references to dance? Further, what about the practices of the past already exists inside our dance knowledge? Methodologies of oral history, autobiography, phenomenological analysis of movement, and movement genealogy all help us sense the rich flamenco world beyond official accounts.

In her inspired theorization of the conflicting histories of swing at the Hollywood Canteen, Sherrie Tucker describes the dynamics of "torque" as a mechanism of dancing the lindy and jitterbug, but also as a method of writing the complex histories of those who participate. Like flamenco scholarship, jazz studies, and particularly accounts of swing music and dance, are enmeshed in a fraught, romanticized narrative of race, gender, class, and national identity in the United States. Tucker recounts her process of "tangling with" narratives of dancing and democracy at the Hollywood Canteen[60]:

> Diverse memories and narratives jostle and bounce one another around the room when they *take* to this crowded iconic space, yet in doing so we are somehow never completely free from a simple "coherent" national version. Writing—even historical writing—is embodied. Dancing—even social dancing—inscribes subjects, democratically or otherwise. And remembering one's body in motion is different from remembering "what happened."[61]

Tucker applies the physical properties of torque in swing dancing—the exchange of weight and momentum, the push and pull around a point of connection—to the process of writing history. She invokes the position of "choreocritic" from tango scholar Marta Savigliano, and the challenge to "imagine stories about people who move for and against each other, articulating webs of power."[62] Tucker also builds upon dance improvisation scholar Danielle Goldman's theories of contradictory narratives, concluding that

"Assumptions of 'sameness' in dance experience blocks [sic] one's ability to appreciate the political power of dancers' interactions within constraints and therefore 'the possibility for meaningful exchange.'"[63]

Certainly, swing culture developed in a different context than flamenco, but, as discussed in several essays in this volume, there are key connections and resonances between the histories and tensions in the different forms. Jazz and flamenco share a cross-cultural presence and dialogue on the world's stages from the early twentieth century through the present, creating complex narratives of race, gender, national identity, and power. They privilege improvisation in practice, as well as an appreciation of the counterbalancing play of weight and torque. Just as the lindy or jitterbug couple relies on the countertension of the embrace and the breakaway, the solo flamenco dancer grounds the lower body while resisting gravity through the upward arch of the spine and articulation of the arms in oppositional tension, pressing down into one leg to lift the other to deliver the strike of a heel against the floor. Musicians and dancers enact a similar exchange of weight and momentum as they speed up, slow down, fill in, ornament, support, and drive the performance forward. Rather than ignore these pushes and pulls, physically or methodologically, the collection of authors in this book, writing from different disciplinary foundations and in varying historical and cultural contexts, contribute to what Tucker imagines as "a different kind of critical engagement."[64]

It is this desire for "meaningful exchange" and "a different kind of critical engagement" in flamenco scholarship that impels this book forward. Not only do methodological perspectives outside of flamenco studies enrich our scholarship, but the integrity of the research in the historiography of flamenco offers researchers in other disciplines potential insights into complex problems. Gathering these essays and authors into a single volume has yielded the kind of productive tensions that bring new information into the chronology, fresh perspectives on age-old themes, and a deeper analysis of recurring tensions that will, hopefully, allow us to imagine new paradigms for the consideration of flamenco as a cultural practice. That which discomfits us and knocks us off balance requires us to equilibrate, to reconsider our position in the world and how we make meaning within a tradition and in the fullness of the world around us.

Notes

1. Mario Bois, *Carmen Amaya ó La Danza del Fuego* (Madrid: Espasa Calpe, 1994), 177–178.
2. Federico García Lorca, Christopher Maurer, and Catherine Brown, "Preciosa y el aire," in *Selected verse* (New York: Farrar, Straus and Giroux, 2004), 207.
3. This resonating stereotype of the Spanish dancer echoes the haunting figure of the "angel of history" in Walter Benjamin's "Theses on the Philosophy of History," in Walter Benjamin, Hannah Arendt, and Harry Zohn, *Illuminations* (New York: Harcourt, Brace & World, 1968), 257.
4. For a detailed analysis of depictions of the dancing body in flamenco by authors in English, see Michelle Heffner Hayes' *Flamenco: Conflicting Histories of the Dance* (Jefferson, NC: McFarland, 2009), particularly the chapters "Purism, Tourism and Lost Innocence" (53–74) and "Imagining Andalusia" (75–96).
5. Marco Jesús Bertrán, "Madroños, caireles y faraláes: divagaciones de indumentaria femenina," in *Hojas selectas* (Barcelona: Salvat y Cia, 1902), 33–48; Susannah Worth, "Andalusian Dress and the Andalusian Image of Spain, 1759–1936" (PhD diss., The Ohio State University, 1990), 48–55.
6. See, for example, Rocío Plaza Orellana, *Historia de la moda en España: el vestido femenino entre 1750 y 1850* (Córdoba: Almuzara, 2009).
7. On Puellae Gaditanae, *Juvenalis et Persii Satirae*, ed. George Long (London: Whittaker and Co.,

1857), 267. Padre Juan de Mariana, *Obras del Padre Juan de Mariana: Historia de España, tratado contra los juegos publicos,* vol. 2 (1598; rpt. Madrid: M. Rivadeneyra, 1854), 433.

8. "Salió Preciosa rica de villancicos, de coplas, seguidillas y zarabandas..." in Miguel de Cervantes Saavedra, *Obras de Cervantes* (Madrid: Gaspar y Roig, 1865), 130.

9. Judith Etzion, "The Spanish Fandango from Eighteenth-Century 'Laciviousness' to Nineteenth-Century Exoticism," in *Anuario Musical* 48 (1993): 232. Marie Catherine Le Jumel de Barneville d'Aulnoy, *The Ingenious and Diverting Letters of the Lady's — Travels into Spain Describing the Devotions, Nunneries, Humours, Customs, Laws, Militia, Trade, Diet, and Recreations of that People* (London: Printed for S. Crouch, 1692), 45–46.

10. Hugh Thomas, *Beaumarchais in Seville: An Intermezzo* (New Haven: Yale University Press, 2006), 120–121; Giacomo Casanova and Willard R. Trask, *History of My Life,* vols. 9 and 10 (New York: Harcourt, Brace & World, 1966), 321.

11. Swinburne, *Travels through Spain,* vol. 1, 354. For more on eighteenth-century tourism in Andalusia, see Rocío Plaza Orellana, *Los caminos de Andalucía: memorias de los viajeros del siglo XVIII* (Sevilla: Universidad de Sevilla, 2008).

12. Jerónimo de Alba y Diéguez, "El Bachiller Revoltoso," in *Libro de la gitaneria de Triana de los años 1740 a 1750 que escribió el Bachiller Revoltoso para que no se imprimiera,* ed. Antonio Castro Carrasco (Seville: Coria Gráfica, S.L., 1995), 9–13. For more on the gran redada ordered by Ferdinand VI and carried out by the Marquis of Ensenada on July 30, 1749, see María Elena Sánchez Ortega, "Evolucion y contexto historico de los gitanos espanoles," in *Entre la marginacion y el racismo: Reflexiones sobre la vida de los gitanos,* ed. Teresa San Roman (Madrid: Alianza Editorial S.A., 1986), 40–44; Alfaro A. Gómez, *La Gran Redada De Gitanos: España, La Prisión General De Gitanos En 1749* (Paris: Centro de Investigaciones Gitanas, 1993); Antonio Zoido Naranjo, *La Ilustración contra los gitanos: antecendentes, historia y consecuencias de la Prisión General* (Sevilla: Signatura Ediciones de Andalucía, 2009).

13. Don José de Cadalso, *Cartas marruecas, por el Colonel Don José de Cadalso, Caballero del Hábito de Santiago, Nueva edición, revista y cuidadosamente corregida* (Paris: J. Smith, [1789] 1827); Luis Suarez Ávila, "Jaleos, Gilianas, versus Bulerías," *Revista de Flamencología* 10, no. 20 (2004), 3–18.

14. Rocío Plaza Orellana, "Spanish Dance in Europe: From the Late Eighteenth Century through Its Consolidation on the European Stage," in this volume.

15. See "Performing Bizet's *Carmen*: John Singer Sargent, *El Jaleo,* and the *Cigarreras* of Seville," in Mary Elizabeth Boone, *Vistas de España: American Views of Art and Life in Spain, 1860–1914* (New Haven: Yale University Press, 2007), 115–146.

16. James Parakilas, "How Spain Got a Soul," in *The Exoticism in Western Music* (Boston: Northeastern University Press, 1998), 166.

17. Campanera's birth and death dates: Manolo Bohórquez, "La Campanera o los brazos de la Giralda," *La Gazapera,* January 26, 2013, http://blogs.elcorreoweb.es/lagazapera/2013/01/26/la-campanera-o-los-brazos-de-la-giralda/ (accessed November 26, 2014).

18. Gerhard Steingress, *... y Carmen se fue a París. Un estudio sobre la construcción artística del género flamenco (1833–1865)* (Córdoba: Almuzara, 2006); Rocío Plaza Orellana, *El flamenco y los románticos. Un viaje entre el mito y la realidad* (Sevilla: Bienal de Flamenco, 1999).

19. Lynn Garafola, *Legacies of Twentieth-Century Dance* (Middletown, CT: Wesleyan University Press, 2005), 91. For more on Spanish dance on the stages of Europe, see Rocío Plaza Orellana, *Bailes de Andalucía en Londres y París (1830–1850)* (Madrid: Arambel, 2005).

20. Francisco Javier Mora Contreras (Kiko Mora), *Las raíces del duende lo trágico y lo sublime en el cante jondo* (Columbus, Ohio: Ohio State University, 2008) http://rave.ohiolink.edu/etdc/view?acc%5Fnum=osu1196980354 (accessed September 18, 2014), 13–14.

21. Parakilas, "How Spain Got a Soul," 160; Lisa Arkin and Marian Smith, "National Dance in the Romantic Ballet," in *Rethinking the Sylph: New Perspectives on the Romantic Ballet,* ed. Lynn Garafola, 11; Gerhard Steingress, "Ambiente Flamenco y Bohemia Andaluza," in Cristina Cruces-Roldán, ed., *El Flamenco: Identidades Sociales, Ritual y Patrimonio Cultural* (Jerez: Centro Andaluz de Flamenco, 1996), 92.

22. For more on Schuchardt, see Gerhard Steingress, *Sociología del Cante Flamenco* (Jerez: Centro Andaluz de Flamenco, Biblioteca de Estudios Flamencos, 1991), 138–154.

23. Emilio Cotarelo y Mori, *Colección de entremeses, loas, bailes, jácaras y mojigangas desde fines del siglo 16 à mediados del 18* (Madrid: Bailly Ballière, 1911). Emilio Cotarelo y Mori, *Bibliografía de las controversias sobre la licitud del teatro en España: contiene la noticia, extracto ó copia de los escritos, así impresos como inéditos, en pro y en contra de las representaciones; dictámenes de jurisconsultos, moralistas y teólogos; consultas del consejo de castilla; exposiciones de las villas y ciudades pidiendo la abolición ó reposición de los espectáculos teatrales y un apéndice comprensivo de las principlaes disposiciones legislativas referentes al teatro* (Madrid: Est. de la "Rev. de archivos, bibl. y museos," 1904).

24. Samuel Miklos Stern, "*Les vers finaux en espagnol dans les muwassahs hispano-hébraïques. Une contribution à l'histoire du muwassah et à l'étude du vieux dialecte espagnol 'mozarabe,*'" in *Al-Andalus Revista de las escuelas de estudios árabes de Madrid y Granada XII* (1948), 299–346. For more on these

topics, see Cristina Cruces-Roldán, *El flamenco y la música andalusí: Argumentos para un encuentro* (Barcelona: Ediciones Carena, 2003).

25. Lynn Matluck Brooks, *The Art of Dancing in Seventeenth-Century Spain: Juan de Esquivel Navarro and His World* (Lewisburg, PA: Bucknell University Press, 2003).

26. Lynn Matluck Brooks, *The Dances of the Processions of Seville in Spain's Golden Age* (Kassel, Germany: Ed. Reichenberger, 1988).

27. F. García Lorca, "Teoría y juego del duende," in *Prosa* (Madrid: Alianza Editorial, 1969), 169–189.

28. Mora Contreras, *Las raíces del duende*, 20.

29. Ricardo Molina and Antonio Mairena, *Mundo y formas del cante flamenco* (Madrid: Revista de Occidente, 1963).

30. José María Castaño Hervás, "Jerez y Sus Familias Cantaoras," in *La Nueva Alboreá*, http://flun.cica.es/revista-alborea/n0067/salida03.html (accessed October 31, 2012). For translation, Brook Zern, http://www.flamencoexperience.com/blog/?p=335 (accessed November 28, 2014).

31. See also Gerald Howson, *The Flamencos of Cádiz Bay* (London, Melbourne, Sydney, 1965); D. E. Pohren, *The Art of Flamenco* (Jerez de la Frontera, Spain: Jerez Industrial, 1962).

32. Mora Contreras, *Las raíces del duende*, 21.

33. Ibid., 16.

34. Ibid., 21–22.

35. José Luis Ortiz Nuevo, *Pepe el de la Matrona: recuerdos de un cantaor sevillano* (Madrid: Ediciones Demófilo, 1975); José Luis Ortiz Nuevo, *Las Mil y una historias de Pericón de Cadiz* (Madrid: Demófilo, 1975); José Luis Ortiz Nuevo and John C. Moore, *A Thousand and One Stories of Pericón de Cádiz* (2012).

36. Bennahum, Ninotchka, *Carmen, a Gypsy Geography* (Middletown, CT: Wesleyan University Press, 2013).

37. Alexander Dumas is famously reputed to have declared, "Africa begins at the Pyrenees." This often-used aphorism, though never published by Dumas, nonetheless succinctly expresses the widening gap between Spain and the ascendant colonial powers of Europe and the United States. Thus, in his 1816 account of the Peninsular War, French ambassador and archbishop Dominique Dufour de Pradt said, "blood, manners, language, the way of life and making war, in Spain everything is African…If the Spaniard were Mohammedan, he would be completely African; it is religion that has kept it in Europe." Dominique Dufour de Pradt, *Mémoires historiques sur la révolution d'Espagne* (Paris: Rosa [etc.], 1816), 168; trans., Kalabeul, "The True Origins of 'Africa Begins at the Pyrenees,'" in "Anythingarian Rants & Rambles from the Land of the Fretting Nun," February 5, 2010, http://oreneta.com/kalebeul/2010/05/02/the-true-origins-of-africa-begins-at-the-pyrenees/ (accessed November 23, 2013). And in 1899, William Ripley wrote, "Beyond the Pyrenees begins Africa…. The Iberian population, thus isolated from the rest of Europe, are allied in all important anthropological respects with the peoples inhabiting Africa north of the Sahara, from the Red Sea to the Atlantic." William Z. Ripley, *The Races of Europe: A Sociological Study* (New York: D. Appleton and Co., 1899), 272–273.

38. Roger Bartra, *The Cage of Melancholy: Identity and Metamorphosis in the Mexican Character* (New Brunswick, NJ: Rutgers University Press, 1992).

39. José María del Olmo Gutierrez, *Historia del racismo en España*. Córdoba: Almuzara, 2009), 192.

40. Maria Elena Sánchez Ortega, "Evolucion y contexto historico de los gitanos espanoles," in *Entre la marginacion y el racismo: Reflexiones sobre la vida de los gitanos*, ed. Teresa San Roman (Madrid: Alianza Editorial S.A., 1986), 20.

41. K. Meira Goldberg, "Border Trespasses: The Gypsy Mask and Carmen Amaya's Flamenco Dance" (PhD diss., Temple University, 1995), 136–137.

42. See Cristina Cruces-Roldán, "Normative Aesthetics and Cultural Constructions in Flamenco Dance: Female and Gitano Bodies as Legitimizers of Tradition," in this volume.

43. Parakilas, "How Spain Got a Soul" 139–140.

44. Ibid.

45. Ibid., 138.

46. Ibid., 139.

47. It should be noted that Noel's use of the "picturesque" here is negative and sarcastic. Eugenio Noel, *Señoritos Chulos, Fenómenos, Gitanos y Flamencos* (Madrid: Renacimento, 1916), 194. Translation by Michelle Heffner Hayes.

48. Federico García Lorca, in *Obras*, ed. Miguel García-Posada (Madrid: Akal, 1980), 328; Federico García Lorca, ed. and trans. Christopher Maurer, *In Search of Duende* (New York: New Directions, 1998), 49.

49. Enrique Baltanás, "The Fatigue of the Nation," in *Songs of the Minotaur*, 161–162. See also Cristina Cruces-Roldán, "El flamenco y la política de patrimonio en Andalucía. Anotaciones a los registros sonoros de la Niña de los Peines," http://www.iaph.es/export/sites/default/galerias/patrimonio-cultural/imagenes/patrimonio-inmueble/atlas/documentos/ph30-130_El_flamenco_y_la_polxtica_de_patrimonio.pdf.

50. For a discussion of the intellectual ramifications and failings of *mairenismo*, see for example "1.1 Orientación y significado del presente proyecto en el marco de investigaciones anteriores," in Gerhard

Steingress, *La presencia del género flamenco en la prensa local de Granada y Córdoba desde mitades del siglo XIX hasta el año de la publicación de los cantes flamencos de Antonio Machado y Álvarez (1881)*, Ref. OAF/2007/26 (Sevilla: Libro Blanco del Flamenco. Instituto Andaluz del Flamenco, 2008), 22, http://www.juntadeandalucia.es/culturaydeporte/redportales/comunidadprofesional/la-presencia-del-genero-flamenco-en-la-prensa-local-de-granada-y-cordoba-de-gerhard-steingre (accessed August 22, 2015).

51. "The Gipsy in Andalusian Folk-Lore and Folk-Music," in *Proceedings of the Musical Association* 62nd Sess., (1935–1936): 1–20.

52. Steingress, "Aparicion del Cante Flamenco en el Teatro Jerezano del Siglo XIX," in *Dos Siglos de Flamenco: Actas de la Conferencia Internacional, Junio 21–25, 1988* (Jerez de la Frontera: Fundacion Andaluza de Flamenco), 362; Starkie, op. cit. In his chapter "Ambiente Flamenco y Bohemia Andaluza," in Cristina Cruces-Roldán, ed., *El Flamenco: Identidades Sociales, Ritual y Patrimonio Cultural* (Jerez: Centro Andaluz de Flamenco, 1996), Steingress addresses the very complicated relationship among flamenco (defined as a fiction fabricated partly by and for the objectifying and exoticizing gaze of French Romanticism) as a national symbol, nationalism, and fascism: Popular culture, understood as a synonym of national culture, began to express itself in folklore as a ... modern interpretation of the more-or-less lost traditional culture of Andalusia ... a confluence of realistic description and interpretive imagination.... Under the influence of the fashion for *costumbrismo* [interest in local custom]...popular culture acted not only as literary stereotype but also as a model of conduct and a space where broad social classes could identify, and in that commons the ideas of a "folk" and its "soul" as superhuman entities in which later would arise the "mass psychology," pseudo-anthropology, and the full gamut of modern nationalists (1996, p. 92 [translation K. Meira Goldberg]).

53. Goldberg, "Border Trespasses: The Gypsy Mask and Carmen Amaya's Flamenco Dance," 136–137.

54. Michel Foucault, "The Subject and Power," in Hubert L. Dreyfus and Paul Rabinow, *Michel Foucault: Beyond Structuralism and Hermeneutics* (Chicago: University of Chicago Press, 1982), 225.

55. Steingress, *La presencia del género flamenco en la prensa local de Granada y Córdoba.*

56. George Borrow, *The Zincali, or, an Account of the Gypsies of Spain with an Original Collection of Their Songs and Poetry, and a Copious Dictionary of their Language* (London and New York: John Lane, [1841] 1902), 15; thank you, Clara Chinoy, for this reference. See also Lieve Vangehuchten, "¿Qué canta y baila, corta y vuela, y viene del norte a la vez? El flamenco: un complejo problema de homonimia/polisemia," in *Revista de Dialectología y Tradiciones Populares* 59, no. 2 (2004): 127–143.

57. One of the first mentions of flamenco as a form of music and dance is in an article by Eduardo Velaz de Medrano in the Madrid *Gacetilla*, dated February 18, 1853. Faustino Núñez, "Música flamenca, Madrid 1853 y 54," El Afinador de Noticias, July 25, 2011, http://elafinadordenoticias.blogspot.com/2011/06/musica-flamenca-madrid-1853.html (accessed October 6, 2013).

58. For more on these topics, see Sancho de Moncada, "Restauración politica de España y Deseos Publicos que escribió en ocho discursos el Doctor" (Madrid, 1619), quoted in Luis Suárez Ávila, "El Romancero de los Gitanos Bajoandaluces: Del romancero a las tonás," in *Dos Siglos de Flamenco*: Actas de la Conferencia Internacional, Junio 21–25, 1988, (Jerez de la Frontera: Fundacion Andaluza de Flamenco, 1989), 43–44; and Fr. de Sales Mayo, *El Gitanismo* (Madrid, 1870), quoted in Bernard Leblon, *El Cante Flamenco: Entre las Musicas Gitanas y las Tradiciones Andaluzas* (Madrid: Editorial Cinterco, 1991), 137; and Antonio Zoido Naranjo, *La Ilustración contra los gitanos: antecendentes, historia y consecuencias de la Prisión General* (Sevilla: Signatura Ediciones de Andalucía, 2009).

59. "*Jaleo de Jerez* and *Tumulte Noir*: Primitivist Modernism and Cakewalk in Flamenco, 1902–1917," in this volume.

60. Tucker's proposal to "tangle with" these histories borrows from Marita Sturken's concept of "entangled" cultural memory and history in *Tangled Memories: The Vietnam War, the Aids Epidemic and the Politics of Remembering* (Berkeley: University of California Press, 1997), 2–4.

61. Sherrie Tucker, *Dance Floor Democracy: The Social Geography of Memory at the Hollywood Canteen* (Durham, NC: Duke University Press, 2014), 3.

62. "Fragments for a Story of Tango Bodies (on Choreocritics and the Memory of Power)," in *Corporealities: Dancing Knowledge, Culture and Power*, ed. Susan Leigh Foster (London: Routledge, 1996), 200.

63. In Tucker, *Dance Floor Democracy*, 16; Danielle Goldman, *I Want to Be Ready: Improvised Dance as a Practice of Freedom* (Ann Arbor: University of Michigan Press, 2010), 54.

64. Tucker, *Dance Floor Democracy*, 15.

Part I. Mapping Spanish Dance on the International Stage

Three Centuries of Flamenco
Some Brief Historical Notes
Marta Carrasco Benítez
Translation by K. Meira Goldberg

Flamenco's history is lost in the night of time. There is no one way to explain the birth of this art so singularly representative of Spanish culture. Some scholars take us back to the Spain of the Arabian era, because the modulations and melismas that define the flamenco genre may have emerged from the monochordic Islamic chants. Other scholars attribute the creation of this music to the Gitanos, a people from India whose wandering ways scattered them throughout Europe. Gitanos entered Spain at the beginning of the fifteenth century, seeking a more welcoming climate than they had experienced on the subcontinent. We must not forget the various musical legacies inherited by the Andalusians. In southern Spain there had long been psalmody melody and the Jewish musical system, the ionian and phrygian modes inspired by Byzantine chant, the ancient Hindu musical systems, the Muslim songs, and the popular *Mozarabic* songs (those of Iberian Christians living in Islamic realms of the Peninsula), out of which the *jarchas* (in medieval Andalusian music, short ending strophes in Romance, the precursor of Spanish) and zambras probably emerge.[1] Without making value judgments about which theory is strongest—and other theories exist, although they are not as widely accepted—we can be sure that flamenco is born of the people. It has clear folkloric roots, although, as it has filtered through the throats of outstanding creators it has indisputably become an art form.

The Earliest Writing

In the beginning, there was no *baile* (flamenco dance) or guitar, only *cante* (flamenco song). Many believe that the first *palo* (flamenco rhythm) was the *toná*, and that this sung form took root in the triangle between Triana (the Gitano neighborhood of Seville), Jerez de la Frontera, and Cádiz. Yet, in "La Gitanilla," written by Cervantes in the early seventeenth century, we observe that—unless the celebrated writer was telling an imaginary story—the first flamenco discipline was baile. This is ratified by the story's principal character, "Preciosa," a young *bailaora* (dancer) who earned her living dancing Andalusian dances that were accompanied by music and song woven together into what are sometimes called *corridos gitanos* (Gitano ballads).[2] At the beginning of this *Novela Ejemplar*, which represents the first non-oral document of flamenco's origins, we read: "Salió la tal Preciosa la más única bailadora que se hallaba en todo el gitanismo, y la más hermosa y discreta que pudiera hallarse, no entre los gitanos, sino entre cuantas hermosas y discretas pudiera pregonar la fama." ("This Preciosa entered, [she was] the most unique *bailadora* in the Gitano world, and the most beautiful and discrete to be found not among Gitanos, but among all those discrete beauties whose fame precedes them.")

We should also note that around 1740 a manuscript by the so-called "Bachiller Revoltoso" (a pseudonym meaning "rebellious student") chronicled that the granddaughter of Baltasar Montes (the eldest Gitano in Triana) went to dance with chord and percussion instruments to the houses of Seville's nobility. The same author described how cruelly the Castillian army treated the population of Triana during the *Prisión General de los Gitanos* (General Imprisonment of Gitanos), decreed in 1749.[3]

José Cadalso's 1789 *Cartas marruecas* features a series of epistles that Gazel Ben-Aly wrote to his friend Ben-Beley.[4] The writer describes a *juerga Gitana* (Gitano party) on a ranch with "Tío Gregorio"; this piece of information, along with the anterior sources cited above, confirms the existence of a unique and different kind of popular music in Andalusia. This is corroborated by the appearance of a newspaper notice in Cádiz around 1820 announcing that Antonio Monge would sing, in the Teatro del Balón, the four *polos* (flamenco forms): *de Ronda*, *de Tobalo*, *de Jerez*, and *de Cádiz*; (evidence also shows that in 1885 "Señorita Sejuela" would dance *por soleá*, a flamenco form related to the polo, in the Salón Barrera in Seville).[5] Finally, Serafín Estébanez Calderón's *Escenas Andaluzas*, of 1838, describes a "Baile en Triana," in which we encounter the celebrated *cantaores* (flamenco singers) "El Planeta" and his student "El Fillo."[6] With this date, we conclude that the flamenco genre is over two hundred years old, which is confirmed by Antonio Machado y Álvarez "Demófilo," the founder of flamencology, in his 1882 *Colección de Cantes Flamencos*.[7]

Flamenco: A Contested Word

Another aspect that adds to flamenco's mystery relates to the origin of the word "flamenco." Of the multiples theories, perhaps the most widely known is that argued by Blas Infante in his book *Orígenes de lo flamenco y secreto del cante jondo (1929–1933) (Origins of Flamenco and Secret of the Cante Jondo)*. According to Infante, the word derived from the Arabic terms "Felah-Mengus," which together mean "wandering peasant."[8] A curious theory that has acquired many adherents claims flamenco was a kind of *cuchillo* or *navaja* (knife). The *sainete* (picaresque one-act farce or tidbit) *El Soldado Fanfarrón* (*The Braggart Soldier*), written by González del Castillo in the eighteenth century, reads: "El militar, que sacó para mi esposo un flamenco." ("The soldier, that drew a flamenco on my husband.")[9] In addition, a verse discovered by Rodríguez Marín says: "Si me s'ajuma er pescao / y desenvaino er flamenco / con cuarenta puñalás / se iba a rematar el cuento." ("If my fish were to get smoked / and my flamenco were to come out of its scabbard / with forty stabs / the story would end."). The theory that the word "flamenco" came from the flamingo—the bird—has few adherents. The theory put forward by experts such as Hipólito Rossy and Carlos Almendro is that the word "flamenco" derives from the polyphonic music of sixteenth-century Spain that grew in the Netherlands, that is, in what was called Flanders ("flamenco" means "Flemish" in Spanish). This theory was advanced, with varying details, by the Romantic-era visitor to Spain, George Borrow, and by Hugo Schuchardt, among others.[10] According to those writers, it was once believed that the Gitanos were from Germany, which explains why they would be called "flamencos." Finally, there are two hypotheses that are less widely known but nonetheless quite interesting. Antonio Machado y Álvarez "Demófilo" said, "los gitanos llaman gachós a los andaluces y estos a los gitanos los llaman flamencos, sin que sepamos cuál sea la causa de esta denominación." ("The Gitanos call the Andalusians '*gachós*' [the widespread term throughout the Romani diaspora for 'non–Roma'] and they call the Gitanos 'flamencos,' although we don't know why they use these denominations.")[11] And musician Manuel García Matos claims: "Flamenco procede del argot empleado a finales del siglo XVIII y principios del XIX para catalogar todo lo que significa ostentoso, pretencioso o fanfarrón o, como podríamos determinar de forma genéricamente andaluza, 'echao p'alante.'" ("Flamenco comes from the argot used at the end of the eighteenth and beginning of the nineteenth centuries to describe something that is ostentatious, pretentious, bragging, or, as the Andalusians would say, 'forward.'")

Professional Flamenco

Flamenco's popularity with audiences made Madrid a hub of cante (flamenco song) by the early twentieth century. Most well-known artists settled there in order to further their careers, and thus theatrical presentations of flamenco proliferated. With flamenco's surge in popularity after the first Concurso de Cante Jondo in Granada in 1922 (organized by outstanding personalities such as Federico García Lorca, Andrés Segovia, Juan Gris, and Manuel de Falla), the impresario of Madrid's Teatro Pavón, located on the Calle Embajadores, created the so-called Copa Pavón, an award that would advance the prestige of the winning cantaor. El Niño Escacena, Pepe Marchena, El Cojo de Málaga, El Mochuelo, and Manuel Vallejo participated in the first contest on August 24, 1925, with Vallejo judged the winner. Other figures who emerged out of this "boom" included Juan Valderrama, a great connoisseur of all flamenco styles, Manolo Caracol, and Pastora Pavón Cruz "La Niña de los Peines," who founded a school still venerated today. Other artists, including Porrina de Badajoz, Angelillo, and José Cepero also gained fame during this era.

In flamenco's fruitful decade of the 1920s, posters announcing shows began to advertise with a polemic label: "*Opéra flamenca*" (Flamenco Opera). This label, however, was a legal maneuver by an impresario named Vedrines who, with his brother-in-law Alberto Montserrat, took advantage of a ruling in the Tax Code of 1926. According to the rule, public spectacles such as variety shows and *cafés cantantes* (venues specializing in flamenco performance) had to pay a tax of ten percent, whereas instrumental concerts and opera paid only three percent. That seven percent difference prompted Vedrines to call his shows "Opéra flamenca," an intelligent commercial subterfuge that opened flamenco performances to grand spaces: bullrings were at their height of popularity as performance spaces.

And in baile (flamenco dance), the era was graced by figures of the stature of Antonia Mercé "La Argentina," Pastora Imperio, Vicente Escudero, and Encarnación López "La Argentinita," a generation that would be followed by that of Pilar López, Carmen Amaya, and Antonio Ruiz Soler.[12] It should be pointed out that the artists of flamenco baile were fully integrated into the vanguardist currents of the time, along with intellectuals such as García Lorca and Manuel de Falla ("La Argentina" and "La Argentinita"), Jean Cocteau, and the Parisian avant-garde (Vicente Escudero and "La Argentina"). In the 1960s there was a dearth of academic study on flamenco, but dance critics and specialists such as Sebastián Gasch preserved personalities like Carmen Amaya for future audiences.

From the Nineteenth Century to Granada 1922: Falla, Lorca ... the Concurso de Canta Jondo

In Spanish politics, the final third of the nineteenth century was a convulsive period marked by revolutionary uprisings, civil war, military coups d'état, and so on. These tensions manifested in a weakness that culminated in Spain's loss of the last of its colonies in 1898. Such events provoked reflection in intellectuals of the day, who saw Spain's loss of political status in relation to its lack of development with respect to the industrialization of northern Europe. Among the host of explanations put forth by the intellectuals of the *Generación del 98* (Generation of '98) was *flamenquismo* (flamenco-ism), a conceptual category that contained Gitano customs, cante flamenco, bullfighting, and other elements of popular Andalusian culture, which was vilified at the same time Galician or Catalonian intellectuals were promoting the recovery of their respective national customs.

The members of the Generation of '98 were thus *antiflamenquistas* ("anti-flamenco-ists"), with the exception of the brothers Antonio and Manuel Machado who, as Sevillians and sons of the famous folklorist Antonio Machado y Álvarez "Demófilo," had a more nuanced vision. But fortunately for flamenco, out of the generation that followed—the *Generación del '27* ("Generation of '27")—arose a wave of professional cantaores, bailaores, and *tocaores* (flamenco guitarists), and segments of the intellectual class who feared the extinction of *lo puro* ("pure" flamenco). Personalities such as Manuel de Falla and Federico García Lorca had an apocalyptic vision of flamenco and believed flamenco should be an art of the people, of the Andalusian minority, and not a commercial style. The fear of losing of what they called *pureza* ("purity") led them to create the 1922 Concurso de Cante Jondo in Granada, mentioned above, in which the only requirement of the contestants was that they be unknown, men of the people, and not figures already consecrated in the cafés cantantes. The winner of the contest was a singer from Morón de la Frontera resident in Puente Genil: Diego Bermúdez Cala "El Tenazas." Honorable Mention was made of a thirteen-year-old boy named Manuel Ortega Juárez, who would later gain renown as "Manolo Caracol."

The Evolution of Flamenco Baile: La Argentina

As the cante achieved great heights, the baile would as well. From its first appearances in the cafés cantantes, conjugating with the so-called *Bailes de Escuela Andaluza*

(Dances of the Andalusian School), nearly always boleros, flamenco dance became a popular favorite. Among the most important sources on the evolution of flamenco baile are the narratives of Spain's visitors from abroad. Andalusia is prominent in their descriptions of dances, street festivities, and spontaneous and intimate performances in family settings. The descriptions give detailed evidence not only of the dances but also of the social environment that produced them. Henry Swinburne, in his *Travels through Spain, in the Years 1775 and 1776,* spoke of the dancing artistry of the inhabitants of Cádiz:

> In an instant, as if roused from the slumbers of enchantment by the magic touch of a fairy's wand, every body started up, and the whole house resounded with the uproar of clapping of hands, footing, jumping, and snapping of fingers.[13]

Old-school flamencologists always begin their origin-stories of flamenco dance with the passage from Martial in which he extoled the *puellae Gaditanae,* the sensual young women from Cádiz who danced with their *crótalos* (castanets).[14] But from the ancient Roman times, many centuries would pass before flamenco baile was born. In the elaboration of flamenco forms, the *escuela bolera* (bolero school), born in the eighteenth century of the absorption into dance academies of old popular dances—including *panaderos, zapateados, oles,* boleros, *seguidillas, fandangos, jaleos de Jerez, malagueñas, el vito,* and *la cachucha*—played an important role. The boundaries between these popular dances and the truly flamenco dances are quite blurry.

During the first third of the nineteenth century, references to flamenco dance are scarce and not explicit regarding their technical components.[15] However, the extant data between the years of 1831 and 1870, seen in their totality, give us a clear idea of what flamenco dance was like during this period. The most significant record is the 1862 account of French Baron Charles Davillier (*Voyage en Espagne*), with illustrations by Gustavo Doré.[16] The second-most important source of information comes from Serafín Estébanez Calderón in *Escenas Andaluzas* (Andalusian Scenes): "Un baile en Triana" ("A Dance in Triana") of 1831, and *Asamblea General de Caballeros y Damas de Triana...* ("General Assembly of the Gentlemen and Ladies of Triana...") of 1846, which adds to the extensive information later provided by Davillier.[17]

This first period documents a dance of the common people, situated in working-class and Gitano neighborhoods, far from the metropolitan centers. In Cádiz, for example, the nucleus of baile and of *juerga* (flamenco parties) was, according to González del Castillo (1790), in Puerta Tierra; in Seville it was in the Barrio de Triana, and in Granada in the Sacromonte. Social gatherings took place in taverns and in *botillerías* (establishments that served drinks and ices, popular in the late eighteenth and early nineteenth centuries), preferably in the interior patios, which were adorned with beautiful plants, as is customary in Andalusia.[18]

By the mid-nineteenth century, Andalusian dance treaded the noblest of stages. Impresario Miguel de la Barrera advertised rehearsals open to the public at his dance salon in Seville's hotels; one of the most important students in his academy was the famous Amparo Álvarez "La Campanera," drawn by Gustave Doré (see Figure 1). Dance academies had already been used as performance venues more than a decade earlier. On August 3, 1850, the Sevillian periodical *El Porvenir* announced:

> In the accredited academy directed by Don Manuel de la Barrera, Calle Pasión near the *Anfiteatro,* today Saturday there are extraordinary public rehearsals of national dances,

Figure 1: Amparo Álvarez, "La Campanera," by Gustave Doré, 1862. In Charles Davillier and Gustave Doré, *Spain* (London: Sampson Low, Marston, Low and Searle, 1876).

assisted by the disciples of the director and the best boleras of this city, dancing *La Malagueña, La Redova, El Vito* and *Jaleos de Cádiz*.[19]

The golden age of the cafés cantantes featured such mythical figures of flamenco dance as Juana Vargas "La Macarrona," "La Malena," Concha "La Carbonera," the Antúnez sisters, "Las Coquineras," Trinidad Huertas "La Cuenca," Enriqueta "La Macaca," Rita Ortega, Salúd Rodríguez "La hija del Ciego, "Miracielos, Lamparilla, Antonio Bilbao, and El Estampío, to name just a few.[20] Of La Macarrona, for example, Fernando el de Triana wrote, "She has reigned for years in the art of dancing flamenco, because God gave her all that is necessary for that to be the case: a Gitana face, a sculptural figure, flexibility of body, grace in her movements and contortions, simply inimitable."[21]

The worldwide diffusion of flamenco dance was so great that in 1909 the bailaor Francisco Mendoza Ríos "El Faíco" gave classes, accompanied by guitar, in New York, a photograph of which was on exhibit in "Prohibido el cante: flamenco y fotografía" at the Centro Andaluz de Arte Contemporáneo in 2009 in Seville.[22] But the internationalization of flamenco had been in process long before then. There is documentation from the nineteenth century of performances all over the globe by bailaores and bailaoras. La Macarrona performed in Berlín in 1895; Antonia Mercé "La Argentina" had by 1914 toured France, Great Britain, and Russia; Serge Diaghilev's *Ballets Russes* brought the dancer Félix Fernández García "El Loco" to London to assist in the production of *The Three-Cornered Hat* (although it was Léonide Massine who would dance the famous "Farruca del Molinero" at the 1919 premiere).[23] As flamenco scholar José Luis Ortiz Nuevo documents, the first exports of flamenco dance might date from 1879: "And it was in Paris, in the Hippodrome, where a fabulous Spanish fiesta was celebrated in order to raise funds for the victims of flooding in Murcia and Almería: and it was in that grand fiesta where flamenco was presented, perhaps for the first time, in the city of Paris."[24]

The Twenty-First Century

Without abandoning theaters but leaving polemics aside, flamenco dance adapted to new stages in the 1950s and 1960s. Festivals, *peñas* (flamenco societies), and *tablaos* (flamenco clubs) inspired a return to tradition, accentuating *jondura* (depth, as in *cante jondo*, or "deep song") in all facets of flamenco. This was the era of dancers like Enrique el Cojo, Tía Juana la del Pipa, the legendary trio Los Bolecos (comprised of Farruco, Matilde Coral, and Rafael el Negro), Manuela Vargas, Merche Esmeralda, Manolete, Güito, and more. The companies of Luisillo, José Greco, Pilar López, and later Antonio Ruiz Soler, Antonio Gades, María Rosa, and Rafael de Córdova triumphed. Some of the companies formed in the latter part of the twentieth century were, curiously, characterized by the optimistic and forward-looking values that had been nurtured in the Ballet Nacional de España when it was under the direction of Antonio Gades, Antonio Ruiz Soler "El Bailarín," and José Antonio. In 1976, Mario Maya premiered an iconic flamenco work, *Camelamos naquerar*, with text by the poet José Heredia Maya from Granada. Its production marked the first time that the protest against the marginalization of Gitanos in Spain appeared on stage. Following that work was *¡Ay jondo!* with text by Juan de Loxa. Flamenco dance bridged dramatization and traditional values. Reinvention is a continuous and unstoppable process—the inherited obligation of each generation in turn. Companies like those of Antonio Canales and of Joaquín Cortés emerged, followed by those of Carmen Cortés, Javier Barón, Sara Baras, María Pagés, Eva Yerbabuena, Antonio el Pipa, Manuela Carrasco, Farruquito, Joaquín Grilo, and others, whose histories are still being written.

Flamenco was also turned around with the support of the Bienal de Flamenco de Sevilla in 1980, created as the world's largest flamenco festival and committed to staging major new aesthetic developments. Artists dare to do more and to do better in making incursions into the avant-garde as their predecessors did in the Europe of the 1920s. Dancer Israel Galván, who adapts the disciplined masculinity of Vicente Escudero into a new conception of flamenco, premiered *Zapatos rojos* (Red Shoes) in 1998 at the Bienal de Flamenco de Sevilla—the work was a turning point for flamenco dance. Nurtured in the dance academy of his father José Galván and later in Mario Maya's company, Galván overlays his very flamenco way of dancing with a compositional aesthetic aligned with the avant-garde art world. He is joined by figures rooted in the world of traditional flamenco, such as Belén Maya, Rafaela Carrasco, Andrés Marín, Rocío Molina, Isabel Bayón, "La Choni," Marco Vargas, and Amador Rojas.

Companies like those of Angel Rojas/Carlos Rodríguez, Antonio Najarro, and Estévez/Paños pick up the baton of flamenco's development by incorporating Spanish classical dance. At the same time, dancers such as Rocío Molina bring music and dance aesthetics from other genres in order to reinvent flamenco dance. Along with them, other dancers of several generations continue to uphold the old and deeply rooted flamenco traditions, such as Antonio Márquez, Joaquín Grilo, Antonio el Pipa, Mercedes Ruiz, Juana Amaya, Luisa Palicio, Pepa Montes, Manuela Carrasco and, in the youngest generation, Jesús Carmona, Patricia Guerrero, and Rubén Olmo, among others.

Flamenco has broken with folklore and is now a protagonist on the world's principal stages, from the Théâtre du Châtelet in Paris to the Sadler's Wells Theatre in London. It is part of major dance festivals, such as those of Montpellier (France), Festival Internacional de Itálica (Seville), Festival de Marsella (Marseilles), among many others. In 2011, Israel Galván became the only flamenco artist ever to be in residence in a European theater, at the Théâtre de la Ville in Paris, a milestone placing flamenco at the highest artistic level.

Many non-flamenco artists have taken an interest in the genre as well. Patrick de Bana dances a pas de deux with Eva Yerbabuena, who in turn dances the choreography of the great Pina Baush; María Pagés and Sidi Larbi Cherkaoui are preparing a show together; in 2014, Israel Galván was collaborating with the British-Bengali choreographer and dancer Akram Khan. The new aesthetics and knowledge of other dance forms gives bailaores a necessary footing in what they consider to be part of their twenty-first century culture. Flamenco dance is alive and reinvented every day. Today's artists are well trained and knowledgeable, although a danger is that they might create ill-considered fusions, out of a lack of awareness of their own roots. The future of this inimitable art is yet to be discovered.

Notes

1. See Cristina Cruces-Roldán, "Normative Aesthetics and Cultural Constructions in Flamenco Dance: Female and Gitano Bodies as Legitimizers of Tradition," in this volume.
2. Miguel de Cervantes Saavedra, "Preciosa La Gitanilla," in *Novelas Ejemplares* (Buenos Aires: Editorial

Losada, S.A., [1613] 1938), 21–91. The following passage, which I coauthored, is reproduced with revisions from "Primeros referencias escritas," *Andalucía: flamenco* http://www.andalucia.org/es/flamenco/primeras-referencias-escritas/ (accessed September 30, 2014).

3. Jerónimo de Alba y Diéguez ("El Bachiller Revoltoso"), *Libro de la gitaneria de Triana de los años 1740 a 1750 que escribió el bachiller revoltoso para que no se imprimiera*, ed. Antonio Castro Carrasco (Seville: Coria Gráfica, S.L., 1995); see also Antonio Zoido Naranjo, *La ilustración contra los gitanos: antecedentes, historia y consecuencias de la Prisión General* (Sevilla: Signatura Ediciones de Andalucía, 2009).

4. Don José de Cadalso, *Cartas marruecas, por el Colonel Don José de Cadalso, caballero del hábito de Santiago, nueva edición, revista y cuidadosamente corregida* (Paris: J. Smith, [1789] 1827).

5. For more on the polos of Antonio Monge, see Faustino Nuñez, "Bohorquez descubre 'El Planeta,'" *El afinador de noticias*, February 21, 2011, http://elafinadordenoticias.blogspot.com/2011/02/bohorquez-descubre-el-planeta.html (accessed September 30, 2014).

6. Serafín Estébanez Calderón ("El Solitario"), "Un Baile en Triana," in *Escenas Andaluzas* (Buenos Aires: Espasa Calpe Argentina, S.A., [1838] 1941), 108–118.

7. Antonio Machado y Álvarez (Demófilo), *Colección de Cantes Flamencos recogidos y anotados por....* (Madrid: Ediciones Demófilo, [1881] 1975).

8. Blas Infante, *Orígenes de lo flamenco y secreto del cante jondo: (1929–1933)* (Sevilla: Junta de Antalucia, Consejería de Cultura, 1980).

9. Juan Ignacio González del Castillo, *Saynete 7 7* (Isla de Leon: Periu, 1812), 179.

10. George Borrow, *The Zincali, or, an Account of the Gypsies of Spain with an original collection of their Songs and Poetry, and a Copious Dictionary of their Language* (London and New York: John Lane, [1841] 1902), 15; Hipólito Rossy, *Teoria del cante jondo* (Barcelona: CREDSA, 1966); Hugo Schuchardt, *Los cantes flamencos* (Seville: Fundación Machado, 1990).

11. Antonio Machado y Álvarez and Enrique Jesús Rodríguez Baltanás, *Colección de cantes flamencos: recogidos y anotados por Demófilo* (Sevilla: Signatura Ediciones, 1999), 73.

12. On Antonia Mercé, see Ninotchka Devorah Bennahum, "Spanish Dancers in Love and War, 1913–1945: Meditations and Female Embodiment and Populist Imagination," in this volume; on Carmen Amaya, see Montse Madridejos, "Carmen Amaya, 1947: The (Gypsy) Beloved of America Reconquers Europe," in this volume; on Vicente Escudero, see Ryan Rockmore, "Dancing the Ideal Masculinity," in this volume; on the *opéra flamenca*, see John C. Moore, "Purity and Commercialization: The View from Two Working Artists, Pericón de Cádiz and Chato de la Isla," in this volume.

13. Henry Swinburne, *Travels through Spain, in the Years 1775 and 1776*, vol. 1 (Dublin: S. Price, R. Cross, J. Williams, et al., 1779), 355.

14. See Kathy Milazzo, "Ancient Dancers of Cádiz, *Puellae Gaditanae* and Creations of Myth," in this volume.

15. See Kiko Mora, "Some Notes Toward a Historiography of the Mid-Nineteenth Century *Bailable Español*," in this volume.

16. Jean Charles Davillier and Gustave Doré, *Voyage en Espagne* (Paris: Hachette, 1862); English edition: Charles Davillier and Gustave Doré, *Spain* (London: Sampson Low, Marston, Low and Searle, 1876).

17. Serafín Estébanez Calderón ("El Solitario"), "Un Baile en Triana," and "Asamblea General de los Caballeros y Damas de Triana y toma el hábito de la órden de cierta rubia bailadora," in *Escenas Andaluzas: bizarrías de la tierra, alardes de toros, rasgos populares, cuadros de costumbres y artículos varios* (Madrid: Baltasar González, 1847), 203–215 and 243–272.

18. Luis Moncín, Antonio Valladares de Sotomayor, Vicente Rodríguez de Arellano y el Arco, José Villaverde Fernández, Juan Pablo Forner, Luis Moncín, et al. 1790, *Teatro espanõl del siglo XVIII* (Madrid: Valencia, etc., 1790); Wiki "botillería," http://es.wikipedia.org/wiki/Botiller%C3%ADa#cite_note-1 (accessed October 3, 2014), cites Diccionario Enciclopédico Abreviado (Madrid: Espasa-Calpe, 1957), tomo II, 190.

19. "En la acreditada academia que dirige don Manuel de la Barrera, calle Pasión junto al Anfiteatro, hay ensayos públicos extraordinarios de bailes nacionales hoy sábado, al que asistirán todas las discípulas del director y además las mejores boleras de esta ciudad, bailándose la Malagueña, la Redova, el Vito y jaleos de Cádiz" in José Blas Vega, *Los cafés cantantes de Sevilla* (Madrid: Cinterco, 1987), 13. Miguel de la Barrera y Quintana "El Platero," and Manuel de la Barrera y Valladares were not related. Manuel Campos, "Los célebres hermanos de la Barrera no eran si quiera primos," *El cante...que jondo y profundo*, July 8, 2012, http://elcantejondo.blogspot.com.es/2012/07/los-celebres-boleros-hermanos-de-la.html (accessed November 20, 2014).

20. See K. Meira Goldberg, "*Jaleo de Jerez* and *Tumulte Noir*: Primitivist Modernism and Cakewalk in Flamenco, 1902–1917," in this volume.

21. "Es la que hace muchos años reina en el arte de bailar flamenco, porque la dotó Dios de todo lo necesario para que así sea: cara gitana, figura escultural, flexibilidad en el cuerpo, gracia en sus movimientos y contorsiones, sencillamente inimitables." Fernando el de Triana, *Arte y artistas*, 148.

22. José Lebrero Stäls, Inmaculada Abolafio, and Isabel Garcés, *Prohibido el cante: flamenco y fo-*

tografía: 3 abril–30 agosto 2009, Centro Andaluz de Arte Contemporáneo, Sevilla (Sevilla: Junta de Andalucía, Consejería de Cultura, 2009). http://www.caac.es/programa/prohib09/frame.htm (accessed October 24, 2014).

23. See Goldberg, "*Jaleo de Jerez* and *Tumulte Noir*: Primitivist Modernism and Cakewalk in Flamenco, 1902–1917" in this volume, and Joan Acocella, "The Critical Reception of *Le Tricorne*" in this volume.

24. "Y fue en París, en el Hipódromo de París, donde se celebró una fabulosa fiesta española para recaudar fondos a beneficio de los pobres damnificados (de inundaciones en Murcia y Almería): Y fue en esa fiesta, pudo ser en ella que se presentase, por su primera vez, el flamenco en la ciudad de París." José Luis Ortiz Nuevo, "*¿Se sabe algo?*" *Viaje al conocimiento del arte flamenco según los testimonios de la prensa sevillana del XIX. desde comienzos del siglo hasta el año en que murió Silverio Franconetti (1812–1889)* (Sevilla: Ediciones el Carro de la Nieve, 1990), 323.

Ancient Dancers of Cádiz, *Puellae Gaditanae* and Creations of Myth

KATHY MILAZZO

Seville, this marvel of Baetica, the *Zeviya de me alma* [Sevilla of my soul] of the Andalucians, being a place of easy access and of many attractions, it is more visited than most cities of Spain: accordingly the demand of foreigners has created a supply of that useful personage the regular lacquey de place, who is rarely to be met with in other towns. Among them, *Antonio Bailly*, to be heard of at the Reyna, or at his house, No. 5, Calle Reynoso, can be recommended, not only as a good guide for the town, but for a courier or travelling servant throughout Spain: he has much experience in that line, and makes a capital factotum and dragoman to those who cannot discourse eloquent Spanish. Antonio is fat and good-humoured, speaks English well, and can sing a good Andalucian song, manage to get up a good gipsy *funcion en Triana*, &c., &c. This dance is the real thing, and the unchanged exhibition of the *Improba Gaditanae* of antiquity.[1]

This passage, written by British traveler Richard Ford, published originally in 1845, makes a fairly outrageous claim that fellow travelers could still witness an unchanged exhibition of dance dating back to Roman times. All one has to do is find a certain fat, good-humored Antonio to take them to a "gipsy" function in Triana, the *barrio* (neighborhood) situated across the river in Seville in Spain's southwest corner. In her book *Flamenco: The Art of Flamenco*, Barbara Thiel-Cramér begins her discussion on the historical background of the art form with an account of these *puellae Gaditanae*, the famous and seductive dancers from the Spanish city of Cádiz. She positions these dancers as the first contributors to what would eventually become flamenco song and dance. She is one of many writers who begins contemporary flamenco histories in this way.[2] Compounding the complexity of the literature surrounding the *puellae Gaditanae* are the myriad perspectives that have positioned them as differing icons.

The puellae Gaditanae began as notorious dancers in Roman times; they were subsequently portrayed as treacherous women in early modern times, but were transformed into icons of desire in the Romantic Age, and have been incorporated into flamenco histories ever since. Such a changing paradigm begs for an academic analysis in order to understand the mechanisms behind the disparities in, and persistence of, these interpretations. This essay, therefore, begins with the original sources that first mention these dancers—the Roman poets and historians who were captivated by the sensuality of the female bodies. The focus then moves to the early seventeenth century when references to these dancers resurfaced in religious texts authored by Catholic priests. Their actions encourage an examination of the aims of the Church when Spain was the world's most formidable imperial power. Finally, it addresses how these puellae Gaditanae dancers were portrayed in the nineteenth century, the Romantic Era, when they were transposed onto images of the ideal Spanish female dancing body.

Puellae Gaditanae

Marcus Valerius Martialis, a Spanish poet/writer living in Roman times, is famous for his twelve books of epigrams—short paragraphs or poems designed to make a succinct point. "Martial," as he is known in English, is one of the best sources available for information on the puellae Gaditanae due to literary confessions of his torrid affair with Telethusa, a dancer that has since acquired infamy for her seductive movements. His most frequently cited passage describes her as:

> She who was cunning to show wanton gestures to the sound of Baetic castanets and to frolic to the tunes of Gades [ancient Roman name for Cádiz], she who could have roused passion in palsied Pelias, and have stirred Hecuba's spouse even by Hector's pyre—Telethusa burns and racks with love her former master. He sold her as his maid, now he buys her back as mistress.[3]

In this passage, Martial confesses that his desire for Telethusa propelled him to make her his mistress after witnessing her wanton, rhythmic movements measured by her castanet playing. In another epigram, he mentions how many cups of wine he will drink if she is delayed or detained:

> If Telethusa comes and proffers me her promised entertainment, I shall confine myself Rufus, for the sake of my mistress, to the third part of the letters in your name; if she delays, I shall indulge in seven cups; if she disappoints me altogether, I shall, to drown my vexation, drain as many cups as there are letters in both your name and hers.[4]

Fourteen cups of wine is a great deal, so hopefully Martial was not disappointed.

What can be gleaned from Martial's prose is that he was quite possibly in love with her because he acquired her as his mistress, a costly perspective at any time. Also, the slightly desperate, poetic praise of his passages indicates that the puellae Gaditanae were enslaved dancers who entertained in more ways than by dancing and were obviously adept at their work. Other sources state that their dances were originally part of sacred rites in religions emanating from the eastern Mediterranean around 1,000 BCE, such as rites honouring Astarte, a goddess of fertility. Lillian Lawler's work on dance in ancient Greece notes that dances for such deities in the early days of Greek civilization were often performed with frenzied and enthusiastic movements by votaries in Greece and Asia Minor.[5] By Roman times, according to A.T. Fear in the periodical *Greece & Rome*, these women were either personal slaves or were hired out for performances like those of Telethusa and were, therefore, prostitutes.[6] This explains Martial's anguish while waiting for Telethusa to appear with "her promised entertainment." If she delayed too long, she was likely offering her services to someone else. While Martial's quotes indicate that Telethusa excelled at wanton gestures and inspired torrid tributes, the question remains as to how these women danced.

Martial's fellow poet and satirist, Juvenal, notes that: "You may look perhaps for a troupe of Spanish maidens to win applause by immodest dance and song, sinking down with quivering thighs to the floor."[7] Wanton gestures and quivering thighs suggest movements more akin to Middle Eastern forms of dance than to flamenco. These dancers were entertainers, rather than votaries bound by spiritual vows, and the historical conceptions of sacred dancing that underlie Middle Eastern dance, including belly dancing, were buried. Indeed, Fear cites another ancient text in which dancers "so tremulously move her thighs, so alluringly gyrate."[8] Therefore, the puellae Gaditanae of ancient Rome, who most likely originated as worshipers of a fertility goddess, can also be envisioned as enslaved dancers who were available for hire and were coveted for their abilities to dance in a frenzied, seductive fashion in a manner that positioned them as objects of sexual desire. The dances they performed emphasized gyrating and shaking movements in the thighs. This is the material from which future writers would use to describe these ancient dancers, either inspiring flights of fancy or drawing other, less favorable, interpretations.

The Honorable Padres of the Seventeenth and Eighteenth Centuries

After the fall of the Roman Empire in the late fifth century, the soul was deemed more important than the body in Christian religious tenets. The value and agency of human beings were rediscovered in the Italian Renaissance through a movement known as Humanism, whose philosophers revived studies into ancient Greek and Roman literature. In imperial Spain, however, these progressive works were subject to the power of the Catholic Church and its interpretation of Christian liturgy. The Spanish state, through its belief in absolute monarchy, distrusted tenets of Humanism and instead supported a mandate to protect its people and to preserve the purity and political power of the Church.

Padre Mariana, a Spanish Jesuit priest wrote his *Tratado contra los juegos públicos* (Treatise Against Public Games) in 1609. He devoted an entire chapter to a dance called the *zaraband*a, which he identifies as the same shameful dance of the Gaditanae that was seen by the Romans. He utilized both Martial's and Juvenal's quotes to cite the evils in the dance's lascivious movements, noting that it was performed in Roman times. Mariana is quick to point out that the women who executed this "dishonest" dance were called *gaditanas*, from Cádiz.[9] He despairs of "this dance [the zarabanda] ... which left hell to give a grave offence to our Father" and warns of the shame it causes the country.[10] Padre Mariana perhaps can be blamed for creating this myth in print in this early Modern Age source; this is the earliest reference to the dancers of Cádiz that I have located in post–Roman literature. Padre Mariana's descriptions, however, seem to define something other than the Middle Eastern dance forms from which the puellae Gaditanae's dances were historically based. In his view, the zarabanda was performed as a couple dance "with wiggles and words with the intention of very stupid and dirty acts that happen in bordellos, displaying hugs and kisses with the mouth and arms, and the whole body pressing together."[11] One hundred years later, in 1712, a priest named Padre Martín witnessed a performance of another dance, the fandango, in the streets of Cádiz:

> Now I saw and censored ancient customs and praised our modesty. I am aware that this dance from Gades has been famous forever for its obscenity. And I contemplate the same dance today as this *baile gaditano* in all the crossroads of the city, in every salon, with incredible applause by those present, not only among *negros* and common people, but also among very honourable women, born in a noble cradle. The dance is executed in the following form: Danced with a man and a woman, two by two, or more. The bodies move to the sound of the cadences of the music, with all the excitation of passion, with extremely voluptuous movements, heelwork, looks, jumps, all the figures brimming with lascivious intentions. You can see the man ingratiate himself and the woman emits moans and wiggles her hips with as much grace and elegance that can appear in the foolishness and vulgarity of the buttocks of the Golden Ass.[12]

Like Padre Mariana, Padre Martín is also witnessing a couple dance, and he, too, despairs of its foolishness and vulgarity. His passage points to the dance's swift popularity in that the fandango had already spread throughout the city of Cádiz. Descriptions of the zarabanda and the fandango not only differ from each other (the fandango seems to exhibit traces of early flamenco, which is observed in Henry Swinburne's letters from 1775 in which he describes wheelings of arms and a wriggling body),[13] but also differ from accounts of the Roman dance despite protestations of it being the "same." Both priests disregard this fact in order to utilize references to the puellae Gaditanae for purposes of moral education. Their discourses mention the "same" lascivious movements to stress that the zarabanda and the fandango will lead practitioners to spiritual risk, which essentially creates a myth to reflect the Padres' objectives.

Roland Barthes has undertaken extensive research in sociology and lexicology in his 1972 *Mythologies*, through which he addresses the signification of mythologies. Barthes views myths conveyed through discourse as messages that function to transform meaning into other forms or with other histories in order to render them naturalized by other preferences.[14] In other words, myths serve to erase the original meaning of something in order to create another interpretation that, through persistence, becomes natural and "true." Padre Martín attempts to highlight the dangers of the fandango when he states that "one could see the man ingratiating himself with the woman emitting groans and contorting herself so gracefully and elegantly that one can well see in her foolishness and rudeness the buttocks of the Golden Ass."[15] By alluding to a Greek myth in which the protagonist has an insatiable desire to practice magic, Martín constructs a strategy for illustrating the difference between good and evil. As a priest, he was engaged in raising moral standards. His awareness of Humanist philosophy and his knowledge of Greco-Roman literature are motivated by the same Catholic zeal that informed Padre Mariana a century earlier. While Spanish philosophers of the eighteenth century were addressing the advantage of virtue and trust in building a nation,[16] Padre Martín seems to be advocating for a return to values of the previous century when politics were grounded in ethics and theology.

Both Padre Martín and Padre Mariana express despair at the immorality of the dances they witnessed, raising the question about why well-known Greco-Roman myths were used as a means to transform perceptions. Barthes observes that the best defense against mythology is to mystify it in order to produce an artificial myth.[17] The priests, by referring to the negative reputation of the puellae Gaditanae, stress the shameful qualities that kept the old legends circulating and ignore the dance itself and its possible religious associations. They attempt to reinterpret the story as a cautionary tale for moral behavior, warning of the dangers of idolatry by emphasizing sins.

The puellae Gaditanae were positioned as fallen, pagan women. The Golden Ass was a man turned into an ass because of his stupidity for playing with magic and his idolatry for joining a cult of Isis when he finally resumed his human form. By situating dance in a pagan, pre–Christian past, the danger and ill repute of perilous dance performances (such as Salomé's dance leading to the beheading of John the Baptist) are inferred by transforming the image of the dancer into a deadly femme/homme fatale. The action of subjugating females associated with fertility goddesses seems to have occurred when male priests gained political power in the ancient world. Ninotchka Devorah Bennahum, in *Carmen: A Gypsy Geography,* observes, "It is a stunning political move on the part of ancient Mesopotamian priests and kings, inventing a new religious and cultural system and reinventing the image and symbolism of women, to hide and subjugate them."[18] Subversive actions on the part of these Catholic clerics continued the work of the Mesopotamian priests, and female dancing bodies were transformed into Eves caught in the act of luring Adam to bite the apple. They were transformed into the sirens of Odysseus, symbols of the treacherous temptation embodied by women constantly throughout Christian theology. And, of course, dangerous female dancing bodies upset political and spiritual powers, because men were perceived as having been "seduced" against their will.

Desired Women of the Romantic Age

These attitudes underwent a radical shift in the nineteenth century after the Napoleonic Wars in Spain removed the French Bourbon regime and ushered in a struggle for Spanish nationalism and identity. Myths of the puellae Gaditanae were about to experience a transformation from symbols of dangerous women to coveted icons of sensual Spanish dancers. Richard Ford, the English author whose quote begins this essay, wrote his *Handbook for Travellers in Spain* based on his travels between 1830 and 1833. According to anthropologist Allen Josephs, Ford, "with his own mixture of salt and gall, turned Telethusa and the puellae Gaditanae into the most interesting *andaluza* of antiquity."[19] Ford was well versed in Greco-Roman literature and was erudite in finding links, both real and imagined, between ancient times and Spain of the 1830s. He was clearly able to fulfill his fantasies in Cádiz. Ford noted:

> This is the spot for the modern philosopher to study the descendants of those *Gaditanae*, who turned more ancient heads than even the sun. The "ladies of Cádiz," the theme of our old ballads, have retained all their former celebrity; they have cared neither for time nor tide. Observe, particularly ... the Gaditanian walk, *El Piafar*, about which everyone has heard so much.... The Gaditana has no idea of *not* being admired.... Her "pace" is her boast.... Her *meneo* [wiggle] is considered by grave antiquarians to be the unchanged *crissatura* of Martial.[20]

Ford's work is liberally peppered with such references to the Gaditanae; his persistent repetitions reinforce the connection between ancient and contemporaneous women in

Cádiz as they subsequently influenced many fellow travelers and travel writers. It seems, however, that he deliberately chose to romanticize in his images of the women of Cádiz much of the pervasive poverty and amateur dancing that he witnessed throughout Andalusia. Other writers were a bit more frank.

Théophile Gautier, the leading French Romantic dance critic, had long been an admirer of classical, theatrical Spanish dance performed by the highly trained professionals he saw in Paris.[21] Gautier made two trips to Spain: one in 1840 after which he published letters under the title, *Wanderings in Spain*, and another in 1847 for a royal wedding.[22] Gautier was appalled when he first arrived in Spain because the dancing he witnessed was considerably inferior to what he had seen in Paris. He wrote that he was dismayed when the first dancers he saw were "more used-up, more worn-out, more toothless, more bleer-eyed, more bald, and more dilapidated,"[23] which quickly made the Spain of the "Romancero, of the ballads of Victor Hugo, of the tales of Merimée, and the stories of Alfred de Musset, fade before [him]."[24] In his opinion, the dancers in northern Spain did not even look Spanish[25] and the Spanish themselves "most strenuously disavow the Spain of the Romancero and the Orientals; they almost invariably assert that they are neither poetical nor picturesque, and their assertion is, alas! But too well-founded."[26] Gautier's observations of dance in southern Spain bring doubt to the veracity of Ford's rapturous account of the "ladies of Cádiz." Nevertheless, Ford's work was hugely influential and is considered to have inspired Merimée's *Carmen*.[27]

Two other important travelers chronicled their experiences in Spain. Baron Jean-Charles Davillier—a French art scholar, collector, writer, and traveler[28]—journeyed to Spain with Gustave Doré. Born in Strasbourg in 1832, Doré was a prolific artist who, by the early 1860s, "was unchallenged as the foremost illustrator in France."[29] Like Ford, Davillier and Doré were also escorted across Seville's Guadalquivir River into the Gitano *barrio* of Triana to witness an "authentic" evening of local dance. Davillier conjures an ultimate Romantic scene by describing being led to Triana by Colirón, a local resident, through dirty, dark streets to a *botillería* (house where alcoholic beverages were sold and served). There, a performance was held in a patio built in Arab times, intoxicating with its sea of fragrant flowers.[30] Figure 1 depicts Doré's sketch of this memorable event.

If this event was staged to draw foreign travelers like Doré and Davillier, then Doré chose not to depict them among the audience members. Except for two men immediately to the left of the male dancer on the left side of the sketch, all of the other patrons at the botillería are wearing Spanish hats and dress. As Ford had noted, Triana was the most desirable place to see Spanish dance. Davillier, who presented himself as quite knowledgeable in the history of Spanish dance, would naturally desire to see such an "unchanged exhibition" in Triana. While it cannot be determined how accurate Doré was in this sketch, he complies with the Romantic paradigm by "realistically" depicting the local scene with Arab arches, peopled with costumed Spaniards. Doré was a commercial artist who was commissioned by a magazine to create aesthetically pleasing work that could be experienced by an armchair traveler. The two female dancers in the foreground are staged on the floor in dramatic, erotic poses that call attention to their loss of control, poses that a proper woman would never assume.

By commodifying, and ultimately fetishizing the image of the puellae Gaditanae, Ford, Davillier, and Doré align the dancers they saw in the 1800s as heirs of the traditions

Figure 1: A dance performance in the neighborhood of Triana by Gustave Doré, circa 1860. *Un Baile de Candil en la Barrio de la Triana*, in Gustave Doré and Jean Charles Davillier, *Danzas Españolas* (Sevilla: Bienal de Arte Flamenco y Fundación Machado, 1988).

dating from Roman times and infuse them with sensuality, rather than with the un-Christian immodesty attributed by the padres. As Eric Hobsbawm and Terence Ranger argue in their seminal work, *The Invention of Tradition*, invented tradition is "a set of practices normally governed by overtly or tacitly accepted rules and of a ritual or symbolic nature, which seek to inculcate certain values and norms of behaviour by repetition, which automatically implies continuity with the past."[31] Myths transform the past and allusions to tradition lend credibility. While it is unknown when the "tradition" of equating modern-day dancers from Cádiz with the puellae Gaditanae began, Ford's travel book was influential in constructing the myth of the puellae Gaditanae as erotic symbols of an exotic past. Doré's sketch enhances Davillier's account by depicting the dance event in Triana as a continuation of the ancient tradition that these dancers evoked by staging it as an exotic commodity disconnected from the poverty that actually prevailed in Seville. This raises doubts as to the accuracy of Doré's work, leading to a conclusion that he emphasized Romantic qualities that were of value to a paying public.

Most of the Romantic writers who wrote about Spain were American, French, or English, but Serafín Estébanez Calderón was a Spaniard born in Málaga in 1799. He was educated in the humanities, having studied philosophy, Greek, rhetoric, and the *Bellas letres*.[32] In 1846, he published *Escenas Andaluzas*, a book containing anecdotes, essays, and poetry drawing from scenes of life in Andalusia in the 1830s; it is known that he met Davillier in his travels. Estébanez Calderón's work is significant because he avows that dance in Seville is not, in his opinion, the "unchanged exhibition" attested to by Ford and Davillier. Estébanez Calderón displays irritation at foreigners who ascribe ancient origins to Spanish dance and ignore historical evidence provided by the Spaniards themselves.[33] Unfortunately, within a few decades after he published his protestations, Spaniards, too, adopted the rhetoric of foreign travelers, claiming that Spanish dance, especially flamenco, could be traced back to Roman times. This solidified "tradition" and exists to the present day.

Foreign Romantic travel writers in the nineteenth century rewrote the myths developed by the Padres. They were likely first drawn to the puellae Gaditanae because of their scandalous reputations, but they changed their mythical meaning from symbols of danger to icons of desire. In other words, they developed another artificial myth in order to remove the meaning set forth by the Padres. As Barthes observes, a myth "writer's language is not expected to represent reality, but to signify it."[34] Myths are discourse, either written or spoken. They seek to elicit emotions rather than offer facts. The Romantics objectified the Spanish dancers they saw by identifying them as a type of petrified exoticism amenable to the world of legend or romance. The only name utilized by Ford is Telethusa, rendering nameless the real women he saw. "One can easily see in an object at once a perfection and an absence of origin ... a *silence* which belongs to the realm of fairy tales."[35] This deprivation of history allows the truth to evaporate so all one has to do is enjoy the beautiful object without wondering where she actually came from.

Conclusion

The mythology of the puellae Gaditanae, as utilized by the Padres and the Romantics is a subjective interpretation of historical accounts written by Roman authors. It does not address the belly dance type of movements described by Juvenal but instead focuses on the reputation of the women and their overt sexuality. Therefore, stating that the zarabanda, the fandango, and the dances witnessed by Ford and Davillier are the same dances performed by the puellae Gaditanae over 2,000 years ago is a fanciful statement. This subsequently questions the accuracy of tracing flamenco's history back to Roman times. The puellae Gaditanae can be considered the spiritual ancestors of flamenco in that Cádiz has a history of infamous dancers, but the evidence points to no correlation except in mythical beliefs.

Notes

1. Richard Ford, *A Handbook for Travellers in Spain*, 3rd ed. (London: John Murray, 1855), http://www.books.google.com/books?id=XDcdAAAAIAAJ&printsec=titlepage (accessed July 10–13, 2010), 166.
2. Barbara Thiel-Cramér, *Flamenco: The Art of Flemenco, Its History and Development until Our Days* (Lidingö, Sweden: Remark AB, 1991). See also Gustave Doré and Charles Davillier, *Danzas Españolas. Viaje por España* (Sevilla: Bienal de Arte Flamenco y Fundacion Machado, 1988); Frederico García Lorca, *In Search of Duende* (New York: New Directions Books, 1998); Allen Josephs, *White Wall of Spain: The Mysteries of Andalusian Culture* (Gainesville: University Press of Florida, 1990); José Luis Navarro García, *de Telethusa á la Macarrona: bailes Andaluces y flamencos* (Seville: Portada Editorial, 2002); Fernando Quiñones, *What Is Flamenco?* (Madrid: Editorial Cinterco, 1992); and Claus Schreiner, ed. *Flamenco* (Portland, OR: Amadeus Press, 1990).

3. Martial, *Epigrams*, Book VI, LXXI, trans. C. A. Walter, The Loeb Classical Library, http://www.archive.org/stream;martialepigramso/martiala (accessed November 4, 2013).
4. Martial, *Epigrams*, Book VIII, LXIII, trans. C. A. Walter, The Loeb Classical Library, http://www.archive.org/stream;martialepigramso/martiala (accessed November 4, 2013).
5. Lillian B. Lawler, *The Dance in Ancient Greece* (1964; Middleton, CT: Wesleyan University Press, 1984), 96.
6. A.T. Fear, "The Dancing Girls of Cádiz," *Greece & Rome* (Cambridge University Press), 2nd ser., 38, no. 1 (April 1991), http://www.jstor.org/stable/643110 (accessed November 4, 2013), 75.
7. Juvenal, *The Satires*, trans. G.G. Ramsay, http://www.tertullian.org/fathers/juvenal_satires_11,htm (accessed November 4, 2013).
8. A.T. Fear, "The Dancing Girls of Cádiz," *Greece & Rome* (Cambridge University Press), 2nd ser., 38, no. 1 (April 1991), http://www.jstor.org/stable/643110 (accessed November 4, 2013), 76.
9. Jose Luis Suárez García, ed. *Juan de Mariana: Tratado contra los juegos públicos* (Granada: Editorial Universidad de Granada, 2004), 187–188.
10. Ibid., 188.
11. Ibid., 186.
12. José Luis Navarro García, *Semillas de ébano: El elemento negro y afroamericano en el baile flamenco* (Seville: Portada Editorial, 1998), 202.
13. Henry Swinburne, *Travels Through Spain in the years 1775 and 1776* (London: J. David, 1787), http://www.books.google.com/books?id=U6hJAAAAMAAJ&printsec=titlepage&dq=henry+swinburne&source=gbs_summary_r&cad=0#PPP11,M1 (accessed 19 February 19, 2009), 70.
14. Roland Barthes, *Mythologies*, trans. Annette Lavers (New York: Hill & Wang, 1972), 129.
15. José Luis Navarro García, *Semillas de ébano: El elemento negro y afroamericano en el baile flamenco* (Seville: Portada Editorial, 1998), 202.
16. Anthony Pagden, *Spanish Imperialism and the Political Imagination* (New Haven, CT: Yale University Press, 1990), 71.
17. Roland Barthes, *Mythologies*, trans. Annette Lavers (New York: Hill & Wang, 1972), 135.
18. Ninotchka Devorah Bennahum, *Carmen, a Gypsy Geography* (Middletown, CT: Wesleyan University Press, 2013), 76.
19. Allen Josephs, *White Wall of Spain: The Mysteries of Andalusian Culture* (Gainesville: University Press of Florida, 1990), 70.
20. Ibid., 71.
21. Théophile Gautier, "Théophile Gautier on Spanish Dancing," ed. and trans. Ivor Guest, *Dance Chronicle* 10 (1987): 11.
22. Ibid., 2.
23. Théophile Gautier, *Wanderings in Spain* (London: Ingram, Cooke, & Co., 1853) http://www.books.google.com/books?id=JjUBAAAAQAAJ&printsec=frontcover&dq=gautier+spain&lr=#PPR1,M1 (accessed December 2013), 23.
24. Ibid., 13.
25. Ibid., 22.
26. Ibid., 54.
27. Bennahum, *Carmen, a Gypsy Geography*, 14.
28. Gustave Doré, *Doré's Spain: All 236 Illustrations from Spain* (Mineola, NY: Dover Publications, 2004), v.
29. Ibid.
30. Gustave Doré and Charles Davillier, *Danzas Españolas. Viaje por España.* (Sevilla: Bienal de Arte Flamenco y Fundacion Machado, 1988), 74.
31. Eric Hobsbawm and Terence Ranger, eds., *The Invention of Tradition* (Cambridge: Cambridge University Press, 1983), 1.
32. Serafin Estebénez Calderón, *Escenas Andaluzas: bizarrias de la tierra, alardes de toros, rasgos populares, cuadros de costumbres y artículos varios* (1847; Madrid: Extramuros Edición, S.L., 2007), book cover.
33. Ibid., 28.
34. Roland Barthes, *Mythologies*, trans. Annette Lavers (New York: Hill & Wang, 1972), 137.
35. Ibid., 88.

Hopeful Futures and Nostalgic Pasts
Explorations into Kathak and Flamenco Dance Collaborations
Miriam Phillips

Dance Encounters: Spain and India

Saying one is a flamenco dancer often conjures up strong visual images and kinetic responses from others. When I pass dance colleagues in the hallway or run into former professors I have not seen in a while, I am often greeted with a series of quick-fire gestures: defiantly stamping feet thrust downward, while the chest lifts and tightens; arms wrapping around the torso, accompanied by twists of the wrists as one arm is thrown overhead; and ending abruptly with a toss of the chin. This split-second sinuous and subversive gesticulation encapsulates the essence of Spanish flamenco dance, and like many stereotypical images, there is some truth to it—even if it is not the whole truth.[1] While dances from countries other than one's own may seem hard to understand—as if they were a foreign language—there is something about flamenco's combination of power and grace, intense rhythms, and unabashed expression of human emotion that has far-reaching appeal. In many ways, like ballet and hip-hop, flamenco has become a "global physical culture" practiced and adapted well beyond the boundaries of southern Spain, its nascent land.[2]

Far from Spain, another dance form exists. Instead of wearing high-heeled shoes with one hundred nails driven into the soles, dancers wrap strings of one hundred bronze bells compactly around each ankle. Firecracker-like sounds of the dancers' bare feet hitting the floor poke through the dense jingling of the bells, creating tapestries of syncopated rhythms. This form, known as kathak, was birthed in north India. Kathak dancers also maintain a regal, uplifted torso that supports gesticulating arms that trace ornate geometric patterns through the air as their wrists loop in figure eights and fingers articulate in response. Mathematically intricate dance phrases are drummed out with precision, force, and elegance, and end with body shapes formed on incisive stops. When the final foot slap culminates the phrase, the dancer simultaneously tosses one arm overhead, framing the face as the other arm glides swiftly to a forward low diagonal, with the palm flipping over as the fingers unwind and the eyes catch a point in space. In the United States, identifying oneself as a "kathak dancer" does not usually generate the immediate kinetic reactions as "flamenco dancer." Although kathak is lesser known than flamenco, at least in the United States, the dance form has gained wide recognition, which was illustrated by the 2009 guest appearance of a kathak dancer on the American dance competition television show, *So You Think You Can Dance*.[3]

Performance encounters among dancers representing traditions from different parts of the globe are occurring at an increasingly rapid pace. Motivations to create collaborative performances have shifted over the decades as people have gained greater exposure to dance communities and styles once considered obscure. Technological and global circumstances have contributed to the following phenomena: increasing ease of international travel and trade; the expansion of the Internet, including social media sites; and the ability to see a wide variety of global movement practices through YouTube and television reality programs such as *Dancing with the Stars*, based on the British TV series *Strictly Come Dancing*, with its many international offshoots, including *Jhalak Dikhhla Jaa* (India) and *¡Mira Quién Baila!* (Spain).

The pairing of kathak and flamenco is a popular combination and co-productions incorporating the two styles are currently experiencing a renaissance. In the same program, dancers might represent their respective forms separately, alternating one style with the other, as well as create choreographies that blend elements of the two styles. Such collaborations contain features distinct from other dance partnerships, which, in part, contribute to their popularity. This essay explores ways in which kathak and flamenco align choreographically within a shared performance space and considers how these alignments reveal certain aspects of each dance culture's history and the concerns for belonging and identity. Despite the increasing number of cross-cultural dance collaborations, little has been written about why and how dances are paired together, and much less about the creative process behind such works. The essay offers an initial look at cross-cultural artistic relationships, focusing on kathak-flamenco collaborations, and adds to the small body of literature on comparative dance studies.

Mirrors Across the Globe

Although kathak and flamenco originated in lands over 6,000 miles apart and have evolved in distinctly different ways, they share a significant number of characteristics, more than other percussive foot-stamping dances.[4] Dance critics, historians, and dancers in various parts of the world have noted their similarities for decades. While observing the company of celebrated kathak guru Birju Maharaj in 1974, New York's *Village Voice* dance critic Deborah Jowitt noted: "the straight, fairly narrow stance of the dancers, the emphasis on rhythmically complex stamping, and the relaxed, weaving arm gestures that accompany the footwork are so like Spanish flamenco dancing."[5] Upon witnessing a kathak-flamenco collaboration directed by Pratap and Priya Pawar, a *Times of India* reporter observed, "while watching, one could note a marked resemblance in the footwork, hand movements and gestures. The swirls shared the characteristic of '*chakkars*' [pivot turns] in kathak and the sudden finishing of a rhythmic cycle on the '*sam*' [culminating beat of a phrase, but also count one of the rhythmic cycle] with a static pose helped in maintaining the uniformity of movements in duet numbers."[6] Publicity on the recent collaboration between contemporary kathak and flamenco dance giants Akram Khan and Israel Galván articulates "similarities between the two forms are evident: feet striking the ground, circular movements of the arms, and direct and essential interaction with the musicians."[7]

Other techniques common to the two forms include the use of a proud, upright body stance, with arm movements radiating from or encircling around a strong vertical axis as wrists twirl and fingers fan. In addition to the many body positions, arm movements, and foot rhythms that emulate one another, as well as the aforementioned similarities in phrasing patterns, flamenco and kathak are both solo forms that traditionally use a noticeable degree of improvisation.[8]

Their many similar attributes, along with some loosely proven linguistic and historical ties, have spawned numerous collaborations between kathak and flamenco dancers over the last several decades. I first came across similarities between the two styles within my own dancing body when, already as an avid student of kathak, I found flamenco. This led me on several trips to India and Spain over the years to study dance and its surrounding culture. I also began a process to compare the features of kathak and flamenco and to discern how the histories, values, and aesthetics of their respective cultures are embedded in each dance.[9] Since my early training and research on these forms, I have collected much information and video footage of collaborative choreographies—including one of my own from 1981—created by kathak and flamenco artists. Recently, I began exploring these kathak-flamenco collaborations to understand how the characteristics of each style were being represented, and I questioned how aspects of each culture's worldview might have been altered. Experimentation in cross-cultural theatrical dance productions between flamenco and classical Indian dancers may have occurred in the 1930s as there is evidence of artistic interactions between the early twentieth-century choreographers Uday Shankar (India) and Vicente Escudero (Spain), who are considered pioneers of a modernist approach to the staging of their respective dance forms and contributed to their international circulation.[10] Since the early 1980s, however, I have noticed a proliferation of dancers creating kathak-flamenco collaborations, with a further boom occurring in the early decades of the twenty-first century. Collaborators range from amateurs to internationally acclaimed artists who claim various countries of origin and residence.[11]

Tradition-Based Collaborations versus Fusion or Hybridization

In collaborations between traditional dance artists, the intention is to keep the respective dance forms intact in order to highlight shared themes. This is distinct from "fusion" or "hybrid" works that blend discrete aesthetic or stylistic features that can be shaped into new forms or structures, whether temporarily or permanently. Here, a cross-pollination process takes place between forms, such as that which occurs widely in the global music industry.[12]

Notions of fusion or hybridization are culturally specific, however. Exploring the works of contemporary Indian dance choreographers, literary scholar Ketu Katrak describes fusion as "a collaging of different movements without evolving a distinctive style," whereas "hybrid work involves a reworking from within the traditional dance forms [...] and other movement vocabularies that a dancer has mastered. Multiple movements may flow or be referenced with sharp disjuncture in innovative choreography."[13] In flamencologist and performance theorist Gerhard Steingress's discussion on contemporary flamenco musical fusion, he notes that "flamenco is basically the result of fusion and hybridization. Indeed, the Spanish term *flamenquización* ("flamencization") refers to this process." Although Steingress distinguishes fusion from hybridization, he considers flamenco "a genre that both appeared and developed as a series of different hybridizations" when distinct local, national, and international musical styles interacted.[14]

Artists whose interests lie in expanding or breaking tradition use cross-cultural dance collaborations to explore new hybrid forms. Contemporary dance choreographer Akram Khan, whose base is kathak, and *nuevo flamenco* artist Israel Galván assimilate modernist ideas into a postmodern choreographic aesthetic, thereby widening each form's expression of its traditional movement vocabularies. Their 2014 collaboration *TOROBAKA* explores elemental principals of voice and gesture in their respective forms. It has been described as "*NOT* an exchange between ethnic traditions or an exercise of global dance."[15]

In tradition-based collaborative works, artists representing distinct dance forms create a joint choreographic production. Often, repertoire from one tradition is interwoven with repertoire from the other tradition, with interludes or grand finales in which dancers from each tradition perform side by side, such as in the productions directed by Pratap and Priya Pawar.[16] Toronto-based flamenco dancer Esmeralda Enrique, who had a collective partnership called "Firedance" from 1996 to 2004 with kathak dancer Joanna DeSouza, describes their process: "We explored how a movement or esthetic of kathak might compliment or juxtapose a similar one in flamenco and vice versa. We worked on creating duets where we actually danced together as opposed to, 'you do something and then I will do something.' In this way the juxtaposition was more delicate and nuanced. Of course we also kept in mind the historical context of how and why movement, music and form developed in the ways that they did for each form."[17]

While performers in tradition-based collaborations might explore fusing certain elements of both styles in some of the presented repertoire, they generally keep the movement vocabulary close to the traditional form but may alter the dance structure. York University graduate student Catalina Fellay-Dunbar describes "Firedance": "the similarities between the mirrored aesthetics and structures of flamenco and kathak provided fertile ground for creation. DeSouza and Enrique aimed to work with these similarities while retaining the individual integrity of each form."[18]

In such collaborations, artists focus on common themes between the individual styles. These themes may relate to general historical relationships; specific movement techniques; spiritual, social, or literary subjects; or, more recently, may accentuate how "aesthetic and ideological meeting points occur onstage."[19] Intentions are not about fusing elements, such as might be found in "kathamenco," or becoming the same, but exploring likeness within different cultural expressions.[20] A tradition-based collaborative dance performance "represents the idea that beyond race, age, class, culture, political or religious beliefs, we can share the same passion with two completely different styles."[21] Ultimately, it is about discovering a shared humanity through the identification of thematic commonalities.

Collaborative Alignments

Why are particular dance styles paired in a shared performance? How are they aligned on stage and represented in program publicity? What is specifically going on in kathak-flamenco collaborations? To explore these questions, I draw upon Benedict Anderson's *Imagined Communities: Reflections on the Origins and Spread of Nationalism*.[22] Anderson explores how geographical places were considered "new" or "old" depending on the ways people thought of themselves in relation to other people and places. I map his theory of "diachronic and synchronic alignments" onto the pairing of dance styles in tradition-based collaborative productions.

In examining place names derived from other place names (toponyms), Anderson outlines two orientations, or "alignments." In a diachronic alignment, people associate one geographical location with another in terms of its chronological development. For example, New York is "diachronically aligned" to an original (older) York in England (named to honor the Duke of York). Anderson explains, "Already in the sixteenth century, Europeans had begun the strange habit of naming remote places, first in the Americas and Africa, later in Asia, Australia, and Oceania, as 'new' versions of (thereby) 'old' toponyms in their lands of origin.... In these names 'new' invariably has the meaning of 'successor' to, or 'inheritor' of, something vanished... [and] appears always to invoke an ambiguous blessing from the dead."[23] In dance, one form can have a diachronic relationship to an older form. For example, the dances associated with the Afro-Brazilian religion *Candomblé* have a diachronic relationship to Nigerian Yoruba dances since some of their roots developed from dances that were transported by enslaved Africans.[24]

"Synchronic alignment" came about when innovations such as shipbuilding, navigation, cartography, and printing expanded, making it possible for people to be in one place yet simultaneously feel linked to others far away, living parallel lives. Anderson writes, "What is startling in the American namings of the sixteenth to eighteenth centuries is that 'new' and 'old' were understood synchronically, coexisting within homogeneous, empty time. Vizcaya is there *alongside* Nueva Vizcaya, New London *alongside* London: an idiom of sibling competition rather than of inheritance.... One could be fully aware of sharing a language and a religious faith (to varying degrees), customs and traditions, without any great expectation of ever meeting one's partners."[25] Competitive Irish step dance offers an example of a dance style whose practitioners are "synchronically aligned" because "they are a part of a worldwide Irish dance diaspora, which encompasses members from Ireland, to the U.S., U.K., Australia, Canada, New Zealand, even South Africa."[26]

Anderson's alignment model serves as a lens to understand the history of dance more comprehensively. The development of a style can be outlined in terms of its chronological development (diachronically) as well as its relationship to other historical events and artistic trends (synchronically). This model can also be used to consider the reasons behind cross-cultural collaborations.

In relating Anderson's diachronic/synchronic alignment model specifically to cross-cultural dance collaborations, one type of pairing links dances evolved from older styles or historical or cultural interactions, such as pairing dances of West Africa to those of the African diaspora. These types of collaborations place dance forms in diachronic alignment as they celebrate the inheritance of a once-faded connection. They stress nostalgic longings for the past by eliciting the memory of a people's lost homeland, identity, roots, or ways of life.

Synchronically aligned dance collaborations highlight particular features shared between styles. They demonstrate how people from very different parts of the world use similar motifs or subjects, thus transmitting a strong message of "global interconnectedness." A popular endeavor juxtaposes dance styles that emphasize percussive footwork. For example, the Broadway show *Riverdance*, which debuted in 1995, featured Irish step dance and included other percussive dances such as flamenco and tap; in 2008, virtuosos Chitresh Das and Jason Samuels Smith collaborated on *India Jazz Suites: Kathak Meets Tap*.[27]

Kathak and flamenco collaborations are unusual in that they can be perceived as both diachronically and synchronically linked. For example, flamenco is sometimes seen as having developed from kathak. Although this view is oversimplified, it presumes they have a diachronic relationship to one another. Additionally, as mentioned earlier, both dance styles have in common several movement and rhythmic elements. Focusing on these shared features without reference to historical context highlights their synchronic relationship. A brief understanding of each dance style's history helps to better comprehend how these types of alignments play out in kathak-flamenco collaborations.

Historical Thorns–Dance History Narratives

Often a synthesis of numerous artistic and cultural influences, dance styles evolve in response to social, political, ideological, and economic shifts. Because many dance forms are passed down through oral tradition and kinesthetic transmission, it can be challenging to pinpoint concrete influences and historical facts. Written historical accounts and practitioners' conceptions of history may erroneously consider dances as evolved from a seamless, unbroken tradition. A dichotomy can exist between what dancers understand about the history of the dances they practice and what scholars discover through scrupulous research. With this in mind, the following brief historical overview outlines commonly held beliefs about significant cultural elements understood in the formation of kathak and flamenco dance.

Historical Roots: Kathak

Generally considered an amalgamation of several dance heritages with influence from varied folk and religious traditions, kathak's early influences came from traveling storytellers, or *kathakas*, who performed in village and temple courtyards using mimetic gesture, song, and recitation to propagate Hindu ideology.[28] Another early influence was the now two thousand-year-old tribal dances of Rajasthan, a desert region in northwestern India where many Roma (Gitano) tribes originated.[29] One of kathak's three main stylistic lineages (*gharānās*) also developed in Rajasthan.[30] The form coalesced and artistically flourished in the lavish courts of Hindu maharajas and Mughal Nawabs from the sixteenth to the nineteenth centuries. Some maharajas promoted a syncretic

Hindu-Muslim culture, becoming great patrons of the visual and performing arts. During this period, kathak absorbed into its music and dance forms Persian and Islamic stylistic features. Dancers developed techniques that included mathematically sophisticated footwork and repertoire based on Urdu sung poems. The court structure patronized coteries of performing artists, including the celebrated and highly cultured courtesans.[31]

Kathak's status as an elevated art form waned during India's British colonial rule (1858–1947) because of the association of the courts as sites of lascivious behavior. In the early 1900s, kathak drew the attention of renowned European and American theatrical dancers such as Anna Pavlova and Ruth St. Denis, largely due to their tours to India and Indian artists' tours to Europe and the United States, particularly that of Indian-born art student, turned self-made dancer-choreographer Uday Shankar. Experimentation in combining classical Indian dance genres with other dance styles occurred in the early 1920s and many point to Uday Shankar as India's first modern choreographer and dancer as well as contributor to the renaissance of classical Indian dance within India and abroad during the 1930s.[32] After the end of colonial rule, the government of India began to recognize and reshape its artistic cultural treasures, and by 1952 endorsed kathak as one of the official classical dances of India. Kathak has undergone enormous changes in the last few decades due to India's loosing restrictions on international trade, expansions of communication networks and technology, and a saturation of media and consumer culture. Notions of "innovation" and "fusion" have inundated Indian dance communities as dancers with foundational training in classical dance reach for a new modernity. Noted kathak scholar Pallabi Chakravorty explains:

> The new discourse on globalization and innovation is resulting in many new experimental and collaborative ventures that go beyond the rigid classicism of the past. Several innovative choreographies, both in India and in the diaspora, now include intercultural fusions or cross-styles such as Kathak and Tap, Flamenco, or modern dance ... among classical dancers, "innovation" within tradition is the new catchword to attract the new kind of audience. The word captures the spirit of the shifting terrain where India's new modernity is being renegotiated.[33]

Historical Roots: Flamenco

Historians debate the history and development of flamenco quite aggressively. Commonplace perceptions tend to over romanticize and elevate certain features while diminishing others. Because of this, general understanding of flamenco history is often at odds with academic interpretations.[34] Flamenco's history is often and reductively divided into two significant historical moments: the ethnic and social groups that impacted the art form, and the modernist artists who transported it from the pueblos and small urban corners of Andalusia to the global stage. Although flamenco song and dance forms blended stylistic elements from earlier cultural influences, flamenco did not materialize as an art form until the nineteenth century, long after the end of Islamic Moorish rule in Spain when in 1492 the Nasrid dynastic leader Abu Abdalla Mohammad XII ("Boabdil") surrendered Granada to the Catholic monarchs Ferdinand and Isabella. During Muslim rule in southern Spain, generically referred to as Al-Andalus, many believe that Sephardic Jews, Muslims, Christians, and Gitanos lived a short period of generally peaceful coexistence (*La Convivencia*), and that Andalusia prospered culturally and economically.[35] Yet, decades later, the lingering repercussions of post–Inquisition Spain's political and economic upheaval spawned an illiterate and poverty-stricken population in Andalusia, consisting of impoverished Andalusians and persecuted and oppressed Gitanos.[36] Many assert that flamenco emerged from these anguished human conditions.

Popular history, fueled by European Romanticism, mythologizes a "Golden Age" of flamenco. Between the late nineteenth and early twentieth centuries, wealthier people who once shunned flamenco and its "bawdy" lifestyle began to embrace it as a means of counteracting the repressive societal norms of middle class life.[37] As flamenco developed, it expanded from private community gatherings to lucrative nightclub stages called *cafés cantantes* (singing cafés). Here, Andalusian songs became "Gypsified" (*gitanizado*) and Gypsy dances "andalusianized" (*andaluzado*)—or as informants described to me, "non–Gypsified" (*engachonado*).[38] Over the years, different social and political groups seeking a form of expression popularized the malleable form of flamenco.[39]

By the late twentieth and early twenty-first centuries, artists sharing a deep interest in Andalusian Spanish and Gitano culture incorporated dances from these traditions as material for modernist expression. According to performance theorist Ninotchka Devorah Bennahum, the first of these modernist choreographic and dramaturgical innovators was Antonia Mercé, "La Argentina" (1888–1936), who became instrumental before the Spanish Civil War in "developing a syntactical, feminist choreography rooted in Gitano flamenco dance and fused with the Spanish 'new school' compositions. La Argentina was followed by Vicente Escudero, Encarnacion Lopez, La Argentinita, Pilar Lopez, and Jose Greco, all of whom on stage and screen contributed to a global circulation of ideas in the press and published literature about the significance of flamenco as the people's art.... Flamenco artists became increasingly sophisticated, reflecting on the global stage a search both for possible aesthetic and geographic origins, as well as an artistic interest in new vocabularies of the body."[40]

Following thirty-six years of dictatorship and censorship under General Francísco Franco (1939–1975), Spain experienced a cultural renaissance that continued to flourish until it joined the European Economic Union in 1986. To adapt to a changing artist mentality and public demand, flamenco strived to become a "popular" genre aimed not just at a minority of connoisseurs but new audiences with younger generations.[41] This propelled tremendous change in dance style, choreographic structure, and production design. It also spawned new genres and collaborations with international artists. Old artistic and ideological debates about what constitutes authentic flamenco (*flamenco puro*) intensified. Flamenco historian Gerhard Steingress noted, "As a reaction to the growing dissidence in flamenco during the seventies, flamencologists and flamenco fans expressed their disapproval by considering any kind of fusion as the effect of the influences of 'foreign music fashions.'"[42] Consequently, flamenco artists began to search for musical elements and traditions that were associated more closely with the origins of flamenco.[43] The search for origins pointed to the Gitanos, specifically to their "Oriental" heritage. Looking to flamenco's "roots" of Eastern ancestry impels us to look at the "routes" crisscrossing India to Spain—the threads, however frayed, that tie kathak to flamenco. Despite being an ambiguous cross-cultural link, it is one that many kathak-flamenco collaborations depend upon.

Historical Routes Between Kathak and Flamenco

Intrigued by how two dance styles so geographically remote from one another share so many visual features, dance critics, historians, and performers often point to the Gypsies (Gitano or Roma) as the source. I have named this "The Gypsy Link Theory," which weaves actual facts with romantic imagination to create a seamless explanation that lacks critical examination.[44] It highlights the knowledge that the Roma migrated from northwest India (specifically, the states of Punjab and Rajasthan) but also presumes that these Roma practiced kathak and thus carried with them when migrating westward to Spain concrete movements that entered into flamenco.[45] There are two main problems with this theory.[46] While it is known that aspects of Rajasthani folk dances influenced kathak, there exists at this time no evidence that Indian Roma dances specifically influenced the form. Furthermore, there are many peripatetic tribes in Rajasthan that get mixed in with those who have actual Roma genetics, thus further obscuring the understanding. More important, footwork is the element most often used as proof of the link between kathak and flamenco, yet footwork did not develop as part of kathak until after the sixteenth century, long after the Roma left India in a series of migrations spanning the fifth through ninth centuries.[47]

Another theory that could explain the reasons for some kathak and flamenco similarities is what I have termed in previous works as "The Muslim-link Theory."[48] This theory, which is rarely acknowledged in texts describing kathak and flamenco historical connections, relates to the Muslim expansion. The spread of Islam from Arabia occurred in waves, with one migration radiating westward and culminating in the founding of the Moorish Empire in southern Spain (Al-Andalus) in 711, and another emanating eastward, resulting in the formation of the Mughal Empire in north India in 1526.[49] Sharing a similar lineage, both dynasties cultivated the arts and offered patronage to performing artists in their courts. Although written accounts attach Muslim cultural influence to both kathak and flamenco, hypotheses that dance influences are responsible for the bridge between kathak and flamenco are rarely considered. Ethnomusicologist Peter Manuel considers that kathak and flamenco dance represent outer boundaries of a vast but stylistically linked realm, one which shares some commonalities with classical and popular Persian and Middle Eastern dance and music.[50]

Choreographic Alignments

Within the spectrum of global dance partnerships, kathak-flamenco collaborations are unique in that the two dance forms are diachronically and synchronically aligned (although the diachronic elements are conjectural). Kathak is presented as flamenco's older sibling, with north India being a symbol of the Gitano's lost place of origin—the diachronic alignment. From a flamenco perspective, kathak represents one link to flamenco roots. Curiously, in the publicity for several kathak-flamenco performances that I analyzed, the Gypsy-link narrative is used as a selling point. Titles and program descriptions such as "India to Spain—Roma/Gypsy concert"[51] or "The Gitanos who wandered away from Rajasthan in India took the Flamenco with them to Andalusia"[52] imply the veracity of this link, yet the performances do not actually communicate that narrative choreographically. Nonetheless, flamenco artists themselves see similarities to kathak and often recount the tale of this historical link. In an interview with the late Gitano choreographer Mario Maya, who appeared along with kathak guru Birju Maharaj in the 1992 film *On the Edge: Improvisation in Music*, Maya states, "The subconscious influences we [the Gitanos] brought with us date back to India because we emigrated from there centuries ago. And though we've lived here for five hundred years, it's still possible to see Hindu influences. There is the way we move our hands, and the sounds we make [shows finger-snapping]. The way our feet are deeply rooted in the soil, always touching the ground just like Indian kathak. Always in counterpoint, always improvising in cross-rhythms."[53]

Baltanás describes how, with a loss of national independence and increasing value placed on the wider European Union, Spain is developing a "new flamenco tend[ing] towards a great universality, towards an international and cosmopolitan expansion; but at the same time this new flamenco keeps inventing its own set of identities, either from the classic and well-known groups (Gypsy, Jewish, Moorish, Christians, etc.), or from additional, ad hoc ones."[54] I would argue that one of the "ad hoc identities" is this Gitano-tribal link to Rajasthan, India, and the notion of tangible elements entering into flamenco.[55]

Emphasizing visual and rhythmic similarities, kathak and flamenco can also appear alongside each other creating, as Anderson stated, "an idiom of sibling competition rather than inheritance"—the synchronic alignment. For flamenco, kathak offers a link to the past; for kathak, flamenco offers a gateway to the future, to modernity, and to wider recognition. Flamenco becomes a mechanism for kathak to acquire a more universal appeal, similar to that which flamenco has enjoyed for some time.[56]

In asking kathak guru Birju Maharaj about his collaboration with Mario Maya, I was struck by how he focused on formal structures rather than historical connections as Maya had. He noted shared footwork technique and rhythms, but because the feet are adorned with *gunguroos* (bells) versus hard-soled shoes, very different sounds are produced.[57] While on tour in the United States, Maharaj's closest disciple, Saswati Sen, expressed a desire to bring kathak into "the mainstream."[58] Despite Birju Maharaj's "star status" in India, his U.S. tours are largely organized at a grassroots level by and for the Indian diaspora communities. I understood Sen's interest in bringing kathak into the "mainstream" to mean expanding its appeal outside of the Indian community. The Italian kathak dancer Rosella Fanelli shared a similar desire to extend kathak's appeal. Describing a collaboration she worked on with flamenco dancers, she said, "besides the artistic challenge [of our collaboration], I also wanted to use this as a private challenge to bring more people into the theatre because here in Italy kathak is very new; it's not popular like flamenco. And in fact I had the [theatre] packed for all the shows."[59]

These two alignments are further epitomized in similar types of concert titles I have seen used multiple times within the past ten years: *Kathak Meets Flamenco* (usually produced by Indian kathak dancers), and *Memories of India* (produced by flamencos). Here we perceive kathak going *to* somewhere, and flamenco as coming *from* somewhere. In one there is a motion forward, in the other a motion backward.

The uniqueness of kathak-flamenco collaborations rests in their ability to be both diachronically and synchronically aligned. For kathak, the alignment to flamenco serves as a hope for a more accessible, mainstream, and global future, or as Chakrovorty describes, "to belong to a 'public modernity' that includes transnational and global communities."[60] In flamenco, the alignment to kathak acts as a nostalgic link to the past—one that reinitiates an old need to (re)discover roots. The metaphor of "the Gypsy originating in India" becomes a symbol of distinctiveness in a time of blurred identities where the "idea and existence of nations is threatened on all sides."[61] Kathak and flamenco collaborations expose aspects of each dance's cultural history and each community's quests for distinctiveness in a swiftly changing globalized world.[62]

Notes

1. See Nigerian novelist Chimamande Adichie, "The Danger of a Single Story," TED Talks: TED Conferences LLC, TEDGlobal 2009, http://www.ted.com/talks/chimamanda_adichie_the_danger_of_a_single_story.html (accessed February 15, 2014).
2. Helena Wulff, "Ethereal Expression: Paradoxes of Ballet as a Global Physical Culture," *Ethnography* 9, no. 4 (2008): 518–535.
3. Amrapali Ambegaokar appeared on Season 5 of *So You Think You Can Dance*, https://www.youtube.com/watch?v=O9AxyLY3iRo (accessed January 18, 2014). She won a Solo Silver Medal in NBC's *Superstars of Dance* and performed on NBC's *Today Show* and *The Tonight Show with Jay Leno* [http://www.imdb.com/name/nm1728201/bio?ref_=nm_ov_bio_sm]. Amrapali is the daughter of Anjani Ambegaokar, a prominent kathak guru based in southern California, who, along with Pandit Chitresh Das, based in northern California, established the first large-scale kathak schools in the United States.
4. Miriam Sarada Phillips, "Becoming the Floor/Breaking the Floor: Experiencing the Kathak-Flamenco Connection," *Ethnomusicology* 57, no. 3 (Fall 2013): 405.
5. Deborah Jowitt, "Squeezing Out All the Good Drops," *The Village Voice*, April 11, 1974.
6. Himani Pande, "Delightful Jugalbandi: Kathak and Flamenco," *The Times of India*, December 18, 1987.
7. *MC2: Saison 13–14*, promotional brochure (Grenoble, France, Season 2013–2014): 76 (author's translation), http://www.mc2grenoble.fr/media/client/saison/13-14-brochure-formulaire_bdef.pdf (accessed January 15, 2014).
8. The kathak comparisons I make to flamenco are based on the kathak repertoire known as *nrtta* (pure dance) rather than the storytelling forms. For more detailed movement analyses, including comparisons to choreographic structure, see Miriam Phillips, "Both Sides of the Veil: A Comparative Analysis of Kathak and Flamenco Dance" (PhD diss., University of California, Los Angeles, 1991).
9. Ibid.; see also Miriam Phillips, "Becoming the Floor/Breaking the Floor," 396–427.
10. While further research is necessary to know if Uday Shankar and Vicente Escudero ever collaborated on a theatrical production, historical accounts document both artists touring in the same places during roughly the same time period. Judith Chazin-Bennahum recounts how Rene Blum, the artistic director of the noted French theatre Théâtre de Monte Carlo, brought dance companies, such as those of Uday Shankar and Vicente Escudero, to Monte Carlo in 1931. See Judith Chazin-Bennahum, *Rene Blum and The Ballets Russes: In Search of a Lost Life* (Oxford: Oxford University Press, 2011), 101. Additionally, the Russian émigré Sol Hurok, a leading American-based performing arts impresario and manager, also brought Shankar and Escudero to the United States (see Dance Heritage Coalition's "100 Dance Treasures: Sol Hurok, http://www.danceheritage.org/hurok.html). Curiously, Spanish film director Jaime Chavarri is currently producing a film that centers on Shankar and Escudero. He describes the film, *Sangam*: "The film, apart from depicting the Indian dance and Flamenco dance, will also have a fictional love story of Flamenco dancer Vicente Escudero and Indian dancer Uday Shankar with a girl called Kala. "Our film 'Sangam' will also have a little fictional angle to it when Vincente Escudero who had visited Rajasthan to go deeper into the roots of Flamenco dance which he believed originated India." See *IFFI Daily*, Goa, India: 41st International Film Festival of India, (November 29, 2010), 5, (http://iffi.nic.in/akalpdf/iffidaily29112010.pdf (accessed June 10, 2014). Both Christine Leboutte, a musician in the 2014 touring kathak-flamenco production TOROBAKA, and Spanish film director Carlos Saura recounted to me recently about a film in production with a similar story line (personal communications with the author, June 27–28, 2014). I wait to see if it is the same film as Chavarri's; Saura and Chavarri have worked together in the past.
11. Some of the more prominent productions include the following. Foremost kathak guru Birju Maharaj and acclaimed Gitano choreographer, the late Mario Maya, worked on a production related to their appearance in *On the Edge: Improvisation in Music, Part 2* (Harcourt Films Production, 1992); this film, part of a four-part series made for U.K. public broadcasting, traced the effects of migration (mostly musical) on improvising links across continents. Indian-born, U.K.-based kathak dancers Pratap and Priya Pawar collaborated on the kathak-flamenco piece *Jugalbandi* in the late 1980s with U.K. flamenco dancer

Juani Garcia, who trained in Spain; this work blossomed into larger-scale productions, which toured cities in the United Kingdom with the titles "Flames and Fire" and "Heritage." Toronto-based kathak dancer Joanna De Souza and flamenco dancer Esmeralda Enrique created "Old Roads/New World" in 1996 with the follow-up performance "Firedance" in 1999. Italian-born kathak dancer Rosella Fanelli created "Journey of the Rhythm from India to Spain" in 2006 with Reina Lopez ("La Blanca") and Massimiliano de Pasquale. In 2009, the Polish musical group "Indialucia" participated in a kathak-flamenco collaborative production at the *Festival des Andalousies Atlantiques* in Morocco with artists from Geneva, Switzerland. In 2008, American-born kathak dancer Janaki Patrik and Egyptian-American flamenco and Middle Eastern dancer and singer La Conja created *Andalusia Hindustan: A Kathak-Flamenco Duet*, performed in New York. La Conja is one of several prolific dance artists to negotiate these movement languages and since 2008 has performed with kathak dancers at prominent venues in New York City and recently in Mumbai, India, with a series of Indian Kathak dancers. In 2012, the production *Las Huellas* ("The Footprints") appeared in Seville in Spain's largest flamenco festival, *El Bienal de flamenco*, featuring world-renowned Gitana artist La Farruquita and Indian kathak dancer Anu Arjun Misra. In 2014, two more large-scale productions were underway. *TOROBAKA*, by choreographers Akram Kahan (kathak) and Israel Galván (flamenco), though known for their work in contemporary interpretations of their traditions, had its world premiere in Grenoble, France, on June 2, 2014, and its Spanish premiere on June 27, 2014, in Madrid. Currently in production is a performance and film project related to kathak and flamenco interchanges by internationally acclaimed Spanish film director Carlos Saura (known for his flamenco dance trilogy: *Blood Wedding* [1991], *Carmen* [1983], and *Love, the Magician* [1986]). On September 27–28, 2014, Pandit Chitresh Das and Antonio Hidalgo Paz performed *Yatra: A Journey from India to Spain*, in San Francisco.

12. In flamenco music, this notion is referred to as *mestizaje* or "crossbreeding." See Gerhard Steingress, "Flamenco Fusion and New Flamenco as Postmodern Phenomena. An Essay on Creative Ambiguity in Popular Music," in *Songs of the Minotaur—Hybridity and Popular Music in the Era of Globalization*, ed. Gerhard Steingress (Münster, Germany: Lit Verlag, 2002), 171.

13. Ketu Katrak, *Contemporary Indian Dance: New Creative Choreography in India and the Diaspora* (New York: Palgrave Macmillan, 2011), xix, 6.

14. Steingress, "Flamenco Fusion and New Flamenco as Postmodern Phenomena," 175–176.

15. Program notes, TOROBAKA, XXXI Festival de Otoño a Primavera, Teatros del Canal, Madrid, Spain, June 27, 2014 (author's translation). Performance theorist Ninotchka Devorah Bennahum believes that productions such as this are the inheritors of the early twentieth-century experiments of Antonia Mercé ("La Argentina"). She describes the process as "Brechtian—the further away, the closer you come" (personal communication with the author, August 5, 2014). I believe that in addition to Mercé, other noted Indian choreographers also paved the way for contemporary artists to explore these types of hybrid productions, namely Uday Shankar (1900–1977), who created some of the earliest large-scale theatrical stagings of Indian dance, and Chandralekha (1928–2006), pioneer of the new Contemporary Indian Dance movement of which Akram Khan is beneficiary.

16. For example, see Pratap and Priya Pawar quartet with flamenco dancers, http://www.youtube.com/watch?v=Sf92tX7usnk&feature=related (accessed February 1, 2014).

17. Esmeralda Enrique, personal communication with the author, February 1, 2014. "Firedance" was the name of the collective between Esmeralda Enrique and Joanna DeSouza, and also the name of one of their choreographic works. See *Firedance: Kathak/Flamenco collaboration*, https://www.youtube.com/watch?v=FoNjpIezVVQ (accessed January 20, 2014).

18. Catalina Fellay-Dunbar, "Firedance: Sharing a Flame Between Flamenco and Kathak," (proceedings, Canadian Dance Studies Conference 2012: "Collaboration: Intersections, Negotiations, Mediations in the Worlds of Dance," Toronto, Society for Canadian Dance Studies, April 14, 2013).

19. Stacey Prickett, "Tradition and Innovation in Cross-Cultural Creativity: Defying Britain's Tick-Box Culture: Kathak in Dialogue with Hip-Hop," *Dance Research Journal* 30, no. 2 (2012): 169.

20. Pallabi Chakravorty, "Dancing into Modernity: Multiple Narratives of India's Kathak Dance," *Dance Research Journal* 38, no. 1/2 (Summer–Winter, 2006): 128.

21. Jason Samuels Smith, cited in Darrah Carr, "Rhythm Mash-Ups: Percussive Dance Hybrids Send New Sounds Across Globe," *Dance Magazine* (May 2010): 30–31. Tap dancer Smith collaborated with kathak dancer Pandit Chitresh Das on *India Jazz Suites: Kathak Meets Tap*, which debuted in 2008.

22. Benedict Anderson, *Imagined Communities: Reflections on the Origins and Spread of Nationalism*, rev. ed. (1983; London: Verso, 2006), 187–192.

23. Ibid., 187.

24. Barbara Browning, *Samba: Resistance in Motion* (Bloomington: Indiana University Press, 1995).

25. Anderson, *Imagined Communities*, 187–188.

26. Kathleen Spanos, personal communication with the author, March 24, 2014.

27. Another example of a synchronically aligned collaboration is when two different dance cultures share a religious ideal or traditional text, such as in the production *Heritage* (2010), a collaboration between San Francisco Bay Area companies Gamelan Sekar Jaya (Bali) and Abhinaya Dance Company

(south Indian *bharatanatyam*), based on the Hindu epic, the Ramayana. See http://www.gsj.org/content/heritage-gsj-performs-abhinaya-dance-company-sunday-oct-24-4pm (accessed January 6, 2014). In working on this essay, I began to consider that there perhaps is a third alignment that has sprung up in relation to artistic collaborations due to massive culture shifts in the way people behave and interact with others, especially related to social media. Although this is the subject of another paper, I wish to note the idea here. I have observed collaborations containing new and unusual pairings of dance styles cropping up that explore social issues shared by particular groups of people in ways that were never possible before (for example, stereotyping, prejudice, identity, belonging, diaspora, women, people of color, and so on) as exemplified in productions such as *Kathakbox*, which integrated kathak, hip-hop, African Caribbean, and contemporary dance to "explore around, inside and between the 'boxes' we use to define art forms/ourselves." See Prickett, "Tradition and Innovation in Cross-Cultural Creativity," 170.

28. While this is basic common knowledge written about in most historical texts on kathak, two sources that offer more details are Norvin Hein, *The Miracle Plays of Mathura* (New Haven, CT: Yale University Press, 1972); and Mekhala Natavar, "New Dances, New Dancers, New Audiences: Shifting Rhythms in the Evolution of India's Kathak Dance" (PhD diss., University of Wisconsin, Madison, 1997).

29. *Gypsy*, a misnomer for the word "Egypt," is a derogatory term coined by sixteenth-century Europeans to indicate this group of dark-skinned people's supposed place of origin. While "Gypsies" in other countries, particularly those of Eastern Europe, prefer to identify themselves as Rom, Roma, or Romani (the latter being the name of their language), in Spain they tend to call themselves *Gitanos*, the Spanish word for Gypsies. For this essay, I use the terms Gypsy and Gitano interchangeably when referring to this ethnic group in Spain; however, when referring to Gypsy tribes in India, I use the term Roma (see also note 31).

30. For further detail, see Mekhala Natavar, "New Dances, New Dancers, New Audiences," 1997.

31. For a well-researched study on kathak, with specific details on the role courtesans played in the development of kathak and why their histories were erased, see Pallabi Chakravorty, *Bells of Change: Kathak Dance, Women and Modernity In India* (Calcutta and London: Seagull Books, 2008).

32. Joan L. Erdman, "Dance Discourses: Rethinking the History of the 'Oriental Dance'," in *Moving Words: Re-Writing Dance*, ed. Gay Morris (London and New York: Routledge, 1996); and "Who Remembers Uday Shankar?" http://www.mukto-mona.com/new_site/mukto-mona/Articles/jaffor/uday_shanka2.htm (accessed August 10, 2014).

33. Chakravorty, *Bells of Change*, 57, 87.

34. For critical reflections on the layered social nuances and historical debates within flamenco discourse, see Timothy J. Mitchell, *Flamenco Deep Song* (New Haven, CT: Yale University Press, 1994); Enrique Baltanás, "The Fatigue of the Nation: Flamenco as the Basis of Heretical Identities," in *Songs of the Minotaur—Hybridity and Popular Music in the Era of Globalization*, ed. Gerhard Steingress (Münster, Germany: Lit Verlag, 2002); and Steingress, "Flamenco Fusion and New Flamenco as Postmodern Phenomena," 2002. Also see Ninotchka Devorah Bennahum, *Carmen, a Gypsy Geography* (Middletown, CT: Wesleyan University Press, 2013), Chapter 4.

35. Vivian B. Mann, Thomas F. Glick, Jerrilynn D. Dodds, eds., *Convivencia: Jews, Muslims, and Christians in Medieval Spain* (New York: George Braziller and the Jewish Museum of New York, 1992 [reissue 2007]).

36. Bertha B. Quintana and Lois Gray Floyd, *!Qué gitano! Gypsies of Southern Spain, Case Studies in Cultural Anthropology* (New York: Holt, 1971).

37. Mitchell, *Flamenco Deep Song*, 1994.

38. *Gachó* is a name in Gitano argot for "non-Gypsy."

39. Baltanás, "The Fatigue of the Nation," 152.

40. Ninotchka Devorah Bennahum, personal communication with the author, August 5, 2014. See also Ninotchka Devorah Bennahum, *Antonia Merce, "La Argentina": Flamenco and the Spanish Avant Garde* (Middletown, CT: Wesleyan University Press, 2000).

41. Baltanás, "The Fatigue of the Nation," 156.

42. Steingress, "Flamenco Fusion and New Flamenco as Postmodern Phenomena," 200.

43. Ibid., 200.

44. Miriam Sarada Phillips, "Both Sides of the Veil: A Comparative Analysis of Kathak and Flamenco Dance" (master's thesis, University of California Los Angeles, 1991), 42–45.

45. Although linguistic and genetic studies commonly point to northwest India as the source of Roma origin, the specific histories of people identified as "Roma" or "Gypsy" are complex with divergent theories about exact origins and the social context for their departures from India.

46. For additional issues, see Phillips, "Both Sides of the Veil," 56–59; Phillips, "Becoming the Floor/Breaking the Floor," 415–418; and Bennahum, *Carmen*, 95–110.

47. There are also different opinions about when westward Roma migrations took place, although most use the range of fifth to ninth centuries, but some use as late as the fifteenth century. See Radu Iovițţă and Theodore G. Schurr, "Reconstructing the Origins and Migrations of Diasporic Populations: The Case of the European Gypsies," *American Anthropologist* 106, no. 2 (2004), 275–278; and Phillips, "Both Sides of the Veil," 42–45.

48. Phillips, "Both Sides of the Veil," 45–50.
49. For more information, see Ira M. Lapidus, *A History of Islamic Societies* (1988; Cambridge and New York: Cambridge University Press, 2002); and Bennahum, *Carmen*, 118–127.
50. Peter Manuel, personal communication with the author, 2011, cited in Phillips, "Becoming the Floor/Breaking the Floor," 418.
51. From a spring 2010 performance of Texas-based musician Oliver Rajamani, with dancers Olivia Chacon (flamenco) and Reetu Jain, who appears to be a hybrid Indian dancer mixing kathak with other classical and popular forms, http://www.youtube.com/watch?NR=1&feature=endscreen&v=Go7Cxmez EsA (accessed October 25, 2012).
52. From the Music Ensemble of Benares, http://www.benares-ensemble.de/benares-Kathak-flamenco-engl.html (accessed October 25, 2012).
53. *On the Edge: Improvisation in Music, Part 2: Movements in Time*, producer/director Jeremy Marre and writer/narrator, Derek Bailey (Harcourt Films Production, 1991).
54. Baltanás, "The Fatigue of the Nation," 159.
55. A performing arts festival in Rajasthan begun in 2012 further advances this link. Although not specifically kathak, The Jodhpur Flamenco and Gypsy Festival "aims to promote and nurture the ties between Rajasthani and Flamenco folk cultures" (http://jfgfestival.com/ (accessed March 15, 2014).
56. In a recent Google.com search (English language websites), the keywords "kathak dance" yielded 1,570,000 results, whereas "flamenco dance" generated 7,480,000 (accessed March 23, 2014).
57. Birju Maharaj, personal communication with the author, September 28, 2012.
58. Saswati Sen, personal communication with the author, September 28, 2012.
59. Rosella Fanelli, personal communication with the author, February 3, 2014.
60. Chakrovorty, *Bells of Change*, 15.
61. Baltanás, "The Fatigue of the Nation," 159.
62. Thanks to undergraduate research assistants, Aishwarya Subramanian for literature gathering, and Morgan R. Askew for her sharp editorial eye, and recognition to the University of Maryland's Center for Undergraduate Research that offered a gateway for them to find me. I give appreciation to Ana Farfán for lively dialogues on the CORD conference paper from which this essay developed, and I offer special gratitude to Sudesh Mantillake for being a resonant sounding board to my preliminary ideas and for his astute reflections. Thanks to fellow dancers Rosella Fanelli, Joanna DeSouza, and Esmeralda Enrique for providing contextual background and for their enthusiasm to relive their kathak-flamenco collaborations in response to my questions. And always, with awe and gratitude, to my teachers, Pandit Birju Maharaj, Saswati Sen, and La Familia Farruco, among others, whose spirits, teachings, and wisdom fall out of my body on every page I write.

From the *Jácara* to the *Sarabande*
Ana Yepes

In the sixteenth and seventeenth centuries, *Jácara* was a brief poetic composition: the *entr'acte Jácara* (*Jácara entremesada*) was a ballad that made up part of a theatrical performance.[1] "Jácara" also signified the characters—the *jacos*, or ruffians—depicted in those works. In addition, it referred to a *son* (musical genre) that was sometimes danced. Not least, it was a *baile* (dance) associated with the *Zarabanda* (see Table 1).[2] In this essay, I discuss three complete extant choreographies of the Jácara. The first two are compositions by the dance masters Juan Antonio Jaque and Francesc Olivelles, respectively, and the third is taken from an anonymous manuscript of the late seventeenth century.

In his *Tesoro de la lengua castellana* of 1611, Sebastian de Covarrubias gives the etymology of the word "jácara": "those who play chess"; from "Jaque," and in criminal slang, "ruffian."[3] In his play *El Rufián dichoso* (*The Lucky Ruffian*) of 1615, Miguel de Cervantes Saavedra describes the Jácara universe. His character Lagartija mentions a "jácaro" song sung "in a rare and jaco style," and later describes how, from the great tenement of the Olmos, "the *jacarandina* of knaves, / emerges Reguilete the jaque / marvelously attired."[4] Juan de Esquivel Navarro, in *Discursos sobre el arte del dançado* (*Treatise on the Art of Dancing*) (1642), says that the Jácara and the Zarabanda are "pieces" danced in schools, and that "the *Rastro*, Jácara, Zarabanda, and *Tárraga* ... are one and the same thing; even if the Rastro has its different *mudanzas* (a sequence of dance steps) and a different style.[5] This reference leads to the important insight that the Jácara and the Zarabanda are "the same."

In the mid-seventeenth century, the Jácara was a son, a musical genre. Sebastián Rodríguez de Villaviciosa, in his *entremés* (a short comic piece performed during theatrical interludes in sixteenth- and seventeenth-century Spain) titled *Extremés de los Sones* (1661), mentions "melodies that carry the air of ... the Castilian Jácara." Calderón de la Barca, in his 1669 *Loa para la Compañia de Escamilla* ("loa" is an introductory monologue or dialogue) for Antonio de Escamilla's company, says, "the Jácara being the tone, from *Gallarda* are the steps."[6] But in José de Cañizares's "Mojiganga de los Sones" (a *mojiganga* was a short burlesque satire, often performed to music) of 1701, the Jácara had not lost its associations with the underworld: "Out comes the Jácara with *mantilla* (lace shawl typical of a Spanish gentlewoman) and a dagger and castanets."[7]

In the *Diccionario de la lengua castellana* (1726), the Real Academia Española described the interwoven meanings of Jácara as referring to the ruffian world, to a musical genre, and to a dance form:

> *Xácara.* f.f. Poetic composition.... Much used in the singing of same among those known as *"jaques,"* from whom the name could be taken.... Also understood to mean the *tañido* (strumming pattern on a guitar) that is played for singing or dancing.... Also refers to a kind of *danza* (dance); fashioned to the tañido or son belonging to the Jácara.... Also understood to mean the gathering of young people, and happy people, who walk about by night making noise and singing in the streets. Said because they generally walk about singing some Jácara.[8]

By 1793, Felipe Roxo de Flores in his *Tratado de recreación instructiva sobre la danza* listed the Jácara among dances of which "there is no other memory than that of their name."[9]

Table 1: Sources for the *Jácara*

Year	Author	Title	Reason
1611	Sebastian de Covarrubias Orozco	*Tesoro de la lengua castellana*	origin of the name
1615	Miguel de Cervantes Saavedra	*El Rufián dichoso*	origin of the name
1642	Juan de Esquivel Navarro	*Discursos sobre el arte del danzado*	cited as a "piece" danced in the dancing school; Zarabanda family
1661	Sebastián de Villaviciosa	*Entremés de los Sones*	cited as a "dance"
1669	Calderón de la Barca	*Loa para la Compañía de Escamilla*	cited
ca. 1680	Juan Antonio Jaque	*Libro de danzar*	choreography
ca. 1680	Anonymous	*Jácara*	choreography
1701	Choreography Francesc Olivelles, transcribed by his pupil Joseph de Potau y de Ferran	*Memoria de las danzas*	choreography
1701	José de Cañizares	*Mojiganga de los Sones*	cited as a character
1726 ff.	Real Academia	*Diccionario de la lengua castellana (Diccionario de Autoridades*	complete definition
1793	Felipe Roxo de Flores	*Tratado de recreación instructive sobre la danza*	disappearance

Three Jácara *Choreographies*

There are three known choreographies of Jácaras, two from the end of the seventeenth century and a third from 1701 (see Table 2):

Table 2: Three *Jácara* Choreographies

Author	Date	Distribution and context	Instructions for arms	Instructions for space
Jaque	ca. 1680	—For one person? For a man? —A school choreography?	no	yes
Anonymous	ca. 1680	—For one person? For a lady? For a couple? —A theater choreography?	yes	yes
Olivelles	1701	For a couple? —A ballroom dance or school choreography?	no	yes

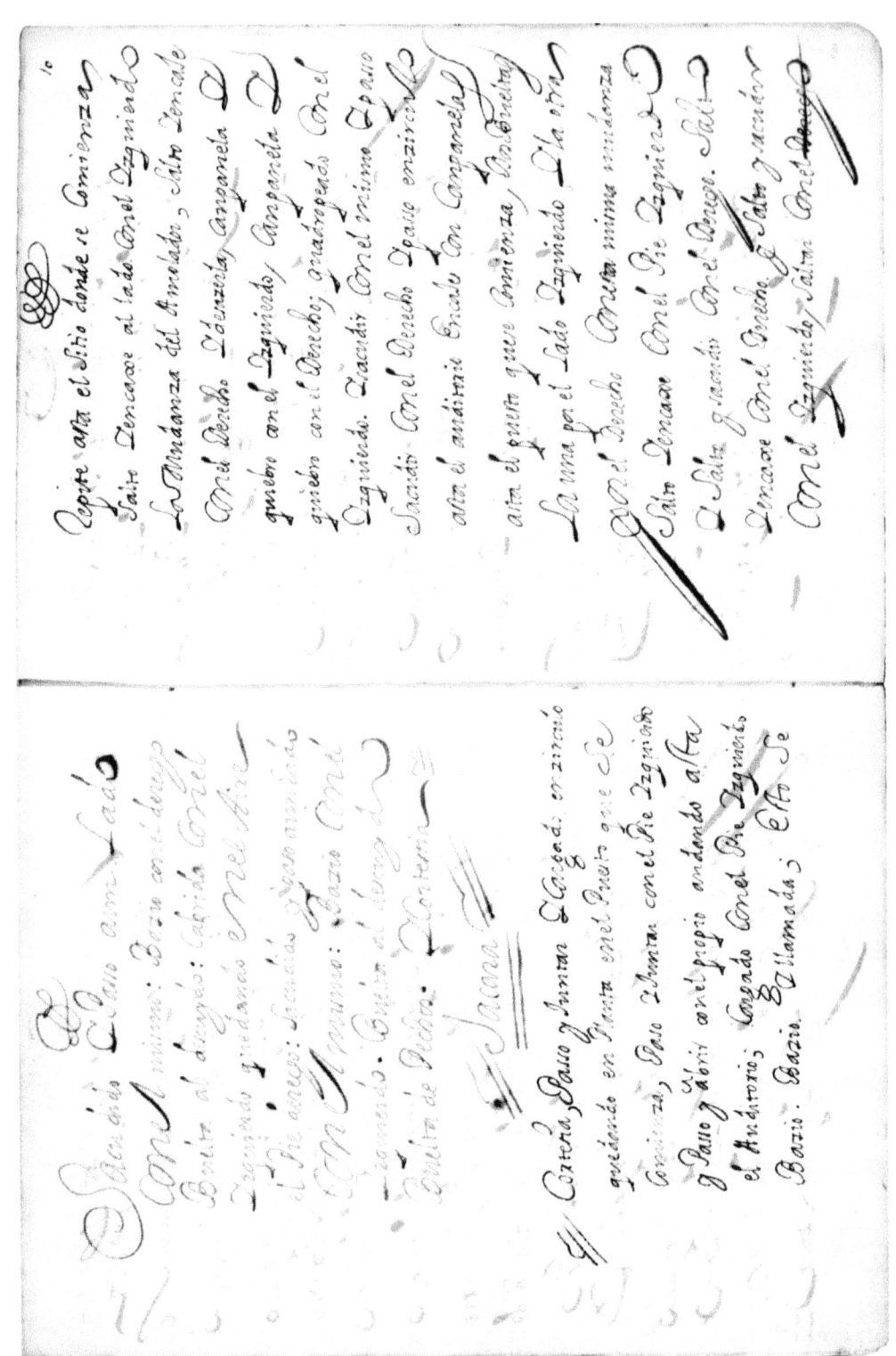

Figure 1: "Jácara," excerpt from *Libro de danzar de Don Baltasar de Rojas Pantojah*, by Juan Antonio Jaque, 1680 (collection of Ana Yepes).

All three choreographies present the dilemma of having no corresponding music and not a single rhythmic instruction that specifies the beat to which the steps need to be executed—nor do they include the quantity of steps that each mudanza comprises.[10] These missing elements create considerable obstacles for those attempting to reconstruct the dances in question. Nevertheless, a common feature of these Jácaras is the inclusion of some spatial instructions, an extraordinary exception among recorded dance works of this period (see Figure 1).

Figure 1 shows the first of two pages of Jaque's description of the "Jácara" in his *Libro de danzar* of c. 1680. It includes a list of steps and some instructions for the use of space, but there is no reference to the movement of arms. The use of several technically complicated steps, such as the *vueltas de pecho* (in the seventeenth century they were turning *saltos*, or jumps), leads me to believe that this choreography could only be for a man, and is, therefore, a choreography taught in a dance academy. Here are some extracts from this choreography:

> *Cortesía, paso*, and *juntar* and *cargado* in a circle ending in *planta* at the starting place, paso and juntar with the left foot and paso and *abrir* with same walking toward the hall, cargado with the left foot *vacío*, vacío and *llamada*, this being repeated until back at the starting place.[11]
>
> ... paso and *romper* and paso and romper with the other in a circle until back in the starting place.[12]

A small series of steps is repeated several times, creating a pattern in the space. This form of choreography is found only in the "Jácara" and the "Paradetas," which are the only extant choreographies by Jaque that contain spatial instructions. The others are simply lists of steps. In his "Jácara," Jaque mentions a specific mudanza, the *mudanza del amolador* (the knife grinder's move):

> salto and *encaje* to the side with the left, the mudanza del amolador, salto and encaje with the right and *deshacerla* [do the mudanza on the other side].[13]

This passage suggests that this mudanza was a variation known by everyone. The *amolador* was a person who sharpened knives with a pedal-operated grindstone. The same mudanza appears in Jaque's "Paradetas." In 1745, Ferriol y Boxeraus describes the mudanza del amolador as part of the series of movements used in *contradanzas* (the Spanish variant of English country dances taken up by French dancing masters in the late seventeenth century):

> The amolador consists of making circles with the hand and index finger, at the same time that the foot on the same side lowers and lifts, while also imitating with the mouth the sound that the stone makes in this practice.[14]

Ferriol incorporated this mudanza into the figure called "*Redonda* [Round] 7": "the first couple dances *floreo*, and, grasping hands, makes a circle, the amolador, and a circle back to the same spot."[15]

El Amolador was also the title and subject of an entremés of 1643 by Luis Quiñones de Benavente, in which Juana, a noblewoman, says,

> Ageda, then you know me, / nothing need I say: / my whole life has been hurly-burly / since the day I was born. / With *rastreadas mudanzas* (Rastro [a dance]-type variations) / and *chaconil* (Chacona [a dance]-like) spirit / I will dance for forty days / without eating or sleeping.[16]

Philologist and folklorist Margit Frenk gives this chorus from the *Baile de el Amolador*, illustrating the sexual suggestiveness of the grinding motion: "Oh, grinder, dear little grinder! / Oh, sharpen me that knife!"[17] Cotarelo y Mori remarks that many French knife grinders roamed about Spain in the seventeenth century; perhaps this indicates another level of reference—to the long-standing aesthetic and political rivalry between Spain and France, and to Spain's view of French sexual mores, implicit in this mudanza.[18]

"Jácara," Anonymous (c. 1680)

This "Jácara" is an undated manuscript that composer and music theorist Francisco Asenjo Barbieri copied from a book in the library of his friend Don José de Sancho Rayón, noting that the handwriting was from the end of the seventeenth century.[19] The anonymous author, in addition to listing steps, indicates paths and positions in space and describes a few very precise arm movements.

Some feminine past participles might indicate that the dancer was a woman: "until you end in half-profile" or "stay in place turned in profile" (unfortunately, these gendered participles are impossible to render in English translation), but they might simply refer more generally to *"una persona"* (a person), which in Spanish is "feminine."[20] I do not know whether this choreography was for one person or two. Only at one point does the text suggest there might be two dancers: "and undo it [the mudanza] with *voladillo*, passing in front."[21] This spatial instruction conjures the idea of passing in front of someone, an indication that a couple might be dancing, although there is no specification as to whether the couple consists of a man and a woman or two women. The fact that women didn't dance in schools, along with the presence of some stage directions in the manuscript, leads me to speculate that this choreography could well be a theater baile.

I see some similarities to the two other Jácaras here: in the anonymous choreography, a series of steps is performed while on a fixed path, and the formula for performing mudanzas is also followed. However, the steps mentioned in this Jácara are quite different from those described by Jaque. It contains some new steps that are repeated, such as several *quiebros* in succession that are danced to the same side. Such steps do not appear in earlier Jácaras. An example of one such a new mudanza is that of *"el borracho"* ("the drunkard"):

> [A]nd the *mudanza del borracho* all around and on arriving at the starting place, the mudanza of arms in and out entering the right foot back and putting it out making a circle all around until holding in profile the left shoulder up.[22]

"Jácara," by Olivelles (1701)

This manuscript was found recently in the archives of the Barcelona Library. I am currently working through it and reconstructing its dances. Like Jaque's "Jácara" of circa 1680, Olivelles' "Jácara" consists of a list of steps, a few instructions for the use of space, and no reference to arm movements. It contains many steps identical to those described by Esquivel in 1642, and to those that we encounter in Jaque, including similar phrase combinations of steps. We know, however, that this choreography was meant for a couple. Therefore, I believe it is more of a society baile. Olivelles' "Jácara" states:

Jácara begins with the man at one end of the room and the lady at the other, and in front of her making two pasos to one side, and *romper en el aire*, and a *cuatropeado*, and *media* [*cabriola*?], and change place with two pasos and romper en el aire and change place with cuatropeado, and media or a vacío afterwards.[23]

This choreography is the only Jácara in which a dancing pair is mentioned.

The Zarabanda

Numerous sources discuss the possible origins of the Zarabanda but, unfortunately, I have not found a Zarabanda choreography from seventeenth-century Spain.[24] In *Le tour du monde*, financier Baron Charles Davillier, who toured Spain in 1862, accompanied by illustrator Gustave Doré, describes how, as in Esquivel's day (1642), and despite evidence in Roxo de Flores (1793), that the Jácara survived in name only. Jácara and Zarabanda were still identified with each other in popular tradition, hinting that Jácara may have survived into the nineteenth century:

> The songs that accompany the Zarabanda [orig. Sarabande] had different names, such as Jácaras, *Letrillas* (short verses), *Romances* (ballads), *Villancicos* (folk songs), etc. These popular poetic forms, a fair number of which have made their way to us today, were not well defined and, in general, only the refrain that was occasionally repeated with each verse gave an indication of how they would end.[25]

This explanation corroborates Esquivel's reference to the Jácara and the Zarabanda as being related insofar as they were one and the same form.

The same author quotes the Countess d'Aulnoy from her book *Voyage en Espagne en 1679*, in which she describes seeing a Zarabanda ["Sarabande"] being danced:

> The Entre'actes were intermingled with dances to the sound of the harps and guitars: The actors had castanets, and a little hat on their heads, without which they never dance, and then 'tis a Sarabande; they seem not to walk, they slip along so lightly. Their manner is wholly different from ours: they move too much their arms and often pass their hands [over] their hats and face, and that with no ill grace; they play admirably well on the castanets.[26]

Countess d'Aulnoy's description of actress-dancers moving their arms above their heads is similar to the arm movements described in the contemporaneous anonymous "Jácara" (the only couple dance) of circa 1680. It also confirms that castanets were played as part of the Zarabanda. From these sources, I conclude that the seventeenth-century Jácara and Zarabanda were bailes with arm movements, and that, in all likelihood, the tañido and the rhythm of the Jácara arrived in France with a Zarabanda son and perhaps for that reason was called "Sarabande."

The Sarabande

Although Jean Boyer's 1642 *Livre des Chansons à danser et à boire* includes several Sarabandes, I am not aware of documentation of French Sarabande choreography before those found in Feuillet's *Recueil de Dances composées par Mr. Feuillet* (1700). However, in his 1671 *Dictionnaire Royale*, Jesuit scholar Père François Pomey provides a description of a danced Sarabande that—although he doesn't mention specific steps—refers to numerous actions, rhythms, contrasts, and graces. Here are two brief excerpts:

> Then, rising up with more poise and carrying the arms to half-height and half open, he performed the most beautiful steps ever invented for the dance.... Sometimes he would glide imperceptibly, with no apparent movement of his feet and legs, and seemed to slide rather than step. Sometimes, with the most beautiful timing in the world, he would remain suspended, immobile, and half leaning to the side with one foot in the air; and then, compensating for the cadence that had gone by, with another more precipitous one he would almost fly, so rapid was his motion.
> ... And certain circles of the arms and body, nonchalant, unfinished and passionate, made him appear so admirable and so charming that throughout this enchanting dance he won as many hearts as he attracted spectators.[27]

This quote describes a Sarabande as danced by a solo man in France. It details some arm movement, including the circles with the arms already cited in the anonymous "Jácara" of circa 1680. The speed and gliding quality of certain steps recall the movement described in the Countess d'Aulnoy's 1679 letter recounting the Zarabanda in Spain.[28]

Jácara and Jean-Baptiste Lully's **Sarabande:** *Between Seventeenth-Century Spanish and French Courts*

Ana María Mauricia, Archduchess of Austria, who was born in Valladolid, Spain, on September 22, 1601, and died in Paris on January 20, 1666, was known as Anne of Austria. She was the daughter of Spain's King Philip III (1578–1621) and Archduchess Margaret of Austria (1584–1611) and, therefore, the sister of King Philip IV of Spain. As the wife of Louis XIII, she was Queen of France from 1615 to 1643; from 1643 to 1661 she was acting regent during the minority of her son Louis XIV, who was King of France and Navarre from 1638 to 1715. She learned to dance in Spain before her marriage in 1615 and her subsequent forty-four-year reign in France and Navarre. Her ladies-in-waiting, actors, and guitarists traveled with her to France. In 1660, Marie-Therese of Austria (b. Madrid, September 10, 1638; d. Versailles, July 30, 1683), daughter of Philip IV and Elizabeth of Bourbon (1602–1644), married her cousin, King Louis XIV. Like Anne of Austria, Marie-Therese had learned to dance in Spain prior to her marriage. She reigned in France from 1661 until her death in 1683.

Marie-Therese's wedding to Louis XIV established peace between France and Spain after the Thirty Years' War. To celebrate the union, Spanish dramatist Pedro Calderón de la Barca wrote the allegorical *auto sacramental* (eucharistic play) *La Paz Universal o El Lirio y la Azucena*. Spanish minister Don Luís de Haro hired the theater company of Sebastián de Prado to perform the piece, and Prado's troupe then traveled to the French court, where they took up residency for some six months. At the same time, Cardinal Mazarin, Chief Minister of France from 1642 to 1661, also commissioned a play to commemorate the wedding: *Ercole Amante*, performed in 1662 with a libretto by Francesco Buti, music by Cavalli, and ballets by court musician Jean-Baptiste Lully (1632–1687).

Four Sarabandes, Choreographies of Le Bourgeois Gentilhomme *(1670)*

On October 14, 1670, at the court of Louis XIV, Jean-Baptiste Poquelin, "Molière" (1622–1673), debuted a five-act satirical *comédie-ballet* (a play incorporating dance, music, and song) called *Le Bourgeois Gentilhomme* (*The Bourgeois Gentleman, or The Would-Be Aristocrat*), with music by Lully. This play included a "Ballet des Nations" ("Ballet of the Nations"), which contained a Sarabande, "Premier Air pour les Espagnols" ("First Spanish Air"). Four different Sarabande choreographies set to this melody survive (see Table 3).

Table 3: Four choreographies of Lully's *Sarabande*

Reference Catalogue F. Lancelot	Choreographer	Title of Choreography	Source	Editor	Dancers
FL/1700.1/05	Feuillet	*Sarabande pour femme*	Recueil de danses composées par Mr. Feuillet	Feuillet	1 woman
FL/1700.1/06	Feuillet	*Sarabande pour homme*	Recueil de danses composées par Mr. Feuillet	Feuillet	1 man
FL/1704.1/01	Pécour	*Sarabande pour une femme*	Recueil d'entrées de ballet de Mr. Pécour	Feuillet	1 woman
FL/Ms17.1/05	Favier	*Sarabande de Mr. Favier*	Descan		1 man

The first two choreographies (FL/1700.1/05 and FL/1700.1/06), from Feuillet's "*Recueil de Dances par Mr. Feuillet*" (1700), were reprinted in Descan's French manuscript in 1748 without any changes. The manuscript contains reprints of all of Feuillet's choreographies as well as other versions of the Sarabande set to the same tunes. Such is the case of the fourth example presented here, a solo for a male dancer choreographed by Favier.[29]

These four choreographies are comprised of French dance steps from the court of Louis XIV, which indicates that they are in a different style from those described in Spain.[30] There is, nonetheless, an essential element common to both the Jácara and this Sarabande (as well as to many other French Sarabandes): the rhythmic-harmonic form of the *hemiola*.

Throughout the seventeenth century, Spanish dance appears to have pleased the French, since Sarabandes and *loures* (slow gigues) were written and choreographed in the Spanish style. Circles of the wrist and elbow were introduced in a dance style that included arm movements, and musical forms like Jácara, Zarabanda, and Chacona, were imbued with Spanish rhythms, such as the influential hemiola.

The Hemiola

The hemiola is a shifting of rhythmical accentuation in the ratio of 3:2, as when, for example, two groups of three eighth notes (6/8) alternate with three groups of two eighth notes (3/4). In Spanish danzas and bailes such as the Jácara, and in the French Sarabandes of the Baroque period, the fundamental rhythm of this alternating pattern tends to be the three-note groups, while the irregularity tends to be provided by the two-note groups (see Table 4).[31]

The hemiola, an omnipresent aspect of the music and dance of Spain, Central America, and South America in the sixteenth, seventeenth, and eighteenth centuries, is found in numerous popular dances of the present day. We also find it in the French Sarabandes of the Baroque period.

In the specific case of the seventeenth-century Spanish Jácara and Zarabanda, we are confronted with rhythmic schemes identical to the *bulerías*, *alegrías*, and *soleá* of present-day flamenco. This is why I contend that the Jácara and the Zarabanda are nascent flamenco, or what we call "ancient" or "historical" flamenco. All Jácara music follows this scheme, and it pervades pieces by numerous authors, including those by Gaspar Sanz (1640–1710), Juan Antonio Mendoza (seventeenth century), Francisco Guerau (seventeenth century), Antonio de Santa Cruz (seventeenth century), Lucas Ruiz de Ribayaz (c. 1650 to early eighteenth century), and Santiago de Murcia (1673–1739), among others. The Sarabande "Premier Air des Espagnols" of the *Ballet des Nations* in *Le Bourgeois Gentilhomme* contains the same rhythmic and formal structure as the Jácaras by Santa Cruz or Gaspar Sanz. Reminiscences of this structure can be found in other French Baroque dances, such as the concluding hemiola in the Sarabande, chaconne, *passacaille*, and *menuet*, and so on.

Table 4: Hemiola

Beats	2	3	1	2	3	1	2	1	2	1	2	1
Accents						>		>	>	>		>>
3/4 (notes)	♩	♩	♩	♩	♩	♩	♩	♩	♩	♩	♩	♩
flamenco counts	1	2	3	4	5	6	7	8	9	10	–	–
Accents			>			>		>		>		>>

Figure 2: Hemiola Chart.

Spanish Arm Movements

I would like to clarify a detail with regard to the arm movements in Spanish dance. In his *Discursos*, Esquivel's only instructions about the arms are that they must be "dropped down, such that the hands are in the pockets at the sides, without winding them around the body, but rather moving them very little and carelessly."[32] He describes the steps that were used in dances in academies, and he speaks very little of the arms, presumably because they are school dances. But popular or theatrical danzas or bailes, such as the Zarabanda described in 1679 Spain by Countess d'Aulnoy, employed arm movements.

Concerning the arm and castanet movements that were used in the Spanish bailes of the seventeenth century (and eighteenth century, for that matter), here are a few excerpts from the Anonymous "Jácara" of circa 1680:

- turn in profile ... turning the right arm around to one
- ... pass the right hand in front of the face
- do three *quiebros* to the left side, making a circle with the right arm on each one
- two pasos to the side with arms out *sostenido* and quiebro with arms in
- sostenido and quiebro to the left side with arms in, two vacíos with arms out, and another sostenido and quiebro with the right and arms in
- two pasos to the right side with the left and making a circle with the left arm and throw out the foot along with the arm.[33]

These descriptions of circular arm movements, such as "making a circle with the left arm," "turning the arm around" in two directions, and "with arms in ... with arms out," are reminiscent of certain arm movements used today in flamenco dance. To complete the picture, here is a description of arm movements and castanet playing from the *Españoleta* by Minguet (1737):

> Whosoever should try dancing the *Españoleta*... must be advised on how to hold the arms in order to play the castanets for this *paseo*: upon starting to do the pasos, they are held down at the sides, without playing the castanets; but upon doing the *sacudido*, one must lift the arms the same amount, bringing the hands up to the chest, and at the moment of doing the *carrerilla* open them outwards the same amount, striking the castanet with both hands at one time, then one must again lower the arms until the other sacudido, and must do the same thing on the *vuelta al descuido*, and all this must be done in the time of one complete tañido for the *Españoleta*: all the mudanzas occur within the time of a half tañido, and the *deshecho* within the other half.[34]

The arm movements described here are much more contained or restrained than those described in the anonymous "Jácara." For this reason, I am convinced that, on some occasions at court, it was also possible to dance with arm movements while playing the castanets, and that this is the type of arm movement practiced in the danzas, or rather, in the dances at court, as well as in the dance schools. Curiously, it reminds me of the arm movements described by Rameau for the French *Menuet*, the court dance par excellence.

Jácaras and Zarabandas as Ancestors of Flamenco

The continuities of arm movements, steps, and the hemiola rhythm from seventeenth-century Jácaras and Zarabandas to today's flamenco are striking. The arm movements described above were part of popular dance along with castanets by the seventeenth century—perhaps even earlier. In 1737, Minguet documents that the use of arms and castanets has been incorporated into some courtly dances.

At the same time, I sense that one of the Spanish contributions to French dance was the integration of the circular motions of the arms and wrists described above, adapted and codified by the Académie de Danse created by Louis XIV in 1661; a second contribution was the use of castanets that eventually developed in France.

In his *Maître à Danser* (1725), Pierre Rameau (the French dance master to Elisabetta Farnese, Queen Consort of Spain 1714–1746) describes in detail the arm movements in courtly dances. Only circles and half circles of the wrists and elbows were used in these dances. In contrast, Feuillet, in his *Chorégraphie* (1700), additionally offers notation for recording circles and half circles of the shoulders. The circular arm movements from the shoulder imply that the arm lifted over the top of the head, as in the Jácara, the Zarabanda, and the original French Sarabande. These higher arm movements were used in dances for the theater. Feuillet also presents a system for annotating the castanet rhythms, an indication that castanets were often played while dancing.

Thus, I conclude:

1. Early Spanish dance used arms and castanets, in diverse ways. In the court and dancing schools, as described by Esquivel, the arms would have been constrained and noble, but in popular dances like the Jácara and the Zarabanda, performed in theaters, the arms circled in front of the face and even over the top of the head.
2. The difference between danza and baile can be found in the use of the arms and the castanets, but the same piece could combine both (see Appendix 1).
3. Flamenco forms such as alegrías and bulerías echo the hemiola, armwork, and expressive ethos of baroque dances like the Jácara and Zarabanda (see Table 5). Moreover, a kind of French Sarabande derives directly from the Spanish Jácara or Zarabanda, perhaps imported to the court with the Spanish queens. It is easy to imagine that seventeenth-century Spanish dances performed at court and in theaters might evolve through the eighteenth century into the style known today as the *escuela bolera*. However, French academic dancing in the seventeenth and eighteenth centuries ultimately became classical ballet.

Table 5: Terms in relation to the *Jácara*

Spanish	→	English	→	Spanish
Jácaras	→	Merry Songs	→	Canciones alegres (Alegrías)
Alegrías	→	Happy Moments	→	Momentos felices
Joglorio	→	Merriments	→	Alegría

Appendix 1: Danza vs. Baile

One question all researchers of historical Spanish dance ask is what constitutes the difference between danza and baile, especially since both words were used in Spanish to describe the act of dancing. Many scholars have researched and written on this topic, and various conclusions have been reached. Here are some examples of usage on this subject as offered by Minguet in his *Danzas a la española para los que las han sabido, y se les han olvidado*, from the 1737 edition of *Arte de danzar a la francesa*:

- In the *Pavana*: "The Pavana is danzada, which means the castanet is not played while dancing."[35]
- In the *Gallarda*: "The Gallarda is danzada like the Pavana."[36]

- In the *Españoleta*: "Whosoever should try *bailar* (to dance) the *Españoleta*, the first thing one must do is to place oneself firmly in the position, as has been indicated in the other danzas [...]."[37] Does this quote mean that it is perfectly clear that the Españoleta is a baile, but that it simply begins in the same way as the danzas described beforehand? Or that the terms danza and baile are confusing and used in an indistinguishable manner?

In the *Villano* (dance of the villagers), castanets are used from time to time, but Minguet does not call it either a danza or a baile. This is an example in which castanets are used with the arms down.

- I advise that ... when doing the paseo at each floreo, one must strike the castanets, all at one time, both arms down at the sides for the whole Villano, and that the striking of the castanets is not more than for the pas[e]o; but played constantly in the rest of the mudanzas.[38]

In the *Imposibles*: "The Imposibles are *bailados*, only the *entrada* (entrance) is danzada."[39] In the *Hermosa*:

- "*Medio tañido es danzado y medio bailado.*" The Hermosa is half *tañido danzado* and half bailado, and this is done with the cortesía up to the middle of the first entry, it has four tañidos, and within them eight mudanzas are performed, four danz[ad]as with the hat in the left hand, and four more bailadas with castanets.[40]

This coincidentally provides a possible clue concerning rhythm: four tañidos equals eight mudanzas, and there is regular alternation of mudanzas danzadas and mudanzas bailadas:

- This first mudanza is danzada and serves as entrada.... The second mudanza is bailada.... The third mudanza is danzada.... The fourth mudanza is bailada.... This mudanza (the fifth) is danzada.... The sixth mudanza is bailada.... The seventh mudanza is danzada.... The eighth mudanza is bailada.[41]

These examples seem to indicate that, on the one hand, the relationship between danza and baile can be that of a movement without use of the arms, with more constrained steps in the case of danzar, and with use of the arms and/or castanets in the case of bailar. On the other hand, the relationship between these two modalities is not well defined, since we already find an alternation between both terms within the same choreography.

Appendix 2: La Jácara de Domingo Gonzaléz

I have just recently discovered the existence of a manuscript on Spanish dance that contains a detailed description of a Jácara, with elements similar to those of Jaque's "Jácara." The manuscript, in two parts, is *Choregraphie figurativa y demostrativa del arte de danzar en la forma española* by Don Nicolás Rodrigo Noveli, and *Escuela por lo bajo* by Domingo González, a contemporary of Juan de Esquivel Navarro, author of

Discursos sobre el arte del danzado. Both studied with Antonio de Almenda, who was the Dance Master for Felipe IV. For this reason, I believe that the so-called González school should be dated from the mid-seventeenth century.[42] I plan to publish this manuscript, along with all the others discussed above, in Spanish, English, and French, in the first volume of a collection called *La danza del siglo de oro español—FUENTES*.

Notes

1. This essay is an adaptation of my article "From the *Jácara* to the *Sarabande*," in "All'ungaresca—al espanol," die Vielfalt der europäischen Tanzkultur 1420–1820. Proceedings of the 3rd Rothenfels Dance Symposion, June 2012, ed. Uwe Schlottermüller, Maria Richter, and Howard Weiner, 227–244. Reprinted with permission.
2. On the distinction between *baile* and *danza*, see Appendix 1.
3. In Sebastián de Covarrubias Horozco, *Tesoro de la lengva castellana, o española* (Madrid: Por L. Sanchez, impressor del rey n.s.; 1611), 487: *Jaque*. Term for those who play chess, when one advises an opponent to move the king from its position or protect it with another piece: Arabic word of Hebrew origin from the verb חק; *jacah, audere, obedire, obtemperare*. / *Jaque y mate*. When one and the other are done simultaneously, making "check" and "mate." Skilled players often make bets as to which of two pieces will give "check" and which will give "mate." / *Jaque* [orig. *Xaque*]. With "X" can mean "old person," "governor," "sir," and in criminal slang "ruffian." / *Jacarandina*. Criminal slang or language belonging to ruffians known as *"jaques."*
4. In Miguel Cervantes Saavedra, *El Rufián dichoso* (Madrid: Por la Vda. de Alonso a costa de Juan de Villarroel, Mercader de Libros, véndese en su casa en la Plazuela del Angel, 1615), lines 173–180: Reveal something about him to me? / The whole unprofitable brain / of Apollo closes in on him. / It is a jácaro romance, / that I equal and compare him / to the best ever made; / the rest made of the underworld / in a rare and jaco style; Ibid., lines 204–207.
5. In Juan de Esquivel Navarro, *Discursos sobre el arte del dançado, y sus excelencias y primer origen, reprobando las acciones deshonestas* (Seville: Iuan Gomez de Blas, 1642), fol. 30v: it is all that is danced in schools: and although there are the Rastro, Jácara, Zarabanda, and Tárraga, these four pieces are one and the same thing; even if the Rastro has its different mudanzas (a sequence of dance steps) and a different style.
6. Sebastián Rodríguez de Villaviciosa, entremés *Los Sones*, cited in Emilio Cotarelo y Mori, *Colección de entremeses, loas, bailes, jácaras y mojigangas desde fines del siglo 16 à mediados del 18*, vol. 1 (Madrid: Bailly Ballière, 1911), cclii; Pedro Calderón de la Barca, *Loa* for Antonio de Escamilla's company, cited in Cotarelo, *Colección de entremeses*, ccxxxii. On Antonio de Escamilla, see Hugo Albert Rennert, *The Spanish Stage in the Time of Lope de Vega* (New York: Hispanic Society of America, 1909), 465.
7. José de Cañizares, *Mojiganga de los Sones*, cited in Cotarelo, *Colección de entremeses*, cclii.
8. Real Academia Española, *Diccionario de la lengua castellana en que se explica el verdadero sentido de las voces ... con las phrases o modos de hablar, los proverbios o refranes y otras cosas convenientes al uso de la lengua*, vol. 6 (Madrid: Francisco del Hierro, 1726), 532.
9. In Felipe Roxo de Flores, *Tratado de recreacion instructiva sobre la danza: su invencion y diferencias* (Madrid: En la Imprenta Real, 1793), 118: The character of Spanish dances can be understood without too much difficulty through the music with which they are executed, as much those familiar to us as those of which there is no other memory than that of their name, such as the *Caballero*, the *Rugero*, *Jácara de la Costa*, *Mariona*, *Tarantela*, *Batalla*, *Gelves*, and *Piegibado*.
10. In the collection *Dance in the Spanish Golden Age: III. Choreographies*, which I am working on, volume 4 is devoted to Jácaras and Zarabanda, with a special emphasis on these three choreographies.
11. Jaque, *Libro de danzar*, fol. 9v.
12. Ibid., fol. 10v.
13. In Real Academia Española, *Diccionario de la lengua castellana*, vol. 1, 271: "*Amolador*. f. m. One who grinds and sharpens tools on a whetstone. Spoken language from the verb '*amolar*' [to grind]. / *Amolar* v. a. To sharpen, to hone, put an edge on a weapon or cutting instrument of some kind"; Jaque, *Libro de danzar*, fol. 10v.
14. Bartolomé Ferriol y Boxeraus, Joseph Testore, and Santiago Perez Junquera, *Reglas utiles para los aficionados a danzar: provechoso divertimiento de los que gustan tocar instrumentos: y polyticas advertencias a todo genero de personas: adornado con varias laminas: dedicado a la S.M. el Rey de las Dos Sicilias, &c*. (Capoa: A costa de Joseph Testore, mercador de libros, à la Calle Nueva, 1745), 47.
15. I conclude that this Jácara mudanza from Jaque's treatise of 1680 survived well into the eighteenth century, incorporated into the contradanzas imported from France with the arrival of Louis XIV's grand-

son Philip V in 1700. Thanks to this later description it is possible to imagine the movement—unless, of course, it already is a deformation of the original movement? The answer to this question remains open. Ibid., 59.

16. Luis Quiñones de Benavente, *El Amolador*, 754, cited in Cotalelo, *Colección de entremeses*, cl.

17. In Margit Frenk Alatorre, *Nuevo Corpus de la antigua lírica popular hispánica: (siglos XV a XVII)*, vol. 1 (México: Colegio de México [u.a.]., 2003), 803: *¡Ay, amolador, amoladorsillo! ¡ay, amúelame acueste cochillo!* Frenk's sources are Quiñones de Benavente, *El Amolador* (1643), fol. 11, which she identifies as a baile and not as an entremés, and *Nuevos entremeses* (or Juan C. Gonzlez Maya, *Entremeses nuevos?*), Alcalá, 1643.

18. Cotarelo, *Colección de entremeses*, cl, cites the *Entremés del niño* by Francisco de Quevedo.

19. Don José Sancho Rayón, the owner of the original manuscript, was co-author, together with Marqués de la Fuensanta del Valle and Don Francisco de Zabalburu, of *Colección de documentos inéditos para la historia de España*.

20. Anonymous, "Jácara," fol. [2]r, line 6; ibid., fol. [3]r, line 10.

21. Ibid., fol. [3]r, line 3.

22. Ibid., fol. [3]r, line 12.

23. Whenever the word "media" (half) is used in this manuscript, it clearly refers to the abbreviated name of a step. I imagine that it could be the abbreviation of media cabriola. Francesc Olivelles, *Memòria de les danças, que don Joseph Fausto de Potau y de Férran aprèn ab mestre Francesc Olivelles en Barcelona y yuntamén després à ecrits y notats los moviments se fan en ellas segons sa doctrina y esceñansa, avent començat a aprendren lo dia de 8 de abril de 1701*. MS A-30. Barcelona: Unpublished manuscript, Arxiu Històric de la Ciutat (Barcelona), 1701: 195.

24. The principal sources on Zarabanda will be included in my collection, *Dance in the Spanish Golden Age: Danzas and Bailes, Sources and Analysis and Commentary*.

25. In many eras, it was customary for foreign writers to translate the names of Spanish steps and dances into their own language, which is why in the original French Davillier and Doré refer to the Zarabanda they saw in Spain as the Sarabande, just as Jean Boyer did two centuries earlier. Davillier, *Le tour de monde*, 396.

26. Marie Catherine Le Jumel de Barneville d'Aulnoy, *The ingenious and diverting letters of the Lady's—travels into Spain describing the devotions, nunneries, humours, customs, laws, militia, trade, diet, and recreations of that people* (London: Printed for S. Crouch, 1692), 21. Cited in Davillier, *Le tour de monde*, 396.

27. Père François Pomey, *Le Dictionnaire Royale* (22). Reproduced and translated in Patricia M. Ranum, "Audible rhetoric and mute rhetoric: the 17th-century French" in *Early Music: Early Dance Issue* 14, no. 1 (February 1986): 34–35.

28. There are also three choreographic descriptions of the Sarabanda in Germany at the end of the seventeenth century in Johann Georg Pasch's *Anleitung sich bei grossen Herrn Höfen und andern beliebt zu machen*. These consist of a list of steps organized in "strophes" with "verses" (lines) numbered from 1 to 8 (except for one strophe made up of ten lines) and with one step per line or "verse." They describe body orientations and directions of steps, but provide no information on possible shapes in space. This treatise gives no indications of who is dancing, nor does it provide any musical transcriptions. However, the possible eight-bar musical structure would correspond to the two Zarabandes found in German musician and theorist Michael Praetorius's *Terpsichore*, a compendium of more than 300 instrumental dances published in 1612. Michael Praetorius and Friedrich Blume, *Gesamtausgabe der musikalischen Werke: Terpsichore* (Wolfenbüttel: Möseler, 1612), Sarabandes XXXIII and XXXIV.

29. The *Sarabande pour une femme* by Feuillet (FL/1700.1/05) is also listed in the Derra de Moroda Dance Archives, Salzburg, in an anonymous *Recueil de Danses* (catalog no. 113) and dated before 1720, but as it happens, the page is totally blank. Listed in Lancelot: La Belle dance, FL/Ms02.1/19.

30. It is curious that a comparison of the names of Spanish steps with the movements transcribed in Feuillet yields many intriguing parallels. This goes beyond the scope of this essay, but is a subject I will address in a future publication.

31. There are also rhythmic foundations consisting of two-note groups, with a three-note group providing the irregularity for the cadence, as in, for example, the French *courante*.

32. Juan de Esquivel Navarro, *Discursos sobre el arte del dançado, y sus excelencias y primer origen, reprobando las acciones deshonestas* (Seville: Iuan Gomez de Blas, 1642), fol. 21v, line 13.

33. Anonymous, "Jácara," fols. 1r–4v.

34. Minguet è Irol, "Danzas a la española para los que las han sabido y se les ha olvidado" in *Arte de danzar a la francesa, adornado con quarenta figuras, que enseñan el modo de hacer todos los diferentes passos de la danza del minuete, con todas sus reglas, y de conducir los brazos en cada passo: Y en quatro figuras, el modo de danzar los tres passapies. Tambien estàn escritos en solfa, para que qualquier musico los sepa tañer* (Madrid: P. Minguet, en su casa, 1737), 61.

35. Ibid., 53.

36. Ibid., 58.

37. Ibid., 61f.
38. Ibid., 65.
39. Ibid., 67.
40. Ibid., 69f.
41. Ibid., 71f.
42. Rodrigo Noveli, *Chorégraphie figurativa y demostrativa del arte de danzar en la forma española*. MS. Madrid, 1708. In the second part of this manuscript we find *Escuela por lo bajo* de Domingo González, circa 1650, which consists of nine choreographies described in prose.

Spanish Dance in Europe
From the Late Eighteenth Century to Its Consolidation on the European Stage
Rocío Plaza Orellana
Translation by K. Meira Goldberg

From Seville: Manuela Perea, Petra Cámara, Amparo Álvarez. From Cádiz: Josefa Vargas and María Mercandotti. And dance maestros Antonio Ruiz, Félix García, Félix Moreno. All are part of the history of Spanish dance. But Frenchwomen Marie-Guy Stéphan, Lise Noblet, and Paulina Duvernay, Irishwoman Lola Montes, and Austrian Fanny Elssler also belong to this legacy. These names, together with those of many others, well beyond the limits of this essay, are links that form a continuous chain of dance in Spanish history, from the early nineteenth century to this day. Adventures and misadventures, chance, tenacity, and talent are woven together in the story of dance on the Spanish stage (see Figure 1).

Boleros, Fandangos, and Seguidillas

Although dance was always part of the performances staged in the *corrales de comedias* (theaters with open-air central patios) of the sixteenth and seventeenth centuries, international recognition of Spanish dance did not arrive until the eighteenth century.[1] For this acclaim to occur, a series of factors needed to come together. On the one hand was the influx of foreign tourists visiting Spain from all over Europe, but especially from England and France, who for political or social motives saw Spain as a place of diversion and/or economic exploitation. On the other hand, Spanish dance was part of the beginnings of a progressive renewal of dance that led, by the early 1830s, to the Romantic ballet. We should view this process in context: moral and religious proscriptions governed dancing in public, and the unique characteristics of Spanish theater during these years were decisive in elaborating new modes of performance. Finally, the role of Spanish dance in the development of the Romantic ballet must be seen from the perspective of Spain's early nineteenth-century political forecast. The country was embroiled in a covert civil war and, at the same time, was a crucial battleground in the struggle between the Napoleonic Empire and its enemies in 1808.

During these years, the representative repertory on any stage in Spain was composed of three dances: *boleros, fandangos*, and *seguidillas*. The most interesting of them for foreign tourists, particularly the British, who recorded their memories in influential travel diaries, was the fandango. Joseph Baretti, Casanova, Joseph Townsend, Christian August Fischer, Henry Swinburne, and Richard Twiss are among those who wrote down their observations on the performance of this dance. In meticulous and conscientious detail, including descriptions of dance steps, their convoluted language attempts to extract every drop of emotion they experienced in its contemplation. Shocked by the dance's sensuality, they provide stories and legends of the fandango's struggle to survive in a land bound by decency and morality. Anecdotes shared by native Spaniards, or plots of *sainetes* (picaresque one-act farces or tidbits) confused with real events, surround the fandango in the travelers' accounts that bewitched England, France, and Germany.[2]

Thus, the fandango became the characteristic dance of Spain. It was a performance, of unknown origin, of seduction between man and woman, a dance in which both partners took an active part in the aim of beguiling the other. Following the fandango came the bolero and the seguidillas. The bolero played the part of the fandango's heir: the history of one blends with that of the other. Over the course of the nineteenth century, the bolero became the protagonist of staged Spanish dance, with many variations created by resident choreographers and dance masters of theater companies.[3]

Figure 1: Daguerrotype of a dancer of the escuela bolera, with combs and castanets, about 1850. Photographer unknown (courtesy Fototeca de IPCE Instituto de Patrimonio Cultural de España, Madrid).

Ballet d'Action and Spanish Dance

At the same time, in Europe, a silent revolution of progressive change was engendering genuine reform. Figures such as French choreographer and maestro Jean-Georges Noverre (1727–1810), together with his followers, invented a new plasticity onstage, shaping all theatrical elements in service of a plot. They created new choreographies and new modes of performance. They rid theater stages of all the extraneous elements—the hairpieces, wigs, corsets, and masks—that interfered with the true beauty of dance:

the dancer's body, seen as an expression of feeling generated by the choreography's dramatic action. This premise, with the advent of Romanticism, became the future of theatrical choreography.

This small legion transformed dance. Noverre's students, and rivals, also played a contributing role in the introduction of Spain and its dances to the choreographic panorama on the international stage. In fact, the first steps leading to public acceptance of national dances on stage were taken in 1786, opening the door to a history that led to the decisive success of Filippo Taglioni's *La Sílfide* in 1832. Between 1786 and 1832, national dances were introduced into the *ballets d'action*, becoming a fundamental element of their choreographic productions. The first instance of this innovation might be *The Whims of Cupid and the Ballet Master* (*Amors og Balletmesterens Luner*, 1786), with music by Jens Lolle and choreography by Vincenzo Galeotti (1733–1816), an influential director of the Royal Danish Ballet and a former pupil of Noverre's.[4] Its plot revolved around the contretemps of a naughty Cupid who capriciously launched his arrows every which way, rendering the whole world love struck. In the service of this plot, several national dances were staged—they were something new—and they filled the tired neoclassicism of the eighteenth century with color and dynamism. But Noverre's contemporary, Franz Anton Christoph Hilferding (1710–1768), dancer and dance master at the Viennese court, had anticipated Galeotti, incorporating Tyrolean and Hungarian villagers in traditional costumes in his first ballet of 1742.[5]

From then on, other ballets followed, characterized not only by the presence of characters costumed as peasants of some other nation but also by novelties that would lay the foundation for the incorporation of Spanish dance. Another student of Noverre's, Jean Dauberval (1742–1806), choreographed *La fille mal gardée*, which debuted in 1789. This enduring work filled the stage with a variety of commoners—ordinary people—denizens of the Parisian streets who were individuals with unique particularities. With the enormous popularity and many revivals of *La fille mal gardée*, Paris became accustomed to seeing people onstage who had previously been considered unworthy of the noble art of dance.

Dauberval's work was followed by a one-act ballet by Jean-Louis Aumer (1744–1833), *Les pages du duc de Vendôme*, which debuted at the Académie Royale de Musique—the Paris Opéra—on October 18, 1820.[6] This ballet became a popular favorite, revived and restaged through the years. Aumer created an atmosphere with Spanish steps and an amorous plot that took place in Spain, where the Duke was fighting. Upon its premiere, the press was sprinkled with reviews criticizing the *divertissements*, in which Spanish dances like the bolero appeared. Critics faulted these dances for being interminable and breaking the momentum of the onstage action, and for being repetitive and monotonous. But the audiences liked them. *Les pages du duc de Vendôme*, which Aumer had debuted in Vienna on October 16, 1815, continued its European tour, opening at the Teatro San Carlo in Naples on November 19, 1825, with the title *I Paggi del duca di Vendôme*. In that production, the role of the page was danced by Fanny Elssler, a young ballerina who ten years later would consecrate the Spanish *cachucha* throughout Europe.[7] In any case, beyond the first reviews, which were colored by the general furor caused by the opening of the Salle Favart at the Académie Royale de Musique, this ballet remained continuously in production through the 1830s as a dependable source of box office receipts.

A Romantic Hybrid of Spanish Dance and Danse Comique

In addition to the incorporation of Spanish dance in the infancy of the Romantic ballet, there were other important transformations in dance during the 1820s. All of the novelties that followed one after the other had met with varied responses from audiences who, taking their time to form an opinion, accepted or rejected these dances in a seemingly capricious manner. The innovations that triumphed were adopted at the end of a bitter struggle between those who sought change and those who, with fierce commitment, fought any alteration in what they considered the unquestionable foundations of dance. Among the pillars that some wished to demolish were the classifications of ballet. According to their training and physical characteristics, ballet dancers were cast as *noble, demi-caractère,* or *comique*.[8] But this long and contentious battle would also be won, the old categories worn away, with seeming inevitability. Ballet dancers found themselves surrounded by novelties that were already considered essential, and with which they could not share the stage.

Ballet master Pierre Gardel (1758–1840) had dominated the Paris Opéra stage until well into the 1820s.[9] Despite his advancing age, he fought to uphold the standards of his training from before the French Revolution. His fiercely held positions meant that the rigid classifications of dancers would not be finally softened until his retirement from the Opéra. As ballet historian Ivor Guest describes in his book *The Romantic Ballet in Paris*, a *danseur noble* had to be tall, with an elegant, well-proportioned, and flexible body. Attaining this elite rank required impeccable technique, defined as a majestic projection of "solemn elegance." But it was difficult to draw precise boundaries between the noble dance and that of the *danseur demi-caractère*. This category demanded dancers of medium stature, who were slim and elegant. Their movement had to be "brilliant and intrepid," yet executed with "a certain restraint."[10] And finally there was the *genre comique*. "National dances such as the bolero, the tarantella and the allemande came within their province, and according to Blasis, 'the *pas Chinois*, the *pas de Sabotiers, l'Anglaise*, steps of caricature,' belonged to the lower comic style."[11]

The consequence of this process of hybridization, which had begun with the inclusion of national dances as part of the comic genre, was the elevation of these dances in the balletic hierarchy. Once national dances were integrated into the branch of demi-caractère dance (which was already blending with the noble dance), the traditional class distinctions of ballet began to fall away. The disappearance of the noble genre and its pursuant categories brought about another consequence and novelty that favored Spanish dance: the declining importance of male dancers as principal protagonists and the ascension of the famous ballerinas they partnered. This was exactly what the great ballet masters of the Paris Opéra—Pierre Gardel, Louis Jacques Milon (1766–1849), and Jean-Louis Aumer—most feared, and they lost the battle. This was the prelude to the Romantic ballet, inaugurating a period of feminine dominance on stage. Only ballet master Jules Perrot (1810–1892) succeeded in stealing some light from those blazing stars. In these days, Spanish dances occasionally appeared, stamping on stages ready to receive them with sustained applause, ready for their definitive disembarkation in 1834.

Spanish Dance at the Paris Opera

In this preamble to Filippo Taglioni's *La Sílfide* of 1832, a new truth for dance had been forged, and there was no place for artificiality or falsification. The balletic genres that impeded mobility and pigeonholed dances and dancers were gone. The role of the male dancer had been reduced to that of a simple *partenaire* for the ballerina. Choreography was spiced with what was thought of as "local color": national dances with their typical costumes and popular characters.[12] With all this came the divertissements of the grand ballets, the Spanish dances in *Les pages du duc de Vêndome* or Aumer's 1821 *La Fête hongroise*.[13] Others ballets followed, becoming part of a complex process of transformation. What emerged was a spectacle reinventing itself to hold the eye of a new audience, an audience that created new fashions out of an incessant search for models and pathways to a new identity: the nineteenth-century bourgeoisie.

The year 1834 marked the arrival of the first Spanish dance company to achieve success on the Paris Opéra stage. The men danced with unabashed masculinity, seducing their partners on stage. Their costumes were unlike anything seen before, made of rich and heavy velvets, frosted with spangles, and adorned with frogging and fringes. Their dances were daring and energetic, accompanied by the constant sound of an ancient and simple instrument, the castanets.

But before this moment could arrive, on the other side of the process that transformed ballet, we should note the efforts of those who, while the new spectacles were being formulated, familiarized audiences with the steps of the Spanish *escuela bolera* and passed them on to their disciples. This is the history of dancers who filled the pantomimic balletic dramas being developing at the end of the eighteenth century with Spanish dances and Spanish characters. This labor was carried out by Charles Le Picq and, especially, by the Vestris family.

In 1780, the great dancer Charles Le Picq, a pupil of Noverre's and responsible for publishing Noverre's *Lettres sur la danse* in Russia, performed at the Madrid theater Los Caños del Peral. His partner was Geltruda, or Margarita Rossi, who later changed her last name to Le Picq when she became his second wife.[14] The bolero and the fandango then began their tour of Europe; in 1782, Le Picq became ballet master at London's King's Theatre, and inserted these two Spanish dances in *Le tuteur trompé*. The ballet, based on Beaumarchais's story *The Barber of Seville*, opened on January 12, 1783; Ivor Guest said the couple danced a seguidillas and Mme. Rossi danced a fandango solo.[15] Later the same year, on April 10, Mme. Rossi again danced a fandango solo and a seguidilla with her husband.[16] Thus, Spanish dance was incorporated into theatrical choreographies in London, and later in St. Petersburg when the couple moved there in 1786. Le Picq also choreographed Spanish dances for Charles Didelot (1767–1837), Guymard, Duquesnay, and Auguste Vestris (1760–1842).[17]

Vestris was another maestro who, with his wife, ballerina Fortunata Angiolini, and their son, Armand, contributed to the incorporation of Spanish dance on the late eighteenth-century European stage. With the denomination "Spanish," Vestris created numerous divertissements, such as *Les Follies d'Espagne* in 1791 for the King's Theatre. Fortunata Angiolini was considered the most talented dancer of the Spanish bolero until the arrival of Cádiz native María Mercandotti (1801–1863) in 1820.[18] Armand

Vestris debuted at the King's Theatre in London in 1809. Following the fashion for inserting Spanish dances in ballets, he interpreted a bolero in *Don Quijote.*

The Vestris family members, with Auguste as patriarch, were the principal protagonists in a story of decisive mastery in the Paris Royal Academy of Music during the first decades of the nineteenth century. For nearly forty years Auguste danced at the Paris Opéra, and also became a dance master at the Paris Opéra ballet school. Among his students were Didelot, Perrot, August Bournonville (1805–1879), and Fanny Elssler (1810–1884). He passed on to them not only his own style but also his unique concept of dance. The definitive success of Spanish dance on the European stage, consecrated with Fanny Elssler's cachucha in Jean Coralli's *Le Diable boiteux* of June 1836, remits to Vestris. In Paris of the 1830s, two completely different ways of thinking about dance coexisted within the Royal Academy of Music. On one side was Filippo Taglioni, battling against cloaked meaning with a permanent state of candor. On the other side was Vestris, as remembered in Paris Opéra director Louis Véron's *Memorias de un burgués de París*, teaching graceful seduction and sensuality, and demanding provocative smiles, poses, and almost indecent attitudes.[19] Step by step, the old maestro taught the time-honored dances of the Spanish bolero school, giving them his own personal stamp and nurturing disciples such as María Mercandotti and Fanny Elssler, who established Spanish dance within the choreographic offerings of the Paris Opéra.

Tourists who journeyed to Spain before 1830 provide evidence of this gradual shift. One of the most interesting examples of this testimony is that of British diplomat William Jacob, who came to Spain in 1809 during the Spanish War of Independence. After seeing these Spanish dances performed in a theater in Cádiz, Jacob wrote that they were not nearly as attractive as those he had seen in theaters in London or on the Continent.[20]

The Spanish War of Independence, kindled by the Napoleonic invasions between May 2, 1808, and 1814, played a crucial role in the dissemination and evolution of Spanish dance in Europe. Spain became one of the most important theaters of war of the era. Contingents of soldiers from diverse nations, fighting for and against Napoleon, faced each other on Spanish soil. Britain and Spain allied against France. The results were numerous travel accounts, written by foot soldiers and officers and published throughout the first half of the nineteenth century, documenting, among other things, the national Spanish dances.

Out of this war came one of the most important stories of Spanish dance: that of María Mercandotti—child of Cádiz—and the aristocratic officer James Duff, Fourth Earl of Fife (1776–1857). After the war, Duff brought Mercandotti and her mother to London. With Duff as her protector, Mercandotti debuted at the King's Theatre in London on July 12, 1814. She danced a cachucha, a dance hitherto unknown outside the Iberian Peninsula, which had been created during the war, possibly during the siege of Cádiz. Soon Mercandotti was sent to Paris to study ballet under Vestris, establishing herself as a dancer in 1821.

That same year, another crucial event unfolded between the stages of London and Paris, with Mercandotti as its central protagonist. At the end of the war, the treaties following the lifting of the siege of Cádiz reestablished relationships that allowed artists to travel between London and Paris. In 1821, the Royal Academy of Music in Paris contracted with the King's Theatre in London to hire the Parisian dancers for the season, bringing about an exchange between the two companies (Lord Fife was on the government committee that organized this arrangement). María Mercandotti thus returned to London, bringing with her a repertory of Spanish dances already well established on the Paris Opéra stage, and adding castanets to her cachucha, boleros, and very successful *guaracha*.[21] In 1823, Mercandotti suddenly left the British stage to marry the aristocrat Edward Hughes Ball and retire from performing.

The programming at the Opéra continued without Spanish dancers, but premiered and revived many pieces filled with Spanish dance. Among these ballets, whose attractiveness derived from fictionalized history and splendid staging, were *L'Orgie* of 1831, and *La Révolte au sérail*, set in Andalusia and sprinkled with national dances.

It was not until 1834, more than a decade after Mercandotti's departure, that Spanish dance was performed again by Spanish dancers on the Paris Opéra stage. A small company, made up of Dolores Serral, Manuela Dubiñón, Francisco Font, and Mariano Camprubí, had been hired by Opéra director Louis Véron to animate the dances at the Carnival of 1834. The Opéra faced financial difficulty, which motivated Véron to propose a series of measures, some innovative and some well established, to generate new income. The imported Spanish dances generated excitement in audiences and acclaim in the press.[22] Véron was enthusiastic about the response, and contracted them to perform at the Opéra, where they danced fandangos, boleros, *zapateados,* and *corraleras* on January 15 and January 24, 1834. From Paris, they travelled with similar repertory and with similar success to the Teatro de la Monnaie in Brussels in March, and to the King's Theatre in London later that year. Aside from the need to make up the economic shortfalls at the Paris Opéra, the European tour of this small company also owed its invitation to Seville native Alejandro Aguado, a crucial and influential figure in the daily life of the Opéra, who had become a patron in 1831.[23] Dubiñón, Serral, Camprubí, and Font never returned to the Opéra, but they continued to dance in Paris during the following years, earning varied levels of public recognition. They performed in smaller theaters such as Variétes and the Palais Royal, which were more accessible to the working-class segments of the public.

Fanny Elssler's Cachucha

Not until June 1, 1836, when Austrian ballerina Fanny Elssler debuted in Coralli's *Le Diable boiteux*, would the success of Spanish dance at the Paris Opéra be repeated.[24] At the opening of the third act came the cachucha that Coralli had imagined for Elssler. This marks the definitive arrival of the fashion for Spanish dance in Europe and America. As a fashion, it ebbed and flowed, capricious, tempestuous, and volatile, but it survived throughout the nineteenth century.

Aside from the dance's sensuality, critics praised the staged image that the Opéra's costume designers had fabricated. The *peina* (decorative comb), the rose in hair pulled back, the bodice with sparking decorations, the pink satin skirt, tight to the waist and weighted at the hem, the ample ruffles of black lace, the silk stockings, the open and luminous neckline, the black shoes, and the castanets knotted over the fingers illustrated the image of the Spanish dancer as well as that of Spanish fashion. This dress, with some variations in color and fabric, enjoyed a long trajectory in Spanish fashions of the following decades, which recognized in it Spanish airs born in the costume shop of the Royal Academy of Music in Paris. In its first sixteen performances, *Le Diable Boiteux* took in 95,000 francs in box office receipts. In December of 1836, the Drury Lane Theatre in London presented the ballet, danced by Pauline Duvernay, also with great success. The cachucha, now danced in principal theaters from one corner of Europe to the other, became a piece whose music was part of the cultural landscape of nineteenth-century Europe. In 1840, the cachucha traveled to America with the dancing feet of Fanny Elssler. By the time Elssler toured the United States, the Paris Opéra had already presented *Le Diable Boiteux* seventy times.

Fanny Elssler's Coattails

The cachucha's tremendous success in June of 1836 cast a long shadow that created opportunities for the arrivals of other Spanish dances and Spanish dance companies in European theaters. It also opened a path to others seeking to take advantage of the fashion for Spanish dance, including Lola Montes in London in 1843 and in Paris in 1844. Manuela Perea, Petra Cámara, Félix García, Antonio Ruiz, and Félix Moreno also were successful on the stages of London and Paris.

Manuela Perea "La Nena" and Félix García opened at Her Majesty's Theatre in London on April 10, 1845. Perea came from the Teatro Principal de Sevilla, where she had been performing for several years in different categories as a dancer in the corps de ballet.[25] She brought Spanish dances such as *El Bolero de la Caleta*, *El Bolero de la Cachucha*, *Seguidillas Manchegas,* and *El Olé* to European stages. Known in the press as the "Andalusian Venus," Perea returned to Madrid to continued success, to Paris in 1851, and in 1854 to London, where, thanks to the work of John Buckstone, she kept the Haymarket Theater open during the summer months, becoming one of the theater's highlights until 1862. For eight years, Perea introduced to London theaters new dances being invented and transformed by Seville's dance masters, especially beginning in the late 1840s. These were little choreographies that told stories of Spaniards in fairs, inns, bullrings, and patios, with names like *The Star of Andalusia, The Gallician Fête, The Bullfighter, El Gambusino, The pretty gipsie and the bullfighter,* and *La Cigarrera de Sevilla*.

To the applause garnered by Perea we must add that which was received by Petra Cámara in Paris on May 13, 1851, at the Théâtre du Gymnase-Dramatique, with a program in three *cuadros* (scenes), which included *El Olé gaditano, La Feria de Sevilla,* and *El Polo del Contrabandista*. From Paris, Petra Cámara traveled to London to perform in Her Majesty's Theatre, hired by Benjamin Lumley as a headliner for the World's Fair.[26] Her repertory included *El Vito, La Manola, Jaleo de Jerez, Fantasía española, Seguidillas Gitanas, La Jerezana, Jaleo de la Pandereta,* and *Danza Valenciana*: divertissements in premieres such as *La Feria de Sevilla, Curra la Gaditana o Los Toreros de Chiclana,* and *La Gitana en Chamberí*.

Cristina Mendes, Pepita Oliva, Lola de Valencia are among other illustrious names in this history. These are artists who contributed definitively to the growth in popularity of Spanish dances, which were derived principally from the escuela bolera. Following the 1870s, when flamenco dances were now performed in private parties and *cafés cantantes* in cities such as Seville, they transformed again into a new artistic manifestation of the traditional and already long-lived fandangos, boleros, and seguidillas that had built a bridge to the hearts of European audiences.

Notes

1. J. Jean Sentaurens, "Bailes y entremeses en los escenarios teatrales sevillanos de los siglos XVII y XVIII: ¿géneros menores para un público popular?" in *El Teatro menor en España a partir del siglo XVI* (Madrid: CSIC, 1983), 67–87.
2. For more on visitors to eighteenth-century Andalusia, see Rocío Plaza, *Los caminos de Andalucía: memorias de los viajeros del siglo XVIII* (Sevilla: Universidad de Sevilla, 2008).
3. For more on the developing role of choreographers in early nineteenth-century Spanish dance, see Kiko Mora, "Some Notes Toward a Historiography of the Mid-Nineteenth Century *Bailable Español*," in this volume.
4. Michael Cherlin, Halina Filipowicz, and Richard L. Rudolph, *The Great Tradition and its Legacy: The Evolution of Dramatic and Musical Theater in Austria and Central Europe* (New York: Berghahn Books, 2003), 157–158.
5. Artemis Markessinis, *Historia de la danza desde sus orígenes* (Madrid: Libr. Deportivas Esteban Sanz Martier, 1995), 91.
6. This was a one-act ballet by Jean-Louis Aumer, with music by Adalbert Gyrowetz, sets by Pierre Luc Charles Ciceri, and costumes by Hyppolite Lecomte. The dancers' roles included: Aumer as the Duke of Vendôme; Louis Jacques Milon as Count Muret; Louis Mérante as Marimon; Godefroy as Pedrillo; Émile Bigottini as the Page Víctor (in travesty); Fanny Bias as Élise; Louise Élie as Madame de Saint-Ange; Adelaïde as Madame Pedrillo; Marinette as Rosine Bertine and Coelina as pages. Other dancers included Antoine Paul, Antoine Coulon, Seuriot, Lise Noblet, Julie Aumer, and Virginie Aulin. Ivor Guest, *The Romantic Ballet in Paris* (Middletown, CT: Wesleyan University Press, 1966), 38.
7. Ivor Guest, *The Romantic Ballet in Paris*, 161.
8. Ibid., 18–20.
9. Ibid.
10. Ibid.
11. Guest, in *The Romantic Ballet* (20), cites Carlo Blasis and R. Barton (trans.), *The Code of Terpsichore: The Art of Dancing, Comprising its Theory and Practice, and a History of Its Rise and Progress, from the Earliest Times* (London: E. Bull, 1830), 91–92.
12. Guest, *The Romantic Ballet*, 39.
13. Ibid.
14. Phillip H. Highfill, *A Biographical Dictionary of Actors, Actresses, Musicians, Dancers, Managers & Other Stage Personnel in London, 1660–1800* (Carbondale: Southern Illinois University Press, 1991), 11.
15. Ivor Guest, *The Romantic Ballet in England* (London: Phoenix House, 1954), 122.
16. Ibid.
17. According to Ivor Guest in *The Romantic Ballet in England*, both the ballet *Le Tuteur trompé*, and the Spanish dances it incorporated were restaged in following seasons. The last iteration was a *pas de trois* titled *Les Folies d'Espagne*, danced by Charles Didelot, Madelaine Guimard, and Duquesnay in 1789. It was danced by Auguste Vestris and ballerinas Hilligsberg and Monzon in 1791. Deshayes, who was *primer bailarín* (first dancer) in Madrid in 1799, revived the work in 1807, dancing with his wife, and Señorita Parisot, repeating it in 1810 and again in 1814. Thirty-one years after Le Picq and Mme. Rossi's interpretation, the ballet was danced for the last time (121–122).
18. "When Etruria (a client state of Napoleonic France established in Tuscany 1801 and disestablished 1807) was obtained by the Spanish Prince Louis, grandson of Phillip of Parma and son of Queen María Luisa Teresa de Parma, María Mercandotti, an Andalusian of Italian origin and heir to the Italian Fortunata Angiolini's talents as a bolero dancer, was born." Marie-Catherine Talvikki Chanfreau, "Les Apports étrangers a l'identité culturelle espagnole (XVIIIe–XXe siécles). L'Italianisme de l'école bolera," in *Le métissage culturel en Espagne*, ed. J. R. Aymes and S. Salaü (Paris: Sorbonne Nouvelle, 2001), 58.
19. Louis Véron, *Mémoires d'un bourgeois de Paris* (Paris: Gonet, 1854), 301.
20. William Jacob, *Viajes por el sur. Cartas escritas entre 1809–1810* (Sevilla: Portada Editorial, 2002), 65.
21. Rocío Plaza Orellana, *Los bailes españoles en Europa. El espectáculo de los bailes de España en el siglo XIX* (Córdoba: Almuzara, 2013) 38–39; Ivor Guest, *The Romantic Ballet in England*, 46–47.
22. Gerhard Steingress, *...y Carmen se fue a París. Un estudio sobre la construcción artística del género flamenco (1833–1865)* (Córdoba: Almuzara, 2006), 88–89; Rocío Plaza Orellana, *Bailes de Andalucia en Londres y París (1830–1850)* (Madrid: Arambel, 2005), 74–77; Plaza Orellana, *Los bailes españoles en Europa*, 70–75.

23. Plaza Orellana, *Los bailes españoles en Europa*, 63–67.
24. Coralli's two-act ballet was based on a libretto by Edmon Burat de Gurgy and Adolphe Nourrit, with music by Casimir Gide. The cast included Hippolyte Barrez (the devil Asmodée), Joseph Mazilier (Cléophas), Louis Montjoie (Bellaspada), Élie (Don Gilès), Châtillon (the dance master), Viaud (the orchestra director), Charles Petit (the doctor), Eugène Coralli (the hairdresser), Péqueux (*l'avertisseur*), Vincent (the rehearsal director), Simon (the inspector), and Paul (a valet). The Gitanos were danced by: MM. Simon, Quériau, and Cozzo. The Gitanas were danced by Mlles. Fanny Elssler (Florinde), Therese Elssler, Mlle. Legallois (Dorothée), Leroux (Paquita), Baptiste Albrier (Hélène), and Roland (the chamber maid). The *Pas de quatre* was danced by Mmes. Noblet, Alexis-Dupont, L. Fitzjames, and María. The *Pas de deux* was danced by Mlles. Blangy and Carrez. First act: MM. A. Albert and A. Mabille/ Mlles. Julia and L. Fiitzjames. Mmes. Noblet, Alexis Dupont, L. Fitzjames. Second act: Mlles. F. and Th. Elssler. Cachucha: Mlle. Elssler. Third act: Mlle. Lerouz/ Mm. Simon, Quériau, and Cozzo; Mlles. Roland, Brocard, and Florentine (Conard).
25. Rocío Plaza Orellana, *El flamenco y los románticos. Un viaje entre el mito y la realidad* (Sevilla: Bienal de Flamenco, 1999), 606.
26. Gerhard Steingress, *...y Carmen se fue a París*, 155–158.

Fandangos and Bailes
Dancing and Dance Events in Early California[1]
ANTHONY SHAY

> *A Californian would hardly pause in a dance for an earthquake, and would renew it before the vibrations ceased.*[2]

It would be simplistic to say that the *Californios* loved to dance. Travellers to Alta California remarked upon the intense passion and interest in dance in almost every account of life in Spanish (1769–1821) and Mexican (1821–1848) California.[3] Dancing fulfilled a number of very real needs of a society politically and economically isolated from the gravitational centers of Mexico City and Madrid, and was characterized by rigorous social customs and segregation of the sexes.

Many descriptions of early colonial California attests to the near fanatical love of dancing, to the numerous occasions when the Californians danced, and to the importance and prestige accorded to an outstanding dancer. Dance as an important activity claims a crucial space in the reminiscences of early Californian residents. Feminist Chicana historian Antonia I. Castañeda notes, "Dance was especially important as a medium of individual and group expression and allowed both men and women to demonstrate their skill, talent, and grace. Special dances were performed by children and adults, groups and couples and married and single people. Women and men danced both together and separately."[4]

Nineteenth-century missionaries and merchants, seafarers and sailors who traveled to California also noted this passion for dance. In 1832, Thomas O. Larkin said that the men on his ship participated in early Californian social and recreational activities while onshore, "hunting wild Deer or dancing with tame 'Dear,' both being plentiful in and around Monterey. With the flagship's splendid band, there were as many balls as there were Sundays, with 'Waltzes, *Quadrilles, Hotas* [jotas], *Sons* [sones], *Arabes* [jarabes], *Bolero* with castaneta, Etc.'—some who had never danced before 'danced here.'"[5]

For an understanding of Walter Colton's oft-quoted remark, which opens this essay, and which depicts the passion and intensity with which the Californians danced, two factors must be taken into account. The first key to understanding the early Californians and the society in which they lived is isolation. Isolation—geographic, economic, cultural, and social—greatly shaped the social conditions that existed in early California. One must remember that Monterey, the largest settlement in Alta California was, in fact, small: "by the 1830s [it] was a settlement of nearly six hundred souls: two hundred men, fewer women, more children, two dozen Indians, and twenty-six to thirty *extranjeros* [foreigners]" lived there.[6] Because of this socioeconomic and cultural isolation, Californios had to fall back on their own resources for entertainment and art.[7]

For travelers of the eighteenth and nineteenth centuries who came to California under the auspices of the colonial Spanish and Mexican governments, California was considered a far western outpost. Spain, especially, was interested in defending its territories in the north against the English and the Russians, and was eager to expand its business interests in a land as rich as California. As historian David Weber notes, "Still another economic framework might place Spanish North America beyond the periphery of the world economic system, and even beyond the fringes of empire."[8] The first Spanish-speaking women did not arrive in California until 1774, when eight women came with a small number of men to join the "Sixty Spanish, mestizo and other *casta* soldiers dispatched to defend the frontier against European incursions" who had arrived in 1769.[9] Thus, 1769 marked the time when "Spain had planted a slight and uncertain colony on the northwest coast."[10]

The settlers who came to California during the period of Spanish rule (1769–1821) were not necessarily of aristocratic Spanish blood. As in other colonial outposts, these agents of the Spanish crown who supposedly introduced Andalusian folk songs and dances in their secluded ranchero patios (so beloved of the early Anglo American chroniclers) were recruited from the lower classes, and were rarely Spaniards, but rather Mexicans. "According to the 1793 census of colonial New Spain, Alta California's population of *gente de razón*—the Spanish-speaking Christians of all ethnic backgrounds—was 1,066 persons, of whom only thirty (or 3%) were actually European Spaniards. The remaining 1,036 were soldiers, settlers, and artisans born in Mexico."[11] Aside from the occasional wife of the governor or a high-ranking military officer, the majority of the population of California from the late eighteenth to the late nineteenth century resembled the complex racial and socioeconomic population of Australia, England's penal colony. As Castañeda explains,

> Artisan wives, or women from what may be considered the middle strata of eighteenth-century colonial Mexican society, did not settle in California. The women who came to stay belonged instead to the lower socioeconomic classes of New Spain. They were the mothers, wives, daughters, and kinswomen of leather-jacket soldiers who staffed the frontier presidios of New Spain, of impoverished settlers who lived in the adjoining civilian pueblos, and of convicts from Mexico and Guadalajara sentenced to Alta California in lieu of other punishment.[12]

Many travelers, until setting foot on American soil, imagined Spanish California as consisting mainly of large ranchos. However, the Spanish colonial period in California, as in New Mexico and Arizona, was vast and complex, resulting in the founding of the mission system (forced conversion of Native Americans), military presidios, and two ultimately successful civil settlements: Los Angeles and San José. There were no more than twenty-five land grants given during the entire fifty-two-year Spanish colonial period. "The first private land grant in Alta California, a small tract of land near Mission San Carlos in present-day Carmel, was awarded in 1775 by California Governor Rivera to Manuel Butrón and his Indian wife.... Only about twenty-five grants were awarded during the Spanish period from 1769–1821."[13]

Many more such ranchos were granted during the Mexican regime, in a much shorter period of time: "about eight hundred—were awarded during the Mexican period, from 1821 to 1848."[14] "They became the most prominent feature of California society."[15] Thus, ironically, it was during the Mexican period, not the fondly remembered Spanish period, that the late nineteenth- and early twentieth-century writers looked back to as the halcyon days of pastoral California rancho life filled with music, dance, and fiestas.

The extreme popularity of dancing and music also owes a good deal to the status of women in traditional Spanish society. Spanish Catholic religious and social values confined women to the domestic sphere; at the same time, the economics of rancho life meant that aristocratic Spanish society was largely equestrian. This was also true of the English gentry, but in Spanish society, women rarely rode and were more sequestered. In addition, the presence of a large Native American labor force, and the disdain for manual labor by most of the settlers, reduced the physical exercise opportunities for women. It is important to note that the most onerous forms of "Spanish labor systems had been abolished by 1769," however, "treatment of the Native Americans amounted to slavery in some instances," according to Steven Haskel in "Land, Labor, and Production" (122).

An apt description from one of the elite women of early California tells us:

> The ladies of Monterey in 1828 were rarely seen in the street, except very early in the morning on their way to church. We used to go there attended by our servants, who carried small mats for us to kneel upon, as there were no seats. A tasteful little rug was considered an indispensable part of our belongings and every young lady embroidered her own.... One of the gallants of the time said that "dancing, music, religion, and amiability" were the orthodox occupations of the ladies of Alta California.... We were in many ways like grown-up children. Our servants were faithful, agreeable, and easy to manage. They often slept on mats on the earthen floor, or, in the summer time, in the courtyards. When they waited on us at meals, we often let them hold conversations with us, and laugh without restraint. As we used to say, a good servant knew when to be quiet and when to put in his *cuchara* (or spoon).[16]

The above quotation illustrates the ways in which New Spain's colonial notions, which were embedded in the racialist casta paintings depicting the dangerous results of racial and class mixing, and the formation of twenty-four named racial categories that marked the society of New Spain, also characterized early Californian society, but on a smaller scale.

Male-oriented horseback riding and such rough-and-tumble sports as bullfighting and bear- and bull-baiting relegated women in this society to the role of observers, although *toreras* (female bullfighters) were celebrated in Spain throughout the nineteenth century. "There were some skilled horsewomen, but not many. When a woman rode, it was side-saddle, with a wooden or straw platform on which her feet could rest. A protective male sat just behind her on the crupper, one arm holding her and the other handling the reins."[17] This, coupled with the Spanish tradition against manual labor for aristocrats and the large number of indentured neophyte (Native American) labor, restricted the activities of the elite California woman to embroidery and the management of servants in the household. Thus, the only physical activity open to women of the leisure class, beyond walking about the ranch, was dancing. One observer noted,

> I was astonished at the endurance of the California women in holding out, night after night, in dancing, of which they never seemed to weary, but kept on with an appearance of freshness and elasticity that was as charming as surprising. Their actions, movements and bearing were as full of life and animation after several nights of dancing as at the beginning, while the men, on the other hand, became wearied, showing that their powers of endurance were not equal to those of the ladies. I have frequently heard the latter ridiculing the gentlemen for not holding out un-fatigued to the end of a festival of this kind.[18]

It should come as no surprise that the men, after a long day in the saddle overseeing their extensive land holdings, were not as eager to dance for long hours as were the women, who had few other physical outlets.

Living conditions in early California were quite rudimentary in the first few decades: "Life on an Alta California ranch in the late eighteenth and early nineteenth century was arduous and lonely."[19] By the 1830s, with the establishment of more populous small towns and outlying working ranches, life became somewhat easier. In the Mexican Californian period, many wealthy families were able to import into Alta California the elegancies of life alongside basic necessities without which they had lived for decades. "The unexpected, but profitable, development of the hide and tallow trade and the subsequent connection with world markets revolutionized ranchero life in Alta California. Ranching, that had generally been a subsistence life style, was irreversibly changed by the wealth derived from the new trade ... the rancheros were able to afford new material comforts. The wealthier rancheros built better homes, furnished them with articles purchased from the Boston merchant ships that regularly plied Alta California's coastline, and began to adopt European dress styles."[20] The stratification of society along Spanish caste lines accompanied this growth and expansion, which is discussed in further detail below.

The difference between the Spanish period's tiny ranches, allotted mostly to retired military, and the ranches of the Mexican period, during which some 800 probably existed, was in size and scope. Tallow and hides, the most important products of the Mexican period, enabled the rancheros to enjoy a much higher standard of living.

Although change was resisted on many levels, the Californios avidly adapted to it, as far as they were able, in dancing and clothing; however, change was slow, and the major agents of change were new colonists. The Padres-Hijar ranch/colony in the Mexican California of 1834, for example, inaugurated new dances and new clothing innovations because several well-educated persons of social rank lived in the colony.

The occasions for dancing and the types of dance events in early California were many and varied. For our purposes, they can be essentially divided into two categories: formal and informal. The difference between formal and informal dance events was reflected in their scope and functions, such as the dances that were performed, who danced and at what point in the evening or during the fiesta, the required European ideas of etiquette, and other elements.[21]

Usually, informal dance events were for the entertainment and amusement of the participants. Beyond this, the ramifications on a social level were few. Informal dance parties also served an important pedagogical function as learning environments for children, who are never mentioned as attending formal dance events. Indeed, matters of age were important; the elderly were held in great honor and younger men and women did not dance without their consent. Not until the strains of the stately minuet and *contradanza* died away were the vivacious dances played that appealed to the younger participants. In informal dance events, etiquette was greatly relaxed. Anglo American Hubert Bancroft, a well-known chronicler of life in early California, observed:

> Dancing was a passion with the Californians. It affected all, from infancy to old age; grandmothers and grandchildren were seen dancing together; their houses were constructed with reference to this amusement, and most of the interior space was appropriated to the *sala*, a large, barn-like room. A few chairs and a wooden settee were all its furniture. If a few people got together at any hours of the day, the first thought was to send for a violin and guitar and should the violin and guitar be found together in appropriate hands, that of itself was sufficient reason to send for the dancers.[22]

Another nineteenth-century chronicler, Dr. Platon Vallejo, recalled:

> The evenings were given over to pure merriment. Every hacienda had its stringed band of several pieces, the harp, the guitar, and violin—once in a while a flute. And every night, rain or shine—except at times of death or sorrow, there was a *baile*. In this, every one had his part. The elder people stepped the stately *contradanza*. The budding generations enjoyed the waltz and the beautiful Spanish folk dances to the accompaniment of the *castanetas*, and even the little ones had their own figures to romp through. In short, the occasion was one for all-around pleasure of the natural unconscious style, without restraint or starchiness, where not a few, but everyone enjoyed themselves.[23]

These descriptions are a far cry from the rigid etiquette enforced at more formal balls, or *bailes*. Formal dance events, which represented one of the socially sanctioned occasions when marriageable men and women could meet, had far-reaching socioeconomic implications in early California. It is certain that much matchmaking took place during the events, since the parents could look over the crop of eligible bachelors and maidens. The young, especially those who were not formally declared marriageable, were not permitted to attend these formal dances.

> The respect in which our parents and elderly persons generally were held was so great that no young man ventured to dance in their presence without first having received permission. From 1831 to 1832, customs became less strict; dances became more exclusive and were usually given in the homes of private persons.
>
> What I have said about dances I learned at long distances from them, for I was never permitted to attend one of them until I was twenty or twenty-one years old. All the other young men were in the same situation…. I confess that even when I reached an age when I could attend dances, I went to them merely out of curiosity and never danced or sang.
>
> Dances were generally opened by older persons … and the young people were not permitted by any chance to take part in them unless they happened to be married; and even then, it was not often allowed. But when the hour came for the old folks to retire, the older of the young fellows began to enjoy the dance.[24]

During the earliest colonial period until 1830, the population was so small that formal balls and events were open indiscriminately to all European social classes (that is, *gente de razon*—Spanish-speaking people).[25]

> Social relations between different classes of society were very equitable, since a sizable part of even the lowest class had claims to better origins (ordinary soldiers had such names as de la Cruz, Mercada, and de Roca Verde), from the outside society did not exhibit that sharp cleavage between different classes that we see in other countries.

Figure 1: A scene of dancers in a cantina, most likely performing a *fandango*, from *Trajes Mexicanos*, lithograph, unknown artist, about 1834 or 1835 (collection of Anthony Shay).

> External official relations always seemed to be on an equal footing, and even the lowest class behaved with dignity before high officials. At parties given by the Russian officers or Spanish authorities everyone entered the dance hall without difference in rank and without a special invitation, except a general announcement that there would be a fandango (the name of a certain dance). Single girls of all classes straightaway joined the circle of dancers equally with the highest members of society; married women and widows sat in the first unoccupied seats, and the men placed themselves in the corners and at the door, standing or sitting unceremoniously on the floor.[26]

This same freedom to attend public events, however, did not extend to converted and unconverted Native Americans. Their restricted access to social events was confined to their usefulness as mission-trained musicians who accompanied services and other religious social functions.

Formal dance events were prearranged affairs and their formality was marked by the presence of a master of ceremonies, or dance master, known as *el tecolero* or *el bastonero*. The tecoloro inaugurated the dancing with a *son*, a highly improvised dance accompanied by a myriad of tunes. His role was also to mediate between men and women, ensuring that every woman had an opportunity to take a turn on the dance floor and, thus, be seen by potential male suitors. The improvisational nature of the son allowed those with exceptional choreographic prowess to make themselves known. In formal dance events, couples were always segregated, except during the public event of dancing.

> The *señoras* and *señoritas* occupied a platform on one side (of the *enramada*, or outdoor arbor), the men remaining entirely separate. If there were many ladies and all the

seats were occupied by them, the men had to stand outside the door of the arbor, which was very wide. Some were on foot and some on horseback. The musicians occupied a place assigned to them in the center of one of the sides. There was one individual called the *tecolero* (master of ceremonies) who went around the edge, keeping time with his feet, and taking out the ladies to dance.

The manner of inviting a lady to dance was by making some pirouettes or dance steps before her, accompanied by clapping of the hands.... The lady who went out to dance returned to her post when she was ready and the tecolero went on making his pirouettes and taking out the ladies one by one until they all had danced. Anyone who was not familiar with the dance, or was not able on account of some illness, arose, took a turn, and sat down again in her place.[27]

"In the sones, the tecolero stepped out, keeping time with his feet and stopping in front of the first woman in the row while we clapped hands.... As soon as she finished her dance, she sat down and he led out another, until the last one had danced."[28] At this point in the dance, if a woman was very skilled, the tecolero would honor her by placing his hat on her head as she danced, and the other men would then follow suit.[29]

[W]hen a lady was prominent for her skill and grace in *El Son* or *El Jarabe*, the men placed their hats on her head, one on top of the other; and when she could carry no more, they threw them at her feet. Then they threw their *mangas*, or wraps, on the floor for her to honor them by dancing on them.

The musicians again commencing a lively tune, one of the managers approached the nearest female and, clapping his hands in accompaniment to the music, succeeded in bringing her into the centre of the room. Here she remained a while, gently tapping her feet upon the floor, and then giving two or three whirls, skipped away to her seat. Another was clapped out, and another, til the manager had passed the compliment throughout the room. This is called a *son*, and there is a custom among the men, when a dancer proves particularly attractive to any one, to place his hat upon her head, while she stands thus in the middle of the room, which she retains until redeemed by its owner, with some trifling present.[30]

As the population grew and social stratification created more complex fissures between rich and poor, native and immigrant, the Californios reverted to a reflection of Spanish society: a two-tiered caste system. This occasioned a division in society unknown in the earlier period that resulted in a concomitant division into two types of dance events: the *fandango* and the *baile*. By the 1830s, the term "fandango" was separated out from the "baile" and used to describe only dance events accepting of the working poor. Thereafter, fandangos increasingly became unruly events in which drinking and partying sometimes resulted in death and injury.

Formal balls were by invitation only and these exclusive events were now called bailes. In contrast, the fandango, which in its beginnings had been an open party event to which all were welcome, gradually became a public dance event of the lowest order. By the time the Gold Rush began, fandango "houses," where one could purchase drinks and dance, were the rage and were notorious for their rough atmosphere, similar to that of cowboy saloons. As often as not, wild brawls ensued, ending in killings. A fandango house was, in effect, a low-class cantina. "Beneath" the fandango were the dances of the people of the poorest class, the dances being the same [as the upper classes], but much exaggerated and unrestrained. These affairs generally ended in blows, wounds, accidents with horses, or at least with dirty and insulting words.

Throughout the mid-nineteenth century, the structure of dance events shifted further, moving in tandem with socioeconomic and political currents. During the administrative rule of José María Echeandía (twice the Mexican governor of Alta California, 1825–1831, 1832–1833), it was usual for a party organizer to place an armed guard at the front door. The balls for "respectable" people were generally held in the *sala* of the government house, within the square of the old presidio. Invitations to families were issued by an appointed committee and entrance was permitted to only invited guests, who now had to present invitation cards to the guard upon entrance. All of the "respectable" families were invited whether they were poor or rich. By the end of the nineteenth century, dance events such as these were in decline; the best families withdrew. From then on, there were instituted dances of "tone" at which were present only those who hosted the dance. Despite this, new "modern" dances that were emerging in Europe and the Afro-Caribbean made their way with travelers to California and were seen on the dance floors up and down the coast. The contradanza, the waltz, and the cotillion became a California craze.[31]

It is probable that civil authorities tried to control some of the more excessive behavior of some dance events. The local authorities of the presidios and pueblos began demanding permits and fees.

> The permission of the authorities had to be obtained to hold a ball and illumination; as for instance, the one at Carrillo's house, in honor of Fitch's return with his bride in 1830.
> In 1837, at San Jose, a fandango required the permission of the alcalde. Owners or occupants of the house were held responsible, jointly with authors of the ball, for disorders. In a non-licensed dance, the first offense was a fine of $20 and the stoppage of the festivity.[32]

Formal dance events were extremely important to wealthy Californios and were marked by prior notice in the form of a public or announcement or private invitation. All important occasions, such as the arrival of a governor or other official or important visitor, the arrival of a ship, a religious Catholic holiday, or a secular rite of passage such as a wedding, engagement, or christening were marked by a dance. The participants to these important occasions often traveled long distances.

Very few California residents who have memories of these old fandango days and the journeys taken from suburb to town in order to participate in them are still alive. Doña Petra Pilar Lanfranco used to tell me how, as a young girl, she came up from the old Palos Verdes ranch house in a *carreta* (wagon), chaperoned by a female relative. On such occasions, the carreta would be provided with mattresses, pillows, and covers. Well-strapped at the carriage's end was the trunk containing the finery to be worn at the ball. To reach town, even from a point that would now be regarded as near, a start was generally made by four o'clock in the morning. It often took until late the same evening to arrive at the Bella Union [a hotel located in the downtown area of Los Angeles], where final preparations were made.[33]

The variety of locations in which dance events were held is intriguing. Aside from the large halls (salas) found in most private homes and the halls of the government in the presidios, Californians also danced in the open-air spaces of large ranches for which a unique temporary structure, the *enramada*, was built. Dancing in the enramada was almost always for formal dance events, for it took several days of preparation to ready the dance floor's surface. This was sometimes a platform, or earth that was watered and pounded for days to create an evenly hardened surface.

> The Californios had still other diversions—such as the fandangos or dances that took place at all kinds of fiestas, religious or profane.
>
> For these dances, a great arbor was constructed in front of the house that was chosen for the function. The inside of the arbor was covered with white goods and some ornaments, such as ribbons, artificial flowers, etc. The arbor was closed in on three sides; the one left open was for the men on horseback, who placed themselves there, that side being well guarded with palings, or posts to keep out the horses. On the inside the ladies sat down on seats placed around the sides. The music, which consisted of a violin, a guitar, and two or three singers, was placed at one end, in order not to be in the way.
>
> The master of ceremonies, or leader was given the name of tecolero. He, at once, placed himself in the center of the arbor to organize the dance.[34]

Weddings lasted at least three days, during which there was almost nonstop dancing. Thus, a good floor became necessary to maintaining a healthy body.

> The married couple then enters the house where the near relatives are all waiting in tears to receive them. They kneel down before the parents of the lady, and crave a blessing, bestowed with patriarchal solemnity. On rising, the bridegroom makes a signal for the guests to come in, and another for the guitar and harp to strike up. Then commences the dancing, with only brief intervals for refreshment, but none for slumber: the wedded pair must be on their feet.[35]

Figure 2: An example of costumes for men and women. The woman's costume is an early version of a *china poblana* (a seventeenth- to nineteenth-century mode of dress with chemise, skirt and shawl [*rebozo*]). From *Costumes of Early California*, lithograph, unknown artist, about 1835 (collection of Anthony Shay).

The difference between the informal and formal dance events in town and on the ranchos is well illustrated by Davis:

> The rancheros and their household generally retired early, about eight o'clock, unless a *valsecito casero* (little home party) was on hand, when this lasted till twelve or one. They were fond of these gatherings, and almost every family having some musician of its own, music and dancing were indulged in, and a very pleasant time enjoyed. I have attended many of them and always was agreeably entertained. These parties were usually impromptu, without formality and were often held for the entertainment of a guest who might be stopping at the house. The balls or larger parties were of more importance, and usually occurred in the towns. On the occasion of the marriage of a son or daughter of a ranchero they took place on the rancho, the marriage being celebrated amid great festivities, lasting several days.
>
> Fandango was a term for a dance or entertainment among the lower classes where neighbors and others were invited in, and engaged themselves without any degree of formality. The entertainments of the wealthy and aristocratic class were more exclusive in character; invitations were more carefully given, more formality observed, and of course, more elegance and refinement prevailed. An entertainment of this character was known as a baile.
>
> In November 1838, I was a guest at the wedding party given at the marriage of Don José Martínez to the daughter of Don Ygnacio Peralta, which lasted about a week, dancing being kept up all night with a company of at least one hundred men and women from the adjoining ranchos, about three hours after daylight being given to sleep, after which picnics in the woods were held during the forenoon, and the afternoon was devoted to bullfighting. This programme was continued for a week when I myself had become so exhausted from want of regular sleep that I was glad to escape. The bride and bridegroom were not given any seclusion until the third night.[36]

Toward the end of this period, with the great influx of foreigners, balls and fandangos began to be held in rented public halls. At first, this was a respectable amusement.

> ... Only for the first few years after I came was the real fandango—so popular when Dana [author of *Two Years Before the Mast*] visited Los Angeles and first saw Don Juan Bandini execute the dance—witnessed here; little by little it went out of fashion, perhaps in part because of the skill required for its performance. Balls and hops, however, for a long time were carelessly called by that name. When the fandango rally was in vogue, Bandini, Antonio Coronel, Andrés Pico, the Lugos and other native Californians were among its most noted exponents; they often hired a hall, gave a fandango in which they did not hesitate to take the leading parts, and turned the whole proceeds over to some church or charity. On such occasions not merely the plain people (always so responsive to music and its accompanying pleasures) were the fandangueros, but the flower of our local society turned out en masse, adding to the affair a high degree of éclat.[37]

As Horace Bell lamented, "The old-fashioned fandango is a thing of the past. Reader, let us go to a fandango in 1853. Before we start, let us examine where we elbow our way through the dense crowd of Indians, peons, and pelados, the riff-raff, scruff and scum of our angel population, and amid jibe and jeer we gain the corridor or veranda."[38] Bell clearly enunciates the racist attitudes toward Mexicans and Native Americans that still exist in the blatant attempts to turn the Santa Barbara Spanish Days festival into a celebration of European rather than Mexican and/or indigenous contributions to California history. Needless to say, Bell observed the crumbling of a society that he and other Anglo Americans venerated but also helped destroy, and that society probably never had the rosy halo imagined.

Early California Dances

The actual dances performed by the Californios were numerous, and their names and musical compositions, as well as first-person reminiscences by pioneer descendants, are available.[39] These dances were of three types and correspond to the kinds of dance events and social environments in which they were performed: play party games; formal, patterned ballroom dances; and highly improvised solo and couple dances of Mexican, and perhaps, Spanish origin, requiring technical skill.

The play party games described in many sources were performed almost exclusively in the informal, family-oriented social gatherings for which early California became famous. In the largely rural, religiously conservative society of that period in which no other form of entertainment was available or church sanctioned, young and old, male and female could derive much pleasure and amusement from the many innocent play party games performed. In the play party games characterized by miming, especially animal movements, singing and dance movements were equally important. The skills required were minimal; anyone could join in. These games were impromptu, requiring no musical accompaniment other than the performers' singing, although literature and memoirs emphasize that in virtually every household there were musicians: guitarists, violinists, harpists, pianists, and/or flutists. Some popular and typical play party dance games were: *el borreg* (the lamb), *el caballo* (the horse), *la canastita de flores* (the little basket of flowers), *el burro* (the donkey), and *la zorrita* (the vixen). Many of the same games held different names in Europe than in the United States. When the first foreigners arrived, some games were already familiar to them, and they, too, could join in the festivities. Hence, dance and music helped absorb and assimilate recent arrivals to California more swiftly, opening a symbiotic exchange between "native" Californians.

> Spanish dances, especially in America, included many dramatics; the combination of the dramatics, the music, the singing, and the improvisations made them more like excerpts from a theatrical performance than proper dances.... There was always general animation, especially with dramatic dances presented as if they were excerpts from operas. Everyone, even the old men and women, joined in the singing and followed the course of activities with the greatest interest.[40]

In contrast, the skills required in the dancing of the *jota aragonesa*, a son, a *jarabe, la bamba,* or the fandango, were considerable. Rivalry erupted among the most outstanding dancers, especially among the women, to literally out dance, outshine, and outlast all of the others. As Esteban de la Torre, writing in 1930, noted,

> At the time when I came from Loreto to San Diego I was very fond of dancing, and was considered the best dancer in the country. I also sang in the Church of the Presidio of Loreto. One Chepa Rodriguez and I danced together at Santa Barbara. Chepa was much lauded as a great dancer. We danced the jarabe, and she got tired and sat down, leaving me still dancing. I also beat another lady who was a famous dancer. A challenge was sent out as far as Monterey for dancers to come and compete with me, but nobody came. That was on the occasion of the blessing of the Church at Santa Barbara.
>
> When I was young, I danced everything—sones, jarabes, *pontorico, medio catorce,* fandango, *la zorrita. Las pollitas,* and *el caballo.*[41]

As one can see, for many Californios dancing was not merely a lighthearted diversion but an activity upon which they expended many hours. A fine dancer of la bamba, for example, could perform a vigorous *zapateado* (stamping, rhythmic footwork associated with flamenco) with a glass of water balanced on her head. Castanets seemed to have been employed for several of the dances as well. These improvised, competitive dances were performed both for formal and informal dance events. It is clear that the expertise in these dances was acquired by the young at home, since many years of practice and exposure are required for the skilled performance of these dances and the playing of castanets.

It is also clear that these dances were the first to disappear with the arrival of large numbers of Americans beginning in the 1840s, and other non–Spanish Europeans, since these newcomers lacked the background and training for their performance. By the 1850s, dances that once governed the social structure and leisure time of early rancheros had fallen out of favor. Some had been changed, such as the total transformation of the jota aragonesa to a simple-patterned ballroom dance whose steps retained fewer elements of the original dance; others, such as la bamba and the jarabe, disappeared altogether. Nevertheless, the many rich descriptions left in memoirs, coupled with our knowledge of current Mexican and Spanish folk dances, opens a rich cultural history of early Californians, whose love of dancing governed daily life.

More complex is the question of the European, Mexican, Caribbean, and American origins of the dances. The dance called the jota in early California is clearly not the vigorous Aragon variety: "However, some dancing was unlike the Spanish style, wherein women always take a spirited part. For instance, the jota, is similar to the Virginia reel in that men and women faced each other in long lines, the women remained almost motionless while the men danced exuberantly around them in circles."[42] This descriptive analysis brings to the surface the circulation of dances within the United States as European lands were colonized alongside Native American land and subsequently entered into U.S. territory.

The third type of dance, the ballroom dances of early California, were performed most often in formal dance events, and tended to be introduced long after their fashionableness had waxed and waned in Europe. "The minuet was fully preserved, although it was mainly danced by elderly people," one observer noted in 1824.[43] The waltz, forbidden by the Church under threat of excommunication, was not performed in California until 1830, nearly two decades after its social acceptance in Europe, at the close of the Napoleonic Wars. The most often mentioned ballroom dance of early Californians was the contradanza that is still performed by descendants of the early Californios, as well as patriotic folk dance groups.

In conclusion, one can see that the types of dances and dance events answered many requirements of the people of early California: entertainment, physical exercise, aesthetic outlet, societal control, and social interaction. The types of dances and dance events changed slowly over time with the concomitant changes in social environment, economy, government, power of the missions over daily life, and ethnic composition of new immigrants, especially the takeover by the Anglo Americans who dispossessed the Hispanic population of their land titles and, therefore, their social economies. Thus, the rich dances and dance events that once formed an integral part of daily life in nineteenth-century California faded, leaving their descendants the opportunity to write memoirs detailing what was lost.

Notes

1. The original version of this essay appeared as "Fandangoes and Bailes: Dancing and Dance Events in Early California," in *Southern California Quarterly* 64, no. 2 (Summer 1982): 99–113, © 1982 by the Regents of the University of California, published by the University of California Press. For this book I have added considerably to the notes to reflect the more recent scholarship concerning early California. It has taken years for scholars to come to grips with the historical romancing of early California and its inhabitants by early Anglo-American boosters of the state such as Charles Loomis and Hubert Bancroft, who portrayed early California as a pastoral paradise, as if only Spaniards lived here, Mexicans were an inconvenient presence, and Native Americans were erased or turned into docile and silent servants in the style of *Ramona*. But early California was overwhelmingly Mexican, with very few Spaniards, aside from one or two governors and a couple of priests; the vast majority of the population of mixed white, African, and Indian mestizos came from Sinaloa and Sonora. Together, in rancho, mission, and presidio, the Hispanic population treated the Native population terribly.

2. Walter Colton, quoted in Nellie Van de Grift Sanchez, *Spanish Arcadia* (San Francisco: Powell, 1929), 314.

3. *Californios* is the Spanish term for those who lived in California and spoke Spanish. The term applied to those who lived in both Alta (Upper) and Baja (Lower) California, territory that today is the state of California in the United States and one of the states of Mexico, respectively.

4. Antonia I. Castañeda, "*Presidarias y Pobladoreas*: The Journey North and Life in Frontier California," in *En Aquel Entonces: Readings in Mexican-American History*, ed. Manuel G. Gonzalez and Cynthia M. Gonzalez (Bloomington: University of Indiana Press, 2000), 11–12.

5. Thomas O. Larkin, quoted in Neal Harlow, *California Conquered: The Annexation of a Mexican Province, 1846–1850* (Berkeley and Los Angeles: University of California Press, 1982), 11.

6. Harlow, *California Conquered*, 14.

7. Alta California, at least the settled part, was smaller than the current state of California, consisting principally of the coastal region up to San Francisco, and the valleys adjacent to the coast. Despite the fact that Mexico owned the entire Southwest, California was isolated from colonies in Arizona, New Mexico, and Texas.

8. David J. Weber, *The Spanish Frontier in North America* (New Haven and London: Yale University Press, 1992), 11.

9. Castañeda, *Presidarias y Pobladorias*, 6.

10. Harlow, *California Conquered*, 18.

11. Antonio Ríos-Bustamante, "The Barrioization of Nineteenth-Century Mexican Californians: From Landowners to Laborers," in *En Aquel Entonces*, 73.

12. Castañeda, *Presidarias y Pobladorias*, 9.

13. Fredrico A. Sánchez, "Rancho Life in Alta California," in *En Aquel Entonces*, 30. A full description of the economy of Alta California, and especially the labor of the California Native Americans, is beyond the scope of this essay. California remained agricultural, and the most important source of cash, and only during the Mexican period was tallow and hides. I refer the interested reader to Steven W. Hackel's excellent survey of the economy of early California: "Land, Labor, and Production: The Colonial Economy of Spanish and Mexican California," in Ramon A. Gutiérrez and Richard J. Orsi, eds., *Contested Eden: California Before the Gold Rush* (Berkeley and Los Angeles: University of California Press, 1998), 111–146.

14. Ibid.

15. Harlow, *California Conquered*, 21.

16. Brigida Briones, "Domestic Life in Monterey in 1827," in *Sketches of Early California*, comp. Donald DeNevi (San Francisco: Chronicle Books, 1971), 43–44. For an especially penetrating analysis of gender roles in patriarchal early California, see Castañeda, *Presidarios y Pobladorias*.

17. Lynn Bowman, *Epic of a City* (Berkeley: Howell-North, 1974), 52.

18. William H. Davis (1822–1909), "Indian Insurrection and Treachery," in *Sketches of Early California*, comp. Donald DeNevi (San Francisco: Chronicle Books, 1971), 39.

19. Sánchez, "Rancho Life," 30.

20. Ibid., 33–35.

21. See Anthony Shay, "Function of Dance in Human Societies" (master's thesis, California State University, Los Angeles, 1970), Chapter Two.

22. Hubert Bancroft, *California Pastoral 1768–1848* (San Francisco: History Co. Pub., 1888), 408.

23. Dr. Platon Vallejo, quoted in Lucille Czarnowski, *Dances of Early California Days* (Palo Alto, CA: Pacific Books, 1950), 19. It should be noted that many Anglo Americans attempted to call every dance and song in early California "Spanish" as opposed to "Mexican," with its lower social status. This is what the eminent California historian Carey McWilliams termed the "heritage fantasy," that is, the romanticizing of a white, European "Spanish" heritage in place of the actual racially mixed Mexican population,

largely recruited from the Mexican states of Sinaloa that settled California. As historian David Weber states, "From Texas to California, Anglo Americans were shocked to meet a predominantly mestizo population" (Weber, *The Spanish Frontier*, 327). For example, the documentation of the music and songs they labeled Spanish folk songs were, in fact, salon music current in Mexico City in the nineteenth century. In 1991, I attended an National Endowment for Humanities-sponsored summer scholars' seminar titled "Latin American Music in its Historical and Cultural Context," directed by Professor Gilbert Behague at the University of Texas, Austin. After tracking down every anthology of "Spanish" folk songs that American aficionados of "Spanish" California collected from Californios, Dr. Behague and I concluded that none of them were of Spanish origin.

24. Don José del Carmen Lugo, "Life of a Rancher," trans. T. Savage, *California Historical Society Quarterly* 32 (September 1950): 235–236. The original ms., in Spanish, is in the Bancroft Library, Berkeley, CA. It was recorded in 1877.

25. According to historian Douglas Monroy: "Positively defined in Mexican California, the phrase *gente de razón* came to refer to anyone who was Catholic, Spanish-speaking, and who renounced instinctual behavior in favor of service to work, community and the Crown. Negatively, it came to contrast a resident of California with anyone who behave like and 'Indian,' or how an Indian was imagined to be.... This notion, not the actual qualities of the Indians and their cultures, formed the primary caste distinction in Alta California. The mulatto and mestizo Don Pio Pico, or the mestizo Governor José Figueroa, or one like Don Manuel Domínguez, who was so dark that he was banned from testifying in court after the American conquest were all considered de razón. *Sin razón* were the Indians tyrannized in the missions, raiding in the wild, or alcoholic in the pueblo; the uncouth lower-class immigrants known as *cholos*; and the vulgar American trappers who wandered into California" (Monroy, "The Creation and Re-creation of Californio Society" in *Contested Eden*, 179). It is important that the reader keep in mind the highly racialized atmosphere of California, at its height through the 1960s. Mexican Americans who wandered into white areas of Los Angeles risked being beaten, or worse.

26. Dmitry Zavalishin, "California in 1824," translated from Russian and annotated by James R. Gibson, *Southern California Quarterly* 55 (Winter 1973): 395. This passage, written by a Russian officer who visited Monterey, feeds into the heritage fantasy, and one imagines that there existed spacious, gracious homes. The reality was different. Historian David Weber more accurately notes: "The Californios of the Spanish era had lived in simple one-story adobes, many with flat, tar-covered roofs, and few with wooden floors, glass windows, fireplaces, or tree-shaded landscaping. Anglo Americans reimagined those modest structures as elegant two-story, red-tile-roofed structures, with carved woodwork and cantilevered balconies that looked into tree-filled patios where water played in fountains...This architectural style, which came to be called Mission Revival, had its origins in California in the 1880s, but its vocabulary of stucco walls, red tiles, arched logias, and bell towers spoke to the nation as well as the state after 1893 World Columbian Exposition in Chicago gave Mission Revival a wide audience" (Weber, *The Spanish Frontier*, 343).

27. Esteban de la Torre, "Pre-American Monterey," *Touring Topics* (October 1930): 30.

28. Eulalia Perez de Guillen, "Keeper of the Keys," *Touring Topics* (January 1929): 25.

29. The custom of placing multiple hats on the heads of women as they danced must have been common in several parts of Mexico, because Amalia Hernandez, the former choreographer and artistic director of Ballet Folklorico de México, uses it in her suite of dances from Vera Cruz.

30. Alfred Robinson, *Life in California* (New York: Da Capo Press, 1969), 63.

31. Bancroft, *California Pastoral 1768–1848*, 408.

32. Ibid., 450.

33. Harris Newmark, *Sixty Years in Southern California, 1853–1913* (1916; Los Angeles: Zeitlin & Van Bruge, 1970), 136–137. The Bella Union was the largest hotel in Los Angeles in the 1840s and 1850s and was about fifteen miles from the Palos Verdes Rancho.

34. Antonio Coronel, "Things Past," *Touring Topics* (September, 1929): 22.

35. Walter Colton, *Three Years in California* (New York: Barnes, 1850), 164.

36. Davis, "Indian Insurrection," 39–40.

37. Newmark, *Sixty Years in Southern California*, 136–137.

38. Horace Bell, *Reminiscences of a Ranger* (Los Angeles: Yarnell Press, 1881), 195– 203.

39. Lucille Czarnowski, in her 1950 *Dances of Early California Days*, provides descriptions and instructions for many of the patterned dances from 1850 and beyond. There were groups of descendants still performing them at museums and other settings, but these were not the exciting improvised dances like el son and el jarabe that were fiery and challenging.

40. De la Torre, "Pre-American Monterey," 53.

41. Ibid.

42. Bowman, *Epic of a City*, 52.

43. Zavalishin, "California in 1824," 397.

Hispanomania in Nineteenth Century Dance Theory and Choreography

CLAUDIA JESCHKE *with* ROBERT ATWOOD

Flamenco emerged in the late nineteenth century, only one of many manifestations of a rich tradition of Spanish-influenced dance history that threaded through both the social and theatrical dance worlds of western and central Europe.[1] Evidence of this tradition and its importance to the repertoire and aesthetics of nineteenth-century ballet, and summed up by today's dance historiography under the collective term *escuela bolera*, comes from nineteenth-century theory (the writings of contemporary dance makers, critics, scholars, and *aficionados*), and from traces of practice (the descriptions, depictions, and notations of the actual steps used by the choreographic record of the period).

The first part of this essay explores Hispanomania and its diversity between 1800 and 1860, offering a brief insight into current research on the escuela bolera, which is then followed by a—similarly cursory—chronology of Spanish dance in what nineteenth-century dance masters considered contemporary literary sources. The second part of the essay deals with the interrelationship of choreography, composition, and the notation of Spanish dances, by examining two ballets with Spanish content as case studies: *Les Conscrits espagnoles* and *Les Folies espagnoles*, each notated and staged by Henri Justamant, one of the many highly productive choreographers of the time.[2]

Dance Theory—la Escuela Bolera

Spanish dance was handed down—in the consensus of current dance research—especially as the bolero, a dance for couples in three-quarter time that became popular in the second half of the eighteenth century in ballrooms and theatres. It developed from the *seguidillas manchegas*, a dance from La Mancha whose structural and musical composition can be detected in many dances of other Spanish cities as well.[3] Frequently used as an interlude during theatre performances in cities and in the countryside, the bolero, from the beginning, presented a composite of movements derived from steps of the *fandango, polo,* and *tirana,* but also from movement material of older dances, such as, for example, turns from the *chaconne* and the *bureo*.[4] As choreography, the bolero is part of longer dance sequences, which means that it is executed together with other Spanish dances, for example, with *cachuchas* or *jaleos*.[5]

At the beginning of the nineteenth century, the bolero was popular among all social classes, as described by Fernando Sor in 1835 in the Parisian *Encyclopédie pittoresque de la musique*.[6] The dance was also present in dance theater, where it evolved into a more "artificial" form, one that retained the conventions of French and Spanish theatrical artifice.[7] Its cultural and aesthetic success as well as its technical requirements marked the bolero as the representative example of Spanish national dance, monopolizing onstage depictions of Spanish culture. It is important to note, however, that already by 1800 the bolero's importance was "multivalent" in that the dance expressed a peculiar Spanish national feeling; the precise nature of the bolero performed was determined equally by indigenous traditions and foreign—that is, English, French, and Italian—fashion.[8] Over time, the bolero became more "Frenchified," especially in the wake of the Napoleonic invasion of Spain.[9] Sor refers to the interculturality of the bolero by highlighting the performance excellence of an Italian ballerina, Marie Taglioni, who dominated the French theatrical stage:

> *Je ne conçois pas qu'en Espagne on puisse se méprendre sur le véritable caractère du Bolero, puisqu'il se trouve encore dans la haute société plusieurs personnes qui le dansent avec une grâce et une noblesse que mademoiselle Taglioni, seule, a pu me rappeler.*[10]
>
> I don't conceive of the fact that in Spain, one can deceive oneself of the true character of the Bolero—as in high society, there are still several people who dance it to a degree of grace and nobility of which only Mademoiselle Taglioni has been able to remind me.

In 1820, dancer Antonio Cairón published detailed instructions on Spanish dance and especially on the bolero, under the title *Compendio de las principales reglas del baile*.[11] Bolero researchers Javier Suárez-Pajares and Xoán M. Carreira state that the characterization of the bolero provided by the most influential nineteenth-century dance theorist, Carlo Blasis, in his well-known treatise *The Code of Terpsichore* (1828) was derived from Cairón, and that the reception of the bolero in Europe was influenced decisively by the mediation of this work. They also call attention to Cairón's version as the Spanish-French synthesis of the dance from the time of the Napoleonic invasion. Cairón describes the bolero as the aesthetic and compositional highlight of Spanish dance history; other dances, for example the *Folías Espagnoles*, the fandango, or the seguidillas manchegas, he considers as completed with the development of the bolero, which is the "most famous Spanish dance and at the same time the most graceful and difficult one which ever was invented":

> *[El bolero] Este es el baile español mas célebre, el mas gracioso y el mas difícil tal vez de cuantos se han inventado: en él se pueden ejecutar todos los pasos, tantos bajos como altos; en él se puede mostrar la gallardía del cuerpo, su desembarazo, su actividad en las mudanzas, su equilibrio en los bien parados, su oído en la exactitud de acompañar con las castañuelas; y en fin, todas las gracias naturales de que se halle adornada la persona del ejecutor: hasta el propio vestido (que debe ser ajustado y ceñido al cuerpo) contribuye á descubrir la forma de las piernas, el aire del cuerpo, el torneo de los brazos [...]. La serenidad en los pasos y mudanzas difíciles es la primera cosa que se debe observar en este baile: nada hay mas ridículo que el ver á un bailarín haciendo esfuer-*

zos y contorsiones para ejecutar cualquier paso, y particularmente en el bolero, en donde es preciso poner todo el cuidado par que las mudanzas sean de una composición des pasos brillantes.[12]

The Bolero is the most famous Spanish dance and at the same time the most graceful and difficult one which ever was invented: all steps can be executed, the high ones as well as the low ones, one can show the galliard of the body, one's casualness, one's flexibility in the changes and one's equilibrium at rest, one's sense of hearing for the exactness of the castanet accompaniment; and finally, the natural comeliness which every dancer should be adorned with: that is, the well-fitting dress (which closely clasps to the body) which takes its share in showing the suppleness of the body, the turns of the arms [...]. The essence of this dance is the mastery of the steps and the difficult changes: for there is nothing more ridiculous than a dancer who undertakes all manner of exertion and twisting around in order to execute a step, especially in the Bolero where the greatest attention to precise positioning is imperative, for the changes are made up of brilliant steps.

Figure 1: *The Fandango at the Theatre San Fernando, Seville*, by Gustave Doré, 1862. In Charles Davillier and Gustave Doré, *Spain* (London: Sampson Low, Marston, Low and Searle, 1876).

He describes with exactness both the gracefulness of the dance and the difficulty of the step sequences, and stresses the complex coordination of the complicated leg movements and steps with the soft and flowing action of the arms that is hard to execute. Thereafter, he lays out the choreographic structure of the bolero in detail.[13] According to Cairón, the dance consists of three equal parts: (1) the three *coplas* in thirty-six measures (and four lines of text), always ending in a pose, the so-called *bienparado*; (2) each copla is followed by the so-called *estribillo*, which consists of a *mudanza* (step sequence) of nine measures; and (3) a *pasada* (change of places) of three measures. Cairón provides exact descriptions of the arrangement and execution of the mudanzas as well as the spatial organization of the pasada. He writes about a bienparado that has to be executed "in narrow space" and "with weight," interestingly also considered a fundamental component of the bolero.[14] With the differentiation of the choreographic and technical categories of space and weight, Cairón implies that the bolero's kinesthetic posturing indicates tension and containment of the trunk and pelvis movements and, thus, classifies the actions of the extremities as secondary.

Simultaneously with the development of the escuela bolera, descriptions of the *chica* or (with equivalent meaning) the *fandango*, considered "predecessors" of the bolero, were published in central and western European dancing manuals. Among the first evidence of the chica is in *De la danse* (1803) by Médéric Moreau de Saint-Méry, who transfers its origin to the Congo. He suggests that from there it traveled to the Antilles and became very important on the whole "Continent de l'Amérique espagnole."[15] Its strong, rhythmic aspect was typical for a "danse nègre." The female dancer had to hold either a handkerchief or her skirt with both hands, thus keeping her upper body steady, while the area below the waist was mobile. In the original choreography, the male dancer approached the female, withdrew, and approached again with charm and seductiveness.[16]

Identical descriptions of the chica were provided by German dance theoreticians Theodor Hentschke and Paul Bruno Bartholomay, as well as by Italian Carlo Blasis. Hentschke and Bartholomay also mention the division of the body into upper and lower parts. Further, they comment upon the body's lack of peripheral movements—that is, apart from the manipulation of the handkerchief or the hands fixed to the skirt, there are few conspicuous arm movements. Due to the dance's high speed, few extensive actions of the legs occur, indicating that the pelvis is the center of movement. Perhaps most interesting, all three theorists mention erotic interaction between the dancers.[17]

Moreau de Saint-Méry not only notes the African influence in South America but also in Europe and especially in Spain, where, due to the Moorish influence, the fandango— "qui n'est autre chose que le chica, seulement un peu moins développé, parceque le climat ou d'autres circonstances lui auront été moins propices" ("which is nothing but the chica, only a bit less developed because the climate or other circumstances have been less favourable")—could establish itself.[18] Moreau thus sees the decisive factors leading to the development of a dance characterized by nakedness, peacefulness, sexuality, and "toute cette gradation de desires" ("all those gradations of desires") in climate and mentality.[19]

The chica undergoes a questioning of its morals in Blasis' dance theories, and can be seen in both *The Code of Terpsichore* (1828) and *Notes upon Dancing* (1847). This is then followed by similar scrutiny from Hentschke and Bartholomay, along the lines of their reading of Blasis. In his *Notes*, Blasis introduces the literal quotes from Moreau de Saint-Méry about origin, movement vocabulary, and expression of the chica, adding that the chica is an immoral dance. In both of his major writings, this deprecatory assignation is also directed at another contemporary variant of the chica in Egypt.[20] Such a reference to "indecency and degeneration" of the chica and fandango, not only in Egypt but also in China, does not appear in Hentschke but is found in Bartholomay's *Tanzkunst*.[21]

The writings of Cairón and Blasis on the subject of Spanish dance offer an interesting contrast. With Blasis' focus on the "moral" dimension, one can say that he coarsens Cairón's choreographic descriptions. Blasis views the movement material and execution of the bolero and Spanish dances in general mainly in their "spectacular" and, therefore, morally and aesthetically condemnable dimension. At the same time, he remains interested (as are the German dance theoreticians) in that same uncommon and somewhat salacious element of the spectacular as a theatrical and performative category.

[The Spanish dances] represent the generous sentiment of an absolute protection of the object beloved, at other times they describe with vivacity the tender feeling it inspires, and the sincerity of the avowal. The eyes, oftentimes directed towards the feet, glance over every part of the body, and testify the pleasure which symmetry of form inspires them with. The agitation of the body, the footing, the postures, the attitudes, the waverings, whether they be lively or dull, are the representatives of desire, of gallantry, of impatience, of uncertainty, of tenderness, of chagrin, of confusion, of despair, of revival, of satisfaction and, finally, of happiness.

Choreographies of the Spanish

The choreographer Henri Justamant notated numerous Spanish dances and probably staged them on the basis of his notations. In *Les Conscrits espagnols* (1851), he describes the choreographies of a fandango, a bolero, a "funny" *Gala Gada,* and a *jota*; in *Les Folies espagnoles* (1885), he notates a Gala Gada, a jota, and a seguidilla.[22]

Before exploring the choreographic content of the notation, some general remarks on Justamant's investigational concept of movement description might be helpful. In the directorial notes of his *livrets de mise en scène,* the choreographer combines pictograms that connect body views of the dancers and birds'-eye views of the dance space with written information on the vocabulary of the movement employed. Moreover, he makes verbal notes concerning mime. No hierarchy of information exists; any data is equally valid. The stick figures only suggest body positions. The musical score does not play a relevant part in the notation. Time is recorded as numbers (the numbers of measures allotted to the designated movement phrase). Duration is expressed relatively by the length of movement lines. Thus, without clear rhythmical assignation, the experience of time becomes experimental, as does the dancer's encounter with space. The floor plans give spatial orientation but do not require exact placement.

Dance theorists claim that the reception of Spanish dances in the first half of the nineteenth century mainly dealt with dances such as the chica, fandango, and bolero. The latter two, fandango and bolero, also appear in Justamant's earlier livret but not in the later notation. There is no mention of the jota in dance treatises of the nineteenth century. Jotas appear to be less fit for theory than for practice—an interesting point given the complexity with which "Spanishness" was received and perceived in Western Europe.[23] According to his notation, Justamant frequently used Spanish dances as divertissements, employing the jotas—contrary to the majority of other Spanish numbers—as group dances.

The two jotas share a commonality in that the choreographic content of the dance figures changes with every couplet, thus assuming typical bolero requirements of Spanish dance theoretician Cairón. With the employment of simple steps and place changes, the mudanza and pasada stand out and can also be interpreted as Spanish influenced. At the end of both jotas, Justamant notates with verbal instructions as well as with drawings the poses Cairón held to be characteristic (and that originated from the genre of character dance), *pose grotesque.* Postures and interactions between the couple dancers are similar in the two temporally remote scripts, even when they do not appear in the identical sequences. Especially noteworthy is the use of the parallel, slanted postures of the individual couples; Justamant's dancers execute them twice in a row in different directions so that they can be seen once in profile and once *en face*. In the later script, they appear in profile only once, and with slightly different steps. We can conclude from Justamant's variation of the steps in space that he is less interested in the microstructure of the step selection than in the implicit spatial—that is, interactive—directness between the dancers involved. The postures, with the arms lifted over the head, convey the aggressive quality ascribed to Spanish couple dances. Apart from that, no "Spanish" arm movements are found in the two jotas. The reason for this can only be speculated. The jotas in our examples were employed as parts of divertissements and were preceded and succeeded by other Spanish dances, executed either as solos or by the entire cast. In those dances, Justamant notates typical arm postures. Thus, the jotas as group dances with their clear spatial emphasis must be seen as choreographic variety.

In both case studies, the Spanish dances are constructed into divertissements and show a variety of groupings: solo appearances, dances in smaller groups, and the full cast in the finales. That cast, as well as the stage space, builds on contrast. And it is obvious that the structural and dynamic variety of the individual dances employs movement repertoire including traditional ballet as well as folk dance steps, mostly (but not always) linked to significant expressive movements of the arms, the torso, and the whole body. Repetitions of these expressive elements function as performative and dramatic references to Spanishness. Justamant's choreography offers a combination of sophisticated technique and simple steps and arm movements, as well as a mixture of "the other" and traditional movement elements.

Summary

It is a truism of dance historiography that theory does not explain practice. Similarly, practice does not necessarily exemplify theory. Both constitute knowledge practices and cultures relatively independent of one another, each working within a different context. But leaving aside direct comparison, one can recognize strategic procedures in both fields—theory and the practice—that suggest a wide range of concepts and formations of the "Spanish" in nineteenth-century dance theatre. If Cairón, in 1820, dealt with the musical and choreographic structure, especially of the bolero, in contrast, the Spanish dances in dance theories after Cairón are used in unspecific ways. Spanish dances became symptoms for Otherness, owing to mentality, not to "authenticity"; they stand as synonyms (or metaphors) for sensuality and desire, an erotically charged form of couple dance with an unusual movement vocabulary. They can be discussed as examples of a new understanding of body, space, and time—just like the choreography, the composition of movement sequences, the recording of dancing. The concept of the Spanish—as exemplified in the work of Henri Justamant—opens the view to the structural level and the craftsmanship in the theatrical presentation of "Spanish." Justamant's choreography, as well as his technique of notating, allow for the experience of physicality. As devices of theatrical operations, both subvert the aesthetic dichotomies and moral stereotypes as they appear in the dance theories.

Spanish dances are not only an instrument toward the redefinition of national, cultural, and societal foundations and self-conceptions. They also place dance identities in the gaps between ethnography, artistic demands, and strategies of embodiment. They render possible a wider discussion about social status and the potential of dance aesthetics, technique, style, expression, dramaturgy, and narration. Dancers' bodies—space and time unclear—constantly accommodate "pre-," "con-," and "re-" figurations in a complex and virtuoso way. On the one hand, Hispanomania is the discursive stage on which the changes become apparent; on the other hand, it can be identified as program and skill—as examples for mobile structures that were applied, in the words of Christopher Pinney, "more than local, less than global" and, as well, during the entire second half of the nineteenth century.[24] In the dance theories, "Spanish" calls out for more intimate movement vocabularies and stories. In solo dances, such as the bolero, Hispanomania mainly operates in the shape of stereotype body and movement aesthetics; in group dances, abstraction and technique as choreographic categories are relocated to the spatial level without neglecting body technique as such. Spanish dances enable structural and aesthetic changes on all scenic levels; they function as a motor of theatrical design techniques. We would like to mark these (as yet, hypothetically and exemplarily) as typical practices of the late nineteenth century. These practices—the motor-kinetic professionalisms—after 1850 move in the semantic field of the significance of the Spanish, just as it sometimes accepts and mostly "denies" to cater to the geographically or temporally allocatable in "the Other" (the Spanish). Due to the collusion of different choreographic systems and standards, the choreographic practices become undefined, open, and elastic.

Notes

1. This essay is reprinted, with revisions, from Claudia Jeschke, Gabi Vettermann, and Nicole Haitzinger's *Les Choses Espagnoles: Research into the Hispanomania of 19th Century Dance* (München: epodium, 2009).
2. "Les Conscrits Espagnols ou le récrutement Forcé. Ballet Comique en un acte Par Mr. H. Justamant. Musique de Mr. Jozet. Representé pour la première Fois à Lyon au le grand théâtre en mars 1851. Representé au théâtre royal de la monnaie à Bruxelles," [no date]; cf. Paul Ludwig, *Henri Justamant (1815–1890). Kommentiertes Bestandsverzeichnis seiner Ballett-Notationen in der Theaterwissenschaftlichen Sammlung Schloß Wahn* (Universität zu Köln, 2005), 27. On Henri Justamant's biography and the contents of the two ballets, see Gabi Vettermann, "In Search of Dance Creators' Biographies: The Life and Work of Henri Justamant" and, respectively, Claudia Jeschke, "Spanishness and Dance Libretto" in Claudia Jeschke, Gabi Vettermann, and Nicole Haitzinger, *Les Choses Espagnoles: Research into the Hispanomania of 19th Century Dance* (München: epodium, 2009).
3. Javier Suárez-Pajares and Xoán M. Carreira, eds., "The Origins of the Bolero School," in *Studies in Dance History. The Journal of the Society of Dance History Scholars* 4, no.1 (Spring 1993), 7. See also Nancy Lee Chalfa Ruyter: "La Escuela Bolera," *Dance Chronicle* 16, no. 2 (1993), 249–257.
4. Without specifically examining the traditional dances of Spain named here, it can be claimed that they shared great popularity, if sometimes short-lived due to their associated dancing behavior that was considered morally questionable and, in most cases, their proximity to song.
5. The bolero technique contains batteries and elevations, while the other dance parts are earthbound.
6. Fernando Sor, "Le Bolero," in *Encyclopédie pittoresque de la musique*. Ed. Adolphe Ledhuy and Henri Bertin (Paris: H. Delloye, 1835), 83–97, here 93ff., also printed in Marina Grut, *The Bolero School* (London: Dance Books, Ltd., 2002), 115–119. See also Brian Jeffery, *Fernando Sor: Composer and Guitarist* (London: Tecla Editions, 1994).
7. Fernando Sor, in Grut, *The Bolero School*, 10f.
8. Details of this development can be found in Grut, *The Bolero School*, 77ff.
9. Not without justification, Marina Grut (in *The Bolero School*, 8) indicates that the aspect of "Frenchification" not only seems to be founded in the acceptable aesthetics of the "new" Spanish dance but can also be explained through power structures: "It is amusing that he [Sor] says she [Mme Lefebvre] changed the way that the Spanish dances were performed and yet was applauded by the Spaniards; so her changes

must have been acceptable. Yet, those who applauded were amongst the conquered, and one can imagine that they probably had little choice, or wanted to flatter the invaders." The aspect of this early influence, especially of France (and also of other European dance cultures), on Spanish dance is underrepresented in historiography. The influence in the other direction, that is, from Spain to France, is quoted more frequently: performances of the bolero dancers Dolores Serral, Mariano Camprubí, Francisco Font, and Manuela Dubinon during the carnival balls at the Parisian opera in 1834 have found their way into dance history books. (A second Spanish "wave," partly with the same artists, can be observed in France after 1850.)

    10. Sor, "Le Bolero," 83–97, here 97, printed in Grut, *The Bolero School*, 115–119, here 119.

    11. Suárez-Pajares and Carreira, "Origins of the Bolero School," 15. According to the two historians, Cairón's descriptions refer to the bolero entry in the *Diccionario de la lengua castellana / por la Real Academia Espanola* from 1817 (Madrid). This statement cannot be verified after perusing the lexicon mentioned above, which only contains an entry of five lines on the bolero (140). Apart from that, it remains unexplained why Cairón remarks in the title of his work that he has translated it from the French; strangely, Suárez-Pajares and Carreira do not go into this peculiarity.

    12. Antonio Cairón, *Compendio de las principales reglas del baile* (Madrid: Impr. de Repullés, 1820), 103; Grut, *The Bolero School*, 111; Cairón, *Compendio de las principales*, 103–105.

    13. On the musical and literary structure of the bolero, see Brian Jeffery, *Fernando Sor: Composer and Guitarist* (London: Tecla Editions, 1994), 21ff.

    14. Cairón, *Compendio*, 106–108; see also Grut, *The Bolero School*, 111.

    15. Médéric Louis Élie Moreau de Saint-Méry, *De la danse* (Parma: Bodoni, 1803), 50–61. *De la danse* was reprinted several times. I am quoting from the third edition (published after the 1796 edition [Philadelphia] and the 1801 edition [Parma, Italy]).

    16. Moreau de Saint-Méry, *De la danse*, 51f.

    17. Theodor Hentschke, *Allgemeine Tanzkunst. Theorie und Geschichte, antike und moderne (gesellschaftliche und theatralische) Tanzkunst und Schilderung der meisten National und Charaktertänze* (Stralsund: W. Hausschildt, 1836), 252: "Ein dem Mittelafrika eigenthümlicher und sehr ausgebreiteter Tanz ist der Tchéga oder Chica, den die Neger über alles lieben und überall hin verpflanzt haben. Von ihm scheint der Fandango herzustammen, der nur weniger als dieser die Geheimnisse der Liebe entschleiert, und durch Steigerung ein mehr empörendes als angenehmes Schauspiel bietet." ("In mid–Africa there is a typical and popular dance called Tchéga or Chica, that the black men love very much. They have shifted this dance everywhere. It is obviously the origin of the Fandango which unveils the secrets of love only less than the Chica and—climacticly—presents a more scandalous than pleasant spectacle."); similarly, Paul Bruno Bartholomay, *Die Tanzkunst in Beziehung auf die Lehre und Bildung des wahren Anstandes und des gefälligen Äußeren* (Gießen: beim Autor, 1838), 215ff, here 217: "In Cairo, [...] der Hauptstadt Egyptens, wo kein Theater vorhanden ist, gibt es eine Art von Akteurs und Tänzern, welche, wie auch in China, in Privathäuser gehen und dort theatralische Vorstellungen geben; bei denen die indecentesten und obscönsten Dinge eine sehr große Ähnlichkeit mit dem Chica [...] haben." ("In Cairo, the capital of Egypt, where there is no theater, there is a sort of actors and dancers who, as in China, go into private residencies where they present theatrical spectacles, in which the most indecent and obscene things have a close similarity with the Chica."); also see Carlo Blasis, *The Code of Terpsichore* (London: James Bullock, 1828), 28ff.; and Carlo Blasis, *Notes upon Dancing, Historical and Practical* (London: M. Delaporte, 1847), 23ff.

    18. Moreau de Saint-Méry, *De la danse*, 55.

    19. Ibid., 56f.

    20. Blasis, *Code*, 30; and Blasis, *Notes*, 25.

    21. Bartholomay, *Die Tanzkunst*, 217.

    22. Moreover, *Les Folies* contain an interesting narrative sequence that is implemented by means of mime and dance, the "imitation de la course aux taureaux" ("imitation of a bullfight").

    23. See Ilse Lipschutz, "Théophile Gautier et la danse espagnole" in *Bulletin de la Société Théophile Gautier* 8 (1986), 153–178.

    24. Christopher Pinney, http://www.ucl.ac.uk/anthropology/people/academicstaff/cpinney (accessed November 12, 2014).

Some Notes Toward a Historiography of the Mid-Nineteenth Century *Bailable Español*

Kiko Mora

Translation by K. Meira Goldberg

The Autonomy of Spanish Dance on Stage

Beginning with the French occupation of Spain in 1807, "national" or Spanish dances assumed a privileged place in the *entr'actes* of theatrical works, gradually becoming independent from the comedies into which they had usually been inserted, and evolving into the *bailable* (literally, "danceable")—a self-contained performance of Spanish dance.[1] Although Spanish nationalism and traditionalism, present across the spectrum of all the arts of this period, arose in part as a reaction against the fashions and customs of the Napoleonic invaders, this evolution in Spanish dance parallels that of ballet in France. Having been a decorative interlude for opera since the seventeenth century, by the end of the eighteenth century ballet had gained greater independence, its growing prominence entailing a concomitant evolution in the training of all ranks of dancers at the Académie Royale de Musique et de Danse, the Paris Opéra.[2] In the Spanish performing arts, nationalistic response to foreign political and cultural incursions took place on three levels: folkloric-styled pieces and Andalusian songs resisted vaudeville and French popular song; *zarzuela* (Spanish light opera) opposed Italian opera; and the *escuela bolera* (popular Spanish dances taught and elaborated for the stage in dance academies) and flamenco resisted ballet and the French cancan.[3]

The emergent autonomy of dance on stage, the growing demand for artists, and the consequent need for professionalized preparation led to the establishment of a new figure in the field of the escuela bolera, arising in imitation of the *maître de ballet* (dancing master), who would acquire fundamental importance over the course of the nineteenth century: that of dancer-director-composer-choreographer. This autonomy of dance and the enlightened consecration of the role of "choreographer" on the theater stage parallels the ballet reforms of Jean-Georges Noverre and is itself a reflection of the shifting concepts of art itself, in which literature, music, painting, sculpture and theater "were grouped together ... as having something essentially in common which distinguished them from other human skills."[4]

Spanish dance's growing autonomy also paralleled the deterioration of Spain's colonial empire. The breaking away of overseas Spanish colonies is often dated from 1810, with the declarations of independence by Mexico and Venezuela. These events, along with Napoleon's invasion of Spain three years earlier, provoked a crisis of national identity that would mark the entire nineteenth century. The escuela bolera (which appealed to the bourgeoisie) and flamenco (which appealed to popular taste) constitute some of the responses to this crisis. Named choreographers and titled dance pieces gained increasing prominence in the press. The choreographer was seen as a genius artist, the dancing incarnation of Romanticism and, simultaneously, as the quintessence of the soul of the folk, a paradigm of Spain's new national identity.

José Rojo was the first to occupy the post of "choreographer" in Seville's Teatro Cómico in the 1820s. Rojo codified the *bolero* as an academic dance form and invented new variations that situated it as the preeminent style of theatrical dance through the mid-nineteenth century.[5] The bolero had existed as a social dance since the eighteenth century and was, along with the *fandango*, among the popular "national" dances, emblematic currents of traditionalism and nationalism, taken up by *majismo* (the fashion among the aristocracy for imitating the dress and customs of common people). It already had been performed on stage in 1800, but choreographers such as Rojo used the bolero as a language with which to "definitively oust the 'educated' maestros of Italian and French dance."[6]

As in French ballet, men dominated the profession.[7] Although on stage male dancers served as *porteurs* to lift and thereby highlight the talents of female

Left: Figure 1: "Doña Pétra Cámara y Don Antonio Ruiz en un paso de salida de los bailes nacionales," engraving, artist unknown. In *La Ilustración* (Madrid), April 5, 1851 (Biblioteca Nacional de España).

Right: Figure 2: "Manuel Guerrero dans La fantacia espanola," engraving, Boetrels, 1850 (Bibliotheque Nationale de France).

dancers, control over the codification of staged dances was, at least in principle, in men's hands. Manuel León followed José Rojo; León and his partner Madame León were the first Spanish bolero dancers to perform in London in 1815.[8] And two of Rojo's outstanding students, Miguel de los Santos and Manuel Guillén, advanced into careers as dancers, directors, composers, and choreographers, as did other artists like Antonio Cairón, Ladislao Luengo, José Guillén, Félix Moreno, Manuel Casas, and Ambrosio Martínez.[9] By the 1850s, the most important dancing masters to develop the bailable were already well established: Carlos Atané, Antonio Ruiz, Manuel Guerrero, Ángel Estrella, Manuel de la Barrera, José Núñez, Ricardo Moragas, Manuel Pérez, and José Carrión (see Figures 1 and 2).

As dance historian Rocío Plaza Orellana has articulated, during the years of the Liberal Triennium (1820–1823, during which the Constitution of 1812 was reinstated) dance began to be perceived as a meritorious endeavor, and the beginnings of popular dance pedagogy benefited from the short-lived government's enlightened educational reforms. Emerging performance genres absorbed this new interest in universal (public) education and in the creation of educational centers supported by the local populace, as was demonstrated by the many benefits for new schools held during this period.[10] The creation of a stable bolero school at the Teatro de la Cruz in Madrid is indicative of the growth in cultural institutions directed toward satisfying the demand for national dances. Popular support and increasing interest among key players in the theater world permitted by the mid–1830s the establishment of numerous academies and dance salons oriented initially toward teaching social dances. By the 1840s, these dance schools also taught and promoted the escuela bolera, the populist and nationalist counterpart to what for "cultivated" music would entail the founding in Madrid of the first Royal Conservatory of Music, clearly influenced by Franco-Italian models.[11] These locales became not only meeting places for enthusiasts, and necessary in building an audience within a new artistic domain, but also a source of performers, many from Andalusia, who nourished the *corps de ballet* of the most reputable theaters of Madrid. Dance, which until the mid-eighteenth century was considered a minor art within courtly diversions and masques, or, among the common folk, as celebration in carnivals and country fairs, began to acquire a novel prestige with the appearance of what philosopher Gilles Lipovetsky has called "a new sensitivity to ephemera ... offering new ways of valorizing phenomena that had previously been unworthy of notice."[12] It is not by chance that the emerging figure of the choreographer coincided with the legitimization of other minor arts, such as fashion and gastronomy, and with the social ascent of professions such as couturier and chef.

The Birth of the Bailable Español

During the 1840s, Andalusian and creole songs like soledades, polos, seguidillas, romances, cañas, tangos and habaneras began to infiltrate theatrical dance.[13] The dance academies were the places where these songs "found a workshop setting in which they could be adapted to a danceable rhythm, becoming dance solos or duets which recreated the song's narrative."[14] It was in this vibrant, artistic context that, at the close of the 1840s, in Madrid there appeared a new type of theatrical presentation, an assemblage of pantomimic dances whose immediate antecedent was the *ballet d'action*, sharing a single stage set, with highly stereotyped characters, titles, and plots. Based on earlier Spanish theatrical forms such as *comedias de costumbres* (comedies of manners), *tonadillas* (sung theatrical interludes), *sainetes* (picaresque one-act farces or tidbits), *pasillos* (short sainetes), *juguetes cómico-líricos* (short, sung comic sketches), zarzuelas (operettas), and songs, most of these short pieces depicted a vernacular Andalusian setting.[15]

Flamenco theorist and cultural historian Gerhard Steingress has argued that the formulation of "Andalusian dance" as a theatrical genre during the first half of the nineteenth century occurred on two levels. One was flamenco itself, and the other

> was a variant in which the dances monopolized by the escuela bolera predominated.... The fruit of this artistic effort was a new genre which utilized the earlier national dances as material for productions based on personalized choreographies, danced in short (one-act) theatrical pieces as an entr'acte within comedies, sainetes, dramas and, in the second half of the nineteenth century, the novel zarzuelas that fascinated the modern audience.[16]

But while French Romantic ballet—ethereal, technical, and focused on the pointwork executed solely by ballerinas—delighted in presentations of exotic characters and librettos extracted from classical Greek and Nordic mythology or from the glories of a medieval past, the *bailable español*—earthier, dramatic, and focused on the figure as a whole—exploited above all the typical folkloric ethos of Andalusia, in taverns, inns, tenements, shipyards, and country fairs.

I will cite an example that illustrates the conceptual genesis (textual and intertextual) of these bailables, titled *El polo del contrabandista* ("The Smuggler's Polo").[17] It owed its namesake to a song by the celebrated musician and tenor Manuel García, originally titled "Yo que soy contrabandista" ("I who am a Smuggler"). The piece debuted in 1805 in the Teatro de los Caños del Peral in Madrid within an opera-monologue by the same author titled *El poeta calculista* ("The Calculating Poet"); in 1813, it would become an independent, stand-alone dance work.[18] Widely toured by respected bolero dancer Antonia Molino throughout the second decade of the nineteenth century, in 1822 a *"bolero nuevo"* (new bolero) was presented with the same title, now danced by a couple: Gertrudis Pérez and Vicente Lapuerta.[19] Although, as flamenco historian José Luis Navarro has explained, the dance could indeed have been performed with other titles ("Los majos de Cádiz," "El caballito de Cádiz," or simply "El jaleo"), the piece not to have been performed again with its original title until 1842, when it appeared within an *"escena gaditana"* ("Scene of Cádiz") at the Teatro del Liceo in Barcelona.[20] By 1849, *El polo del contrabandista* was performed as an independent number, part of an ensemble of staged dances. One year later, it was a one-act comedy.[21] There is no documentation as to the choreographer of the 1849 debut of *El polo del contrabandista* as a bailable. However, one month after the opening of the comedy, Carlos Atané presented the piece with dancers Pepa Vargas and Adela Guerrero, immortalized by Gustave Courbet.[22]

Historian Basilio Castellanos de Losada, writing about the choreographer Carlos Atané, takes note of the novelty of these performances in Spain's capital:

> [Carlos Atané] is responsible for reviving the enthusiasm for our national dances in the theater in Madrid, where they have been lately viewed with disdain, through the novelty with which they contrived to present them at the Institute in 1850, beginning in that year to stage the national dance as a grand spectacle, with showy costumes of the country, happy tambourines and other effects, and within those effects allowing for a pantomime, a new kind of dance that with these effects the knowledgeable professors of choreography have also succeeded in preserving.[23]

Without entering into a lengthy discussion of sole-authored choreographic attribution, it is clear that the first pieces of this artistic genre to be performed in Madrid in 1849 clearly belonged to Atané. That year, again with choreography by Atané, all at the Teatro de la Comedia, the bailables titled *Los panaderos de Cádiz* ("The Bakers from Cádiz"), *El Jaque* ("The Bandit"), *Un día de feria en Mairena* ("A Day at the Fair in Mairena"), *La gitanilla y el curro* ("The Gypsy Girl and the Fop"), *La hija de Manuel Rayo* ("Manuel Rayo's Daughter"), *El sol de Andalucía* ("The Sun of Andalusia"), *La peña de la gitana* ("The Gypsy Woman's Hill"), *La sal de Andalucía* ("The Salt of Andalusia"), *El Tripili*, *Los toreros de Chiclana* ("The Bullfighters from Chiclana"), and *La linda Manola* ("The Beautiful and Feisty Woman") were given.[24]

Nonetheless, there is no doubt that choreographer Antonio Ruiz, of Granada, achieved greater success on the stages of Europe during the first years in the evolution of the bailable español.[25] A writer for the Madrid newspaper *La Ilustración* noted the inventions that Ruiz, along with several noted Spanish dancers—Petra Cámara, Pepa Vargas, and Manuela Perea "La Nena"—had understood his work to constitute a significant, new ensemble of already existent national Spanish dance with its iconography of *Spanishness*:

> To perfect with study the special nature of Spanish dance, to dramatize it more with the creation of pantomimic compositions, to cultivate pomp on stage in costumes and sets (*coreado* [sic]); to add often the pleasing accessories of song, tambourine, castanets, fan, hat, *mantilla* (lace head-covering); and offer consequently such a pleasing and picturesque ensemble, so characteristic of sunny Andalusia, that all Spain and the capital at the forefront has responded with enthusiasm for a truly characteristic and popular performance (see Figure 3).[26]

The mid-century birth date of these performances coincided with the immigration of artists from southern Spain to Madrid theaters, where Andalusian and Gitano styles had taken root. Anthropologist and historian Julio Caro Baroja noted as early as 1969 the relationships between Andalusian cities, especially Cádiz, and the capital of Madrid.[27] The fashion for Gitano mimicry, descended from eighteenth-century majismo, was a response to the dynamic of social change engendered by the emergence of an urban proletariat, originally of rural origin, demanding entertainment that resonated with its sensibility and values. But this minstrelizing fashion also responded to the desires of the bourgeois populist and nationalist project as a subtle means of masking its dependence on both the nobility of Spain's *Ancien Regime* and the more robust, emergent capitalism of other European nations.[28] This class sought to identify its interests with those of the nation and to conceal any class conflict that could threaten its privilege.[29] The Andalusian genre of performance was, therefore, a propitious space for revealing the dialectic between performance forms that simultaneously reflected and constructed new, troublesome realities. More than any other art form performed in foreign countries, the bailable embodied this process perfectly.

A Show for Export

Antonio Ruiz created his own choreographic version of *El polo del contrabandista*, touring it to the Gymnase Dramatiç de París in May of 1851, and probably adapted it

124

TEATRO PRINCIPAL.

Grande y Estraordinaria Funcion para el Lúnes 1º de Mayo de 1854.
A las 7 y media de la noche.

A beneficio del público. Entrada general 2 rs.

NOVENA Y PENÚLTIMA FUNCION en que tomará parte la célebre bailarina española

DOÑA PETRA CAMARA.

Deseando la Empresa de este teatro proporcionar al público que con tanta constancia la favorece, toda clase de novedades, y procurando al mismo tiempo que estas estén al alcance de todas las clases de la sociedad, ha resuelto presentar este dia en escena á la CELEBRE BAILARINA SEÑORITA CAMARA, abaratando de un modo considerable los precios, tanto de entrada como de localidades, á pesar de los escesivos gastos que de esto se la originan.

ORDEN DE LA FUNCION.

1º Una escogida sinfonia.
2º La comedia en un acto, titulada

LA PENA DEL TALION.

En la que desempeñará el principal papel la primera actriz doña Matilde Duclós.

3º El baile español en un acto, compuesto por el director de bailes nacionales don Manuel Guerrero, titulado

UNA FIESTA EN EL CABAÑAL,
ó danza valenciana.

Por la señorita CAMARA el señor Guerrero y cuerpo de baile.

4º La comedia de gracioso en dos actos, arreglada á la escena española por don Luis de Olona, nominada

PIPO, O EL PRINCIPE DE MONTE-CRESTA.

Desempeñando el protagonista el primer actor del género cómico DON PEDRO GARCIA.

5º El baile español en un acto, música del señor Gaztambide, composicion de don Manuel Guerrero, cuyo título es

PETRA LA SEVILLANA.

Bailables de que se compone.

1 Introduccion por el cuerpo de baile.— 2 ZAPATEADO de las Capas, por cuatro parejas.— 3 PASO DE ACCION por la señorita CAMARA, el señor Guerrero y cuerpo de baile.— 4 SOLEDAD, por las señoras Martin, Ojeda, Fernández y Andrés.— 5 Jaleo de la SEVILLANA, por la señorita CAMARA.— 6 VITO, por las señoras Martin y Ojeda.— 7 LA ZAMBRA por la señorita CAMARA y el señor Guerrero.— 8 Bailable final por la Srita. CAMARA, el señor Guerrero y todo el cuerpo de baile.

6º y último. La graciosísima comedia en un acto, escrita en valenciano por el señor Baldoví, titulada

PATAQUES Y CARAGÒLS.

Desempeñada por las señoras doña Matilde Duclós y los señores Garcia (don Pedro), Pastrana, Torromé, Rodriguez y Toné.

NOTA. A los que abonaren 24 rs. se les dará un palco 2.º y 6 entradas.— A los que abonaren 18 rs., un palco 3.º con id.— Y á los que tomaren 6 entradas, se les dará gratis un palco de 4.º piso.

Las puertas del REAL y de CUARTE se abrirán á los que de fuera vengan á ver la funcion, segun órden de S. E. el Sr. Capitan General.

Los señores que gusten adquirir localidades con anticipacion, pasarán á Contaduría á las horas de costumbre.

Valencia, Imp. de J. Ferrer de Orga, á espaldas del teatro.

Figure 3: Teatro Principal (Valencia), benefit performance featuring Petra Cámara. Program, May 1, 1854 (Universitat de Valencia/Parnaseo).

as a bailable at Her Majesty's Theatre in London that July.³⁰ These representations, commonly called *bailable español* within Spain, *ballet espagnol* in France, and "Spanish divertissement" or "Spanish ballet" in English-speaking nations (note the ethnocentrism of the non–Spanish denominations), all had a marked Andalusian and Gitano accent.³¹ In these dances, the figure of the choreographer, along with important *bailarinas* (ballerinas) like Petra Cámara, Adela Guerrero, Rosa Espert, Josefa Vargas, Pepita Oliva, and Perea Nena, emerged globally as institutionally responsible for the creativity and innovation of national dances (see Figure 4). From this personalized transformation of national dances, rooted in folklore and in the escuela bolera, grew an authored performance, spurred on by the originality and virtuosity of its creators, and constructed "through a series of stylistic *mestizajes* or hybridizations across Spanish regions and cultures."³²

New York City's French-language daily, *Le Courrier des Etats-Unis,* reported on Sevillian dancer Pepita Soto's 1855 performance in New York City's Metropolitan Theater. The description, probably of a dance entitled *La maja de Sevilla*, offers an excellent opportunity to understand the choreographic language and shape of a *bailable*:

> Hello. I stand before a muleteers' inn at the gates of Seville; with the mule drivers and smugglers, hats over one ear, a cape over the shoulder, a fist on the hip and a cigarette between the lips, waiting for the manola to dance for them. Listen. The orchestra plays a prelude in a minor key. She appears. Ah! She enters not from behind a flowering rosebush: she descends the stairs of the hostel, and steps on to solid ground like a girl nurtured by something other than the tears of the night in the calyx of volubilis.³³ Her twisting hips make us pray to Saint Anthony; she smiles at one, and then at another, conquers this one with a glance, and perhaps sends a furtive kiss to another, and then stops in the middle of the circle. She will dance! Dance!
>
> The orchestra explodes in a happy song to a triple-time *allegro*. The tambourines tremble with pleasure, and the castanets

Figure 4: "Doña Josefa Vargas en el Ole," engraving, J. Vallejo, c. 1850 (Biblioteca Nacional de España).

chatter as they are struck one against the other; all this to arouse the enthusiasm of the public. This is how I feel and enjoy the dancer, and you will call her what you will: la manola, la maja, la madrileña, la cachucha, la jota, la sevillana...—whatever you wish, *tra la la*. Her skirt is decorated with happy-sounding bits of metal, and all the lace, all the bows, all the trinkets and all the soutache braid, gathered everywhere: in the shoulders, the bodice, the waist, on the skirt, and all this laughs, dances, flies, filling with joy the heart of a man hung the day before.

What would you like those gallant majos, whose costume adds such color to this scene, to do? They should dance as well, and this time a man can dance without fear of seeming ridiculous. His dance signifies something else, although it does not signify too much. It is very fitting to call this "character dance," as character is the one thing not lacking.

Mlle. Soto possesses all the aptitudes of Spanish dance. She doubtless lacks the immodest ardor of La Dolores [Serral], and the seductively serpentine air of Petra Cámara; but nonetheless she has an advantage over both in her beauty on stage, which is quite rare in dancers. There is a strangeness in the glance of her black eyes, concentrated beneath the double arch of her brows. Her smile, to which her white teeth lend a brilliant and youthful touch, never seems forced, even though she has the same happy air in dancing that the spectators do in watching her. And it is a lot.

Note here that all of the above corresponds only to her head, and without dwelling on the other details that each may appreciate in his own way, allow me to highlight the elegance of this artist's waist, the modeling of her legs, her curved foot, all that is highly valued in a ballerina.

Now, take all this to heart with an inspiration ... from the South, a *dæmonio meridiano* (noonday devil), as the Latin text says; the impulses of body and the turns of the hips, the movement of the legs and the circling of the arms, the sudden stops that would turn a Quaker congregation into pagans, and you will understand how Mlle. Soto brings jubilance to the Metropolitan Opera House every night.[34]

In the middle of the nineteenth century, Madrid became a transitory residence for artists who, poorly paid, sought economic well-being in foreign lands, on long tours that would take them to Europe's most cosmopolitan, and often faraway, cities: Paris, Luxemburg, Stockholm, London, Vienna, Berlin, Budapest, Prague, Saint Petersburg, and Constantinople. The nomadism of bohemian artists became an activity inherent to the development of the dance profession, generated by technical advances in transportation, the increasing dependence of performers on publicity and the patronage of a wide audience, and the commoditization of art.[35] The birth of these spectacles obeyed the rules of a market that benefited from a growing tourist industry, which drew foreign members of the cultural and economic elite to Spain's interior.[36]

Although, as in the case of Manuel León, bolero dances interpreted by Spanish artists found the international stage by the second decade of the nineteenth century, the bailable español offered a longer self-sufficient dance work for the entr'actes that could contain various dances, capturing and holding viewers with the thrust of narrative realism. The sainete and the comedia de costumbres, however, rarely appeared in Europe because of the obvious restrictions imposed by a text not only in Spanish but often containing Andalusian dialect mixed with Gitano slang. The only exceptions were those moments when a local immigrant Spanish audience of artists, the independently wealthy, businessmen, diplomats, and political exiles came together.

The bailables, whose titles left the program open with regard to the number, length, and types of dances, perfectly complied with the demands of an emerging mass culture by allowing flexible combinations of repertory that could be adapted with great flexibility to the dramaturgy of each new show. These performances translated an image of Spain simply and effectively without the mediation of language, which satisfied an audience keen for local color. Thus, the bailable español, as a recurrent reflection, embodied the stereotypical image of Spain that European Romantic writers had forged in the collective imagination of foreign audiences. The bailable español was the vessel out of which arose a new aesthetic experience tied to Romanticism and known as "picturesque." The iconography of the pure picturesque, a Romantic return to pre-industrial communitas, enabled audiences now mired in urbanity and industrialization to gaze with nostalgia toward rural life. As philosopher Robin Collingwood affirms,

> The picturesque is the spectator's sense of a gulf between the object and his own habitual surroundings and activities.... The industrializing of our civilization has produced a new form of the picturesque, and has concentrated our feeling for natural beauty upon the spectacle of a rural society living in the pursuit of traditional arts and deeply rooted in a landscape which has in part created it and [is] in part created by it.... And when that event had divorced us from this state of things, our civilization began to feel its own industrialism as artificial and the pre-industrial society of the countryside and the little town as natural and, therefore as endowed with all peculiar qualities of natural beauty.[37]

The Bailable Español in the United States

Although the presence of Spanish dance in the United States dates to the Spanish conquest of the American Southwest from the sixteenth through the eighteenth centuries,[38] the consolidation of Andalusian dance on U.S. stages during the 1830s and 1840s was affected by Europe's most important touring dancers: Fanny Elssler, Madame Celeste, James Sylvain, and Paul Taglioni. These artists brought techniques of Andalusian dance to American dancers such as Paul Hazard, Augusta Maywood, George W. Smith, Julia Turnbull, and Mary Anne Lee. Aside from Cuba, still part of Spain's empire, the most renowned Spanish boleras did not travel to the Americas during this first phase of the bailable's development. European touring allowed Spanish boleras to maintain close contact with their native land and provided them with a comfortable living, thus dissuading them from risking a long and dangerous transatlantic journey. The touring of Spanish performing artists reflected more general migratory patterns: Andalusian dance and song as performed by Spaniards arrived in the Americas, from Río de la Plata (Uruguay, Argentina) to the United States, by way of artists who had not garnered sufficient recognition to stay in Europe.

The Llorente family in 1851 was the first Spanish troupe to introduce bolero dances to the United States (California).[39] The following January, Lola Montez and George Washington Smith presented the bailable in New York City. Advertised as a "Grand Spanish ballet divertissement," the opening at the Broadway Theatre was titled *Un jour de Carnival à Seville* and included a *zapateado* (footwork dance), *pas de L'Andalousian* (Andalusian dance), *la sivigliana* (sevillanas), and a *pas de matelot* (sailor dance).[40] The overwhelming personality of Montez failed to hide the imperfections in her dance from U.S. aficionados, and not until the arrival of Sevillian dancer Pepita Soto in 1852, did the bailable educate American audiences, thereby becoming a regular number in shows that included popular Spanish dance numbers of the day like "El Jaleo de Jerez," "El Jaleo de Santiago," "La Cachucha," "La Manola," "El Bolero de Cádiz," "La Malagueña," "El Zapateado," "La Madrileña," "La Jota," "La Gitana," "El Olé" and "El Vito."[41] In the course of two long sojourns in the United States (1852–1855 and 1857–1858), Soto, accompanied by dance masters like George W. Smith, F. Mège, and Giuseppe Carrese, presented the bailables *The Carnival of Seville, Rosita, La Maja de Sevilla, La Belle de L'Andalusia,* and *La Perla de Andalucía.*[42]

Unlike what occurred with the *bailable andaluz* (Andalusian bailable) created by Spanish choreographers and exported to Europe, the bailable andaluz presented in the United States, a collaboration of Spanish dancers and North American *maestros*, generated a more mixed reception.[43] Rather than taking inspiration from Andalusian genre theatrical productions, as was the case in Spain, in the United States, bailables drew from librettos from the Romantic ballet; choreographers exploited the sets of English and French farces and comedies with Spanish themes. The ethnic and cultural diversity of the United States affected a repertory whose performers, sensitive to the demands of a new public, began to combine Spanish dances and boleros with other dances of foreign origin and popular roots, like *polkas, tarantelas, schötish, napolitanas, sicilianas.* Curiously, the juxtaposition of the glorious Spanish past in comedies, farces, and in the plots of romantic ballets, alongside the presence of modern Spanish dances in contemporary costumes made of the nineteenth-century bailable a heterochronic and heterotopic collage that, even without enjoying critical favor at times, must have produced an aesthetic shock of extraordinary novelty for an avid public.

Finale

Mutual influences between the escuela bolera and flamenco, mediated by the performances of Gitano artists in the bailables españoles, have yet to be documented. Although the presence of Gitano artists in the dance academies and salons of this era is well documented, it seems that Spanish theaters denied them entrance to the stage, paradoxically defining a "Gypsy world" without "Gypsies."[44] On the international stage, the bolero and flamenco schools, developing alongside other types of dance and adapting to foreign musical styles and audiences, were marked by a world of transnational fusions and hybridizations. In Spain, the bailable entwined the bolero dances of Rosa Espert, Francisca Bueno, Conchita Ruiz, Isabel Argüelles, and Antonia Martínez with the Gitano dances of Josefa Vargas, Adela Guerrero, Petra Cámara, and Manuela Perea. The latter, who have yet to be closely studied, were equal masters of the bolero dances as of dances clearly related to flamenco.[45] Similarly, the bailable blended academic musical compositions on popular themes with vernacular-styled performances by musicians, singers, and dancers such as Francisco Pardo, José Villegas, Santolio, and Manuel Guerrero.[46] Guerrero and Pardo gained fame by promoting flamenco dances and songs from the Iberian Peninsula, and for adapting Hispano American songs and dances to the Andalusian style.[47] Thus, the choreographers of Spanish bailables catalyzed unique dance styles by creating personalized and original interpretations of national dances. In so doing, they mediated between two distinct conceptions of Andalusian music and dance, one of which—flamenco—was fighting for legitimacy on the theater stage. The artists of the bailables, many of whom were Andalusians, closely tied to the popular culture of their region, were sensitive and astute enough to balance the expectations of bourgeois taste with the formal and expressive demands of flamenco. The academic escuela bolera and vernacular flamenco styles grew along distinct paths, but neither remained the same after this period of contact in the bailable español. The bailable drew elements of flamenco song, dance, and guitar to the stage. When the *cafés cantantes* began to proliferate in the 1860s, their performances absorbed these disparate fragments, gathering them in a unified spectacle, now at last with Gitano protagonists, and ready to tour the world.[48]

Author's note: This essay is dedicated to the memory of my father.

Notes

1. Rocío Plaza Orellana, *El flamenco y los románticos. Un viaje entre el mito y la realidad* (Córdoba: Almuzara, 1999), 504.
2. John V. Chapman, "The Paris Opera Ballet School, 1798–1827," *Dance Chronicle* 12, no. 2 (1989): 200. See also Rocío Plaza Orellana, "Spanish Dance in Europe: From the Late Eighteenth Century to its Consolidation on the European Stage," in this volume.
3. As Terence McMahon Hughes wrote of an 1845 performance in Triana, "The *Olé*, the most charming of dances, is announced, and by a genuine Gitana. All is hushed ... Rubí glided to the middle of the floor ... Round and round she bounded, her arms elegantly arched, her figure magnificently sustained, the *agaçante* castanet answering sharply to every movement of her twinkling feet. Now she proudly bore herself back, now eagerly forward, now turned within narrow compás on the floor, waving her haunches like a true Gitana, and flinging out her feet alternately to a stupendous height—for the dance, a compound of the fandango and cachucha, is more absorbing than either." I am grateful to K. M. Goldberg for this reference. Terence M. Hughes, *Revelations of Spain in 1845*, vol. 1 (London: Bradbury and Evans, 1845), 420.
4. Raymond Williams, *Culture and Society 1780–1950* (New York: Anchor Books, 1960), xiv.
5. Plaza Orellana credits José Rojo with having introduced the seguidillas manchegas to the stage, and with being the probable inventor of the cachucha. Plaza Orellana, *El flamenco y los románticos*, 302–303, 340–342.
6. Ibid., 340–341, 720.
7. There were some exceptions, such as Amparo Álvarez, "La Campanera." José Luis Navarro and Eulalia Pablo Lozano, *El baile flamenco. Una aproximación histórica* (Córdoba: Almuzara, 2005), 36–43.
8. Manuel León, from either Cádiz or Seville, was part of the company at the Teatro del Príncipe in 1816 ("Avisos al público," *Diario de Madrid* [May 19, 1816], 2, 4). In 1815, a certain "Mons. and Madame León" danced the bolero "La casaque" in the finale of the first act of *Le Grand Bazar du Caire* at the King's Theatre (*Morning Post,* [July 7, 1815], 2). In that same theater in 1816 a ballet titled *Gonzalve de Cordove*, choreographed by Armund Vestris, debuted, with music by Frèderic Venua and based on the (Moorish) novel by Jean Pierre de Florian of the same title. This ballet featured "a *pas seul* of Madame León with the guitar, which she plays with fine effect" (*Morning Chronicle* [March 8, 1816], 3).
9. Antonio Cairón's *Compendio de las principales reglas del baile* (Madrid: Repullés, 1820) is an important resource for understanding the dance of this period.
10. Plaza Orellana, *El flamenco y los románticos,* 370.
11. Reputable dance academies in Madrid included the Academy of Luis Vensano, la Academia Andaluza de Carlos Atané, the Academy of the Calle de las Infantas, and the Academies of the Teatro del Circo and the Teatro Real; in Barcelona were the Academies of José Alsina and of Antonio Biosca; in Seville were the Academy of Calle Jimios, and the Salons de Oriente, de la Aurora, de los Descalzos, and del Recreo. In Seville, the work of Miguel de la Barrera and Manuel de la Barrera was crucial in the transformation of these academies and salons into sites for public performance: the *cafés cantantes*. For more on this topic, see José Blas Vega, *Los cafés cantantes de Sevilla* (Madrid: Editorial Cinterco, 1987). Manuel Bohórquez in his blog *La Gazapera,* June 16, 2012, disproved the long standing belief that the two dancers were brothers.
12. Gilles Lipovetsky, *The Empire of Fashion: Dressing Modern Democracy* (Princeton, NJ: Princeton University Press, 2002), 71.
13. For more on this topic, see Celsa Alonso, *La canción lírica Española en el siglo XIX* (Madrid: ICCMU, 1998).

14. Plaza Orellana, *El flamenco y los románticos*, 602.

15. Pasillo is the diminutive of *paso*, or *entremés*, which in Spain's golden-age theaters were one-act comic pieces, without music, and interspersed within a larger work and protagonized by common folk. Their European equivalent is the farce, but in Spain the term *farsa* refers to any theatrical representation of this era.

16. Gerhard Steingress, *La presencia del género flamenco en la prensa local de Granda y Córdoba desde mitades del siglo XIX hasta el año de la publicación de* Los cantes flamencos *de Antonio Machado y Álvarez (1881)* (N.p., 2008), 169, http://www.juntadeandalucia.es/culturaydeporte/comunidadprofesion al/sites/default/files/presenciaflamencoprensagranadacordoba.pdf (accessed October 30, 2013).

17. Polo was an eighteenth-century song and salon dance that the Conde de Noroña described in 1779 as being danced and sung in a "new tone" and "in a whining manner" by Gypsies. By 1838, Estébanez Calderón described Antonio Monge Rivero "El Planeta," a "veteran singer" widely considered to be one of the earliest flamenco singers, as the "King of Two Polos." Today, the polo is a flamenco song in the family of soleá. Gerhard Steingress, *Sociología del cante flamenco* (Sevilla: Signatura, 1991), 90, 210, 350; Serafín Estébanez Calderón and F. Lameyer, *Escenas andaluzas: bizarrias de la tierra* (Madrid: B. Gonzalez, 1847), 259. Regarding the date Estébanez Calderón wrote "Un baile en Triana," see Andres Raya, "Poniéndole un año a 'Un baile en Triana,'" Flamenco en mi memoria, January 24, 2012, http://memoriaflamenca.blogspot.com/2012/01/poniendole-el-ano-un-baile-en-triana.html, (accessed January 5, 2014).

18. Manuel García led the first European opera company to perform on a U.S. stage in 1825. "Teatros," *Diario de Madrid* (July 10, 1813), 8.

19. "Teatros," *Diario de Madrid* (March 11, 1822), 4.

20. José Luis Navarro, *De Telethusa a La Macarrona. Bailes andaluces y flamencos* (Sevilla: Portada Editorial, 2002), 153–154. Malibrán interpreted his father's original version of the song in the Teatro Italiano de París ("Teatro Italiano de París," *El correo literario y mercantil* [August 4, 1828], 2); "Espectáculos," *El Constitucional* (June 17, 1842), 4.

21. Plaza Orellana, *El flamenco y los románticos*, 742; "Teatros," *Eco del Comercio* (November 11, 1849), 4; "Espectáculos," *La España* (March 7, 1850), 4.

22. "Diversiones públicas," *Diario Oficial de Avisos de Madrid* (May 14, 1850), 4.

23. Basilio S. Castellanos de Losada, *Glorias de Azara en el siglo XIX*. Segunda parte (Madrid: Imprenta de D. B. González, 1852), 877; cited in Faustino Nuñez, "Carlos Atané: un olvido injustificado" September 27, 2012, *El afinador de noticias*, http://elafinadordenoticias.blogspot.com/2012/09/carlos-atane-un-olvido-injustificado.html (accessed December 28, 2013).

24. Panaderos is also a dance of the escuela bolera; for more on the figure of the Jaque, see Ana Yepes, "From the *Jácara* to the *Sarabande*," in this volume; "salt" refers both to the production of salt on Cádiz Bay from antiquity and to the flavor and value which this mineral imparts to the region; "El Tripili" is the name of a popular tirana (song) of about 1812, which would later become a bailable; Chiclana is a town near Cádiz; a manola is a female figure associated with the cultural ethos of majismo, a common woman who is brazen and sassy.

25. The first choreography of Antonio Ruiz in Madrid dates from December of 1849. It was a *bailable* titled *El rumbo macareno* ("The Path of the Man from the Macarena—a neighborhood in Seville"), which debuted at the Teatro Español ("Diversiones públicas," *Diario Oficial de Avisos de Madrid* [December 19, 1849], 4). Petra Cámara and the choreographer had arrived from Seville just days before to form part of the stock dance company ("Diversiones públicas," *Diario Oficial de Avisos de Madrid* [December 16, 1849], 4).

26. Perhaps the writer meant "*decorado*." "Baile español," *La Ilustración* (April 5, 1851), 8.

27. Julio Caro Baroja, *Ensayo sobre la literatura de cordel* (Madrid: Istmo, 1990), 257.

28. On minstrelized performance: ethnic studies and performance theorist Jayna Brown uses the concept of "racial mimicry" to analyze "forms of race delineation, with and without cork, as enacted by white women," in burlesque and minstrel shows on the global stage. They are applied here to a similar fashion in nineteenth century Andalusian theater performances. For more on this topic, see Jayna Brown, *Babylon Girls: Black Women Performers and the Shaping of the Modern* (Durham: Duke University Press, 2008). On emergent capitalism: Marx and Engels considered that, at a social level, each epoch is compounded by a number of dominant and subordinate classes. The definition of these classes depends on their relationship to the ownership or means of production, capital considered central to the economy of the era. The nomenclature offered is quite simple and is formed by three social classes: bourgeoisie (upper middle class), petty bourgeoisie (lower middle class) and proletariat (working class). According to the authors, since the petty bourgeoisie—small tradespeople, shopkeepers, retired tradesman, artisans and peasants—is in the process of disappearing (having been forced out of traditional guilds that protect them), their capital, now separated from them, forces them into the proletariat. Two other castes, the nobility and the *lumpenproletariat*, are mentioned only peripherally. However, with regard to Spain, the latter classes are important to take into account. Since the Napoleonic invasion was aborted, the nobility in Spain was able to hold onto its power longer than in other European countries. The *lumpenproletariat*, defined by Marx

and Engels as "the social scum, that passively rotting mass thrown off by the lowest layers of the old society," will become an important social force for the development of flamenco. For more on this topic, see Karl Marx and Frederick Engels, *The Communist Manifesto* (New York: International Publisher Co., 2014), 8–17. For more on the participation of a *lumpenbohemia* in the formation of flamenco, see Gerhard Steingress, *Sociología del cante flamenco* (Sevilla: Signatura, 2005 [1991]), 342–345.

29. On the peculiar weakness of the Spanish bourgeoisie as an emerging social force, see Antonio Elorza, *La modernización política en España (ensayos de historia del pensamiento político)* (Madrid: Endymion, 1990), 141–145.

30. "Programme des Espectacles," *Le Nouvelliste* (May 5, 1851), 2; *Morning Chronicle* (July 7, 1851), 4.

31. The generic term *bailable español*, would, by 1857, become simply "baile español" and its presence on Spanish stages would continue through the 1870s. During this period, there was a range of generic referents for these pieces. In Granada there were notices of a *cuadro andaluz bailable* (Andalusian scene bailable) titled *La perla de Andalucía* ("The Pearl of Andalusia") in April of 1853; a *bailable andaluz* titled *Marinos gaditanos* ("Sailors from Cádiz") in October of 1857; and a *gran baile lírico bailable* (grand lyric dance bailable) titled *La gitana en Chamberí* ("The Gypsy Girl in Chamberí") in January of 1861. There are notices in Córdoba of a *cuadro español bailable* (Spanish scene bailable) titled *La noche buena en Valencia* ("Christmas Eve in Valencia") in October of 1860, and of a *bailable de costumbres andaluzas* (bailable of Andalusian customs) titled *La ponderosa* ("The Potent Woman") in April of 1866 (Steingress, *La presencia del género flamenco*, 18, 21, 50, 105, and 123). Lavaur called this genre a *cuadro bailado* (danced scene), but the term "cuadro," which came into widespread usage in reference to flamenco in the early twentieth century, was not used during this period (Luis Lavaur, *Teoría romántica del cante flamenco* (Sevilla: Signatura, 1999), 160).

32. Steingress, *La presencia del género flamenco*, 172.

33. The newspaper reviewer contrasts the idealistic iconography and topics of romantic ballet to the more realistic ones of Spanish *bailable*.

34. "Cronique de New-York", *Courrier des Etats-Unis*, August 20, 1855, 1.

35. Gerhard Steingress, "La creación del espacio socio-cultural como marco de la *performance* híbrida: el género del canto y baile andaluz en los teatros de Buenos Aires y Montevideo (1832–1864) in *Trans-Revista Transcultural de Música/Transcultural Musical Review*, no. 17 (2013): 13.

36. Caro Baroja, *Ensayo sobre literatura de cordel*, 303.

37. Robin G. Collingwood, *Outlines of a Philosophy of Art* (Bristol: Thoemme Press, 1994), 60.

38. Ninotchka D. Bennhaum, "Early Spanish Dancers on The New York Stage," in *100 Years of Flamenco in New York City*, ed. Ninotchka D. Bennhaum and K. Meira Goldberg (New York: New York Public Library for the Performing Arts, 2013), 29. See also Anthony Shay, "Fandangos and Bailes: Dancing and Dance Events in Early California," in this volume.

39. "Amusements," *Daily Alta California* (October 4, 1851), 3. California, with its large Hispanic population, had just become the thirtieth state of the Union and was experiencing a strong demand for shows as a consequence of the flood of immigrants, from within and without the United States, lured by the Gold Rush. For more on this topic, see Kiko Mora, "Pepita Soto: una historia del sueño americano (1852–1859)," *Revista de investigación sobre flamenco La Madrugá* 8 (2013): 212–213.

40. "Amusements," *New York Times* (January 5, 1852), 5. G. W. Smith probably based this bailable on the plot from a fantasy novel by Jacques Cazotte, *Le Diable Amoureux* (1772), whose story takes place between Spain and Italy. One of the scenes is staged in the Carnival of Venecia. Smith knew well the ballet by Mazillier based on the same novel.

41. Mora, "Pepita Soto," 188–189.

42. Ibid., 225–230.

43. During this period, the bailable was also performed in the United States by the Rousset family, and two years later Isabel Cubas would bring the bailable as well. By the end of the twentieth century, the bailable was still a point of reference for Spanish dancers performing in the United States, although with a slightly altered format.

44. For more on this topic, see José Luis Ortiz Nuevo, *¿Se sabe algo? Viaje al conocimiento del arte flamenco en la prensa sevillana del XIX* (Seville: El carro de la nieve, 1990), 33–64.

45. Examples include *seguiriyas gitanas*, *olés gaditanos*, *vitos*, *zapateados de Cádiz*, *soleares*, and *jaleos del arandito*.

46. Composers of such music included Cristobal Oudrid, Mariano Soriano Fuertes, Francisco Asenjo Barbieri, Hipólito Gondois, and Joaquín Gaztambide,

47. Some of these included *tangos americanos*, "Zapateado del Dengue," "Zapitusé (Tango del Chupa que Chupa)," "La Neguita" [sic], and "Tango de la Mamita." The verse of Zapitusé goes like this:
> Si tu boquita fuera ciruela verde
> Toda la noche anduviera muerde que muerde
> Si tu boquita fuera terrón de azúcar
> Toda la noche estaría chupa que chupa
> If your little mouth were a green plum

> All night long I would bite and bite it...
> If your little mouth were a sugar cube
> All night long I would suck and suck it

This verse, sung by flamenco singer Pepe de la Matrona in the second decade of the twentieth century, makes evident the relationship between this song and flamenco tangos and bulerías. "Revista Coreográfica Musical," *La España* (April 30, 1848), 4.

48. Akin to the *cafés-chantant* in France and the music halls of England and the United States, these establishments offering drinks and performance are often thought of as the locus of flamenco's development in the nineteenth century.

Antecedents of Carmen in the History of Spanish Dance

GERHARD STEINGRESS

Translation by K. Meira Goldberg

The Figure of Carmen

The figure of Carmen is neither fully real nor merely fiction; she is the product of a socio-aesthetic construction in which Andalusia as much as the rest of Europe participated during the nineteenth century. The protagonists of this romantic configuration were the common folk and their heroes: bullfighters, bandits and smugglers, women working in the cigar factories, Gitanos, and Moorish women.[1] The Alhambra, castles and ruins, mountains, bridges, and taverns made up the stage. European fantasy, frustrated by the convulsions of revolution and frightened by the social change brought about by industrialization, turned its gaze toward the great South, that corner of the old continent beyond the Pyrenees. An unknown and mysterious land, exotic and erotic, both attractive and frightening—upon superficial glance, Spain was the unknown object. It is therefore not surprising that the first incarnations of Carmen were the product of imagination outside Spain, the projection of a collective fantasy.

The first Carmen, the *Carmen* of Prosper Mérimée, of Valencia, of literature, was born in 1846. The tragic fate of the Gitano woman as a fictitious construction motivated an entire generation of romantic tourists to endure hard travels over the mountain paths and plains of Spain. Théophile Gautier and Alexandre Dumas were the first, followed by Richard Ford, Jean Charles Davillier, Gustave Doré, and many more. As they searched for traces of their Carmen, the fulfillment of their dreams, the legend of the sensual and seductive flamenco woman emerged. Whether they found her or not, what did it matter? They got to better know Spain and her people, they got to know the real Gitano woman, obstinate and rebellious, even if later they would transform her into a misleading representation. The next version, the operatic character of the still young, yet already dying, Georges Bizet, was fused in an 1875 narrative with music inspired by Giuseppe Verdi, giving the figure of Carmen an added dimension of sensuality.[2] The vibrant voice of the mezzo-soprano, her serpentine movements, and the force of destiny tied her to her Don José (see Figure 1).

Without doubt, beyond literature and opera, one more Carmen was needed to

Figure 1: "Gipsy Dancing the Vito Sevillano," by Gustave Doré, 1862. In Charles Davillier and Gustave Doré, *Spain* (London: Sampson Low, Marston, Low and Searle, 1876).

close the dramatic cycle: that of dance. That version arrived, although late, with Antonio Gades, who, as he said, made her Spanish again.[3] He gave her the perfection of professional interpretation, telling a story through movement; he made her a *bailaora* (flamenco dancer), "a woman who prefers death to losing her freedom ... a woman who never loses herself, who is always allied with her own class ... a woman who does not believe in feeling as private property. When she loves, she loves. And when she ceases to love, she says so. She is noble."[4] Perhaps he drew inspiration from that well-known seductress Gustave Doré drew in the outskirts of Seville: the one who dances on a narrow tavern table, surrounded by brutes who devour her with their eyes.

But the image does not necessarily depict a prostitute, as one might imagine, for the dance is not simple seduction. Beyond seduction, we remember Gades's words, "is to squeeze out feeling through movement, and anyone can do that." In other words, his Carmen could also do that. To express feeling in public, to share private sentiment, and even to pretend emotion in order to produce *duende* (the magic of flamenco), that is art. The *tablao* (flamenco club) was born out of this impulse, and Gades understood how to broaden it, transposing it for the concert stage, where collective anonymity and the heroine are caught in a web of tense, corporeal action, that of the dance (*baile*—roughly, popular dance—or, if you will, *danza*—roughly, concert dance.)[5]

Fallen Woman, Resigned Andalusia

Up to this point, fantasy has art as its visible expression. But reality is something else—it was different: its roots predate the birth of the fantasy of the *Gitana* (Gypsy), and it should be considered as a product of the hard work of many artists: *tiples* (guitarists), *bailarines* (classical dancers), and flamencos. Gades's Carmen is everything but the personification of a fallen woman and of a resigned Andalusia. Rather, she is the desire for freedom, the incarnation of a Spain incontestably rooted in the South. Alberto González Troyano expresses this well when, in his attempt to reclaim the Andalusian origin of the character, he points out that Carmen "has endured in a disquieting way, and the character has been disassociated from her origins, but the perfect pitch sounded by both Prosper Merimée and Bizet was to give voice to the desire for artistic enlightenment."[6] But, one might object, the Carmen of the stage is not only an Andalusian character: she is a symbol of the nation, tightly linked to Spain's nineteenth-century Europeanization and its changing cultural and territorial configuration. She is the projection—of course unconscious—of the idea of Spain as a historical and cultural unity; she is a variant of the "Motherland" born in the fog of the Peninsular War (1807–1814): an aesthetic construction opposed to the red hot political struggles of the era. Carmen's faithful and sensitive vanguard formed within the art world—as much in Spain as in other countries—and throughout her existence she has been represented many times in literature, music, dance, theater, and film.

This artistic field, in which flamenco dance must be included after approximately 1860, was formed over the course of more than two centuries. From it, some key characteristics emerge: it reflects the height and later the decadence of the *escuela bolera* (bolero school) from the end of the eighteenth into the mid-nineteenth century; its legacy and evolution as flamenco dance toward the end of the nineteenth century; and the complete professionalization of the flamenco ballet during the twentieth century. These three periods, which serve as organizing principles, contain a sociological and artistic dimension that explains the significance and enduring value of Gades's work. If his vision of Carmen resonated—and continues to resonate—it also had antecedents that lead to the understanding that Gades did not invent his Carmen from thin air. As Gades himself confessed, his Carmen had two principal sources: popular tradition and hard work.[7] With respect to tradition, Carmen gestures toward flamenco as "the culture of an entire people," not only the Andalusian people, but rather as the synthesis of his study of every place Gades visited: she is the "Spanish" Carmen. With respect to work, she is born of hard work; she has no improvisation and no ease, and no innate genius: "Flamencos who say they taught themselves are lying."[8] She is an artistic construction out of the material of popular Spanish culture. Curiously, with this Antonio Gades revived an aesthetic and cultural lineage already present on Spanish and European stages during the first half of the nineteenth century. The logic of his dance reveals the logic of the historical and aesthetic development of Spanish dance itself. The following provides observations and conclusions from my research into the genre of Andalusian dance and song and its representation and perception in Europe during the Romantic era.

Flamenco Ballet

Flamenco ballet began taking shape in the second half of the eighteenth century, yet far removed from what would later become flamenco dance. It began with the invention of new dances created by dance teachers whose techniques eventually became the escuela bolera, and its principal centers of activity were theater stages and ballrooms.[9] This project or mode of recycling the old medieval dances, both courtly and popular, was the nucleus of a brilliant constellation that—influenced by the winds of revolutionary populism and nascent pastoral romanticism—led to a new conception of both academic and popular dance (danza and baile).[10]

The professionalization of dance, its integration into the theater, and its impact on the social life of the middle and upper classes were reflected in the popularity of *sainetes* (picaresque one-act farces or tidbits) and *tonadillas* (sung theatrical interludes). In those performances, the piquant combination of verse, music, and dance found a singular aesthetic that culminated in a word synthesizing all the varieties of *seguidillas, fandangos,* and *tiranas* (popular "national" dances, emblematic of currents of traditionalism and nationalism, taken up by *majismo*—the fashion among the aristocracy for imitating the dress and customs of common people—and incorporated into the repertory of the escuela bolera): "baile."

Without doubt, the role of eroticism in these dances must be highlighted as one of the most important "secrets" to their success. Liberated from courtly etiquette and from the roughness of the campfire, male and female bodies were molded under the supervision of the dance maestros, with the goal of stimulating and expressing the fantasies of the dancers and their audiences. Once these longings became an artistic standard, the step from the populism of *majos* and *majas* to the popularization of new dances yielded a new aesthetic culture, a vulgarization that condemned and categorized the bolero for some time as a low-class diversion. Nonetheless, after the decadence of light theater in the eighteenth century, and once the haze of the reign of Fernando VII (1808 and 1813–1833) had cleared, Spanish dance became a trademark on most stages of Romantic Europe, especially in Paris and London.[11]

As the press in theater magazines of the period and music and dance performance programs show, the public was familiar with a wide range of dances. Although the French school of ballet predominated, between 1833 and 1856 more and more Spanish dances, called "boleros" or "national dances," invaded the stage. The *boleras* (Spanish ballerinas), with their stylized folkloric costumes, ballet slippers, and an apparent spontaneity and voluptuousness that made the male Parisian world tremble, triumphed over the cool rationalism of French ballet with its pointe shoes and tutus. In this era, Spanish dance, as a differentiating characteristic, took up the magic of "squeezing a feeling out through movement," to reiterate Gades's idea. Let us read one of Gautier's many commentaries on Spanish dance in Paris:

> The Spanish dancers, although they lack the polish, the requisite correctness and the elevation of the French are, in my view, far superior to them in grace and enchantment. As they work little and do not submit themselves to those exercises in agility that make of a dance class a torture chamber, they avoid the leanness of a trained horse that gives our dances a macabre and excessively anatomical aspect; they preserve the curves and roundness of their sex; *they look like women who dance rather than like ballerinas*, which is completely different. Their way of dancing has not the faintest similarity to the French School.[12]

The curves of the dancers were, of course, similar to those of Carmen, although in this case Gautier was speaking of dance professionals, such as Dolores Serral, accompanied by Mariano Camprubí, both Catalonians converted for greater appeal into "Andalusians," who returned to perform in 1843 at the Teatro des Varietés de Paris, ten years after their first success at the prestigious Teatro de la Opéra.[13] It was doubtless insufficient to be a Spanish ballerina or bolero; besides, a dancer had to be Andalusian, or better yet, Gitana. These were the "pretend Andalusian Gitanas," the fruit of avaricious lies, which culminated in the iridescent character of peripatetic Carmen as the destiny of the boleras. Nonetheless, the performing tours of Pepa Vargas, Petra Cámara, Pepita Oliva, Manuela Perea "La Nena," Lola de Valencia, and others demonstrate a sociologically important fact: art and spectacle traveled together. The radius of performance lengthened rapidly because of European hunger for diversions and leisure, and with improvements in both travel conditions and performance contracts.

"I found my style among the Spanish people"

Around 1860, public interest in Spanish dance significantly declined, a fading of the aesthetic represented by the escuela bolera. Dance passed from theater stages and ballrooms to "the street," where—once again—it was enriched by an aesthetic hidden among the people and newer and more modern expressive forms, like the French *cancan*. In this way, while preserving the goal of reviving supposedly ancient traditions, Spanish dance differentiated itself from the escuela bolera from which it had emerged and began to represent a series of new styles based on contemporary poetry, music, and choreography. Its most distinctive products were the *copla* (sung poetry popular in eighteenth-century Spain and Latin America) and the flamenco genre as new manifestations of the old peculiarities of the Andalusian and the Gitano. These developments were not simply the consequence of a saturation of possibilities for boleras to continue within an existing framework of dance aesthetics. There were also changes in Spain: although theaters continued offering ballets inspired by picturesque Andalusian themes, the nation's economic crisis and revolutionary political turmoil emerging around 1868 left their mark on Spanish stages. Increasing urbanization, industrialization, and democratization provoked diversity in kinds of establishments and in taste. Many theaters either closed or began focusing on works and genres more suited to the "elegant classes," reducing or abandoning pieces typical of light theater. So-called "national dance" was now merely a diversion for the audience between dramas, comedies, or *zarzuelas*. On July 22, 1865, Jerez's local *El Guadalete*, in reference to celebrated *cantaor* (flamenco singer) Silverio Franconetti's first performance there after his return from Uruguay, wrote:

> The elegant world goes to the beach or hides in order to pretend that it has emigrated. And the world which is not elegant—oh! They are a frank and simple folk, whose intelligence and taste seek out certain pastures, and are only enthusiastic about great drama, or about Silverio.
>
> Silverio, the *cantador*, not the *cantor*, because God has not permitted us to call he who gargles indefinable notes in that monotonous cadence that is precious and full of sentiments when exhaled from a sweet and harmonic throat a *cantor*. But it is true that Silverio has filled the theater once, twice, three times. And three nights the muses of dramatic arts have been mourning.[14]

The complaint does not seem an exaggeration, in light of another of the characteristics about which Gades spoke a century later with respect to his way of comprehending and working within dance. Flamenco dance, and so his own dance, was nourished by the people; they are popular in the same measure as that with which they tell a story, a story of the people, through movement, although in this case we are dealing with art gilded with hard labor: "If it is true that flamenco should be danced with a certain spontaneity, this absolutely does not imply relaxation, nor even improvisation."[15] There is little doubt that the critic of Silverio's performance was unaware of the artistic character of the emerging flamenco genre, that it was the fruit of an effort, of the work of discipline and of knowledge of the disdained *cantador*. In contrast, Hugo Schuchardt and Antonio Machado y Álvarez ("Demófilo") observed in their studies of the new genre that flamenco is not popular in the active sense but rather in the passive sense: it is not the song and dance of the people, it is not folklore, it is a genre belonging to cantaores, an art built upon the sensibility of the artist to the feelings and the reality of the folk.[16] Gades expressed it in this manner: "I found my style among the Spanish people, and to them I owe everything.... I respect the dance and above all the tradition of the people, and I respect the people because they taught me everything I know."[17]

Antonio Gades: Syntheses and Innovation

The artistic experience of Antonio Gades as a dancer brought him toward intelligent postures with respect to the character of Spanish dance and flamenco. But the dancer's experience is not merely personal—it is not only a staging of the sentimental history of the Spanish people. Rather, it reflects the logic of the artistic field as a whole: it is a way to express the universal character of human dance. More concretely, Gades's assertions correspond to a high degree with the history of Spanish dance and flamenco. That he was able to drink from the font of tradition as well as from his surroundings, Gades demonstrated that he had comprehended the essence of his art. In this way, he was able to create and renew an aesthetic-cultural tradition deeply anchored in the history of Spanish art and of the Spanish people. For this reason, he can be considered a legitimate heir to a rich tradition and as one of the few personifications (until now) of its highest level. Gades inherited an art that came into existence during the second half of the eighteenth century and that yielded diverse and fascinating manifestations. It is an expression of universal character, which in all cases offers itself to us—by way of a precise and critical gaze (not a folkloristic or mystifying gaze)—as a synthesis of the best of Andalusian and Spanish culture.

Notes

1. This essay is a revision of "Antecedentes de la *Carmen* de Gades en la historia de la danza española," in *Carmen/Gades. Veinticinco Años. Twenty Five Years. 1983–2008*, ed., Elna Matamoros (Madrid: Fundación Antonio Gades/Ediciones Autor, 2008), 113–124.
2. See Gerhard Steingress, "Nietzsche y el caso Carmen," *ABAO-OLBE 08–09*, ed. María Carmen Rodríguez Suso y Willem de Waal (Bilbao: ABAO-OLBE, 2008), 178–181.
3. Antonio Gades, "Nuestra Carmen y el significado de la danza en mi vida," *Carmen/Gades. Veinticinco años. Twenty Five Years. 1983–2008* (Madrid: Fundación Antonio Gades, 2008), 23.
4. Ibid., 22.
5. For more information on baile versus danza, see Ana Yepes's "From the *Jácara* to the *Sarabande*," in this volume.
6. Alberto González Troyano, *La desventura de Carmen. Una divagación sobre Andalucía* (Madrid: Espasa-Calpe, 1990); Fundación Antonio Gades, *Antonio Gades,* (Madrid: Fundación Antonio Gades, 2005), back cover.
7. *Antonio Gades.*
8. Ibid.
9. See Kiko Mora's "Some Notes Toward a Historiography of the *Bailable Español*" in this volume.
10. Serafín Estébanez Calderón, *Escenas Andaluzas*, ed., Alberto González Troyano (Madrid: Cátedra, 1985), 76ff; Don Preciso, *Colección de las mejores coplas de seguidillas, tiranas y polos que se han compuesto para cantar a la guitarra* (Jaén: Ediciones Demófilo, 1982), 7–27.
11. Gerhard Steingress, *...y Carmen se fue a París. Un estudio sobre la construcción artística del género flamenco (1833–1865)* (Córdoba: Almuzara, 2006).
12. Théophile Gautier, *Viaje por España*, prólogo de M. Vázquez Montalbán (Barcelona: Taifa, 1985), 254. My emphasis.
13. Steingress, *...y Carmen se fue a París*, 88ff.
14. *Cantor* and *cantaor* translate as "singer," but *cantaor* (*canta'or*) is *cantador* spoken with an Andalusian accent. As in the difference between *bailarina* and ballerina, and *bailaora* versus *baila'ora* (flamenco dancer), the "*ador/a*" ending references a working-class ethos in contrast to the elegance of the *cantor/bailarina*. Gerhard Steingress, "Nietzsche y el caso Carmen," *ABAO-OLBE 08–09*, ed. María Carmen Rodríguez Suso y Willem de Waal (Bilbao: ABAO-OLBE, 2008), 178–181.
15. *Antonio Gades.*
16. Hugo Schuchardt, *Los cantes flamencos*, ed., trans., and commentary, Gerhard Steingress, Eva Feenstra, Michaela Wolf (Sevilla: Fundación Machado, 1991 [1881]); Antonio Machado y Álvarez, "Demófilo," *Colección de cantes flamencos recogidos y anotados por...* (1881; Madrid: Ediciones Demófilo, 1975).
17. *Antonio Gades.*

Part II—Becoming Flamenco: Gitano Embodiment and Modernist Subjectivity

Jaleo de Jerez and *Tumulte Noir*
Primitivist Modernism and Cakewalk in Flamenco, 1902–1917

K. MEIRA GOLDBERG

> She rose from her chair with the majestic dignity of a Queen of Sheba. Arrogantly. Magnificently. She raises her arms over her head as if to bless the world ... grave, liturgical, she parts her unpainted lips and shows her teeth, reddish like those of a wolf, tinged with blood.... She is like a peacock, white, magnificent and proud. Over her face the color of smoke-stained ivory, the aggressive and dirty whites of her eyes, and in her black and matte hair faints a carnation which falls, defeated by the shivers of the final *redoble* of those marvelous feet wearing carmine slippers, as if there were a pool of blood at her feet. The audience is silent and eager, with almost religious fervor, while the feet of La Macarrona measure out her dance. The chords of the guitar now have an appalling quality. Because La Macarrona dances to the rhythm of her barbaric heelwork.... La Macarrona transfigures herself. Her black face, harsh, with dirty skin, crossed by fugitive shadows, from within which her eyes and teeth strike like lightning, is illuminated by the harmonious line of her body. The beauty of her bodyline is so great that the ugliness of her face is swept aside.
>
> —Pablllos de Valladolid, on Juana Vargas, "La Macarrona," 1914[1]

Blood—spilled by a lover's hand—seeping into sand, swarthy faces and glittering eyes—flamenco imagery has always revolved around the Gitano.[2] Flamenco's representation of the Gitano archives a complex history of power and identity negotiations in Spain. It bears traces of relationships, alliances, and densely interwoven analogies between, as Andalusian poet Federico García Lorca put it, "those who are persecuted: the Gypsy, the black, the Jew ... the Moor we all carry inside us."[3] Even before Ferdinand and Isabella's 1492 reconquest of the Iberian Peninsula from the so-called "Moors" ignited the twin holocausts of the Inquisition and the Atlantic slave trade, the Andalusian popular dances leading to flamenco were characterized by the signifiers of blackness. Wanton, lascivious, and animated by noisy confusion and ruckus (*bulla* and *jaleo*), they ostentatiously danced the metaphorical blackness of "moral turpitude" and "original sin."[4] Baltasar Fra Molinero, historiographer of the image of blackness in Spanish Golden Age theater, explains that early modern theologians justified slavery on the basis of this state of spiritual confusion and disorder in which they thought Africans lived. Confusion, uproar, and wanton sexuality swirl together in the ideations of jaleo—synonymous with flamenco's iconic ¡Ole!—the tumult that defines flamenco-ness.[5]

Juana Vargas, "La Macarrona," (1870–1947) was one of the greatest flamenco dancers of all time (see Figure 1). And, yet, as a Gitana she was perceived outside the flamenco world as primitive, bestial, essentially rhythmic, and essentially lascivious (so much so that in France her performances at the 1889 Exposition Universelle were remembered for more than a decade in burlesque impersonations).[6] The centuries of repeated representations of Gitanos, Afro-Iberians, and other socially marginalized groups in terms of tumult and jaleo undergird the lie of the disturbing stereotype of the compliant, "lighthearted slave."[7] The long tradition of Spanish dances portraying the "blackness"

Figure 1: Juana Vargas "La Macarrona." Photographer unknown, c. 1889. In Fernando el de Triana, *Arte y Artistas Flamencos* (Madrid: Editoriales Andaluzas Unidas, S.A. [1935] 1986).

of the so-called Moor carried "the germ of an unconscious rebellion against the system within which [they] had been born."[8] Cacophony and confusion voice veiled resistance.[9] Jaleo and bulla, which in the early modern era carried racialized significations of promiscuity and sinful disorder, bequeath to flamenco this dimension of resistance and social critique. As Cristina Cruces says, "that which we call 'tradition'—classical, orthodox flamenco, what we call '*flamenco puro*'—was in its day just another form of disobedience."[10]

In looking at flamenco's absorption of the "cakewalk," the first international jazz dance craze, in the early twentieth century, I am examining how flamenco, as a form born of the racy tumult of popular Andalusian dance, reinterpreted the cakewalk's complicated performance of blackness for the twentieth century. The terms of these exchanges reveal much about how Spain invented a modern identity for itself, using flamenco as analogous to jazz in providing the body language for Spanish modernity.

Flamenco's absorption of cakewalk and jazz in the first decades of the twentieth century also reflects the role of Spanish dance on both U.S. and European stages as intermediate between "blackness" and "whiteness," which were conceived as absolute, ontological categories.[11] Coming out of a "long nineteenth century" bracketed by the Napoleonic invasions of 1808–1814 and the loss of Cuba to the United States in 1898,

Spain's status vis-à-vis the ascendant Americas was reduced to that of "Other." In the performances of race that ethnicity theorist Jayna Brown says "had everything to do with articulating the modern world," flamenco reveals folklore caught in transition, wavering between Herderian *Volkgeist*, Orientalist eroticism, and a dawning Primitivist Modernism, heralding the Jazz Age.[12]

A Patio in Seville, July 1917

In the spring of 1916, with World War I raging, Ballets Russes director Serge Diaghilev accepted an invitation from Spain's King Alfonso XIII to bring his company to perform at Madrid's Teatro Real. In Spain, principal dancer and choreographer Léonide Massine, whose choreography was of seminal importance to Diaghilev's radical modernization of ballet, was introduced to flamenco. Massine recalled,

> Once we were firmly established in Madrid I began to spend my free evenings in the local cafes, watching the flamenco dancers. I was fascinated by their instinctive sense of rhythm, their natural elegance, and the intensity of their movements. They seemed to combine perfect physical control with flawless timing and innate dignity, something I had never seen before in any native folk-dancing.[13]

That year, Massine and Diaghilev met composer Manuel de Falla and flamenco dancer Félix Fernández García, "El Loco," who became their guides on several tours through Spain.[14] Falla was from Granada and already interested in flamenco; like his friend, the much younger poet Federico García Lorca, with whom he would organize the first Festival of *Cante Jondo* (Deep Song) in Granada in 1922, Falla was part of a Modernist circle seeking to reenvision and reclaim flamenco from the hostility it had faced among Spain's educated classes at the turn of the twentieth century.[15]

In 1915, Falla had composed his first flamenco ballet: *El amor brujo* (Love the Magician)—a *Gitanería* (performance of Gitano-ness) sung and danced by the famous flamenco artist Pastora Imperio and conceived as a vehicle for presenting flamenco on a wider stage than that of the *café cantante*.[16] Flamenco had been born on the stages of the café cantantes in the second half of the nineteenth century, but by the turn of the twentieth century these venues struggled to compete with the influx of new entertainment such as vaudeville, film, and American jazz.[17] Describing the winter of 1916–1917, which he spent in Rome creating his Futurist ballet *Parade* (1917), Massine said "our studio in the Piazza Venezia in Rome was the meeting place for an ever-widening circle of artists," including painter Pablo Picasso, poet Jean Cocteau, and composer Eric Satie.[18] "Cubism was at its height," and Satie's music was a "subtle synthesis of jazz and ragtime."[19] Massine continued,

> Picasso … was at that time trying to transpose and simplify nature in much the same way as primitive African sculptors in carving their powerful wooden figures and masks. By dissolving surface barriers and clearing away sentimental layers of association, he widened his vision to encompass previously unknown perspectives.[20]

Against the backdrop of this Modernist impulse, Massine went looking for authenticity.[21] Back in Spain in the spring and summer of 1917, and following the April 7 premiere in Madrid's Teatro Eslava of Falla's pantomime *El corregidor y la molinera*,

Diaghilev and Massine decided to adapt Falla's piece for the Ballets Russes. The resulting ballet, *The Three-Cornered Hat* (in Spanish, *El sombrero de tres picos;* in French, *Tricorne*), premiered July 22, 1919, at London's Alhambra Theatre. The sets and costumes were by Picasso; the libretto was by Gregorio Martínez Sierra, who had also written *El amor brujo.*

Falla wrote flamenco airs into his *Three-Cornered Hat:* the *Farruca del Molinero,* the *bulerías* in the first verse of *Casadita, Casadita* and the *fandango* in *La danza de la Molinera.* Massine prepared for his choreography of these flamenco forms by first studying with Félix and then with Félix's teacher, José Molina.[22] In July 1917, Massine filmed Juana Vargas, "La Macarrona," with a 16-millimeter camera he had bought in Rome the previous winter. He also filmed another dancer who I surmise is Juana's sister Maria Vargas, "La Macarrona," (b. 1865), and Juana's partner, their cousin Antonio López Clavijo, "Ramírez," (1879–1927).[23] This spectacular footage is the only film of Macarrona's dancing, or of any of the late nineteenth-century flamenco greats, of which I am aware. It is certainly one of the most important extant records of this early period of flamenco dance.[24]

The silent film encompasses four segments: one of Ramírez dancing on a sunny rooftop, and three of Juana and María. In the first of the three, Juana dances what we now call bulerías rhythm. In the second segment, Juana dances *alegrías* with a train, a *bata de cola.* Although her train is very short, a *colín,* Juana's use of the bata is comparable to the techniques of today; both dancers initiate and brake their turns with a *"golpe de cadera"* ("hit with the hip"), a sharp twist of the hips.[25] Fernando el de Triana (pseudonym for Fernando Rodríguez Gómez) described how, following a quick turn with a firm stop, Juana's "feet are softly wrapped in the train of her bata, like a beautiful sculpture atop a delicate pedestal."[26] The third clip features María dancing in the rhythm of *tangos*.[27]

It is striking to the film's viewers how similar the dance is to that of today. Juana employs the lifted and majestic posture, punctuated by deep breaks in the hips and leans, that epitomize today's flamenco. She dances with her hands and arms in tension, with stretch and sensuality. An easy stateliness distinguishes Juana's dance from that of her sister, who is more agile and whose head and torso are more mobile, less held. Both dancers seem to improvise, taking basic elements and recombining them in various ways, signaling calls and breaks with arm gestures (an inward circle of the arms) and foot patterns (the *recoje*, three steps backward), as we do today. Juana travels playing countertime *palmas* (rhythmic hand-clapping) against every beat; essentially, she is dividing the eighth notes of the 6/8 in half, playing sixteenth notes. With this intricate articulation she controls the tempo, demonstrating the shift from the steady beat of popular dances in communal festivities toward flamenco as a virtuosic concert form protagonized by artists who are "stars," a development whose beginnings were in the cafés cantantes of the late nineteenth century. Both Juana and María, foreshadowing techniques of the legends of later generations of dancers, including Carmen Amaya (1918–1963) and Antonio Montoya Flores, "El Farruco" (1935–1997), play constantly with changes and displacements of weight.[28]

In both dancers, much of the movement vocabulary—the jumps, leaps, turns, *redobles* (quick stamping patterns), and little lifts of the body (*pellizcos*)—are just like in today's flamenco. As we do now, they incorporate steps from the *escuela bolera*: *jerezanas, carrerillas, panaderos,* and *seasé con tres pasos por detras*.[29] Toward the end of Juana's alegrías, María starts to stamp her feet while bringing up the tempo. With a series of *llamadas* (calls), Macarrona performs the now old-fashioned ending for alegrías, the *ida* (exit), which Carmen Amaya used in her iconic interpretation of this dance two generations later.[30] In her bulerías, Juana always calls at the halfway point in the two-measure cycle of 6/8—the 6 rather than the 12 in flamenco counts—just as is the current style in Jerez de la Frontera, the sisters' birthplace.[31]

But María performed the gesture that most intrigued me: in a clip that lasts only one minute and eight seconds, she trembled her open palms and fingers—"jazz hands"—twice in her tangos.[32] This hand gesture is not part of the fundamental ornamental twirlings of fingers and wrists that today echo the sonic layer of the song's continuous melisma, nor of the emphatic hand gestures that punctuate the *cante* (song).[33] This hand gesture is performed in quotation marks: it is pantomimic (although not narrative). It evokes the sonic specter of a trumpet's high brassy trill: it evokes jazz.

Pantomimic allusion is among the expressive techniques used by dancers to illuminate and comment on the cante, to proclaim their presence as free, autonomous, and powerfully subjective beings. In performance, flamenco dancers are not simply objects of gaze: they see, and they represent. Interestingly, alongside characteristic flamenco hand-gestures evoking the movements of the bullfight, a *torero*-like thrust forward in the hips, palmas, *pitos* (finger snaps), jumps, bravura walks on the knee, and footwork, Massine also choreographed this gesture into his *Farruca del Molinero* from *The Three-Cornered Hat*.[34]

Jazz had arrived in London with the 1897 *Oriental America* and in Paris with John Phillip Sousa at the 1900 Exposition Universelle. Jazz dance—the cakewalk—arrived in Paris in 1902 with the show *Joyeux Nègres*, and appeared in Spain that same year.[35] Spain now faced a reversal, the colonizer now colonized by jazzy (as Eva Woods Peiró says, "racy") representations of American blackness.[36] Jody Blake describes the Parisian art scene of 1905–1906, when painters such as Picasso, Matisse, and Andre Derain began to study and acquire African masks and figures: "the discovery of things '*negre*' by the European avant-garde was mediated by an imaginary America, a land of noble savages simultaneously standing for the past and future of humanity—a perfect affinity of primitive and modern."[37] Primitivism was a "process of beginning over again.... Archaic Africa ... came to Paris by way of the future—that is, America."

Falla, Lorca, Massine, Diaghilev, and Antonia Mercé, "La Argentina," (1890–1936) sought to elevate and dignify flamenco as an international art form. As Joan Acocella explains, British critic Edward Dent wrote in 1921 that Spain "sets before us the ideal of a grave and passionate nobility'—something altogether different, he adds, from the 'American vulgarity' that is currently degrading Northern European music."[38]

Flamenco figured into this Modernist narrative as a rebuttal to African American jazz, and this resistance was enacted in the mimicry of the Gitano.[39] Ironically, as seen in Macarrona's "jazz hands," flamenco simultaneously absorbed this danced mimicry of blackness.[40] What follows here is an exploration of how this came to be.

Cakewalk Arrives in Spain, 1902

> The cakewalk is one of most savage dances, which is being introduced in the aristocratic salons of Paris. Some American blacks invented and

danced it during the period of legalized slavery; it is danced to the rhythm of a barbaric music, which is sufficient to drive those of refined spirit mad, making their bodies dance feverishly.... The voluble Mlle. Mariette Sully, applauded actress, will soon debut this dance in the Trianon, accompanied by two cakewalk stars, Fred and Elks, who have been her teachers.

—J. Pérez Jorba, "Cháchara pariense: Baile de última moda," *El Globo*, December 24, 1902[41]

Jayna Brown maintains that the cakewalk's history "catches all of the dubious ironies produced from the terms of exchange by which an ex-slave populace teaches the new elite its dance of wealth."[42] The cakewalk was received in Spain as "American," a dance of modernity, yet originating in the dances of slaves. The irony of this reversal escaped none of the Spanish press. In fact, acid descriptions of the "emperor's lack of clothes" served to resist both American and French cultural imperialism, asserting the superior refinement and civilization of Spanish aesthetics.

For Spain at the turn of the twentieth century, "America" was a slippery concept, wavering between the poles of Spain's former colonies and the United States. For example, an article of January 1903 read,

Europe, *chic* Europe, *smart* Europe, the Europe that "holds the reins,"... dances to the music and rhythm of the most degenerate and ridiculous American dance. Which, in turn, is not exactly American, because it is a dance in an African mode, which is the blackest. What a way to dance the twentieth century![43]

In "Racing for Modernity: From Black Jazz to White Gypsy Folklore," with its deep analysis of the 1926 film *El negro que tenía alma blanca* (The Black Man who had a White Soul), Eva Woods Peiró writes,

When black jazz entertainers came from the United States and Latin America, their "return" was not as former colonial subjects but as exuberant bearers of modernity. With talent and tuxedos and being far more educated and worldly than any middle-class Spaniard could hope to be, they created a confusing dilemma: if these performers were modern, wherein lay Spanish modernity, and what did modernity mean?[44]

The cakewalk's blackness, employed as a token of white privilege, reminded Spaniards of their subordinate, exoticized status in the eyes of Europe: Spaniards *shared* with Americans of African descent the "aspiration and inability to be European and modern."[45]

On February 3, 1903, in its Madrid debut at the Salon de Actualidades, Señorita Pura Martini and "el excéntrico *Sebas*" danced the cakewalk.[46] The costumes were based on designs from Chicago, and the dance was staged by Maestro Segura, who, according to the announcement, had seen *Joyeux Nègres* in Paris.[47] A February 15 article on society dances reiterated confusion about the cakewalk's origins: it was an African American dance, but it was really African, danced by Afro-Cubans and Afro-Puerto Ricans.[48] A "symbolic pantomime," the couple "demonstrates their happiness upon being together" by "*haciendo dengues*" (doing *dengues*). The dengue, like the *guineo* and the *zarabanda*, was an early modern Spanish dance, and I read in this phrase something like "*bailar el guineo*" (to dance the guineo) or *hacer negrillas* (to do little black things), which in fifteenth- and sixteenth-century Spanish literature were euphemisms for sex.[49] In other words, Spain received the cakewalk through the prism of its own history of sexy performances of blackness.

A Modernist Becoming: Tango, Farruca and Garrotín

> In vain new songs and dances of distinct, though always delicious and lascivious, ancestry arrive in Cádiz from the two Indies; they will never acclimate there, if before passing through Seville they do not leave behind in vile sediment whatever exaggerations are too stupid, tiresome and monotonous. A dance ... leaves the school of Seville, as from a crucible, purified and dressed in Andalusian style....
> —Serafín Estébanez Calderón, 1847[50]

American stars, like the vaudeville team of Bert Williams, George Walker, and Aida Overton Walker, did not, to my knowledge, perform in Spain during this first decade of the twentieth century. Spain made its own version of the cakewalk. Antonio de la Rosa, "El Pichiri," was a singer and dancer from Cádiz, listed in a 1901 article in *Alrededor del Mundo* among the "celebrated flamencos" (along with both Macarronas) of the era.[51] Its description of Pichiri read:

> [He is a] *bailaor de chufla*, that is, of dances analogous to those of the blacks, tangos, etc., burlesque dances, but not so clownish and distorted as those of today, which are a mix of flamenco, *baile inglés*, and the lewd and ridiculous clownish contortions that have been imported to Spain in all the *couplet* and *danse du ventre* productions.[52]

"Baile ingles" is, literally, "English dance," but I believe the author alludes to dances of the English-speaking world, including, perhaps especially, the United States. Using the non–Spanish spelling "couplet" (in Spanish, *cuplé*), the writer refers to the early twentieth-century incorporation of flamenco into Spanish *varietées*, or vaudeville. Likewise, *danse du ventre* is belly dance, but the author pointedly uses the French term. *Chuflas*—comic dances—are "analogous to those of the blacks"—"tangos"—but these American tangos were in 1901 so thoroughly nativized that Spaniards saw Pichiri's performance as an answer to, a rebuttal of, the "exotic" dance ideas of Spanish varieties. This perception of tangos as "native" focused the Spanish response to the cakewalk in this rhythm. That is, Spain's response to the cakewalk of 1902 was to adapt the old tangos de negros, which had become tangos gitanos, into new flamenco forms: *garrotín* and *farruca*.[53]

Russell Meriwether Hughes, "La Meri," one of the earliest and most significant American teachers of Spanish dance in the United States, traveled to Spain to study in the 1920s. She studied in Granada with "La Bisca," a Gitana Charleston champion, and in Seville with Maestro José Otero, dance teacher for the royal family and founder of a well-known dance academy. Of the encounter between cakewalk and flamenco, La Meri wrote:

> Early in the twentieth century the "baile flamenco" appeared in the music halls of Spain. And the reason for its debut was this: Up to that time the professional dancers had depended largely on the Bolero, the Fandango, etc., for repertoire. But one day a Negro from the United States appeared in a Barcelona "cafetín" dancing the Cakewalk.

Inexplicably his success was immediate and overpowering. The popular native dances lost caste. The Spanish public desired nothing but the Cakewalk. According to Otero, it was a professional Spanish dancer displaced by the high-stepping colored boy, who went to the "cuevas" ... of the "gitanos" ... for new repertoire.

This is what Otero says in his treatise of 1912:

> First came the *Cake Walks*, first seen in the black *Joyeux* in Barcelona. That dancer was from New York, the homeland of this dance, and throughout North America ... the dance is popular, especially among people of color. After this black dancer several Spanish duos came out, leaving behind their classical dances and launching themselves into the art world with only the cakewalk.... Around that time I was maestro at the [Madrid] Teatro del Duque [1903] and I didn't know what to invent to give variety to so many dances ... whose music and rhythm was all the same [See Figure 2].[54]

The rhythm Otero is referring to is the 4/4 rhythm of jazz, tangos, farruca, and garrotín, as opposed to the Spanish 6/8.

Maestro Otero tells us that after the cakewalk became the rage in Spain in 1903, Francisco Mendoza Rios, "El Faíco" (c.1870–1938), wanting to escape the misery of his native Triana, fused cakewalk with the "very flamenco" "*Tangos Gitanos*" "of his ancestors"—"putting flamenco dance movements to a different music."[55]

> Although the *Tango* is an old dance it has just become widespread in the last eight or ten years. In Cádiz the *Tango* was always danced among the working classes, as it was their favorite dance, and here in Seville, in the cafés cantantes, there have been several occasions of *Tango* dancers coming from Cádiz.... Two classes of *Tango* were known, one called the *Tango gitano*, very flamenco, and which could not be danced just anywhere, because of its postures, which were not always those required by the rules of decency, and others called the *Tango de la vecindonas* or *de las corraleras* [neighborhood girls], but in a thousand girls you would find one who dared to dance this one, even if she knew how to do the silly things that those less worried about their reputation usually used to adorn this dance.[56]

The French and Spanish alike characterized tangos gitanos, even as danced by Macarrona at the Paris Exposition Universelle of 1889, as "voluptuous" and "bestial."[57] Likewise, the use of the hips was characteristic of Gitano dance long before the advent of cakewalk. An 1845 description of a Gitana named Rubí dancing in Triana says: "Now she proudly bore herself back, now eagerly forward ... waving her haunches like a true gitana."[58]

From Faíco's fusion came the garrotín, danced with the proverbial elegant hat of the cakewalk, and the farruca. Otero taught them both in Seville by 1906.[59]

> The Farruca ... is a dance similar to the Garrotín and to the Tango.... When Faíco left for Madrid, with a contract from ... the Café de La Marina ... talking with some friends he said that he wanted to invent something new, to see whether in that way he could become an artist of a different class. His friends approved of the idea and working with a good maestro of the guitar, they arranged the Garrotín and the Farruca.
>
> Faíco danced Tangos quite well and ... what he did was to mold the movements of the flamenco dances to a different music. The success of the Garrotín, Farruca, and his Tangos was so clamorous that he was soon hired to perform at the Edén Concert in Barcelona; from there he got a contract to perform in Paris, and later, London and other places abroad.[60]

The "good maestro" with whom Faíco created farruca and garrotín was none other than the renowned Ramón Montoya Salazar (1879–1949), who was performing in Madrid's

Figure 2: Encarnación Hurtado, "La Malagueñita," and Les Mingorance. In *Eco artístico*, May 25, 1911 (Biblioteca Nacional de España).

Café de la Marina.⁶¹ The garrotín, "the *Bonitos tangos del garrotín que se cantan en el Café de La Marina* became famous, and were sold as sheet music."⁶² And this song, with its chorus "Con el garrotín, con el garrotán/ De la vera, vera, vera, va," accompanies the dance to this day.⁶³ Dancer Aileen Passloff, who learned a garrotín from Frasquillo's daughter Mercedes León and her husband and partner Albano de Zúñiga, recalls that, using a hat as a prop, it employed an "exaggerated backward lean and butterfly knees.... For me it's straight vaudeville."⁶⁴

The farruca was invented at the same time, as singer Pepe de la Matrona recalled:

> This is the café where Montoya and Faíco made up the farruca, which became popular as a cante, and hearing the cante they began to study it and invented the farruca as a dance. Then it became fashionable and later people continued dancing it and adding to it what Faíco had not.⁶⁵

Alongside Faíco and his cousin Mojigongo, Antonio Ramírez (Macarrona's partner and cousin, filmed by Massine in 1917) further developed the farruca.⁶⁶ And at this time (1906) in Madrid's Café de la Marina, another male dancer appeared, Antonio de Bilbao, who would become known for developing spectacular footwork techniques. Flamenco Modernist Vicente Escudero (1888–1980) called him "a colossus of macho flamenco dance" and maestro: "at his side I learned the mystery of flamenco."⁶⁷

In 1912, Otero commented, "Today, dance academies have to teach differently than they did 12 or 14 years ago ... every dance teacher has to teach lots of footwork, even if he knows how to do [the fanciest] beats."⁶⁸ This emphasis on footwork was integral to making the old tangos, whose blackness was signified by burlesque tumult and waving haunches, a response to the cakewalk that would be suitable to royal ballrooms and middle class dance academies. Dancing tangos before King Alfonso XIII and Queen Victoria Eugenia, Otero realized, "for bailes to be agreeable it is not necessary to add grotesque movements; all the Andalusian dances have many charming movements that do not stray from morality."⁶⁹ "Today," he continued,

> there is no one, of any class, who learns to dance without asking to learn the *Tango*; and as it has become the obligation of the dance maestros to teach this dance, what has happened is that I have situated it within the rules of dance by using footwork (*trabajo de pie*), and not with indecent postures.⁷⁰

In substituting footwork for lascivious swaying, Otero alludes to the many imbrications, and to the slippage, between these minstrelized performances, as seen in an advertisement from 1911 for an elegant "cosmopolitan" couple (that is, performing foreign dances) dancing "transformed" (that is, in blackface) and specializing in flamenco footwork (see Figures 2 and 3).

¡Ole to Blondeness!

> If the cakewalk is a Negro dance caricaturing certain white customs, what is that dance when, say, a white theater company attempts to satirize it as a Negro dance? I find the idea of white minstrels in blackface satirizing a dance satirizing themselves a remarkable kind of irony—which, I suppose, is the whole point of minstrel shows.
> —Amiri Baraka (Leroi Jones), *Blues People*⁷¹

In 1904–1905, La Macarrona began dancing and singing a *tientos-tanguillos*—a *tango del sombrero*—wearing a hat to one side.[72] In 1908, she traveled to Paris to perform with Faíco, who is ruefully described by a Spanish journalist as jumping onto a table and dancing a frenzied tango, while Macarrona, giving "a tap on the brim of her hat," gives "the gentlemen in the audience a wink" and makes an "infernal racket" with her hands and feet. An African aristocrat in the audience throws his hat at her feet, exclaiming, "'¡Ole to blondeness!'" The Spanish correspondent remarks with irony, "What an idea—La Macarrona is darker than a shoe!"[73]

What is the legacy of cakewalk's absorption into flamenco in the first decade

Figure 3: Hermanos Gavilan. In *Eco artístico*, May 25, 1911 (Biblioteca Nacional de España).

of the twentieth century? The cakewalk's comic procession, a continuation of the walk-around of blackface minstrelsy (itself, according to many, a continuation of the Ring Shout, the sacred danced observance that originated among enslaved plantation laborers), certainly is echoed in the comic processions that conclude many flamenco shows.[74]

Zapateado, footwork, seems to be evolving at this precise moment, and in this precise context. As seen in the 1911 advertisement above (Figure 3), *zapateado flamenco* (flamenco footwork, here in blackface) seems, like tangos, garrotín, and farruca, to reference the racy representations of cakewalk and jazz.[75] In the same publication, for example, Encarnacion Hurtado, "La Malagueñita," is called "Soberana del Baile Flamenco" (Queen of Flamenco Dance) and "the authentic creator of 'farrucas,' ... 'tangos' and 'garrotíns,'" yet she is pictured in a tuxedo, holding a cakewalk cane (see Figure 2, top row, second and fourth images).[76] On the same page is an advertisement for "Les Mingorance, eccentric international dancers"—she is dressed as a Spanish dancer, he is in blackface and wearing a dirty, broken-down riff on George Walker's plaid suit and top hat from *In Dahomey* of 1903, calling himself the "creator of the tango bearing his name" (see Figure 2).

Footwork also seems to reference the essential rhythmicity that was so emblematic of the Primitive for Modernists. Dance critic John Martin, writing in 1929 about Vicente Escudero's upcoming appearance in New York with La Argentina, and probing the differences between Argentina's "classic" dances and Escudero's "flamenco" ones, articulated the (fictional) image of Escudero as "a full-blooded gitano," a "son of the soil," whose "gypsy dances" run in his blood. For Martin, this equated to Escudero's *a cappella* "Rhythmes," "whose fame has traveled most quickly across the ocean." Martin continues, "Naturalness is an innate quality of his art. Every movement has the appearance of spontaneity. Can it be that there is a certain amount of improvisation in his dances?"[77]

1917 Again: The Politics of Improvisation

> I finally made up my mind to shout my blackness. Gradually, putting out pseudopodia in all directions, I secreted a race. And this race staggered under the weight of one basic element. *Rhythm!*
> —Frantz Fanon, *Black Skin, White Masks*, 1952[78]

Part of cakewalk's jazziness was improvisation: "figures ... one more strange and fanciful than the other."[79] "This latitude for individual invention and improvisation was considered one of the major attractions of the cakewalk ... the cakewalk was nothing but 'the wildest frolics' and 'the triumph of personal improvisation.'"[80] And the dilemma for white dancers of absorbing these dances without, as Charles Gregory's cakewalk theory from the 1902 *Joyeux* says, "appearing ridiculous or foolish," gestures toward the multiple layers of meaning embodied in cakewalks' buffoonery.[81] I believe this dilemma leads us to the crux of the politics of race and national identity inherent in the slippery contestations between Gitanos and non–Gitanos in Spain's absorption of cakewalk into flamenco.

In her introduction to *Los Ballets Russes de Diaghilev y España*, Delfín Colomé quotes Russian composer and musicologist Boris Asafyev writing on the "*teatro de la España rusa*" (the theater of Russian Spain): "'This theater ... could only be born in Russia ... where people dreamed of ... sun, passion, and liberty.... Spain is ... duende ... the *feu sacré slave* [fiery sacred slave], as they said in Paris.'"[82] In her chapter "The Choreography of *Le Tricorne*" in the same volume, Lynn Garafola quotes this passage from Massine's memoirs, writing about his Farruca:

> "Throughout the dance my movements were slow and contorted, and to the style and rhythm which I had learned from Félix, I added many twisted and broken gestures of my own. I felt instinctively that something more than perfect technique was needed here."[83]

Massine continued,

> "it was not until I had worked myself up into a frenzy that I was able to transcend my usual limitations.... For one moment it seemed as if some other person within me was performing the dance."[84]

Duende *as Rhythmic Rapture and Manifest Freedom*

> Who had the right to be Florence? Certainly not Florence.
> —Jayna Brown, on Irene Castle's 1923 blackface impersonation of Florence Mills[85]

Macarrona helped give birth to flamenco dance in the cafés cantantes of the late nineteenth century. These music hall stages featured alternating vignettes—*cuadros*—that were literally plucked from the dance academies on the one hand, and from Gitano street performance on the other. In Spain, this was the moment of emergence of Gitano performers onto the stage. And yet, similar to the way "black female dancers were barred from the U.S. white stage, although their creative innovations formed the backbone of what would make black vernacular dances emblematic of urban popular entertainment," until Spain's 1936 outbreak of Civil War catapulted Carmen Amaya onto the stage of the Teatro Variedades of Buenos Aires, Gitano performers rarely graced the international stage.[86]

Instead, flamenco's absorption of cakewalk became the terms of Modernist abstractions, a matrix of contestations of race and national identity. As nineteenth-century Orientalism slipped toward twentieth-century Primitivism, "Africa"—as a representational concept of blackness that lent Spain its uniquely ambiguous situation vis-à-vis the rest of Europe—was characterized in movement by ideas that we find at the heart of flamenco dance. In the 1902 advent of cakewalk in Spain, and its absorption into the flamenco canon, I read Primitivist Modernism's performance of blackness. Its signifiers were what novelist François de Nion, writing in 1889, called the "dance *par excellence*" of the African continent, and what Otero termed the tango's "indecent postures": "dislocations of the torso" and "movement of the hips with their brutal jolts."[87] And footwork, essentialized rhythmicity. And improvisation, linked to flamenco as "*duende*": an ecstatic trance, a rhythmic rapture, a conduit to the manifest freedom of the sublime.[88] This is the Dionysian revelry that for Lorca evoked duende—"the mysterious creative force, dear to performing artists, that can 'lash open the eyes of a poem' and help the audience understand it 'at the speed of the voice.'"[89] As Brown says, the "'hypnotic, seductive, potentially unmanning' pleasures of possession were symbolized by jazz."[90] Possession was "a trope for the mimetic contact Europeans sought."[91] In the illicit moral and aesthetic values of the tangos via which flamenco absorbed cakewalk, we find the interwoven images of the black Moor, the enslaved African, and the Gitano as minstrel figure.

Figure 4: "Le Cake-Walk—Dansé au Nouveau Cirque. *Les Nègres*." Postcard of cast member of *Joyeux Nègres*, c. 1902 (collection of K. Meira Goldberg).

The word "flamenco" means different things to different people, but as an adjective, for me at least, it evokes the overwhelmingly salty-acid taste of grasping a radical incongruence, a "Topsy"-turvy inversion. When contemplating images of the cakewalk, the one that leaped out to me as the most flamenco was that of Charles Gregory's partner in *Joyeux Nègres* (see Figure 4). I see it as all reversals, all minstrel mask, yet all shining person-ness. In this image, the vitality and strength of the black man's body is cloaked, and yet, solo, facing the audience with an inviting crease in the lap, the lean breaking in the hip sideward, with a relaxed, not arched, neck, yet he is upright, forthright, frank, and full of self—he is receptive, yet regal.[92]

Macarrona, as Amaya would be two generations later, was known as the "Queen of the Gypsies." What does that mean? Flamenco performance, "endowed with qualities like bravery and integrity of spirit," took up the image of the marvelous, powerful, and unfettered black dancing body, as Fanon said, demanding consideration on the basis of its desire and "contradictory activity … fighting for the birth of a human world, in other words, a world of reciprocal recognitions."[93] As the seminal interpreter of Modernist Spanish dance, Antonia Mercé, "La Argentina," said in 1935, "Everything now is jazz."[94]

Notes

1. Pablillos de Valladolid, "El conservatorio del flamenquismo—Baila la 'Macarrona,'" *Por Esos Mundos* 15, no. 238 (November, 1914), 525–526. All translations are mine, unless otherwise noted.

2. I would like to thank Sybil Cooksey for recommending to me Jayna Brown's *Babylon Girls: Black Women Performers and the Shaping of the Modern* (Durham and London: Duke University Press, 2008), and for fascinating conversations on black phenomenology, and on mothers—bringing to mind my own mother, Marjorie Joan Weinzweig, who was a feminist and a phenomenologist and whom I wish to remember here. I began the endeavor of digging into flamenco's Africanist presences in the late 1980s as I began my doctoral work under Brenda Dixon Gottschild at Temple University. That phase of my work culminated in a 1995 dissertation titled (in reference to Houston Baker Jr.'s 1987 *Modernism and the Harlem Renaissance*) "Border Trespasses: The Gypsy Mask and Carmen Amaya's Flamenco Dance." I began studying the absorption of the cakewalk into flamenco in 2012 while co-curating, with Ninotchka Devorah Bennahum, the exhibit *100 Years of Flamenco* at the New York Public Library for the Performing Arts, and I wrote about Macarrona in my chapter on Carmen Amaya in that catalog.

3. Federico García Lorca and Miguel García-Posada, *Obras, VI. Prosa, 1: primeras prosas, conferencias, conferencias-recitales, alocuciones, homenajes, varias, vida* (Barcelona: Akal, 1994), 506. Cited in Lemuel Johnson, *The Devil, the Gargoyle and the Buffoon: The Negro as Metaphor in Western Literature* (Port Washington, NY: Kennikat Press, 1971), 66; and in Christopher Maurer, "Federico García Lorca: His Life in Brief," García-lorca.org, Un poeta en Nueva York, http://garcia-lorca.org/Federico/Biografia.aspx (accessed October 11, 2013).

4. Baltasar Fra Molinero, *La imagen de los negros en el teatro del Siglo de Oro* (Madrid: Siglo XXI de España, 1995), 13–15, 17. The depiction of blackness in terms of scandalous racket is ubiquitous in the literature of Spain's Golden Age. See, for example, historian Aurelia Martín Casares' discussion of Francisco de Quevedo's early seventeenth-century burlesque poem *Boda de negros* (Negro Wedding), in "Comba y Dominga: la imagen sexualizada de las negroafricanas en la literatura del cordel de la España Moderna," *La esclavitud negroafricana en la historia de España. Siglos XVI y XVII*, ed. Martín Casares y Margarita García Barranco (Granada: Comares, 2010), 178–179, 176n8; and Francisco de Quevedo, "Boda de negros, Romance XVIII," in *Obras festivas*, ed. Pablo Antonio de Tarsia (Madrid: F. de P. Mellado, 1844–1845), 307–308. I have explored these ideas in K. Meira Goldberg, "Sonidos Negros: On the Blackness of Flamenco" *Dance Chronicle* 37, no. 1, 85–113; see especially the section "The Blackness of Bulla," 98–102. For more on these topics, see Lemuel Johnson, *The Devil, the Gargoyle and the Buffoon*, especially his chapter "The Spanish Metaphor," 66–83; and Mar Martínez Góngora, "La invención de la 'blancura': el estereotipo y la mímica en "Boda de negros" de Francisco de Quevedo," in *Modern Language Notes* 120, no. 2 (2005): 262–286.

5. This genealogy was described in Luis Suárez Ávila's noted article, "Jaleos, gilianas, versus bulerías," *Revista de Flamencologia*, vol. X, no. 20 (2° Semestre 2004): 8.

6. See, for example, press accounts of soprano Jeanne Granier's impersonations of Macarrona, such as "le principal 'clou' de *Paris-Exposition*," in *Le Monde Illustré*, November 30, 1889. I have written a full ac-

count of the wave of burlesque imitations that followed Macarrona's 1889 appearances at the Paris World's Fair, in K. Meira Goldberg, *"Jaleo de Jerez* and *Tumulte Noir*: Juana Vargas 'La Macarrona' at the Exposition Universelle, Paris, 1889," a chapter in the monograph I am writing: *Sonidos Negros: On the Blackness of Flamenco*, forthcoming from Oxford University Press.

7. Hans Nathan, an historian of early blackface minstrelsy, quotes historian Francis Parkman writing in 1846: "'None are more gay and active then [sic] the two fellows chained together.'" Hans Nathan, *Dan Emmett and the Rise of Early Negro Minstrelsy* (Norman: University of Oklahoma Press, 1962), 188.

8. Gerhard Steingress, "Aparicion del Cante Flamenco en el Teatro Jerezano del Siglo XIX," in *Dos Siglos de flamenco: Actas de la Conferencia Internacional*, Jerez, 21–25, June 1988 (Jerez de la Frontera: Fundación Andaluza de Flamenco), 362.

9. See, for example, the figure of the *Jaque*, or outlaw, in early modern Spanish literature. For an exegesis of this representational trope, see Bronwen Jean Heuer, "The Discourse of the Ruffian in Quevedo's "Jácaras,'" PhD. diss., State University of New York at Stony Brook, 1991, abstract (ProQuest: UMI Dissertations Publishing, 1991 [9128566]); and Felipe Pedraza Jiménez, "De Quevedo a Cervantes: la génesis de la jácara," in *La comedia de caballerías: Actas de las XXVIII jornadas de teatro clásico de Almagro, 12, 13 y 14 de julio de 2005* (Almagro: Ed. de la Univ. de Castilla–La Mancha, 2006), 77–88. For more on flamenco as jácara, see K. Meira Goldberg, "Sonidos Negros," 2014. For more on the baroque dance named for this outlaw, see Ana Yepes, "From the *Jácara* to the *Sarabande*," in this volume.

10. See Cristina Cruces-Roldán, "Normative Aesthetics and Cultural Constructions in Flamenco Dance: Female and Gitano Bodies as Legitimizers of Tradition," in this volume.

11. Frantz Fanon, *Black Skin, White Masks* (New York: Grove Press, 2008), 89–90. For more on Spanish dance on the nineteenth-century U.S. stage, see Ninotchka Devorah Bennahum, "Early Spanish Dancers on the New York Stage," in Ninotchka Devorah Bennahum and K. Meira Goldberg, *100 Years of Flamenco in New York City* (New York: New York Public Library for the Performing Arts, 2013), 27–57; and Kiko Mora, "Some Notes Toward a Historiography of the Mid-Nineteenth Century *Bailable Español*," in this volume.

12. Jayna Brown, *Babylon Girls*, 6, 125, cites Michel de Certeau *The Practice of Everyday Life* (Berkeley: University of California Press, 1984), 37.

13. Léonide Massine, *My Life in Ballet* (London: Macmillan, 1968), 89. For more on Massine's "neo-primitivist method" of choreographing *Tricorne*, combining "authenticity and stylized gesture," and "reworking ... a familiar nineteenth-century story as modernist narrative," see Lynn Garafola, "The Choreography of *Le Tricorne*," in Vicente García-Márquez, Yvan Nommick, and Antonio Alvarez Cañibano, eds., *Los Ballets Russes de Diaghilev y España* (Granada: Archivo Manuel de Falla, 2012), 89–95. Quotations are from page 91.

14. Vicente García-Marquez said in his biography of Massine: "Massine's autobiography is not accurate in its chronology of events. It was during the 1916 trip that he met Félix in Seville; he re-encountered him in Madrid in 1917, the year Félix joined the company." Vicente García-Márquez, *Massine: a biography* (New York: Knopf, 1995), 400n14.

15. For more on the *antiflamenquismo* of Eugenio Noel and the Generation of '98, see Michelle Heffner Hayes, "Choreographing Contemporaneity: Cultural Legacy and Experimental Imperative," in this volume.

16. In 1925, Antonia Mercé, "La Argentina" (1890–1936) choreographed her iconic reinterpretation of this work. For more detail, see Ninotchka Devorah Bennahum, *Antonia Merce, "La Argentina": Flamenco and the Spanish Avant Garde* (Hanover, NH: University Press of New England, 2000).

17. For more on flamenco's emergence and development in the nineteenth and early twentieth century, see Marta Carrasco Benítez, "Three Centuries of Flamenco: Some Brief Historical Notes," and Clara Chinoy, "The First Academy of Flamenco Dance: Frasquillo and the 'Broken Dance' of the Gitanos," in this volume.

18. Massine, *My Life*, 101; Garcia-Marquez, *Massine*, 80–81.

19. Massine, *My Life*, 101.

20. Ibid., 106.

21. While in Rome that winter, Massine acquired first editions of eighteenth- and nineteenth-century dance treatises by Raoul Feuillet (*Chorégraphie*, 1700), Louis Pécour (*Recueil de danses*, 1700), Jean Philippe Rameau (*Le Maître à danser*, 1725), Malpied (*Traité sur l'art de la danse*, 1770), and Carlo Blasis (*The Code of Terpsichore*, 1830). For a detailed discussion of the trends and countertrends in the "polarization between the avant-garde and the inheritors of nineteenth-century romantic realism" as related to Orientalism and Primitivism in the critical reception of *Tricorne*, see Joan Acocella, "The Critical Reception of *Le Tricorne*," in this volume.

22. García-Márquez, *Massine*, 111; Daniel Pineda Novo, *Juana, "la Macarrona" y el baile en los cafés cantantes* (Cornellà de Llobregat [Barcelona]: Aquí + Más Multimedia, 1996), 43; Massine, *My Life*, 117–118; Alfonso Puig, Flora Albaicín, Sebastià Gasch, Kenneth Lyons, Robert Marrast, Ursula Patzies, and Ramón Vives, *El arte del baile flamenco* (Barcelona: Ed. Poligrafa, 1977), 68; Fernando el de Triana, *Arte*

y artistas flamencos (Madrid: Editoriales Andaluzas Unidas, S.A., [1935] 1986), 174, 222, 224. The catalog from the exhibit at the National Gallery of Art in Washington, D.C., May 12–October 6, 2013, includes a page from Massine's notes from these lessons in Spanish dance (Jane Pritchard and Geoffrey Marsh, *Diaghilev and the Golden Age of the Ballets Russes 1909–1929* [London: V & A Publishing, 2013], 84).

23. Throughout this chapter, "Macarrona" refers to Juana, whose fame eclipsed that of her sister, María. As Fernando de Triana said of Maria, "This good dance artist was on the way to becoming a star. But as she was almost there, she became interested in singing and neglected somewhat that path which, in my judgment, she should have taken" (el de Triana, *Arte y artistas*, 148). Nonetheless, as knowledgeable students of this footage, such as Susana Lupiañez Pinto "La Lupi," have noted, María's dancing, while very different than that of her sister, is not only excellent, but her lines and much of her movement are echoed and elaborated in Carmen Amaya's seminal dance style. Pineda, *Macarrona*, 9; Daniel Pineda Novo, *Antonio Ramírez, el baile gitano de Jerez* (Jerez de la Frontera: Centro Andaluz de Flamenco, 2005), 21. The sisters were first cousins of López Clavijo's grandmother (first cousins twice removed) (Pineda Novo, *Ramírez*, 23). I am grateful to Juan Vergillos for sending me both of Pineda's books.

24. A donation of the Léonide Massine Estate, the footage is held in the collection of the Jerome Robbins Dance Division at the New York Public Library for the Performing Arts. I am most grateful to Léonide Massine's heirs, Tatiana Weinbaum, Lorca Massine, and Theodor Massine, for their generosity in allowing my work on Macarrona to be published. I am also grateful to François Bernardi for helping me capture these images.

25. Renowned dancer Matilde Coral (b. 1935) lists this as a fundamental technique for controlling the bata de cola. Matilde Coral, Angel Álvarez Caballero, Juan Valdés, and Rocío Coral, *Tratado de la bata de cola: Matilde Coral, una vida de arte y magisterio* (Madrid: Alianza, cD. L. 2003), 152.

26. Fernando el de Triana, *Arte y artistas*, 148. For more on the bata de cola as an extention of the body, see Cruces-Roldán, "Normative Aesthetics and Cultural Constructions in Flamenco Dance: Female and Gitano Bodies as Legitimizers of Tradition," in this volume.

27. I propose these identifications based on the following: guitarist Curro de Maria, studying the guitarists' hands, helped me identify the rhythms and tonalities. With François Bernardi, I captured still photos from the Massine footage, which led me to realize there were two dancers in the film, staged in what seems to be a family setting, with two women, two men, and seven or eight children. The only photo of which I am aware that positively identifies María is that in Fernando el de Triana's *Arte y artistas* (75); Triana also included two photos of Juana (72 and 73, my Figure 1). The sisters often worked together as "Las Macarronas." In the Massine footage, one dancer has a distinctive facial shape, with very wide cheekbones. Comparing the two with known photos of Juana, such as that from the Kursaal published in *ABC* on March 27, 1921 (see Chinoy, Figure 2, in this volume), and noting that the first dancer dances in two clips, while the second dancer, shot later in the day, dances in only one, led me to this conjecture. As part of my research, I have added a soundtrack of palmas and a visual box showing the counts to the first and third Macarrona clips, at both 50 percent and 100 percent speed (which is slowed slightly to compensate for the fewer frames per second in 1917 film technology). These modified clips will be available at the New York Library for the Performing Arts. Blas Vega, *Los cafés cantantes de Madrid (1846–1936)* (Madrid: Ediciones Guillermo Blázquez, 2006), 126–127, 258–259.

28. For a deep analysis of Amaya's play with weight, see K. Meira Goldberg, "Border Trespasses: The Gypsy Mask and Carmen Amaya's Flamenco Dance" (PhD diss., Temple University, 1995). For more on Carmen Amaya in this volume, see Montse Madridejos, "Carmen Amaya, 1947: The (Gypsy) Beloved of America Reconquers Europe."

29. On jerezana, see Marcellus Vittucci, "Matteo," with Carola Goya, *The Language of Spanish Dance* (Norman and London: University of Oklahoma Press, 1990), 121–122; Marina Grut, Alberto Lorca, Ángel Pericet Carmona, Eloy Pericet, and Ivor Forbes Guest, *The Bolero School: An Illustrated History of the Bolero, the Seguidillas and the Escuela Bolera: Syllabus and Dances* (Alton, Hampshire, UK: Dance Books, 2002), 159; and Eulalia Pablo Lozana and José Luis Navarro García, *Figuras, pasos y mudanzas: claves para conocer el baile flamenco* (Córdoba: Almuzara, 2007), 72. On carrerillas, see Lynn Matluck Brooks, *The Art of Dancing in Seventeenth-Century Spain: Juan de Esquivel Navarro and His World* (Lewisburg, PA: Bucknell University Press, 2003), 101–102 (in Spanish original, 228); "Matteo," with Carola Goya, *The Language of Spanish Dance*, 52, 119; Eulalia Pablo Lozana and José Luis Navarro García, *Figuras, pasos y mudanzas*, 54. On panaderos, see "Matteo," with Carola Goya, *The Language of Spanish Dance*, 142–144; and Grut, *The Bolero School*, 142. On seasé, for those readers who know the Sevillanas, this is the first *mudanza* (step) of the third *copla* (verse), and Juana performs it in her bulerías, shifting into Sevillanas' characteristic rhythmic feel, the *pam tarrián tarrián pám pám* that Spanish dancer and New York maestro Juan Martínez called *tiempo de bolero* (bolero rhythm). Mariano Parra, personal communication with the author, March 26, 2013; "Matteo," with Carola Goya, *The Language of Spanish Dance*, 223–224.

30. For a detailed analysis of Carmen Amaya's alegrías, see Goldberg, *Border Trespasses*.

31. That is, Macarrona employs odd numbers of 6/8 measures, dancing in sixes rather than in pairs of sixes, or twelves. Many thanks to Hanaah Frechette, company manager, and to Leslie Roybal, director of the Center for Flamenco Arts, at Flamenco Vivo Carlota Santana, for helping me with this process,

and to Leslie for performing Macarrona's tangos in my conference presentation "Tumulte Noir and Jaleo de Jerez: Modernist Primitivism, Cakewalk and La Macarrona's Flamenco Dance" (60-minute lecture-demonstration) at the New Perspectives in Flamenco History and Research Symposium at the University of New Mexico, Albuquerque, June 8–9, 2014.

32. The jazz hands appear at timestamps 00:43–00:49 and 00:53–1:02 of the third filmed Macarrona segment. Juana Vargas (La Macarrona)—Antonio López Ramírez (Ramirito), NYPL Performing Arts Research Collections—Dance, MGZHB 2–1000, no. 268.

33. In Massine's footage, although there is always guitar accompaniment and *palmas*, or handclapping, and the guitarist seems to sing in the tangos, there is no sign of a singer. In this era, women often sang and danced at the same time, and men often sang *alante*—at the front of the stage—in a solo recital format. For more on this transitional moment in the development of flamenco cante (song), see Cruces-Roldán, "Normative Aesthetics and Cultural Constructions in Flamenco Dance: Female and Gitano Bodies as Legitimizers of Tradition," in this volume.

34. In the New York Public Library's 1937 film of Massine and Tamara Toumanova dancing *The Three-Cornered Hat* with Col. W. de Basil's Ballet Russe de Monte Carlo at the Chicago Opera House, Massine performs this gesture in his *Farruca del Molinero*, at 15:00 and again at 15:25, and again, after defeating the Corregidor, at 21:40. MGZHB 12–1000, no. 291–293, http://digitalcollections.nypl.org/items/dacd5830-e366-0130-d583-3c075448cc4b (accessed October 31, 2014). For more on the hand gestures of masculinity, see Michelle Heffner Hayes, "Choreographing Contemporaneity: Cultural Legacy and Experimental Imperative," and Ryan Rockmore, "Dancing the Ideal Masculinity," in this volume.

35. I have given the following conference presentations and talks on this: March 28, 2013, "Meet the Curators of *100 Years of Flamenco in New York*," Bruno Walter Auditorium, Library for the Performing Arts at Lincoln Center; November 16, 2013, "Tumulte Noir and Jaleo de Jerez: Cakewalk, Tango and Jazz in La Macarrona's Flamenco Dance," presentation at the joint conference of the Congress on Research in Dance and Society of Dance History Scholars, Riverside, CA; March 9, 2014, "Tumulte Noir and Jaleo de Jerez: Cakewalk, Tango and Jazz in La Macarrona's Flamenco Dance," Philadelphia Flamenco Festival, Philadelphia, PA; and the above-cited presentation in Albuquerque in June 2014.

36. Eva Woods Peiró, *White Gypsies: Race and Stardom in Spanish Musicals* (Minneapolis: University of Minnesota Press, 2012), 112.

37. Blake, *Tumulte Noir*, 40. Thomas L. Riis concurs, saying "Blacks from the turn-of-the-century shows, and probably from earlier theatricals also, were identified with this essential aspect of Americanness" in Thomas L. Riis, "The Experience and Impact of Black Entertainers in England, 1895–1920," *American Music* 4, no. 1 (1986): 56–57.

38. Acocella, "Critical Reception of *Le Tricorne*," in this volume, who cites Edward Dent, "Manuel de Falla," *The Nation & Athenaeum* (May 28, 1921), 335.

39. José Otero Aranda, *Tratado de Bailes de Sociedad, regionales españoles, especialmente andaluces, con su historia y modo de ejecutarlos* (Seville: Tip. de la Guia Oficial, 1912), Lista no. 1, 211–213, 219–220, 226.

40. For more on the cakewalk as a globalized mimicry of blackness, see José María García Martínez, *Del fox-trot al jazz flamenco: el jazz en España [1919–1996]* (Madrid: Alianza, 1996); and Nadine George-Graves, "Just Like Being at the Zoo' / Primitivity and Ragtime Dance," in Julie Malnig, ed., *Ballroom, Boogie, Shimmy Sham, Shake: A Social and Popular Dance Reader* (Urbana: University of Illinois Press, 2009), 55–71.

41. J. Pérez Jorba, "Cháchara pariense: Baile de última moda," *El Globo*, December 24, 1902, 1.

42. Brown, *Babylon Girls*, 135.

43. Mariano de Cávia, "Cake-walk," *El Imparcial*, January 22, 1903, 1.

44. Woods, *White Gypsies*, 102.

45. Ibid., 108.

46. "Diversiones públicas," *La Época*, February 7, 1903.

47. This is possibly Maestro José Segura, well-known dance maestro and contemporary of Maestro José Otero Aranda. José Luis Ortiz Nuevo, *Coraje, del Maestro Otero y su paso por el baile: según las huellas recogidas en la prensa sevillana de su época* (Sevilla: Bienal del Flamenco, 2012), 22.

48. "Bailes de sociedad—El cake-walk," *Vida Practica—Suplemento mensual de La Última Moda*, no. 789 (February 15, 1903), 11–12.

49. The dance's name may contain a reference to Denguele, on the Côte d'Ivoire, as the guineo to Guinea, the *Fulanis* to the Fulani, and the *mandingoy* to the Mandinka people. The dance was a burlesque, and in the nineteenth century existed in Cuba, related to a guaracha and also a minuet. José Luis Navarro García, *Semillas de ébano: el elemento negro y afroamericano en el baile flamenco* (Sevilla: Portada Editorial, S.L., 1998), 155, cites Tony Ebora, *Orígenes de la música cubana* (Madrid: Alianza, 1997), 239; Aurelia Martín Casares, "Comba y Dominga," 180.

50. Serafín Estébanez Calderón, *Escenas Andaluzas ... el Solitario: Edicion de lujo adornada con 125 dibujos por Lameyer* (Madrid: Balt. Gonzalez, 1847), 204–205.

51. José Blas Vega and Manuel Ríos Ruiz, *Diccionario enciclopédico ilustrado del flamenco y maestros*

del flamenco (Madrid: Cinterco, 1988), 603; Roberto de Palacio, "Los flamencos: bailaoras, cantaoras, y cantaores célebres," *Alrededor del mundo* 5 (November 21, 1901): 325–326. Portions of this article were reproduced in "Especiales: Reportaje historico—Los Flamencos ("Alrededor del mundo," 1901), https://www.flamenco-world.com/magazine/about/flamencos1901/eflamenco19012508082.htm (accessed August 31, 2014).

52. For an excellent introduction to the early twentieth-century Spanish cuplés, see Daniel Pineda Novo, *Las folklóricas* (Sevilla: J. Rodríguez Castillejo, 1990); Palacio, "Los flamencos," 326.

53. Otero, *Tratado de bailes*, 211–213, 219–220, 226. On tangos de negros, see Milazzo; Milazzo and Shay.

54. Ibid., 211–213; Ortiz Nuevo, *Coraje*, 152.

55. Otero, *Tratado de bailes*, 211–213.

56. *"Vecindonas"* are the neighborhood girls, and *"corraleras"* refer to the *corrales de vecinos*: in Andalusia, multi-family dwellings built around an open central patio. Otero, *Tratado de bailes*, 223; for more on the corrales de vecinos, see Francisco Morales Padrón, *Los corrales de vecinos de Sevilla (informe para su estudio)* (Sevilla: Universidad de Sevilla, 1990).

57. Alberto Rodríguez, "María la Bonita (y II)," June 12, 2010, http://flamencodepapel.blogspot.com/search?q=macarrona (accessed August 15, 2014), reproduces Monday, "París, 13 de Junio" *El Imparcial*, June 15, 1891.

58. Terence M. Hughes, *Revelations of Spain in 1845* (London: Bradbury and Evans, 1845), 420.

59. Otero, Tratado de bailes, 213.

60. Otero, *Tratado de bailes*, 219–220. Faíco performed with La Argentina, Antonio de Bilbao, Realito, and Encarnación Hurtado, "La Malagueñita," in the show *Embrujo de Sevilla* in London's Alhambra in 1914.

61. Blas Vega, *Los cafés cantantes de Madrid*, 259, cites an interview with Montoya by Fernando Castán Palomar, *¿Qué hizo usted ayer?, Revista Dígame*, November 25, 1947.

62. Blas Vega, *Los cafés cantantes de Madrid*, 260, cites *Madrid*, Imprenta Universal, Cabestreros, 5.

63. Blas Vega, *Madrid*, 260–261.

64. Aileen Passloff, personal communication with the author, August 18, 2013. See Clara Chinoy, "The First Academy of Flamenco Dance: Frasquillo and the 'Broken Dance' of the Gitanos," in this volume.

65. Blas Vega, *Los cafés cantantes de Madrid*, 260, cites José Luis Ortiz Nuevo, *Pepe el de la Matrona. Recuerdos de un cantaor sevillano* (Madrid: Demófilo, 1975), 217. In his discussion of Guajiras, which he calls a "popular song from Cuba" and the last dance to develop in response to cakewalk, Otero also mentions the use of songs to invent new dances: "as today it is in fashion to put dance to all the flamenco songs," Otero, *Tratado de bailes*, 233.

66. Blas Vega, Los cafés cantantes de Madrid, 260.

67. El de Triana, *Arte y artistas*, 164; Blas Vega and Ríos Ruiz, *Diccionario enciclopédico*, 105; Escudero, *Mi baile* (Barcelona: Montaner y Simón, 1947), 51–52. See also Chinoy, "Frasquillo," in this volume.

68. Otero, *Tratado de bailes* 211–213.

69. Ibid., 225.

70. Ibid., 223–224.

71. Amiri Baraka (Leroi Jones), *Blues People* (New York: W. Morrow, 1963), 86. Paraphrased and cited in Brooke Baldwin, "The Cakewalk: A Study in Stereotype and Reality," *Journal of Social History* 15, no. 2 (1981): 212.

72. Pineda Novo, *Juana, "la Macarrona,"* 30. See the photo of Macarrona with a hat, in Fernando el de Triana, *Arte y artistas*, 72.

73. José Juan Cadenas Muñoz, "Escenas Parisienses—Las mañanitas del 'Pre-Catalan,'" *Blanco y Negro* (July 11, 1908), 10; reproduced in David Pérez Merinero, "Faíco y La Macarrona en París," January 30, 2010, http://www.papelesflamencos.com/2010/01/Faíco-y-la-macarrona-en-paris.html, (accessed October 21, 2014).

74. Baldwin, "The Cakewalk," 211–212, cites Eileen Southern, *The Music of Black Americans: A History* (New York, 1971), 272; Samuel A. Floyd, Jr., "Ring Shout! Literary Studies, Historical Studies, and Black Music Inquiry," in Gena Caponi-Tabery, ed., *Signifyin(g), Sanctifyin' & Slam Dunking: A Reader in African American Expressive Culture* (Amherst: University of Massachusetts Press, 1999), 135–156.

75. A generation later, dancer Antonio García Matos, "Antonio Triana," who would partner Encarnación López, "Argentinita," her sister Pilar López, and Carmen Amaya, adventured to the United States in search of fame and fortune. In the late twenties, Triana spent time with "the great black American tap-dancer John Bubbles, of Buck and Bubbles, in the smoking car of a Pullman train. There the two compared and traded foot rhythms and wailed their sorrowful combination of Blues and Flamenco, as the speeding train carried them into the night." Rita Vega de Triana, *Antonio Triana and the Spanish dance: A Personal Recollection* (Chur, Switzerland: Harwood Academic Publishers, 1993), 68.

76. "Les Mingorance," and "Encarnación Hurtado 'La Malagueñita,'" *Eco Artistico* 3, no. 56 (May 25, 1911), 2. Thank you, Estela Zatania, for bringing La Malagueñita to my attention.

77. John Martin, "The Dance: A New Spanish Invasion," *New York Times*, July 28, 1929, x7.

78. Frantz Fanon, *Black Skin, White Masks*, 101–102. The term *tumulte noir* is an homage to Jody

Blake's book, *Le Tumulte Noir*; she took the title from artist Paul Colin's 1929 album of lithographs, *Le Tumulte noir*. Jody Blake, *Le Tumulte Noir*, 9.

79. E. Antréas, "*Le Joyeux Nègre (The Happy Coon): Cake Walk and Two Step, avec théorie par Charles Grégory du Nouveau-Cirque et de Parisiana, Professeur de Cake Walk, Conforme au Cake Walk dansé par Charles Grégory dans la Grande Pantomime Américaine Nautique Joyeux Nègres*" (1903).

80. Blake, *Tumulte Noir*, 21, cites "*Américain-noir*, célebre cake-walk, par William Schitt's," *L'Actualité française étrangère artistique et litéraire illustrée* 4 (February 15, 1903), 1781; and C. C. B., "Le Cakewalk," 30.

81. Charles Gregory was a member of the cast of *Joyeux Nègres*, the 1902 show that introduced cakewalk to Paris. His published cakewalk theory, absorbed by Parisian dance master Henri de Soria, was by 1903 translated and disseminated throughout the Spanish press. On Gregory's cakewalk theory, see Antréas, "*Le Joyeux Nègre*. For examples of mentions of Soria's cakewalk instructions in the Spanish press, see E.P., "Cake-walk (danza nueva)," *Actualidades*, Madrid, no. 6 (February 8, 1903), 6–7; "El baile de moda—el 'cake-walk,'" *Por Esos Mundos*, no. 97 (February 1903), 135–141.

82. Delfín Colomé, "Presentación," in Vicente García-Márquez, Yvan Nommick, and Antonio Alvarez Cañibano, eds., *Los Ballets Russes de Diaghilev y España*, 18–19.

83. Garafola, "The Choreography of *Le Tricorne*," 92, cites Léonide Massine, *My Life*, 141.

84. Léonide Massine, *My Life*, 142.

85. Brown, *Babylon Girls*, 211–212.

86. Ibid., 164. Faíco, as detailed above, was a notable exception.

87. Annegret Fauser, *Musical Encounters at the 1889 Paris World's Fair* (Rochester: University of Rochester Press, 2005), 242–243n56, which cites Francois de Nion, "Theatre," *Revue Indépendante*, September 1889, 504.

88. When I began working on articulating the sublime in flamenco, I was unaware of Kiko Mora's important 2008 dissertation "Las raices del *duende*: lo trágico y lo sublime." I am very pleased to enter into a dialogue with him now about these ideas. Francisco Javier Mora Contreras (Kiko Mora), "Las raíces del *duende* lo trágico y lo sublime en el cante jondo" (PhD. diss., The Ohio State University, 2008), http://rave.ohiolink.edu/etdc/view?acc%5Fnum=osu1196980354 (accessed September 18, 2014).

89. "It was while reciting his New York poems that Lorca first developed his theory of *duende*—the mysterious creative force, dear to performing artists, that can 'lash open the eyes of a poem' and help the audience understand it 'at the speed of the voice.'" Christopher Maurer and Andrés Soria Olmedo, curatorial statement displayed in *Back Tomorrow: Federico García Lorca / Poet in New York* (exhibition, New York Public Library, April 5–July 20, 2013).

90. Brown, *Babylon Girls*, 255–256.

91. Brown, *Babylon Girls*, 255, cites Hal Foster, *Compulsive Beauty* (Cambridge: MIT Press, 1995), 4, citing Breton, "Le message automatique," *Minotaure* 3–4 (December 14, 1933), trans. in André Breton, *What is Surrealism? Selected Writings*, ed. Franklin Rosemont (New York: Pathfinder, 1978), "The Automatic Message," 105, 109.

92. I am grateful to Thomas DeFrantz for his suggestions on how to approach this image.

93. Ricardo de la Fuente Ballesteros, "Los gitanos en la tonadilla escénica," *Revista de Folklore* 4, no. 40 (Fundación Joaquín Diaz, 1984): 126; Fanon, *Black Skin, White Masks*, 193, 205. A different translation of this passage is quoted in Awam Amkpa, "Floating Signification: Carnivals and the Transgressive Performance of Hybridity," in May Joseph and Jennifer Natalya Fink, eds., *Performing Hybridity* (Minneapolis, London: University of Minnesota Press, 1999), 103.

94. From a 1935 souvenir program for Columbia Artists, in the collection of Mariano Parra. For more on Argentina in this volume, see Ninotchka Devorah Bennahum, "Spanish Dancers in Love and War, 1913–1945: Meditations Female Embodiment and Populist Imagination."

The First Academy of Flamenco Dance
Frasquillo and the "Broken Dance" of the Gitanos
Clara Chinoy

> With the wings of Saint Michael in his legs and hearing in each foot ... [Frasquillo] combines perfectly the movement of the arms with wonderful filigrees that he executes with his feet....[1] Neither tall nor short, a marvelous figure to wear the *traje corto*, unlimited flexibility and most unlimited self-esteem in his artistry, he can't hear them applaud another *bailaor* (male flamenco dancer) without procuring, with his skill and temperament, the ovation which he always manages to elicit.[2] In the *zapateado* and the *alegrías*, he embroiders Almagro lace with his feet; and in the bulerías he has an infinity of details of his own creation with artistic contortions, which always arouse public enthusiasm for his grace and flawless execution. This is Frasquito! The only one maintaining the old artistry in the male dance.[3]
>
> —Fernando el de Triana

Flamenco is a relatively young art, dating from the second half of the nineteenth century, and the formal teaching that transformed flamenco into the art it has become is even more recent. Francisco León Fernández (1898–1940), called "Frasquillo" because he died young, is known as "one of the most important bailaores of his day."[4] He was also the first person to formally teach flamenco independently from other Spanish dance styles.[5] Though his initiative in teaching flamenco separately was not practiced by others for another decade, his development of the flamenco academy was a significant step in defining and establishing the vocabulary, repertory, and learning process of flamenco dance. His legacy was carried on by his widow Francisca González Martínez (1905–1967), known as "La Quica," then by their daughter Mercedes León González (1923–2000) and her husband and dancing partner Albano Zúñiga (1923–2002), and finally by their granddaughter, Mercedes Zúñiga León (1952–).

Spanish Dance in the Nineteenth Century

Flamenco as such did not exist in 1808 when the first academy of theatrical dancing opened in Madrid "in defense of the national styles."[6] Nor was it taught yet in the academies that opened in Seville in the 1840s; these were largely schools of social dancing with little division between teaching and performances among students, family, friends, and visitors. Perhaps best known of these academies was that of Don Manuel de Barrera, where, "Said director teaches all types of society dances with the perfection and taste with which he is accredited as well as the castanets."[7] The "society dances" were the waltz, polka, mazurka, or *"bailes nacionales"* (national dances). The latter were either *"los bailes boleros"* (the bolero dances), which included turns, difficult jumps, and complex foot patterns, or *"los bailes de palillos"* (the castanet dances), which were more earthbound and included rhythmic footwork.[8]

The famous *bolera* Amparo Álvarez (1828–1895), known as "La Campanera," taught bolero dances in her school in Seville to the three most important maestros of the next generation: Angel Pericet Carmona (1828–1895), called "Maestro Pericet"; Manuel Real Montosa (1877–1944), called "Maestro Realito"; and José Otero Aranda (1860–1934), called "Maestro Otero."[9] Pericet and his descendants were responsible for the codification and survival of the *escuela bolera*.[10] Realito, "who taught Sevillanas to high society of Seville to liven up their parties," organized dance groups.[11] Otero, partner to well-known boleras of the 1890s, is considered the creator of the *cuadro* (literally, "square" or "painting"), made up of performers in a semicircle within which individuals perform. The cuadro is best known in relation to the *cuadro flamenco* still practiced today; in the late nineteenth and early twentieth centuries, the *cuadro bolero* was equally important.[12] In mentions of his academy in the press in 1902, Otero's major talent was "not to dance as he knows how to do, but ... to bring together a group of pretty girls who can dance to make even the most bored tourist approve."[13]

But flamenco was not theatrical, folkloric, or ballroom dance, and those who performed this developing style did not

Figure 1. Francisco León Fernández, "Frasquillo," c. 1930. Published in Alfonso Puig Claramunt, *El Arte del Baile Flamenco* (Barcelona: Ediciones Polígrafa, S.A., 1977).

learn it in academies. In addition to the students and professional boleros, Gitano dancers and singers were often hired to perform in the early academies.[14] Their particular way of dancing was described as *a lo Gitano* ("in the gypsy style") or *"a lo flamenco"* ("in the flamenco style") in the nineteenth-century press and performance programs.[15] Drawing on steps, rhythms, techniques, and positions of other styles, these performers often diverged from the established rules of line, aesthetic, choreographic, or moral standards of the day. Other dancers imitated this "flamenco" styling, developing increasingly complex footwork variations and combining them with steps from folk dances as well as with the more formal, balletic carriage of upper body and arm positioning from escuela bolera. "Flamenco" came to refer to the repertory of dance forms that developed along with the repertory of song forms called *cante* or *cante flamenco*.[16]

At the turn of the twentieth century, the distinction between these styles was unclear, although Realito and Otero taught choreographies considered flamenco. Otero has been called "the first to define how flamenco should be danced ... his treatise set a series of guidelines so that the flamenco baile could enter into society, that is, be represented in the theater."[17] Yet, of the twenty-five social dances and thirteen regional Spanish dances Otero describes in his *Tratado de bailes de sociedad* (1912), he specifies only three—*tangos, farruca,* and *garrotín*—as flamenco. He does not include alegrías, which is surprising, as it was a mainstay of flamenco repertory at the time.[18] Nor does Otero include the zapateado, although he describes the footwork techniques of other dances.[19] *Soleá*, which became one of the most important flamenco dance forms, is described as a couple dance, as is the *peteneras*. Furthermore, it seems there were then, as there are now, significant differences between bailes studied in the academy and intended for the theater, and the more natural, spontaneous, and nonacademic style appropriate to a *fiesta* or *juerga* (flamenco party).

Frasquillo was already well known as a bailaor (specifically and exclusively a flamenco dancer) when he began teaching in Seville sometime between 1917 and 1920. He did not learn his dance in an academy, and he undoubtedly taught what he danced, which has been described as "wonderful filigrees that he executes with his feet" and "artistic contortions of his own creation" perfectly coordinated with arm movements and performed with grace and skill. The limited information we have available tells us that, while dancers studied folk or bolero styles from Otero and Pericet, they turned to Frasquillo for flamenco. Enrique el Cojo (Enrique Jiménez Mendoza, 1912–1985), who later became the most famous flamenco teacher of Seville, says, "I went to learn.... Flamenco ... with a maestro who was called Frasquillo, the only one who had a flamenco academy in Seville."[20]

Frasquillo the Bailaor

Francisco León Fernández was born May 26, 1898, in Utrera.[21] His first notions of flamenco came from the Gitanos of the town.[22] Frasquillo also played the guitar.[23] The oldest of several siblings, he did not want to follow in his father's trade of shoemaker, though his family was so opposed to his dancing that they burned his dancing clothes at least twice. Frasquillo's granddaughter, Mercedes, estimates that by his early teens he had left home to make his way in the *cafés cantantes* of Seville. He and his friends would bring the Seville train station guard a bottle of wine so that they could practice their steps in the unused trains parked on the sidings.[24] Singer Fernando el de Triana, whose 1935 book *Arte y artistas* is a unique historical document of photographs, biographies, and descriptions written by someone who participated directly in the developmental period of flamenco, wrote, "I started to see him dance twenty-five years ago in the Café Novedades, really still a child." This places Frasquillo in Novedades around 1910 at the age of twelve.[25] In his book, de Triana identifies the three major elements that distinguished flamenco as a separate and important dance style: a base of complex rhythmic footwork, refined with arms and upper body placement of escuela bolera, and inspired and colored by the style of the Gitanos. Frasquillo was not Gitano, but his artistic contortions mimicked their "broken" dance.[26]

Frasquillo himself said he entered the Café Novedades in 1917 at the age of 19. From then on, he shared the stage with all the great flamencos of his day.[27] In 1919, he formed part of the cuadro flamenco in Seville's Salón Variedades, located on a street called Amor de Dios. In tune with public demands of the time, the venue "alternated flamenco with variety shows and those of a frivolous character."[28] It appears that Frasquillo had already started teaching by then, and on June 5, 1919, he and his student Antonio Triana (Antonio García Matos, 1906–1989), with other regular artists from Salón Variedades, appeared in a benefit performance for the celebrated and aging singer Antonio Silva ("El Portugués").[29] In 1920, Frasquillo, with his soon-to-be wife La Quica and Antonio Triana, joined the cuadro flamenco of the Café Novedades. All the important artists of the time performed in the cuadro flamenco, in a "permanent parade of all the best in cante and baile."[30] Frasquillo and La Quica both appeared in 1921 in the cuadro flamenco of the Café el Kursaal, made up of many of the best artists from Novedades and, by the end of the decade, directed by Frasquillo[31] (see Figure 2).

A Marriage of Flamenco and the Escuela Bolera

Frasquillo met his future dancing partner and wife Francisca González Martínez (1905–1967), called "La Quica," when she came to him to learn flamenco, possibly as early as 1917.[32] They had probably seen each other previously, as La Quica was "an authentic bolera" who started frequenting the professional dance world when she was only eleven years old (see Figure 3).[33] La Quica had performed escuela bolera as partner to Antonio Triana, her classmate in the academy of Maestro Otero, and possibly went to study with Frasquillo under Antonio's influence. She and Frasquillo soon became engaged, and within a short time both she and Antonio Triana were performing with him.

Fernando el de Triana stated that while Frasquillo had wonderful footwork, his skill in placement and use of upper body and arms was initially lacking, though eventually he corrected this imperfection.[34] La Quica said this defect came from the Gitano influence and, with her training in escuela bolera, she was instrumental in perfecting Frasquillo's upper body placement; at the same time, she learned from him the choreographic patterns and footwork techniques that, increasingly, distinguished flamenco from other styles.[35] At some point, she also learned to play the guitar. Around this time Frasquillo, now 23, and La Quica, age 14 or 15, were married and became inseparable (see figure 4).[36]

Figure 2. Cuadro del Kursaal, 1921. Photograph by "hijo de P. Romero," published in *Blanco y Negro*, March 27, 1921. Far left, Antonio Ramírez (Antonio López Clavijo, 1879–1927); center, guitarist Javier Molina (1868–1956); fourth from right, Juana Vargas, "La Macarrona," (1870–1947); far right, La Quica. La Quica, pictured here in male dress, danced *farruca* in this costume. The dancer to the guitarist's right is probably Rita Ortega, and Malena Seda Loreto, "La Malena" (1872–1956) is probably the dancer seated to La Quica's right. Other artists in the cuadro were Carmen de José María, Concha la Roteña, Juana Junquera, María la Roteña, María Heredia, Rosarito Ortega, Rosario la Coriana, and possibly La Sordita, six out of eight of whom are in the photograph, as well as Pepe el Ecijano and Frasquillo (not in the photograph) (courtesy Mercedes Zuñiga León).

Figure 3. La Quica, 11 or 12 years old, circa 1917, winner of a competition of *escuela bolera*. Photograph by Casa de Fotografía La Campana, Sevilla (courtesy Mercedes Zuñiga León).

Frasquillo, Flamenco Dance Maestro

By 1920, Frasquillo apparently had set himself up formally as a flamenco teacher, perhaps to ensure support for his family, on Seville's Calle Pedro Miguel in a *corral* called the Corral del Cristo.[37] One of his students was Antonio Ruiz Soler (1921–1996) of the dancing duo known as Rosario (Florencia Pérez Padilla [1918–2000]) and Antonio. After learning bailes boleros and regional Spanish dances from Otero and Pericet, "for the flamenco dances, Rosario went to the home of Juana la Macarrona, and Antonio to the school of Frasquillo."[38] Enrique el Cojo describes Frasquillo's academy in his memoirs:

> At that time flamenco was a low-class thing.... So we went to ... the Calle Amor de Dios, to talk to.... Frasquillo.... He charged us five pesetas a week, and charged in advance two or three weeks because he made no money and he was broke.... I began to learn flamenco, there in the Calle Pedro Miguel ... to the left was the academy ... just one room, with benches all around.... Real aficionados gathered there.... Esteban Sanlúcar came to play, Antonio Moreno came.... One could hear good rhythm and ... really good guitarists" (see Figure 5).[39]

Informal gatherings in Frasquillo's studio included Gitanos, whose art was not learned in an academy, and *aficionados*, some professional, some not. But his students came to learn and hear flamenco, not *bailes de sociedad* (society dances), folk dances, or bolero dances. Frasquillo's daughter, Mercedes, recalled standing in front of the class to demonstrate when she was only seven or eight years old.[40]

In addition to teaching, Frasquillo and La Quica continued performing. As additional entertainment during the 1925 competition of Cante Jondo in Córdoba, they provided "the flamenco note in the Salón San Lorenzo." Frasquillo performed in a benefit

Figure 4. La Quica, left, Frasquillo, right, and possibly Esteban Sánlucar (Esteban Delgado, known as "El Niño de Sanlúcar"), with whom Frasquillo worked frequently and who is mentioned in Fernando de Triana's book *Arte y Artistas Flamencos*. Circa 1921–22 (courtesy Mercedes Zúñiga León).

Figure 5. Frasquillo with students, Seville, circa 1920–1925. The ruffles of la Quica's skirt are visible on the far left (courtesy Mercedes Zúñiga León).

in 1927 for the guitarist José Flores, organized by the Sociedad Benavente.[41] By the end of the 1920s, Frasquillo and La Quica, like many other flamenco artists, made the transition from cafés cantantes to the larger stage, performing in bullrings of villages and cities throughout Spain, and in "troupes" called "Conciertos de Opéra Flamenca," organized by impresario Carlos Hernández (known as "Vedrines").[42] They shared the stage with top names such as the bailaor Estampío, *cantaores* (flamenco singers) La Niña de los Peines, Manuel Vallejo, and Antonio Chacón, and guitarist Ramón Montoya.[43] They also toured Madrid and the provinces in "Solemne Fiesta Andaluza," headed by Don Antonio Chacón, performing before thousands in the bullring of Jerez on August 4, 1928.[44]

Frasquillo danced in 1929 in the "Semana Andaluza" of the Exposición Universal in Barcelona in a group organized by Maestro Realito, along with renowned bailaoras La Macarrona, La Malena, and Rafaela Ortega, Realito's cuadro bolero, and a *zambra* (group of flamenco performers) from the Gitano caves in the Sacromonte of Granada.[45] In 1929–1930, Frasquillo and La Quica formed part of the first Les Ballets Espagnols of Antonia Mercé (1890–1936), known as "La Argentina," in the Opéra Comique of Paris, where Frasquillo danced the "Farruca del Molinero" as well as alegrías and zapateado. While in France, Frasquillo also performed with Carmen Gómez, known as "La Joselito."[46]

Madrid: 1934–1940

It appears that Frasquillo had a *caseta* (booth) in the Seville Fair in 1931, which suggests a certain amount of professional and financial success.[47] However, according to Frasquillo's granddaughter, Mercedes, he was an irascible and temperamental man, and after a disagreement with a colleague and leaving the stage in anger, he took a break from performing, though he still enjoyed the occasional juerga with friends.[48] In 1934, he left for Madrid, claiming that Seville was too small for him. On the road to Madrid, Frasquillo showed his temper again, arguing with the driver and making his family get out of the car. They made it to Madrid by walking and hitching rides.[49]

Because Frasquillo was a noted flamenco dancer, his arrival in Madrid merited press attention. According to the *Heraldo de Madrid* of December 5, 1934, Frasquillo came to the city in search of opportunities for his talented daughter, Mercedes, in spite of his own needs as a "reclusive and exclusive flamenco." Upon arrival, he presented his cuadro—Frasquillo, La Quica, his student Rafael Cruz, young Mercedes, cantaor Bernardo de los Lobitos and guitarist Manuel Bonet—in a private event for the newspaper. The reviewer tells us Frasquillo "has all his faculties and is at the height of his powers," and his daughter is "no longer a promise of 'Gypsy style' dancing, but a splendid reality (see Figure 6)."[50]

Frasquillo did not lack for work in Madrid's varied venues offering flamenco. He performed at the luxury club "El Gong ... one of those select environments of the Madrid nightlife of the 1930s ... where the men of high society drank imported whiskey."[51] He also choreographed an *opéra flamenca* with the singer El Niño Talavera in the Teatro Pavón, which had been presenting flamenco shows and competitions since 1925.[52] In 1935, the cuadro of Frasquillo closed La Argentina's recital celebrating the publication of Fernando el de Triana's *Arte y artistas flamencos*.

But teaching remained a major interest for Frasquillo and La Quica. Mercedes says her grandparents always had the concept of an academy, and Frasquillo's move to Madrid was made with the specific intention of opening one with La Quica and his disciple, Rafael Cruz.

In 1930s Madrid, two other important flamenco dancers, both older than Frasquillo and reaching the end of their performing careers, were also teaching. Estampío (Juan Sanchez Valencia y Rendón Ávila [1879–1957]) started an academy, which lasted until the 1950s, around the same time as Frasquillo opened his.[53] The great bailaor Antonio el de Bilbao had started an academy just seven months before Frasquillo's came to Madrid. In an odd stroke of fortune, Frasquillo's arrival coincided with his death.[54] Frasquillo recounted, "At Antonio de Bilbao's funeral were gathered the only three bailaores of flamenco who are truly that—Don Antonio de Bilbao, who unfortunately can no longer dance, Juan Sánchez 'El Estampío,' and myself."[55]

Frasquillo's first student in Madrid was Jovino Ruiz, father of the well-known contemporary bailaor Joaquín Ruiz (1959–). A waiter at the club El Gong, Jovino was relaxing with the artists after work one night and showed Frasquillo some tap-dance steps he had taught himself. Frasquillo offered him flamenco classes for twenty-five pesetas a week, not an insignificant sum in 1935. Jovino studied with Frasquillo for a year before the outbreak of the Spanish Civil War in July of 1936.[56]

Frasquillo and La Quica operated several academies in Madrid, first renting a studio

Figure 6. "Frasquillo, el gran bailaor, nos da una gran fiesta de arte flamenco en nuestra redacción," *Heraldo de Madrid*, 5 December 1934 (Biblioteca Nacional de España).

at Calle Relatores 20, then moving to the Calle Cartagena. Jovino, who also worked as a night watchman and knew the neighborhood, found a semi-basement ideal for a dance studio at Calle Toledo 132, near their home. Because Frasquillo had no money for rent, Jovino arranged for a loan of three hundred pesetas through a friend in the Banco de España. The war broke out a few months later, and Frasquillo never repaid the loan.[57]

Shortly after the war began, Frasquillo was denounced for "dealing with aristocrats," possibly his contacts with "men of high society" in El Gong or the Banco de España, and jailed. Contact with the upper classes, important patrons of the arts, was inevitable for any flamenco artist; however, Frasquillo was a complicated and temperamental man, and his arrest may have provided a useful pretext for adversaries or rivals. As Pilar López said of this period: "If someone doesn't like you, or is envious of you, and they denounce you, they came to your house at night and they took you away by the ear."[58] Frasquillo spent almost the entire war in jail. Though released a few months before its end in 1939, he never recovered from the experience. Weak and ill, he suffered from depression and nightmares and spent most of his time in bed until his untimely death on July 1, 1940, at the age of 42.

An Enduring Legacy: The Flamenco Academy

Frasquillo taught the repertory that he danced, which he considered the "only four true flamenco dances ... zapateado, alegrías, tangos, and bulerías."[59] The bulerías was initially considered to be a series of joking contortions, the "broken dance" of the Gitanos. It was not taught by Realito or Otero, but since then it has been fully incorporated into the academic dance repertoire. Navarro García claims that Frasquillo's ability in the bulerías helped make this style acceptable.[60] Enrique el Cojo commented that he knew nothing of *cante jondo*, nor did he realize how complex and difficult flamenco was until he studied with Frasquillo. Though he had seen the Gitanos dancing bulerías, he didn't understand it until he practiced with Frasquillo's students.[61] Well-known dancer Luisa Triana commented that her father, Antonio Triana, always said he learned to dance *por derecho*, in correct, masculine style, from Frasquillo.[62] Both Frasquillo and La Quica played the guitar in their classes, another distinguishing element in the development of flamenco; this contrasts to the piano arrangements included for the dances described as flamenco in Otero's book.[63]

At the beginning of the twentieth century, the distinction between styles of Spanish dance was still quite blurry. Frasquillo was of a younger generation than Antonio el de Bilbao and Estampío and had danced in the variety shows, the opéra flamenca, and the more refined theatrical productions, such as those of La Argentina. But he had learned and performed in Seville's historic cafés cantantes where flamenco dance developed. Like the older bailaores, he was a direct heir of the original creators of what is now considered flamenco dancing. Frasquillo was not Gitano, but neither was he trained in the academic dances, the escuela bolera, and the national dances taught by Otero and Realito. He brought his mastery of the "broken" Gitano style into the relatively formal context of the dance academy, giving it legitimacy and making it accessible for future, non–Gitano generations. His was the first academy of flamenco dance, and he was the first to teach this nonacademic style, with its elaborated footwork and "artistic contortions." He pioneered the process that distinguished flamenco from other Spanish dance forms, defining and establishing it as a wholly independent style of dance.

La Quica, left on her own with three children to support after Frasquillo's death, taught for many years in basement studios in the Rastro of Madrid, and later in the Plaza Tirso de Molina, 20. She was known especially for her arms and upper body technique and her use of the *bata de cola* (dress with long train).[64] Mercedes and Albano taught continuously from 1960 until Mercedes's illness in 1999, when their daughter, Mercedes Zúñiga, known professionally as "Mercedes León," "continued teaching nearby in her own studio at Calle Relatores 20 until 2003."[65] As Jovino Ruiz said in his memoirs, "One learned Spanish dance in an irregular manner, and it was Frasquillo and La Quica who would make history institutionalizing the teaching of flamenco."[66]

Notes

1. "Las alas de San Miguel" (literally, "the wings of Saint Michael") refers to a kind of knife with a wing-shaped blade, so this comparison has a double meaning as both fast and sharp.

2. The traje corto is the traditional suit for a bailaor. It could be considered a stylized version of the traditional suit of an Andalusian cattle trader, which consisted of high-waisted trousers that end at mid-calf and a short jacket, usually over a fitted vest, and worn with boots. The pants of the bailaor extend to the ankle. A scarf around the neck is also common.

3. Fernando el de Triana, *Arte y artistas flamencos* (1935; Madrid: Editoriales Andaluzas Unidas, S.A., 1986), 154, 156.

4. José Luis Navarro García, *Historia del baile flamenco*, vol. 1 (Sevilla: Signatura Ediciones, Sevilla, 2008), 76.

5. Bailaor, (feminine form: *bailaora*) is the Andalusian pronunciation of *bailador*. It is used to refer to a dancer of only flamenco, as opposed to *bailarín* (feminine form: *bailarina*), which refers to any other kind of dancer (Navarro García, *Historia del baile flamenco*, 76).

6. The Academia Oficial de Baile Teatral (Official Academy of Theatrical Dance) was created as the result of the suggestion to the Madrid city government by the Marquis of Perales "in defense of the real Spanish dances." Beatriz Barceló, "La Escuela Bolera," Portal sobre la cultura escénica en España, n.d., http://www.eter.es/dn/artic/artic.php?id=2 (accessed May 20, 2014).

7. José Blas Vega, *Los cafés cantantes de Sevilla* (Madrid: Editorial Cinterco, S.A., 1987), 14. Unless otherwise stated, all translations are mine.

8. The Spanish boleros are not to be confused with the form of mainly Latin American romantic music of the same name. For more on the transition from bolero to flamenco dance on the concert stage, see Kiko Mora's "Some Notes Toward a Historiography of the Mid-Nineteenth Century *Bailable Español*" in this volume. "Expediente de la escuela bolera para su Declaración como Bien de Interés Cultural," n.d., http://www.juntadeandalucia.es/culturaydeporte/comunidadprofesional/sites/default/files/expediente_de_la_escuela_bolera_para_su_declaracion_como_bien_de_interes_cultural.pdf (accessed May 20, 2014), 5–6.

9. Specialists in the bolero dances were called boleros or boleras, and this style was gradually elaborated into what is known as the escuela bolera. One might consider the escuela bolera Spain's response to nineteenth-century ballet. For more on relationships between the escuela bolera and nineteenth-century ballet, see Rocío Plaza's "Spanish Dance in Europe from the End of the Eighteenth Century through its Consolidation on the European Stage" in this volume. "La Campanera o los Brazos de la Giralda," *La Gazapera: El blog de Manuel Bohórquez*, January 26, 2013, http://blogs.elcorreoweb.es/lagazapera/2013/01/26/ (accessed May 20, 2014); José Luis Navarro García, *De Telethusa a la Macarrona, bailes Andaluces y flamencos* (Sevilla: Portada Editorial, 2002), 322, 364, 366.

10. According to Eloy Pericet, grandson of Maestro Pericet, "My grandfather was the first to create in Spain a method which ordered the learning of the bolero dance in chronological (*sic*) order, according to the grade of difficulty." Mercedes Albi, "Interview with Eloy Pericet," *Danza Eter*, http://www.eter.es/dn/notis/albinoticia.php?id=12550 (accessed May 20, 2014).

11. Rafael Salama Benarroch, "Rosario: aquella danza española," *El Mundo*, 1996, http://www.elmundo.es/larevista/num123/textos/rosario1.html (accessed May 20, 2014).

12. For more on the decline of the bolero school in the late nineteenth and early twentieth centuries, see Marta Carrasco Benítez's "Three Centuries of Flamenco: Some Brief Historical Notes" in this volume.

13. José Luis Ortiz Nuevo, *Coraje, del maestro Otero y su paso por el baile*, (e-book: http://www.labienal.com and www.librosconduende.es, 2013), 29.

14. I use the Spanish *Gitano* rather than "Gypsy" because Gitano refers specifically to the branch of the Romani people from the Iberian Peninsula (the Gypsies of Spain), some of whom were important in the development of flamenco, whereas Gypsy is a broader term that includes many other groups of Romani throughout the world who have nothing to do with flamenco.

15. Certain Gitanos in the provinces of Seville and Cádiz call themselves flamencos. George Borrow in the 1840s was the first to mention Gitanos referring to themselves as such: "by which they are known in various parts of Spain." *The Zincali, an Account of the Gypsies of Spain*, facsimile edition (Sevilla: Extramuros Edición, 2007), 38. Arie Sneeuw, in *Flamenco en el Madrid del XIX* (Córdoba: Imprenta San Pablo, 1989), 20, 23, cites the use of the term in *La España*, February 1853, in reference to Gitano artists from Andalusia in Madrid, and Pedro Peña Fernandez in *Los Gitanos flamencos* (Córdoba: Editorial Almuzara, 2013), 16, defines Gitano as "the human group which forms a notable contingent of Gypsy families, settled in the provinces of Seville and Cádiz."

16. The actual steps of both the bolero school and flamenco essentially came from the folk dances, but the aesthetic choices, expressive intention, and general flavor of the two styles went in opposite directions. The history of flamenco dance and the history of flamenco music, particularly the singing, follow quite different, though overlapping, paths. The history of the singing is beyond the scope of this essay; therefore, unless otherwise specified, I use the general term "flamenco" to refer specifically to dance. The role of the Gitanos in the origins of flamenco has been greatly debated, and the relationship of flamenco to Gitano, and baile flamenco to baile Gitano (or, for that matter, cante flamenco to cante Gitano), has a complex and lengthy history, full of controversies and sharply differing opinions, and as far as I know, as yet unwritten. For more on the Gitanos in flamenco, and on the differentiation between baile and cante in flamenco, see Cristina Cruces-Roldán's "Aesthetic Norms and Cultural Constructs in Flamenco Dance: Female Bodies and Gitano Bodies as Legitimizers of Tradition" in this volume. For more on antecedents to the escuela bolera, see Ana Yepes's "From the *Jácara* to the *Sarabande*" in this volume.

17. Antonio Zoído Naranjo, cited in Margot Molina, "El 'Tratado de bailes' de 1912 se reedita por

suscripción popular," *El País*, August 10, 2012, http://ccaa.elpais.com/ccaa/2012/08/10/andalucia/1344621472_779945.html (accessed May 20, 2014).

18. Pilar López (1912–2008) said of her time working at the Kursaal, one of Seville's major flamenco venues in the 1920s: "Even if there were ten women in the cuadro, all ten danced alegrías." Ángel Álvarez Caballero, *El baile flamenco* (Madrid: Alianza Editorial, 1998), 92.

19. For more on Otero's commentary on footwork, see K. Meira Goldberg's "*Jaleo de Jerez* and *Tumulte Noir*: Primitivist Modernism and Cakewalk in Flamenco, 1902–1917" in this volume.

20. José Luís Ortiz Nuevo, *De las danzas y Andanzas de Enrique el Cojo* (Sevilla: Imprenta Escandón, S.A., 1984), 30.

21. According to his passport, Frasquillo was born in Utrera, a small town in the province of Seville. Though I have no documentary evidence, his granddaughter reports family lore that he moved to Seville as a young adolescent, probably on his own, in order to dance. Mercedes Zúñiga León, various interviews with the author, 2010, 2013, 2014.

22. The town of Utrera is recognized for a long line of Gitano flamenco artists, professional and non-professional. An important figure in this community at the turn of the century was Fernando Peña Soto (1863–circa 1930), known as "Pinini" and creator of the cante "*las cantiñas de Pinini.*" His household was filled with flamenco, and his descendants—cantaoras Fernanda and Bernarda de Utrera, among others—are well known in the history of flamenco. Clara Chinoy, "Los Gitanos Flamencos, Un estudio de caso: los Pinini de Lebrija," (manuscript, Diploma de Estudios Avanzados, Universidad de Sevilla, September 2013). Manuel Rios Vargas tells us, "It seems that he [Frasquillo] was taught to dance by Manuel Vega Villar of [the town of] Benacazón who was also the father of the excellent fandango singer 'El Carbonerillo.'" Manuel Rios Vargas, *Antología del baile flamenco* (Sevilla: Signatura Ediciones, 2002), 134. Manuel Vega García (1906–1937) was an itinerant *carbonero* (coal salesman) generally considered to be Gitano. Manuel Bohorquez, "El Carbonerillo de la Macarena," 2010, http://blogs.elcorreoweb.es/lagazapera/2010/03/18/el-carbonerillo-de-la-macarena/ (accessed February 19, 2013).

23. Mercedes Zuñiga León, interviews, 2010, 2013, 2014.

24. Ibid.

25. El de Triana, *Arte y artistas flamencos*, 172.

26. The expression "broken dance" was used to describe this Gitano style by Jovino Ruiz, Frasquillo's close friend and father of the well-known bailaor Joaquín Ruiz.

27. For more on the dancers at Novedades in the early twentieth century, see K. Meira Goldberg's "*Jaleo de Jerez* and *Tumulte Noir*: Primitivist Modernism and Cakewalk and Flamenco, 1902–1917" in this volume. Interview with Frasquillo in "Frasquillo, el gran 'bailaor' nos da una gran fiesta de arte flamenco en nuestra redacción" (*El Heraldo de Madrid*, December 5, 1934), 6, http://hemerotecadigital.bne.es/issue.vm?id=0001071482&search=&lang=es (accessed January 12, 2010).

28. Blas Vega, *Los cafés cantantes*, 93.

29. The other artists were singers Joaquín Vargas ("Cojo Málaga"), Fernando el Herrero, José López Cepero, José Rodríguez ("El Colorao"), Manuel Vallejo, Las Hermanas Pompi, and El Niño Gloria, and the guitarists Antonio Moreno, Pepillo El Jerezano, Manolo el Moreno, Currito ("El Niño de la Geroma"), and Manolo el Carbonero. Manolo el Carbonero, for whom this was his debut performance, later became known as "Niño Ricardo" and as one of the greatest of flamenco guitarists. The *cuadro coreográfico* was under the direction of the maestro of bolero, Rafael Pericet (Blas Vega, *Los cafés cantantes*, 93). On the mid-twentieth-century links between cante and baile, see John C. Moore's "Purity and Commercialization: The View from Two Working Artists, Pericón de Cádiz and Chato de la Isla" in this volume.

30. Blas Vega, *Los cafés cantantes*, 71.

31. *El Heraldo de Madrid*, April 23, 1929, in Ángeles Cruzado, "La Malena, la elegancia de una bailaora de la vieja escuela (1)," http://www.flamencasporderecho.com, September 13, 2013 (accessed May 14, 2014).

32. Frasquillo's granddaughter said Frasquillo and La Quica met when La Quica was twelve years old, around 1917; in another conversation, she said they met when La Quica went to study with Frasquillo, which implies that he was already teaching by 1917.

33. It appears that La Quica's family was more open-minded—or financially needier—than that of Frasquillo, in letting their daughter pursue a career as a dancer. Furthermore, the escuela bolera was not associated with the Gitanos and therefore probably considered more respectable than flamenco (Mercedes Zuñiga León, interviews, 2010, 2013, 2014).

34. El de Triana, *Arte y artistas*, 174.

35. Mercedes Zuñiga León, interviews, 2010, 2013, 2014.

36. While the couple was working in Malaga's Café de Chinitas in July of 1923, their daughter, Mercedes, who became a well-known dancer and teacher in Madrid, was born. They had two other children, neither of whom became professional artists, though Manuel played the guitar and Paquita, who was sickly, helped in the studio (Mercedes Zuñiga León, interviews, 2010, 2013, 2014).

37. A corral is a building made up of many usually small rooms in which working-class families lived. The rooms opened onto a large patio where families shared common facilities for cooking, washing, and

general living space. Typical in the nineteenth century and previously, there are still many such buildings in Seville (Ortiz Nuevo, *De las danzas*, 30).

38. Learning in a Gitano family environment such as home of La Macarrona is a different process than that in a formal academy and is worth investigating but is beyond the scope of this essay. Ángeles Cruzado states that la Macarrona, however, opened an academy in Seville's Alameda de Hercules in the mid–1920s (Cruzado, "Juana la Macarrona, la estrella de los cafés cantantes," http://www.flamencasporderecho.com/juana-la-macarrona-ii/, April 5, 2013 (accessed May 14, 2014); Navarro García, *Historia del baile flamenco*, 219).

39. For more on the importance of rhythmic fluency in the development of flamenco dance in the 1950s and 1960s, see John C. Moore's "Purity and Commercialization: The View from Two Working Artists, Pericón de Cádiz and Chato de la Isla," in this volume; Ortiz Nuevo, *De las danzas*, 30, 85.

40. Ortiz Nuevo, *De las danzas*, 30.

41. "El Diario de Córdoba," September 3, 1925, http://flamencodepapel.blogspot.com/2009_12_01_archive.html (accessed March 24, 2010); *El Heraldo de Madrid*, December 5,1934, http://hemerotecadigital.bne.es/issue.vm?id=0001071482&search=&lang=es (accessed January 12, 2010).

42. *El Heraldo de Madrid*, 1934. For more on the transition from cafés cantantes to *variedades*, see Marta Carrasco Benítez's "Three Centuries of Flamenco: Some Brief Historical Notes" in this volume.

43. José Manuel Gamboa, "Por qué la denominación opéra flamenco," *13 Festival de Flamenco de Ciutat Vella*, http://www.deflamenco.com/revista/noticias/13-festival-flamenco-ciutat-vella-1.html#.Ur8jeMa A1jp (accessed March 12, 2010); Manuel Bohorquez, "¿El año de Manuel Vallejo?" January 31, 2010, http://blogs.elcorreoweb.es/lagazapera/2010/01/ (accessed February 21, 2010).

44. The singers were La Niña de los Peines, Manuel Vallejo, José Cepero, Guerrita, Chato de las Ventas, Bernardo el de los Lobitos, and El Niño de Sevilla. Guitarists were Ramón Montoya, Luis Yance, Manuel Martell, and Manuel Bonet. Bailaores were Carmen Vargas, El Estampío, Frasquillo, La Quica, and Carmelita Borbolla. *El Diario de Córdoba*, September 3 and September 5, 1925, http://flamencodepapel.blogspot.com/2009_12_01_archive.html (accessed March 24, 2010).

45. There were twenty-four artists in the zambra. Navarro García, *Historia del baile*, 399.

46. *Le Correspondant*, 1929, cited in Cruzado, Ángeles, "La Joselito, el alma de Andalucía en París (III)," March 3, 2014, http://www.flamencasporderecho.com/la-joselito-iii/ (accessed May 14, 2014).

47. A caseta is a small, temporary facility used for purposes of entertainment in popular festivals such as *ferias*, or town fairs. Seville's Feria de Sevilla is considered the largest and most important feria of Andalusia. To have your own caseta in the Feria de Sevilla is expensive and indicates a certain amount of social prestige. Ortiz Nuevo, *De las danzas*, 43, 44.

48. The term *juerga* is considered archaic and has been largely replaced by the more general *fiesta*, or party. Zuñiga León, 2010, 2013, 2014; *El Heraldo de Madrid*, 1935.

49. Mercedes Zuñiga León, interviews, 2010, 2013, 2014.

50. *El Heraldo de Madrid*, 1934.

51. Juan José Rivas González, "Rojo Vino, historias de una Vida, Esbozos de una generación," in "Historia de la vida de Jovino Ruiz, padre del bailaor Joaquín Ruiz," (manuscript, Madrid, 2010).

52. Rivas González,"Rojo Vino"; Vicente Vela-Hidalgo, "El Madrid Flamenco de los Años Veinte," *La Caña*, no. 11 (n.d.): 28–31.

53. El de Triana (*Arte y artistas*, 326) speaks of Estampío's "inimitable play of arms," and as a bailaor he was celebrated for his domination of the alegrías, but his greatest legacy as a teacher was his choreography of the zapateado. Teresa Martínez de la Peña says his "was perhaps the most advanced academy in didactic method, as the ... exercises of footwork were ordered in groups from lesser to greater difficulty" ("Treinta Años de Academias de Madrid," *La Caña*, no. 12 [n.d.]: 41). Mercedes Zuñiga describes the zapateado of Estampío as a "compendium of footwork steps," which her parents, Mercedes and Albano, used for teaching purposes, in contrast to that of her grandparents—which was a shorter, more musical choreography designed for the theatrical stage.

54. Vicente Escudero interviewed in *El Heraldo de Madrid*, 1935.

55. *El Heraldo de Madrid*, 1934.

56. Rivas González, "Rojo Vino," 19, 20.

57. Ibid., 21.

58. Miguel Mora, interview with Pilar López, *El País* (January 10, 2006).

59. *El Heraldo de Madrid*, 1934.

60. Navarro García, *Historia del baile*, 391.

61. Ortiz Nuevo, *De las danzas*, 85.

62. Luisa García Garrido ("Luisa Triana"), interview with the author, December 20, 2013.

63. Otero provides sheet music for piano for the tangos, farruca, and garrotin, all listed as flamenco dances. Mercedes Zuñiga León, interviews, 2010, 2013, 2014; José Otero Aranda, *Tratado de bailes de sociedad 1912 (Edición conmemorativo del centenario)* (Sevilla: Secretariado de Publicaciones de la Universidad de Sevilla, 2012), 220, 223, 226.

64. Frasquillo's disciple Rafael Cruz taught at the end of the hall, and in the next basement down was

the studio of the younger maestro Antonio Marín Delgado, also from Seville and extremely important in training the next generation of dancers in Madrid. Gloria Mandelik, interviews with the author, March 10, 2010, and December 12, 2013.

65. Margarita Hsu ("Margarita la China"), telephone interview with the author, December 19, 2013. Calle Relatores 20 housed Madrid's oldest dance and rehearsal studio, and it is where Mercedes's father, Albano Zúñiga, had studied with Antonio el de Bilbao shortly before Bilbao's death in 1934.

66. Rivas González, "Rojo Vino," 20.

The Critical Reception of *Le Tricorne*

Joan Acocella

An account of the critical reception of the Ballets Russes' Le Tricorne, *from its London premiere in 1919 to its Spanish premiere in 1921. The ballet was a popular success in England and France, and in general it was well received by the reviewers, though critical opinion, especially of Pablo Picasso's sets and costumes, was conditioned by the degree to which modernism had been accepted in the two countries. An important issue for English critics was the music of Manuel de Falla, who was still relatively unknown in England. Many critics found* Tricorne's *Spanish "exoticism" appealing. Others lamented the Ballets Russes' abandonment of its prewar Russian primitivism, and of its Russian music. For Spanish critics a more pressing concern was* Tricorne's *relationship to Spanish culture and to the question of Spain's position vis-à-vis the rest of Europe. Nationalist critics complained that Falla had succumbed to the modernist chic of the North and that* Tricorne *caricatured Spanish culture. Others replied that art transcended national borders, that beauty was universal. This quarrel is reminiscent of similar disputes in Russia at the turn of the century and also of debates in many countries today, as ethnic styles are assimilated into an increasingly unified culture.*

Le Tricorne, in its Diaghilev years, was a great popular success and, in general, it was a success with the daily reviewers as well.[1] Not all the critics admired it, however, especially in the intellectual journals. Or if they admired it, it nevertheless raised critical problems that they then had to solve on the page. I want to concentrate on this thornier side of *Tricorne's* history, for it is there that we can best read the mind of the period. As with the Ballets Russes itself, what was said of *Tricorne*, back and forth, from one journal to the next, constitutes a sort of intellectual cat's cradle: trend and countertrend, purpose and cross-purpose, all intersecting in a dense web. The intellectual life of Europe in the years following World War I was a complicated matter, and the reception of *Tricorne* helps us to map those complications.

Tricorne premiered to an audience heavily disposed in its favor. Beginning in September of 1918, the Ballets Russes performed in London, with only brief interruptions, for over a year, and though the company had been warmly received there from the time it first arrived in 1911, now, in the postwar period, Londoners really took the Russian dancers to their hearts. Two weeks before *Tricorne*, the premiere of *La Boutique Fantasque* had been a *succès fou*: "the applause was deafening," writes Lydia Sokolova in her beautiful memoir, *Dancing for Diaghilev*, "and the stage was piled with flowers."[2]

The reception of *Tricorne* was not quite equal to this, but it was very hearty. Serge Grigoriev, the company's *régisseur*, says the new ballet "took the audience by storm."[3] *The London Times* also registered a rapt response. According to the *Times* reviewer, the choreography "left one helpless with amusement and excitement," while the score was "a wonderful maze of rhythmical dexterities."[4] Ernest Newman, the great Wagnerite, who was generally unsympathetic to the Ballets Russes, wrote a far more negative review, and complained in particular that Tamara Karsavina was miscast as the Miller's wife. She looked, he said, like "a racehorse being set to take a caster's cart to the Derby"—in other words, she was too refined for the role.[5] Others echoed this complaint. But there was almost no one who did not praise Léonide Massine's dancing as the Miller. He "went beyond anything he has yet done," wrote Richard Aldington in *The Sphere*, and everyone agreed.[6] There was much that they disagreed on, however. Of the many intellectual struggles going on in England at this time, the one that most directly affected the reception of *Tricorne* was, expectably, the quarrel over modernism. In no country did modernism have an easy birth. But, in England, the polarization between the avant-garde and the inheritors of nineteenth-century romantic realism was especially violent. To quote John Rothenstein's history of English painting: "In 1914, a man was either 'of his time,' a progressive, or else he formed part of the menacing shadow that stood between mankind and the sun."[7] In the years leading up to 1914, some of London's young intellectuals tended to take the Ballets Russes less than seriously as art because, among other reasons, its decors seemed to them *passé*, with all those Russian colors deliquescing in the *symboliste* miasma. Accordingly, when the Ballets Russes returned to London after the war with a new, modernist art program, with André Derain and Pablo Picasso, these intellectuals, and Bloomsbury in particular, fell into its arms. For his work on *La Boutique Fantasque*, Derain became the darling of Roger Fry and Clive Bell, Bloomsbury's arbiters of pictorial taste. Osbert Sitwell, a rather cold witness to this change of heart—for he had loved the company from the beginning—says that the very cows in the pastures surrounding the Oxfordshire home of Ottoline Morrell, the Bloomsbury hostess, put aside mooing and said "Derain" instead.[8] As for representatives of other intelligentsias, Ezra Pound, who had been living in London for several years and had ridiculed the prewar Diaghilev company, wrote in *The New Age* that *Boutique* was "worthy of a permanent place in the art of ballet," particularly on the grounds of Derain's contribution.[9]

So it should come as no surprise that Picasso's set for *Tricorne* was warmly received. "M. Picasso had the curious experience of hearing his picture clapped," writes Aldington.[10] Clearly, the public found it beautiful. For certain writers, however, what was thrilling in the set was not just its beauty, but its sheer, daring modernism. Of *Boutique* and *Tricorne*, Osbert Sitwell says, "I shall never forget the excitement of first seeing truly modern works of scenic art upon the stage."[11]

The costumes were far less admired. And while it is possible to say that this is because they were not as good as the set, reactions to modernism may also have played a part. The public might be ready for a modernist set, which, after all, could be thought of as a big painting, but clothing was another matter. England had not seen the theatrical experiments of the futurists—the work of Fortunato Depero and Giacomo Balla—which, as Lynn Garafola has shown, influenced Diaghilev's postwar costuming.[12] Nor, to stay closer to home, had they seen *Parade*, the Ballets Russes' first and more radical Picasso ballet. Though *Parade* premiered in Paris in 1917, Diaghilev did not let London see it until the end of 1919. The experimental approach in question—the dehumanization of the actor—had strong roots in England, in Gordon Craig's theory of the *Übermarionette*. But Craig remained something of a fringe character; his influence was greater outside England than in. And to the despair of forward-thinking theater artists, realism was still stubbornly entrenched on the London stage. An École de Paris set, particularly in a ballet, was all right, even desirable, perhaps. But to dress pretty women in avant-garde constructions—headdresses that looked like cones, stiff skirts that seemed to move all in one piece—this, for many, was going too far. The writer J. Middleton Murry, discussing *Tricorne* in *The Nation & Athenaeum*, described the costumes as "purely arbitrary."[13] And W. A. Propert, in his 1921 *Russian Ballet in Western Europe*, remarked irritably on

> those noisy dresses, dresses that never seemed to move with the wearers or answer the changing curves of their bodies, that looked as if they were cut in cardboard, harshly barred and rayed, with all their contours heavily outlined in black. One or two such queer garments might have been forgiven, but multiplied to ten or twenty, they became merely ugly.[14]

The "barred and rayed" aspect—the loud stripes with which Picasso decorated the costumes—bothered many critics.

At the same time, the elements of abstraction in *Tricorne* appealed to precisely those writers who, holding up their end of Gordon Craig's tradition, were seeking a non-realistic, poetic theater. Of special interest in this regard are T. S. Eliot's essays on the company. Describing the new Massine ballets of the 1918–1919 London seasons, he says, "we greeted [them] ... as the dawn of an art of the theatre." While the prewar company may have had better ballet dancers, the postwar repertory "is more sophisticated, but also more simplified, and simplifies more; and what is needed of art is a simplification of current life into something rich and strange."[15] In a later article in *The Criterion*, he describes Massine as "the greatest actor whom we have in London." What makes him great is his hieratic, inhuman quality. "The difference," Eliot says, "between the conventional gesture of the ordinary stage, which is supposed to express emotion, and the abstract gesture of Massine, who symbolizes emotion, is enormous," and it is the latter that will be the mark of acting in the poetic theater. "Massine," Eliot writes, "the most completely unhuman, impersonal, abstract, belongs to the future stage."[16] So here we see essentially the same critical loop-the-loop as with the decor and costumes. Massine's jerky choreography and his stylized stage presence put off some people, but to minds dissatisfied with traditional theater, these things looked like modernism in action.

Another aspect of *Tricorne*'s appeal, quite separate from modernism, was its mere foreignness, the charm of its Spanish ways. In particular, the Spanish music added immeasurably to the work's prestige. Before *Tricorne* Manuel de Falla had received some attention from French music critics, for he had lived in Paris for a number of years, and his *La Vida Breve* was produced in Nice and Paris in 1913. But little had been written about him in England. Now, with *Tricorne*, the English critics went to work, and it is interesting to see them trying to come to terms with him. A representative sample is a series of three articles that Edward Dent wrote on Falla in the period following *Tricorne*. In August of 1919, in a review in *The Athenaeum*, Dent seems to be trying to explain to himself Falla's peculiarities. "The orchestration," he says, "is not always felicitous"— a charge that was to be repeated by others, but not as often as Dent's next critical maneuver, which was to compare Falla with Stravinsky. At this moment Stravinsky was the reigning young genius of the European musical world, and like Falla, he had entered the center of that world from a peripheral tradition. Hence the comparison was almost inevitable, and here as elsewhere, the resulting conclusion was that Falla was milder, less daring. "Intellectual" is the word Dent uses here, "by contrast with the barbaric style of Stravinsky."[17]

But the following year, in *The London Mercury*, Dent makes a certain advance on the Falla question by comparing him not to Russians, but to Spaniards—to Albéniz, Granados, and Turina—thereby discerning a pattern in Spanish music and showing how Falla, though he might seem less radical than his young counterparts in other countries, is nevertheless truly modernist within the Spanish school: "He is modern, in the sense that he is ... anti-sentimental, as compared with Albéniz."[18] So Falla is now being seen within his own tradition.

A year later, in 1921, in *The Nation & Athenaeum*, Dent takes a further leap in this direction. What seemed at first a weakness of construction in Spanish music, he says—recall his complaint about *Tricorne*'s orchestration—was really a failure on our part to understand that Spanish music has different principles of construction, and it is these structural principles that we must uncover in foreign music, for it is they, and not folk tunes, that define a national tradition:

> The primitive peasant art of a country, whether foreign or our own, may have a momentary charm, and a sentimental association, but it cannot suffice as the expression of cultivated ... modern minds. The really important difference between the men of our country and those of another lies not in their folk songs but in their methods of handling music as an elaborated art[19]

—that is, in their structure. And what makes Spanish music so fundamentally different from the German-based musics of the North is that the structural principles of Spanish music derive from the guitar.

For those of us who imagine that the artistic confusions of living in a "global village" belong uniquely to our generation—that we are the ones who have to learn our ideas of the beautiful only to unlearn them again in the face of competing traditions—this set of three articles is a touching statement. For here we see Dent coping with the very same problems: the quest for a relativism that would not exclude values, the search for deep structure rather than surface idiosyncrasy to define national difference. He ends on a note of reverence: Spain, he says, "sets before us the ideal of a grave and passionate nobility"—something altogether different, he adds, from the "American vulgarity" that is currently degrading Northern European music.[20] Relativism goes only so far.

Dent's remarks bring us to another critical force that intersects with the quarrel over modernism, and that is primitivism, the idea that things less civilized, or presumed to be less civilized, are more wholesome, vigorous, and truthful. Next to orientalism, with which it overlaps, primitivism was perhaps the greatest stylistic selling point of the prewar Ballets Russes. And *Tricorne*, together with *Boutique Fantasque* and *The*

Good Humored Ladies, seemed to many English critics to signal the end of the Ballets Russes' primitivism. What the critics saw in these ballets was an appropriation of foreign national styles as opposed to a delving into Russian style—a cosmetic putting-on, as opposed to self-expression—and this grieved them. Several of the music critics lamented the abandonment of Russian music, a loss which in certain cases led them to disprize the Diaghilev company's new music, including that of *Tricorne*. "The Three-Cornered Hat has an excellent setting by Picasso," wrote W. J. Turner in *The London Mercury*, "but the music, though clever, is mediocre." "The best ballets," he says "are the old ones: *Petroushka, Children's Tales, Thamar, Scheherazade, Prince Igor*, every one of which is Russian and has the advantage of exceptionally fine music."[21] As for the new ballets, "Novelty has been sought rather than originality." This is not the first time such a charge was leveled at the Ballets Russes, but it is an early example. As the years passed, the complaint would be heard again and again: that once the company went from its Russian to its international period, it abandoned itself to thinness, chic and pastiche.

But however much primitivism, or its abandonment, may have figured in the English response to *Tricorne*, it figured more heavily for the French, or at least for the company's prewar intellectual fans in France. *Tricorne* had its Paris premiere on January 23, 1920, six months after the London premiere, and as in London, it was very warmly received: "long ovations greeted each of the entrees," said the review in *Le Figaro*, and the reviewer praised the ballet in elaborate, if conventional terms.[22] But the reaction of the intellectual press was more mixed, and the company's turning away from a Russian identity was crucial in this regard. No group of critics was more attached to the presumed simplicity of the Ballets Russes' prewar Russian soul than the French intellectuals. In the essays of Henri Ghéon, Jacques Rivière, André Suarès, and Fernand Gregh, writing in the *Nouvelle Revue Française* and elsewhere from 1909 to 1914, one finds the Russians described as innocent, instinctive artists, devoid of narcissistic individualism and therefore endowed with a sort of automatic access to spiritual truth.[23] The greatest essay ever written about a Ballets Russes' production, Rivière's November 1913 essay on Nijinsky's *Rite of Spring*, was founded on that belief.

In the context of this attachment to the company's Russianness—and also in the context of the grim mood of postwar Paris, with its strikes and shortages—*Tricorne*, together with the other novelties of the season, *La Boutique Fantasque* and *Le Rossignol*, came as jarring news. In place of the great well of truth that had been *The Rite of Spring, Petrouchka* and *Prince Igor*, now the critics were faced with what to many of them seemed mere playthings, and all of them decorated with up-to-the-minute École de Paris painting, the kind of thing they could see by going to a local gallery. Nothing could have been more disheartening. Rivière in particular could not comfort himself over what he saw as the loss of the company's prewar profundity and especially over the loss of Nijinsky. "His absence is almost visible," Rivière writes. As for Massine, "His profile may be charming, but nothing ever emerges from it. It does not move beyond him; it does not grow."[24] Rivière admires Massine as a dancer. He even goes so far as to say that in *Tricorne's* "Farruca," Massine seemed almost an "hallucination of Nijinsky." But he can find no depth in him or, for that matter, in his choreography, which looks to Rivière thin and cramped. Falla's score he regards as simply lightweight, "slavishly attached to its Spanish-folklore inspiration" and—that complaint again—harmonically undistinguished.[25] Elsewhere in the review, speaking of Derain's decor for *Boutique*, he says,

"Its primitivism is a bit superficial."[26] Those words encapsulate his reaction to the season as a whole.

As regards the music, Rivière's reaction was shared by Jean Marnold, writing in the *Mercure de France*. Marnold decried what he called the "narrow 'nationalism'" of the score, in which, as he saw it, Falla's forcing himself into a collective "folk" mode resulted in banality.[27] But like everyone else, Marnold admired the dancing. André Levinson, who, from what I can discover, never wrote at length on *Tricorne*, paused in the middle of a later indictment of Massine's choreographic style to praise *Tricorne's* "Farruca" as an inspired exception.[28]

The critical situation in Spain, as one can imagine, was somewhat different. Whatever their emphases, the English and French critics had common concerns: modernism, Russian primitivism versus internationalism, questions about the future of the theater. The Spanish critics were not indifferent to those matters, but they had another, more pressing concern: *Tricorne's* relation to Spanish culture and, by extension, Spanish culture's relation to Europe. In Spain as in other European countries, including Russia, the major historical forces of the nineteenth century—industrialization, democracy, and national unification—had resulted in a reevaluation of national artistic heritage. Folk art was no longer taken for granted but culled and collected, even as its survival was threatened by an increasingly international culture. The more removed a country was from the center of that international culture, the more difficult the questions involved. On the one hand, artists did not want to live in a backwater. They wanted to be part of what was new, part of the grand exchange of ideas. They wanted to be sophisticated, *au courant*. On the other hand, they knew well that the closer they moved to the center of European trends, the greater the danger that their national culture, more removed from those trends than, for example, French or German culture, would vanish into the folk-art museum. They also knew that in the international exchange, not everyone's coin had equal value. Ideas and styles from less powerful countries tended, of course, to be the assimilated rather than the assimilator.

One of the finest examples of this phenomenon is Russia, where, in the late nineteenth century, there were fervent efforts to preserve folk traditions and to base new art on old. Diaghilev, the great internationalist, in some measure emerged from this nationalist movement. Its two greatest patrons at the end of the century, Savva Mamontov and the Princess Maria Tenisheva, provided the money for him to found the magazine, *Mir Iskusstva*, that brought him into a position of real power in the Russian art world, the base from which he later launched the Ballets Russes. Another country where the conflict of national versus international culture was especially pressing is Spain. Again, to cite only the most pertinent facts, most of the best Spanish musicians of the nineteenth century were historians of their country's music as well as makers of it. Felipe Pedrell is the obvious example. Falla was a pupil of Pedrell and became, like his master, a lover of Spanish musical history as well as an expert on it. *Tricorne*, a product of that love and knowledge, is thus the child of a great, overarching cultural movement, full of strife and passion—a phenomenon linked to the Generation of 1898—and when *Tricorne* finally had its Spanish premiere at Madrid's Teatro Real on 5 April 1921, it fed right back into the conflict.

Actually, it began doing so long before its Spanish premiere. In 1919, when it had its world premiere in London, the great Spanish music critic—and Falla's friend—Adolfo

Salazar was in attendance and wrote back, in *El Sol*, of his great joy in the thought that Falla was raising Spanish music to a level where it could compete with the modern music of the North. Even in 1914, when Falla returned to Spain from France, says Salazar, he "stood for the renewal of our music. In him were fused those trends by virtue of which Spanish music was going to enter into a new period and achieve a standard worthy of comparison with the most vital of foreign contemporary art."[29] He adds that since Albéniz, Falla is the Spanish composer who has been taken most seriously by foreign critics.

One can guess what these remarks might have meant to Salazar's more nationalist colleagues. Indeed, Salazar's learned and proud essay may have intensified their annoyance, once *Tricorne* arrived in Spain, over the ballet's dubious Spanish credentials. In his first-night review in *La Epoca*, Victor Espinós complained that *Tricorne*, if it wished to be Spanish, was inaccurate, for it combined styles of different regions: "Andalusia? Galicia? Mallorca? It's all the same." Not only was the ballet inaccurate; it was insulting. By exaggerated makeup and other grotesqueries, it subjected Spanish characters to "absurd futurist jokes" and thereby caricatured Spanish culture. "We cannot condone an art that consciously holds us up to ridicule," Espinós concluded.[30]

This review states the themes—inaccuracy, ridicule, and modernist snobbery—that the other hostile reviews will also sound, each with its own special emphasis. *La Acción*'s reviewer stresses the snobbery. Falla, he says, by virtue of his long sojourn in France, has been converted to northern modernist chic. He is not making true Spanish art, but art for export, art for northerners, and to this end he has renounced the "fluidity, clarity and atmosphere" natural to Spanish music.[31]

The critic in *La Voz* is more torn. He recognizes *Tricorne*, he says, as a "masterpiece of color, of movement, of comic feeling," but "Gentlemen! Let us not lose our heads and start asking ourselves whether this marvel is Spanish. It is simply admirable. But all that it has that is ours is the music and the dance rhythm." As for the rest, what are we to call it? he asks: "Universal? Grotesque? Fantastical? Cubist?"[32] Implied here, as in the other reviews, is a prickly irritation at being condescended to by foreign sophisticates, however talented.

Other critics tried to create a bridge between *Tricorne* and national feeling. M. Muñoz in *El Imparcial* says that though the ballet lacks the kind of sentimental picturesque so prized by the guardians of *españolismo*, it is Spanish in a deeper way. Its colors are not the gaudy contrasts of souvenir-shop Spanish works, but the browns of the dry plains and a "certain ashen tone that recalls somewhat the dull silver of the olive trees—so very Spanish!" *Tricorne*, then, is not inauthentic: "None of its lines, its gestures, its colors ever ceases to be absolutely Spanish; they are condensed, however, into fixed characteristics, shorn of the vagueness and repetitiveness of the real-life models."[33] In other words, this is an authenticity raised to universality.

Others simply dismiss the whole issue of authenticity as a provincialism and make the art-for-art's sake argument: that *Tricorne* should be valued simply because it is beautiful. Not surprisingly, this is Salazar's approach in his review of the Spanish premiere. *Españolismo*, he says, is what *El corregidor y la molinera* had, and most charmingly. In *Tricorne*, on the other hand, you are looking at a great work of art. *El corregidor* is a comedy; *Le Tricorne* is a grotesque, with dark depths of which *El corregidor* is innocent. "*Españolismo*?" he asks. "Alarcón? Haven't we had enough of these catchwords?"[34]

Juan de la Encina, art critic of *La Voz*, makes essentially the same argument with respect to the decors. Many people, he says, would have preferred a Zuloaga to a Picasso, and have charged Picasso with distortion. Here we see the authenticity problem overlap with the quarrel over modernism, and Encina has the same answer for both of them: that artists do not have to be true to anything—to history, to regional difference, or to "objective reality." They need only be true to themselves. "If Picasso has taken liberties with regional clothing styles, there is no reason to reproach him.... We are not concerned here with truth or falsehood, or with a course in the history of costume, but rather with ... a work of plastic art ... with the discovery of combinations and harmonies and accents that give us pleasure."[35]

As I mentioned above, the debate in Spain recalls the intellectual quarrels from which Diaghilev evolved his aesthetic in turn-of-the-century St. Petersburg. Indeed, the Spanish nationalists, with their bristling pride and their charges of snobbery, sound very much like the Slavophil writers of Russia's late nineteenth century, and Salazar sounds like their opponents, the Westernizers. In fact, the Westernizer he at times resembles most eerily is the young Sergei Diaghilev. We have art reviews written in the 1890s by Diaghilev in which he calls upon Russian painters to enter the grand tournament of European painting, just as Salazar expresses the hope that Falla will place Spanish music in a position compared with northern music. Both are internationalists; both love art more than any extra-artistic use to which it might be put.

At the same time, one can sympathize with the nationalists' unhappiness at seeing their art appropriated by an international company, and with their indignation at the suggestion that they should feel honored by this. Likewise, in the United States jazz artists have repeatedly accused other musicians of taking what they wanted from jazz, this often brooding and individualistic art, and using it to produce a more comestible mainstream product. As the poet Langston Hughes put it, "They've taken our blues and gone." Of course, the situation of black jazz musicians in relation to American culture is quite different from that of early twentieth-century Spain in relation to Europe. Yet the two have this dilemma in common. In a culture to which everyone has access, regional or ethnic conservatism often spells lack of prestige, lack of support. At the same time, to watch precious local arts be used as a piquant raw material for a broader, blander international culture is a wrenching experience—and one that we are not finished with.

Notes

1. This essay is reprinted, with revisions, from Yvan Nommick and Antonio Álvarez Cañibano, eds., *Los ballets Russes de Diaghilev y España* (Granada: Fundación Archivo Manuel de Falla and Centro de Documentación de Música y Danza, 2000).
2. Richard Buckle, ed., *Dancing for Diaghilev* (London: John Murray, 1960), 139.
3. S. L. Grigoriev, *The Diaghilev Ballet, 1909–1929*, trans. and ed., Vera Bowen (London, 1953; repr., New York: Dance Horizons, 1974), 148.
4. "'The Three-Cornered Hat.' Russian Ballet at the Alhambra," *The Times* (London, July 23, 1919), p. 10, column 6.
5. In *The Observer*, July 27, 1919, quoted in Nesta Macdonald, *Diaghilev Observed, by Critics in England and the United States, 1911–1929* (New York: Dance Horizons; London: Dance Books, 1975), 232.
6. "The Russian Ballet," *The Sphere* (August 16, 1919), 160.
7. *Modern English Painters*, rev. ed. (New York: St. Martin's, 1976), vol. II, 142.
8. *Laughter in the Next Room*, vol. 4, *Left, Hand, Right Hand! An Autobiography* (London: Quartet, 1977), 149.

9. "At the Ballet," *The New Age* (October 16, 1919), 412.
10. "The Russian Ballet," *The Sphere*, 160.
11. *Laughter in the Next Room*, 148–149.
12. Lynn Garafola, *Diaghilev's Ballets Russes*, (New York and Oxford: Oxford University Press, 1989), 76–97. I am extremely grateful to Lynn Garafola for help in gathering reviews of *Tricorne* and in translating the Spanish reviews.
13. "The Art of the Russian Ballet," *The Nation & Athenaeum* (September 10, 1921), 834.
14. W. A. Propert, *The Russian Ballet in Western Europe, 1909–1920*, (New York: Blom, 1972), 55.
15. "London Letter," *The Dial* (August 1921), 214.
16. "Dramatis Personae," *The Criterion* (April 1923), 305.
17. "A Spanish Ballet," *The Athenaeum* (August 1, 1919), 692.
18. "Modern Spanish Music," *The London Mercury* (February 1920), 508.
19. "Manuel de Falla," *The Nation & Athenaeum* (May 28, 1921), 335.
20. Ibid., 336.
21. "Drama," *The London Mercury* (August 1921), 424.
22. Beranger, "Courrier des théâtres," *Le Figaro* (January 24, 1920), 3. All translations in this essay are mine.
23. For a discussion of the role of primitivism in the French response to the prewar Ballets Russes, see my "Reception of Diaghilev's Ballets Russes by Artists and Intellectuals in Paris and London, 1909–1914" (PhD diss., Rutgers, 1984), 323–331.
24. Jacques Rivière, "Les Ballets Russes à l'Opéra," *La Nouvelle Revue Française*, vol. 78 (1920), 463.
25. Ibid., 465.
26. Ibid., 464.
27. "Musique," *Le Mercure de France* (April 1, 1920), 224.
28. André Levinson, "Grandeur et decadence des 'Ballets Russes,'" in *La danse d'aujourd'hui: études, notes, portraits* (Paris: Editions Duchartre et Van Buggenhoudt, 1929), 52.
29. Adolfo Salazar, "Triunfo del arte Español. Manuel de Falla y 'El sombrero de tres picos.' Exitos y duelos," *El Sol*, 1919, undated clipping. I am extremely grateful to Vicente García-Marquez for the loan of his collection of Spanish reviews of *Tricorne* and for his help in interpreting them.
30. "Los bailes Rusos. 'El sombrero de tres picos,'" *La Epoca* (April 6, 1921).
31. "Música," *La Acción* (April 6, 1921).
32. P. Victory, "Anoche en el Real. 'El sombrero de tres picos,'" *La Voz* (April 6, 1921).
33. "Teatro Real. Los bailes Rusos. 'El sombrero de tres picos,'" *El Imparcial* (April 6, 1921).
34. "Los bailes Rusos. Estreno de 'El sombrero de tres picos.' Un gran exito en el Real," *El Imparcial* (April 6, 1921).
35. "Critica de arte. 'El sombrero de tres picos,'" *La Voz* (April 6, 1921).

Purity and Commercialization
The View from Two Working Artists, Pericón de Cádiz and Chato de la Isla
John C. Moore

Introduction

This essay explores two related themes that have received considerable attention among flamenco aficionados and scholars: purity and professionalism. It is based on the oral histories and artistic trajectories of two early- to mid-twentieth-century singers—Pericón de Cádiz and El Chato de la Isla—and conveys their personal observations of *cante flamenco* (flamenco song).[1] While some, such as Timothy Mitchell, suggest that purity is largely an intellectual construct superimposed on flamenco discussions through *mairenismo*, I suggest that this concept is actually attested in a more nuanced fashion in the Pericón stories, and that it predates the influence of Ricardo Molina and Antonio Mairena.[2] Chato also addresses this, albeit more indirectly. Similarly, commercialism and professionalism, which are sometimes held in opposition to purity (as, for example, in Donn Pohren's work), are, nevertheless, essential to those who make a living from flamenco.[3] Pericón and Chato's ability to feed their families, as their histories attest, depended on being paid for their art. Though some may find it ironic, both of these artists, whose cante is generally considered to be on the pure side, achieved a semblance of middle-class comfort only with the commercialization of flamenco in the advent of *tablaos* and as a consequence of flamenco's role in an emerging tourist economy. This essay, therefore, considers the development of cante for dance in a tablao setting.

Purity and Professionalism

The first theme, purity, is difficult to characterize precisely and, thus, has been the subject of endless debate. It often comes up in discussions of what types of flamenco are highly valued, that is to say, authentic and original. Often *flamenco puro* is contrasted with examples of things that are less valued: those that may be popular, cheap, lightweight, and so on. One might infer that some forms are purer than others—for example, *cante jondo* (deep song) might be considered purer than *cante chico* (light song). The situation is more complex, however, as forms often characterized as cante chico, such as *bulerías* and *rumbas,* might at times be considered pure flamenco, while, at others, some of the more *jondo* forms, such as *malagueñas* and *fandangos,* are considered corrupt.[4] The concept of purity is, therefore, orthogonal to the depth of emotion, but seems to relate more to a vague concept of flamenconess.[5] It is precisely this vagueness that ensures a lack of consensus with respect to what constitutes authentic flamenco. Published discussions often center on the views of nonartists (aficionados and intellectuals, such as José Luis Ortiz Nuevo), *mairenista* artists, and, sometimes, non–Spanish aficionados such as Mitchell and Pohren.[6] This essay presents a novel perspective: that of two professional twentieth-century singers whose careers spanned both the *opéra flamenca* and mairenista periods. We will see that their views are both nuanced and not entirely consistent. I will suggest that this reflects the dynamic nature of the construct.[7]

The issue of professionalism in flamenco overlaps that of purity. There is a romantic tradition among some aficionados that views professionalism as inevitably leading to commercialization, and, ultimately, to corruption. This view guided the famous cante contest organized by Federico García Lorca, Manuel de Falla, and other intellectuals in Granada in 1922. Under the assumption that only nonprofessional singers represented pure flamenco, professionals were barred from the competition (although the judges included professional artists such as Antonio Chacón). The result was a mediocre line up, and first prize was awarded seemingly by default to a former professional, Diego el Tenazas.[8]

The romantic and exoticizing attitude of the contest organizers ignored the fact that the best flamenco of the time was sung by professionals (again, some of whom served as judges) and that flamenco had been a professional art form since its beginnings. Any art form requiring such technical skill and knowledge cannot thrive without dedicated professionals. Nevertheless, one might maintain a correlation between professionalism and commercialization. Under this view, commercialized flamenco appeals to a common denominator of public taste, and is, therefore, inferior (a view presented by Pohren).[9] Given that flamenco, like any living art form, changes over time and is subject to trends, it is difficult to objectively distinguish cheap commercial tricks from honest artistic innovations.

Pericón and Chato

Juan Martínez Vílchez (1901–1980), known as "Pericón de Cádiz," was born in Cádiz to an impoverished family; his father was disabled, but the family survived from the work of his mother (who had a meat stand) and his and his siblings' contributions. Because of his stubborn and unruly nature, he was removed from elementary school and spent a childhood living by his wits (for example, standing guard for illegal gambling games, organizing a street gang, and raiding dumpsters). He claimed to have never learned to read or write.[10] Pericón began singing as a young child. Around age ten, he sang on coaches and in mobile *fiestas* (parties), and, at some point, had a job selling candies with a *pregón*.[11] By age twelve, he was singing in baptisms and in cafés in neighboring towns, and eventually in Seville. Throughout this period he also sang for private fiestas, a common venue for flamenco singers of the era. Wealthy men (*señoritos*)—either from old money or *petite bourgeois*—hired several such artists for often marathon debaucheries. Pericón's stories describe this power dynamic in detail—the indignities the artists suffered at the señoritos' whims, the variable and insecure payment, the tricks artists used to increase their income and reign in the parties, and more.[12] Pericón also found work in touring variety shows, performing in bullrings and theaters. This was the primary venue of opéra flamenco.[13] In the years before the Spanish Civil War, he toured with Pepe Marchena, the most famous and influential singer of opéra flamenca.[14]

Pericón participated in a cante contest in Madrid in 1936, winning first prize for *soleá* and *siguiriyas*, for which he was to be paid 1000 *pesetas*; however, the prize money never materialized. He toured with the other prize winners, collecting pay erratically. He litigated and prevailed in his case, but returned to Cádiz when the Civil War began that year, still without collecting his contest earnings. His economic situation, like that of millions during the war, became desperate, exacerbated by his fear of arrest due to his having sung two left-leaning verses during the tour, not out of political conviction but because he was told he would receive applause and, thus, avoid being upstaged by the young singer El Chiquito de Triana, whose short pants and child's voice brought the house down.[15] In the difficult postwar years, Pericón worked with Conchita Piquer as she restaged the production *Las Calles de Cádiz* ("The Streets of Cádiz").[16] When its run ended, he again tried to live on earnings from private fiestas, but this was a sparse existence during a lean period.

Around 1950, Pericón went to Madrid to seek work with the larger, wealthier señorito class and became friends with guitarist Manolo de Bádajoz, who had pull in the Villa Rosa, a large establishment that facilitated private fiestas.[17] Pericón was successful in the fiestas there, and in 1954 guitarist Perico del Lunar convinced him to accept a nightly engagement in La Zambra—Madrid's first tablao. Pericón's one-month contract continued for thirteen years; he earned a weekly paycheck as well as money from associated private fiestas and tours. This stability and income allowed Pericón and his family to achieve something akin to a middle-class standard of living.[18]

José Llerena Ramos (1926–2006), known as "El Chato de la Isla," was born in La Isla de San Fernando—an island in the saltwater marshland located some ten miles south of Cádiz, in Las Callejuelas, the same humble neighborhood where El Camarón de la Isla was born almost twenty-five years later. Chato's father was a sporadically employed fisherman, who often had to feed his family with what he was able to catch on his own. Chato was one of twenty-four children, although only four survived infancy and only three made it to adulthood. At age eight, his family moved to Villalata, a shantytown on the outskirts of the city. This area had no electricity, so the nights were lit with *mariposas*.[19]

Chato had about two years of schooling, attaining a basic level of literacy. Because of reports of mass executions in the neighborhood, the family hid out in the salt flats during the outbreak of the Civil War.[20] Chato's father passed away shortly after the war, leaving Chato to provide for the family through selling salt, agricultural work, and singing for tips on the San Fernando–Cádiz trolley.

Because San Fernando was situated on the main highway between Cádiz and the rest of Andalucía (the current bridge, Puente de Caranza, did not open until 1969), there were *ventas* (roadside inns), which, unlike most bars, remained open all night (ostensibly as truck stops). They became primary venues for private fiestas, and Chato became a regular performer at several of them, including the famous Venta de Vargas (where Camarón also began his career). He eked out a precarious living from the ventas, fiestas in Cádiz nightclubs, and other occasional performances during the difficult postwar years. By the 1960s, eight of his ten children had been born.[21]

In 1961, Chato was contracted to sing in the Madrid tablao Las Brujas. As was the case with Pericón, well-paying private fiestas spun off tablao performances. Chato was eventually able to bring his family to Madrid and, through the influence of a Housing Authority minister, to buy an apartment in Fuenlabrada, a working-class suburb to the southwest. Chato continued at Las Brujas until it closed in 1982; he then worked for periods in two other tablaos, Los Canasteros and Café de Chinitas, until his retirement in the 1990s.

Purity: Two Artists' Perspectives

In *Lives and Legends of Flamenco*, Pohren writes of Pericón:

> Like nearly all artists, he has his detractors, who claim that he was a border-line "opéra flamenca" singer in the past. Were this true, Pericón would have been part of the commercial movement generated by Pepe Marchena. I can detect no trace of this.[22]

Pericón is associated with the Cádiz school of cante, in the tradition of Enrique Mellizo and his sons, Antonio del Mellizo and Enrique el Morcilla; however, his stories suggest that he may have participated in popular trends of the time. One aspect of the opéra flamenca movement was the incorporation of Argentinian-influenced songs, such as *milongas*, into the flamenco repertoire:

> They gave me the name "The king of Argentinian cante," even though I wasn't Argentinian at all. I got the name because I sang an Argentinian song called, *Mi Noche Triste* ("My Sad Night")—a kind of tango—that I had made into a flamenco-ized version. Every night I had to sing it because people wanted such lousy things.[23]

He also discusses a tear-jerking milonga, *Pobre Vieja* ("My Poor Mother"), that made all the dance-hall girls cry: "Between this verse, my falsetto voice, and the things I did with it, they all cried their eyeliner off."[24]

These quotes suggest that Pericón was willing, albeit reluctantly, to participate in the commercial style associated with the opéra flamenca movement. This is not particularly surprising as music is subject to trends that must be negotiated by professional artists. Perhaps intellectuals and aficionados (foreign aficionados, in particular) tend to hold a harder line than working artists who need sufficient public approval to make a living.

The comment regarding the Argentinian tango suggests disdain for a current style. In other places, Pericón prides himself on his command of the traditional Cádiz canon of cante:

> Even though I was just a kid, I already sang good cantes: soleá, malagueña del Mellizo, fandangos, alegrías, bulerías.[25]

In two other stories, Pericón contrasts his style of cante with commercial trends of the time. In describing his tour with Pepe Marchena, Pericón recounts how Marchena, though an idol throughout Andalusia, often left his artists waiting until the early morning in the bullrings and theaters. Marchena would simply disappear.[26] Fed up, Pericón quit the tour but was later advised that he must perform with Marchena when he was in Cádiz. Perhaps as a form of retribution, Marchena changed the order of the performances in the program at the last minute, forcing Pericón to sing after Marchena (something no one wanted to do, given Marchena's popularity). Pericón received a great ovation when he said:

> Dear public, dear public, since I'm in my own town and, until now, no one has sung real flamenco, I'm going to sing soleá, I'm going to sing siguiriyas, I'm going to sing malagueñas del Mellizo. Then I'll sing alegrías, and then whatever you ask me to, because I'm in no hurry.[27]

On another occasion, speaking of the 1936 Madrid cante contest, Pericón notes that everyone sang fandangos. This form, based on a folkloric Andalusian song and dance, can range from quite deep to rather light, depending on the interpretation. It was a staple of the opéra flamenca repertoire and a specialty of Marchena's, whose interpretation included long falsetto filigrees. When Pericón's entry was announced, the audience made fun of his name by pronouncing "Cádiz" in an exaggeratedly effeminate manner (Cádiz has a reputation as a large gay community). Pericón responded by equating the style of fandangos of the era with a lack of *machismo*, resulting in another ovation and first prize for soleá and siguiriyas:

> Ladies and gentlemen! I, being from Cádiz, have noticed so far that no one has sung real *macho cantes*. And I, being from Cádiz, am going to sing macho cantes for you.[28]

While Marchena was probably the most popular singer of the first half of the twentieth century, it is clear that Pericón identifies his own cante with the Cádiz tradition. In his depictions of the masters, Pericón lauds Cádiz singers (Mellizo, Mellizo's sons, and Aurelio Sellé), Antonio Chacón, Manuel Torre, Manolo Caracol, and Tomás Pavón.[29] Most of these *cantaores* would pass purist muster by any standard, except perhaps Chacón who pioneered several *libre* forms (flamenco song styles without a marked *compás* or rhythmic measure) and the use of falsetto, and Caracol, who ran the gambit between hard-core *cante gitano* (Gypsy style) and commercial songs with orchestral accompaniment. Nevertheless, both Chacón and Caracol are widely regarded as giants of the late nineteenth and early to mid-twentieth centuries.

Chato does not directly address issues of purity. Like Pericón, he professes a preference for the cantes from Cádiz. On some of the Latin American–inspired cantes, he says:

> Now those cantes that are called *ida y vuelta* (round trip), like milonga, *vidalita*, and such. Really, I don't find them to have any flamenco flavor.[30]

More so than Pericón, Chato was a follower of Caracol; many of his recordings strongly resemble Caracol's delivery. They were close friends.[31] Chato describes several singers with whom he interacted, including Marchena. However, he has nothing to say about Marchena's singing, only his good manners. He describes in favorable terms Juanito Valderrama, another opéra flamenca figure who "sings splendidly, no matter what people say," but may do so with faint praise.[32] He also describes his friendship with the noted fandangos singer, Rafael Farina, but says nothing about his singing.[33] Aside from Caracol, Chato speaks glowingly of Terromoto de Jerez, a hard-core Jerez singer of cante gitano, and Camarón, Chato's compatriot who helped usher in the *flamenco nuevo* movement and is, therefore, controversial, but considered the most influential flamenco singer of the late twentieth century. In both Pericón and Chato, we find an attitude toward flamenco that is inclusive and authentic. This suggests that concepts of purity are not just the product of nonartists, as Mitchell argues, but that a traditionalist vein is present among working artists as well.

In addition to their regionalist preference for cantes from their homeland, both Pericón and Chato emphasize *compáss* (rhythm), an essential element of tablao performance. While it is the job of the guitarist to keep time, singers vary in their ability to mesh with the guitarist's rhythm. Those with a superior sense of time and who can play with the compás are the most exciting. To Pericón:

> Cante flamenco is the only thing on planet Earth that, if you learn it without compás, you sing well, but still can't sing because you lack the most important thing—which is the compás.[34]

To Chato:

> Compás is everything. For the rhythmic forms it's everything, because if you go out of compás, you mess up.[35]

Tablaos

Tablao flamenco, a revival of the earlier *café cantantes* and a flamenco venue for the emerging tourist market, first appeared in Spain in the 1950s. El Guajiro opened in Seville in 1952 and La Zambra in Madrid in 1954.[36] Others followed, including Madrid's El Corral de la Morería in 1956 and Las Brujas in 1960.[37] Soon, Madrid and Seville each boasted several such venues; these thrived through the latter part of the twentieth century, but waned around the turn of the millennium. Because of their high cover charge, tablaos catered to tourists, gaining a reputation for second-rate, commercialized flamenco.

Tablaos featured flamenco dance. A typical performance included a large *cuadro* with each dancer (usually an attractive woman) dancing a short solo. The cuadros alternated with an *atracción*—a featured artist, usually a dancer. The atracción might highlight one of the dancers from the cuadro, a fixed artist who did not dance in the cuadro, or a guest artist. The cuadro embodied an artistic culture in which dancers, singers, and guitarists performed without rehearsal, guided by a series of unwritten signals between the artists. A dancer led, calling in the singer and initiating tempo changes and stops. Once the singer entered, a shift occurred, with the dancer following the tempo and feel of the cante; the guitarists follow the dancer and singer throughout the performance. Cuadro members execute *palmas*, or intricate hand claps. Thus, while individual dancers might perform set choreography, the rest of the cuadro displays a degree of improvisation and spontaneity. This is possible due to the dancers' signals, but also because of the musical/choreographic structure associated with tablao dances.[38]

Woven into Spain's tourist industry, tablaos have been considered the epitome of low-quality, tourist flamenco. Even many tourists are aware of this and seek out more authentic venues ("where can we go to see the *real* flamenco?"). Noted flamencologist Ángel Álvarez Caballero writes that attractive women who "barely knew how to dance" populated the large cuadro in Las Brujas.[39] While it is true that performers may not have given their best night after night (grueling touring schedules have caused some to sleep through a performance) to uncomprehending, foreign audiences, tablaos also presented top-quality artists (see Appendix in this essay). Indeed, most of flamenco's major dancers and singers of the 1970s used tablaos as training grounds, and several artists, such as Rosita Durán and Blanca del Rey, have made their entire careers in tablaos.[40] The local professional flamenco community sometimes attends tablao performances; for example, in the 1980s I witnessed a performance at Los Canasteros in which La Tati was the featured guest artist. The Madrid flamenco community, including most of her rival professionals, was out in force. In addition, tablaos offer steady work in larger Spanish cities, allowing artists who live in these areas to earn a living without having to tour coastal resorts. Great performers have given top performances in tablaos, despite the venue's less than ideal conditions.

Pericón and Chato came to work in tablaos in the initial stages of the venue's development and had to transform from *cante p'alante* to *cante p'atrás*, that is, from being the center of attention to playing a supporting role in dance performances. Neither artist had much experience with dance; Pericón noted that there was virtually no dance scene in Cádiz fiestas.[41] His singing for dancers in *Las Calles de Cádiz*, mentioned above, would have been a rehearsed performance. When he came to La Zambra, he sang for Rosita Durán's atracción.[42] Nevertheless, Pericón's excellent sense of compás was an important asset in singing for dance. Of his transition, Chato says:

> When I came to Las Brujas I hadn't sung much for dance, as my thing had always been cante p'alante. But since compás held no secrets for me, I quickly adapted to what had to be done—sometimes I sang p'alante, and sometimes in the cuadro. Because everyone knows that one can sing better or worse for dance, but what you can't do is fail in compás.[43]

Thus, an interesting point from both Pericón and Chato's accounts—cante-centric though they are—is the transition of the first generation of tablao singers from the fiesta ambience to cante p'atrás. Flamenco, as a professional art form, is shaped by market forces; while singers from the early twentieth century were molded by the requirements of fiestas, in the second half of the century, singers were trained in tablaos. Twentieth-century recordings reveal a much stronger sense of compás in the later period. I believe this is a consequence of the dance-related training. The singers who successfully made the transition between these periods were those like Pericón and Chato for whom compás held no secrets.

Conclusion

In examining the notions of purity and commercialism, and by reading the accounts of two twentieth-century artists, we can conclude:

1. While notions like purity are trend driven, there is a conservative vein among artists. Their tastes may be more eclectic than those of nonartist aficionados

and intellectuals, but they maintain strong opinions about what is good versus poor flamenco.
2. Singers need to make a living. In the fiesta period, their flamenco had to meet the demands of señoritos; in the tablao period, they had to learn to support dancers. Even when they did not favor current trends, they sometimes participated in them.
3. The much-maligned commercialization of tablaos led to a new flamenco culture that transformed the art, placing a premium on compás. Tablaos had liabilities for performers, but perhaps not to the extent their detractors suggest. Commercialization and purity are not inconsistent.

Appendix

Veteran tablao guitarist and cooking enthusiast Félix García Vizcaíno (1929–1998), known as "Félix de Utrera," dedicates several pages of his memoirs, which were interspersed with recipes and published posthumously, to the history of Madrid's flamenco scene, including tablaos and other venues.[44] He includes in his descriptions lists of artists who performed at each venue (Félix himself worked at Corral de la Morería for 31 years). While these lists are by no means complete, they give an excellent idea of the range of artists performing in over a dozen venues during the second half of the twentieth century.

La Zambra (FOUNDER: Antolín Casares); DANCER: Rosa Durán; GUITARIST: Perico del Lunar; SINGERS: Juanito Verea, Rafael Romero, Manolo Vargas, Pericón de Cádiz

El Corral de la Morería (FOUNDER: Camorra family [Manolo del Rey, José María del Rey, José del Rey]); DANCERS: Pastora Imperio, Regla Ortega, El Farruco, Los Pelaos, Lucero Tena; GUITARIST: Félix de Utrera; SINGERS: La Paquera de Jerez, Porrinas de Badajoz, Beni de Cádiz

Torres Bermejas (FOUNDER: Felipe García); SINGER: Camarón de la Isla

El Duende (FOUNDERS: Pastora Imperio, Gitanillo de Triana); DANCERS: Gitanillo de Jerez's daughter, La Cañeta de Málaga, Sole y Pipo, Diego Pantoja, Alejandro Vega; GUITARISTS: Paco Aguilera, Manolo Garzón; SINGERS: Sernita de Jerez, Chano Lobato, José Salazar, El Lebrijano, Los Hermanos Reyes

El Café de Chinitas (FOUNDER: Verdasco family); DANCERS: La Chunga, La Chunguita, Dolores la Pescaílla, Toñi, Tere Maya, Maruja Baena, Ricardo el Veneno, Faiquillo; GUITARISTS: Victor Monge "Serranito," Andrés Heredia, Manolo Sisón, El Entri, Monchi

El Corral de la Pacheca DANCERS: Los de Utrera, Paloma, Yolanda; GUITARIST: Juanele Maya; SINGER: Antonio Maya

Cuevas de Nemesio GUITARIST: José María Pardo; SINGERS: Pepe Aznalcóllar, El Sevillano, Porrinas de Badajoz, Hermanos Toronjo, El Chato de la Isla

El Arco de Cuchilleros (FOUNDER: Alfonsos Valdavia y Estévez); DANCERS: Alejandro Vega, Maleni Loreto, Mari Carmen La Debla, Juan Antonio, Luisa

La Escuela Flamenca (FOUNDER: Gloria Librán, Paco Reyes); DANCERS: Regla Ortega, Paloma; GUITARIST: Pepe Romera; SINGER: Jarrito Montoya

Las Brujas (FOUNDERS: Luis Sabell, Paquito); DANCERS: La Polaca, La Contrahecha, Merche Esmeralda; GUITARISTS: Alberto Vélez, Antonio de Cordoba, Antonio Pucherete, Paco de Antequera, Manolo Sanlúcar; SINGERS: El Chato de la Isla, Romerito, Terremoto de Jerez, Calderas de Salamanca, Dolores de Córdoba, Miguel Fernández

Los Canasteros (FOUNDER: Manolo Caracol); DANCERS: Manuela Carrasco, Manuela Ortega, Manolo Soler; GUITARISTS: Melchor de Marchena, Manolo Heredia, Tito Losada; SINGERS: Manolo Caracol, Luisa Ortega, Adela La Chaqueta, Diego Pantoja, Fernando Gálvez, Dolores de Córdoba; PIANIST: Arturo Pavón

La Venta del Gato (FOUNDER: Rafael Pantoja); DANCERS: Faíco, Antonio "El Camborio," La Gitanilla de Bronce; SINGERS: Gabriel Cortés, Pansequito

Caripén (FOUNDER: Lola Flores); PIANIST: Felipe Campuzano; SINGERS: Las Grecas

Casa Sara (FOUNDER: Sara Lezana); DANCER: Sara Lezana; GUITARISTS: Paco Izquierdo, Rafael Andújar; SINGERS: Antonio "Cuquito" de Barbate, Pepe el Malagueño

Caracol (FOUNDER: Antonio Benamargo)

Casa Pata (FOUNDER: Antonio Benamargo)

Notes

1. José Luis Ortiz Nuevo, *Mil y una historias de Pericón de Cádiz* (Barcelona: Barataria, 2008 [Madrid: Demófilo, 1975]); English edition: José Luis Ortiz Nuevo, *A Thousand and One Stories of Pericón de Cádiz*, trans. by John Moore (Licking, MI: Inverted-A Press, 2012; Salvador Aleu Zuazo, *El Chato de la Isla, entre la vida y el cante* (San Fernando: ISPREN, 1995).

2. Timothy Mitchell, *Flamenco: Deep Song* (New Haven: Yale University Press, 1994); Ricardo Molina and Antonio Mairena, *Mundo y formas del cante flamenco* (Madrid: Revista de Occidente, 1963). Mairenismo emphasizes older flamenco forms most closely associated with Gitano (Gypsy) artists of Lower Andalucía (particularly, the provinces of Cádiz and Seville), hence, de-emphasizing forms derived from regional fandangos. Mairenismo was partly in reaction to opéra flamenco, a popular trend that favored stylized interpretations of fandangos and Latin American–inspired forms, often delivered in a falsetto voice (as opposed to the rougher flamenco voice quality associated with flamenco gitano). Opéra flamenca was popular from the early twentieth century until about the 1950s. Poet Ricardo Molina and Gitano singer Antonio Mairena's co-authored work represented the mairenista manifesto. Mairenismo dominated many aspects of the flamenco community from roughly the mid–1950s until the advent of flamenco nuevo in the 1970s and 1980s. For many, mairenismo and opéra flamenca represent opposing poles of flamenco purity. In this essay, "gitano" is lowercase when it is used as an adjective (cante gitano, for example), but uppercase when it is used as an ethnic label for Spanish Roma.

3. D. E. Pohren, *The Art of Flamenco* (Shaftesbury: Musical Services Limited, 1984 [Jerez: Industrial, 1962; Madrid: Society of Spanish Studies, 1967, 1972, 1990; Westport, CT: Bold Strummer, 1990, 2005]); D. E. Pohren, *Lives and Legends of Flamenco: A Biographical History* (Madrid: Society of Spanish Studies, 1988 [1964]).

4. Flamenco is organized into a number of song (cante) forms (palos), each of which has its distinctive melodic and rhythmic characteristics. Cante jondo and cante chico refer to forms that are respectively deeper and lighter (in terms of emotion). Typical cante jondo forms include siguiriyas, soleá, and, for some, malagueñas, and some fandangos; common cante chico forms are alegrías, tangos, bulerías, and rumbas. See Pohren, *The Art of Flamenco*, 104–159, for descriptions and classifications.

5. For example, some might consider the popular rumba *La pared*, sung by Bambino, very flamenco, but might not describe the similarly popular rumba *El porompompero*, sung by Manolo Escobar, as such. The same might be said of a fandango sung by Rancapino versus another by Antonio Molina.

6. Mitchell, *Flamenco: Deep Song*; Pohren, *The Art of Flamenco*; José Luis Ortiz Nuevo, *Alegato contra la puereza* (Barcelona: Barataria, 2010).

7. Clearly, purity is a constructed concept, and its particulars will differ depending on whose construct is employed. The list of contenders is diverse and includes upper-class Spanish aficionados, under-class Spanish and Gitano flamenco artists, foreign aficionados (some of whom also participate as artists to varying degrees), and intellectuals. It is beyond the scope of this essay to examine the different nuances of purity among these groups.

8. Diego Bermúdez Cala (1850–1933), known as "El Tenazas de Morón," is believed to have been a singer in the café cantantes (nineteenth-century flamenco clubs), including possibly Café Silverio, but he

had not sung in thirty years at the time of the contest. Singer Pepe el de la Matrona recounts Antonio Chacón's recollection:

> Como ahí no se presentó nadie a concursar, nada más que Tenazas, y exigían los cantes antiguos, pues mejor o peor el hombre salió cantándolos, y si no se equivoca en la serrana—que se equivocó en la letra—, pues le tengo que dar todo el dinero; porque allí exigían los cantes antiguos, y el único que los cantó fue él, y a él se lo tenía que dar. Claro, como se equivocó y el premio había que darlo, pues yo lo que traté de conseguir es de ir de la infancia a la vejez, y por eso le di la mitad a Caracol y la mitad a Tenazas.
>
> Since no one turned up to compete, no one except Tenazas, and they required old cantes, well, for better or for worse, the guy came out singing them. Didn't he ever mess up the serrana—he got the verse wrong. But I had to give him all the money because they required old cantes and he was the only one who sang them, so I had to give it to him. Of course, he messed up, but the prize had to be awarded, so what I tried to do was go from infancy to old age—giving half to Caracol and half to Tenazas [José Luis Ortiz Nuevo, *Recuerdos de un cantaor Sevillano: Pepe de la Matrona*, 102]. [All translations from Spanish are my own.]

Manolo Caracol (1909–1973) was a teenager in the Granada contest and was awarded a youth prize. He went on to become one of the best known and most influential professionals of the twentieth century. His cante ranged from traditional cante gitano to ultra-commercial popular music, with orchestral accompaniment.

9. Pohren, *The Art of Flamenco*, 180–181.

10. Illiteracy remained common among Spain's lower socioeconomic classes well into the late twentieth century.

11. Until the mid-twentieth century, it was common for Spanish street vendors to sell their wares with a *pregón,* a singing advertisement. Pericón notes that he was fired from this candy job because he collected money for his song but did not sell any candy. Some pregóns became famous and are sung by flamenco artists today, such as the candy pregón by Cádiz singer Macandé. See Eugenio Cobo Guzmán, *Pasión y muerte de Gabriel Macandé* (Madrid: Colección el Duende 4, Demófilo, 1977), or the *mirabrás* verse *Venga usted a mi puesto Hermosa...* ("Come to my stand beautiful..."). Pericón demonstrates his pregón in the *Rito y Geografía del Cante Flamenco* television series.

12. Using several of Pericón's accounts as primary data, this tradition is discussed and documented in detail in Mitchell, *Flamenco: Deep Song*.

13. As mentioned in note 2, opéra flamenca was associated with a particular style of cante. However, at that time the term referred to a type of flamenco variety show (regardless of the singing style). The term *opéra* did not refer to the nature of the singing; rather, it was a designation that producers employed to take advantage of a tax loophole reserved for *bel canto* performances (Ortiz Nuevo, *Alegato contra la puereza*, 252).

14. Pepe Marchena was probably the most popular flamenco singer of the first half of the twentieth century; however, his legacy is controversial and polarizing. While most acknowledge his fandangos creations (see Fernando el de Triana, *Arte y artistas flamencos* [Madrid: Caln, 1952], 24), aficionados remain divided over the quality of his artistic merit (see Anselmo González Climent, *"Pepe Marchena y la opéra flamenco" y otros ensayos* (Madrid: Demófilo, 1975); Pohren, *Lives and Legends of Flamenco;* Eugenio Cobo Guzmán, *Vida y cante del Niño de Marchena* (Córdoba: Virgilio Márquez, 1990); and Mitchell, *Flamenco: Deep Song*). In his biography of Marchena, Cobo Guzmán (*Vida y cante del Niño de Marchena,* 73) notes that he was unable to confirm Pericón's tour through promotional material. It is likely that the tour occurred in the early 1930s.

15. See http://www.elartedevivirelflamenco.com/cantaores615.html for photos of Luis Algaba Valdivia (1921–1987), known as "El Chiquito of Triana." Also included is a discussion of his participation in the 1936 contest and a link to an audio recording of the maudlin fandangos verse. El Chiquito married Antonia Amaya, sister of the famous Carmen Amaya. Their granddaughter, Karime, is now a well-known dancer. José Luis Ortiz Nuevo's one-man theater production, *Por dos letras* ("Because of two verses"), weaves several of Pericón's stories around the theme of his terror during the war (see http://www.youtube.com/watch?v=Ez3PsmzUTns). There are two accounts of fascist militia coming to Pericón's house—both were terrorizing but ultimately benign. Pericón's son, Antonio, told me a different version of one of the accounts, and that they were actually coming to arrest Pericón. José Luis Ortiz Nuevo, in a 2012 interview (available at http://www.youtube.com/watch?v=ETBsu2u7sio), notes that there were several versions; he suspects that the militias periodically came to scare Pericón for the fun of it.

16. This work, a theatrical enactment of the flamenco streets of Cádiz, had been originally produced in 1933 by dancer Encarnación López (1898–1945), known as "La Argentinita," one of the major pioneers of theatrical Spanish and flamenco dance. Conchita Piquer (1908–1990) was a famous singer of *copla,* a popular genre of typically Andalusian songs.

17. The Villa Rosa, situated at the corner of Madrid's Plaza de Santa Ana and Calle de Nuñez de Arce, has been a flamenco center since the early twentieth century. See Pepe el de la Matrona's description (in Ortiz Nuevo, *Recuerdos de un cantaor Sevillano*) of the fiestas there and at its competitor Los Gabrieles (on the nearby Calle de Echeguray). The Villa Rosa later became a tablao, closed for several years, and has

now reopened again as a tablao. Los Gabrieles declined in the 1970s and 1980s and no longer exists. Both establishments featured impressive murals made from painted tiles.

18. Pericón's success included achieving home ownership with the purchase of an apartment in the Puerta de Ángel area of Madrid, where his son, Antonio, continued to live until his death in 2012.

19. Aleu Zuazo, *El Chato de la Isla*, 32. With respect to mariposas ("butterflies," but in this case, a type of oil lamp), Chato alludes to the famous *bulería de Cádiz* verse:

Dicen que van a poner	They say they'll put up
Una fuente iluminosa	An illuminated fountain
En la Plaza de las Canastas	In the Plaza de las Canastas
Se alumbran con mariposas	They light up with oil lamps

This bulerías started off as a *tanguillo de Carnaval*, which is typically satirical and often deals with local politics (and public works). Catalina León Benítez, in *El flamenco en Cádiz* (Córdoba: Almuzara, 2006), 3, attributes it to the 1896 group *Los Viejos Cooperativos*, and the first line was *Van a poner en Puerto Chico* ("They'll put up in Puerto Chico"). Thus, in this verse, they get a nice illuminated fountain in Puerto Chico, while the poor Gitano neighborhood of Santa María (where the Plaza de las Canastas is located), is forced to use mariposas, makeshift lamps that consists of a saucer of oil and a wick, the same technology used since Phoenician times.

20. The outbreak of the Civil War was particularly brutal in Andalusia, which was on the front line as nationalist troops moved in from Morocco. Nationalist general Emilio Mola engineered a campaign of mass executions, *"eliminando sin escrupulos a todos los que no piensen como nosotros"* ("eliminating without scruples all those who don't think like us"). Carlos Jerez-Farran and Samuel Amago, eds., *Unearthing Franco's legacy* (Notre Dame: University of Notre Dame Press, 2010), 175.

21. Gerlad Howson, *The Flamencos of Cádiz Bay* (Westport, CT: The Bold Strummer, 1994; [London: Hutchinson & Co., Ltd., 1965]), 155–173, provides a dismal picture of the living conditions of two other flamenco artists in San Fernando during the 1950s. One can imagine that Chato's situation would have been similar. Chato himself discusses constant poverty and hunger during this time.

22. Pohren, *Lives and Legends*, 126.

23. Me pusieron de nombre "el Rey de cante argentino," sin ser argentine ni na'. Me pusieron este nombre porque yo había cogío una copla argentine mu' melosa, como tango, y lo había puesto a mi forma de flamenco. "Mi noche triste" se llamaba la canción, y toas las noches tenía que cantarla, porque me pedían una cosa mala. (English: Ortiz Nuevo, *A Thousand and One Stories of Pericón de Cádiz*, 15; Spanish: Ortiz Nuevo, *Mil y una historias de Pericón de Cádiz*, 33).

24. Y entre este y el falsete y las cosas que yo le hacía, acababan toas chorreando rímel (English: Ortiz Nuevo, *A Thousand and One Stories of Pericón de Cádiz*, 15; Spanish: Ortiz Nuevo, *Mil y una historias de Pericón de Cádiz*, 34).

25. Y entonces, a pesar de ser un chiquillo, ya cantaba yo cantes güenos: la soleá, la malagueña del Mellizo, fandangos, alegrías, bulerías (English: Ortiz Nuevo, *A Thousand and One Stories of Pericón de Cádiz*, 13; Spanish: Ortiz Nuevo, *Mil y una historias de Pericón de* Cádiz, 32).

26. Pericón's son, Antonio, told me that Marchena would have picked up a woman on these occasions. This picture of Marchena contrasts with the usual depictions of him as a perfect gentleman (see Cobo Guzmán, *Vida y cante del Niño de Marchena*, and Chato's description in Aleu Zauzo, *El Chato de la Isla*, 179–180).

27. Respetable público, respetable público, como estoy en mi tierra y hasta este momento no se han cantao cantes güenos, ahora voy a cantar por soleá, voy a cantar por seguiriyas, voy a cantar la malagueña del Mellizo, después voy a cantar por alegrías y después lo que ustedes me pidan, porque no tengo prisa (English: Ortiz Nuevo, *A Thousand and One Stories of Pericón de Cádiz*, 19; Spanish: Ortiz Nuevo, *Mil y una historias de Pericón de Cádiz*, 39).

28. ¡Respetable público, respectable público! Yo, que soy de Cádiz, no he visto que hasta esta hora se hayan cantao cantes machos ... y yo, que soy de Cádiz ... yo, que soy de Cádiz, voy a cantar cantes machos (English: Ortiz Nuevo, *A Thousand and One Stories of Pericón de Cádiz*, 20; Spanish: Ortiz Nuevo, *Mil y una historias de Pericón de Cádiz*, 41).

29. English: Ortiz Nuevo, *A Thousand and One Stories of Pericón de Cádiz*, 146–164; Spanish: Ortiz Nuevo, *Mil y una historias de Pericón de Cádiz*, 236–265.

30. Ahora bien, a esos cantes que le dicen de ida y vuelta, como la milonga, la vidalita y esas cosas, la verdá es que no le encuentro yo er sabó der flamenco (Aleu Zuazo, *El Chato de la Isla*, 134).

31. Nevertheless, Caracol enjoyed playing rather cruel practical jokes on Chato, who was an easy target due to his short stature, slight build, and pug nose.

32. Aleu Zauzo, *El Chato de la Isla*, 130.

33. Rafael Antonio Salazar Motos (1923–1995), known as "Rafael Farina," was a Gitano singer from Northern Spain (Salamanca), noted for his personal fandangos. Pohren (*Lives and Legends*, 139) dismisses him as a *fandanguero* in the vein of other opéra flamenca singers, although many flamenco artists respected him (Camarón, for example). His nickname "Farina," shared also by the lame dancer Juan Farina from Chiclana (see Howsen, *The Flamencos of Cádiz Bay*), was given to boys with dark complexions in

mid-twentieth-century Spain. This practice originated in the popularity of 1930s dubbed versions of the *Little Rascals* movies, in which the African American character "Buckwheat's" name was translated as "Farina" (Aleu Zuazo, *El Chato de la Isla*, 67).

34. El cante flamenco es lo único que no se aprende en el planeta Tierra y el que no sabe hacer compás puede cantar bien, pero no sabe cantar porque le falta lo principal, que es el compás (English: Ortiz Nuevo, *A Thousand and One Stories of Pericón de Cádiz*, 168–169; Spanish: Ortiz Nuevo, *Mil y una historias de Pericón de Cádiz*, 269).

35. Que er compás es er tó. Pa los cantes de ritmo es er tó ... porque si te vas de compás ... la liaste (Aleu Zuazo, *El Chato de la Isla*, 131).

36. Paco Sevilla, *Queen of the Gypsies: The Life and Legend of Carmen Amaya* (San Diego: Sevilla Press, 1999), 314, 321; English: Ortiz Nuevo, *A Thousand and One Stories of Pericón de Cádiz*, 36–38; Spanish: Ortiz Nuevo, *Mil y una historias de Pericón de* Cádiz, 63–66).

37. Félix de Utrera, *La cocina flamenca: Memorias y guisos* (Madrid: Celedte Ediciones, 2000), 28; Areu Zuazo, *El Chato de la Isla*, 114. See the Appendix in this essay for Félix de Utrera's description of many of Madrid's tablaos (de Utrera, *La cocina flamenca*, 27–33).

38. See K. Meira Goldberg, "Border Trespasses: The Gypsy Mask and Carmen Amaya's Flamenco Dance" (PhD diss., Temple University, 1995), 323–324, for a description of the structure of an alegrías dance.

39. Ángel Álvarez Caballero, *El baile flamenco* (Madrid: Alianza, 1998), 318. Las Brujas had a special relationship with Seville impresario Ricardo Pulpón, who, according to Felix de Utrera, sent them "the tallest and prettiest girls" (de Utrera, *La cocina flamenca*, 31).

40. On tablaos as training grounds, see José Luis Navarro García, *Historia del baile flamenco*, Volume III (Seville: Signatura, 2009); on Blanca del Rey and Rosita Durán, see Álvarez Caballero, *El baile flamenco*, 318–324.

41. English: Ortiz Nuevo, *A Thousand and One Stories of Pericón de Cádiz*, 82; Spanish: Ortiz Nuevo, *Mil y una historias de Pericón de Cádiz*, 132.

42. Paco Sevilla (*Queen of the Gypsies,* 321) notes that Fernán A. Casares founded La Zambra with the idea of presentando pure flamenco to a paying public and eschewed artists associated with the opéra flamenca movement. This is generally true, although La Zambra singers Juanito Varea and Jarrito Montoya each had a foot in both camps.

43. Cuando llegué a Las Brujas poco había cantao pa bailá porque lo mío había sío siempre, er cante p'alante. Pero como lo der compás pa mí no tenía secreto pues rápidamente me hice ar cante que allí había que hacé, que unas veces era p'alante y otras veces le tenía que cantá al cuadro. Porque como sabe tó er mundo pa bailá se puede cantá mejó o peor, pero en lo que no puedes fallá es en er compás (Aleu Zauzo, *El Chato de la Isla*, 114).

44. de Utrera, *La cocina flamenca*, 27–33.

Carmen Amaya, 1947
The (Gypsy) Beloved of America Reconquers Europe

MONTSE MADRIDEJOS

Translation by K. Meira Goldberg

Carmen Amaya (1918–1963) left Spain as a *bailaora cañí* (Gitana flamenco dancer) in 1936 upon the outbreak of the Spanish Civil War, and she returned in 1947 as a star of stage and screen.[1] Building on her success, first in Argentina and then on tour throughout South and Central America (in addition to Argentina, Amaya performed in Uruguay, Brazil, Mexico, and Cuba between 1937 and 1940), her consecration as the most renowned Gitana dancer took place in the United States. She attracted huge audiences, first to the Beachcomber, a New York supper club, and later to venues such as New York's Carnegie Hall and Los Angeles' Hollywood Bowl between 1941 and 1945.[2]

On August 11, 1947, having been absent from Spain for eleven years, Amaya, along with her sisters Antonia and Leo, and the singer Pepita Llácer, flew from Montevideo to Madrid's Barajas airport. As soon as the KLM flight landed, she knelt on the runway to kiss the ground. Amaya then greeted welcoming friends and family, including her beloved aunt Juana La Faraona.[3] After having toured the most prestigious stages of North and South America and now part of the circle of Hollywood celebrity, she was enjoying and showering upon her family stratospheric salaries. But Amaya was returning to an impoverished Spain, internationally isolated by the dictatorship of Francisco Franco, and to a Europe that was rising, literally, from the ashes.[4]

Between August 1947 and August 1949, audiences and critics alike received Amaya's performances across Europe as an apotheosis. Journalists viewed her as a "personality," and dwelled on the luminous legend that had reached the suffering Spanish society in bits and pieces. Carmen Amaya was, for most Spaniards, a dancer who had triumphed in Hollywood. She was an artist who had danced for U.S. President Franklin Delano Roosevelt and had moved him to such an extent that he gifted her a diamond-embroidered vest. Amaya was a woman who traveled with her large company by plane, who owned more than one car, and who had bought various houses across the Americas. She was a Spanish artist who was a millionaire.

Carmen Amaya's 1947 arrival in Madrid was filmed by NO-DO (Noticiario y Documentales Cinematográficos: News and Cinematic Documentation), the propaganda arm of the Franco regime, informing Spaniards of the return of this internationally known artist.[5] Despite this, the press coverage of Amaya's return was somewhat sporadic and unusual. Journalist Alfredo Marquerie, who had greeted her at Barajas, confessed,

> I am ashamed to say that I am the first and the only journalist to have welcomed her, but this is true. My esteemed colleagues decided not to get up early, perhaps because it is Monday, or perhaps they thought they would interview her later at her hotel.[6]

Another of the few Madrid journalists who interviewed Carmen Amaya was José Luis Gómez Tello for the magazine *Primer Plano*. As Marquerie had predicted, he interviewed her at her hotel. Gómez Tello did not scrimp on superlatives in his biographical summary of her triumphant career:

Figure 1: Carmen Amaya, from a 1948 souvenir program from the Théatre des Champs Elysées. Photograph by Armand de La Habana (courtesy Centro Andaluz de Flamenco).

> Great dancer, great artist, a Gypsy Queen with all the marvelous *duendes* of her soulful dance, Carmen Amaya is once more with us. For twelve years the *bailaora's* [flamenco dancer] inimitable and breathtaking feet have traced dancistic circles across the skin of the Americas: New York, San Francisco, Los Angeles, Mexico, Puerto Rico, Cuba, Venezuela, Colombia, Brazil, Peru, Chile, Argentina, Ecuador, Uruguay, have served as pedestal for the star among stars of the Gitano dance, who smiles to find herself once more in Madrid. Tiny, fragile, lively, with midnight hair and the mournful eyes of Granada, there is something in her which explains how she could have shaken audiences at the Roxy, at the Opera House, of the great American stages, to their foundations—something deep in an incorruptible race that never disappears even in the vestibule of the great Madrid hotel where I speak with her. The twentieth-century armchair in which Carmen Amaya sits immediately acquires the aspect of throne of the Queen of the Gypsies. Marvelous gold bracelets, with dangling coins tinkle on her arms: each coin recalls a triumph in Caracas or in New York or in Bogotá. Despite the atmosphere and the simple suit she wears, Carmen is a living image of a Gypsy. The civilization of the frigidaire, airplane travel and two luxurious automobiles that she had to leave behind in Buenos Aires have not altered the well of ancient dance, filled with wisdom, that lays within the body and the eyes of this bailaora.[7]

Amaya was reunited with her extended family and the rest of the company on August 20 in Barcelona, where the transatlantic ocean liner *Cabo de Buena Esperanza* arrived from Buenos Aires (Pepita Llácer, Amaya's sisters, and her brother Paco had arrived in Barcelona with Amaya three days earlier). From that moment on, notices of her return reverberated through the press; the journalist Sempronio dedicated an extensive article to her in the magazine *Destino* on August 23.[8]

Less than a month later, on September 20, Amaya's show *Embrujo Español* premiered at Madrid's Teatro Madrid. The company was made up principally of songstress Pepita Llácer (Antonio Amaya's wife), all of Amaya's brothers and sisters (Paco, Antonia, Leonor, Antonio, and María), her aunt La Faraona, *cantaor* (flamenco singer) Chiquito de Triana (Antonia Amaya's husband), the dance couple Teresa y Luisillo (Teresa Vieira Romero and Luis Pérez Dávila), La Pillina, Teresa Maya, Agustín de Triana, and Lorenzo Contreras. The guitarists included Paco Amaya, Antonio González, Ramón Gómez, and Manuel Flores. They were accompanied by actor Juan José reciting poetry; the musical director was Maestro Ruíz de Azagra, with designs by Muntañola and created by Viñals, and with sets by Ferrer y Fontanals. The program, with only slight variability, included[9]:

> First Act:
> —**En los tiempos de Goya**
>> *Intermedio de Goyescas, Soleá* by Ros, *Con mi abanico, Panaderos, Vito, Danza no. 5* by Granados, *¡Olé Catapum!, Romance Sonámbulo* by Federico García Lorca, *Así canta Aragón, Malagueña* by Lecuona
>
> —**Evocación de Ravel**
>> *Cuadro de la inspiración, Bolero* by Ravel
>
> Second Act:
>> *Sinfonía por la orquesta, Romance de la luna* by Federico García Lorca, *Sacromonte* by Turina, *Zambra*, Recitación, *Capricho Español* by Rimsky Korsakov, *Aires flamencos, Fiesta en la cueva, Romance de los 7 niños*

Of those numbers, Carmen Amaya danced the *Danza no. 5* by Granados, *¡Olé Catapum!*, Ravel's *Bolero*, García Lorca's *Romance de la Luna*, the *Fiesta en la cueva*, and the *Romance de los 7 niños*.[10]

The positive reviews for the show began in Madrid. The September 22, 1947, review in the *Hoja del Lunes* said:

> After some years' absence from our stages, finally Carmen Amaya returns, this time to the coliseum of the Plaza del Carmen, with a show about which there is much to say in little allotted space. *Embrujo Español* is the climax of Carmen Amaya's artistry. The night of the debut, the applause was resounding, delirious. She gives her dances an impact and an air that accredit her with the most prestigious artistic enterprises. We were afraid we would be attending an *españolada* [a parody of Spanishness], or that we would find ourselves witnessing a so-called folkloric show, but we were pleasantly surprised. The choreography was frankly good. It cannot be denied that Carmen Amaya is an astonishing artist.[11]

On October 20, the Asociación de la Prensa (Press Association) organized a farewell event in Amaya's honor, and Alfredo Marquerie heaped praises:

> Last night in Madrid the Asociación de la Prensa celebrated a farewell in honor of Carmen Amaya. This astonishing artist, at once *bailarina* [classical dancer] and bailaora, has made Spanish dance as expensive as it is difficult. After the choreographic revelations of herself and her company there is room no longer for simulations or pastiche, more or less charming poses and more or less acrobatic jumps. One needs to know how to dance! Carmen Amaya's triumphs abroad are perfectly justified, because to the *salida* [entrance onto stage] and the *desplante* [in bullfighting, a sudden stance of defi-

ance; in flamenco dance, a striking step], in exchange for the *cambio al paso* [change of step] and for the characteristic *mudanzas* [movements] of our dance she has added strength and attack, rhythm which is passionate and which also inspires passion, and style born of the fire of inspiration and the total and absolute mastery of choreographic sensibility.[12]

Notable performers at the event included Trío Los Calaveras, Mexican folkloric singer Irma Vila y sus mariachis, Spanish actors and singers Carmen Morell and Pepe Blanco, famous "operatic"-style flamenco singer Juanito Valderrama, and Mexican baritone Mario Gil Ojeda, with the Prieto orchestra.[13]

After these four triumphal weeks in Madrid, Amaya performed for a week at the Teatro Cervantes in Seville, opening on October 23 to a sold-out house:

> Last night the locale on Calle Amor de Dios presented one of its great events. It was sold out, with many people waiting outside [for the opportunity to enter]. The performance began with an air of expectation. And when in the *Cuadro goyesco*, illuminated orchestrally by Barbieri's figures, Carmen Amaya appeared, the first steps had to be suspended, because the audience, who had longed for her for many years, hailed her with a great ovation that made this Gypsy artist's face turn pale.[14]

Bailaor and dance maestro José de la Vega, a child then, remembers the performance vividly:

> An hour before the performance began I was at the door of the theater. When they opened the doors, those like myself who had tickets to the uppermost balconies competed with sharp elbows to grab a good seat. I stayed in the lobby to watch the artists arriving: Lola Flores and Manolo Caracol, La Macarrona, La Malena, Estrellita Castro, La Niña de los Peines, Eloísa Albéniz, Arturo Pavón father and son, Pepe Pinto, Manuel Vallejo, Juanito Valderrama…. I slipped between the knots of people to listen to their commentary. In other words, this was for me the beginning of a performance that I knew would be revelatory. Suddenly the chimes sounded and I scooted upstairs, to the nosebleed section. The curtain rose and Carmen Amaya appeared, dancing Ravel's *Bolero*, dressed in pants [which at this time would be quite shocking in Seville], descending a ramp hanging from the left side of the stage until she arrived center stage at the large drum upon which Amaya continued beating on Ravel. This performance has remained indelibly in my memory. The theater was in flames. I have never seen anything like it….
>
> That dance had nothing to do with the bailaoras that I applauded in the 1940s. If Andalusian bailaoras promenaded in the *Rosas de las Alegrías*, with their characteristic bombast: *braceando hacia afuera* [opening their arms outward], *tronchás hacia atrás* [backwards cuts], tracing the righteous and exclusive arabesques of the feminine hand that seem, as writers say, like doves on the wind…. Carmen Amaya's dance was completely the opposite. Carmen's dance was vertical, she moved her arms inwards, like the old-time farruca dancers like Faíco, El Gato o los Pelaos.[15]

Amaya also brought *Embrujo Español* to Barcelona, opening at the Teatro Tívoli on December 18, and staying for four weeks, until January 18, 1948. In the *ciudad condal* it seems that Amaya's arrival had an extra degree of interest for the press. One of the most interesting interviews that Amaya gave during this period was with journalist and caricaturist Manuel del Arco:

> *Gitanísima* [the most Gypsy] Carmen Amaya is here once more.
> —Carmen, during the past few years much "folklore" has been danced, but it seems to me little flamenco. Why is that?

—Flamenco is indecipherable; good flamenco is timeless.
—Has your style changed?
—Since I started here, (and I am from the Barceloneta) when I was four years old, and at the Teatro Español, performing in the Catalan company of Santpere, until today, I dance the same. The only difference is that now I dance with common sense, knowing what I do.
—In other words, no one taught you?
—No one; didn't I tell you that I began dancing when I was four years old? And the first *parné* [money, in Caló] that I earned was the coins that the audience threw onto the stage for me.
—You say you dance with common sense. What is your foundation, or, where is the truth of flamenco?
—In three things: *colocación* [placement, body line], *zapateo* [footwork] and *brazos* [armwork]; and that all of this, when it is done well, should motivate the audience to say ¡olé!
—When you see a bailaora, how do you assess her performance?
—I watch to see if she places her arms in the proper way, if she does footwork and lifts her arms, and if she turns properly, and [if so], I say, "This is excellent, she is phenomenal." But to move one's hands without reason, to thrash one's skirt as if to shake out the dust, and to let the audience see what should not be shown, aside from the Spanish style of movement, this is not flamenco.[16]

In the following weeks, an intense dialogue on Amaya emerged in the Catalonian press. Among these journalists were writers and critics Sebastià Gasch, one of the first to write about Amaya; Néstor Luján, who, like Gasch, wrote for the magazine *Destino*; theater critic Josep Maria Junyent, who chronicled Amaya's appearances in the conservative (and Carlist) periodical *El Correo Catalán*; Enrique Rodríguez Mijares, who wrote for the *Diario de Barcelona*; José del Castillo, who wrote in *Solidaridad Nacional*, the organ of the Falange (Franco's fascist party) in Barcelona; and M. Costa, whose review in the magazine *Lecturas* was illustrated with watercolors by Pere Clapera.[17]

Junyent was among the first to emphasize the specificity of Amaya's Gitano artistry. In a review filled with praise, following up on one from the previous day, he wrote[18]:

Carmen Amaya's footwork, clean, and without useless baroquism, without bastardized preciousness, resounding and mathematical, creates the curious complexity of her art, in which crossbreeding has no place, in space and time.

The balance in her waist. Her quick, frenetic turns. The energetic movement of her body gives value to her personality as an artist. In Amaya, Spanish dance is not a symbol enclosed within the borders of our nation. It projects abroad, because it possesses the spirit of near genius. Possibly, the secret, the formula, consists in simply regulating, compressing the ardor, the delirium, calculating its explosive force, building tension and letting shattering moments escape in a climate of emotional exasperation. It is something that only Latins can do, and more still when they are of the Gypsy race, because then the paroxysm beats through their very veins.[19]

Gasch continued as her faithful champion:

Time stands still for Carmen Amaya. Despite eleven uninterrupted years of brutally kicking stages in performances across the Americas, Carmen Amaya has resisted the weight of time with more elegance than some of her contemporaries, some of whom are scourged with ailments. Her turns have not lost any of their wildness, nor has her footwork lost any of its ferocity. Carmen Amaya dances with the fury that she always has.

> If the principal aim of art is to produce emotion, Carmen Amaya's dance produces tremendous, intense emotion that lifts one out of their chair, leaving him breathless. And that is, at the end of the day, what matters.[20]

In contrast, Néstor Luján criticized, with gusto, both Amaya's performances and those of another star of the era, Lola Flores, as "folkloristic":

> Of Barcelona's twelve theaters, three of the most important run on dead nature—guitar *cordobés* [Córdoba hat], *bata de lunares* [polka-dot dress], and the soapy language of folklore. The problem with these folkloristic performances in terms of dance demands immediate clarification, in all senses of the word. We need to recall the path of Antonia Mercé, which is the same as servile imitation, frozen in the topical, and which has been practiced till this day, because both extremes are terrible. Antonia Mercé intelligently used the best musicians, painters and librettists that she could find. The list of her collaborators is a litany of prestigious names. But Spanish dance, not to mention great flamenco, is not an affair of anecdote and *zarzuela* [light, folkloristic opera]—in the most provocative sense of the word—it can't be danced out of charming ignorance, neither from God-given talent. The moment has arrived, as these shows enjoy such great favor in the eyes of audiences that see them as a substitute for the lost zarzuelas, which in their day were the extraordinarily respectable backbone of popular Spanish music, for prominent aficionados to solve this problem as best they can.[21]

Luján, however, concluded his article with a beautiful description of flamenco dance ("that mysterious Andalusian dance"):

> The only dignified thing that a dancer of today, like Carmen Amaya, should do onstage is to appear alone with a guitarist before a severe backdrop and dance the men's dances: her unforgettable *soleares*, her *alegrías*, her *farruca*, her *zapateado*. In that way, as a consolation we can dedicate to her a gallant homage to those extraordinary tempers she occasionally emits, embodying that mysterious Andalusian dance, whose ancient form flickers like fire.[22]

Another prestigious critic, Armando de María y Campos, also attacked the out-of-place arrangements of some of Amaya's dances:

> And as the international airs have obligated her to give her presentations the prestige of ballet, she has returned to Spain looking like someone who never puts on an evening gown without doing her hair first....
>
> The dance costume is similar to the way she has left the guitar behind in order to try her hand with Albéniz and Granados. A new exponent of "intellectual illiteracy!" Good grief, what a *Danza V* by Granados! Full out, without rhythm, making a racket over those delicious melodies to which Antonia Mercé created her immortal choreographies! It's like when "jazz" irreverently decides to take hold of Chopin or Schubert and grind them in a pot, changing their rhythms and trampling on their musical lines.[23]

It could be that Carmen Amaya's choreographies did not reach the same level of excellence as her flamenco dances, but the few critics who dared judge her choreographies as "Americanized" were, in fact, failing to appreciate their modernity. As an example, let us recall the review in the magazine *Ritmo*, which specialized in classical music:

> We went to see the outstanding artist, and frankly we were disappointed. We conceive of Spanishness—and Andalusianness—in a completely different way [than Amaya]. Carmen Amaya returns "Americanized." There were moments in which we saw her do tap dance. And those brusque moves, those vertiginous turns may have a great deal of merit as gymnastics, but we are far from believing they have anything to do with the

rite, the reverie that everything Andalusian holds within. Carmen Amaya speaks to us of music made movement, of the gesture, the angry grimace made music. Everything about this show is speed, frenzy, whirlwind, hyperesthesia, in sum, abnormal. We are convinced that Carmen Amaya and her Gypsies—faithful disciples of their maestra— use and abuse a tic that perhaps in America electrifies the crowd, but that, at least upon us, has the opposite effect: it is the barrier that impedes our view into the emotional pulse of any of our most typical dances.[24]

After Barcelona, Amaya toured with her *Embrujo Español* without pause through numerous other Spanish cities. On January 29 and 30 of 1948, she performed at the Gran Teatro Jovellanos de Gijón, on February 6 and 7 at the Teatro Lope de Vega in Valladolid, on February 9 and 10 at the Nuevo Teatro de Zamora, and on February 16 and 17 at the Teatro Menacho in Badajoz.[25] From March 8 to 19, she and her company returned to the Teatro Fuencarral de Madrid.[26] It was at this time that Amaya and the great cantaor Antonio Mairena, who had worked together in the 1936 film *María de la O*, were briefly reunited. Mairena recalled,

> I accepted [the gig at the Fuencarral] and I was with her for the period we had agreed upon. Carmen's dance was a lot of dance for the audiences who came to see the show at that theater, who were not prepared to absorb all of her greatness and the full dimensions of the genius of that extraordinary bailaora, and she felt that. Nonetheless, the success was huge every day, especially in the forge number, which had been staged dancing and singing a poem from Lorca's *Romancero gitano*.... That forge number was our hit. As I sang, she, turning on her left foot, wrapped and wrapped herself in the tail of a very long bata [de cola], until it was completely coiled around her, with all that unparalleled artistry that she had. Then she made a brusque move and sent the end of the bata flying far away. Finally I finished off the song, as she brought the tempo up, doing desplantes and dragging that long tail.
>
> > *Yo te quería.*
> > *Ya no te quiero.*
> > *Tengo en mi casa*
> > *géneros nuevos.*
>
> And she did a spirited, elegant, and spectacular exit that caused a sensation in the audience. It brought the house down.[27]

Despite the excellent chemistry between Amaya and Mairena, Amaya continued using Chiquito de Triana (her sister Antonia's husband) as the principal cantaor for the rest of the European tour.

On March 24, Amaya was operated on for appendicitis in Barcelona, which prevented her from fulfilling her contract to return to Barcelona's Teatro Poliorama, as had been announced.[28] Finally back on stage, from April 25 to May 5 she and the company conquered Paris and then blazed a triumphal trail through Great Britain, Belgium, Scandinavia, and the Netherlands.[29]

In September of 1949 they returned to Buenos Aires, Argentina, with a new show, *Esto es España*, but that is another story.

Notes

1. Since Amaya's death in 1963, it was thought that she had been born in 1913, but this has been proven incorrect. In 2013, documents were unearthed indicating 1918 as Amaya's probable birth year. Among these are a 1930 Barcelona census listing Carmen Amaya as age 12; a 1920 painting by Julio Moisés, which

depicts Carmen Amaya as a baby; and the appearance of Carmen Amaya as a young girl in 1929 in Paris in the film *La Bodega*, by Benito Perojo and starring Conchita Piquer. See Montse Madridejos and David Pérez Merinero, *Carmen Amaya* (Barcelona: Edicions Bellaterra, 2013), 20–71; and http://www.papelesflamencos.com/2012/06/carmen-amaya-en-un-filme-de-1929.html (accessed October 7, 2014). The title of my essay is inspired by the article by TIM in the *Diario de Zamora*, February 8, 1948, titled: "Carmen Amaya. La bailaora con duendes. 'La novia de América' está reconquistando España" ("Carmen Amaya. The Bailaora with *Duendes*. 'America's Beloved' is Reconquering Spain" (a reference to Federico Garcia Lorca's 1933 essay on flamenco aesthetics titled "Theory and Play of the Duende"). *Duende* translates roughly as a blend of soulful and bewitching. *Cañí* has been used since the 1920s to refer to "Gypsiness" as the essence of pure-blooded, authentic, folkloric Spain.

2. For more information on Carmen Amaya's arrival and debut in the United States, see K. Meira Goldberg, "The Latin Craze and The Gypsy Mask: Carmen Amaya and the Flamenco Aesthetic (1913–1963)," in Ninotchka Devorah Bennahum and K. Meira Goldberg, eds., *100 Years of Flamenco in New York City* (New York: New York Public Library for the Performing Arts, 2013), 68–99; Montse Madridejos, "Carmen Amaya *star* de Hollywood," *Revista de Investigación sobre flamenco. La Madrugá* no. 6 (June 2012), http:/www.revistas.um.es/flamenco (accessed September 14, 2014).

3. Alfredo Marquerie, who was there to greet Amaya, wrote that he also was part of the welcoming committee for the great guitarist Ramón Montoya. "Informaciones y noticias teatrales y cinematográficas," *ABC de Madrid*, August 12, 1947.

4. In New York, Amaya earned $2,000 per week, and in Rio de Janeiro $14,000, as she confessed to the journalist Sempronio in "Tan gitana como se fue. Carmen Amaya pisa de nuevo la calle barcelonesa," *Destino*, August 23, 1947.

5. The footage appears at the beginning of NO-DO, no. 242, versión A, AÑO V, http://www.rtve.es/filmoteca/no-do/not-242/1468010/ (accessed February, 2014). Although the original film had sound, this copy in the archive of the Filmoteca Española with RTVE does not have audio.

6. Marquerie, "Informaciones y noticias teatrales y cinematográficas."

7. José Luis Gómez Tello, "Carmen Amaya. Aquella gitana ha vuelto y va a trabajar en el cine español," *Primer Plano*, August 17, 1947.

8. Sempronio, "Tan gitana como se fue."

9. In the notes for the performance in Gijón on January 29, 1948, is a handwritten addition to that day's performance of the "Danza del Molinero de Falla" (from *The Three-Cornered Hat*).

10. Announcement in *Imperio* de Zamora, February 6, 1948.

11. *Hoja del Lunes*, September 22, 1947.

12. In today's flamenco, a cambio is a hemiola, a duplet rhythm superimposed on a triplet, used as a syntactic element signaling a change of chords in the guitar accompaniment to the song, or, in dance, as a change between quietly marking time while the singer sings to a desplante. Alfredo Marquerie, "Despedida en el Madrid de Carmen Amaya, en function patrocinada por la Asociación de la Prensa," *ABC de Madrid*, October 21, 1947.

13. For more on the "flamenco opera," see John Moore's "Purity and Commercialization: The View from Two Working Artists—Pericón de Cádiz and Chato de la Isla" in this volume.

14. Gil, "Embrujo Español," *ABC de Sevilla*, October 24, 1947.

15. José de la Vega, "El baile flamenco en Cataluña a través del esplendor de Carmen Amaya," *Revista Cronopio*, no. 43 (September 9, 2013), http://www.revistacronopio.com/?p=11223, (accessed January 1, 2014). We know that the reported presence of Juana Vargas "La Macarrona" in the audience is apocryphal: she died on April 12, 1947. See Daniel Pineda Novo, *Juana,"la Macarrona" y el baile en los cafés cantantes*. Cornellà de Llobregat [Barcelona]: Aquí + Más Multimedia, 1996), 152. For more on Macarrona, see K. Meira Goldberg's essay in this volume.

16. Manuel del Arco, "Vd. dirá," *Diario de Barcelona*, December 18, 1947.

17. The first article to signal Carmen Amaya's talent to the public was written by Sebastià Gasch in the magazine *Mirador* in 1931: "In the Taurina one must be lucky to arrive on the right day. Because some nights, just a few, Carmencita dances. It is difficult to find words to describe this marvelous artista. Imagine a young Gitana, around fourteen, seated on the stage. Carmencita remains impassive and statuesque, haughty and noble, with the indefinable nobility of her race, hermetic, absent, detached from everything and everyone, her body *figée* [frozen] in order to permit her soul to fly toward inaccessible regions. Suddenly, a jump. And the Gitanita dances. It is indescribable. Soul. Pure soul." Sebastià Gasch, "Andalusia a Barcelona. Avez-vous-vu dans Barcelone," *Mirador*, May 21, 1931, in Madridejos and Merinero, *Carmen Amaya*, 25. Enrique Rodríguez Mijares, "Carmen Amaya," *Diario de Barcelona*, December 19, 1947; José del Castillo, "Carmen Amaya, la bailarina española que triunfó en Hollywood," *Solidaridad Nacional*, December 18, 1947; M. Costa, "Carmen Amaya," *Lecturas*, February 1948.

18. Josep Maria Junyent, *El Correo Catalán*, December 19, 1947.

19. Josep Maria Junyent, "Carmen Amaya en Embrujo Español," *El Correo Catalán*, December 20, 1947.

20. Sebastià Gasch, "Presentación de Carmen Amaya," *Destino*, December 27, 1947. In 1932, Gasch

had written: "We begin with Carmen Amaya, that fourteen-year-old Gitanita already known to our readers. We have already written that Escudero considers her one of the best Spanish dancers, and wants to take her to America. This girl is a product of nature. Like all the Gitanas, she must have been born dancing. Hers is the antithesis of schooled, academic dancing. Everything she knows, she knew from the moment she was born. 'La Carmela' grabs the spectator with the energetic conviction of her face, with her prodigious hip dislocations, with the abandon of her pirouettes *a la segunda* [in second position], in which animal ardor allies with Russian precision, with the rabid beating of heals and the varied play of her arms, sometimes rising excitedly, sometimes falling as if abandoned, dead weight around her body, only moved from the shoulders. She is a complete dancer, the most impressive thing about her is that she is ready to explode, engendering pathetic shocks, her blood, her violence, his savage fire of a born dancer." Sebastià Gasch, "La dansa, Cuadro flamenco," *Mirador*, June 30, 1932. In Montse Madridejos Mora, *El flamenco en la Barcelona de la Exposición Internacional (1929–1930)* (Barcelona: Edicions Bellaterra, 2012), 163–164.

21. Néstor Luján, "El problema del folklore," *Destino*, December 27, 1947.

22. Ibid.

23. Armando de María y Campos, *Un ensayo general sobre el teatro español contemporáneo visto desde México* (Madrid: Ed. Stylo, 1948), 210.

24. "Carmen Amaya y sus gitanos," *Ritmo*, November 1, 1947.

25. This is according to the leaflet of the same day and from *Voluntad*, February 1, 1948; *Diario Regional*, February 3, 1948; *Diario de Zamora de la FE de las JONS*, February 9, 1948; and *Hoy*, February 17, 1948. The information about Carmen Amaya in Badajoz was provided to me by researcher and writer Manuel Iglesias.

26. *ABC de Madrid*, March 7, 1948.

27. Alberto García Ulecia, *Las confesiones de Antonio Mairena* (Sevilla: Universidad de Sevilla, Colección de bolsillo, núm. 53, 1976), 123–125.

28. *ABC de Madrid*, March 25, 1948.

29. They performed at the Princess Theatre in London from June 15 through August 7, 1949; on May 5, 1949, they were on the cover of the magazine *Le Soir Illustré* in Brussels; on July 13, they performed in Valkenburg (Netherlands); and July 17–23 in Rotterdam.

Flamenco
The Real Stories
Brook Zern

I seem to think I recall that I once overheard in the distance a discussion about flamenco origins and aesthetics. It must have involved one of the few surviving flamenco traditionalists (now widely reviled as "purists" or "The Taliban") and a member of the fast-growing group of flamenco revisionists (now widely admired as "progressives," or, in academic circles, "postmodernist deconstructionists"). In my role as the first pre-conceptualist recreationist, I present here, in dialogue form, a flamenco farce:

Purist: Let's start at the beginning. The earliest forms of flamenco were forged at least three centuries ago...

Progressive: Wait a minute, wait a minute—there are no reports that clearly describe flamenco until the first newspaper accounts in 1850. And don't start telling me some old family stories you heard from old people when you were young. Oral histories aren't worth the paper they aren't printed on. If flamenco existed for many years previously, it would have been reported. Repeat after me: "There were no written accounts of flamenco before 1850 because there was no flamenco."

Purist: Granted, there are no books or newspaper reports before 1850, but flamenco didn't arise fully formed. It must have been created earlier, much earlier. Listen to the words of the earliest songs—they tell of the persecution and the attacks on Gitanos from the victims' perspective. Those old verses were valid documents, validly transmitted. You insist on written documents? Well, how about all those official decrees with their elegant calligraphy, outlawing the Gitano trades, their language, and their wandering ways, and commanding their persecution and imprisonment as galley slaves?

Do you really insist that the old contemporary documents tell the true story? Do you get all your information about the Lakota Indians from the U.S. Cavalry reports on the people they were trying to exterminate—the "cruel and cunning savages," to use the government's official words? If one group can write and the other can't, won't that skew the next century's findings a bit? You give zero credibility to accounts passed down within one despised group, and you trust the other group for its fair and balanced reporting—the history as written by the winners?

Progressive: There you go again. Why are you already talking about the Gitanos? Why do you think Gitanos created those early songs? In fact, why are you so sure that the Gitanos really exist as a distinct group in Spain? Identity is a luxury—but in Andalusia, where all but a few people were desperately poor and often literally starving for centuries, how can a group remain cohesive and distinct? The Gitano language was lost long ago in Spain—what else was lost?

Purist: As I was saying, the earliest songs were forged in the Gitano ghettos of Seville and Jerez, where outsiders were not invited inside. It was a hermetic environment where the families created this living testament to an ethnic trauma. When the official persecution finally eased around 1800, the previously concealed music gradually emerged into the light and by 1850 you started getting public events and newspaper reports.

Progressive: And your proof that there was a secret or hermetic period—your "proof" is that there is absolutely no record of such a period anywhere?

Purist: Well, after all, it was hermetic, so yes, it happened and no, there's no proof, by definition—hey, why are you laughing?

Progressive: Was it that obvious? Sorry. But has it ever occurred to you that French tourists were coming to Spain centuries ago, hoping to meet Carmen herself even though that Spanish Gitano was a French creation? So dancers in Spain started dressing up like Carmen and giving off the same femme fatale vibe for big bucks, or big francs?

Has it further occurred to you that those allegedly tragic "deep song" styles—boy, that sounds like a great marketing name—might have been created because long ago, people like you with insanely romantic ideas about the Gitanos went to Spain. They kept insisting that the Gitanos must have a secret tragic music, until finally the Gitanos decided to cook up a lot of weeping and wailing noises that you'd pay a lot to hear? At last, you could say you heard the songs the Gitanos sing after the tourists go home, even though (a) you were the tourists, and (b) you had not gone home.

Figure 1: Augustín Castellón, "Sabicas" (1912–1990), right, with Brook Zern, early 1980s (collection of Brook Zern).

Purist: You know, you're better than some of your friends. You admit that the Gitanos might have created those great songs. A lot of scholars think your precious documents show that the Gitanos didn't create anything—that they just stole them because, hey, that's what Gitanos do, isn't it?

You know, the Gitano people are still being persecuted today. I'd say the main charge seems kind of ironic: that they are undocumented aliens—using the lack of documents against them. But today, Spain is the country that seems to do best in respecting Gitanos' rights and traditions.

Anyway, after the Gitanos created the three forms called *cante jondo,* or "deep song"—the *martinetes,* the *siguiriyas,* and the *soleá*—they created two light and festive styles, the *tangos* and the *bulerías.* But there are more than forty other styles of non–Gitano flamenco song—some light, like the *alegrías* and the *fandangos de Huelva,* and some quite serious and moving, though not as tragic and terrifying as the deep song styles. Those include the *malagueñas,* the *tarantas,* the *serranas,* the *caña*—so most flamenco is Spanish rather than Spanish Gitano art. Just give us those few we claim.

Progressive: We? As Tonto once said, "What you mean we, white man?" You seem to have your own identity issues; maybe you're a little too close to your subject to claim objectivity.

The documented fact is, flamenco was created around 1850 by a varied bunch of people—including the equivalents of urban sophisticates, bohemians, Eurotrash, and, yes, maybe some Gitanos who hung out with those folks. One of the legendary singers of your allegedly Gitano forms was Silverio Franconetti, who wasn't Gitano and whose father was Italian. He started the first places where people could go to hear flamenco—the *cafés cantantes* where Gitano and non–Gitano singers worked together and inevitably started mixing their approaches and their melodies and verses—again, assuming there was a distinct Gitano identity at all.

This new music was not a backward-looking lament; it was a hip, modern art form that immediately found an audience in lots of Andalusian cities and in Madrid and Barcelona. But it needed a backstory, because at that time there was a rage for an imaginary quality called "authenticity" in Europe—as if one person could somehow be more "authentic" than another person. It was a time when farmers in Sussex decided they were Celts, or better yet, Druids, and every shopkeeper in Bavaria suddenly carried the blood of Wagner's Nordic gods. In Spain, the first book about flamenco came out in 1881, *Cantes Flamencos* by Machado y Álvarez, insisting that the deep songs were flamenco's sacred texts and they were a Gitano creation.

You don't seem to think that particular written document is unreliable. In fact, you think it's holy writ, but the author was just another storyteller. He was creating the tragic-romantic Spanish Gitano identity, taking cues from a German named Kraus who fostered this kind of racial mythologizing. And the great composer Manuel de Falla fell for that mythmaking and its phony IDs. Then Lorca fell in love with the whole fabrication, and in the 1960s the great singer Antonio Mairena concocted a nasty blood-based theory of gitanísmo or Gitanoism called "incorporeal reason" that insisted only Gitanos could properly interpret certain songs and dances. It was just too much. People finally woke up from this insanity about twenty years ago. Present company excepted, of course.

Purist: Look, pal. That old book tells the real story, and names the Gitano creators.

In fact, aside from Silverio—the first person to market flamenco as a public event—all the other early singers were Gitanos. The proof is that all the early deep song variants still bear their names—the soleá of La Serneta, for example, or the siguiriyas of Loco Mateo and El Planeta. They created the core component of flamenco, the deep songs, and the two great light styles.

But don't get me wrong. There are far more non–Gitano flamenco styles, and they added another necessary dimension that made flamenco the perfect and the emblematic Spanish art. That's why it is such a shame to see some artists today breaking all the rules that made flamenco so distinctive, and fusing it with absolutely everything from hip-hop to jazz to bagpipe tunes.

Progressive: For Pete's sake, flamenco has always been fusion music. It started as a mix of Arab, Jewish, Spanish, and other styles. Why do you insist that it reached an ideal state some decades ago? Do you realize that the most successful singers are the ones with the sweet voices, starting with the fabulous Don Antonio Chacón and continuing with the *cante bonito,* or pretty song, of Pepe Marchena? Do you really wish that Camarón de la Isla's fresh songs and Paco de Lucía's reinvigorated guitar had never happened?

Purist: First, flamenco fusion is a new phenomenon, not a continuation of a process. Yes, all emergent musical forms come from pre-existing styles, but that isn't the same process as a Spanish wannabe homeboy suddenly declaring himself El Flamenco Hip-Hopero. People know when an artist can't do one or the other, but if you mash them together and call it fusion, who will have the nerve to point out that it's both invalid and incompetent? Flamenco song is called a "minoritory" art because the general public doesn't like it. Fuse it with a "majority" art that lots of people love, and maybe somebody will listen to you. As for the great Don Antonio Chacón, his singing was brilliant and consistently beautiful. But he knew that on the list of flamenco priorities, those qualities are valued slightly below the qualities of being wildly erratic and—though only at certain rare and unpredictable moments—terrifyingly intense.

So Chacón, flamenco's ultimate Apollonian artist, constantly took the money he earned from his gorgeous singing and gave it to the greatest singer of all time, Manuel Torre, on the off chance that the fire-breathing Dionysian Torre just might attain the mysterious Gitano state of becoming the art itself, the moment when the *duende* floods the room and…

Progressive: Can you skip the ecstatic transport business and get to the point, if any?

Purist: Okay. When the incredible Gitano Camarón started singing with saxophones and and electric basses and the Royal Philharmonic Orchestra and still called it flamenco, or when the incomparable non–Gitano Paco de Lucía insists that playing guitar as part of a jazzy sextet is more flamenco than playing alone—well, maybe something's gained, but something else is certainly lost. The flamenco is lost. Because you can't stretch it forever—at some point, it breaks and becomes something else.

Too many great flamenco dancers have stopped dancing flamenco. Instead, they are creating elaborate and expensive spectacles that subordinate flamenco dance to a story line, or to expressing some cockamamie abstruse concept like time or memory. Israel Galván and Rocío Molina, probably the most hugely gifted dancers of our time, spend much time in recent shows emerging from and dancing upon a coffin while masked, and lying on a dimly lit pile of rocks for a very, very long time, respectively.

You may think it's better than flamenco, but I don't. It may be trendier, but it's just a faddish flavor-of-the-month music. To call it flamenco is theft—you steal the cachet and gravitas that flamenco has paid for in blood and suffering, and trade it for nothing. You sell flamenco down the river. You take a glorious art that glows in a few hard-edged primary colors, and you water it down into an endless pallet of soft pastels. Keep adding new shades and you'll end up with a dull grey.

Progressive: This is quite entertaining, assuming you are actually serious. Your frozen, fossilized flamenco can't breathe. Do you really want young artists to sing the way their grandfathers did? Haven't you noticed that Spain today is politically more progressive than America? Who are you to tell them they are making a mistake?

Purist: Okay, buddy. You wanna play rough? I sentence you to listen to the best-selling fusion records—starting with Pitingo's allegedly flamenco version of Roberta Flack's "Killing Me Softly," and continuing with "Mammy Blue" as performed by the greatest living master of deep song, José Mercé. After that, you can move on to...

Progressive: Well, I'd love to but I have a pressing engagement. But what are you looking for in your strange, idealized, and pathetically limited vision of flamenco?

Purist: That's easy. I'm looking for a quality that permeates valid flamenco. Let's call it musical truth.

Progressive: And just how would you define this clearly subjective so-called "musical truth?"

Purist: First, it's objective, not subjective. It's palpable. Maybe it can't be defined, but you know it when you hear it. A musical truth is anything performed by Leadbelly or Edith Piaf or Oum Kalsoum or Billie Holiday or Robert Johnson or Jerry Lee Lewis or Amália Rodrigues or Charlie Parker or Miles Davis or Ray Charles or, for that matter, by the late Amy Winehouse. A musical lie is anything performed by Britney Spears or Steve and Edie Gorme or Frankie Avalon or Justin Beiber. A musical half-truth is anything performed by, say, El Chocolate and the Belmonts, or Fernanda de Utrera and the Mitch Miller Orchestra, or Antonio Mairena and Kenny G, or Paco de Lucia and his Hot Six. In fact...

Progressive: Enough. Flamenco is moving on, despite people like you standing in the road. Because young artists have courage and vision...

Purist: Ah, yes. The noble non-savages, courageously blazing new paths to extend the art. Let's talk about money, or as you academics call it, the phenomenon of commodification. Because fusion is where the money is.

Progressive: I thought you'd never bring it up. Because your vision of flamenco keeps focusing on those *juergas* and fiestas and other intimate gatherings among friends. But flamenco, unlike actual folk music, has been performed for money since the start. It wasn't something that everybody could do, like normal folk music. It took uncommon talent that commanded respect and could earn more money than picking olives. Fusion is simply the current way to keep flamenco profitable for its artists, while respecting the tradition and its deep roots.

Purist: You know, a 1964 tape recording surfaced recently. It's the last recording, the swan song, of La Niña de los Peines, the greatest *cantaora* in history, singing brilliantly at the wedding of the singer Lebrijano. Speaking in the abstract, it was immediately recognized as a priceless cultural treasure. Speaking in the concrete, no commercial record company was willing to issue it, because they saw no demand for it. But they are bidding like crazy for kids who do flamenco hip-hop, or flamenco jazz, or flamenco rap, or, god help us all, flamenco chill-out—flamenco to relax by.

Okay, I can deal with that. But here's the kicker: when these hip young mixmasters are interviewed, they say that they have the utmost respect for their predecessors. They've heard Paco de Lucía insist it's necessary to listen to the great artists of the past before trying to create the flamenco of the future. But they don't understand that he's referring to artists from an early era—they think that Paco and Camarón *are* the past, the starting point of flamenco. They don't say that, of course. They say that they listen to La Niña de los Peines, because that's the name their PR people have made them memorize.

Progressive: You and your pals lost this debate years ago. Get used to it. Did I mention that I have a pressing engagement? Sorry, gotta run.

Purist: Fine. Oh, just one more question: Could you tell me about the most memorable flamenco event you've witnessed. I assume it was a tightly rehearsed dance troupe doing a perfectly synchronized choreographic routine during a huge stage production in a world-renowned theater...

Progressive: Hey, pal, I didn't just fall off the turnip truck. I've got friends and connections in this art, too—why, during my last sabbatical I was invited to a private midnight fiesta in the back room of the Venta de Vargas off the old Cadiz road. Three great singers, one funky dancer, and a guitarist who really knew how to accompany. Man, at noon the next day it was still...

Purist: Wow. Sounds terrific. What did the press coverage say about it?

Progressive: Coverage? Don't be ridiculous. There weren't any reporters there. That would have messed up the whole thing. This was strictly among friends...

Purist. This is really disappointing. You know, until now I thought you had respect for the truth. But this whole thing was clearly the product of a fevered romantic imagination.

Progressive: Have you lost your mind? I was there. And I can introduce you to other people who were there.

Purist: Sorry, but ten minutes ago you proved that the idea of a "hermetic" period of concealed flamenco genesis was laughable, because there are no published reports of flamenco prior to 1850. I respect your high standards of verifiability. Therefore, in the absence of proof that your alleged event happened—except for your inherently unreliable oral history—I must conclude you are either confused or deluded.

Oh, and is it possible you'd had something to drink during the event? In that case, we would all agree that your judgment and recollection was impaired. Sorry, but I must be going. I have a previous engagement.

Progressive: Wait! Come back! Okay, maybe I had a few drinks, or a lot of drinks, but I know what I saw. And a month before that, I was at a Gitano wedding fiesta in Granada. Honest! And then there was this baptism in the Barrio Santiago in Jerez... (fades out).

Wait, wait—don't tell me you're one of those people who sit through shows by great dance troupes, ignoring the stars and going wild during the encore when the guitarists and hand clappers get up and do a few moves that have been carefully choreographed to appear spontaneous?

Spanish Artists in Love and War, 1913–1945
Meditations on Female Embodiment and Populist Imagination

NINOTCHKA DEVORAH BENNAHUM

> For the European, even today, America represents something akin to exile, a phantasy of emigration and, therefore, a form of interiorization of his or her own culture. At the same time, it corresponds to a violent extraversion and therefore to the zero degree of that same culture. The whole foundation of America is a response to ... a radicalization of the utopian.... To land in America is to land in ... the way of life. America is the original version of modernity.[1]
>
> —Jean Baudrillard, *America*, 1986

Introduction

"Dance configures relationships between body, self and society."[2] Ideals of citizenship, power, spiritual belief, and inner (somatic) awareness emerge as one studies the historical relationship between dancing and Spanish history, and between pre- and post–Spanish Civil War art.[3] Had flamenco not emerged at this specific time in history—had its modern creation been part of another time and place—the political nature of its modernity would have looked quite different. But as its modern genesis occurred simultaneously with the Bolshevik Revolution, World War I, the Great Depression, the Spanish Civil War and World War II, flamenco bears the mark of its time: syndicalist radicalism, global violence and partisan survival.

The socio-political richness of *el baile español*—Andalusian, Galician, Catalan and Castilian—helps scholars to uncover the deeper significance of Spanish dance as part of a global circulation of ideas about democracy, authenticity and art. Spanish dance's influence is far-reaching, filled with resistant and populist imagery. Flamenco's material/architectural survival in the bodies of Gitana(o) and Spanish artists offers an avant-garde radicalism that can be perceived as a call for a democratic Spain.

While many Spanish dance artists survived the long-lived dictatorship of General Francísco Franco, many did not. Here are their contributions to history, suspended within

Spain herself between the end of the Spanish Civil War in 1939 and the death of Franco in 1975, re-absorbed body-to-body in dance studios and on street corners throughout the country. Today, the assimilation of Spanish dance-theater's vanguard radicalism into the post- and neo-modern virtuosic art of Rocío Molina and Israel and Pastora Galván must be seen in this light: as conscious, political iterations of the work begun by Antonia Mercé, La Argentina (1888–1936) and Encarnación López Júlvez, La Argentinita (1898–1945).[4]

Spanish Modernism

With the global circulation of nationalist ideologies sweeping the world between the First and Second World Wars, a rich discourse surrounding democracy, art and modernist tendencies surfaced in Europe and America. Rooted in the political and aesthetic radicalism of the Russian avant-garde and the French, Spanish and Italian Cubist, Dadaist, Futurist and Surrealist movements, definitions of art and modernity, performance and political theory—art as a resistant subject—rose to the surface of civic life.

Flamenco developed as a globally-recognized modern art in the first decades of the twentieth century. An art form whose great gift is the act of vital aliveness embedded in a physical architecture of the dancing body. Its sways, articulations and deep backbends are rooted in the nomadic cultures of South Asia and the ancient Middle East, with a classical torso born of the aristocratic courtier of early modern Europe. Flamenco artists fused song to dance, ancient to prescient being. Much the way Balanchine's "Americanization" of Tsarist ballet was achieved by combining the grounded, Africanist jazz body with the controlled and erect dance-steps of Renaissance Europe, flamenco's nervous energy and rhythmic explosions emphasize inherently Africanist values: individualism, anarchy, self-isolation, and syncopation. A projection of physical aggression as urban cool, flamenco symbolizes modernity.[5] While modernism exists in all cultures at any moment in time, early twentieth-century modernism was an anti–Romantic, anti-escapist, transatlantic movement that praised self-consciousness and anti-authoritarianism. With roots in European literature and painting, modernist art critics appeared in Europe and the U.S. in the 1910s, religiously separating the "old" from the "new," and praising the anarchy of contemporaneity, and rejecting the rule-bound academy.[6]

Spanish dance artists sought freedom and self-knowledge—a conscious movement into the unknown. Their dance art flourished with touring solo careers in which each artist, in her/his own way, made radical, public statements about the human body. The new performative spaces opened between the 1880s and the 1920s led specifically to a transformation of the bolero tradition, from academic and refined to ethnographic and interpretive.

The tumultuous, syncopated nature of jazz seeped into Spanish dance acts in many ways. In more contemporary, evening-length works, the jagged, masculinist cool of African American jazz, architecture, and civic space could be felt resonating with quicksilver accented beats accompanied by increasingly complex ways of mobilizing limbs and inhabiting space. This stage was a solo female paradise where, like the American modern dance pioneers, a woman could feel free, the intellectual equal of artists throughout history. Early twentieth century Spanish dance artists contributed to an evolving modernist discourse, mining the rich trove of Spanish dance and opening the form to an aesthetic conversation surrounding feminist consciousness, art and corporeality. Each, in her own way, fell in and out of love with aspects of modernity, their experimentation rooted in self-exploration and desire.

Writers and artists evolved a constantly shifting body of aesthetic principles used to define the "value" of a work of art. Historians cite many "birthdates" for the term "modernism." Clement Greenberg, one of the most distinguished early twentieth-century American critics, identified three historic moments in the history of Modernism as a philosophical movement: the eighteenth-century enlightenment writing of Immanuel Kant; 1860s France and its escapist, Romantic embrace of *la vie bohème* alongside the writing of Charles Baudelaire ("never before the 1860s in France had the difference between newness and everything else shown itself so strikingly in high art."[7]) and Italian Futurism, "the first manifestation connected with the avant-garde to win public attention immediately.... [The Futurists] were the first to think in terms of avant-garde*ness*, and to envisage newness in art as an end in itself; and they were the first group to adopt a program, posture, attitude, stance that was consciously 'avant-garde.'"[8] They were the first if one leaves out Loïe Fuller, Isadora Duncan, Ruth St. Denis, Ted Shawn and La Argentina.

Shaping Spanish Modernism in the U.S.

How can we enlarge Greenberg's definition to include dance and, more specifically, Spanish dance? Is the dominant Greenbergian vision of modernism all that greeted Spanish artists on this side of the Atlantic Ocean as they stepped onto the stages of the Metropolitan Opera, the Maxine Elliott Theatre, Town Hall, Carnegie Hall and various theaters along Broadway? Greenberg's notions of modernism are shaped by painting and sculpture, not by the body. Can we enlarge this somewhat narrow view to include Hispanic or Spanish modernist tendencies praised in New York City between 1915 and 1945 and shaped by the Hispanist poetic writings of Guillaume Apollinaire; Spain's poet-laureate Federico García Lorca; the chief music critics of *The New York Times*, Carl Van Vechten and Olin Downes; and John Martin, America's first major dance critic?[9] Van Vechten reviewed the earliest performances of La Argentina and Escudero. But it was Martin who enlarged Americans' understanding of modern dance with his pointed reviews of Mary Wigman, Humphrey-Weidman and Martha Graham, whose dancing, he argued, enlarged the global rhetoric of modernist ideology. Graham's emphasis on distorted line, distillation of form and content, America's frontier, and a Spartan use of color and stage design reflected for him a "true, American spirit."[10] And it was Graham's *esprit du corps*, her intrinsic American being, that educated Martin to receive Antonia Mercé, La Argentina's experiments in Spanishness in much the same way.

European modernist aesthetic terms used by art, music and, subsequently, dance critics to identify certain aesthetic tendencies and organizing principles came to define the art world of New York City at the beginning of the twentieth century. Imported by writers, art and music critics, museum curators, and visual and performing artists who had spent significant time in Paris just after its famous *Salon d'Automne* of 1907 at which Pablo Picasso's *Les Demoiselles d' Avignon* was exhibited alongside Paul Cézanne's many experiments with planar perspective, modernist ideas came to dominate how New York City identified and understood art. With the opening of New York's first modernist art exhibition in 1913—the Armory Show—at which William Merritt Chase's grand portrait of a dancing Spaniard, Carmencita, was prominently displayed, a specifically American consciousness was raised about the new American body in art.[11]

Flamenco as a modernist form of art, be it by Spanish and/or Gitano practitioners, can only be understood in the postwar era (1918–1929) as part of a global shift in artistic sensibility. Rooted in African and African American tradition, flamenco played a central role in the formation of a modernist and civic cultural identity and artistic sensibility in Europe and America. Flamenco became a vehicle, like early modern dance, through which various Spanish artists imagined themselves, deconstructing issues of authenticity and socio-political identity vis-à-vis a country—Spain—that was in its final stages of industrialization.

Dance benefited from bold new theories of the dancing body exemplified by Loïe Fuller, Isadora Duncan, Mary Wigman, Ruth St. Denis, Ted Shawn and Martha Graham.[12] Literate in Freudian notions of the unconscious mind and desire, these radical dance theorists privileged inner psychological awareness and ecstasy over pictorial representation and social hierarchy—educated audiences and critics alike. Duncan "sought to establish a link between inner feeling and outward gesture," an established quality in flamenco and Spanish dance."[13] For Europeans and Americans, Duncan's theory of the natural dancing body goes further than any other dance artist in freeing the body (in this case, the female dancing body), from the strictures of technique and of the academy. Duncan saw the dancing body as a transparent representation of the soul, a medium of expression divorced from traditional balletic iconography and dramaturgy. Duncan's and, subsequently, Michel Fokine's concomitant dethroning of classical ballet's embedded hierarchy and storytelling devices radicalized stage performers and directors to look inside, to the psyche and inner experience, for material with which to shape, conceive of and execute a dance. American modern dancers, like Spanish dancers, rebelled "against having to be somebody else."[14] They wanted to move as sculptural figures with rhythmic and/or percussive support. This "constant awareness of space," John Martin revealed, "turned the surrounding space into a 'dramatic antagonist' by making gravity one's partner."[15]

American dance artists whose values were broadly shared by Spanish dance artists brought forth a focus on the spatial environment surrounding their movements. The sustained consciousness of artists to art-making—the creation of a bold, new syntax and language of moving that led to the "expression of inner feeling"—began with concomitant revolutions in ballet and early modern dance. The individualism inherent in jazz and Dadaist art—ready-made or found art (discovered internally or on the street)—radicalized flamenco artists' approach to the body in space and the materiality of the concert stage as an object in and of itself.

When Spanish dance artists La Argentina and, later, La Argentinita arrived on American shores, Duncan-influenced music and dance critics viewed them through the lens of American modern dance.

La Argentina—Modernism in Spanish and American Dance, 1913–1929[16]

It is something less than adequate to describe La Argentina as a Spanish dancer for, although she bases her art on Spanish forms, it is universal in its character. [Her] superb artistry ... sacrifices nothing of the splendor of its tradition, but rather, enlarges it to a wide significance.[17]

We also remember very vividly, my wife and I, an evening with Federico at a performance by La Argentina, Antonia Mercé, the most finished of all the Spanish dancers, a truly great artist whose stature grows in the memory. Federico and Maroto talked as freely, unashamedly and continuously as they had been in an open-air café ... but they, too, were silent when those marvelous castanets began ... always a supreme moment. After the performance, Federico said he wanted to introduce us to his good friend La Argentina, who loved him very much, so we all started backstage where there was a crowd. Some policeman tried to stop Federico and their gestures emphasized their words, but the impetuous young poet could not imagine anyone keeping him from greeting a fellow Andalusian in New York, so he plowed straight ahead with the three of us in his wake until La Argentina, wrapped in an old grey wooly bathrobe, saw him at the door.

There were shrieks of greeting and immediately afterward a flurry of embraces and back-pattings, before the presentations that followed. We had often seen La Argentina and had heard our beloved maestro Enrique Fernandez Arbós, for so many years a famous conductor in Madrid and elsewhere, and a close collaborator of the dancer.[18]

After we left the theater, we walked along Broadway with the two Spaniards (Maroto and Lorca) who blocked pedestrian traffic at intervals by stopping to discuss with vehemence and gesticulations.[19]

A Spanish craze gripped New York between La Argentina's first performances in 1915 and the death of her prodigious follower, La Argentinita, in 1945. The collapse of Primo de Rivera's dictatorship led the new Spanish government to advertise itself to the world as civilized. Spain opened a costly tourism bureau on Fifth Avenue. Her agencies sponsored Spanish art exhibitions, music concerts and educational exchanges and invited once exiled Spanish intellectuals to speak on Spain's behalf.[20] In the tense years preceding Spain's bloody Civil War, Hispanism became so popular that Columbia University's Spanish Institute became a central location for noted lectures, concerts and philosophical debates. García Lorca, poet-in-residence and English student at Columbia from 1929 to 1930, read from what would become his elegant, posthumous ode to the city, *Poet in New York* (1940). Lorca sang Spanish folk songs and popular Andalusian melodies, accompanying himself on an upright piano.[21] After his brother's murder, Francísco Lorca escaped Franco, at the invitation of Columbia University.

Antonia Mercé, stage named La Argentina, rose out of the dancehalls of Spain and France to become a scion of contemporary art. Born in a Buenos Aires boarding house in 1888, the only daughter of principal dancers at Madrid's Teatro Real, she, much like Loïe Fuller, Isadora Duncan and Martha Graham, would invent herself, imagining a modernist *gesamtkunstwerk* of flamenco and Spanish dance and music, founding and directing a full company (Les Ballets Espagnols) and developing a codified dance technique that synthesized the many forms of Spanish dance into a single, unified expression.

Before her premature death in 1936 La Argentina, with her dance partner Vicente Escudero, wrote the curriculum for the conservatory that would become The Ballet Nacional de España. Drawing inspiration for her aesthetic abstraction from Paris-based

Figure 1: Antonia Mercé, La Argentina, seated with her manager, Arnold Meckel, to her right, at a banquet dinner in the Excelsior Restaurant in Madrid with members of the Spanish artistic and literary vanguard. Federico García Lorca is seated third on the left from the front (collection of Ninotchka Devorah Bennahum, gift of Carlota Mercé de Pavloff).

Figure 2: Antonia Mercé, "La Argentina," dances *El Tango Andalou* at Madrid's Teatro Español, December 1, 1931. At the end of her performance, La Argentina was presented with the Cross of Isabela la Católica by the president du Conseil of the Second Spanish Republic, Manuel Azaña (collection of Ninotchka Devorah Bennahum, gift of Carlota Mercé de Pavloff).

cubist and Surrealist Spanish painters—Pablo Picasso, Juan Gris, Salvador Dalí, Juan Gris and Francis Picabia—and from the Parisian seasons of Les Ballets Russes, La Argentina became not only a self-made modern woman; she shifted (some critics argue replaced) audiences' historic perceptions of Spanish dance by introducing them to *el baile Español* as something modern, politically engaged and *de rigueur*. On the one hand, she was, like Duncan, a spiritualist, and, on the other, a dance theorist who wove music and rhythm into the very core of her being.

Where Duncan's racism would not allow her to accept the Africanist presence in American modern dance into her vision of "America Dancing"—the percussive, syncopated rhythms of jazz, the polyrhythmic relationship of dancer to musical score, and the improvisational "anarchy" and spontaneity (that she called "savage") of American social dancing—La Argentina's choreographic *assemblage* embraced it.[22] As a trained musician, Argentina welcomed percussive instrumentation into her choreographic scoring and her castanet-playing of flamenco and Spanish dance rhythms.[23]

In her hands, the Spanish dancer became a protean spirit, removed from the semiology of Orientalist and Romantic harem spectacle in which a dark-eyed, red-lipped thief named Carmen moves dangerously around a tiny, dark-lit stage like a panther in a cage.[24] In its place, La Argentina substituted the dancer as an intellectual being, arguing that the Spanish body is a historically-minded, sentient figure. She transformed her stage design as well, subtly revealing a modernist ideology grounded in the corporeal: *La Corrida* (1910) offers a spare use of stage design; *Cordoba* (1923) communicates a sense of the dancer as an intellectual being; *El Amor Brujo* (1925), her decade-long collaboration with Manuel de Falla, relays a focus on the materiality of the body as the whole of a dance; *Triana* (1929) engages in a sensibility that a greater truth resides within the body and mind of the performing artist; and *Tango Andalou* (1931), the final work performed in her beloved homeland, negotiates an intense pursuit of individual expression—La Argentina's personal worldview.[25]

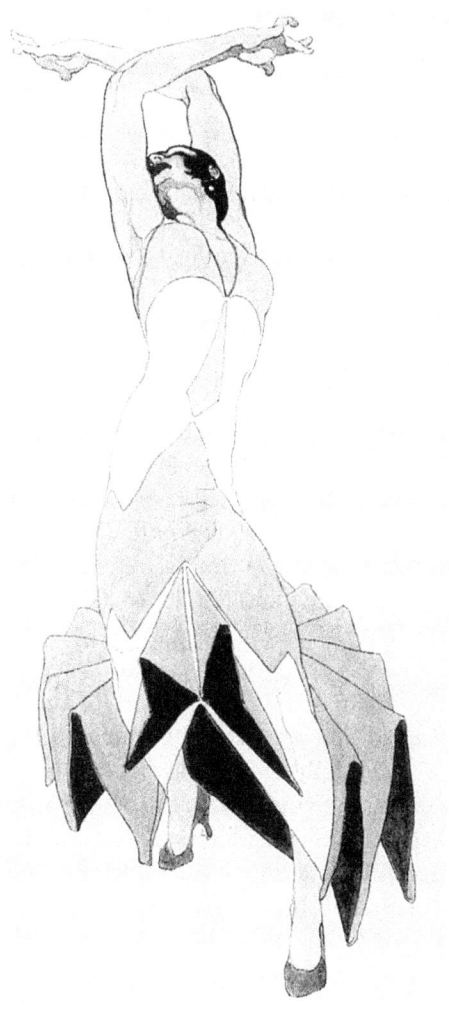

Figure 3: Costume design for *Triana* by Néstor de la Torre. *Triana* premiered May 27, 1929, at the Opéra-Comique. Music by Isáac Albéniz (from *Iberia*) transposed by Enrique Arbós. Sets and costumes by de la Torre (collection of Ninotchka Devorah Bennahum, gift of Carlota Mercé de Pavloff).

Like Balanchine whose ballets *Apollo* (1928) and *Prodigal Son* (1929) premiered in Paris several years after La Argentina's modernist masterpiece, *El Amor Brujo,* she, too, experimented with a new use of dance-steps whose historiography emerged out of the courts of Europe. La Argentina migrated, like Ruth St. Denis, Carmencita and Pastora Imperio, out from under the complex socio-economic yoke of burlesque, vaudeville and music-hall environments where working- and upper-class men smoke and drank, unaccompanied by wives and children. Cutting her teeth as a flamenco and Spanish dancer in the *café cantantes* of Madrid, Barcelona, Lisbon and Paris, she rose to become the first female member of Spain's literary and artistic vanguard—*el Generacíon del '27*—and its first dance artist. Placing dance and the dancing body at the center of avant-garde discourse, Mercé transformed the way Europeans and the intellectual community wrote about and discussed stage spectacle, opening a space for dance and dancers in the creation of a new, democratic, socialist Spain.

In 1905, La Argentina resigned from the Teatro Real de Madrid, a job most dancers longed for, instead seeking short contracts in dancehalls, movie theaters and flamenco clubs throughout Spain. The next year, she accepted an important but short-lived touring engagement with a respected *bailaor*, Antonio el de Bilbao. They toured Portugal, England and Spain and, slowly, her title rose to star dancer. By 1910, with her mother in tow, she moved to Paris for an engagement at the Tuileries gardens' noted open-air music-hall, Le Jardin de Paris, where she was dubbed "La reine des castanettes," "La reiña de las castañuelas," the queen of the castanets. Rising in stature with the French and Spanish press, La Argentina received an invitation from Moscow's Aquarium Theater where Isadora Duncan, a self-professed Bolshevik, had danced several years earlier. She accepted and traveled to Russia for a brief period in May of 1913.[26] She continued on to London's Alhambra Theatre to star in *El embrujo de Sevilla*, dancing beside flamenco greats La Malaguenita, Faïco, Antonia el de Bilbao and Realito. Finishing at the end of June, Argentina was invited back to Russia with her own small company (her first company) and, upon arrival on July 14, was forced to flee with the start of World War I. A German U-boat arrested her ship's crew and all its passengers. Terrified, they were eventually released and forced to go back to London as Spain declared herself non-aligned and all members of the troupe held Spanish passports. Upon arrival in Madrid, she was invited to dance before the Spanish vanguard, a heroine's welcome.

The following spring, following the arrival of Sergei Diaghilev and the Ballets Russes in Spain and the unsuccessful April 15 premiere of Falla's *El Amor Brujo*, Argentina was again invited to dance for Spain's intelligentsia at its well-known literary club, El Ateneo.[27] At this time she conferred with Falla about the orchestration for *El Amor Brujo*. Soon after, Argentina set sail for South America. While performing at the Teatro Colón in Buenos Aires, she fell in love for the first time. A businessman and owner of *La Prensa* newspaper, Carlos Marcelo Paz was the nephew of the former president of the Argentine Republic, General Roca. He proposed and they wed on 23 June at the Basilica de Nuestra in a civil wedding, she twenty-seven, he thirty-one. Paz gave her gonorrhea, leaving her unable to bear children. Five years later, in 1920, they separated, although Argentina was never able to obtain a divorce. Six years later, Argentina, engaged to dance at the Femina Theater in Paris, met the producer Robert Ochs, twenty years her senior, with whom she fell madly in love and lived the rest of her life, unmarried.

Americans can understand Spaniards ... only Spaniards can be cubists.[28]

The next year, at the invitation of Spanish "New School" composer Enrique Granados, La Argentina traveled to New York City for the first time. Following on the heels of Denishawn, the first company and school to "shape a consciousness about American dance," Argentina arrived to star in Granados' opera *Goyescas* at the Metropolitan Opera House.[29] She arrived to discover that the Met director had given her job to his wife. In an attempt to salvage Argentina's earnings, Granados helped her to rent the Maxine Elliott Theatre, located beside the Metropolitan Opera on 39th Street and Broadway. Argentina engaged the Little Symphony Orchestra and, as a gift, Granados composed *La danza de los ojos verdes,* which he dedicated to her.

Argentina danced a varied repertory of nineteen solo Spanish and flamenco dances, accompanying some with castanets and others with song. Critics wrote rave reviews, noting the emotional expressivity of her dancing that they connected to her use of rhythmic syncopation in footwork and castanet-playing and her articulate use of wrists and head. With its ecstatic emotionalism, translated as an inherent freeing of the body from its implicit rigidity as seen in early experimental work—Ruth St. Denis' *Radha* (1905) and Mary Wigman's *Hexantanz* (1914)—Argentina's performance was significant. For American dancers and audiences, Argentina's dancing reflected the modernist tenets being explored by Wigman, who had been exposed to the rhythmic ideas of Dalcroze in Hellerau, and to Duncan and Denishawn, artists who had grown up under the restrictive yoke of Victorian stoicism and sought release in the music visualizations of François Delsarte. Further, the psychic transformation of the Spanish dancer in long flamenco solos (what García Lorca called *duende*) embodied Wigman's ritualistic ecstasy and St. Denis' revolt against the softness of ballet and adoption of a percussive style with sharp attack. Where classical ballet could carry diffuse gestures that "seemed to float off indefinitely into space," St. Denis and, a decade later, Doris Humphrey and Martha Graham, sought to "center the body and to integrate its movement within its own sphere of action."[30] Duende, like Freud's notion of the death principle, emerges out of Spanish folklore, tied in Lorca's vanguardist imagination to the inner workings of the semiconscious mind of the dancer in motion.

Argentina's aesthetic treatment of Spanish dance contained a modernist slimming down—a honing in on dance's essential qualities. She focused on function already being adopted by modern dance pioneers.[31] Mexico's *El Universal* commented in 1915: "Internal rhythm, poetic emotiveness, elegance, plasticity, everything in Antonia Argentina sings a hymn to grace."[32] Upon her return to New York's Town Hall in 1928, John Martin commented that Argentina's choreographic modernism grew out of her ability "to capture the aliveness of the Spanish body and hold it in the bounds of form," thus fusing the materiality of her dancing with a kinesthetic response to Spanish modernism.[33]

Linking the modernist plasticity of her dancing with an analysis of her musicality, H. Bibaum, writing for *Musical America,* commented: "a perfect sense of rhythm gives her performance an exceptional perfection ... in the liveliness of her dances ... she executes delicately, not by way of vigor or simple muscular control. She is also a virtuosa in the playing of castanets, in which she has never been outdone."[34] This expression of inner feeling that is transmitted—exteriorized—in the form of rhythmic, corporeal visualization resonates with Martin's aestheticizing commentary on St. Denis, Wigman, Graham and Duncan.

La Argentina's solos, or "dance acts," resonated as modernist exploration on multiple levels. They possessed the syncopated quality of Dadaist *assemblage.* This was understood in the 1910s by music critics as a modern-day jazz band: La Argentina's choreographic assembly of castanets, song, footwork, articulate arms and hands atop a centrifugal use of the torso fused into a "ready-made," organic whole that answered modern art's mechanistic call for chaotic liberty. Meanwhile all of the sonic parts of Argentina's corporeal and musical assemblage fused into an electric, integrated collage of resounding body parts. If modern dance and visual art in New York City were testing and, to some extent, undermining traditional definitions of performance as art, then Argentina's visionary world of Spanish dance answered and confirmed their call with a syntax of percussive movement that abolished the escuela bolera's European courtier-like prettiness, while simultaneously opening flamenco to the art of nostalgia.[35]

La Argentina returned to the U.S. six more times before her premature death in 1936. Her choreographic theories of Spanish dance and musical scoring evolved throughout the 1920s and 1930s and, placed beside those of American modern dance pioneer Martha Graham, transformed solo female performance both in the U.S. and in Europe. Argentina, like Duncan and Graham, made radical statements about the dancing female body in public space. In the fall of 1929, Argentina traveled to dance in New York and at the White House, crossing the country to act in a film for MGM, a part she ultimately refused.

On October 29—"Black Thursday"—the New York stock market crashed and the country was reeling from its totemic effects. La Argentina continued performing; she kept late-night company with ardent hispanophiles and Spanish musicians. Their gravitational pull was García Lorca, who would later connect the Andalusian Gitano to the African American who suffered most from the devastating effects of the crash.

Argentina fell ill and was forced to delay her trip home. One evening, she joined Ted Shawn and Ruth St. Denis to see Mary Wigman's first season in America. "At her New York reception, La Argentina and Ruth and I stood at the head of the receiving line," remembered Ted Shawn.[36] Several months later, in February of 1930, her prodigious follower, La Argentinita, arrived with her "secretary," the bullfighter Ignacio Sanchez Mejías, with whom she was madly in love. (Mejías, the best friend of the great toreador Joselito el Gallo, had fallen in love with the dancer. After Joselito was gored to death 16 May 1920, Ignacio made his move.)

La Argentinita, contracted by Broadway impresario Lew Leslie, danced in his musical extravaganza *International Revue.* Her substantial salary of $208,000 was advertised in the New York press as audiences booed her off the stage. New York found her operatic-style singing and cameo Spanish characters superficial and uninteresting. Leslie's attempt to exoticize his female chorus lines with a little "local" Spanish color backfired and Argentinita quit, vowing never to return to New York City.

In an attempt to salvage her name on this side of the Atlantic Ocean, La Argentinita, following in Argentina's footsteps, secured the Maxine Elliott Theatre, dancing and singing a solo program of Spanish and flamenco. Endowed with a soft and lilting voice, a lovely body and a fierce attack of the floor, La Argentinita recovered somewhat from her failed commercial appearance. In the audience for her February solo concert appearances was Lorca, her great friend and admirer, and a number of noted American and

Spanish musicians and hispanophiles: Federico de Onís, Mildred Adams, Andrés Segovia, Enrique Arbós and Gabriel Maroto. Several weeks later, leaving La Argentinita behind, Mejías and Argentina returned by ship together, he to his wife and children and, she eventually to France to dance in a gala benefit at the Paris Opéra.[37]

Deeply concerned for his friend and collaborator's artistic well-being, Lorca "appears to have given new direction to the career of Encarnacíon López Júlvez," whose *bosquejo*—singing, mime and dance comedic sketches—had been received by New York critics and audiences as old-fashioned, lacking the prescience and complexity of modernist art of the 1930s.[38] Argentinita's brightly colored costumes appeared flashy; her melismatic (operatic) singing-style too frilly for desperate times. Critics and friends alike agreed that the artist lacked insight into (and failed to understand) a moment in history.

One night at the home of Federico and Harriet de Onís, García Lorca and Andrés Segovia persuaded Argentinita "that her repertory of songs from zarzuelas and *sainetes*—light opera—was exhausted."[39] Together, working through the night on sandwiches and coffee, they reshaped her repertory, popularizing her material and rendering it at once ethnographic and global. These were "the folk songs that enabled her to renew her career."[40] This unplanned artistic mentorship would have global effects. Upon their return to Spain, La Argentinita and García Lorca recorded ten popular songs, "harmonized by Lorca at the piano for La Voz de su Amo's recording label."[41] Some songs came directly from the streets, from Gitanos, from romanceros, from cafés de Chinitas or from friends who were flamenco singers. The pair rehearsed at Argentinita's house. When the songs were finally performed in theaters and on radio throughout Spain, people loved them because they sounded real—like them—a slice of life. When Argentinita returned to New York's Majestic Theater on November 13, 1938, under the management of Sol Hurok, it was this populist repertory that finally won New Yorkers' hearts.

During the Spanish Civil War, La Argentinita's voice could be heard throughout Spain on radio and in movie theaters; hers was the voice of the people. These populist recordings brought her stage performance gravitas.[42]

> The Nazis do not represent the real people. The real people are American, not European; you must believe me.[43]
> —La Argentinita quoted in the *New York Sun*, 1942

Throughout the 1940s, Argentinita and her sister Pilar rented a home on Manhattan's Fifth Avenue. La Argentinita was said to be earning more than $200,000 per year on tour, one of the highest artist's salaries in the country.[44] She was generous, dancing in wartime benefits for Navy Relief, displaced victims and orphans, and frequently performing in outdoor venues in front of 10,000 people alongside Martha Graham, Paul Draper, Doris Humphrey, Charles Weidman, Erick Hawkins and the Barry Brothers tap team.[45] She became a dear friend of Ruth St. Denis and Ted Shawn and recommended La Meri to them as their Spanish dance professor for their University of Dance at Jacob's Pillow. She also taught for Shawn, joining Jack Cole, Helen Tamiris, Asadata Dafora, Anna Duncan, Irene Castle, and Joe Pilates as summer faculty.

> I feel that in times of great emergency, we must do finer work than ever before. We too must mobilize our skills. I feel that we Americans are fighting to preserve a way of life while we are fighting for it.[46]
> —Ted Shawn, July 1942

Populist at heart with a lifelong commitment to the underserved—the Gitano, the artist, the partisan, the anti-fascist—La Argentinita's art embraced self-consciousness, a prime modernist concern of the concert dancer. With the death of La Argentina in 1936, La Argentinita acquired the spotlight, stepping quite literally into her repertory. Commenting in 1944 upon "her" version of *El Amor Brujo*, performed at the Metropolitan Opera House on a program shared with Ballet Theatre, Edwin Denby wrote: "Her piece was her own version of *El Amor Brujo*, a classic of theatricalized gypsy dancing, famous in the great Argentina's version. This novelty I thought missed fire."[47] Because of Argentina's many tours to America, audiences expected to see concert stage recitals of Spanish dance, paving the way for Argentinita whom Edwin Denby remarked in 1943 "is now a star (at least here)."[48]

Argentinita "borrowed" Argentina's musical scores, the titles of her dances and evening-length works, as well as her choreographic ideas, and reworked them to the great praise of the European and American press. By the 1940s, she would receive high modernist praise:

> Though there is the touch of the earth in her art, there is also the fine reserve of the conscious artist. To have retained the subjective vitality of the material with which she is dealing, while at the same time shaping it selectively into works of form and taste and self-containment is a miracle that makes Argentinita's dance unique.[49]

And while her politics were grounded in a strong sense of justice with an eye to those in need, nowhere, not in any program, press interview, or correspondence, would Argentinita ever thank or memorialize Argentina, whose copyright, ultimately, she had stolen.[50] Argentina and Manuel de Falla, together, in a legal document, forbade her from dancing *El Amor Brujo*; she danced it anyway. Falla inserted a clause into his last living will and testament that detailed how the ballet must be danced. Although Argentina was famous on a global level, xenophobic Spanish scholars more familiar with Argentinita's career—in part because of the longevity and respect commanded by her sister, Pilar Lopez—have nursed rescue fantasies of saving Argentinita from the harsh truth that she stole Argentina's programming, solo performance style, focus on the female body as a central core tenet of her choreography, and global emphasis on dances and music from many parts of Spain. This buried history has been fueled further by a prejudiced historiography, delaying a critical discourse surrounding both women's distinct contributions to the evolution of modernism in Spanish dance as a movement of, by, and for women.

Argentinita danced in the U.S. and South America many times, thanks to the producing efforts of the great impresario Sol Hurok and her lifelong friend Anton Dolin, both ardent supporters since 1930.[51] Unlike Argentina, who lived mostly in France, Argentinita chose to become a refugee artist, exiled from Franco's fascist dictatorship. She moved permanently to the U.S. and Mexico after 1938 and performed for the last time on 28 May 1945 at the Metropolitan Opera House. Argentinita died several months later following a complex surgical procedure. She was just forty-seven years old, one year younger than La Argentina at the time of her death.

José Greco, her dance partner, and, Pilar Lopez, her beloved sister, escorted Argentinita's body back to Madrid.

Argentinita's most seasoned works were those produced after her first New York season, made with her lifelong collaborator, García Lorca, and her lover Mejías: *El Café de Chinitas*, the result of her collaboration with Lorca after visiting the original flamenco *tablao*; *Los calles de Cadíz* for which she also hired an Incan musical trio from Peru after hearing them play at a New York restaurant; and *Capriccio Espagnol*, her celebrated collaboration with Léonide Massine and the Ballet Russe de Monte Carlo, of which a film exists. In each of these dances, critics discovered something new: Argentinita's focus on the body as the core idea, movement radiating out from the center of her body and back in. Whatever costume she wore, it was her dancing body that commanded attention, not the historic props of Spanishness—the comb, the fan, the bata de cola, the zapatos—that constituted the pictorial surface.

Female Embodiment and Populist Imagination

Argentina and Argentinita shared an uncanny, unspoken dialogue, although the two were not friends. Each was born to Spanish parents in Buenos Aires at the end of the Victorian era, although Argentina was ten years older. While Argentina was one of two siblings (her brother, José, joined the Vichy Government during World War II), Argentinita was one of four. She lost her two younger brothers in the Scarlet Fever epidemic of 1903, prompting her heartbroken parents to leave the country forever.

Both families—the Mercés and the Lópezes—settled in Madrid. Argentina was enrolled by her father in Madrid's celebrated Music Conservatory; Argentinita was enrolled by her father in private Spanish dancing lessons that, like ballet classes, took place in her teachers' homes. Both women, although trained in the Bolero School, recognized the moment in which they lived and chose the commercial over the opera stage. And both women, concurrently with Loïe Fuller and Isadora Duncan who were by then working in Parisian music and concert halls, engineered the migration of Spanish and Flamenco dance from the *café cantantes* into respected global venues: the concert hall and opera stage.

Each was a modern working woman. Each became a potent symbol for other young women: of feminist consciousness, of self-will and of self-determination. Each emerged as a solo concert artist in a distinctive way: Argentinita helped along by her musical, collaborative partnership with Lorca; Argentina in her close collaborations with Manuel de Falla and her commissions of Spanish "New School" composers and designers. Each woman danced at a time when women's suffrage was first and foremost on the minds of working women. In 1920, one year after Argentina's first solo concert in New York City, American women gained the right to vote. (They would have to wait until 1931 in Spain and 1945 in France.)

Argentina and Argentinita died young. Neither had children or time for a traditional family life. Both women lived hard lives, touring even though they knew they were ill. Argentina suffered more than a decade from rheumatic heart disease; Argentinita had cancer and refused treatment until it was too late. And each woman built and maintained dance companies, although Argentina's was responsible for dozens of salaries, while Argentinita usually performed with a single male partner—Antonio Triana, Federico Reye, Manolo Vargas, or José Greco—and her sister. Both earned enough to maintain summer homes; Argentinita's, where Carmen Amaya and family came to stay, was in Rye, New York; Argentina's in Bayonne, France.

Their aestheticization of Spanish and flamenco dance brought the female body and notions of corporeality into a discourse about feminism, national identity and exile, educating critics worldwide who came to review and, slowly, to understand the significance of their art. Written into history by a vanguardist intelligentsia, both women asserted themselves in the global rhetoric of modernism, assuring the place of dance and female embodiment beside a broader, international conversation about the place of art in human society. La Argentina's repertoire is housed today in the repertory of the Ballet Nacional de España.

Modernity and Civic Space

Argentina came of age as an artist at a time when the streets of Paris, Barcelona and New York had become a collage of word and image. An explosion of print media in the form of poster art, journals and newspapers and cubist design incorporated "daily" objects into the picture frame itself, and surfaced throughout Europe. The likenesses of La Loïe, Isadora Duncan, Josephine Baker and, by the 1920s, La Argentina— could be seen throughout Paris, in particular: in Metro stations, along city walls and park gates and in front of theaters. Motion, speed, costume design and persona could be experienced in a single glance. La Argentina quickly became a recognizable public figure, her dancing body part of the image portfolio and social space of the City of Lights. Woven into the psyche of urbanites' daily lives, her high fashion chic and noted scholarly afternoon lectures on Spanish dance were all carefully crafted to reveal a modernist ethos reflective of the city itself. Exercising significant control over her public image, she choreographed carefully how, when, and where her facsimile would appear. La Argentina's art became a celebration of the female, and Spanish dance the medium of her subjectivity and self-reflection. The surface vitality of her dancing body lifted her kinetic portraiture and her modernist sensibility away from the view of Spanish dance as a short-lived music-hall "act" and into the realm of modern art.

La Argentinita came of age in Spain, a country that was much slower to industrialize and, except for Barcelona, to take on the look, feel and sensibility of urban France. Argentinita's public image, crafted in part by her singing and, in part, by her folkloric approach to dancing, appeared less urban, more home-grown. It was this sincerity, this folkloric authenticity, that endeared her to audiences worldwide. A skilled performer in her final days, she trained the next generation of great male partners and female dancers who, thanks to her sister Pilar, sought to emulate her after her premature death. (Pilar became perhaps the finest dancer of subsequent generations.) Argentinita, less concerned with the crosscurrents of history and art, concentrated her choreographic aesthetic on the particulars of flamenco rhythm and regional dance style. And while her legacy as a populist singer would never be forgotten, the aesthetic design and choreographic rigor of her dance art never succeeded in advancing Spanish dance beyond the character roles to which she was devoted. Choreographically, Argentinita did not fundamentally transform Spanish dance from the inside out as Argentina had, who forced a reconsideration of the art form itself. Herein lies the real difference between these two magnificent female artists.

Notes

1. Jean Baudrillard, *America* (London: Verso Books, 1988), 27–28.
2. On the subject of power and dancing, please see: Susan Foster, *Choreography & Narrative: Ballet's Staging of Story and Desire* (Bloomington: Indiana University Press, 1996).
3. Gitana(o)s had a relationship to Franco, fascism and the Spanish Civil War. While Gitanos continued to suffer terribly economically, socio-politically (in terms of citizenship) and culturally after 1939, they ironically joined forces with the Falange. For a deepened perspective on this complex issue, see: Paul Preston.
4. On the subject of Israel Galván's recent work, please read: Joan Acocella, "The Refusé," *The New Yorker* (17 March 2014).
5. On the subject of the West African notion of coolness, please see: Robert Farris Thompson, "African Art in Motion," *African Forum* 2 (1966).
6. For a deep analysis of the nationalist modernist hegemony of Alfred Stieglitz and the transatlantic visits of American artists in Paris, see: Sophie Lévie, ed., *A Transatlantic Avant-Garde: American Artists in Paris, 1918–1939* (Berkeley: University of California Press, 2004).
7. Clement Greenberg, "Modernist Painting," in *The New Art: A Critical Anthology*, ed. Gregory Battcock (New York: E.P. Dutton & Co., 1966), 101; Greenberg, "Counter Avant-Garde," the Adolph Ullman Lecture given at Brandeis University, 13 May 1970, 16.
8. Ibid. I add to Greenberg's definitions of modernism in painting and sculpture the significance of Spanish modernism and the writings of Guillaume Apollinaire, who revealed to Picasso in a series of surrealist writings that the master's Spanishness embodied his modernism. Apollinaire revealed Picasso's intertwined Hispanism with machismo revealed in his repeated focus on the bullfight—*la corrida*—and its gendered violence; the goring of the horse (female) by the bull (male) whose horns symbolize the crescent moons (cyclical nature of the moon and woman). It was, Apollinaire argued, Picasso's Hispanic masculinity that was the root source of the artist's modernist sensibility: his use of fragmentation, of dream-state in which women are loved and raped simultaneously.
9. Martin was appointed by *The New York Times* in 1927 and served as chief dance critic until his retirement in 1963.
10. John Martin, *America Dancing: The Background and Personalities of the Modern Dance* (New York: Dodge Publishing Company, 1936), 38–41.
11. For more on American modernism and modern dance, please see: Bruce Robertson, "American Modernism and Dance: Arthur B. Davies *Dances* 1915," Text Curation, Detroit Institute of Art, catalogue forthcoming.
12. John Martin, *The Dance* (New York: Tudor Publishing Company, 1946), 113.
13. Ibid., 116.
14. Ibid., 121.
15. Ibid., 118.
16. An important element that contributed to the rich artistic evolution of early twentieth century Spanish dance as a modernist form of art on the international stage: new music. The Spanish "New School" composers—Isáac Albeníz, Enrique Granados, Manuel de Falla, Joaquín Turina, Ernesto Halffter, Joaquín Nin—and Spanish/Gitano guitarists Andres Segovia, Carlos Montoya and Sabicas offered Spanish dance artists who knew their work a treasure trove of new composition that served as inspiration for new dance. {Segovia and, later, Montoya and Sabicas are credited with introducing New York City audiences and critics to the instrumental richness and abstract expression of the Spanish guitar in their Carnegie Hall performances.}
17. John Martin, "Marvelous Dancer Is La Argentina," *The New York Times*, 10 November 1928.
18. La Argentina hired Fernando Enrique Arbós as her conductor and musical collaborator for her company, Les Ballets Espagnols. The two worked together from the late 1920s until her premature death in 1936, enjoying a rich and fruitful attention to the music of Manuel de Falla, Isáac Albeniz and others in the Spanish "New School" and to the significance of contemporary Spanish symphonic music.
19. Herschel Brickell, "A Spanish Poet in New York," *Virginia Quarterly Review* 21/3 (Summer 1945), 6–7, www.vqronline.org/essay/spanish-poet-new-york (accessed November 22, 2014). Brickell also comments upon a significant fact that might indeed have affected Spanish post–Civil War opinion of *La Argentina*. He claims that Adolfo Salazar, ethnomusicologist and Lorca's travel companion, "argued passionately about the art of Argentina" which they thought "déracinée because of the dancer's long periods of dancing in France." Salazar espoused a xenophobic, post-majismo, anti–French argument that "everything Spanish was corrupted by French influence." I had not given this idea much weight in my book on Antonia Mercé but I now believe that, perhaps, Salazar was more of a force in the erasure of La Argentina from Spanish music and dance history than previously thought. What is odd, or perhaps ignorant, about Salazar's anti–French argument is the fact that Manuel de Falla (1876–1946), whose musical composition Salazar greatly admired, moved to Paris in 1907, remaining until 1914 when he returned to non-aligned Spain where he would compose *El*

Amor Brujo in 1915. Falla wanted to live in the avant-garde capital of the world, beside Maurice Ravel and Claude Debussy, whom he greatly admired. In Paris, Falla met his own countryman, Isáac Albeníz. In 1907, he was introduced to Sergei Diaghilev and Igor Stravinsky whose composition he worshipped. Once he admitted that Stravinsky's composition was more "modern" than his own.

20. Andrés Segovia, José Iturbi, Carlos Montoya and Sabicas all toured America at this time, introducing packed houses to the refined art of the Spanish guitar. In just a few years, Segovia had performed for over 5000 people at Town Hall.

21. Lorca sang in his Whitmanesque free verse style, unearthing profound and magical connections between the plight of the African Americans and that of the Spanish Gitano.

22. For a thorough discussion of Duncan's "creation of an American self" divorced from Africanism, please read: Ann Daly, *Done Into Dance: Isadora Duncan in America* (Middletown: Wesleyan University Press, 2002), 216–219.

23. For a wonderful discussion of the African modernist root of Flamenco, please read: K. Meira Goldberg's essay on *Le Tumulte Noire* in this volume.

24. The concept of semiology comes from the Swiss semiotician Ferdinand de Saussure's *Course in General Linguistics* (1916) and is enlarged by the French-born philosopher Roland Barthes, in *S/Z* (1970). For evidence of historians' orientalizing of Spanish dance, see: J.E. Crawford Flitch, *Modern Dancing and Dancers* (Philadelphia: J.B. Lippincott Company, 1912) and Ted Shawn, *The American Ballet* (New York: Henry Holt & Co., 1926); Havelock Ellis, *The Soul of Spain* (London: Constable, 1926).

25. Marcia B. Siegel, "Modern Dance–Tradition in Process," in *The Living Dance: An Anthology of Essays on Movement and Culture,* ed. Judith Chazin-Bennahum (Dubuque: Kendall/Hunt, 2007), 92–101.

26. It is unclear whether or not La Argentina ever saw the Ballets Russes' production of *The Rite of Spring*, as she left for Russia several days before the 13 May opening of the work. She may have seen a rehearsal or rehearsals as the ballet had been in rehearsal for the preceding months.

27. The 1915 premiere of *El Amor Brujo* played unsuccessfully to audiences and critics alike. The score contained long, burdensome sections of spoken text that interfered with the flow of the music and dramaturgy. Audiences grew restless and critics assailed the work for being clunky and narratively disastrous. Argentina, who had studied music at Madrid's Conservatory and who had graduated with a degree in music and castanet-playing, had taught herself orchestration. Over a ten-year period, with Falla's permission, she cut down the score, took out the spoken dialogue, and condensed the action to dancing scenes only. When she premiered the work on 29 June 1925 at Paris' Opéra-Comique theater, Falla conducted the orchestra. They received standing ovations. The French and Spanish press lauded Manuel de Falla's composition and La Argentina's choreographic synthesis and re-orchestration. For a more complete historiography of *El Amor Brujo*, see: Ninotchka Devorah Bennahum, *Antonia Mercé, "La Argentina": Flamenco & the Spanish Avant-Garde* (Hanover: Wesleyan University Press, 2000), 76–103.

28. Gertrude Stein, *The Making of Americans: Being a History of a Family's Progress* (Paris: Contact Editions, 1923), 62.

29. John Martin, *The Dance*, 126.

30. Ibid., 131.

31. Ibid.

32. *El Universal* (13 June 1915). Scrapbooks: Fundacíon Juan March. Madrid.

33. John Martin, "The Dance: La Argentina," *The New York Times* (23 November 1928).

34. H. Birbaum, "The Argentina Plays the Maxine Elliott Theater," *Musical America* (19 February 1916).

35. For an excellent examination on the percussive nature of Dadaist assemblage, please see: Jody Blake, *Le Tumulte Noire, in Modernist Art and Popular Entertainment in Jazz-Age Paris, 1900–1930* (University Park: Pennsylvania State University Press, 1999).

36. Ted Shawn, *One Thousand and One Night Stands*, 227. Manuscript. Jacob's Pillow Archives.

37. Mejías was gored in the bullring 11 August 1934. He died two days later in Madrid. He was forty-two years old. La Argentinita was devastated. Mejías, although married, was the second love of her life and the second *toreador* to die in the ring. In 1935, Argentinita left Spain for Argentina, to dance in Buenos Aires' famed Teatro Colon in whose lobby a giant portrait of Argentina hung.

38. Correspondence, Harriet de Onís to Mildred Adams, 7 April 1968. Papers of Mildred Adams. Hispanic Society of America. Lorca and La Argentinita had met in Madrid in 1919. He offered her the part of the White Butterfly in his play *El maleficio de la mariposa (The Butterfly's Evil Spell)*, which premiered 22 March 1922 at the Teatro Eslava.

39. José Luis Navarro García, "La Argentinita," *Historia del Baile Flamenco* vol. II (Seville: Signatura Ediciones, 2008), 130–131.

40. Mildred Adams.

41. José Luis Navarro García, 131.

42. La Argentinita Clippings File [La Argentinita MWEZ + N.C. 10, 670]. The Jerome Robbins Dance Division, New York Public Library for the Performing Arts, Lincoln Center.

43. Montgomery Wright, "U.S. Tourists Sway Mexico," *New York Sun* (11 February 1942).

44. Robert Sylvestre, "La Argentinita Speaking," *Daily News* (3 March 1942).
45. "Dance Notes," *New York Herald Tribune* (14 June 1942).
46. Ted Shawn quoted by Walter Terry, *Dance in America* (New York: Hermitage House, 1955).
47. Edwin Denby, *Dance Writings*, 10 April 1944 (New York: Alfred A. Knopf, 1986), 209.
48. Ibid., 103.
49. John Martin, "The Dance: Argentinita; In Praise of the Spanish Artist on Her Return (22 February 1942).
50. In a 1975 televised interview, José Greco acknowledged his debt to La Argentina. See: Conversation with Paul Haakon and José Greco [MGZTL 4-651]. Moving Image Archive, Jerome Robbins Dance Division, New York Public Library for the Performing Arts, Lincoln Center.
51. Anton Dolin, "La Argentinita: A Tribute," *Dance Magazine* (November 1945); Sol Hurok, *S. Hurok Presents* (New York: Hermitage House, 1953), 53–58, 204.

Part III—Disobedient Bodies: Flamenco in the "New" World

Normative Aesthetics and Cultural Constructions in Flamenco Dance
Female and Gitano Bodies as Legitimizers of Tradition

CRISTINA CRUCES-ROLDÁN
Translation by K. Meira Goldberg

Dance embodies the most universal image of flamenco. A fascinating archetype, at once colorful and tragic, sensual and profound, it transports us toward an aesthetic of unbridled, elemental passion. Nonetheless, flamenco's attractive and romantic halo is, from an analytical viewpoint, mostly inexact. Flamenco contains passion and reason—spontaneity and discipline—creativity and reproduction—emotion and learning by the book (see Figure 1).

Baile (flamenco dance) helps us dissect this simplistic opposition between unscientific dreaming and excessive intellectualization.[1] The body becomes a fundamental theoretical category, holding the immediacy of dance and providing a basic system of cultural classification.[2] The body is at once a formal icon and a space of ideological, historical, and political production and reproduction. From this perspective, flamenco dance, as artistic manifestation and aesthetic object, is also a social construction.

We pause here to consider gender and ethnicity as legitimizing principles of sexed and racialized normativity in flamenco dance as art. Flamenco's interpretive modes have been internalized as naturalizing expressions of identity for man/woman and Gitano/not Gitano. They have provided continuity and stability to the plastic forms perpetuated among individuals and groups. They have been, in this sense, normative consensuses and performed imaginaries (representations)—but also arenas of social action.[3]

In what exact moments and in what exact ways did "flamenco," as an assemblage of identity codes, emerge? Two fundamental dimorphisms help describe the codes underlying what is considered "traditional" flamenco. The first, applied to sexuality, refers to a canon of "masculine" and "feminine" flamenco dance. The second, attributed to the Gitano dances, gestures toward spaces of resistance that generate competition with respect to other aesthetic and interpretive conventions. These signs were operational from the moment flamenco was born as performance. Now, they are embedded in interesting processes of redefinition and reinterpretation which, lacking space, I will not address here.

The Birth of Flamenco, as Disobedience of Tradition

A brief history of flamenco—no more than two centuries old—confirms its emergence out of the hybrid and colorful anchorage of varied musical cultures layered in the historical sediments of Andalusia. As the southernmost region of the Iberian Peninsula, Andalusia always oriented toward the Mediterranean and the Atlantic rather than toward northern Europe. Andalusian music and dance grew out of a blend of harmonic keys derived from ancient Mediterranean scales—the basis of the Andalusian scale—as from Middle Eastern modes and melismatic melodies. It recalls some chordophones and percussion instruments of *música andalusí* (the school of Arabic music developed in ninth- to fourteenth-century Islamic Andalusia).[4] Flamenco is an alloy of medieval ecclesiastic music, the Spanish songbook and the regional folklore of the Iberian Peninsula, and the legacy of Gitano performance. Even the dances and music of enslaved Africans disseminated by cultural exchange with America lent various movements and sounds to the musical system of flamenco. Flamenco continues to renew its syntax, accent, and grammar. In a globalized world, interpreters negotiate a delicate balance between "tradition" and the experimental modes that give flamenco's language new meaning.

Figure 1: Ivan Vargas performing in Los Veranos del Corral, Granada, Spain, 2013 (© Joss Rodriguez, all rights reserved).

But that which we call "tradition"—classical, orthodox flamenco, or *flamenco puro*—was in its day just another form of disobedience. A gamut of popular and Gitano songs, instrumental modes, and dances preceded flamenco, which was a fully commercialized artistic genre by the mid-nineteenth century.

Theaters and places where the working class could socialize (*colmaos* and *ventas*) and shows at the caves of the Gitanos in Granada were, during the eighteenth and nineteenth centuries, privileged performance contexts. At the height of Romanticism, echoes and sounds constructed from the early modern stereotypes of Gitanos were exalted as the height of authenticity. The Andalusian aristocracy and bourgeoisie frequently hired Gitano artists to entertain at private parties, as had been customary long before flamenco appeared as a separate genre (Gitanos were celebrated for, among other things, their dances and their fiestas, as Cervantes documented in 1613 with his novel *La Gitanilla*). In the nineteenth-century theaters of Spain, more and less well-known *boleras* (Spanish ballerinas) danced in variety shows that included diverse genres ranging from flamenco to circus acts. Dance academies and ballrooms served as performance spaces and modes of transmission for the *bailes del país*—the national Spanish dances.

In other words, "flamenco" as we know it today was not an independent invention but a reinterpretation of existing dance, song, and music. These subgenres had been previously accessible only in coarser venues or as part of communal festivities: popular couples dances (like *fandangos* and *seguidillas*), *bailes de candíl* (dances lit by oil lamps), boleros, Afro-American musics and dances, Gitano dances, and more.[5] But flamenco found a place onstage as a new musical and artistic system, a new model, a new commercial code, attractive to those who wished to pay admission. The word "flamenco" appeared precisely to denominate this new art, unique and differentiated—although not completely disassociated—from previous forms.

Flamenco crystalized as an independent genre in the *cafés cantantes* of Andalusia, establishments that imitated Parisian and European models and that soon became a presence in Spain's booming cities. The cafés, where *cante* (flamenco song), baile (flamenco dance), and *toque* (flamenco guitar) were differentiated from the festive and rhythmic music and dances of communal, public celebrations and not focused on individual artistic practice, were the setting for the emergence of the first known flamenco artists. A new interpretation of the old rules governing what is often called "*cantes y bailes preflamencos*"—songs and dances that lead to flamenco—arose.

But the cafés also facilitated a hierarchization of social roles that, at least for Spain, has situated cante at the heart of flamenco's symbolic nucleus.[6] In this new hierarchy, *cantaores* (flamenco singers)—usually men—were the principal protagonists of artistic celebrity. A structured system of vocal styles, or *palos*, took the place of the original rhythmic songs, which had been oriented toward dance. These sung creations ennobled and individualized musical expression. On the one hand, structures were refined: the cantes grew slower, losing their rhythmicity and permitting more elaborate vocal expression, and they adjusted harmonically to the guitar with greater refinement. On the other hand, these artists elevated the cante, distilling a polished repertory from "bastard" and "vulgar" popular forms. This new music was quickly enlisted into the budding market for recordings. For a short while there were singers who accompanied themselves on the guitar; this custom has been almost completely lost in the professionalization of flamenco, which has separated these roles.

Cuadros (a semi-circle of seated performers framing and providing musical accompaniment for a soloist) were the most common presentational model for flamenco groups.[7] Made up of a guitarist, one or two singers, and various *bailaoras* (female flamenco dancers), the cuadros in images and photographs of the period document a notably increased feminine presence in dance.[8]

When, as a result of individualized interpretations by celebrated artists, flamenco dance acquired choreographic structures, costume, and imagistic protocols, it was in an abstract rather than a narrative form. Like cante, flamenco dances are based on rhythmic, melodic, and tonal structures (palos) and not "stories," as in ballet. An allusive set is not necessary: the cuadro is divided into artists *de alante* (those who stand out front) and *de atrás* (those who stand behind, as accompanists).

Flamenco can be considered as part of the vanguard of theatrical innovation that shaped other forms of modern dance. These new ways of dancing shed realistic staging in order to reveal the "pure" body, and the performative space was the only container of movement and gesture, which had been stripped of artifice (see Figure 2).[9] Bailaoras who danced *alegrías, soleares, tangos,* or *garrotín* faced the onstage protagonism that potentiated the iconic charge of their bodies alone and without adornment. Unashamed movement, brimming with sensuality, made the bailaoras into the disquieting focus of consumerist gaze. They evoked a mind-body imaginary of deviation from social normativity and from virtue—which made reference to an ethos of unbridled sexuality.

Flamenco women epitomized the physicalization of art, a seductive visual attraction for male audiences who perhaps hoped that this "carnal" performance would not be limited to dance. Urban workers, livestock traders, libertines, soldiers, nocturnal aristocrats, students, and aficionados of different stripes frequented the urban cafés cantantes, often visiting nearby brothels or "houses of ill repute" as well. "Moral" women were excluded as spectators and as consumers of the diversions, environments, and services offered by the "ladies of the night'" or—significantly—"artful women" (*mujeres del arte*).

The women's dance signified at once a transgression of social convention and also a "technique," in the sense in which Mauss used the word: the way human beings learn

Figure 2: Susana Lupiañez Pinto, "La Lupi," in a posture that embodies the curves and adornments of the "baile de mujer," 2013 (courtesy photographer Levent Erutku).

and know "how to use" their bodies.[10] The "artistic" labor and the corporeal dispositions of the new flamenco esthetic became enduring models, incorporated systems managed in the body of the bailaora, in the same sense that Bourdieu applies corporeality to the concept of *habitus*.[11]

Without doubt, this labor lacked prestige. These bailaoras—women, artists, flamencas—danced in establishments censured for their decadence, indecency, and amenability to wine, prostitution, gambling, and rowdiness. And often they were Gitanas. With the exception of famous bailaoras and renowned dancers such as "La Macarrona" (1870–1947), they were considered the dregs of society. The expansion of the flamenco cafés happened, for the most part, at the expense of women, who offered an abundant, interchangeable labor force, and whose vulnerability lay in the least esteemed members of the cuadros.[12]

From this moment on, the normative aesthetics of baile have emanated from two models: On the one hand was the orthodoxy of sexual norms. The birth of the *baile de hombre* (man's dance) and the *baile de mujer* (woman's dance) broke with the parallelisms and consonances that had homogenized pre-flamenco dances. Maestros and maestras—dance teachers—especially from the Sevillian academies, played an important role in formulating and reproducing these new forms, giving birth to *Escuela Sevillana*, flamenco's Seville School. On the other hand, Gitanos and Gitanas protagonized a series of key interpretations that, at least partly, blurred sexual protocol. They developed an expressive and selective "corpus" that continues to be recognized as a dialogic voice in an art whose plurality is reflected in its every performance.

Gender Normativity: Dancing de Cintura para Arriba *(from the Waist Up) or* de Cintura para Abajo *(from the Waist Down)*

The body is an ethnographic map of cultural representations. Theories of anthropology of the body help us understand the specifics of social and historiographic construction in these corporeal geographies, these "maps of power and of identity" that express characterizations, valuations, and essentializing hierarchies in direct and apprehensible form.[13] From this theoretical perspective, concepts such as those developed in Anthony Synnott's *The Body Social*, and in the work of Jeffrey Weeks, Thomas Laqueur, and David Le Breton, reference the body as an historical category. Michel Foucault theorized the body as a political category, and Pierre Bourdieu used the concept of a corporeal "hexis": a repertory of ideas that reveal processes of incorporation and reproduction of embodied systems of socially legitimized behavior.[14] In addition, the notion of "sex-gender systems" reveals the constructed character of gendered social roles.[15] The profoundly gendered roles of flamenco's Andalusian birthplace expressed biological differences between men and women through a dimorphism that functioned historically as a cognitive cartography dominating flamenco bodies. From an etic perspective, we are dealing with cultural systems. But in the emic discourse of the flamencos, masculine and feminine bodies and ways of dancing would be "authentic" somaticizations. The "baile de mujer" (women's baile) and the "baile de hombre" (men's baile) would be the *inevitable* physical testimony and technical strategies responding to behavior, norms, social roles, and even psychological dispositions implicit in the fact of "being a woman" or "being a man."

The romantic opposition of "body-emotion-femininity" vs. "mind-reason-masculinity" was systemized as a basic duality in the emergent sexual division of flamenco labor. The voice and music were the jurisdiction of men, and the criteria of hypercorporeality condemned women to using their bodies as the ultimate frontier of art and professionalism, which meant, simply, that they oriented their careers toward dance. Female singers (cantaoras) were in the minority, in similar proportion to male dancers (bailaores).[16] From the outset, there was a romantic avocation of "femininity" as the essence closest to nature, reproduction, and the body. The body would be made flesh—emotionality, irrationality, intuition, and communication as collective, communal.

We have already situated the first flamencas in the sub-genre of imagery and of movement. But in newly born flamenco, there was also an opportunity for exercising analytic, reasoned, objective, ideational, and cultural capacities, privileged in this social and historical context as "naturally" masculine. It was subordinated by a Cartesian duality that values reason, mind, and consciousness over emotion, intuition, and passion. Voice and music were essentialized as the territory of the "real" professionals: male cantaores and *tocaores*.[17] Composition, creativity, and technique would be "masculine" attributes demonstrating the control of mind over body: individual, not interchangeable, not communal.

The center and the periphery, the trunk and the extremities, are the continents that ground sexual dimorphism. Even within the baroque *gesto* (gesture) and *mueca* (facial expression) of this sentimental art (*del sentimiento*), women took on soft and sinuous, insinuatingly carnal attitudes, in contrast to the linearity, verticality, precision, and strength of bailaores.[18]

Abdomen, arms, hands, bust, head, and face hold the greatest formal density in the "glossary of the body" of the female flamenco dancer—what flamencos call dancing *de cintura para arriba* (from the waist up).[19] The arms hold the essence of the image's loveliness. They are adorned by shoulder shakes, labyrinthine paths, semicircles of the wrists, and arabesque hands that all contribute to a serpentine and curvaceous figure. Gesture, attitude, and the lowered head round out the seductive and provocative arsenal of the feminine dance, conveying coquetry and even a certain boldness.

But the woman's dance articulates an intermediate space between empowerment, exhibitionism, and patriarchal control and domination.[20] The first tool for manipulating female bodies is their appearance, which makes them into idealized erotic objects.[21] Traditional costume and accessories are decorative modes that support the metonymy of morality with physicality. Sleeves and shawls hide the bust. But the greatest symbolic density is hidden beneath rounded hips and wide thighs, symbols of the fecundity of *bailaoras flamencas*—in contrast to the androgynous slim hips and narrow sexuality, seemingly incapable of reproduction, of *bailarinas clásicas* (classical dancers). Swaying and circling pelvic movements are permitted—the genital focus remaining always hidden beneath colorfully patterned skirts with gores and decorated with ruffles, lace, ribbons, and petticoats. In the movement of the flamenco costume, the leg is barely glimpsed, granting access to this focal point of desire only in the imagination.

Flamenco skirts may be lifted to the knee, but the skin is protected by flesh-colored fishnet stockings. Color dominates, and in the image of the bailaora necklaces, earrings, combs, flowers, and bracelets proliferate, symbolizing an anxious expressive overload.[22] To all this is added an excess of makeup, highlighting eyes and lips, and the almost sculptural demands of hairdos. In the dance de cintura para arriba (from the waist up), the shawl, the castanets, the hat, and the fan are the exclusive signifiers of the female body, functioning as hypercorporealized extensions of the arms, the head, and the hands. With the technique of violent dorsal movements used to move it, the *bata de cola* (skirt with a long train) is not conceived of as an accessory, or an external element of the baile, but rather as an extension of the body.[23] The bata is literally "incorporated": it does not embellish the body but alters its proportions, becoming part of a surreally elongated torso and legs.

Although the Seville School favors dance *de la raíz a la copa*, from the ground up, rising from the roots to the tips of the branches, the aesthetic of flamenco dance is "heavy." Concentric movements seek ground, gravity, in contrast to the aerial aspirations of classical dance. Today, flamenco dancers shape their bodies through diet, exercise, and even plastic surgery (a new iteration of "biopower" anticipated by Foucault). But thick flamenco dancers have always been accepted, their careers unfolding as their bodies change, growing bigger or smaller, giving birth, never bound by the rigid anatomical standards of ballet.[24]

In the woman's dance, arching and twisting radiate through all movements of the waist and back. The waist constantly rotates, as in *cambrés* (side bends) and *vueltas quebradas* and *vueltas de pecho* (turns bent at the waist, with the upper body rotating at an angle to the axis of the rotating lower body). The dancing image of the flamenca, as the Andalusian woman was for writers of the Romantic era, is that of spiraling flesh that seems to "have no bones."[25] It is the image of a dancer who, despite flamenco's aggressive bodily stance, dances innocuously, causing no damage and seemingly without effort.

Finally, in the stylized Escuela Sevillana, women limit their footwork to *marcajes* (marking steps), timid stamps in *llamadas* (calls), *carrerillas* (little runs forward), and *escobillas* (footwork sections), emphasizing musicality and refinement over virtuosity. In general, the codes for feminine dance dictate that women limit their footwork to minor exercises or small details, respecting and generously adorning the singing, closing without disturbing the ensemble. The feminine canon is to *bailar al cante*—to dance the song, answer the verses, harmonically embellishing the melodies of the guitar.

In opposition to the fleshiness, the bends and curves, the seduction and decorativeness of women's dance, masculine baile demands total exertion and strength, marking line, angle, and bone (see Figure 3). Bailaores hold their arms at shoulder height in opposition across the body (flamenco's third position), in front of the heart (*a media altura*), or symmetrically overhead (fifth position). They avoid roundness and prefer zigzag, tilted geometries of arms and legs. Their hands do not spiral or pinch, they make fists, with half-open palms (*media palma*), or with open palms. They produce sound: *pitos* (snapping fingers), *palmas* (hand clapping), and body percussion are integral to the masculine dance. The stable and precise structure of the bailaor is sustained by his muscularity and by an austere and monochrome costume that nonetheless displays more than it hides. The pants of the bailaor are tight to his legs and to what is between his legs, highlighted and protuberant. This contrasts with the bailaora, whose voluminous costume restricts her mobility and prevents her from making big movements, promoting instead intimacy and movements that curl inward. Even though flamenco tends to be introverted, the codes for classicism in bailaores allow for more expansive movement. Acrobatic jumps, *vueltas de tornillo o de tacón* (turns on the heel), movements with strong impact, and *desplantes* (in flamenco dance, a striking step) speak to the structural concepts of masculine flamenco dance. This contrasts with the more decorative use of the limbs and of accessories as theatrical devices in the feminine dance. Hats, capes, and canes are rarely used in the baile de hombre (man's dance), which concentrates instead on the armature of the body, the figure, and percussion.

The masculine play of the feet—*zapateaos*, or footwork—concentrates the attention on the dancer: it is an egocentric, individualistic exercise. It displays determination, potency, spiritedness, firmness, rigor, and efficiency and precision of *compás* (flamenco rhythmic schemas), along with countertimes, stamps, combinations of metatarsal, heel, and toe tips, *látigos* (a sounded double brush of the ball of the foot out and in, similar to a shuffle in tap dance), and accelerations. Sound, as much as image, is the aesthetic basis for baile en hombre, described by flamencos as *de cintura para abajo* (from the waist down).[26] One of the transgressions most criticized by flamenco "purists" who advocate strict sexual dimorphism is the generalized use of zapateado by bailaoras, with its wealth of desplantes and percussive exuberance.

Figure 3: Manuel Liñán performing in Los Veranos del Corral, Granada, Spain, 2014 (© Joss Rodriguez, all rights reserved).

Gitanos and Gitanas in Baile Flamenco

Nativism and genetic determinism have sustained the reading of sexualized dance as rule anchored by nature. An analogous essentialization has become dogma for the *baile gitano*.

The historicized construction of this "corporeal ethnic-ness" leads us to the originating germ of *flamenquería*—flamenco-ness. The word "flamenco" has functioned since the mid-nineteenth century as an analog for "Gitano," and it is possible that this association was the reason for the metonymy of the term. Gitanos, a minority population in Andalusia (although greater concentrations of Gitanos live in Andalusia than in the rest of Spain), are a symbolic and perhaps also a statistic majority in flamenco history.[27] Gitanos *caseros* (homebodies, or settled Gitano populations) have long been part of Andalusian neighborhoods, towns, and cities such as Jerez de la Frontera, Granada, and Seville that have high flamenco density.

Since Spain's Golden Age in the sixteenth century, Gitanos have been the essential stereotypes embodied in music and dance. This has been propagated in great measure as a beguiling stereotype by romantic and *costumbrista* (nativist) texts since the eighteenth century.[28] Nonetheless, between their settlement in Spain at the end of the fifteenth century and the last proclamation declared against them in 1783, they were continuously stigmatized because of their customs, their endogamy, and their looks, and for being practitioners of witchcraft and fortune-telling. They were described as diabolical, thieving, beggars, alien to Catholicism and social norms, incestuous, and even cannibalistic. These asocial habits were ascribed to Gitanos, in an exercise in simplification, among other marginalized minorities such as Moriscos (descendants of Islamic-Andalusians who were able to remain in Spain from 1492 to about 1609 by converting to Christianity) and Afro-Iberians. The dances of all these groups were equally characterized as primitive, natural, and lascivious, and were often prohibited. Gitanos, Moriscos, and "negros" were not Church or State. Their bodies were marked, racialized. They represented defining borders with respect to the unracialized "white" bodies that, by the nineteenth century, would define the national citizenry.[29] This was the century in which Orientalism aggregated with the hierarchized and exclusionary discourses of early modern colonialism. This is a phenomenon, as Edward Said, author of the seminal 1978 book *Orientalism*, took pains to note, which "is better grasped as a set of constraints upon and limitations of thought than it is simply as a positive doctrine."[30]

The Gitanos of the *zambras* (performances in Gitano homes in the caves of the Sacromonte neighborhood) in Granada were the perfect synthesis of this romantic image of Andalusia: the myth of the cave in industrial civilization, the last vestige of Arab history in Europe, the captivating enclave of an unredeemed and tribal past that, seen from today's perspective, had already become one of the first tourist centers of contemporary Andalusia. Who better than the Gitanos—shameless and indecorous as they were defined, indomitable, and marked by their physical features, their skin, their dirtiness, and their clothing—to embody the feral archetype of racial purity? Already in descriptions dating from before flamenco existed as a named form of performance, we perceive a Gitano aesthetic normativity applied to dance. This is masterfully exemplified in a poster from 1781 announcing a performance in a tavern in the town of Lebrija: "El demonio duerme en el cuerpo de las gitanas y se despierta con la zarabanda." (The devil sleeps in the bodies of the Gypsy women and wakes with the zarabanda.)[31] The idea of dance as a natural locus of sin highlights the understanding of the "savage" Gitano body as an uncontrollable territory. Classical rationality, political nationalism, and geostrategic colonialism would censure its damned yet fascinating impulses, which spurned the corporeal expectations of procreation and labor of economic liberalism.

That the liberated and Dionysian imaginary envelops the Gitano-ist halo should not lead us to abandon the search for normative consensus on the Gitano ways of dancing. And I use the plural intentionally, because there is no *one* Gitano way of dancing. In fact, one of the foremost representatives of the Seville, or classical, school of flamenco, was Pastora Imperio (1887–1979)—a Gitana. But we can indeed note confluences. Some are keys that are difficult to codify within the closed schemas of the stage and of sexual dimorphism, whose traces have elicited danced reproductions, recreations, and inventions, by bailaoras and bailaores Gitanos, and imitated by those who are not Gitanos.

In the context of the "hypersexualization" of the generic codes of baile, we may speak as well of a "hyperracialized" Gitano flamenco aesthetic that resists and even impugns categories such as technique, style, discipline, virtuosity, appearance, order, and control. The body acquires a capacity for action ("agency," in Gell's words) that bets on spontaneity, radicalism, defiance, intuition, baroque style, and chaos.[32]

A well-defined aesthetic hides beneath this apparent temerity and freedom. In the first measure, Gitano baile is concentrated around the compás, the articulating axis of repertory defined by the hemiola styles (soleares, *seguiriyas*) and the *festero* forms such as *bulerías* and tangos.[33] The compás—more than the unfolding sinuosity or the gestural insinuation—functions for Gitanos and Gitanas as a fundamental mnemonic rule, which imbues its flamenco dynamic with certainty.

Sexual dimorphism becomes less potent in the baile Gitano, where the permeability of movements and steps is proven, and is principally drawn from "masculine" morphology. It is not by chance, for example, that among the first dancers to repudiate conventional femininity by dressing as men on stage, with pants, boots, and a cropped jacket were Gitanas. These artists always seem to resist the limitations in mobility imposed by flamenco feminine vestments, favoring instead the simplicity, dark colors, and unadorned character of male dress, and concentrating on the most fundamental elements: the baile and its emotional expression. Men and women have developed the techniques of zapateado, and have expanded and legitimized the percussion of pitos, palmas, and golpes within the women's dance. In festero dances such as bulerías, acrobatics, sleight of hand, and daring bravura are danced with jumps, riffs, twisted legs, footwork, and vigorous countertime—movements of the pelvis, play of weight, and far-fetched postures. Impelled by the expressionism inscribed in the corporeal "hexis," which values excitement and sensation over sensitivity, the descriptive excellence of arms and hands has historically been de-emphasized in the aesthetic of Gitana bailaoras, who have always used pitos, open hands, and hands closed in fists.

In the sexualized canon of the baile, women's use of space is ideally limited to a few turns about the stage, and to a very circumscribed set of dynamics in terms of choreographic structure. In contrast, the unequivocal stylistic mark of the baile Gitano is its great interpretive density, its ability to concentrate expression *hacia dentro*—that is, with an inward-moving focus—and, simultaneously, to explode outward with a great range and amplitude of steps and centrifugal movements. Both lines of energetic directionality are always contained within the template of compás, which is the sound and the strength of bailaoras.

Tearing oneself apart, coming undone, is a mark of Gitano style that shocks and impresses, but it smoothly negotiates the contentions of the body. *Bailar en una loseta* (literally, "to dance on a single tile") is to dance in a small space, but it refers as well to the concentrated power onstage of stillness, the solemn and profound artistic strategies that charge the silence of Gitano baile with energy and magnetism. An essential aspect of its normativity is the ability to *mandar*—to command the stage, utilizing challenging figures, with defiant movements of the head held high and the torso thrust forward; it is power onstage, an expression of empowerment and resistance.

In any of the Gitano registers, interpretive expressivity functions as a stormy window into shock. Gitano dance opts not for stylistic perfection but for emotional excitement. It implies a search for something other than beauty: to loosen one's hair, to kick the elegant bata out of the way as though it were a rag, to renounce theatrical frontality, to use dance in a Dionysiac worship of the song. It situates the Gitano modes—already permeating the flamenco genre—within representational routines that advocate for a "body in action" as social, ceremonial, and integral fact, not as simply a professional demonstration.

If the bailaoras Gitanas, without abandoning models of so-called "femininity," can genuinely adopt ways of dancing that orthodoxy would dub "masculine," the reverse is not true, at least not in the protocol of the *baile largo*—the long, formal dance. In the *fiesta*—the private party—in what is considered to be the *baile corto*—short dance, domestic, and nonacademic (especially as practiced by Gitanos), provocation and diversion legitimize communal bodies, with inadvertent transferences between "femininity" and "masculinity."

The tangos de Triana, nearly lost because of the forced expulsion of the Gitanos from that neighborhood, contain the inheritance of those *bailes de negros* (Afro-Iberian dances) in which men and women shake their hips and their thighs, touch each others' genitalia, and share the voluptuous and "indecent" charge of the fiesta.[34] The llamadas of the bulerías of Jerez, the marcajes, and the ending *patás* (*patadas*: fancy kicks) permit male bailaores to move their shoulders suggestively, bend at the waist, move the hips, arch the arms, and rotate hands in morphologies recognized as being shared with women. Often, tangos and *patás por bulerías* are expressive fictions transferred onto the stage, dramatizations of this enveloping communal ritual and symbolic communion, with whose archetype we began this essay.

A Note on Bending the Rules

The principals of gender and ethnicity regulating flamenco dance, codified through the dialogic contingencies of style, interpreter, and tradition, have in recent decades been faced with new impertinences. Bailaores and bailaoras seek alternatives, distancing themselves from timeworn social and aesthetic models. Embracing their lineage, some reinterpret the past; others rebel against formal impositions. The most radical, the truly "sacrilegious," resist sex-gender and race-ethnicity normativity with intellectual valor, upsetting traditional forms to the point of destroying them.[35] The bodies of bailaores and bailaoras attain in this context an active character of "lived bodies"—individually antihegemonic. These transgressions, this "embodiment," as defined by Csordas, show that, as Foucault said, power relations inscribed in the body are never univocal.[36]

Notes

1. In flamenco, *cante*, *baile*, and *toque* are terms that, although they follow their own aesthetic systems, correspond in other musical systems to *canto* (song), dance, and instrumentation. In performance, *palmas* and *jaleos* refer to body percussion, spirited exhortations, and the interaction between interpreters called *cantaores/as* (singers), *bailaores/as* (dancers), *tocaores* (instrumentalists), and *palmeros/as* (hand-clapping

percussionists). I use italics on first usage for the terms and expressions particular to the flamenco lexicon, which do not always have a standard equivalence in Spanish.

2. For the author, the social body constrains the way the physical body is perceived. The physical experience of the body, always modified by the social categories through which it is known, sustains a particular view of society. There is a continual exchange of meanings between the two kinds of bodily experience so that each reinforces the categories of the other. As a result of this interaction, the body itself is a highly restricted medium of expression. The forms it adopts in movement and repose express social pressures in manifold ways. Mary Douglas, *Natural Symbols: Explorations in Cosmology* (London: Routledge, 1996 [1970]), 72.

3. Mariella Combi, *Corpo e tecnologie. Simbolismi, rappresentazione e immaginarii* (Roma: Meltemi, 2000), 62 ff.; John Comaroff and Jean Comaroff, *Ethnography and the Historical Imagination (Studies in the Ethnographic Imagination)* (Boulder: Westview Press, 1992), 61 ff.

4. Música andalusí is Arabic music developed in Al-Andalus, as Andalusia was known during the period of Muslim governance between the ninth and fifteenth centuries. It expanded throughout North Africa via commercial and cultural exchange, especially following the expulsions that followed the Christina reconquest of the Iberian Peninsula in 1492. For more on this music, see Cristina Cruces-Roldán, *El Flamenco y la música andalusí. Argumentos para un encuentro* (Barcelona: Ediciones Carena, 2003).

5. *Bailes de candíl* are defined as slang for popular dance by La Real Academia Española in its *Diccionario de la lengua castellana, décimatercia edición* (Madrid: Sres Hernando y Companía, 1809), 119, 205.

6. In fact, on the international stage, flamenco's symbolic nucleus was the feminine dance. Curiously, for flamenco aficionados throughout the world, the cante, especially sung by men, has much more value and prestige than the woman's dance.

7. In Spanish, a *cuadro* is a painting. One contemporary usage of the word is to describe a group of performers who pose together for the audience. The DRAE (Dictionary of the Royal Spanish Academy) since 2012 defines cuadro (Flamenco) as "a group of performers who sing, dance, and play instruments interpreting flamenco music." Real Academia Española, *Diccionario de la lengua española (DRAE)*, 22nd edition (Madrid: Espasa-Calpe, 2011), http://lema.rae.es/drae/?val=cuadro+flamenco (accessed October 6, 2014).

8. This was not a new phenomenon. By the end of the eighteenth century, the *tonadillas escénicas* (danced and sung theatrical interludes)—clear antecedents to the genre of theatricalized *coplas* (verses) and to Andalusian-styled scenes—disproportionately favored women. Of 27 of the most notable performers of this era, 19—more than two thirds—were women. My data analysis is based on lists published in José Blas Vega, *La canción española. De La Caramba a Isabel Pantoja* (Madrid: Calambur Editorial, 1996), 12. On women guitarists in the contemporary flamenco scene, see Loren Chuse's "Las Tocaoras: Women Guitarists and Their Struggle for Inclusion on the Flamenco Stage" in this volume.

9. Salaün says dance is, perhaps even more than song, the most innovative art of the late nineteenth century and accompanies all the vanguard movements of the era. In the eyes of authentic theatrical reformers and intellectuals such as Mallarmé, dance represents an authentic rupture with the naturalist stage tradition in the degree to which it is stripped of all narrative and realist reference. Dance is seen as pure movement that obeys none other than its own rules; it is unimpeded gesture in space. It is the body that is finally free: pure choreographic creation, and pure sensation for the audience. Modern dance (like mime and pantomime that were reborn in the same era) illustrates a new concept of theater, which is based on the stage and on the body—the body of the actor and no longer that of the text. Serge Salaün, "Las mujeres en los escenarios españoles (1890–1936). Estrellas, heroínas y víctimas sin saberlo," *Dossiers Feministes* 10 (2007): 78–79.

10. The idea of the body as site of transgression for contemporary women is developed by Mari Luz Esteban, who builds on the insight that "we as bodies are effectively regulated, controlled, normalized and conditioned by a gender system that discriminates against women through large-scale institutions (publicity, fashion, advertising, sports, medicine). But our corporeality is what we are, it is the body we have, and it can be (in fact, it is becoming) a perfect agent of confrontation, of response, of resistance and of creating new gender relations—just as the sexual/reproductive body was twenty or thirty years ago." Mari Luz Esteban, *Antropología del cuerpo. Género, itinerarios corporales, identidad y cambio* (Barcelona: Bellaterra, 2004), 42. See also Marcel Mauss, "Techniques of the Body," *Economy and Society* 2, no. 1 (1973): 70–89.

11. For an analysis of the relationships between *habitus* and corporeality, see Pierre Bourdieu, *Distinction: A Social Critique of the Judgement of Taste* (London: Routledge, 2010), 187–206.

12. This was a "generally unstable population, constantly renewed as a function of age, of self invention and re-invention (caught between aspirations of fame or of a comfortable 'retirement' from the stage, or threatened with forcible 'retirement'—there were few other alternatives) or as a function of the evolution in the genre itself." Serge Salaün, "La mujer en las tablas. Grandeza y servidumbre de la condición femenina," in *Mujeres de la escena, 1900–1940,* ed. Ma Luz González Peña, Javier Suárez-Pajares, and Julio

Arce Bueno (Madrid: SGAE, 1996), 30. Flamenco women lived with—and sometimes alternated careers with—*canzonetistas, cupletistas, vedettes,* and music-hall variety show performers. Among the iconic images of this period we find, for example, photographs of flamencas from the cuadros dressed as cupletistas, wearing a *bata de cola* (dress with a train), in a *goyesca* costume (Spanish ballet costume representing the fashions of the early nineteenth century), or as bolero dancers. Juan Rondón has documented that the singer Rafael Pareja remembers (at the beginning of the twentieth century) that the top cantaor, Chacón, was paid 30 pesetas; the first guitarist, Maestro Pérez, 17.5; and the top dancer, La Macarrona, 10 pesetas. Other bailaoras earned between 4 and 10 pesetas. The cantaor who earned the least, Niño de Alcalá, received 12 pesetas, and guitarists in general earned 10, in addition to the cost of replacing broken strings. Juan Rondón Rodríguez, *Recuerdos y confesiones del cantaor Rafael Pareja de Triana* (Córdoba: Ediciones La Posada, 2001).

13. This is how Donna Haraway, from the point of view of feminist discourse, analyzes the "cyborg imaginary" as a channel for overcoming the dualisms by which we, as humans, have explained our bodies. Donna Haraway, "A Cyborg Manifesto: Science, Technology, and Socialist-Feminism in the Late Twentieth Century," in *Simians, Cyborgs and Women: The Re-invention of Nature* (New York: Routledge, 1991), 180.

14. Anthony Synnott, *The Body Social: Symbolism, Self and Society* (London: Routledge, 1993); Jeffrey Weeks, *Sexuality and Its Discontents: Meanings, Myths, & Modern Sexualities* (London: Routledge & K. Paul, 1985), Spanish edition: *El malestar de la sexualidad. Significados, mitos y sexualidades modernas* (Madrid: Talasa, 1983); Thomas Walter Laqueur, *Making Sex: Body and Gender from the Greeks to Freud* (Cambridge, MA: Harvard University Press, 1990), Spanish edition: Thomas Laqueur, *La construcción del sexo. Cuerpo y género desde los griegos hasta Freud* (Madrid: Cátedra, 1994); David Le Breton, *Antropología del cuerpo y modernidad* (Buenos Aires: Ediciones Nueva Visión, 2002); Michel Foucault, *The History of Sexuality,* vol. 1, *The Will to Knowledge* (New York: Vintage Books, 1978), Spanish edition: Michel Foucault, *Historia de la sexualidad, 1: La voluntad de saber* (Madrid: Siglo XXI, 1978); Pierre Bourdieu, *Masculine Domination* (Oxford: Blackwell, 2000), Spanish edition: Pierre Bourdieu, *La dominación masculina* (Barcelona: Anagrama, 2002).

15. From a feminist perspective, these authors have recognized the polyphonic relationships between concepts such as "sex," "body," and "cultural practice," deconstructing the ties between biological sex and gender. With respect to biological sex, gender is a cultural construction, which varies within and between cultures. Michelle Z. Rosaldo, "Woman, Culture and Society: A Theoretical Overview," in Rosaldo and Lamphere, eds., *Women, Culture and Society* (Stanford: Stanford University Press, 1974); Ann Oakley, *La mujer discriminada: biología y sociedad* (Madrid: Debate, 1977). For Gayle Rubin, the body is a semiotic object, biologically irreducible, but manipulated in accordance with a wide social and historical range, and the distinct positions of agents of hegemonic processes. Gayle Rubin, "The Traffic in Women: Notes on the 'Political Economy' of Sex," in Rayana Reiter, comp., *Toward an Anthropology of Women* (New York and London: Monthly Review Press, 1974), 157–210.

16. According to Fernando el de Triana, at the end of the nineteenth and beginning of the twentieth centuries, there were a total of 313 flamenco artists, 127 women and 186 men, with a distribution of 97 cantaores (male singers), 96 bailaoras (female dancers), 37 bailaores (male dancers), 30 cantaoras (female singers), 52 tocaores (male guitarists), and just one female guitarist. That is to say that almost a third of the total flamenco artists were male singers (30.9 percent), and a similar percentage (30.6 percent) were female dancers. Nonetheless, while slightly more than half of male flamencos were cantaores (52.1 percent), three-quarters of female flamenco professionals were dancers (75.5 percent). Fernando el de Triana, *Arte y artistas flamencos* (Madrid: Ediciones Demófilo, 1978 [1935]).

17. This dualism has had important repercussions in the social sciences. Turner uses it as factor explaining the historical neglect of the category of "body" within these disciplines. Bryan Turner, "Avances recientes en la teoría del cuerpo," *Revista Española de Investigaciones Sociológicas*, no. 68 (1994), 11–40.

18. Luis Lavaur, *Teoría romántica del cante flamenco. Raíces flamencas en la coreografía romántica europea* (Sevilla: Signatura Ediciones, 1976). In contrast to the theory of Molina and Mairena then in vogue, Lavaur identified developing "operatic" styles with Andalusian flamenco performance in the nineteenth century. He saw them as cultivating both gesture and facial expression, since in both cases they performed "notable elements of the southern 'ethos,' whose dramatic flowering evoked violent fits of romanticism."

19. I use Erving Goffman's expression "body gloss": relatively self-conscious gesticulation an individual can perform with his whole body in order to give pointed evidence concerning some passing issue at hand, the evidence to be obtainable by anyone in the situation who cares to perceive him. Here, then, we have the externalization of evidence ... behavioral gloss, as defined here, gives the impression that the actor is having to make do. *Relations in Public: Microstudies of the Public Order* (New York: Basic Books, 1971), 128.

20. There are two interesting sources for understanding how "femininity" and "masculinity" are defined by their interpreters, as opposed to the interpretations offered from the etic perspective of the researcher. The "Código de la escuela Sevillana de baile" ("The Code of the Seville School of Dance") by Matilde Coral (b. 1935), a principal representative of this school, contains elegant precepts on the tantalizing or

provocative intentionality of dance. "The bailaora must seduce," and "each movement and gesture should be a promise." But this promise should never be explicit: "lift in the waist, and make each *quiebro* [bend at the waist] a feint of hidden sensuality and complicity." The utility of the feminine form, "open, diaphanous and luminous," is outside the limits of women's control: "Try always to be sure the audience does not leave with an overall impression of sadness or depression ... even if they are shaken to the core.... Give yourself body and soul to the vehemence of a forbidden lover." Matilde Coral, "Código de la escuela sevillana de baile," *Pepa Montes*, http://www.pepamontes.com (accessed September 12, 2014). These principles, written in the 1970s, represent the photographic negative of those written by bailaor Vicente Escudero (1888–1980) in his 1951 *Decálogo del buen bailarín* (Decalogue of the Good Male Dancer). Escudero advocated marked accent, style, quietude, and the lack of artifice: "Dance like a man. Sobriety. Turn the wrist from inside to out, with the fingers together. Hips still. Dance grounded and tempered. Harmony of feet, arms, and head. Aesthetic and plasticity without mystification. Style and accent. Dance in traditional costume. Achieve variety of sound with your heart, without taps on your shoes, without fake stages or other accessories. Vicente Escudero, "Decalogue," in Alexandra V. Krinkin, "'Vicente, esto es'; Vicente Escudero, Greatest Flamenco Dancer of This Century, Returns in Triumph," *Dance Magazine* (1955), 18–21.

21. Simone de Beauvoir, *The Second Sex* (London: Vintage, 2009 [1949]), 359–360. For the process of construction of the body-object during puberty, and external appearance as a social requirement exclusively for women, see 586.

22. Oliver Faure, "La Mirada de los médicos," in *Historia del Cuerpo (II) de la Revolución Francesa a la Gran Guerra*, ed. Alain Corbin (Madrid: Taurus, 2005), 23–56.

23. Matilde Coral calls these movements *golpes de cadera*, or "hits with the hip." Matilde Coral, Angel Álvarez Caballero, Juan Valdés, and Rocío Coral, *Tratado de la bata de cola: Matilde Coral, una vida de arte y magisterio* (Madrid: Alianza, 2003), 152.

24. By the mid-nineteenth century, Gautier already noted these differences in standards of beauty as a sign of Spanishness, and more specifically Andalusian-ness: "Spanish dancers, although lacking the finish, the precise technique, and the elevation of French dancers, are in my opinion very superior on account of their grace and charm. Since they practice very little and do not subject themselves to those terrible limbering exercises that turn a dance class into a torture chamber, they avoid the skinniness of a trained horse that makes our ballets seem so macabre and anatomical. They have preserved the curves and contours of their sex. They look like women dancing and not like dancers, which is something very different.... In Spain ... [they] dance with their whole body, they arch their backs, bend sideways, and twist their torsos with the suppleness of an almeh or a grass snake ... their dancing consists of harmoniously lascivious undulations of the torso, hips, and back, with *renversements* of the arms above the head.... most of all in Andalusia." Théophile Gautier, *Un Voyage en Espagne* (Paris, 1843), 283; English translation, Ivor Guest, "Theóphile Gautier on Spanish Dancing," *Dance Chronicle* 10, no. 1 (1987), 7.

25. "The ladies, who seem to have no bones, resolve the problem of perpetual motion, their feet having comparatively a sinecure, as the whole person performs a pantomime, and trembles like an aspen leaf; the flexible form and Terpsichore figure of a young Andalucian girl—be she gipsy or not—is said by the learned, to have been designed by nature as the fit frame for her voluptuous imagination." Richard Ford, *Gatherings from Spain, Selected from the "Handbook of Spain" with Much New Matter* (London: John Murray Albemarle Street, [1846] 1861), 328. http://www.archive.org/stream/gatheringsfromsp00ford/gatheringsfromsp00ford_djvu.txt (accessed September 12, 2014).

26. For more on codes of masculinity and femininity in flamenco dance, see "'De cintura para arriba.' Hipercorporeidad y sexuación en el flamenco," in Cristina Cruces-Roldán, *Antropología y Flamenco: Más allá de la música (II): Identidad, género y trabajo* (Sevilla: Signatura Ediciones de Andalucía, 2003), 167–206.

27. Although the data is inexact, and it is difficult to precisely delimit one population from another, a little over 4 percent of the Andalusian population in 2001 was Gitano (1.5 percent in Spain as a whole): 350,000 in Andalusia, 653,000 in Spain as a whole (*Diagnóstico social de la comunidad gitana en España. Un análisis contrastado de la Encuesta del CIS a Hogares de Población Gitana, 2007*). There is no objective data on the percentage of flamenco artists who are Gitanos, even if it were possible to clearly delimit ethnic boundaries.

28. For a historical survey of the formation of these stereotypes, see Alberto del Campo Tejedor and Rafael Cáceres Feria, *Historia cultural del flamenco. El barbero y la guitarra* (Sevilla: Ed. Almuzara, 2014).

29. I refer here to Carmen Romero Bachiller in "El exotismo de los cuerpos y la fetichización de la mirada en la producción de las 'mujeres inmigrantes' como 'otras'" in *Crítica feminista y comunicación*, ed. Mª José Sánchez Leyva and Alicia Reigada Olaizona (Sevilla: Comunicación Social, 2007), 198. Given the analogous historical models, and for an explication of the relationships between artistic representations of savages, women and workers as subaltern categories, also marked, see Lourdes Méndez, *Cuerpos sexuados y ficciones identitarias* (Sevilla: Instituto Andaluz de la Mujer, 2004).

30. Edward Said, *Orientalism* (New York: Vintage Books, 1979), 42.

31. *Bayles de Jitanos. Aviso.* ("Gypsy Dances. Notice."), in Jerónimo de Alba y Diéguez, *Libro de la gi-*

taneria de Triana de los años 1740 a 1750 que escribió el Bachiller Revoltoso para que no se imprimiera (Book of the Gypsy Neighborhood of Triana of the Years 1740 to 1750 written by the Rebellious Student That It Not Be Published), ed. Antonio Castro Carrasco (Seville: Coria Gráfica, S.L., 1995).

32. Alfred Gell, *Art and Agency: An Anthropological Theory* (Oxford: Clarendon, 1998), 21 ff.

33. "Festive" forms in flamenco have to do with ritual, a gathering, community, and celebration. In flamenco, *festero* relates to the classification of styles. Cantes, tangos and bulerías mostly, sung and danced within the unfolding of the *fiesta* (party), are called festeros because of their musical characteristics in terms of the rhythmic mode of the celebration.

34. The tango's great popularity at the end of the nineteenth and beginning of the twentieth century made it the featured dance in cafés and theaters, to the extent that it was incorporated into the first treatises that combined "flamenco" bailes and society dances, refining its choreographies for the comfort of the upper classes. José Otero, *Tratado de bailes de sociedad, regionales españoles, especialmente andaluces, con su historia y su modo de ejecutarlos* (Sevilla: Tipografía de la Guía Oficial, 1912); facsimile edition: (Sevilla: Asociación Manuel Pareja-Obregón, 1987). Also, the tango was a principal attraction in the *varietées*, or variety shows. Some of those examples are collected in primitive cinematic recordings of Spanish dance and flamenco from the end of the nineteenth and the beginning of the twentieth century in the archives of Lumière, Gaumont Pathé, and the Library of Congress, among others. Cristina Cruces-Roldán, "Presencias flamencas en los Archivos Gaumont-Pathé. Registros callejeros en la Granada de 1905." *Presumes que eres la ciencia: Estudios sobre arte flamenco,* ed. José Cenizo and Emilio J. Gallardo (Sevilla: Centro de Documentación Musical de Andalucía—Libros con Duende, 2014). For an example of this type of dance, see the Tangos del Titi de la serie "Rito y Geografía del cante," http://www.youtube.com/watch?v=gG5sA3Um7-g (accessed October 5, 2014), and the trailer for the recent documentary by Ricardo Pachón "Triana pura y pura," http://www.youtube.com/watch?v=m2TTtkhZbfE (accessed October 5, 2014).

35. For more of my ideas on so-called "new flamenco," and the intellectualization of the art, see Cristina Cruces-Roldán, "El aplauso difícil. Sobre la 'autenticidad', el 'nuevo flamenco' y la negación del padre jondo," in *Comunicación y música II: Tecnología y audiencias,* ed. Miguel de Aguilera, Joan E. Adell, and Ana Sedeño (Barcelona: UOC Press, Comunicación 6, 2008), 167–211; and Cristina Cruces-Roldán, "Hacia una revisión del concepto 'nuevo flamenco'. La intelectualización del arte," in *Interdisciplinary Conference on Flamenco Research—INFLA—and II International Workshop of Folk Music Analysis—FMA* (Sevilla: Universidad de Sevilla, 2012), 13–27. Also, see Michelle Heffner Hayes, "Choreographing Contemporaneity: Cultural Legacy and Experimental Imperative," and Niurca Márquez, "Y Para Rematar: Contemplations on a Movement in Transition," in this volume.

36. Thomas J. Csordas, "Somatic Modes of Attention," *Cultural Anthropology* 8, no. 2 (1993), 135–156.

Las Tocaoras
Women Guitarists and Their Struggle for Inclusion on the Flamenco Stage
Loren Chuse

Cantaoras, women singers, have risen to prominence in flamenco over the past several decades, transforming the long-held social stigma regarding professional flamenco performance for women to an attitude of respect and prestige. Despite the growing prominence of cantaoras, flamenco guitar persists in being the nearly exclusive domain of male performers. The flamenco *cuadro* (ensemble) now regularly includes women singers, but women flamenco guitarists continue to be a rarity. For much of the twentieth century, women guitarists have been viewed as an aberration. Only recently, in the past dozen years, have a handful of courageous women struggled to take their place in the profession. Yet, in the earlier *café cantante* era of flamenco, during the second half of the nineteenth century and the early twentieth century, women guitarists were numerous and highly regarded. This essay examines the issues related to women guitarists, from their high visibility in the nineteenth century to their marginalization during the twentieth century, and to their emergence in contemporary flamenco.

The varied experiences of women guitarists, both Gitana and non–Gitana, and their creative responses to the barriers and marginalization they have encountered, reveal much about their sense of themselves as Andalusians, as women, and as members of the flamenco community. Issues of gender identity are constantly negotiated in the nuanced strategies employed by women guitarists to contest their exclusion from flamenco guitar. These strategies emphasize the important role played by individual agency in the enactment of musical performance.

The discussion of women flamenco guitarists must be framed within larger issues of musical instruments and gender. Veronica Doubleday outlines some of the key issues in the examination of gender and musical instruments in "Sounds of Power: An Overview of Musical Instruments and Gender."[1] Doubleday notes the following characteristics regarding gendered instrumental performance:

1. Male instrumental musicianship typically emerges as the cultural norm, while female instrumentalists are viewed as deviant.
2. Masculine identity is often connected to a particular instrument and

gendered meanings are invested in musical instruments. These notions are evident both in the history of the guitar and in flamenco.

3. There is a perpetuation of power relations. This touches on two important factors: gendered space and male control of public space; and male control of technology and knowledge.
4. That women lack adequate physical strength to play an instrument is an opinion often voiced by those who disapprove of women flamenco guitarists.
5. Attitudes, and the cultural assignments of instruments by gender, are changing on an international scale, fueled by global mass communication and political and social changes.

To begin, a few comments on the history of the guitar are in order. For centuries the guitar existed both as a popular and cultivated instrument but gradually came to be associated with popular songs and dances. This music had connotations of lewd lasciviousness to such a degree that, for example, public performance of the *sarabanda* (a dance with African roots) was outlawed in Spain in 1594. Guitar was associated with the sensual, and by extension, with the female. Gaspar Sanz wrote in his 1674 method for guitar that "the guitar is a woman, to whom the saying look but don't touch does not apply."[2] The idealized female form is seen in the guitar's hourglass shape; likewise, the temperament of the guitar has been idealized in stereotypical notions of the female: moody and sentimental, alternately lascivious and sweet.

Women Guitarists in the History of Flamenco

In the nineteenth-century world of the cafés cantantes and popular theaters in Spain, women were admired as singers, dancers, and guitarists. Many accompanied other singers and dancers on guitar, while some both sang and played guitar.[3] They were highly regarded as artists but suffered the social stigma of public performance in the *demi-monde* nightlife of cafés and taverns. Anilla la de Ronda was a singer and guitarist who continued to perform well into old age. Dolores de la Huerta, the famous interpreter of *fandangos,* accompanied herself on guitar. Trinidad Huertas de Cuenca, who polarized audiences with her bullfighter number in the 1880s, was a singer, dancer, and guitarist. Tía Marina Habichuela, the grandmother of the famed Habichuela clan of guitarists from Granada, accompanied her father when she was a young girl. Mercedes Serneta, known as the "mother of the *soleá,*" was an accomplished guitarist and singer who supported herself later in life teaching guitar to aristocratic families in Madrid. Paca La Coja, the wife of singer Fernando el de Triana (real name Fernando Rodríguez Gómez), was also his accompanist. Fernando documents these performers in his 1936 book *Arte y artistas flamencos,* a valuable compendium of biographies and personal anecdotes of artists of this era in flamenco performance.[4]

This tradition of female guitarists died out in the 1920s and 1930s. There are a number of reasons for this, both musical and social. One key reason was the guitar's growing importance as virtuoso solo instrument, in contrast to its traditional role as accompaniment in flamenco song and dance. Its transformation into solo instrument and its rise in prestige seems to have resulted in the exclusion of women, quite possibly due to the low social status of female performers. The repressive social and political climate of Spain's post–Civil War years and the Franco dictatorship doubtless played a role in taking the guitar out of the hands of women. During this period, women singers all but disappeared from flamenco, with the exception of a few, and women guitarists were nonexistent. In Franco's Spain, women participated in flamenco primarily as dancers. The folkloric films of the 1940s and 1950s are rife with stereotypical representations of flamenco women as sensual and alluring, in imagery evoking notions of exoticism, otherness, and the quintessential Andalusian seductress of literary and operatic fame—Carmen.[5] Since the return to democracy in Spain, women have reappeared as professional singers, and the decade of the 1990s experienced an explosion of successful cantaoras. The world of the guitar, however, has been slow to reflect this social change. When I began my fieldwork in 1996, I found only one professional woman guitarist. Since then, the number of women guitarists has grown slowly in response to social changes and to new contexts for the study of flamenco guitar.

María Albarrán, the first guitarist I met in 1996, grew up in a Gitano family of professional flamenco artists that toured extensively in Europe, Latin America, and New York when she was a child. Her father, singer Ramón de Cádiz, and her mother, dancer La Marruja, formed a company, with their daughters Lucía as dancer and María on guitar. María developed her skills in an ambiance of family friends who were flamenco artists, including the renowned guitarist Sabicas, who encouraged her aspirations in

Figure 1: Maria Albarrán, right, with her mother, Maruja Heredia, center, and sister Lucía, c. 1966, photographer unknown (collection of Loren Chuse).

guitar. She was self-taught, studying the recordings of classic guitarists such as Ramón Montoya and Niño Ricardo. When I interviewed María, she was directing the family troupe and was musical director of its productions.[6]

Maria pursued her career within the family troupe, but she has experienced her share of uphill battles as a female guitarist. She described the difficulties of being taken seriously as a professional, as well as the social complexities of negotiating the male-dominated world of flamenco as a single woman. It is customary in flamenco for guitarists to learn from each other, to share *falsetas,* or melodic passages, and to jam frequently. The gender-separated spheres of traditional Andalusian life made this nearly impossible for María. She recounted how, time after time, when she attempted to join a group, the others became uncomfortable with her presence, made excuses, and one by one dispersed. This was repeated so often that María stopped trying to collaborate with other players. Within the family troupe she was respected, but socially, it was impossible to play music with other guitarists. While not dissatisfied with her professional gains, María Albarrán has resented being marginalized from the larger world of flamenco based on her gender.[7]

When I conducted interviews with cantaoras in 1996 and in 1998, I asked them why there were few women guitarists and if they envisioned this changing. Carmen Linares and Esperanza Fernandez, innovative singers both known for being excellent classic singers and pioneers in their repertoire, commented on the future for female guitarists. Both lamented the discrimination and sexism that has prevented women from achieving in this area and felt strongly that the upcoming generation would produce a few brave souls whose efforts would begin to break down the barriers for women in flamenco guitar.

Pioneering Female Guitarists

Ten years later, I met the first of these brave souls. Antonia Jiménez, a professional guitarist from El Puerto de Santa María in the province of Cádiz, was born in 1972. Antonia began studying the guitar at age fourteen, and a year later she became an accompanist for dancers at local academies. The next year she toured with a professional company to Madrid and Barcelona. She moved to Madrid to continue studying and to work, but she found it discouraging trying to get a foothold in the world of flamenco guitar despite her efforts, finding that she often had to overcome doubt and distrust. The turning point came when she toured for a year in Japan. After this successful year abroad, she returned to Madrid confident and determined to succeed. Today, she is a well-known and respected guitarist who works primarily as an accompanist for dancers and singers in a variety of venues.

Invited to participate in the all-women show *La Diosa Blanca* in March 2005, in honor of International Women's Day, she and guitarist María José Matos, introduced below, accompanied singer Carmen Linares, marking the first time two women guitarists had been featured together in a performance. She has performed as an accompanist for the singer Juan Pinilla at Granada's Peña de la Platería, and in the Festival of Music and Dance in Granada in July 2010. She regularly performs with the innovative flamenco dance company of Marco Flores, which won first place in the 2010 Córdoba

Flamenco Festival with its *De Flamencas*. For this production, in which the male dancer, Marco Flores, was accompanied by an all-female ensemble of guitarists and singers, Antonia both composed the music and played the guitar. She also works as a soloist and performed to critical acclaim in the XIII Festival de Jerez *Mujer Contra Mujer,* a concert series that featured women flamenco guitarists.[8]

Antonia shared a number of interesting observations about women in the world of flamenco guitar. She feels one of the obstacles is that there are few prototypes for women as guitarists and that the public is not used to seeing women play guitar. She has experienced the rejection from male guitarists, and reflected that although she had problems with this early on, she believes attitudes are changing as the public becomes more open-minded. She talked about the tendency of some to regard women guitarists as a novelty and made it clear that she seeks to be judged as a guitarist on her own merits. Antonia noted that the instrumental practice is considered the more intellectual aspect of the tradition, from which women have been excluded. Her comment echoes Doubleday's observations regarding the issues of male exclusivity of instrumental tradition and the control of knowledge. In an interview during a flamenco festival in Berlin, which featured an evening of women flamenco performers, Antonia said: "To make a place for yourself is quite difficult.... I have had to struggle a lot, just as all the others. My case is nothing special, because in all aspects of life we women always have to struggle more. An image of the woman guitarist does not exist, and little by little, I am creating this image."[9]

Guitarist Celia Morales faces the challenges of balancing family life and her career as a guitarist. Born in 1972, the same year as Antonia Jiménez, in Antequera in the province of Málaga, Celia began studying flamenco guitar at eight years old with a teacher at school. She later attended the Conservatory of Music in Málaga, where she studied classical guitar, since flamenco instruction was not available. In 1998, she returned to her pursuit of flamenco guitar, first with Pedro Blanco and later with the esteemed guitarist and composer Manolo Sanlúcar. Like all the other guitarists I interviewed, she has studied the recordings of masters of flamenco guitar and has been profoundly influenced by the musical innovations of internationally renowned Paco de Lucía.

For the past ten years, Celia has earned her living both as a guitar teacher and a performer. She performed as accompanist for singer Antonia Contreras in *peñas* and cultural centers in Málaga in 2005. A year later, she accompanied singer Rocío Díaz in the final concert of a course entitled *Mujeres, sonidos y virtualidad* in Madrid. While Celia works primarily as an accompanist for singers, she also has a solo career. In 2008, she performed in solo concerts in the series *Rutas Flamencas*, beginning with a performance at the Centro Andalúz de Flamenco in Jeréz de la Frontera. In 2009, she performed as part of the University of Málaga summer course honoring the centenary of the birth of Gitano guitarist Diego del Gastor. In the summer of 2010 she was featured as a solo performer in the Córdoba Guitar Festival.

Celia discussed the challenges she faced returning to flamenco after years of playing classical guitar: her need to develop different right and left hand technique as well as strength and a steady *compás* (rhythm). In an interview in the noted flamenco periodical *La nueva Alboreá*, Celia objected to the attitude that women are not physically strong enough to play flamenco.[10] She emphasized that the most important qualities are musical aptitude and much-devoted study, and that strength, endurance, and dexterity come from practice. While she is fortunate to have the support of her husband and manager, Juan Ponce, she has experienced mixed responses in her efforts to succeed in flamenco. She endeavors to be respected and given the opportunities of any other flamenco guitarist. Like Antonia, Celia feels that attitudes are slowly improving for women guitarists.[11]

The experience of María José Matos provides a thought-provoking example of the shifting attitudes toward women guitarists. Born in Huelva in 1963, María José was a founding member of the Peña Flamenca Femenina de Huelva, the flamenco club created in the 1980s by women in response to their exclusion from the other peñas in Huelva, all of which were male-only establishments at that time. She had begun studying guitar at age twelve with one of the guitarists from the peña and was active in performances there. But when they decided to record, there was opposition to including María José, invoking the stereotypical arguments that women are not as strong players as men and that it would look better for a male guitarist to accompany the group. The attitude of the other women of the peña, which reinforced prevailing stereotypical notions of gender, and Maria José's discouragement at the rejection as an instrumentalist, influenced her later decision to leave the profession.[12]

Some of her performance highlights include the 2005 collaboration with fellow guitarist Antonia Jiménez in *La Diosa Blanca* and her participation in *Poesía y Toro*s in September 2006 in Salamanca, but she concluded that a career in performance is too ridden with obstacles. She has continued to teach in private academies in Huelva, including the school associated with the *Peña Femenina,* in which she participates as guitar instructor but not as accompanist of the performing group. In contrast, the generation of female guitarists of a decade later, Antonia Jiménez and Celia Morales, among others, are optimistic about their future as flamenco guitarists despite the obstacles they have faced.

Changing Contexts for Guitar Study Encourage a New Generation of Women

Traditionally, all aspects of flamenco performance (*cante, toque,* and *baile)* were learned within the environment of the family. Flamenco is well known for its famed lineages of flamenco performers who span many generations.[13] In this traditional family context, women generally did not play the guitar. Both Celia Morales and Antonia Jiménez studied with private teachers and learned a great deal from recordings of flamenco masters, such as Ramón Montoya, Sabicas, and Paco de Lucía. In recent years, new contexts are emerging for the study of the guitar and expanding the possibilities for women in flamenco. An invaluable and relatively new center for guitar study, which has enabled more women to enter the profession, is Córdoba's Conservatorio Superior de Música, Rafael Orozco. The conservatory created the first university-level program in flamenco guitar performance, from which a number of women have graduated and gone on to both perform and teach.

Laura González Toledano, born in 1980 in Córdoba, is among the conservatory's graduates. She received the degree of Título Superior de Guitarra Flamenca in addition to a master's degree in music education, and is pursuing a professional career as a teacher and as a performer. We met in July 2008 when she accompanied cantaora Antonia Contreras in a recital entitled *Sólo y nada menos que mujeres* ("Only and nothing less than women"), which was part of the summer course *Mujer en el Flamenco Arte y Género* sponsored by the International University of Andalucía. In this program, Laura and Antonia interpreted songs composed or made famous by women singers such as La Trini, Concha La Peñaranda, La Serneta, and la Niña de los Peines, among others.[14] In addition to accompanying singers, Laura González has performed solo concerts in flamenco festivals, including Nijar's Noches de Luna y Flamenco in August 2008 and the Festival Flamenco de Jerez the following March. Laura's performance and skill in both concerts was praised in the press and by the public. In an interview published in the online journal *El Mirabas*, Laura made several observations about the position of women flamenco guitarists in the profession. She noted that women have been sidelined in flamenco, as in many other fields, but as a consequence of social changes, women are now able to enter into various professions, including the guitar. She expressed optimism regarding the future: "Things are changing and normalizing, and in no time, the flamenco guitar will no longer be only a man's world."[15]

Pilar Alonso is another of the first generation of graduates from the Conservatorio Rafael Orozco. Born in 1966, she is a multifaceted musician who began playing guitar in the *rondillas*, or string ensembles, in her native Baza, near Granada. Like Celia Morales, she began her musical life as a classical guitarist, obtaining a degree in 1994. She went on to study flamenco and received a degree in flamenco guitar from the conservatory in 2006. Pilar's musical career represents the eclectic diversity of her many talents as director, composer, arranger, and guitarist in a wide range of ensembles, from folk music to flamenco. She created and directs the Orquesta de Laúdes Españoles "Velasco Villegas," a folkloric string ensemble, as well as the Escuela Musical de los Coros y Danzas de Caniles, a regional folklore group.[16] Pilar Alonso's flamenco ensembles, both of which she founded and in which she has performed, include the all-female Trajitoma of Granada and the group Al 4 por Medio.

Pilar's teaching career is equally multifaceted. She has been a professor of classical guitar in Granada's Conservatorio Profesional de Música Ángel

Figure 2: Guitarist Pilar Alonso, 2013. Photograph by Marian Munilla (collection of Loren Chuse).

Barrios and in the Conservatorio Elemental de Música in Córdoba. Her flamenco guitar career includes teaching in Córdoba's Professional Conservatory as well as in the Conservatorio Profesional de Música in Granada.[17] In addition to her interests in Andalusian folklore and flamenco, Pilar has explored other world music forms, including collaborating with Moroccan and Greek musicians in Granada. In our interviews during the summers of 2012 and 2013, Pilar shared her enthusiasm for her many musical projects, her profound dedication to teaching, and her varied experiences in the world of flamenco guitar. She has experienced discrimination and sexism, particularly in the traditional venues of the local flamenco peñas, but she responds to these conservative attitudes with her characteristic good humor and confidence.

Elena Castillo, born in 1980 and a native of Córdoba, is a more recent graduate of the Conservatorio Superior de Música program. Since receiving a degree in flamenco guitar, she obtained a master's degree in music education; during her studies, she developed a pedagogy of flamenco guitar instruction.[18] She has taught in the Escuela de Música de Córdoba and currently teaches in one of the city's Conservatorio Intermedios. Elena has performed with the group Flamencas en el Cuadro in a festival organized by the Universidad Complutense in Madrid, and has also given solo recitals in a number of venues in Córdoba.[19] Like Pilar Alonso, Elena Castillo is a multifaceted guitarist with a strong commitment to teaching.

Looking Forward

The women I interviewed or whose stories I researched share a number of elements in common. All have pursued their guitar studies in a less traditional manner than they might have in previous generations, when guitarists learned solely within the family. All have dedicated themselves to years of study, with professional guitarists, privately, in dance academies, or at the conservatories. They have begun their careers in the traditional manner: as accompanists to singers and dancers; yet, most have gone on to perform solo concerts. None of these guitarists have recorded their music. Both Celia Morales and Antonia Jiménez mentioned that they want to compose and do not want to record until they have an individual body of work. However, their conspicuous absence from the recording industry reflects the history of the exclusively male presence in the industry. Women guitarists are still viewed as a rarity and no room has been made for them in the recording studio.

The experiences of these *tocaoras* reflects the gendered status of instruments. During the twentieth century, masculine instrumental musicianship in flamenco guitar emerged as the cultural norm, though in earlier periods this was not the case. The gendered meanings ascribed to the guitar in Spain, however, have a long and well-documented history. Certainly, the idea that women flamenco guitarists are an aberration to the norm has persisted until recently. The perpetuation of power relations and notions of gendered space, along with male control of technology and the music industry, prevail in terms of the opportunities available to women guitarists. Women flamenco guitarists continue to be stereotyped by many as lacking adequate physical strength to play the instrument, despite the examples to the contrary in this essay. But transformation is evident in the flamenco world and reflects changes on an international scale by which cultural assignments of instruments by gender are being erased; this is fueled by increased global communication and by political and social changes. As the number of women guitarists continues to grow and their opportunities expand, we may see an explosion of tocaoras much like we saw in the emergence of cantaoras some twenty years ago. What is certain is that these pioneering women guitarists will have earned their rightful place in flamenco.

Notes

1. Veronica Doubleday, "Sounds of Power: An Overview of Musical Instrument and Gender," *Ethnomusicology Forum* 17, no.1 (June 2008), 3–39.
2. Glenn Kurtz, *Practicing: A Musician's Return to Music* (New York: Knopf, 2007), 104.
3. The café cantante era of flamenco began in the mid-nineteenth century and continued into the early twentieth century. Flamenco as we know it owes much to this period. This was a formative era, both in the development of cante flamenco and in baile flamenco. Much has been written about this fascinating period, as it was well documented in the press, in biographies, and in other sources. For further information on the world of café cantante performers, see José Blas Vega and Rios Ruiz, *Diccionario enciclopédico ilustrado del flamenco*, two volumes (Madrid: Editorial Cinterco, 1988); Ángel Álvarez Caballero, *Historia del cante flamenco* (Madrid: Editorial Alianza, 1981); José Blas Vega, *Los cafés cantantes de Sevilla* (Madrid: Editorial Cinterco, 1980); Loren Chuse, "The Cantaoras: Music, Gender, and Identity in Flamenco Song" in *Current Research in Ethnomusicology: Outstanding Dissertations, Volume 7* (London and New York: Routledge, 2003); José Luis García Navarro and Miguel Ropero Nuñez, *Historia del flamenco* (Sevilla: Ediciones Tartessos, 1996); José Luis Ortiz Nuevo, *Se sabe algo? Viaje al conocimiento del arte flamenco en la prensa Sevillana del XIX* (Sevilla: El Carro de la Nieve, 1990); and Fernando el de Triana, *Arte y artistas flamencos* (Madrid: Imprenta Helénica, 1935).
4. El de Triana, *Arte y artistas flamencos*, 5–30.
5. For further information on flamenco under the Franco dictatorship and on stereotypical imagery in flamenco, see Chuse, "The Cantaoras: Music, Gender, and Identity in Flamenco Song," William Washabaugh, *Flamenco: Passion, Politics and Popular Culture* (Washington, D.C., and Oxford: Berg, 1996); and William Washabaugh, *Flamenco Music and National Identity in Spain* (UK: Ashgate Press, 2012). For information of the folkloristic cinema under the Franco regime, see Helen Graham and Jo Labanyi, eds. *Spanish Cultural Studies* (Oxford and New York: Oxford University Press, 1996). Numerous sources provide an in-depth look at stereotypes of Andalusian culture. See also Pedro Jiménez González, "Lo tópico de la mujer Andaluza" in *Las mujeres en la historia de Andalucía* (Córdoba: Publicaciónes de la Consejería de Cultural y Medio Ambiente de la Junta de Andalucía y Obra Social y Cultural Cajasur, 1994); Gerhard Steingress, ... *y Carmen se fue a París: Un studio sobrela construcción artistic del género flamenco (1833–1865)* (Córdoba: Almuzara, 2006).
6. María Albarrán, interview with the author, May 1996.
7. María Albarrán, interview with the author, July 2009.
8. Eulalia Pablo Lozano, *Mujeres guitarristas* (Sevilla: Signature Ediciones, 2009), 170–174; Antonia Jiménez, interview with the author, July 2008 and July 2009.
9. Pablo Lozano, *Mujeres guitarristas*, 175.
10. "La raíz y la savia nueva," interviews with Antonia Jimenez and Celia Morales, in *La nueva Alboreá* 6 (April–June 2008): 20–21.
11. Celia Morales, interview with the author, July 2009.
12. Pablo Lozano, *Mujeres guitarristas*, 179.
13. Flamenco has been traditionally carried down through families, in particular Gitano families. Some famed lineages whose members have been professional flamenco performers for generations include: the Habichuela clan of guitarists in Granada; the Soto family of singers in Jerez de la Frontera; the Farruco family of dancers and singers from Sevilla; and the Heredia family of singers from Granada, just to mention a few. There is extensive literature in Spanish on these flamenco families, and on individual performers within them. See Blas Vega and Rios Ruiz, *Diccionario enciclopédico ilustrado del flamenco*, for detailed descriptions of these performers; also see Don Pohren, *Lives and Legends of Flamenco: A Biographical History* (Sevilla: Society of Spanish Studies, 1964).
14. Laura González Toledano, interview with the author, July 2008.
15. Pablo Lozano, *Mujeres guitarristas*, 191.
16. Pilar Alonso, interviews with the author, August 2010 and July 2012.
17. Pablo Lozano, *Mujeres guitarristas*, 197.
18. Elena Castillo, personal communication with the author, July 2013.
19. Pablo Lozano, *Mujeres guitarristas*, 198.

Dancing the Ideal Masculinity
RYAN ROCKMORE

The dancing body exhibits more than just movements, shapes, and lines. It also carries a plethora of ascribed meaning, ranging from political histories to sociocultural factors that influence the viewer's perception and the artist's presentation. How we, as audience members or viewers, engage with these identities and embodied histories will determine the varied means of interpretation and understanding of them. In her cogent synthesis of the literature on the politics of dance, Susan Reed emphasizes how "ethnicity, national identity, [and] gender" affect the dance and the dancer.[1] Additionally, there are a substantial number of texts that discuss how these identities relate to the societal construction of the body.[2] The body of concern here is the male flamenco dancer during the dictatorship of Francisco Franco in Spain between 1939 and 1975. More than just a moving body, the male dancer exhibits "kinesthetic and structural characteristics laden with social implications and associations."[3] Furthermore, in certain respects, the dance as a transmitted artistic product by the dancer "is ideological, and it carries inevitable political effects."[4] The dancer, through his medium, can act as an inscripted vessel to convey political ideologies.

Yet, in the case of flamenco, the pre-existing importance of distinct gender roles in the dance prior to Franco's rise to power complicates the notion of a passive dancer as an object of inscription. By already performing a seemingly inherent masculine/feminine binary, flamenco dancers played a very active role in promoting gender ideologies of the time shared by the Falange political party. This essay discusses the symbiotic relationship between the concept of gender during the Franco regime and the aesthetic idea of the *bailaor,* or "male flamenco dancer." The two strengthened one another, perhaps unintentionally, and reified how men should act in both flamenco and society.

The New Spain and Ideologies of Francoism

To understand some of the extreme ideologies of the Franco regime it is imperative to situate them as reactionary to Spain's situation between the turn of the century and the country's Civil War in 1936. Commonly referred to as "*el desastre*" by Spanish historians, 1898 was a disastrous year for Spain. The empire lost its three remaining colonies: Cuba, Puerto Rico, and the Philippines. More than territorial losses, this decline challenged "the nature of Spanishness."⁵ As a former political and economic superpower, especially between the fifteenth and seventeenth centuries, Spain was desperate to enter the twentieth century with a reinvented image on a global scale.

Following the conservative dictatorship of Primo de Rivera, the Democratic Republic of 1931 sought to regenerate Spain through liberal policies such as the separation of church and state, secularization of education, and increased rights for women and workers.⁶ Richard Cleminson, a historian of sexuality in Spain, explains that, in addition, the promotion of sexual liberation, love, and the freedom from the "repressive authority of the Catholic Church" was prevalent in the rhetoric of anarchist collectives during this time.⁷ The bloody Civil War from 1936 to 1939 between the Nationalists, led by Franco, and the Republicans, demonstrated the severe polarization of values

Figure 1: From Ruven Afanador's *Ángel Gitano, The Men of Flamenco* (New York: Rizzoli, 2014) (courtesy Ruven Afanador).

between political parties. Following the Falangist political party victory in 1939, the new dictatorship sought to distance itself as much as possible from what the previous Republic had represented with its socially progressive views. Franco's regime, therefore, needed to change not only the political and economic structures of the country but also its internal spiritual and cultural philosophy.[8]

The first task for the new regime was to create a sense of nationalism that would connect citizens from every corner of the country, unless of course, they were part of the opposition. Localizing and applying Benedict Anderson's influential concepts of imagined communities, Sebastian Balfour and Alejandro Quiroga address how, "like its European counterparts," Franco needed to create such "an imagined community" for Spain.[9] Spain could, through various efforts, present itself to the world as a unified cultural entity. In addition to the promotion of myths and national heritage, Franco's government also had to "eradicate [...] cultural difference"[10] and control "predominantly marginalized social groups."[11] This distillation of Spanish society would then allow the regime to selectively define what the new Spain would be. Dance historian Theresa Buckland reminds us that "'folk culture' had become a resource for asserting specific ethnic and ultimately national identity" throughout Europe, an act that was not uncommon during the nineteenth and twentieth centuries.[12] There is evidence that Spain was no exception and that folk culture and danced played a functional role in creating a national identity, although flamenco was not a national focus at the beginning of the new dictatorship.

This new way of life appropriated from the people was effective partly because it seemed to originate from "natural emanations of the people's spirit."[13] Within Spain, the Coros y Danzas division of the Sección Femenina, founded in 1939 within the Falangist party, was instrumental in collecting such representations of the people in the form of, albeit sterilized, folk songs and dances. What these women acquired would be a "new ideological and instrumental influence for the purposes of the Regime."[14] Even in the early stages, the government displayed a keen interest in exploiting dance as a means to create a sense of Spanish identity. However, with concentrated opposition in the northern provinces of Catalonia, Basque Country, and Galicia, Franco and his ministers turned elsewhere for the source of a pure and passionate national culture, arriving ultimately at the provincial home of flamenco: Andalusia.

The present notions of *hispanidad* and *casticismo* grew out of two principal areas of Spain, the central and southern regions. As part of a regeneration of the country's image, casticismo took form by representing some of the key cultural elements one currently might associate with modern Spain—bullfighting, zarzuela, coplas, and flamenco—most of which have their origins in Andalusia. While various scholars[15] only allude to this growing favoritism towards the South during the early- to mid-twentieth century, Balfour and Quiroga specifically identify the process as an "Andalucization" of the country. As mentioned earlier, with the main separatist groups located in the North, the Franco regime's employment of the South as a cultural marker seems in no way arbitrary. With regards to dance, this reorientation not only had the effect of promoting flamenco as a national art form, which is discussed below, but also prevented other dances from having equal opportunity to contribute to the greater notion of a national character. For example, the Sardana was the target of discriminatory and oppressive policies that limited its practice and performance throughout Catalonia.[16] Through the concurrent processes of promotion and oppression, the regime "systematically promoted certain meanings above others."[17] Franco's policies consequently gave a nationalistic voice to Andalusia by silencing the regional expression of northern provinces like Catalonia.

The Catholic Church was another major influence for Franco's government in creating a sense of nationhood and instilling various ideologies into the Spanish mindset. In addition to reconnecting modern Spain with its powerful status of the Inquisition and Golden Age, the religious institution once again served as a model to cleanse the nation of those who did not fit its ideological mold. Placing "Catholic values as central to their own cultural and social program,"[18] after their previous deconstruction by the Republicans, the Falangists sought to re-inject Catholic conservativism back into education and culture as a regulatory "moral crusade."[19] Education laws subsequently changed to reflect the traditional ideologies surrounding marriage, gender, and sexuality propagated within the Catholic faith. It is important to note that Gabriel Arias Salgado, vice-secretary of Popular Education from 1941 to 1946, later served a significant role in carrying out the regime's strict censorship policies as the minister of information and tourism during the 1950s.[20] One may presume that Catholic ideologies, which once influenced Arias Salgado in education matters, remained fundamental to his positions on censorship and tourism when he oversaw the promotion of flamenco as a principal Spanish commodity.

Ideologies of the Catholic Church became intertwined with those of Fascism during this time, most notably in Spain. The Hitlerian philosophy of strict conservatism served as a final key aspect to "Francoism," which Michael Richards labels more as a "mentality" than an ideology, comprised principally of the aforementioned nationalism, cultural Spanishness, and Catholic values.[21] A commonality between Franco's Falangist philosophy and Fascism was the notion of masculinity and manhood. Influenced by a visit to Nazi Germany in April 1939, General Moscardó, president of the Consejo Nacional de Deportes, incorporated sport into the national propaganda to symbolize and foster "patriotism" and militaristic "discipline" in Spanish men.[22]

Fascism's concept of the "New Man" served as a template to represent men as "virile," "physically strong," and "forceful and vigorous" beings.[23] Similarly, the belief that "men had to be strong, controlling and virile" for the nation to be a world power again was central to the Falangist image of masculinity.[24] In order to define masculinity, both Fascism and Falangism regulated non-masculine behavior in an attempt to extinguish homosexuality from society. The Franco regime tolerated typical "caricature" expressions such as "transvestism [and] harmless effeminacy,"[25] yet homosexuality was still "fiercely repressed."[26] Franco's amendment to the 1933 law, Ley de Vagos y Maleantes, solidified the political party's stance that homosexuality was "dangerous" and that it would, under the same statutes as thieves or the homeless, fall victim to highly subjective interpretations and punishment of the law.[27]

Under these conditions, perhaps the masculine style of flamenco became more pronounced and exaggerated because of the lack of acceptance regarding male displays of femininity. Ramsay Burt supports this notion and suspects that the hypermasculine display of some male dancers—from diverse cultural and stylistic backgrounds—was "to show that they [were] not effeminate."[28] Dancing "manlier" distanced one from signifying representations of homosexuality, femininity, and weakness. There is, however, a more rooted basis to the masculine aesthetic than simply a rejection of or distancing from the feminine.

Embodying the Bailaor

In a review of some of the literature on flamenco history, generally written by non-dancers, it is not difficult to find the widely held belief that the dichotomy between male and female gender performance is fundamental to flamenco.[29] Photos from Fernando el de Triana's *Arte y artistas flamencos* add testimony to this Saussurean approach and reveal an established gender aesthetic, beginning with flamenco's documented history in the nineteenth century.[30] Moving into the twentieth century, the following masters of flamenco dance embodied the traditionally accepted masculine aesthetic and gained prominent status during the Franco era: Vicente Escudero (1887–1980), El Farruco (1935-1997), Antonio "El Bailarín" (1921–1996), José Greco (1919–2000), Mario Maya (1937-2008), El Güito (1942–), Manolete (1945–), and even Carmen Amaya (1913–1963). Escudero presented his "Decálogo del baile flamenco" in 1951, which explicitly codified certain aspects of the pure masculine form. Its main points included:

1. Dance like a man
2. Seriousness
3. Rotate the wrists inwards with fingers together
4. Keep hips still
5. Dance with stability and certainty[31]

The evidence clearly shows that a masculine image of male flamenco dancers existed in the nineteenth and early twentieth centuries; however, Escudero's mandates reveal the form's inherently performative nature. In this prescriptive fashion, each ingredient is combined to ultimately create the perfect recipe of masculine embodiment. In her analysis of Antonio Gades's style, Michelle Heffner Hayes similarly fortifies the idea of a relationship between masculine performance and male gender in flamenco choreography:

> This process first creates gender as an effect of representation, then obliterates that moment of signification. The choreography appears to emerge as an expression of a biologically masculine body: "He is a man, therefore he dances in a masculine style," rather than "Because he is dancing in a masculine style, he can be identified as a man."[32]

Using such "choreographic conventions of masculinity,"[33] the performer gives the illusion of a gender dichotomy and suggests that men must dance a certain way, a process that is compounded through generations of training and correction. Further reifying the existence of gendered performance in flamenco is the ready availability of texts dictating the necessary characteristics to dance like a man: "uncompromising virility," "technical control," and "relentlessly vertical,"[34] and "aggressive," "ferocious," and "steely ferocity, controlling, dominating."[35] While these are contemporary texts, their language applies to the characteristics of the style observed in videos and photos of male dancers from the Franco era. By employing Judith Butler's notion of gender performativity, in which "gender identity is the stylized repetition of acts through time,"[36] and if the previous descriptions were demonstrated, one could dance, and perform, like a male flamenco dancer and, ultimately, a Spanish male. The masculine styles and acts of the artists mentioned above, therefore, served both to construct the notion of the male flamenco dancer and "[crystallize] what it [meant] to be a male member of their culture."[37] With such domination and aggression reflected in the style of the male dancer, flamenco was also the perfect tool for Franco's promotion of the ideal "hombre."

Selling Flamenco and the Masculine Aesthetic

Although available documentation or evidence referencing a specific plan or purpose is lacking, it is generally accepted by dance and flamenco scholars that flamenco became "a propaganda element of the first magnitude"[38] and "a major component in Franco's plan to develop Spain [...] from the tourist industry."[39] With these claims, and a look at the widespread popularity of flamenco during the mid-twentieth century, we can infer the importance of flamenco to Franco's plan for tourism. His regime first had to accomplish two basic tasks: clean up the art form for public display, and promote it. Because flamenco was viewed as an "alcohol-assisted catharsis of the ethnic drinking subculture,"[40] it needed to be altered in order to represent the country on a global scale in the form of an artistic practice. Scholars and flamenco aficionados often refer to this change and elevation of flamenco to a national level as *nacional flamenquismo*, or "national flamencoism." This was the "sneering name they gave to the franquista promotion of meretricious spectacles that celebrated the richness of Spanish art without acknowledging regional differences and economic despair."[41] Rather than a representation of the pain and suffering experienced by marginalized groups in Spanish society, the popularized version of flamenco foregrounded its aesthetic and stylistic qualities.

The *opéra flamenca* era, from 1920 to 1955, was already in full swing, which benefited the regime. During this period, flamenco was increasingly influenced by formalized, academic techniques from classical Spanish dance and an emphasis on theatrical elements such as linear storylines, props, lighting, and costumes. Purists and traditionalists alike vehemently expressed their distaste for this new, "wretched era of the 'flamenco opera.'"[42] Even bailaores, as a collective whole, were not safe from the critiques of established flamencologists and were chastised for the way they were changing forever the face of flamenco. Many of the great male dancers of the time, including Antonio Gades, Mario Maya, José Greco, Manolo Vargas, and Roberto Ximénez, had been trained by the consummate Spanish dancer, Pilar López, which is evidenced by the classical influences in their style and, arguably, softer aspects of the dancing present in various choreographies. This contamination of the pure masculine style was deplored by writers such as D. E. Pohren, who went so far as to say, "thus, from a purely flamenco point of view (not theatrical), a list of good dancers is not relevant. It would be pitifully small."[43] For Pohren, one of the principal issues was the male dancer's loss of "strength" and "virility" from the integration of classical stylization and technique.[44] While his attacks on the effeminacy of bailaores or the commercialization and theatricality of flamenco were plentiful, comparable generalized critiques of the entire male Spanish dancer community did not seem to exist. Yet one needs not look further than the above dancers, renowned for their embodiment of the masculine aesthetic during the early- and mid-twentieth century, to discredit Pohren's views on the emasculation of flamenco. From the present historical point of view, dancers from Escudero and Farruco to Amaya, were truly emblematic in fortifying what is currently understood as the traditional masculine style.

Focusing again on the effects of the opéra flamenca, another advent of the time was the *tablao*. Whereas the *cafés cantantes* mainly contributed to the professionalization of the art form, the fortification of the "baile masculino" and "baile femenino," and the evolution of musical styles into actualized *palos*,[45] the tablaos served primarily as a new performance space for tourists to view stylized representations of flamenco.[46] They also played an important role in providing amateur and professional dancers a venue outside the context of the theatre to test new choreographies, experiment with improvisation, and perform. These venues, which developed in the early 1950s, transformed almost naturally into spectacular, touristy shows, for which they became famous. As flamenco dancers entered the performance space of the tablao with faster footwork, *de rigeur* from the virtuosic ability of Carmen Amaya and Antonio El Bilbao,[47] an established emphasis on costumes, accessories, choreography, and "disciplined regimen of professional training" [my translation] from Spanish dance companies,[48] and a need to attract tourists for revenue, the performance aesthetic of flamenco changed for both bailaores and bailaoras. Through advertisements and marketing, the male flamenco dancer of the tablaos had to exact a certain image by combining increased technical skills and the stylistic qualities of the "baile masculine" established within the cafés cantantes. Flamenco anthropologist Cristina Cruces-Roldán succinctly describes this established masculine style as "the exhaustive displays of energy, the acceptance of acrobatic movements, the insistence on footwork, the verticality of the body, and the austere use of costume attire." The tablao was also unlike the quasi-vaudevillian cafés cantantes, which were criticized as being locales for the "popular classes" and those inclined toward "indecency and drinking." By restricting flamenco to the confines of a touristic, performative environment, the tablao contracted artists to deliver a packaged, aestheticized product to an audience of foreign visitors.

With theatres and tablaos as prominent public locales for flamenco performances, especially for tourists, the Falangist government was able to regulate the art form on a larger scale. For the arts and other sectors, including the press, this regulation took form through censorship, which, starting in 1951, was directed by the previously mentioned Gabriel Arias Salgado in the ministry of information and tourism.[49] Consequentially, with flamenco presumably as a focal point of the government's plan for tourism, the opportunity to shape and control the image of the dance, and dancers, was greater than ever. The characteristic "brutal repression and tight state control [...] affected all the arts,"[50] even without a strictly "co-ordinated cultural programme."[51] For dance and the performing arts, specifically, "local delegates attended dress rehearsals and first nights, making later spot checks," which not only affected the final result but also the pre-production mentality for creating future works.[52]

Finally, one must question the effect on the dancer of Spain's combined focus on tourism, censorship mentality toward the arts, and the required "look" in tourist settings. Similarly related to the issue of gender and dance performance, Jane Desmond asks, "what skills are demanded of each dancer, and what do they imply about desired attributes ascribed to men or to women?"[53] Given the state of censorship and the Falangist beliefs and policies of the time, how a male flamenco dancer performed had significant social and cultural ramifications. Whether consciously or not, male dancers made specific and temporal choices, including those related to gender, given the ideological aesthetic set forth by society and the government.

The Symbiosis Between Francoism and Flamenco

The nature of the symbiotic relationship between the notion of a fundamental gender binary in flamenco and the Franco era ideologies of masculinity remains complex. By implementing frameworks from the biological sciences, the idea of symbiosis as simply a "relationship between organisms of two different species [...] in direct and intimate contact" could privilege three options of sub-classification in this case—mutualism, commensalism, and parasitism.[54] Although some flamenco purists or traditionalists may disagree, I refuse to claim that flamenco was necessarily harmed through Franco's appropriation and nationalistic promotion of the form; while it was transformed, to make this qualitative judgment is highly subjective and nearly impossible. Spain's economy and tourist sector benefited to some extent from flamenco's inclusion in the nationalist image, but one cannot definitively conclude that flamenco changed for better or worse. Also, to say that the Franco regime's views on traditional gender roles and masculinity helped maintain a gender performance dichotomy vital to traditional flamenco is equally problematic. Even with various censorship laws and nationalist rhetoric, it is safe to assume that Francisco Franco and his government were not directly concerned with minute aesthetic details of the art form. It seems that a commensal relationship, allowing room for further discussion, is the most applicable. A dialectic relationship might exist between gender roles of the time and gendered performance on the flamenco stage; however, the suggestion of such a definitive influence is extremely presumptuous given the information presented.

As a result of Francisco Franco's Falangist regime during its various stages between 1939 and 1975, it is possible that the performance of the gender binary was both reified and preserved in traditional flamenco. It is unclear how the performative aesthetic of flamenco might have been affected if the liberal ideologies and policies of the Democratic Republic surrounding gender and sex had continued to gain prevalence. Through the nationalist, Catholic, and Fascist values of Francoism, strict notions of masculinity and Spanishness were reflected through various aspects of culture and society.

Although it is impossible to substantiate any causal relationship between Franco's socio-cultural ideals and the preservation of a masculine aesthetic in flamenco, the persistence of a distinctly male look in the dance from its documented origins until the end of the dictatorship certainly suggests a connection. Using the birth of a democratic Spanish nation in the late 1970s as a point of division, the flamenco of the past may also help to understand certain trends of the present. Since Franco's death in 1975, Spain has opened itself to the world, and a range of influences has flooded the nation, from modern and contemporary dance[55] to progressive ideas surrounding gender and LGBT rights.[56] The style of male flamenco dancers is also changing, and in some respects shifting towards feminine or seductive movement and expression for certain performers. The past can help contextualize and explain the dance's current evolution. The various aesthetics and styles of flamenco will continue to change and reflect the sociocultural environment of the country, but surely the purists, with equal force, will continue the fight to keep distinct gender roles at the heart of the traditional form.

Notes

1. Susan A. Reed, "The Politics and Poetics of Dance," *Annual Review of Anthropology* 27 (October 1998), 505.
2. These include Judith Butler, "Performative Acts and Gender Constitution: An Essay in Phenomenology and Feminist Theory," *Theatre Journal* 40 (1988); Ann Cooper Albright, *Choreographing Difference: The Body and Identity in Contemporary Dance* (Middletown, CT: Wesleyan University Press, 1997); Jane C. Desmond, "Embodying Difference: Issues in Dance and Cultural Studies," in *Meaning in Motion: New Cultural Studies of Dance,* ed. Jane C. Desmond (Durham, NC: Duke University Press, 1997); Helen Thomas, *The Body, Dance and Cultural Theory* (London and New York: Palgrave Macmillan, 2003); Ramsay Burt, "The Performance of Unmarked Masculinity," in *When Men Dance: Choreographing Masculinities Across Borders,* ed. Jennifer Fisher and Anthony Shay (New York: Oxford University Press, 2009); and Andrée Grau, "Dancing Bodies, Spaces/Places and the Senses: A Cross-Cultural Investigation," *Journal of Dance & Somatic Practices* 3 (2011).
3. Cynthia J. Bull, "Looking at Movement as Culture: Contact Improvisation to Disco," in *Moving History/Dancing Cultures: A Dance History Reader,* ed. Ann Dills and Ann Cooper Albright (Middletown, CT: Wesleyan University Press, 2001), 407.
4. Mark Franko, "Dance and the Politics: States of Exception," in *Dance Discourses: Keywords in Dance Research,* ed. Susanne Franco and Marina Nordera (London and New York: Routledge, 2007), 14.
5. Sebastian Balfour, "The Loss of Empire, Regenerationism, and the Forging of a Myth of National Identity," in *Spanish Cultural Studies: An Introduction,* ed. Helen Graham and Jo Labanyi (Oxford: Oxford University Press, 1995), 30.
6. For more information and a detailed review of Spanish society prior to, during, and after the Franco dictatorship, see Jean Grugel and Tim Rees, *Franco's Spain* (London: Arnold, 1997).
7. Richard Cleminson, "Beyond Tradition and 'Modernity': The Cultural and Sexual Politics of Spanish Anarchism," in *Spanish Cultural Studies: An Introduction,* ed. Helen Graham and Jo Labanyi (Oxford: Oxford University Press, 1995), 120.
8. Both Balfour and Richards conduct cogent analyses on the political, cultural, and economic transitions in Spain during the 1930s and 1940s. See Balfour, "The Loss of Empire" (1995); and Michael Richards, *A Time of Silence: Civil War and the Culture of Repression in Franco's Spain, 1936–1945* (Cambridge: Cambridge University Press, 1998).
9. Sebastian Balfour and Alejandro Quiroga, *The Reinvention of Spain: Nation and Identity since Democracy* (Oxford: Oxford University Press, 2007), 17.
10. Antonio Elorza, "Some Perspectives on the Nation-State and Autonomies in Spain," in *Spanish Cultural Studies: An Introduction,* ed. Helen Graham and Jo Labanyi (Oxford: Oxford University Press, 1995), 163.
11. Gerhard Steingress, "Social Theory and the Comparative History of Flamenco, Tango, and Rebetika," in *The Passion of Music and Dance: Body, Gender and Sexuality,* ed. William Washabaugh (Oxford: Berg, 1998), 163.
12. Theresa Buckland, *Dancing from Past to Present: Nation, Culture, Identities* (Madison: University of Wisconsin Press, 2006), 7.
13. Steingress, "Social Theory," 152.
14. Estrella Casero-García, "Women, Fascism and Dance in the Coros y Danzas of the Feminine Division Under the Franco Regime (1936–1977)," in *The Society of Dance History Scholars, 22nd Annual Conference Proceedings* (Riverside, CA: Society of Dance History Scholars, 1999), 81.
15. They include Julian White, "Music and the Limits of Cultural Nationalism," in *Spanish Cultural Studies: An Introduction,* ed. Helen Graham and Jo Labanyi (Oxford: Oxford University Press, 1995); Nèlida Monés, Marta Carrasco, Estrella Casero-García, and Delfín Colomé, "Between Tradition and Innovation: Two Ways of Understanding the History of Dance in Spain," in *Europe Dancing: Perspectives on Theatre Dance and Cultural Identity,* ed. Stephanie Jordan and Andrée Grau (London: Routledge, 2000); and William Washabaugh, *Flamenco Music and National Identity in Spain* (Surrey, UK, and Burlington, VT: Ashgate, 2012).
16. Stanley Brandes's "The Sardana: Catalan Dance and Catalan National Identity" continues to serve as the foundational article, written in English, on the Catalan Sardana. See "The Sardana: Catalan Dance and Catalan National Identity," *Journal of American Folklore* 103 (1990).

17. Richards, *A Time of Silence*, 13.
18. Grugel and Rees, *Franco's Spain*, 131.
19. Ibid., 28.
20. Stanley G. Payne's *Franco's Spain* (London: Routledge and Kegan Paul, 1968) examines various facets of Franco's regime, including plentiful information on Franco's leading officers and secretaries.
21. Richards, *A Time of Silence*, 17.
22. John London, "The Ideology and Practice of Sport," in *Spanish Cultural Studies: An Introduction*, ed. Helen Graham and Jo Labanyi (Oxford: Oxford University Press, 1995), 204.
23. Encyclopædia Britannica Online (2013) provides a sufficient overview on the key facets of fascism and the concept of "The New Man." http://www.brittanica.com/topic/fascism#ref742180 (accessed September 16, 2015).
24. Grugel and Rees, *Franco's Spain*, 134.
25. Christopher Perriam, "Gay and Lesbian Culture," in *Spanish Cultural Studies: An Introduction*, ed. Helen Graham and Jo Labanyi (Oxford: Oxford University Press, 1995), 393.
26. Grugel and Rees, *Franco's Spain*, 134.
27. A copy of the 1954 amendment to the *Ley de Vagos y Maleantes* by Francisco Franco can be accessed at http://www.boe.es/datos/imagenes/BOE/1954/198/A04862.tif.
28. Ramsay Burt, *The Male Dancer: Bodies, Spectacle, Sexualities*, 2nd ed. (London and New York: Routledge, 2007), 11.
29. Authors and their publications include Doris Niles, "El Duende," *Dance Perspectives* 27 (1966); D. E. Pohren, *A Way of Life* (Madrid: Society of Spanish Studies, 1980); and William Washabaugh, "Fashioning Masculinity in Flamenco Dance," in *The Passion of Music and Dance: Body, Gender and Sexuality* (Oxford: Berg, 1998).
30. Fernando el de Triana, *Arte y artistas flamencos,* facsimile ed. (1935; Sevilla: Extramuros Edición, 2009).
31. Vicente Escudero, *Arte Flamenco Jondo* (Madrid: Estades Artes Gráfucas, 1959).
32. Michelle Heffner Hayes, *Flamenco: Conflicting Histories of the Dance* (Jefferson, NC: McFarland and Co., 2009), 104.
33. Ibid.
34. Ibid.
35. Washabaugh, "Fashioning Masculinity in Flamenco Dance," 40.
36. Butler, "Performative Acts and Gender Constitution," 520.
37. Ted Polhemus, "Dance, Gender and Culture," in *Dance, Gender and Culture*, ed. Helen Thomas (London: Macmillan Press, 1992), 11.
38. Monés et al., "Between Tradition and Innovation," 154.
39. Heffner Hayes, *"Flamenco: Conflicting Histories,"* 40.
40. Timothy Mitchell, *Flamenco Deep Song* (New Haven, CT: Yale University Press, 1994), 45.
41. William Washabaugh, *Flamenco: Passion, Politics and Popular Culture* (Oxford: Berg, 1998), 103.
42. Monés et al., "Between Tradition and Innovation," 154.
43. D. E. Pohren, *The Art of Flamenco* (1962; Shaftesbury: Musical New Services, 1984), 68.
44. Ibid., 60.
45. Cristina Cruces-Roldán, *Antropología y Flamenco: Mas allá de la Música (III)* (Seville: Signatura Ediciones, 2003).
46. For a more detailed description of the tourist-oriented nature of tablaos, see Timothy deWaal Malefyt, "'Inside' and 'Outside' Spanish Flamenco: Gender Constructions in Adalusian Concepts of Flamenco Tradition," *Anthropological Quarterly* 71(1998); Hayes, *Flamenco* (2009); and José Luis Navarro García and Eulalia Pablo, *El baile flamenco: Una aproximación histórica*, 2d ed. (Córdoba: Almuzara, 2010).
47. D. E. Pohren, *Lives and Legends of Flamenco: A Biographical History* (Madrid: Society of Spanish Studies, 1964).
48. Cruces-Roldán, *Antropología y Flamenco*, 135.
49. Payne, *Franco's Spain*.
50. Julian White, "Music and the Limits of Cultural Nationalism," in *Spanish Cultural Studies: An Introduction*, ed. Helen Graham and Jo Labanyi (Oxford: Oxford University Press, 1995), 225.
51. Jo Labanyi, "Censorship Or the Fear of Mass Culture," in *Spanish Cultural Studies: An Introduction*, ed. Helen Graham and Jo Labanyi (Oxford: Oxford University Press, 1995), 207.
52. Ibid., 210.
53. Desmond, "Embodying Difference: Issues in Dance and Cultural Studies," 32.
54. Neil A. Campbell and Jane B. Reece, *Biology*, 8th ed. (San Francisco and London: Pearson Benjamin Cummings, 2008), G-35.
55. Monés et al., "Between Tradition and Innovation" serves as a valuable resource for a concise history of dance in Spain during the twentieth century.
56. Perriam, "Gay and Lesbian Culture."

Flamenco in *La flor de mi secreto*
Re-Appropriation and Subversion in a Film by Pedro Almódovar
NANCY G. HELLER

In 1980, the Spanish writer and director Pedro Almodóvar achieved notoriety in his home country with his first feature film, the exuberantly raunchy *Pepi, Luci, Bom*. Eight years later he won international fame with his runaway hit, the zany black comedy *Women on the Verge of a Nervous Breakdown*. Today he is regarded as "the most successful Spanish filmmaker of all time" and "the cultural symbol *par excellence* of the restoration of democracy in Spain, after nearly 40 years of the right-wing military dictatorship of Francisco Franco."[1]

In his nineteen feature films Almodóvar creates particular worlds, characterized by the liberal use of Day-Glo colors, complex plots with equally complex subplots, absurd coincidences, and violations of taboos against depicting subjects such as cross-dressing, transsexuality, incest, and child abuse by Roman Catholic priests.

The director also enjoys creating short pauses in the action of his films, into which he inserts mini-performances. Almodóvar is famous for showing brief movie clips by other directors (often playing on television screens) within his own films. In addition, his principal characters frequently attend performances—of live theatre or, more commonly, vocal music. Occasionally, Almodóvar has even included dance—most notably in the 2002 *Hable con ella* (*Talk to Her*).[2] Much has been written about the brief excerpts from two works by the late German Expressionist modern dancer and choreographer Pina Bausch that frame this film. However, little has been said about the intriguing and unconventional flamenco duet that appears in *La flor de mi secreto* (*The Flower of My Secret*), made in 1995, seven years earlier. In this essay, I argue that the flamenco dance scene in *Flor*—which, at first, seems like a mere *divertissement* (an entertaining but irrelevant break from the principal plotline)—is in fact an important confirmation of the film's focus on personal, and artistic, reinvention.

La flor de mi secreto is about an elegant, middle-aged Madrileña named Leocadia ("Leo," for short, played by Marisa Paredes), the author of a highly successful series of so-called "pink novels," or women's romances. After twenty years of fulfilling her readers'—and her publisher's—desires, the tumult in Leo's life has given her a bad case of writer's block. With a crumbling marriage, plus guilt about her elderly and infirm mother (Chus Lampreave), Leo finds it impossible to churn out steamy bodice rippers with happy endings. In fact, she becomes so distraught that she attempts suicide.

But, by the end of the film, most of Leo's problems seem to have been resolved. She and her husband (Imanol Arias) are getting a divorce, Leo's mother, who has been driving her crazy, has moved from Madrid back to her home village, and Leo has developed a new, and potentially close—though, at her request, platonic—friendship with Ángel (Juan Echanove), a culture editor for the prestigious Madrid daily newspaper *El País,* for which she has started to write serious literary criticism, indicating that Leo is well on her way to becoming a strong, independent, single woman.

Meanwhile, Leo's maid, Blanca (Manuela Vargas), a retired flamenco dancer, and Antonio (Joaquín Cortés), Blanca's would-be-dancer-son, have taken a big step toward defining and/or redefining themselves as flamenco artists, by performing the duet that is the focus of this essay. This two- and one-half-minute sequence appears roughly three-quarters of the way through *Flor.*

The duet is an excellent example of *nuevo flamenco* (new-style flamenco) of the 1990s, involving a combination of traditional and innovative elements, co-choreographed by the two performers. The dance's title (clearly listed on the poster for the show) is *Soleá,* a traditional type of *baile jondo*—a deeply serious, highly emotional flamenco form. And both dancers exhibit the upright posture and carefully controlled *zapateado* (stamped footwork) that is standard in flamenco.

However, traditional flamenco seldom involves duets, since it is an inherently solo dance form. And the music to which they dance is anything but standard. It comes from *Sketches of Spain,* the classic 1960 jazz-fusion album by Miles Davis and Gil Evans.[3] Nor is it usual for flamenco dancers to wear these types of costumes—a plain, floor-length red dress for Vargas, with Cortés in a tight black tee shirt with black satin trousers.

Most obviously, it is anything but traditional for a twenty-five-year-old male dancer to nuzzle the arm, lie between the legs, or caress the hips and breasts of the woman portraying his character's mother. Nor does traditional flamenco include Martha Graham–style pelvic contractions, floorwork that includes kneeling before the audience, or balletic lifts and pirouettes.

Ironically, despite the noteworthy elements of this choreographic sequence, few of the myriad international writers who have commented on this film have mentioned the dance sequence in *Flor.* This is hardly surprising, since it is not a film about dance, or even one in which dance takes up a significant amount of time. Most people who have seen the film only once have probably forgotten that it includes a dance concert. But it does, and that sequence is well worth a closer look.

On one level, this flamenco duet works as a sort of visual and aural palate cleanser, a change of pace and mood, after a great deal of anguished melodrama.[4] Dramatically speaking, the flamenco duet gives Almodóvar an opportunity to show us that Ángel and Leo are now friends who do things together—like go to the theatre. Almodóvar notes:

> The flamenco performance marks another stage in [Leo's] recovery.... I think this is the beginning of her realization that life can be contradictory.... In the blackest period of her life, [Leo] was helping to create something beautiful because someone—the maid's son—was stealing from her in order to finance a work of art.[5]

After the fact, we learn that—without his mother's knowledge—Antonio had taken some jewelry and an unpublished manuscript from Leo's apartment, and sold them to help pay for producing their flamenco show. Almodóvar explains, "It is important for Leo to learn that something can be both destructive and creative," at the same time.[6]

But that does not explain why Almodóvar chose to insert a flamenco duet, versus some other type of dance, into his movie. More specifically, we have to wonder: what did it mean, for a Spanish person to include flamenco dancing in a film during the mid–1990s? Why highlight this particular kind of flamenco dancing? What about the Oedipal implications of the duet? And, finally, why did Almodóvar cast these two particular artists?

Let us consider the last question first. By the time he began writing *Flor*, Almodóvar had wanted to work with Joaquín Cortés for some time. According to a member of Cortés's staff, the two men met in 1992, when Almodóvar invited Cortés to appear in his film called *Kika*. But things did not work out; instead, Cortés made his film debut in *Flor*, three years later.[7]

So, who *is* Joaquín Cortés—and, more importantly, who *was* he in the early 1990s? Cortés is a Gitano, a native of Córdoba in Andalusía, born in 1969. At fifteen, he was accepted into the prestigious National Ballet of Spain, with which he toured the world, eventually reaching the rank of soloist.[8] Then, by the time he was twenty-three, Cortés had established his own troupe, for which he created a series of elaborate, evening-length spectacles. Now, after twenty years, Cortés is an international superstar, a genuine theatrical phenomenon known to almost anyone who follows dance or reads the supermarket tabloids. Flamenco purists despise him, but he continues to sell tickets, filling enormous concert venues all over the globe.

As demonstrated in the sequence from *Flor*, Cortés is a charismatic performer with excellent technique. An exponent of nuevo flamenco, in his work he typically augments—or replaces—the traditional dance accompaniment of voice, guitar, and *palmas* (rhythmic hand clapping) with an array of non-flamenco instruments from trumpets to *tablas*, violins, and electric flutes. While traditional flamenco costumes tend toward the dowdy, Cortés commissioned the noted *couturier* Giorgio Armani to design his company's chic, flattering costumes. And instead of relying on a time-honored movement vocabulary, Cortés combined flamenco steps with elements from modern dance, jazz, and other forms.

There are other charismatic, technically adept and highly successful nuevo flamenco stars in Spain who also have their own large companies and put on elaborate productions.[9] But there is only one Joaquín Cortés, a supremely polarizing figure who long ago moved to the dark side—advertising: appearing in television commercials for automobiles and print ads for high-end luggage, launching his own line of celebrity fragrances, and inspiring a character in a popular Japanese video game. In the United States, Cortés is probably best known for dancing at the White House, performing on the Oscars telecast, and appearing with pop singers Jennifer López and Alicia Keys. He was even a guest performer on *Dancing with the Stars*. It's difficult to imagine many other flamenco dancers being invited, or agreeing, to do these things.[10]

Cortés's signature look is bare chested—in an art form where costumes have traditionally been quite modest. His apparent obsession with showing off his well-toned torso is undoubtedly one reason why Cortés's audiences are typically filled with women, screaming ecstatically, and why one critic dubbed him "the sexiest Spanish icon since Antonio Banderas."[11]

It makes perfect sense that Pedro Almodóvar—himself no stranger to over-the-top theatricality, and the man most responsible for launching Banderas's film career—was intrigued by the young Cortés. By 1995, Cortés already had his own enormous international fan base. In addition, he was interested in a kind of flamenco dance that defies convention, is bold, and takes risks—as Almodóvar does, in all of his films.

What about Manuela Vargas, who died in 2007 at the age of 66 (or possibly 69, depending on which of her published birth years is correct)? When *Flor* appeared, Vargas was well-known to Spain's theatre-going public, but unfamiliar to most foreigners, since her international touring days had long ended.[12]

Like Cortés, Vargas was an Andalusian Gitana—in her case, from Seville—who made her professional debut very early. When she was in her twenties, Vargas led her own flamenco company in frequent, well-received engagements in Madrid, London, and New York, and on extended tours of other parts of Europe, and South America. The quality of Vargas's troupe is indicated by the number of its performers who already were, or soon became, major artists in their own right.[13]

In 1964 and 1965, shortly after winning the International Dance Prize for the Théâtre des Nations in Paris, Vargas raised her professional profile even higher by dancing with her company in the Spanish Pavilion at the New York World's Fair. She also appeared on the popular American television variety program *The Ed Sullivan Show*.[14] Aside from the YouTube footage of those appearances, there are many dramatic, black-and-white still photographs of Vargas from the 1960s. In them, she is heavily made up, her dark hair slicked back into a bun, and wears a flower pinned to the top of her head— in traditional Gitano style, with huge earrings, and a fierce expression.[15]

Most of the journalists who reviewed the dancing at the World's Fair were lavish in their praise of Vargas's troupe. They noted Vargas's youth, her "pure-blooded Andalusian heritage," and her exceptional beauty. American critics used the standard, exoticizing "Latina" stereotypes when describing Vargas: she "smouldered," she was "the tigress of flamenco," her dancing was "fiery and untamed," and so on.[16]

All this makes Vargas sound like a traditional (professional, theatrical) female flamenco dancer of her day—so, initially, it seemed odd that Pedro Almodóvar chose her to dance with Cortés, whose approach to the art form could hardly have been more different. What made Almodóvar think that Manuela Vargas would agree to do—or be capable of doing—something as radical as this duet? Because, well before she appeared in *Flor*, Vargas had changed.

When she was young, there was little choice about what "kind" of flamenco a professional Spanish dance artist could pursue. As many writers have pointed out, Franco effectively appropriated flamenco, one of the principal symbols of Spanish national identity, and used it as a vehicle to create a sense of what one writer has called "false collectivity"—an image of Spain as a single nation, happily unified under the Generalissimo, as opposed to what Spain actually was: a set of geographically isolated, largely impoverished, fiercely proud, and potentially separatist regions—especially Catalonia and the Basque Country.[17] Franco's regime promoted a tourist-friendly, entertainment-oriented version of flamenco. But soon after Franco's death in 1975, once the country was established as a modern democracy, Spanish artists of all kinds were free to work however they wished. Manuela Vargas (like Almodóvar) did so—with a vengeance.

In 1978, Spain's National Ballet was established. Beginning in the early 1980s Vargas was a frequent guest artist with that company, starring in several full-length dance-theatre works, including *Retrato de Mujer* (Portrait of a Woman), about unrequited love, and, most important, *Medea*, in which she played the title role of a woman who exacts revenge on her unfaithful husband by killing their two children. She also starred in *Fedra*, based on another tragic female figure from the ancient world. These parts required Vargas to convey strong emotions and to move in ways that merged flamenco with early modern dance expressiveness and technique. Vargas clearly relished these challenging roles, for which she received excellent reviews. Along the way, she also appeared in five plays—as The Shadow of Death in *Don Juan Tenorio*, and as the murderous Agave, in Euripides's *The Bacchae*. Therefore, it was not much of a stretch for Vargas to act in an Almodóvar film or to dance an anguished, nuevo-style duet with flamenco's bad boy of that era, Joaquín Cortés.[18]

In retrospect, there were several hints that Vargas had always been more interested in flamenco jondo than in tourist fluff. Virtually every critic of her early U.S. and British performances complained that Vargas's programs were too much of the same thing—"serious," or even "anguished" flamenco. Vargas herself was also taken to task, for virtually always having what was variously described as a "tragic," "severe," or "sullen" expression on her face.[19]

Thus, Vargas was a logical choice for *Flor*. But why did the director include a mini-dance concert in this film, in the first place? As noted earlier, Almodóvar enjoys reminding viewers of the artificiality of what they are watching. The device of forcing audiences to watch his characters watch performances, of whatever kind, reinforces this point, and explains two of the abrupt cutaways within the duet.

At the beginning of this scene, for a few seconds we see a man in the theatre's technical booth, emphasizing that this is a performance within a performance. Later, the camera cuts away from the dancers to focus on Leo and Ángel, who are seated in the auditorium, as Ángel drinks furtively from a pocket flask, much to Leo's embarrassment. This amusing moment makes a related point: that, like the film's audience, Leo and Ángel are merely observers. Almodóvar could also have decided to include the avant-garde flamenco duet to indicate that he is re-appropriating this symbol of Spanish national identity—by having his dancers perform a kind of flamenco that would have been impossible during Franco's dictatorship.

Another cutaway suggests that Almodóvar may, in fact, be using this scene as homage to Vargas's long and distinguished career. Right after Cortés leaves Vargas crumpled, face down, on the stage floor, the camera lingers on another female flamenco dancer. She is seated in the wings, watching the performance. A young woman, she is wearing all the standard flamenco elements: a pink dress with white polka dots, a fringed shawl, red earrings, and a big ornamental comb. Dressed, coiffed, and made up to look like an old-school flamenco dancer, the woman's expression remains severe the entire time the camera is on her. It seems likely that she is meant to look like the Manuela Vargas of the 1960s, and that somehow this figure represents Blanca, the maid, confronting her younger self.[20]

The Oedipal element in the duet from *Flor* could refer to Vargas's earlier dramatic roles—Agave, Medea, and Phaedra—legendary, dangerous women who share lethal relationships with their sons. Or it might be there simply because Almodóvar's films often include some reference to deviant sexual behavior, like rape or incest, and in *Flor*—which is generally acknowledged to be the first of his so-called "blue period" films (ones that are more serious and less outrageous than his earlier works)—perhaps he felt the need to include something truly shocking.

That could also explain the brief, almost subliminal, glimpse Almodóvar gives us of two drag queens—one wearing an off-the-shoulder frock, the other decked out in a wonderfully silly, Marge Simpson–esque, tall, hot-pink wig. Before Leo meets Ángel outside the theatre, we see these two men enter. One says, "I'm dead tired," and the other responds, "I'm not surprised, considering your weight."

This strange, and apparently unrelated, snippet goes by so fast that it is difficult to process the first time around. The drag queens never appear again, and they look completely different from the other theatre patrons, who are conservatively dressed. So it is difficult to imagine what purpose they serve here, if not to remind us, once again, that we are watching a film, and that it is by Almodóvar.

Whatever his reason for including *Soleá*, with it Almodóvar has created one of the most powerful parts of *Flor*. He also relates the duet to the rest of the film by using one of the most recognizable sounds of flamenco: rhythmic, rapid-fire stamping. Zapateado is heard under the opening credits; its rhythmic insistence sets the initial mood. Later, footwork is used to emphasize Leo's growing anxiety, after a frustrating phone call to her husband. With typically ironic, postmodern humor, Almodóvar introduces a scene of Leo and her mother enjoying village life with what at first sounds like flamenco footwork, but it turns out to be the clacking together of wooden bobbins used by the local women for their traditional craft of lace making.[21]

Finally, the director runs the ending credits for *Flor* with a hauntingly beautiful recording by one of his favorite artists: the Brazilian singer Caetano Veloso. In the song "Luna llena" ("Full Moon"), a man laments the fact that, just as the moon is starting to wane, his relationship with his lover is also dying—for reasons he does not fully understand. The recording includes flamenco-style palmas to punctuate and enrich the last few moments of the movie.

Veloso's soft, lilting, and evocative song resolves itself into what one listener has described as "a sort of uneasy, post-traumatic calm."[22] This mirrors the final scene of *Flor*, in which Leo—having survived her husband's betrayal, her mother's relocation, a major change in her own career, and a suicide attempt—sits with Ángel in his living-room. They share some wine while relaxing in a matched pair of armchairs before a crackling fire, like a comfortable, long-married couple—or, in this case, two friends. But Ángel also convinces Leo to kiss him, suggesting the possibility of a closer relationship in the future. In other words, the final scene implies hope.[23]

Notes

1. Paul Julian Smith, "Marks of Identification," *Sight & Sound* 21, no. 9 (September 2011): 23; Steven Marsh, "Pedro Almodóvar," *Senses of Cinema* 40 (2006), http://www.sensesofcinema.com/2006/great-directors/almodovar/ (accessed October 8, 2011).

2. For example, Almodóvar's *All About My Mother* includes scenes from Tennessee Williams's *A Streetcar Named Desire*; the Brazilian pop singer Caetano Veloso sings in *Talk to Her* and Penélope Cruz lip-synchs to a recording by flamenco singer Estrella Morente in *Volver*. To my knowledge, Almodóvar's

characters have never visited an art exhibition—though the sculpture of Louise Bourgeois figures significantly in *The Skin I Live In* (2011).

3. The duet from *Flor* is especially surprising, since *Soleá* (which is also the title of the musical segment used here) means "solitude" or "loneliness." The late, great Spanish flamenco/jazz fusion guitarist Paco de Lucía often cited *Sketches of Spain* as an important source for his own musical experimentation.

4. In an interview about *The Skin I Live In*, Almodóvar explains that he briefly paused the action in the film for a song by Concha Buika. He did this, as he did in several earlier movies, because he "wanted to create a moment that bewitches the viewer.... A magical moment"—or so he hopes—that allows him to take the narrative in a new direction. This seems analogous to the way Almodóvar uses the flamenco duet in *Flor*. Maria Delgado, "Flesh and the Devil," *Sight & Sound* 21, no. 9 (September 2011): 22.

5. "Interview with Pedro Almodóvar," Sony Pictures Classics, http://www.sonyclassics.com/flower/ (accessed September 6, 2015).

6. It is ironic, and surely not accidental, that Almodóvar makes the character Antonio a stereotypically "bad Gypsy," a thief and a flamenco dancer who, at one point, offers to repay Leo for his theft by sleeping with her.

7. Isabel Teruel, e-mail communication to the author, September 7, 2011.

8. Despite its name, the Spanish National Ballet (Ballet Nacional de España, or BNE) does not present classical ballet. Instead, it offers a unique mixture of flamenco, modern dance, traditional/regional/folk material, and Spanish classical dance—which combines ballet technique with castanets but does not use pointe shoes.

9. These include Sara Baras, Eva Yerbabuena, María Pagés, and Rocío Molina—all of whom Cortés claims to have influenced, which may well be true.

10. Joaquín Cortés has been featured in advertisements for the Spanish automobile Ibiza, Samsonite and Carpise luggage, celebrity fragrances for men and women (both named 24k), and luxury watches made by Chopard and IWC. His video-game character is Vamp, from the popular *Metal Gear* series. Cortés danced at the White House in 2004; he was part of the Oscars telecast in 1999; he danced with Jennifer López in her first Puerto Rican concert in 2001; that same year he appeared on the Grammy Awards telecast with Alicia Keys; and he performed on *Dancing with the Stars* in 2007. The strong feelings elicited by Cortés's performances is demonstrated by the unusually broad range of critical commentary on his work—from raves to outright insults.

11. Quoted by Kevin Ng in his 2003 interview with Cortés in *Ballet Magazine*, http://www.ballet.co.uk/magazines/yr_03/.../interview_joaquin_cortes.htm (accessed October 8, 2011).

12. It is unclear how or when Almodóvar, or Cortés, first met or learned about Vargas. But there may be a surprisingly direct connection between the two dancers, at least. The company Vargas assembled to perform in Madrid in 1964 included the dancer Cristóbal Reyes, Joaquín Cortés's uncle, whom the younger man has often cited as an important formative influence, and who Cortés later cast in one of his own productions.

13. These included dancers Matilde Coral, El Güito, and Cristina Hoyos, singers Fosforito and El Lebrijano, and guitarists Juan and Pepe Habichuela. In later years, Vargas worked with additional flamenco luminaries, including Mario Maya, El Chocolate, and Enrique Morente.

14. These programs originally aired October 23, 1965, and June 19, 1966.

15. See, for example, the clippings file for Manuela Vargas at the New York Public Library and Museum for the Performing Arts, Jerome Robbins Dance Division, at Lincoln Center. Yet, in the October 15, 1964, issue of *Vogue* magazine, Vargas posed in four different American-designed gowns, alongside the handsome young flamenco dancer Antonio Gades, whose company was also performing at the Spanish Pavilion.

16. The sources for these comments are Saul Goodman, *Dance Magazine* (September 1965), 50; Walter Terry, New York's *World Journal Tribune* (September 27, 1966), 39; and promotional quotes in the printed program for Vargas's 1965 New York World's Fair appearance. Other prominent dance critics who praised Vargas and her troupe included Clive Barnes, Doris Hering, and Richard Buckle.

17. Núria Triana-Toribio, *Spanish National Cinema* (London and New York: Routledge, 2003), 125.

18. *Retrato de Mujer* was choreographed in 1981 by Rafael Aguilar. *Medea* was first
performed in 1984, with choreography by José Granero and music by Manolo Sanlúcar. Vargas also choreographed four nonnarrative items for the Ballet Nacional de España.

19. See, for example, Elsa Brunelleschi, *The Dancing Times* (London), vol. LIII, no. 633 (June 1963), 514; Robert Harrold, *The Dancing Times*, vol. LX, no. 651 (December 1964), 125; and Walter Terry, op cit.

20. Another shot established that there were other flamenco performers in the wings, presumably waiting for their turn to go onstage. This makes sense, since a flamenco performance would not consist exclusively of a brief duet—although in the film we only see posters advertising *Soleá*, with images of a man, clad in black, dancing with a woman in red—clearly representing Vargas and Cortés. Also, earlier in the film, Antonio boasts to Leo that his mother is "the best" flamenco dancer around. Blanca ruefully corrects him, as she cooks Leo's dinner, saying, "I *was* the best."

21. As has often been noted, *Flor* was filmed in a village in La Mancha, very close to the one in which Almodóvar was born and raised, and where he says the local women made lace.

22. This is a typically eloquent comment from Ralph Pemberton, a retired professional translator and teacher of Spanish literature, who has played flamenco guitar for many decades. I thank him for this insightful note, communicated in an e-mail to the author September 21, 2011.

23. Earlier versions of this essay were presented at the 2011 conference of the European Association of Dance Historians in London and at the 2012 Flamenco History Symposium at the University of New Mexico, Albuquerque. I would like to thank the following friends, colleagues, and outside experts who made important contributions to this project: Robert Ackerman, Ninotchka Devorah Bennahum, Marc Dicciani, Paula J. Durbin, K. Meira Goldberg, Tiffany Gordon, Marina Keet de Grut, Michelle Heffner Hayes, Gerry Hooper, Jo Labanyi, Richard Peña, Anna Rubio, Nancy L. Ruyter, Mary Ann Shelton, Paul Julian Smith, Barbara Sparti, Steve Saylor, Michael Solomon, Samantha Soto, Kathleen Vernon, Estela Zatania, and the staff of the University of the Arts Libraries. Research support for this project was provided by the University of the Arts Provost's Fund.

Flamenco Fusion
Cross-Cultural Coalitions and the Art of Raising Consciousness
Jorge Pérez

Flamenco is the only Spanish musical style that has circulated with relative ease within the complex channels of world music, the marketing term corporations created in 1987 to promote music from countries outside the dominant Anglo-American locales.[1] A key component of this international circulation is flamenco's fusion with other global beats. Within flamencology, this process has generated two opposing reactions that match those that Steven Feld identifies for the broader context of world music.[2] On the one hand, "celebratory narratives" of flamenco fusion underscore the benefits of redefining musical styles beyond stagnant purism[3] and the value of fluid identities and hybridization as a sign of transgression and sometimes cultural resistance.[4] On the other hand, "anxious narratives" lambast fusion practices as the deterioration of a traditional musical culture. This is the position held by flamenco purists, popularly known as "mairenistas"—in honor of Antonio Mairena, the flamenco singer who canonized the *cante puro* in the mid–1950s.[5] Flamenco purists condemn what they consider a commodification of ethnicity for profitable purposes. By equating fusion with homogenization and cultural colonization, purists concur with the views of the so-called cultural imperialism theory.[6] Since the 1960s, Marxist-centered critiques of capitalism have appraised transcultural borrowings solely from a binary model that follows a one-way logic: from the center to the periphery, which in the case of popular music means from Anglo-American contexts to the rest of the world. This essay questions the cultural imperialism thesis—and the anxious narratives that adhere to such a thesis—as an insufficient framework to theorize the multifaceted factors and outcomes that pertain to the contexts of production and performance of contemporary flamenco fusion practices. I avoid the oversimplified paradigms that, following the influential views of Theodor Adorno, regard popular music as "mere automatism" due to the "standardization" that musical industries impose.[7] Although our assessment of popular music cannot be removed from the industry in which it appears, it is a mistake to reduce the significance of music to its economic frame and, furthermore, to deprive it of any artistic or ethical agency. I argue that a strictly formal scrutiny of flamenco fusion in terms of its faithfulness to or its deviation from a pure form misses some of the contributions of these innovative practices.

It is imperative to clarify that my critique of the "anxious narratives" is that of an outsider. I am not a flamenco scholar, a musicologist, or a dance specialist; rather, I am a cultural studies scholar whose passion for flamenco comes mainly from growing up in southern Spain. Flamenco reaches out to many people beyond dance and music experts, and for reasons that go beyond its form. This essay focuses on present-day redefinitions of the flamenco cante in examples of flamenco fusion to show that their meaning resides in musical characteristics but also in extra-musical elements, such as the fascinating cultural alliances across national and ethnic boundaries that fusion practices enable.

I am, thus, taking sides with the celebratory narratives but not in an uncritical way. There are challenges created by the circuits of world music. Major music corporations involved in asymmetrical economic practices trigger a domestication of traditional musical forms to adapt them to an international taste that usually involves, as Christopher Paetzold notes, "a certain amount of cultural voyeurism by international audiences."[8] In the case of flamenco, however, artistic innovation is consistently linked to a tense negotiation with the broader capitalistic market that regulates mass culture.[9] Transgression of mainstream culture is, according to Gerhard Steingress, what drives the evolution of flamenco as an art form from its very origins.[10] Flamenco has always been connected to a circuit of economic profit. It has long relied on tourism for its financial viability and currently generates a financial network worth between 120 million and 500 million euros (approximately $164 million and $681 million) per year. The multilayered touristic apparatus around flamenco includes "tourism-related services (teaching, *tablaos* and bars, accommodation), flamenco events (festivals and *peñas flamencas*)" as well as "flamenco-related purchases (recording media, *moda flamenco*)."[11] The complexity of this flamenco economy reveals the "geographic paradox" that contemporary cultural industries face: balancing the desire to maintain a "place-based identity" with the need for "export markets for their survival."[12]

When assessing this paradox and its aftermath—the fusion practices that appeal to an international audience—one should recall the hybrid and multicultural roots of flamenco.[13] Flamenco scholars such as Cristina Cruces-Roldán acknowledge flamenco's hybrid roots but limit them to endogenous hybridizations; they consider flamenco as a blend of several elements from within the Andalusian cultural traditions and, therefore, as an identity marker of Andalusian culture.[14] Other scholars maintain that flamenco has evolved with elements from both endogenous and exogenous sources.[15] The latter view considers that flamenco has evolved and survived thanks to its "capacity for continual reinvention."[16]

Flamenco scholars who examine the innovations fusion practices bring to the art form tend to divide them into two (often interrelated) categories: (1) formal innovations to which flamenco artists contribute by experimenting with new musical elements and (2) sociocultural messages attached to the ethnic origins of those new musical elements.[17] Flamenco fusion practices highlight precisely what is explored in this volume: flamenco as a cultural activity on the global stage. This involves looking at how the impact of flamenco across the world helps the art form to survive. Furthermore, fusion practices enable flamenco to include other types of messages, especially politically charged commentaries with a global scope in mind. Committed messages advocating for marginalized social groups are hardly new to flamenco. For example, flamenco has often promoted the civil rights of Gitanos and it became a vehicle to express political opposition against the Franco regime in the early 1970s.[18] What is new is the global perspective of these sociopolitical commentaries in contemporary flamenco fusion ventures. This point is illustrated in the music of Chambao and Ojos de Brujo, two bands that engage the issue of global migration with a similar sharp critical edge but with disparate end results.

Raising Awareness but Missing the Target

Chambao became renowned for creating a distinctive fusion sound with its debut studio album, *Flamenco Chill* (2002), which popularized the notion of "flamenco chill" and refers to the fusion of flamenco sounds with electronic music. The band enhanced its style with the albums *Endorfinas en la mente* (2003) and *Pokito a poko* (2005), although it was with the 2007 album *Con otro aire* that it achieved considerable commercial support. Most notably, the track "Papeles mojados" reached number one in the singles chart in Spain. Adding to the mix of flamenco and electronic music, this song employs North African beats and words to offer a sympathetic musical elegy to the unsuccessful journeys of undocumented migrants seeking to reach the coasts of Europe. "Papeles mojados" begins and ends with vocals in the Tuareg dialect spoken in Algeria and tells the same story "in an abbreviated manner" as the Spanish part of the track.[19] The use of North African music and vocals in its "flamenco chill" has been a consistent element in Chambao's musical project. Early in the band's trajectory, these transcultural borrowings were appropriated to promote Andalusian regional identity—the track "Ahí estás tú" (*Flamenco Chill*) was used by the Junta de Andalucía (the government of Andalusia) in promotional campaigns.[20]

"Papeles mojados" has a specific geographical grounding—the journeys of migrants in *pateras* (rafts) trying to reach Spain's southern coast—but also a universal message of commiseration with the sufferings migrants often endure in their attempts to make their dreams come true. The phrase *ponte tú en su lugar* ("put yourself in their shoes") encapsulates the central plea of the song: to persuade listeners to empathize with the tragic circumstances of migrants. This plea suggests, albeit in a timid fashion, a call for the right of all human beings to decide where they want to live. The historical context not articulated in the song concerns the sealing of European borders in the last two decades to manage the number of immigrants from the "South." Spain's geographical location as a gate to Europe gives the country a strategic role as a guardian state of European border policies. Within this context, the repeated phrase *tanta injusticia me desespera* ("so much inequality exasperates me") in "Papeles mojados" enunciates and identifies with the migrants' hardships.

While "Papeles mojados" is effective in faulting European governments for the tragedies related to immigration because of inhumane immigration laws, it is far less effective in delving into the profound causes of migratory displacement. In other words, the responsibility of the global "North" in this issue seems to begin only when installing obstacles to the crossing of national borders, but not before. The song fails to articulate that among the main "push" factors that accelerate the European dream of African residents who die tragically in the ocean—*se hunden sus sueños* ("their dreams sink")—one should count the economic and political intrusions from the North. Listeners are left to assume that local deficiencies and destabilizations in the African countries are the only triggers. A similar scenario is heard in the track "Voces," also in *Con otro aire*. In denouncing the problem of abandoned children in underdeveloped countries, "Voces" begins by blaming *sociedades que los ignoran* ("societies that ignore children") and that marginalize them in ghettos full of *pobreza, dolor y sufrimiento* ("poverty, grief, and suffering"). Both "Papeles mojados" and "Voces" condemn African governments and societies yet bypass the European powers—including Spain—that should be held accountable for the aftermath of the colonial past and the repercussions of the neoliberal present. To achieve their full potential as thought-provoking and socially committed music, these songs should include a broader scope in their inquiry, a more profound analysis of the structural causes of migration beyond the demonization of African governments. Otherwise, these flamenco fusion practices, though well intentioned in their attempt to address global social issues, risk reinforcing the neoliberal agenda of the capitalist "North" and, simultaneously, endorsing the "anxious narratives" that criticize world music as a capitalist enterprise with no artistic or ethical value.

Global Alliances, Global Resistance

Not all flamenco fusion ventures that address the issue of immigration fall short in their ethical messages. The Barcelona-based band Ojos de Brujo (1998–2011) proved that the circuits of world music offer challenges and opportunities, and obstacles as well as avenues, for innovation.[21] *New York Times* music critic Jon Pareles fittingly described the nine-member group, led by the charismatic singer Marina Abad, "La Canillas," as "a determinedly independent band."[22] This description refers to Ojos de Brujo's decision to work with complete artistic independence and produce music with its self-created label, La Fábrica de Colores, later rebranded as Diquela Records. Ojos de Brujo was not a "wannabe big band" that struggled to make a splash on the margins of the industry until it landed a major music label. Band members decided instead to produce world music and explore international markets on their own terms. In doing so, they were not only determinedly independent but also determined believers in the potential of world music. Rather than a commercially imposed eclecticism, which I have elsewhere called "postmodernist cul-de-sac,"[23] the fusion of diverse ethnic sounds in Ojos de Brujo was a conscious decision ensu-

Figure 1: Marina Abad of Ojos de Brujo, performing at TFF Rudolstadt in Germany, 2010 (photograph by Schorle).

ing from its will to innovate and to enrich its style, by taking advantage of what Philip Bohlman calls "the space of the encounter" that the circuits of world music enable.[24] This decision paid off; the band sold over 100,000 copies of its second album and received international recognition, including the 2004 BBC Radio World Music Award.

For Susanne Stemmler, Ojos de Brujo created a new hybrid genre that she calls "flamenco hip-hop," a distinctively urban sound that emerges from blending the languages of flamenco and hip-hop as well as the histories of cultural resistance that both musical traditions carry with them.[25] While hip-hop is important in the band's musical project, so are other international beats that Ojos de Brujo adds to its flamenco base: rock, funk, ska and reggae, Afro-Cuban percussion, and even Indian elements. Technically speaking, this is not a musical hybrid but rather a musical fusion. As Gerhard Steingress aptly explains, we should differentiate between fusion, a technique that musicians apply by incorporating diverse musical elements at the level of composition, from hybridization, which entails the creation of a separate art form that becomes independent of the original style "with regard to their formal, semantic and socio-cultural characteristics."[26] Though certainly unique, the sound of Ojos de Brujo is hardly a completely distinct genre.

Ojos de Brujo illustrates the use of commercial music industry networks to create new modes of expression that help to redefine the configurations of local identities and, furthermore, to address sociopolitical concerns at a local as well as global level. The very name of the band, which refers to the "sorcerer's eyes," reveals Ojos de Brujo's intent to look deeper into social issues. Recurrent themes of its music include poverty and social unevenness, the main themes in songs such as "Na en la nevera" and "Con hambre" (*Vengue*), "Naita" (*Bari*), and "Corre Lola corre" (*Techarí*); antiwar and anti-globalization messages in "Piedras vs tanques" (*Techarí*) and "Una verdad incómoda" (*Aocaná*); and the obstacles and adversities affecting migrants in "Tiempo de soleá" (*Bari*), "El confort no reconforta" (*Techarí*) , and "Baraka" (*Aocaná*).

"El confort no reconforta" in *Techarí*, Ojos de Brujos' third album, highlights the global scope of the group's musical messages. The song contains a loud and sound objection to the siren song of material welfare. The critical lyrics of this track, released in 2006, must be framed within the context of a Spain overtly optimistic about its economic rise in the first years of the twenty-first century. With an estimated growth of 4 percent in 2006, the Spanish economy also showed that year its best figures in terms of employment since the late 1970s with an 8.3 percent unemployment rate.[27] These numbers finally aligned Spain, economically speaking, with the first European powers. Simply put, Spain was no longer different than its European neighbors. "El confort no reconforta" alerts listeners to the false conditions created by this economic bubble, which hides structural unevenness and debilitates community values. As if predicting—with sorcerer's eyes—the soon-to-come economic downfall of Spain's economy, Ojos de Brujo denounces the dark side of the economic growth: the violation of human rights at the expense of the most vulnerable people, *personas sin papeles* ("undocumented people"), who serve as cheap labor and live as second-class citizens denied basic rights.

Ojos de Brujo does not merely express sympathy for the exploited immigrants. Unlike Chambao in "Papeles mojados," Ojos de Brujo in "El confort no reconforta" points to the root of the problem: the *megamacromultinacionales* ("multinational companies") that act with the blessing of the political and military powers to become *multiexplotadoras* ("multi-exploitative") and *multicoloniales* ("multi-colonial"). This song elicits a critique of the underlying reasons that trigger migratory movements beyond the usual "push" factors (natural disasters, local wars, extreme poverty, and political corruption in underdeveloped countries) and "pull" factors (jobs in developed countries) typically used to justify migration. Ojos de Brujo does not hide the First World's responsibility in those circumstances. The economic intrusions of the global North induce populations of the poor South to migrate, yet the intrusive North has no qualms erecting *fronteras con muertos de los dos lados* ("frontiers with dead people on both sides").

This global scope of Ojos de Brujo's critique—not merely limited to immigration to Spain—demonstrates that the world capitalist system can only be contested at the same global level at which it operates. In this way, the message of "El confort no reconforta" echoes influential political theories. Michael Hardt and Antonio Negri's concept of "Empire" resonates as a type of power that "cannot be resisted by a project aimed at a limited, local autonomy."[28] A global perspective is imperative because "[a]ny proposition of a particular community in isolation, defined in racial, religious, or regional terms, 'delinked' from Empire, shielded from its powers by fixed boundaries, is destined to end up as a kind of ghetto."[29] The only course of action for a resistant project or movement is to think and act globally. Hardt and Negri contend that practical actions must follow theoretical positions. With this song, Ojos de Brujo offers a defiant gesture. The point of the song is not to passively complain but to incite people to act. *Revuelta y cambio* ("revolt and change") is the only way to construct a better future with collective efforts on a global scale.

The critical message of the lyrics of "El confort no reconforta" works in tandem with key formal aspects of the track. The song employs the verse/chorus/verse/chorus pattern typical in contemporary pop music; however, other musical components of the song, which express a sense of discomfort and restlessness, offset this standard structure. The main counterbalance comes from the combination of flamenco and hip-hop, which in itself highlights countercultural undertones. As a musical style that originated as an expression of subaltern groups—African American communities in New York in the 1970s—hip-hop accentuates in this song the sense of anger and distress. It provides a compelling countercultural vocabulary that transcends the musical features to also include a global subcultural style.[30]

To conceptualize this combination of African American musical elements with a flamenco base, consider the concept of "de/territorialization" coined by Jonathan Xavier Inda and Renato Rosaldo. With this term, Inda and Rosaldo summarize a dual process that occurs in cultural borrowings from other national traditions: those cultural elements are removed from their ordinary, traditional settings and then integrated into a new spatial and temporal matrix. The significance of this concept rests on the slash, which "allows us to separate 'de' from 'territorialization,' thus calling attention to the fact that deterritorialization always contains territorialization within itself."[31] In other words, deterritorialization and reterritorialization partner in this case to provide cross-cultural identifications, formulating a critique of global capitalism and its discontents.

In the song, lead singer Marina Abad raps agitatedly, protesting against multinationals. The song ends with a moaning female voice fading, the signature flamenco *quejío* that crowns the sense of despair the lyrics express. Yet, once again a twist is added to this traditional element: the moaning is remixed. Flamenco meets the DJ's mixing turntables and contemporary urban subcultures. Live performances of Ojos de Brujo further emphasize this sense of fusion. Marina Abad often wears traditional flamenco dresses in combination with other not-so-traditional garments and accoutrements, such as comfortable sneakers and cheap plastic jewelry. As Susanne Stemmler notes, these outfits seek to turn around in ironic style the stereotypes of the "gypsy dancer" and the "oriental woman." Traditional flamenco shoes are replaced by sneakers, "a symbol of today of hip-hop fashion and culture."[32] Unlike the static nature of the flamenco dancer stereotype, inextricably tied to "the exotic spectacle of colonialism,"[33] the aesthetics, the poetics, and the politics of global hip-hop serve here to stir up matters, to present flamenco as an *arte vivo*, a practice in constant development; in short, flamenco is mobilized by de/territorializing it, by inscribing it on a global stage. Flamenco fusion, as Ojos de Brujo conceptualizes it, is no longer just the embodiment of Andalusian Gitano culture but is a vehicle to facilitate transcultural coalitions and to provide a global forum for youth protest.

This global scope coincides with the current push within Andalusia to institutionalize flamenco "as a patrimonial object and marker of Andalusian identity," as stated in article 68 of the 2007 *Estatuto de Autonomía*.[34] A timely corrective measure to counteract Franco's co-optation of flamenco as a heritage object of Spain—which became known as *nacional flamenquismo*—this institutionalization of flamenco in the twenty-first century at the service of regional autonomy also reinforces the purist views of flamenco. The inclusion of flamenco in UNESCO's list of Intangible Cultural Heritage of Humanity in 2010 does as well. Institutionalization entails looking to the past to preserve the cultural patrimony of an enclosed collectivity often defined in essentialist terms—such as a uniform version of Andalusian identity. Enrique Baltanás notes that, despite the efforts of Andalusian nationalist discourse to circumscribe the perimeters of flamenco and to sidestep flamenco practices produced outside the regional borders, flamenco is, paradoxically, "more appreciated beyond our regional borders than in Andalusia itself."[35] This is why I advocate—by examining two examples of flamenco fusion—celebrating rather than neglecting the significance of flamenco on the global stage. The meaning of this is twofold: by appropriating the conduits of the global musical industry and by participating in a network of transcultural exchanges, fusion practices bring international visibility to flamenco and, consequently, enhance its cultural relevance. It also allows flamenco to serve as a vehicle for cultural interventions on issues of global concern, such as migration.

Notes

1. Steven Feld, "A Sweet Lullaby for World Music," *Public Culture* 12.1 (2000): 146; Tony Mitchell, ed., *Global Noise: Rap and Hip-Hop Outside the USA* (Middleton: Wesleyan University Press, 2001), 310.
2. Feld, "A Sweet Lullaby for World Music," 151–154.
3. José Luis Ortiz Nuevo, *Alegato contra la pureza* (Barcelona: Ediciones Barataria, 2010).
4. Jorge Pérez, "The Soundscapes of Resistance: Notes on the Postmodern Condition of Spanish Pop Music," *Journal of Spanish Cultural Studies* 7.1 (2006): 75–91; Gerhard Steingress, "Flamenco Fusion and New Flamenco as Postmodern Phenomena: An Essay on Creative Ambiguity in Popular Music," in *Songs of the Minotaur: Hybridity and Popular Music in the Era of Globalization*, ed. Gerhard Steingress (Münster: Lit Verlag, 2002), 169–216; Susanne Stemmler, "'Sonido ciudadísimo': Black Noise Andalusian Style

in Contemporary Spain," *Sonic Interventions*, ed. Sylvia Mieszkowski, Joy Smith, and Marijke de Valck (Amsterdam: Rodopi, 2007), 241–264.
   5. Antonio Mairena and Ricardo Molina, *Mundo y formas del cante flamenco* (Madrid: Revista de Occidente, 1963).
   6. John Tomlinson, *Cultural Imperialism: A Critical Introduction* (Baltimore: Johns Hopkins University Press, 1991).
   7. Theodor Adorno, "On Popular Music," in *On Record. Rock, Pop, and the Written Word*, ed. Simon Frith and Andrew Goodwin (New York: Pantheon Books, 1990), 302–303.
   8. Christopher Paetzold, "'Singing Beneath the Alhambra': The North African and Arabic Past and Present in Contemporary Andalusian Music," *Journal of Spanish Cultural Studies* 10.2 (2009): 213.
   9. Steingress, "La hibridación transcultural como clave de la formación del Nuevo Flamenco (aspectos histórico, sociológicos, analíticos y comparativos)," *Trans. Revista Transcultural de Música* 8 (2004).
   10. Steingress, "Flamenco Fusion," 174.
   11. Yuko Aoyama, "Artists, Tourists, and the State: Cultural Tourism and the Flamenco Industry in Andalusia, Spain," in *International Journal of Urban and Regional Research* 33.1 (2009): 88.
   12. Aoyama, "The Role of Consumption and Globalization in a Cultural Industry: The Case of Flamenco," *Geoforum 38* (2007): 106.
   13. Aoyama, "The Role of Consumption," 105; Paetzold, "Singing Beneath the Alhambra," 214; Steingress, "La hibridación," 4.
   14. Cristina Cruces-Roldán, *Antropología y flamenco. Más allá de la música (II)* (Sevilla: Signatura Ediciones, 2003), 27.
   15. Steingress, "Flamenco Fusion."
   16. Michelle Heffner Hayes, *Flamenco: Conflicting Histories of the Dance* (Jefferson, NC: McFarland, 2009), 186.
   17. See Luis Clemente, *Filigranas: Una historia de fusiones flamencas* (Valencia: Editorial La Máscara, 1995), for a thorough account of the history of flamenco fusion practices until the mid–1990s from a formal point of view.
   18. Hayes, *Flamenco*, 1.
   19. Silvia Bermúdez, *Rocking the Boat: Migration and the Significance of Race in Contemporary Spanish Music* (Toronto: University of Toronto Press, forthcoming).
   20. Paetzold, "Singing Beneath the Alhambra," 217.
   21. Ojos de Brujo has released five studio albums: *Vengue* (1999); *Barí* (2002); *Techarí* (2006); *Aocaná* (2009); and the compilation *Corriente Vital 10 Años* (2010), as well as an album of remixes, *Barí: Remezclas de la Casa* (2005), and a live album, *Techarí Live* (2007).
   22. Jon Pareles, "Far Beyond Flamenco, a Zest for Rhythms (and Politics)," *New York Times* (June 30, 2007), http://www.nytimes.com/2007/06/30/arts/music/30ojos.html (accessed October 31, 2013).
   23. Pérez, "The Soundscapes of Resistance," 76.
   24. Philip Bohlman, *World Music: A Very Short Introduction* (London: Oxford University Press, 2002), xii.
   25. Stemmler, "'Sonido ciudadísimo,'" 241.
   26. Steingress, "Flamenco Fusion," 210; and "What Is Hybrid Music? An Epilogue," 318–319, in *Songs of the Minotaur*.
   27. "La tasa de desempleo cierra 2006 en el 8.3%, el nivel más bajo desde 1979," *El Mundo*, (January 27, 2007), http://www.elmundo.es (accessed October 20, 2013).
   28. Michael Hardt and Antonio Negri, *Empire* (Cambridge, Mass: Harvard University Press, 2000), 206.
   29. Ibid.
   30. See Lipsitz, *Dangerous Crossroads* (London: Verso, 1994), 23–48, and Mitchell, *Global Noise*, for thorough accounts on the global appropriation of African American musical styles and of hip-hop in particular by urban youth musical subcultures.
   31. Jonathan Xavier Inda and Renato Rosaldo, eds., *The Anthropology of Globalization: A Reader* (Oxford: Blackwell, 2002), 12.
   32. Stemmler, "'Sonido ciudadísimo,'" 244.
   33. Hayes, *Flamenco*, 89.
   34. William Washabaugh, *Flamenco Music and National Identity in Spain* (Surrey, UK: Ashgate, 2012), 5.
   35. Enrique Baltanás, "The Fatigue of the Nation: Flamenco as the Basis of Heretical Identities," in *Songs of the Minotaur*, 161.

Y Para Rematar
Contemplations on a Movement in Transition
Niurca Márquez

And the codes? The grammar?
There's the rub.
For there is no one dance code, no one grammar, but several.[1]
—Valerie Preston-Dunlop, choreographer and scholar

El flamenco es como un tapiz que se construye a partir de varios trocitos de tapices.[2]
—José Luis Rodríguez, flamenco composer and guitarist

We become artists because we have something to say. In many instances, it is not with words but through other mediums that we find release. As dancers, we find the genre, the language that best fits, and we move forward, we articulate, we develop dialogue and discourse. Once we reach a certain point, and if it is our intention to engage our community and our audience, we realize that our contemporary reality demands that we are able to communicate not only with those in our own genre but also with those outside of it. But what of a language that is so highly codified that it is often misunderstood? What of a language that corresponds to a cultural, political, and social reality? Is it possible to simplify the syntax and grammar, take only pieces of it in an attempt to make it accessible? Or does it lose its meaning? And what of dialects, new forms of communicating? These are questions I ask myself on a constant basis and among the reasons I remain in flamenco.

It seems the most pressing question is this: Can we view flamenco as a single art form or are there many flamencos? Which leads me to ask if the confrontation of binary opposites, Gitano or non–Gitano, tradition or vanguard, are necessary in a conversation on flamenco today? They are questions that permeate both formal and informal studies on flamenco, from academics and artists alike. In one such conversation among myself, guitarist Jose Luis Rodríguez, and dancer Juan de Juan, the conclusion was this: "Flamenco is a personal (individual) art form, and for that reason there will always be as many interpretations of it as there are people practicing it. It is an art form of the here and now, not of what happened years ago."[3] There are many directions in which this comment could take us, but we will focus on what this individuality has meant for the art form in the last ten years and the happenings that indicate we may be experiencing the beginning of another movement within the form, similar to the one experienced during the last years of the Franco regime and into the 1980s.[4]

A new generation of flamenco artists is pushing the boundaries of what is acceptable. Simultaneously, journalists and scholars have understood these artistic strategies and have published widely in digital and print media the fact that widespread experimentation is taking place in flamenco, with and without institutional support from the Spanish government and cultural ministries.[5] Among artists, there is an undercurrent of resistance to the established norms of what is "sellable" in flamenco both in and outside of Spain. The phrase that was so common in the late 1990s, *hay que darle lo que les gusta* ("we must give them what they like"), is being challenged by *hago esto porque es lo que tengo que contar* ("I do this because it is what I have to say"). More artists are finding new ways to rescue the idea of a flamenco that is about human experiences: a space to express the realities of a contemporary world.

In a recent interview, Israel Galván, like other experimentalists, noted he was surprised when people found it strange that he "looks like a lot of things, especially modernism."[6] This surprise is shared by many artists who see experimentalism as a natural progression of an art form that has always evolved in response to the cultural, social, and political arena in which it has developed. So for a man who was fascinated by Kafka's *Metamorphosis*, it is not at all strange that his dance, too, would be transformed. Galván, a global phenomenon, claims that attending college, surfing social media sites, and going to the movies are proof of the many educational and cultural sources that surface in his work, as they do in the work of many other cutting-edge experimental artists of his generation.

Such is the case of Juan Carlos Lérida. Born in Germany to Sevillian parents, Lérida is a choreographer and dancer and holds a degree in Choreography and Dance Interpretation from the Institute de Teatre of Barcelona.[7] He is also one of a very small group of artists who is actively writing and concerned with the discourse surrounding flamenco today. To consolidate the work of artists who questioned the parameters of tradition, Lérida curated in 2009 the first Flamenco Empírico Festival, sponsored by Mercat de les Flors.[8] Bringing together for the first time artists of disparate philosophies whose work was considered avant-garde, the festival's theme was to look at the current state of evolution and transformation in flamenco dancing. Was there a unifying "look?" Were there limits to the level of experimentation that was possible? Could a set of markers in stylistic choices that was unanimous across the board be identified? There certainly was no single set of identifiable aesthetic markers governing the works presented. Where one artist experimented with the lack of traditional costuming and music, another experimented with the actual movement vocabulary, while yet another chose to push the boundaries of the very structures that make up flamenco by superimposing compositional approaches and philosophies of other forms such as modern dance or even *butoh* (an experimental form of dance from Japan). The only limit one could pinpoint was the need to keep true to the line of questioning, not from a superficial attempt to equate flamenco to modern dance, but from a true investigation of what exactly makes up the dance.

Lérida identifies three distinct sections of the festival's programming as particularly important in demonstrating the various lines of inquiry pursued.[9] The first was "Tócame las Palmas," a series of improvisational encounters between flamenco artists, many of whom had never met before, with little predetermined structure. In some instances, the artists met for the first time one hour prior to the performance, quickly discussing structure and form. In others, they let chance and the elements of composition borrowed from contemporary dance dictate the development of the hour-long improvisation. For example, Belén Maya, Rocío Molina, Florencio Campo (Cuqui), and Lérida used dice to determine when each would take the floor and with whom they would improvise at any given moment, led by ideas of listening and instant composition. The second, the series "Tapeos," showcased emerging artists from Spain and abroad, which, Lérida states, was a chance to give "visibility to these artists from around the world with an interest in experimentation and to witness flamenco from other perspectives" that approached an understanding of the human experience from a "social, political and cultural" standpoint through the language of flamenco "contaminated by other artistic lines" of inquiry.[10] The third, "Irse por las ramas," short two- to three-day residencies, provided the format that has led to the most questioning in Lérida's experience as it has brought together artists in a laboratory setting to explore the inner workings of the form. These encounters led to collaborations, the establishment of alternate ways of approaching composition, and a reexamining of the corporeal and theoretical discourse that we present when working within contemporary flamenco.

Despite their differences, each presentation awarded viewers an opportunity to approach the art form from a distinct perspective with a unique set of outcomes. None was more notable in illustrating the dichotomy of choreographed versus improvised composition than the space shared by Amador Rojas and Yolanda Heredia, accompanied by Pablo Logiovine on the *bandoneón*. Both Rojas and Heredia are bending in very different ways ideas about what is traditional. Amador Rojas is a dancer who does not blur the line between what has traditionally been considered male and female, but erases it entirely to embody both. His first evening-length work, "Kahlo Caló" (a reference to his Gitano upbringing and to Frida Kahlo, on whose life the work is based), contains numerous layers of subversion as he takes the audience on a journey of cross-dressing and gender-bending that includes traditional flamenco structures set against theatrical backdrops featuring contemporary dance and music. Heredia is a dancer and teacher who borrows elements of Argentine tango to enrich her teaching and understanding of the use of the body with the traditional train dress, the *bata de cola*, in flamenco. She is also a staunch advocate of improvisation in the traditional sense, leading students to learn the *cante* and how to relate to it rather than learning choreography, and always with a clear understanding of our contemporary reality and the search for individuality in each dancer.

A tobacco ceremony led by Heredia opened the show.[11] As she called upon the ancestors and the spirits of the earth and thanked the essence of those present, one could not help but wonder how this differed from calling on the *duende*. The artists then took turns performing their improvisations. Amador Rojas chose to showcase an excerpt from his most recent work at the time, *Mandala,* a staged choreography that follows established flamenco structures. However, his choice of costuming with a black veil tied around his face, his non-gender-specific choice of movement, and the musical backdrop were evidence that even while adhering to set choreographic markers, Rojas is questioning boundaries. Heredia followed with an improvisation accompanied by a recorded version of Esperanza Fernandez's version of *Gelem-Gelem*. Her mastery of the bata de cola, the organic quality of her movements, and the lack of pretense in the performance brought to light the importance of the female figure artistically, socially, and spiritually.[12]

Finally, it was time for the two to share the stage joined by the live improvised accompaniment of the bandoneon. In this last segment, the stage served as a space of truce for the arguments constantly imposed by presenters, scholars, and other artists. It quickly became apparent that what these two artists shared was a search for harmony within the body. The prejudices of what *is* male and what *is* female and what is composed and what is improvised, were absent, and most importantly, it was a clear example of the *anti-guapa* phenomenon. Coined by Belén Maya and discussed at length by Michelle Heffner Hayes, the term refers to artists' resistant strategies concerning beauty and femininity.[13] Rojas challenges the idea of who is allowed to be feminine, while Heredia explores historic definitions of beauty, stretching those to include the sociopolitical nature of performativity and gender politics as artistic strategies. She was elegant, but never superficial, easily expressing the rawness and depth of experiences that have molded her. Both performers shed light on expressions of loneliness, vulnerability, and even ecstasy inside of a movement vocabulary that revealed the unsteady oscillation between tradition and the iconography of modernity.

Flamenco Empírico 2009 was the beginning of an open and rich conversation among artists about what it means to be contemporary within flamenco, as an individual artist and as part of a collective. It explored multiple facets of the field: the implications for programming within the industry of flamenco; concerns faced by artists who were showcasing new work; and most important, it created a platform for performers to meet as a collective, during which time they shared a critical discourse concerning the current spectrum of flamenco.[14] These meetings, like those of the radical Judson Church Movement of the 1960s, illustrate that contemporary artists are mindful of the world in which they live, concerned first and foremost with the backgrounds, ethnicities, and experiences of artists within their discipline, in an overt attempt to interrogate and widen the critical performative discourse surrounding the festival and art-making of flamenco in Spain and abroad. The inclusion of "Tapeos: Flamenco Empírico" in the 2013 London Flamenco Festival bears witness to the fact that these lines of inquiry have become so significant to contemporary artists working today that they have spilled well beyond the Spanish borders and onto the London stage.

In 2010, Flamenco Empírico became part of the Festival Flamenco Ciutat Vella. Although in 2014 it was not included in the festival's programming, its effect on the overall vision of Ciutat Flamenco is apparent in the festival's description of purpose and scope of activities:

> a platform and meeting point for stirring up interest in flamenco, reviewing and experimenting with it. It is a proposal open to other disciplines and, in particular, to the new trends and emerging projects that follow an experimental line of work. A yearly keynote event committed to the most contemporary, trans-cultural and universal vision of national and international flamenco. A week of flamenco offering the premieres of commissioned productions, concerts, workshops, artistic residencies, audiovisuals, exhibitions, competitions, video installations and dance sessions hosted by a DJ.[15]

Lérida is concerned with what it means for the continuation of an open dialogue when a process like this is institutionalized through written manifesto of a government-run cultural platform. But he cites Flamenco Empírico's five-year history as responsible for mainstreaming their prescient concerns, independent of whether or not they follow through with the risks involved. In addition, Lérida credits his curatorial tenure with educating and allowing him the public and private space to reexamine the public attitudes, aesthetic praxis, and intellectual discourse surrounding experimental process within contemporary flamenco:

> And it has also made me question that all artists who work from varying perspectives of flamenco no longer need to be joined because there are multiple lines of focus in these apparently independent attitudes towards traditional flamenco. But that doesn't mean that I have to identify with those artists. Maybe only due to an understanding of belonging to a collective who until now has had to deal tags that label them flamenco or not.[16]

This statement by Lérida illuminates the new spaces opening up for experimentation in flamenco and illustrates how they can be viable and effective platforms for discourse on the form. As a result of concerted, conscious efforts on the parts of various artists, what was once underground and subaltern is now gaining a space within the most notable expository platforms for flamenco. This is evident in "48 Noches. Laboratorio Bienal," a program proposed by the Universidad Internacional de Andalucia (UNIA) and adopted by the Biennale of Seville within its roster of "Actividades Paralelas" (parallel activities), and "Plataforma Independiente de Estudios Flamencos Modernos y Contemporáneos" (PIE.FMC), also a program of UNIA.

Some of the names that appear in the festival's five-year history are to be expected: Israel Galván, Andrés Marín, Belén Maya, Rocío Molina, and Amador Rojas. Others, such as La Chana, Yolanda Heredia, and Carrete are by most accounts considered traditional artists.[17] The latter group raises two questions for artists and scholars alike concerned with the texture and historiography of flamenco art: What is contemporary in flamenco and is the art form itself not contemporary by nature? If it does in fact reflect the reality of a people, then is it not logical that the form of said expression will change in appearance as the reality of said group changes over time? Flamenco Empírico was not the first to tackle

Figure 1: Juan Carlos Lérida, performing in Olga Pericet's *Pisadas*, Festival de Jerez, 2014 (courtesy photographer Paco Villalta).

these questions, but it was the first event to use them as the foundation for its curatorial philosophy.

What about work that not only pushes the improvisational boundaries of flamenco but also reclaims flamenco's use as social protest? Possible answers can be found in the work of Flo6x8, a collective that describes itself as "activist-artistic-situational-performative-folkloric and very *jondo*."[18] The name is an abbreviation of the word *flamenco* and an allusion to the rhythmic patterns in flamenco. Its members employ pseudonyms to remain anonymous. I have spent much time with its members over the years, in class and performance settings, and have talked at length with La Niña NINJA (an acronym for No Income, No Jobs and Assets) about the collective's efforts and the description of what they do as a "flash mob."[19] She stresses that these are not flash mobs; they are not there for entertainment: they are "actions." This charges them with the activism that their proposals espouse. When asked why they utilize flamenco as the basis for their actions, she explains that when they began, it was the natural choice because it was a language the members shared. But, as the work developed, they realized "how appropriate flamenco is as a form of protest."[20] The actions bring the members a collective sense of empowerment in a society where the lines between rights and privileges is constantly blurred and loopholes are efficiently used by governmental institutions to disempower its citizens. Bank lobbies seemed a natural location for the most evident of the protests:

> In addition to representing capitalism and the oppressor, in a bank you are expected to act a certain way, you speak softer, you feel small, you approach it with apprehension at times, and they feel they have all the power when in reality without our money, they can do nothing. They feel powerful and it is important to us to take over their space. It is empowering, even if it's just for a few minutes.[21]

When asked about the role of foreigners in the collective, La Niña NINJA responded that the mix of backgrounds is always a positive as it generates more dialogue, more proposals, and new ideas.[22] When questioned about the performance possibilities that have arisen from these actions, she points out, "We have not been given a space, we have forged it ... we have to be constantly aware of it so that it is not taken from us."[23]

In order to gain a broader perspective on the variety of experimentation undertaken in flamenco today, it is necessary to note that over the past decade a series of artists has emerged who are looking at flamenco as a whole, a complete artistic genre that includes the cante (singing), the guitar, the dance, and, yes, even video, poetry, and visual arts. Flo6x8's work illustrates that this is not only a phenomena of the body, but of the art form as an organic whole, much like the collective spirit of the group itself.

In the cante, it is important to note the contributions of singers such as El Niño de Elche and Tomás de Perrate, whose work challenges both the spaces available to singers and the sonic/corporeal use of the voice/body. Here again we find the juxtaposition of two figures that seemingly belong to different sides of the dichotomy who are experimenting and challenging the limits of commercial flamenco. In the case of Perrate, it is through his most recent collaboration with Pedro G. Romero and Israel Galván in *Lo Real-Le Reel-The Real*, which deals with the extermination of the Gitanos in Europe during the 1930s and 1940s. The work is described as follows in the program notes:

> A degenerated art. Tomas de Perrate sings Hugo Ball's *Karawene* in the Tona style. What does it mean to be Oriental? Strange bedfellows: Jews, homosexuals, Jehovah's

witnesses, communists, gypsies. What meaning can we then give orientalism? *Metastasis*: where Xenakis, anti-fascist, wounded by his allies, defines with precision the form of the anomaly.[24]

In the case of Niño de Elche, it is through a mostly self-generated body of work that explores the limits of the voice/body from different perspectives and pushes the limits of the genre. Elche is committed to an exploration of the voice/body as a means of raw expression rooted in tradition, but in response to a contemporary reality. Among his many works, two in particular illustrate Elche's current radicalism: In his 2011 *VACONBACON*, a multidisciplinary work that searches for a moving and action-filled cante, and based on the works of Francis Bacon, Elche "translates the original force of the body and the emotions of a flamenco cantaor of the here and now"; in *ToCaBa*, his latest collaborative work with Juan Carlos Lérida and Raul Cantizano, the conventions of the *tablao* are disrupted in a postmodern interpretation that dares touch upon the hidden queer in a performance among three men. In *VACONBACON*, Elche tests the body and explores it as a resonator. He sings in the traditional manner, deconstructs the *grito* to illustrate it in pieces, jumps rope until he is almost out of breath to deliver the cante that requires all his strength, closes his mouth with clothespins while still reciting a piece of popular wisdom, and, yes, fries bacon on stage. He pulls freely from the works of T.S. Elliot, Antonio Machado, and others, and does not limit himself to the traditional forms in cante. Rather, he returns to the fullness of the form, utilizing the entire body as a sound source: a "tube filled with secret resonators, sphincters, empty spaces, muscles and huffs."[25]

Elche's solo works and collaborations are extensive and each takes on a different layer of subversion: sometimes subtle, sometimes not. His 2013 CD, *Sí, a Miguel Hernández*, rejects conventional packaging and is instead accompanied by a newspaper with different elements of the life and work of the famed Spanish author and activist and becomes a platform to make the material a viable and pertinent reflection of and reaction to Spain's current sociopolitical climate. For Elche and his collaborators, a newspaper was a logical choice as source of information, a political facsimile, and an element that "flies from one hand to the next."[26] His collaborations with guitarist and composer Raul Cantizano are notable in that they deconstruct preconceived notions about what is possible both in the cante and the guitar, and their heavily poetic content is allowing Elche to open new avenues for presenting the work, most notably in poetry and spoken word festivals.

Raul Cantizano is no stranger to this line of work and inquiry. In 2003, he began a collective with Santiago Barber, "Bulos y Tanguerias," producing an endless number of projects exploring the various parameters of flamenco. The projects varied in scope and purpose and in 2012 it was apparent that this endeavor had moved well beyond the stage and was entering a space of "inter-media." "Bulos y Tanguerias" became "bulos.net," with its focus to create a body of work that showcases the point of intersection between flamenco and other artistic practices and disciplines. The format in which to present the work was expanded to include workshops, articles, conferences, audiovisual projects, and graphic arts. It is an art-making process that in Cantizano's words is "provocative, both in content and form."[27] For example, in *D.E.F. Dialogos-ElectroFlamencos (Electro-Flamenco Dialogues)*, Cantizano approaches the guitar as an instrument that can partake in a dialogue among instruments, bodies, and machines;

the films of José Val de Omar serve as a source of structure and study. Cantizano and Barber describe it as a process that is "intuitive and open to surprise, to the interruption of the unknown and why not, to activate the tremors of the city that takes us in."[28] Their work has a distinct sociopolitical flavor that is supported by a philosophy based on the collective rather than the individual. It is a space where the model of actions undertaken by Flo6x8 has its roots and where it meets the space for questioning and investigation that *Flamenco Empírico* coalesced: yet another example of the cross-disciplinary approaches that these experimentalists are undertaking.

What of our perceptions of flamenco? What are the spaces for experimentation and innovation outside of Spain? Festivals such as Flamenco Festival Dusseldorf repeatedly take risks in their programming, and newer festivals that are often sparked by artists who have been involved with the Flamenco Empírico collective, such as "im Raum Flamenco" (in Flamenco-Space) organized by Julia Petschinka, demonstrate there is a space for practices that push the limits of what is conventional and, most important, that there is interest in these lines of inquiry outside of Spain. There are also artists who have relocated to other countries as a result of the economic crisis in Spain, such as guitarist and composer José Luis Rodríguez, who for many years was musical director of Ballet Cristina Hoyos and has collaborated with both Belén Maya and Juan Carlos Lérida. While the work of bulos.net centers on performance "actions," Rodríguez is searching for the possibilities for expansion existent in the flamenco guitar itself. In 2011, he released *io:Flamenco Abstractions*, a collaborative work with electronic composer David Font that was the first of its kind in the guitar arena. The work is a complete deconstruction of the flamenco guitar, a stripping away of the cante, dance, and *palmas* to highlight the essence of the guitar. Unlike previous explorations in which bits and pieces of flamenco compositions are taken by sound artists and treated electronically, this was the first instance in which live electronics and guitar came together in much the same way that traditional improvisations are approached in flamenco: each came to the table with their codes and structures and they made the experience a meeting of two distinct personalities. Rodríguez takes this approach and incorporates it into his staged works by which he challenges audiences to experience the guitar as a whole, not just as a traditional instrument for accompaniment, but as part of a collective that creates a narrative.

His most recent work, *Resonancias,* includes a sound design that utilizes both prerecorded sounds and live electronic processing with strategies of spatialization and layering to explore content and the placement of sound in space. The work includes full-length guitar compositions as well as video projections and an electro-acoustic collaboration similar to live orchestration. Rodríguez calls his approach *anti-toque*: a deconstruction of conventional forms of playing in favor of a search for hidden meanings and the essence in compositions. He credits this to his many years touring and experiencing different musical forms as well as his time spent composing for companies outside of Spain and learning how flamenco is interpreted, experienced, and understood abroad. This has led him to dismantle its many layers in an attempt to "demystify" the codes that govern and to allow content to take precedence over form.[29] It is yet another example of innovation that is not detached from tradition but instead searches in the essence of the form for elements necessary to comment on today's pertinent issues.

Experimentalists within flamenco have always existed. This is not a new phenom-

Figure 2: José Luis Rodríguez, in *Resonancias*, Miami, Florida, 2014 (courtesy photographer Manuel L. Romalde).

enon and is not one that should be surprising in an art form that is first and foremost a form of expression and commentary for a people. It is also important to note that even what we consider classical or traditional today emerged in the context of specific history. The *seguiriya* as a dance did not exist until Vicente Escudero decided to set movement to the style, and the *silencio* section that is considered standard in a traditional *alegrías* today was first included by Carmen Amaya. Issues of visibility and representation have made it challenging at times to understand the extent to which this kind of work is shaping our understanding of flamenco. One thing is certain: this propensity goes much deeper than the modernist deconstructions of Israel Galván's dance or the musical experimentations of the late Enrique Morente. In the words of Rodríguez, it is as it's always been: "in essence, the necessity of expression in present time."[30]

Notes

1. Valerie Preston-Dunlop, *Looking at Dances: Choreographical Perspective on Choreography* (Binstead, Hampshire, UK: Noverre Press, 1998).
2. José Luis Rodríguez, master class given at Keene State College, New Hampshire, March 4, 2012. "Flamenco is like a tapestry that is made up of pieces of many different tapestries." Translation by the author.
3. Juan de Juan and Jose Luis Rodríguez, personal conversation with the author, Miami, May 2014.

4. I am referring to the contributions made by artists such as Enrique Morente and Manolo Sanlúcar (the inclusion of lyrics by poets who had been censored by the Franco regime), Lole y Manuel (the introduction of forms reminiscent of troubadors), Mario Maya (who was inspired by the civil rights movement in the United States and used innovations in content and lyrics to express the social and economic hardships of Gitanos in Spain), among others. Additionally, one must note the creation of the co-op by Antonio Gades that later became the National Ballet of Spain. This group of innovators was expanded by collaborations with Andalusian rock groups such as Alameda and Triana, the subsequent works of Pata Negra, and of course the best known of the innovators, Paco de Lucía and Camarón de la Isla. Much of the push to challenge content and form that we see among today's generation of experimentalists is similar to that found in the works of the above-mentioned artists.

5. Scholar Cristina Cruces-Roldán, for example, has ample references in her works about what we recognize as the established codes of classical flamenco and how these are broken down by contemporary artists.

6. Joan Acocella, "The Refusé: Israel Galván and the Evolution of Flamenco," *New Yorker* (March 17, 2014), 16.

7. Lérida was the second artist to graduate from this program, the first of its kind. Programs in Madrid and Malaga followed.

8. "Flamenco Empirico 2009 sets bailaores the challenge of experimentation," http://www.flamenco-world.com/noticias/mercat12022009.htm (accessed May 18, 2014).

9. Juan Carlos Lérida, e-mail message to author, June 19, 2014.

10. Ibid.

11. Heredia is a shaman in the Red Road tradition and a sweat lodge leader. In that tradition, sacred tobacco is used for many reasons, among which are the blessing of a space and connecting the individual with himself or herself and the Universe.

12. Heredia refers to the particular train dress worn for the performance as the *bata de las abuelas* (of the grandmothers), a dress whose ruffles are constructed of various print fabrics. She describes it as a reference to the reverence towards those who have come before as a place to begin to innovate. Yolanda Heredia, comments during class with the author, Seville, July 15, 2010. Transcription and translation by the author.

13. Michelle Heffner Hayes, *Flamenco: Conflicting Histories of the Dance* (Jefferson: NC: McFarland & Company, 2009).

14. In 2005, the *Agencia para el desarrollo de la industria del flamenco* (Agency for the Development of the Industry of Flamenco) was created, sparking many debates among artists and presenters about the implications for flamenco of this designation as an industry.

15. "Cituat Flamenco (Flamenco City) 2013," http://mercatflors.cat/en/ciclesifestivals/ciutat-flamenco-flamenco-city-2013/ (accessed May 21, 2014).

16. Juan Carlos Lérida, e-mail message to author, June 19, 2014.

17. In his e-mail correspondence with the author, Lérida states that he included La Chana in the programming when he learned that she had not performed on a stage in over fifteen years and taught all her classes, with full footwork and arm sequences, sitting in a chair. The improvisational performance she presented awarded the audience an opportunity to reflect upon issues of age and the transmission of information from a vital place, the possibility of dancing independent of the conditions.

18. http://www.pieflamenco.com (accessed June 14, 2014).

19. "A Flamenco Flash Mob Performance in a Spanish Bank," and "Spain's Creative Protests: Flamenco Flash Mobs and Supermarket Robin Hoods," http://www.bbc.com/news/magazine-22174456 (accessed August 15, 2012).

20. La Niña NINJA, interview with the author, June 18, 2014, via Skype. Christina Cruces-Roldán states that "in many cases it is not a thought-out process, but reactive as much of the nature of flamenco." Cristina Cruces-Roldán, "De cintura para arriba: Hipercorporeidad y sexuación en le flamenco," *Plataforma independiente de estudios flamencos modernos y contemporaneous,* http://www.pieflamenco.com/investigaciones/de-cintura-para-arriba-hipercorporeidad-y-sexuacion-en-el-flamenco/ (accessed May 27, 2014). Translated by the author.

21. La Niña NINJA, interview with the author, June 18, 2014.

22. A large number of the collective's members are foreign born and raised. La Niña NINJA was born in France to Spanish parents and has resided in Spain since 1997.

23. La Niña NINJA, interview with the author, June 18, 2014.

24. Program notes to *Lo Real-Le Reel-The Real,* which premiered at Teatro Real, Madrid, December 13, 2012.

25. Program notes to *VACONBACON,* which premiered at Centro de la Cultura Contemporánea de Elche, in May 2011, http://bulos.net/vaconbacon-cantar-las-fuerzas/ (accessed June 3, 2014).

26. Francisco Contreras Molina ("El Niño de Elche"), interview with the author, July 7, 2014, via Skype. Translated by the author.

27. Raul Cantizano, interview with the author, July 8, 2014, via Skype. Translated by the author. A full

archive of the collective's various projects and information about the members can be found at http://bulos.net.

28. "DEF DiálogosElectroFlamencos. Sevilla, marzo 2014," http://bulos.net/def-dialogoselectroflamencos-taller-de-creacion-remezcla-partir-del-flamenco-14-15-16-de-marzo-2014/ (accessed May 7, 2014). In my interview with Cantizano on July 8, 2014 (cited in note 27), he pointed out that the intention was to use the films of Val de Omar (who collaborated with Vicente Escudero) not to deify the man and his works, as has often been the case in flamenco, but rather to utilize them as a point of departure.

29. José Luis Rodríguez, interview with the author, March 31, 2014. Translation by the author.

30. Ibid.

Blancanieves, Flamenco and National Identity

WILLIAM WASHABAUGH

A movie's soul, in José Saramago's words, is a box of surprises, as if clowns were always ready to spring out.[1] Rather than being singular and integral, a movie is a congeries, a hybrid object. It is a complex experience "comprised of multiple components irreducible to a single essence."[2] It is chunky thing with parts that stick out at odd angles. Rarely a seamless work of art like a Bach fugue, a movie is usually "ramshackle and rickety.... One can remember only parts of it, irrespective of their original relationship with the whole."[3] True, we may talk about the force of a movie as if it were a unified phenomenon. We can hardly do otherwise. Our talk wants to produce a unity that captures some, if not all, of a film's complexity. But such talk should not seduce us into believing that the movie is itself unified. "If you're honest about what you remember from a film, a film remains three or four moments." So says the Oscar-winning director Danny Boyle.[4]

So as I begin my comments on Pablo Berger's *Blancanieves* (2012), I ask readers to remember that this movie, like most others, is a box with clowns inside. It delivers surprising moments that can be appreciated and discussed independently of plot, character development, and obvious themes. The value of these moments depends on the strength of one's arguments. So, I offer my excitement and my arguments.

The moments that I find riveting in *Blancanieves* have to do less with Snow White, ostensibly the theme of this movie, than with Carmen, flamenco, bullfighting, and the very identity of Spain as a nation.

National Identity in Spain

Spain is an old polity with a fragile sense of its own identity. Looking down at itself, it is hard pressed to recognize the unity of its own body. Currently its seventeen semi-autonomous political regions share few customs and values. Even the national language is contested. Although the Iberian territory was unified in January of 1492, that territorial unification did little to bring about cultural unity. Antonio de Nebrija foresaw the problem and proposed a solution in June of that same year when he published the grammar of Castilian. He contended, in his preface to Queen Isabella, that if she were to promote a common language she could forestall disintegration and promote cultural unity. The grammar was published, but the promised unity never materialized. Instead, Spain has seen more than five hundred years of incessant conflict between villages within provinces, between provinces within regions, and between the seventeen regions that now constitute the nation of Spain. The sources of these conflicts are manifold, not the least being matters of money, history, language, religion, land, and class.

Over the centuries, intellectuals, artists, and politicians have pursued various solutions to the problem of national unity. One in particular, the Carmen-solution, is focal in this present discussion. Let me set the stage.

Andalusia's cultural stock started to become attractive in the late 1700s, and its value continued to rise after 1814 when courageous Andalusians with little training and less weaponry repelled Napoleon's forces in Cádiz. For those looking on from the outside—especially from England and France—Andalusia's star, rising from the South, sparkled brightly as a marker of its indomitable spirit and cultural promise. Thereafter, Spaniards themselves, from all across the peninsula, began to look to Andalusia as a source of cultural unity. Queens started dressing like Andalusian *majas*, commoners began taking pride in their raggle-taggle lifestyle, bullfighting became the rage across Spain, and flamenco took Europe by storm. This trend culminated in Carmen.

"Carmen," here, stands for a tightly knit ensemble of Andalusian cultural features, not the least of which are *majismo*, exotic and defiant femininity, bullfighting, and flamenco artistry.[5] This ensemble took shape with the publication of Prosper Mérimée's story in 1845, became well known by way of the *bailes españoles* popular on Paris stages during the 1850s, and was then well solidified with Georges Bizet's opera in 1875.[6] Thereafter, the character of Carmen became Spain's own tragic identity marker. Spaniards looking into a glass saw their reflection as Carmen.[7]

The irony here is that this image of Carmen, although fashioned by outsiders, was cultivated in Spain during the twentieth century as an autochthonous and authentic insider image, rich with transcendentalist resonance and ripe for use as a symbol of cultural and political identity.[8] It became "a form of shorthand for a notion of Spain as a hot land of primitive passion."[9] This "shorthand" was employed deftly by the Spanish government in the 1950s to quell domestic dissent and attract tourists' dollars.[10]

The Movie

Pablo Berger's *Blancanieves* can be understood as a meditation and critical reflection on this "shorthand." It invites us to rethink Carmen by aligning her with Snow White, and it presents us with this surprising juxtaposition so as to enable us to see strangeness in what we had thought to be utterly familiar. The movie is obviously built around Snow White, but in the end it overwhelms us with its reflections on Carmen.

The reflections work well even though the protagonist of *Blancanieves* differs so strikingly from Carmen. She is neither Mérimée's dangerous coquette nor Bizet's femme fatale. But then Carmen has always loomed larger than these two celebrated sets of characters.[11] She is a topic for historic metaphorics more so than for general literary criticism. She is an image that has traveled through operatic, choreographic, and many

Figure 1: *Teresa Bolsi, Andalucian Torera,* by Gustave Doré, 1862. In Charles Davillier and Gustave Doré, *Spain* (London: Sampson Low, Marston, Low and Searle, 1876).

cinematic performances—roughly eighty, according to Ann Davies—playing with the minds of each new generation as it faces its distinctive challenges.[12] The protagonist of *Blancanieves* earns her place in this discussion by reason of the fact that she is a tragic *torero flamenco andaluza* (Andalusian flamenco woman-bullfighter) courageous enough to defy class and gender conventions. She is Carmen.

Berger shrewdly hides his Carmen behind Snow White's cloak so that all the while we think are watching a Snow White we are sensing the presence of Carmen. The advantages are twofold. On the one hand, the cloaking character resonates with the symbolism of the Grimm tale. On the other hand, the cloaked Carmen transmits a critical response to those who might still be holding onto to the stale "shorthand." Although the movie retells the story of a young girl's courageous handling of her stepmother's villainy, it also tells the story of the tragic consequences of a young girl's devotion to *toreo* (bullfighting) and flamenco. She is Snow White, but she is also Carmen.

Blancanieves opens to scenes of old Seville. The date is April 21, 1910. The camera moves us forward along with well-dressed Sevillian townsfolk as they walk toward the arena El Monumental—historically constructed in 1909, torn down in 1930, and digitally reconstructed for this movie—and to the *corrida* (bullfight) soon to take place there. The featured matador, Antonio Villalta, dispatches five bulls before the sixth one disrupts his moment of truth, leaving him near death. He survives but can never walk again. The disruption may have been provoked by the flash of a journalist's camera, a foreshadowing of the manifold dangers associated with an overly enthusiastic embrace of *toreo*.

Antonio's beloved Carmen de Triana watches as events unfold in the ring. She, a notable *cantaora* (flamenco singer), is well along in her pregnancy, and the sight of the goring throws her into a labor that she does not survive. The child, Carmencita, is taken and raised by her loving grandmother, Doña Concha. Time passes and we next see the young girl in preparation for her first communion. With the sounds of a flamenco guitar in the background, Doña Concha prepares Carmencita's dress as the young girl plays at being a *bailaora* (flamenco dancer). Doña Concha beams during the religious ceremony, and then performs a lively dance in a celebration of the event. She collapses in mid-dance and dies.

With Doña Concha gone, Carmencita is transported to Antonio's lavish country estate, Monte de Olvido, where she is "cared for" by Antonio's new wife Encarna, a nurse who had sidled up to Antonio during his recuperation and then taken control of his estate and affairs after their marriage. Encarna's occupation as nurse worked against her social ambitions, but her marriage to Antonio suits her well because it enables her to leapfrog into a class of Spanish elites. She receives Carmencita coldly, dyes her communion dress black, assigns her the scutwork of the estate, houses her in a dark cellar room, and keeps her wholly separated from Antonio who lives wheelchair-bound on the second floor of the estate.

It is Carmencita's pet chicken who exposes the secret—as Toto did in *The Wizard of Oz*—raising the curtain on Antonio and his second-floor repository of memory. Carmencita embraces her father, visits him regularly but surreptitiously, and there she acquires some of his and her mother's arts, toreo and flamenco. But then the tragedy unfolds. Encarna catches Carmencita with Antonio, cooks and eats her chicken, kills Antonio, and, after a time, sends the butler/chauffer/decorator/lover Genaro to murder her. He fails to strangle her and fails again to drown her in the river to which she has fled.

Carmen, now nineteen years of age, is rescued from the river by the handsome young Rafita, an *enano* (dwarf) who is a member of a traveling troupe called Los Enanos Toreros. Having just come through her near-death experience, she remembers nothing, not even her name. So they call her Blancanieves, after the fairytale, and welcome her into their midst. But the welcome is not unanimous. Jesusín, a toupeed enano with a sour attitude, mutters suspicions and festers fears from the very beginning of their association.

In a chance moment, trying to save that very Jesusín in the bullring, Carmen displays her grace and courage and thereafter becomes the star of the dwarf-show. News of Carmen's beauty and talent spreads across the land. Fatefully, that news displaces Encarna's image from the cover of a glossy magazine that Genaro had assured her would proclaim her "fairest in the land"—here the magazine cover plays the role of the magic mirror in *Snow White*. In a rage, Encarna kills Genaro leaving his body floating facedown in the swimming pool.

If moviegoers should have failed, up to this point, to see that Encarna is delusional, the image of Genaro face down in the swimming pool, reprising as it does the image of Joe Gillis murdered by Norma Desmond in *Sunset Boulevard* (1950), should set matters straight. Encarna is a psychopath who, having acquired wealth and influence, is in a position to poison the whole society. She begins her assault with a passion ... and an apple.

Her poisoned-apple plot unfolds at the Monumental arena where Carmen appears with her troupe precisely nineteen years after her father Antonio had been gored there. An unscrupulous agent-promoter named Carlos Montoya de Val had signed Carmen to a life-long contract of appearances, the first of which was this one at the Monumental. There in the arena, Jesusín skulks about, trying to derail Carmen's career, if not her life. But it is Encarna and her poisoned apple that succeed in bringing Carmen down. She falls to the ground dramatically during her finest moment as the crowd applauds the marvels of her courage and grace. Apparently dead in the sand, she is then carried off to the sounds of a flamenco dirge, therewith to be housed in the promoter's sideshow. Gawkers are charged a dime to try their best to kiss her back to consciousness. Some kisses are hesitant and fastidious, others lecherous, some even homoerotic—this last seems to shock the otherwise unshockable promoter. But no kiss is so sincerely loving as the after-hours kiss delivered by the ever-faithful Rafita. Sadly, not even Rafita's kiss can stir Carmen to consciousness. She is comatose. The movie ends with a tear slipping down Carmen's cheek, a sign that she is stuck in, and immobilized by, her identity as Carmen even if she is not yet clinically dead.

Fleeing Carmen

Blancanieves presents us with an image of Carmen immobilized physically to suggest an image of Spain immobilized culturally. It uses the exaggerated life and death of a *torera flamenca andaluza,* along with the many bizarre characters who bring her down, to highlight the dangers of Spain's clichéd identity marker. It is a cinematic *esper-*

pento—grotesque in the manner of a Valle-Inclán stage play—"of clearly Iberian colors where tauromachy and flamenco are laid out as distinctive and defining elements" in a daring assault on national imagery.[13] As such, it encourages critical reflection on the disturbing political uses to which the Carmen-image has been put for over a hundred years. True, it operates, in part at least, by directing moviegoers' attention to other recent Carmen-related movies that carry heavy political overtones, movies such as Carlos Saura's *Carmen* (1983) and Luis Buñuel's *That Obscure Object of Desire* (1977). But it takes stronger steps than these preceding films to displace Carmen. Whereas Saura—like Buñuel—remains a prisoner of Carmen, "never imagining that it is within his power to destroy" her image, Berger leans right across the horns to thrust a blade to the heart of the cliché with his powerful finale.[14]

Saving Carmen

Having suggested this association between *Blancanieves* and other negatively critical films of the post–Franco years, we should also note that *Blancanieves* alludes to a bundle of other movies that are more positive if not optimistic in their exploration of ways to free Spain from Carmen-marked politics. Berger's own *Torremolinos 73* (2004), for example, features a Carmen who is saddled with many of the miseries that stereotypical Carmens usually face. She is desperately poor, frustratedly childless, and married to a loving but clueless husband. Taking matters into her own hands, so to speak, she saves her family by making bold choices and pursuing an outrageous course of action. Unlike Saura's Carmen, she lives happily to tell the tale.

Her salvation may be related to the fact that she is completely uninterested in and untouched by flamenco and bullfighting. What is more, she is far from exotic and hardly defiant in her relations with others. Instead, she is shrewd but careful, even dainty, in her transgression of sexual mores. She is thoughtful, clear-sighted, and sure-footed, a model for the new body of Spain (although such a suggestion seems almost blasphemous on its face).[15]

Carmens in other movies have pursued similarly courageous but somewhat less scandalous tactics in pursuit of a new life. They often succeed by scuttling the tired symbol of unity fostered by Francisco Franco. For example, Fernando Trueba's *The Girl of Your Dreams (La niña de tus ojos)* (1998) depicts the escapades of an actress named Macarena as she plays the role of "Carmen" in an *españolada* subsidized by the Franco regime. Her "Carmen," like the one played by Imperio Argentina in Florián Rey's *Carmen, la de Triana* (1938), sings and dances on a rough-hewn table in a rustic tavern populated by poor and illiterate Gitanos. But Trueba's movie reveals what Rey's does not, the unsettling underside of this *españolada*. The rustic tavern where Carmen sings has been reconstructed on a soundstage in Berlin in 1938, the only place where film companies could operate while the war raged in Spain. The Gitanos in this movie's movie are played by imprisoned Jews awaiting their fate in camps; Macarena's father is dying in one of Franco's prisons; and Joseph Goebbels himself is incessantly pestering her for sexual favors—Macarena calls him "Go Balls." And more importantly, everyone in the production company, including Macarena's director/lover, is Carmenesque, over-sexed, underfed, often drunk, and always ready for a fight. Macarena confronts all these challenges courageously and imaginatively, using new resources, which lie well beyond those available to a clichéd Carmen, in order to find a way forward. She ends up saving herself—metaphorically rescuing Spain from its ill-fated identity—by leaving all the old stereotypes behind while she boards a plane, bidding farewell Casablanca-style to her lover. With her departure she leaves the tired image of Carmen languishing in a Nazi prison.

One other movie with a twist in its identity-saving plot is *La Lola se va a los puertos* (1993). The date is roughly 1929. Lola is a flamenco singer who crosses class lines and breaks free of traditional gender roles ... as Carmen did. She opens the movie dressed in a flaming red gown, singing a festive flamenco song and forcefully casting aside suitors. She is courted by the elderly and very wealthy Don Diego but comes to love Diego's son José Luis who pursues her despite his engagement to Rosario. One could imagine events turning very ugly, but Lola's unswerving commitments to flamenco song as a quasi-religious experience, to her class, and to her ever-faithful guitarist Herédia lead her forward to a noble resolution of the problems she faces. She shows herself to be honorable as well as passionate, respectful of the wealthy, sympathetic to the working class, and loyal to the community. In a memorable scene, she leads an assembly of political elites in singing the Andalusian anthem accompanied by Federico García Lorca with Blas Infante looking on approvingly.[16] In these moments, she is transformed into a new kind of Carmen, just as bold, but far more altruistic, and decidedly committed to Andalusia.[17] As such, she is fashioned as a marker of regional identity rather than of national identity.

So the female protagonists in these three films effectively sidestep the Carmen-image of Spain. They do so by ignoring it, scuttling it, and redefining its scope. But any way you see it, their target is Carmen.

Palimpsest

Blancanieves remembers all these—and many more—movie precedents. It is a cinematic palimpsest, operating like a magic slate, a "mystic writing pad," that holds the past in its underlying wax tablet after the surface layer has been lifted and the text erased.[18] As a palimpsestic movie, *Blancanieves* brings to mind alternatives for Blancanieves/SnowWhite that are depicted in other films, leaving us viewers to scratch our heads in puzzlement. What to make of the eerie connection between Encarna-like elites in Spain and Norma Desmond in Hollywood? And why can't a Blancanieves live happily ever after like a Snow White? Moreover, it jolts us with hidden experiences that persist in cultural imagination without surfacing in consciousness. Villalta's country estate is a brick-and-mortar reminder of just how much lies hidden. Its name, Monte de Olvido—which translates as Hill of Forgetting, a fairly obvious reference to the *pacto de olvido* (pact of forgetting) associated with the amnesty law of 1977, according to which the war crimes of previous decades were to be left un-investigated—alludes to specters that haunt Blancanieves, her torero/flamenco parentage. Her trauma at the hands of Genaro drives these specters back below, but, they are persistent and surface again as she enters the arena at El Monumental. Like the ghosts in *The Devil's Backbone* (2001) or *Pan's Labyrinth* (2006) or even *Volver* (2006), they persist in making their presence felt despite being invisible.[19]

The forcefulness of ghosts hidden behind consciousness is not easily overestimated, as the film's finale suggests. Carmen, caught in her death-like coma, sheds a tear as if from beyond the grave. Obviously it is easier to talk the talk of a new identity—for example, by having Macarena flee her Carmenesque identity in *Niña de tus ojos*—than to walk a walk that would require an exorcism of Carmen from Spain's cultural-political imagination.

Summary

Some English-language publications have reviewed *Blancanieves*, praising its cinematography but questioning its ambition, for example the *London Film Festival Review* (2012). The suggestion is that Berger would have done better to put his considerable skills to a more significant task than remaking *Snow White*.

My own view runs the opposite way. *Blancanieves* strikes me as an extraordinarily ambitious film, one dedicated to the Herculean—if not Sisyphean—task of refiguring Spanish identity by disengaging it from flamenco and bullfighting. The traditional Carmenesque identity, as it comes down to us, is dangerous because it is a one-size-fits-all solution for national identity in Spain. It imposes a single set of interests, values, and objectives on people who differ from each other.

Every stereotypical identity is dangerous, but especially so when it results, as Carmen does, from an insider-remake of a highly selective outsider-view. Spaniards may be courageous and defiant as the image of Carmen suggests. But they may also be humorous, hospitable, and sophisticated in art, science, and philosophy. About all these latter matters, "Carmen" says nothing.

A number of contemporary film directors have struggled with Spain's stereotyped identity, aptly singling out the tangle of bullfighting and flamenco as distinctly problematic. Directors such as Buñuel, Saura, Trueba, and Pedro Almodóvar are prominent in this regard. But the challenge they face is so daunting that their singular efforts fall short of handling the whole problem.

Blancanieves may gain ground over their efforts because it draws on all their energies while advancing its own way of handling Carmen. It is multifaceted as well as singular, a cinematic palimpsest. It effectively draws on manifold cinematic precedents to illustrate the dangers that have been visited upon the national body by its long association with Romantic celebrations of Gitanos, exotic femininity, flamenco, and bullfighting.

But as the tearful finale should make clear, this disentanglement is still incomplete. Old symbols die hard. A notable case in point is the current program of the Andalusian government, which aims to promote rather than dismantle the links between political identity and flamenco. While other regions are rethinking stereotypical identities, Andalusia aims to strengthen rather than weaken the contribution of flamenco to its political image.[20] True, the government is taking steps to rebalance the interpretations given to flamenco by Romantics of the past. But still the very idea of trying to refresh such a heavily freighted symbol so that it might, in the end, come to symbolize something other than what it has long been taken to mean seems naïve if not misguided. That, I think, is one of the messages conveyed—subtly—by *Blancanieves*. What else are we to make of this movie in which every character who expresses a deep and sincere interest in flamenco and bullfighting ends up dead?

Notes

1. José Saramago, *The Double* (Orlando: Harcourt, 2004), 299. Saramago used these words to describe a human soul, but here they are meant to depict the "soul" of a movie. I am indebted to Catherine Washabaugh, David Monroe, Teresa Zulueta, and Estela Zatania for their helpful comments on earlier drafts of this essay.
2. David N. Rodowick, *The Virtual Life of Film* (Cambridge: Harvard University Press, 2007), 35.
3. Umberto Eco used these words to describe what he called "cult movies" like *Casablanca*. "Perfect movies," like *Stagecoach*, he argued, remain "in our memory as a whole." For my part, I doubt that perfect movies exist, but I'll not argue the point here. It will suffice for me to move forward on the assumption that *Blancanieves* is not a "perfect movie" and that it is therefore a "ramshackle" experience. Umberto Eco, *Travels in Hyperreality* (New York: Harcourt Brace Jovanovich, 1986), 198.
4. Robert K. Elder, *The Film that Changed My Life* (Chicago: Chicago Review Press, 2011), 36.
5. Majismo was a defiant backward looking cultural style that flourished at the end of the eighteenth century. The rude and arrogant behavior of men (majos) and women (majas) enjoyed popular support as a homegrown response to the morally decadent style of the French court that dictated manners in Madrid.
6. For a discussion of the development of the figure Carmen, see Gerhard Steingress, ... *y Carmen se fue a París. Un estudia sobre la construcción artistic del género flamenco (1833–1865)* (Córdoba: Almuzara, 2006), 65–72.
7. Andrés Lema-Hincapié, "Carlos Saura's *Carmen*: Hybridity and the Inescapable Cliché," in *Carmen: From Silent Films to MTV*, ed. Chris Perriam and Ann Davies (Amsterdam: Rodopi, 2005), 159.
8. William Washabaugh, *Flamenco Music and National Identity in Spain* (Surrey, UK: Ashgate, 2012), 66.
9. Ann Davies, "Introduction," in *Carmen: from Silent Films to MTV*, 6.
10. Alejandro Yarza, *Un caníbal en Madrid: la sensibilidad camp y el reciclaje de la historia en el cine de Pedro Almodóvar* (Madrid: Ed. Libertarias, 1999), 17.
11. Ninotchka Devorah Bennahum, *Carmen: A Gypsy Geography* (Middletown: Wesleyan University Press, 2013), 68–92.
12. Davies, *Carmen,* 3. See also Anat Zanger, *Film Remakes as Ritual and Disguise: From Carmen to Ripley* (Amsterdam: Amsterdam University Press), 2006.
13. Aaron Cabañas, "Blancanieves" *Fuera de Campo: El blog de Contrapicado,* 2013, http://contrapicado.net/2013/02/blancanieves-pablo-berger-2012-cameo-2013/ (accessed January 14, 2014).
14. Lema-Hincapié, "Carlos Saura's *Carmen*," 162.
15. She sleeps with a black-robed figure ripped from the frames of Bergman's *The Seventh Seal* (1957). More precisely and twistedly, she makes a porno movie, going all the way, so to speak, despite having been frightened early on by a dreamlike confrontation with her own be-coffined body being carried to a crypt by a troupe of dwarves.
16. Blas Infante Pérez, who, like Lorca, was murdered by fascist thugs in 1936, authored the lyrics of Andalusia's regional anthem. This anthem was recently recorded in flamenco styles intended to represent all the provinces of the region (Washabaugh, *Flamenco Music,* 99–103). The recording was explicitly undertaken in order to demonstrate the ability of flamenco to serve as a unifying symbol for a diverse region. (Coincidentally, the Lola who sings this anthem in Molina's film is Rocio Jurado who was soon to marry to the torero José Ortega Cano.)
17. See Rafael Utrera Macías, *Literatura y Cine: Adaptaciones del Teatro al Cine* (Sevilla: Universidad de Sevilla, 2007), 141–146.
18. Anat Zanger, *Film Remakes as Ritual and Disguise: From Carmen to Ripley* (Amsterdam: Amsterdam University Press, 2006), 38.
19. See Colmeiro, "Rehispanicizing Carmen," 93; and Colmeiro, "A Nation of Ghosts? Haunting, Historical Memory and Forgetting in Post-Franco Spain," *452°F: Electronic Journal of Theory of Literature and Comparative Literature* 4 (2011): 17–34.
20. Bullfighting was banned in Catalonia in 2010, but it continues to be popular in Andalusia. More to the point, flamenco artistry remains not only popular, but politically sanctioned in Andalusia. The region's constitution (*Estatúto de autonomía*), revised in 2007, makes it clear that exclusive power is accorded to the autonomous community of Andalusia regarding the knowledge, conservation, investigation, formation, promotion, and diffusion of flamenco as a singular element of Andalusian cultural patrimony. The political implications of this proposition are discussed at length in Washabaugh, *Flamenco Music,* 2012.

Choreographing Contemporaneity
Cultural Legacy and Experimental Imperative
Michelle Heffner Hayes

> Vanguard and tradition intersect in one of the most confusing common places.... To begin with, how do we explain that in flamenco those two words are not opposites? If anything, the vanguard is the most audacious form of aligning one's self with a tradition that, in any case, never dates back more than thirty or forty years.[1]
> —Pedro G. Romero

The uneasy relationship between innovation and convention underlies flamenco's history as a form recognizable in its codes and resilient enough to sustain itself through continuous change. Practitioners and aficionados often treat "tradition" as static, or as having existed in exactly the same way since the beginning of time. The experience of tradition, however, is quite different.[2] Much of what we learn as dancers is transmitted as an oral tradition, with steps and historical anecdotes imparted from teachers to students. These accounts can vary and contradict each other, creating an unstable ahistorical narrative. The coherence of the narrative requires the exclusion of any information that threatens the legitimacy of one account over another.[3] In order to better understand the interventions of contemporary flamenco choreographers, it is useful to remember how the tradition of flamenco continually reinvents itself.[4]

A look at flamenco's history reveals its capacity to assimilate specific influences and transform in different contexts. Contemporary flamenco, for all its experimental tendencies, recaptures some of flamenco's historic antecedents and imbues them with a new significance. Each departure from the conventions of tradition reveals the mutability of the lines drawn and re-drawn that delimit the boundaries of the form. These fluid yet enduring boundaries allow us to reconsider the constantly changing nature of tradition as it reflects the issues and aesthetic values that define each generation.

Some Historical Tensions

In the traces that remain of flamenco's lived moments—that is, travel diaries, newspaper articles, books, photos, recordings, and other archival materials—change and ideological conflict appear as recurring events in the historical narrative. Most of the evidence available to us about flamenco performance in the mid-nineteenth and early twentieth centuries deals primarily with the music, most frequently the *cante* (flamenco song). Dance, particularly in English sources, receives less attention in terms of detailed description or analysis. The collection of essays in this volume increases access to English-language scholarship on flamenco dance.[5] It is the performance of flamenco as a public spectacle (including music and dance) and the response to those performances that provides a foundation for the analysis of contemporary flamenco in this essay.

By the time flamenco emerged in the mid-nineteenth century, Spain had been occupied by Napoleon, torn apart by civil wars, and had lost most of its colonial territories. Reduced in its status as a global power, and falling behind other European countries in the Industrial Revolution, the nation struggled to recall its former glory. Some of the first images of flamenco and Gitano dance from this period are found in the travel diaries of Europeans.[6] Flamenco's transition from private to public settings in the *cafés cantantes* of the mid-to-late 1800s simultaneously elicited public enthusiasm, evoked a crisis of Spanish national identity on the international stage, and spurred an *antiflamenquismo* (anti-flamenco) movement. Writer Eugenio Noel, a member of a group of intellectuals in Spain called the Generation of 1898, was among the most vocal in his criticism. Noel attributed the decline of Spanish culture and political power to practices that symbolized the stereotypical "Andalucized" Spain, among them Holy Week celebrations, bullfighting, and flamenco. In *Señoritos Chulos, Fenómenos, Gitanos y Flamencos* (1916), Noel lampooned the excesses of Andalusian culture, decrying "Clichés, ya estereotipados, ideas muy bien hechas han divulgado la Andalucía pintoresca" ("Stereotyped clichés, worn out ideas, have disseminated the picturesque image of Andalusia").[7] There were also proponents of flamenco within the Generation of 1898, most notably the poets Antonio and Manuel Machado, sons of Spanish folklorist and flamencologist Don Antonio Machado y Álvarez, also known as Demófilo, one of the first scholars to chronicle early flamenco performance.[8]

Pedro G. Romero, a contemporary director, visual artist, and frequent collaborator with Israel Galván, addresses the accusations made by Noel in the quote that begins this essay. Rather than discredit the attacks made by flamenco's detractors, Romero, in an amusing reversal of tactics, insists "Y es que estos malentendidos hacen grande al flamenco" ("And these misunderstandings made flamenco great").[9] From the moment flamenco became a public practice and commercial commodity, the tradition has torsioned in the tension of dissent among its participants. Audience demands have shaped artistic choices, and even as the conservators of flamenco have attempted to preserve, capture, codify, and isolate the art form from that which is "not flamenco," every conversation about flamenco propels it forward. The "threats" to flamenco lead to its cyclical reconstitution through dialogue.

This concept reemerges periodically in flamenco history at important and productive moments. The transition of flamenco performance from the cafés cantantes to theaters in the 1920s, for example, led to changes in the flamenco repertory. The resulting amalgam of forms called *opéra flamenca* (flamenco opera) threatened to displace what had emerged as "traditional" flamenco in the cafés, a setting already once removed from the private locales where flamenco was and is practiced among families and intimates. In response to the denunciation of flamenco among Spanish intellectuals, but also as a reaction to the perceived degradation of the song forms in the commercial environment, composer Manuel de Falla and poet Federico Garcia Lorca, among others, organized the Concurso de Cante Jondo of 1922 in Granada.[10]

Part of the perceived compromise of flamenco song related to the emergence of dance within the spectacle. In discussing the impetus for the creation of the 1922 Concurso, Génesis García Gómez describes the need to legitimize flamenco song in the wake of the concessions to spectacle in previous years. "In order to compete with the *baile*, the *cante puro* abandoned its depth enjoyed by a few, imposing instead the operatic vocal style: the cante was vulgarized to suit the tastes of a public majority that began to fill the theaters and the bullfighting rings."[11] The endorsement of a "purified" flamenco by a famous composer and a new audience of aficionados offered flamenco a legitimacy it had never before enjoyed, at least in certain circles, but it did not end the debates regarding authenticity and tradition.

In the 1950s, followers of the *cantaor* Antonio Mairena mounted an effort to distinguish "authentic" flamenco (in this case, flamenco categorized as Gitano in origin) from Andalusian and Latin American forms that had crept into the standard repertory. The exclusion of other cultural contributions to the authorship of flamenco exacerbated ideological conflicts concerning authenticity, race, and ownership of the tradition, and reflected other political and social tensions within Spain. Mairena's goal of recognizing the contributions of Gitanos to flamenco and to Spanish culture led to a polarization among subsequent generations, an essentialist configuration of race and reductive analysis of flamenco forms as either Gitano or non–Gitano, and imposed constraints on those artists who would have performed *palos* (song forms) as part of the accepted repertory in prior decades.[12]

Mairena's theories (*Mairenismo*) dominated the flamenco music scene in Spain until the waning of the Franco era, when the *jóvenes flamencos* (young flamencos) of the 1970s began to introduce instruments and styles from other forms of music and dance.[13] According to musicologist Enrich Folch, the legendary Gitano singer Camarón de la Isla's *La leyenda del tiempo* (1979) "caused a great commotion among the public, dividing it between partisans and critics of Camarón's new flamenco schemes." He continued, "Camarón gave a new turn of the screw to the whole of flamenco, and in a second stylistic phase would leave behind the old aesthetic principles and venture into new musical territory."[14] This expansion was mirrored by Camarón's contemporaries, including Paco de Lucía, who explored genres such as jazz through his collaborations with Al Di Meola and John McLaughlin, and popularized the use of instruments unfamiliar to flamenco repertory, including the now well-established Afro-Peruvian cajón.[15]

Although many flamencologists attribute the notion of experimentation to the generations following the jóvenes flamencos of the 1970s, it is clear that change, criticism, and ideological conflict have been present throughout flamenco history. These intervals in flamenco history serve as a frame of reference for the consideration of contemporary flamenco artists and their artistic evolution. The ubiquitous cajón is evidence that what might have been considered outrageous, or simply "not flamenco," by one generation or group may be acceptable to certain audiences at the moment of performance and even celebrated as "tradition" within the span of a few decades. The tradition has never been fixed.

Contemporary Interventions

With few exceptions, artists working within experimental circles of contemporary flamenco do not make arbitrary decisions. Even, or especially, their improvisational decisions are informed by a lifetime of practice and synthesis.[16] These artists work via the careful manipulation of specific codes. For some audiences, these decisions are not immediately apparent and are unintelligible; that is, the decisions either pass unnoticed, or they conflict with a sense of narrative coherence, as in the case of Israel Galván, whose work is discussed below. These choreographers negotiate the legacy of tradition and the experimental imperative through a deep sense of context and a masterful command of syntax, utilizing the language (or rather, languages) at their disposal. They include the vocabulary and compositional strategies of what has been categorized as flamenco, but they also employ classical Spanish, jazz, rap, rock, and other musical forms, experimental theatre, music, and dance, along with images, text, personal histories, flamenco histories, and an explosion of data that emanates from the World Wide Web.

Like their predecessors, contemporary artists such as Israel Galván, Belén Maya, Manuel Liñan, Flo6x8, Pastora Galván, and others rigorously engage with the history of the form even as they are reinventing it for their individual expressive purposes and as a response to the conditions of life that surround them. Ways in which choreographers and dancers manipulate the language of flamenco, their deviations from traditional conventions, the spaces of contention created by these explorations, and the elastic notion of tradition are discussed below.

Flamenco as a Language

So, then, what are the choreographic conventions of contemporaneity? For the purpose of clarity, I divide the seemingly endless interventions employed by contemporary flamenco choreographers into two categories of change: language and context. Language encompasses changes in the flamenco vocabulary, its ordering, and its capacity to make meaning. Context may refer to the juxtaposition of gendered vocabulary on different bodies, changes in physical location of the performance, the re-location of a historic event in a contemporary moment, and the intention to move beyond the "traditional" spaces of meaning in flamenco. Most contemporary artists use a combination of these compositional strategies. Israel Galván deconstructs the flamenco vocabulary at such a high level of sophistication in so many implicit, coded references to the form's history that audiences may need to see a particular work several times to understand his decisions and their effects. As audiences and artists, we rely on the phrase structure in flamenco to lend coherence to the language. His departure from the traditional framework of understanding for "reading" flamenco dance challenges our ability to comprehend what is happening onstage.[17] Galván experiments with this language at the level of its most basic vocabulary but also with its more complicated syntax and phrasing.[18]

Witness the oft-repeated Galván silhouette, en route to becoming part of the fabric of flamenco tradition. Galván exaggerates to the point of distortion the familiar matador-style, masculine placement of the hips, with shoulders seated so far back behind his pelvis he appears on the verge of falling. His hands work in a similar way as he juxtaposes idiosyncratic personal gestures with more "traditional" arm and hand movements. Because his gestures are once removed from traditional movements of *postura* (posture) and *floreo* (hand movements), their "original" source is still visible, perhaps even within the same piece. These are simple examples of the kind of movement invention, a morphing of language that is part of the compositional strategies employed by contemporary flamenco artists.

Traditional flamenco is intelligible by virtue of its recognizable language and syntax. For example, audiences recognize the structure of the *salida del cante* (entrance of the singer), the *falseta* (a short melodic phrase) by the guitarist and then the entry of the dancer through *marcaje* (marking steps) and *pitos/ palmas* (percussive snapping/hand clapping), and the *llamada* (call) signaling a new section. We see and use this order of specific movements within traditional performance settings to frame a dancer's solo. The performance becomes more complicated when Galván employs complex strategies such as repetition, interruption, and disruption of traditional sequence, "cutting and pasting" traditional phrases in unexpected choreographic structures, or substituting movements from other forms into flamenco structures.

Galván frequently uses traditional elements in performance as well, most recently in *Pastora* (2010), choreographed for his sister, dancer Pastora Galván. However, after only a few seconds of viewing an excerpt of *La Edad de Oro*, a solo he performed at the Flamenco Festival London 2011, these choreographic interventions involving the disruption of syntax are visible.[19] At .03, Galván repeats a thrusting gesture with an open palm, emphasized by a *golpe* (a flat-footed strike against the floor) that might be used to signal a llamada, except he performs it not once but several times and without any discernible meter, a radical departure from the tradition of staying within the *com-*

Figure 1: Israel Galván demonstrating his abstracted posture and arm movements in performance, Miami, Florida, 2006 (courtesy photographer Liliam Dominguez).

pás (the rhythmic structure of each song form). At .14, he segues into a short footwork section, much like a traditional *grupo de pies* (short section of footwork), accompanied by the plucking of a guitar. The footwork dissolves without warning as he stands upright and points his finger to the sky at .17. At .20, he performs what looks like marcaje with pitos as he crosses the floor, resolving into another standing position, with his hands splayed behind his back at .24. When Galván presents fragments of phrases in no perceptible order, traditional audiences struggle to find pleasure and meaning in his choreography. Even members of his own family didn't recognize his early experimental works. In a 2011 interview with Pastora Galván in *El País*, his sister recounts, "I remember when he did *Arena* in the Teatro de Maestranza of Seville. My mother covered her face in shame."[20]

What marks Galván's perverse brilliance is his ability to distort the flamenco vocabulary almost to the point of unrecognizable, while simultaneously referring, with scholarly accuracy, to the history of flamenco. This re-presentation of previous events marks a shift, or change, in context. In *La Curva* (2010), Galván was inspired by Vicente Escudero's performance at the Parisian Theatre La Courbe in 1924.[21] His specific reference to an avant-garde flamenco artist of a bygone era speaks to the simultaneity of legacy and experimentalism that characterizes the current generation of flamenco dancers. It also reminds us that the tendency to exaggerate, to deconstruct, to combine flamenco with other vocabularies is not limited to contemporary artists.[22] Escudero's original work contained references to visual artists of the era, tap dance, and Josephine Baker.[23] Such unexpected elements also appear in Galván's *La Curva*, but he extends the idea further to explore the concept of space and the vibration in sound, juxtaposing the cante of Inés Bacán with the experimental jazz piano of Sylvie Courvoisier. The flamenco body serves as a conduit and commentator on these sounds, for we see footwork and distorted but still intelligible silhouettes. However, the syntax of traditional flamenco language is broken, disorientating or discomforting viewers who seek reassurance in recognizable, traditional flamenco performance.

Changes of Context: Gender Play

In addition to experimenting with the language of flamenco, contemporary flamenco choreographers explore and manipulate the context of flamenco, or the placement of that language, in a number of different dimensions. Performers displace flamenco's highly gendered vocabulary onto different bodies, locate the performances outside traditional venues, and expand the possibilities for creative expression beyond the interpretation of the traditional palos. These changes in the context of flamenco performance generate criticism and ideological conflict, but like previous shifts in context, they also generate new audiences and propel the tradition forward.

Evidence of gender play can be seen in late nineteenth- and early twentieth-century photographs of cross-dressing female singers and dancers, such as Trinidad Huertas ("La Cuenca") and "La Malagueñita." Of course, one of the most famous flamenco dancers of all time, Carmen Amaya, dressed in *traje corto* (the men's costume) and performed what have been called "trouser dances," forever changing the expectations of the female role in terms of flamenco vocabulary and repertory.[24] The evidence of male dancers crossing the gender divide in flamenco is more elusive. Ryan Rockmore's "Dancing the Ideal Masculinity" in this volume addresses some of the obstacles to non-traditional masculine gender expression in twentieth-century Spain and illuminates recent efforts by male choreographers experimenting with "feminine" vocabulary and repertory.

Manuel Liñan performed with *bata de cola* (the long, tiered train that is part of the traditional female costume) in Belén Maya's *Los Invitados* and in his own work *Nómada* in the 2014 Festival de Jeréz. Rather than remarking on his cross-dressing, critics such as Silvia Calado of flamencoworld.com instead commented on his technique and mastery displayed in Maya's work; he received "one of the most resounding ovations so far in the festival."[25] Estela Zatania claimed that Liñan is "the first man to dance with a bata in a credible way, because it's impossible to imagine this dance without it, nor would there be the same effect if this were a woman dancer. Everything is possible in the world of Manuel Liñán who gives us traditional flamenco seen through new eyes."[26] Despite its departure from the conventions of gendered vocabulary, Liñán's performance, traditional in its vocabulary but experimental in its context, does not threaten the notion of tradition. It is still recognizable to audiences and critics alike in its adherence to the conventional use of flamenco as a language.

Location as Resistant Context

An example of the use of flamenco in a new context of location is the provocative work of Flo6x8, a collective of artists who perform guerrilla-style interventions in public spaces as a form of protest. They are most famous for their flamenco performances as political actions against the effects of the financial crisis in Spain on working-class people. In the video *Cuatro Trileros-BBVA* (soleá por bulerías), Flo6x8 dancers disguised in dark glasses perform in a bank lobby fiesta style, trading solos and then dancing as a group, accompanied by guitarists, *palmeros* (hand clappers), and singers.[27] The *letra* (lyrics) attack the bank's opportunistic role in the failing Spanish economy: "Twenty billion went to the banks ... not to hospitals or refuges/ Where will I find refuge/when until the day I die/I am in debt to them?"[28] The dancers perform marcaje with *braceo* (armwork) and pitos in time with the compás, using llamadas to announce section changes, performing recognizable steps, and answering the singers with footwork, following the traditional codes for flamenco performance.

Flo6x8's political actions re-locate flamenco outside the context of the *tablao* (flamenco bar), the *peña* (private flamenco club), the *juerga* (private flamenco party), or even the theatre. Their public performances in the banks and on streets attract attention, but their largest audiences for these events encounter them online, through YouTube, Facebook, and similar sites. This world-wide format gives flamenco an unprecedented scale of influence. Although the vocabulary and syntax used in these performances may be traditional, the places in which they perform and the overtly political address of the familiar steps, silhouettes, and sounds mark a shift in context beyond the interpretation of the traditional palos. These activists have shifted the location of flamenco and the intended effects of its performance, from personally affecting the viewer to moving for social change on a grand scale by means of the internet.[29]

New Context, New Meanings

This desire to do more than illuminate the story of the letra or explore the rhythmic possibilities of the compás marks the current generation of experimentalists. In 2008, I interviewed Belén Maya the day after the performance of *Mujeres* at the Festival de Jeréz, which was choreographed and directed by her father, Mario Maya. The work celebrated the contributions of three generations of female dancers, embodied in Merche Esmeralda, Belén Maya, and Rocio Molina.[30] Although it featured contemporary moments, *Mujeres* was overall a sumptuous celebration of traditional flamenco femininity. As the reviews came in, I translated them for myself and marveled at the critics' positively purple prose of adoration. Critic David Fernandez in *Diario de Jeréz* declared, "We could contemplate how they danced in the old days, with a sharp delivery, full of elegance."[31] I expected Belén Maya to be pleased by such praise, but instead she treated me to a rant that was even more spectacular than her performance the night before, which had been stunning. She said, "I'm very happy about the good reviews, but it makes me angry. It's very unjust."[32]

The daughter of celebrated dancers, Mario Maya and Carmen Mora, and immortalized in Carlos Saura's film *Flamenco* (1995), Belén Maya is well known in the Spanish flamenco circuit. Her experimental work, however, has been less favorably received than that which conforms to the notion of "traditional" flamenco. Her work *Souvenir* had been criticized in 2007 by the same authors of the love letters received for *Mujeres* a year later. When we discussed the contrast between the reception of her traditional versus that of her experimental work, she explained:

> At times, I "put on the flower" and dance in a very classical way. But it's like a costume I put on. I can do it, or not. The traditional artists, the critics, the festivals, they always want you to enter that space and stay there, because they believe that tradition is more forceful. When I depart from tradition, it has no value for them.[33]

This exchange led to a longer conversation about women in flamenco and the constraints for contemporary artists dancing the narrowly defined "feminine" role. These include the expectations to "put on the flower," la bata (the long train) and the very weight of the costume, *el abanico* (the fan), and the pressure to be *"la más guapa"* (the most beautiful) at every moment. We also talked about the scope of what can be said, and what feelings or ideas can be expressed. She then added something sublime, inadvertently giving me the title for the final chapter of my book, for which I am most grateful.[34] She said, "We have to renounce beauty. You don't have to be beautiful or marvelous all the time. There are many other things to think, feel, and create. We are the *antiguapas*."[35] To clarify, I am not suggesting that contemporary female flamenco artists such as Belén Maya, or their work, are not beautiful. On the contrary, I think they exceed the narrow strictures of beauty; they are beyond beauty. They negotiate these constraints and balance them with an "experimental imperative," the desire to say more about the world they inhabit in compelling ways.

The choice to dance differently in order to expand the possibilities of creative expression was echoed in my 2008 interview with Pastora Galván, an acclaimed dancer in her own right and a collaborator with her brother, Israel Galván. While Belén Maya speaks from the dual position of choreographer and dancer, Pastora has, to date, focused on the role of dancer, showing herself to be a formidable interpreter of both traditional and experimental flamenco. She spoke about the challenges of performing for the commercial expectations of the industry of flamenco, an aesthetic she describes as *guirilándia*, the tourist-oriented, stereotypical representation of the flamenco dancer "with the castanets who does a *parada* (a turn with an abrupt stop) and the people shout ¡Óle!"[36] She said:

> I do a lot of this work, but I don't want to stay there, because I get bored. I arrive at a performance and one moment I perform soleá por bulerías, the next an *alegrías*, the next a *tarantos*, and by the fourth piece I think, "I want to do La Francesa," or some other performance that departs from flamenco, because I want to take more risks, I want to sweat more. I sweat more in La Francesa than in Casa de Memoria.[37]

About her role in performing her brother's choreography, she added:

> He is my brother, he knows me. In reality it is as if the work is more mine [than choreography by other artists]. He's not going to put his steps on me. He draws from me what is mine, and I am obligated to work harder. In this way I change more, people can see the transformation."[38]

This shift in context allows her to create characters of great depth, with contradictory qualities and the capacity to transmit multiple layers of meaning.

In *La Francesa*, which premiered at the Flamenco Bienal of Seville in 2006, Pastora Galván departs from traditional flamenco to what critic Silvia Calado describes as "the point of absurdity, ugliness, vulgarity. With no fear of ridicule. Shameless."[39] The work turns back on its creator the exotic gaze of the French fantasy that created Merimée's femme fatale Carmen. The Galváns adopt stereotypes of Frenchness, from Edith Piaf, Ravel's *Bolero*, the French national anthem *La Marseillaise*, and the colors of the French flag to the scandal of the head-butting soccer star Zizou, and subject them to a distinctly flamenco satire. As the narrative's protagonist, the flamenco dancer both occupies and disrupts her own stereotype. Calado goes on in her review to declare that "Pastora Galván experiences a metamorphosis which is not only her own, but that of a generation...."[40] Following a 2010 performance of *Pastora*, a headline in *El Correo de Andalucía* claimed "Sevilla ya tiene a otra gran Pastora" ("Seville has another great Pastora"),[41] an implicit reference to Pastora Imperio, the legendary figure of the Golden Age and, according to Matilde Corál, founder of the *escuela sevillana*.[42] This reference to and re-presentation of the past is one of the compositional tools contemporary choreographers use to re-locate themselves within the flamenco tradition.

Tradition Reinvented

In each of these choreographic interventions, the structure of what artists and audiences recognize as flamenco shifts and accommodates new ideas. The outcomes of these manipulations entail that the language and context of flamenco vary according to the intentions of the creator. However threatening to the boundaries of tradition, it should be noted that none of these artists expresses a desire to destroy flamenco even as they deconstruct it. These departures from tradition are usually so heavily layered with specific references to flamenco that they capture flamenco's core values even though it may not be apparent.

It is this rootedness in the past combined with a critical engagement in the moment—the tension between cultural legacy and experimental imperative—that underpin these innovations. As they question conventions and transgress boundaries lovingly maintained by aficionados, these performers remind us that tradition is constantly in flux. Flamenco artists and audiences reinvent the genre through these iterations, reaffirming certain values and giving new life to the form. Tradition is a space that contemporary dancers occupy; it informs their aesthetic, but it is not the entire terrain available to them. When audiences, critics, flamencologists, other artists, and even family members resist those innovations, it is in that space of productive "misunderstandings" described by Pedro G. Romero that the tradition moves forward: responsive, embodied, and alive.

Notes

1. Pedro G. Romero, "Pastora: Lo que hay en los bailes de Pastora Galván," http://www.pastoragalvan.com/esp/espectaculos.php?id=3 (accessed July 13, 2014). My translation, with assistance from K. Meira Goldberg.
2. For an analysis of the "disobedience" embedded in flamenco tradition, see Cristina Cruces-Roldán's "Aesthetic Norms and Cultural Constructs in Flamenco Dance: Female and Gitano Bodies as Legitimizers of Tradition" in this volume.
3. I deal with the historiography of flamenco and the ideologies that underpin its narratives in Michelle Heffner Hayes, *Flamenco: Conflicting Histories of the Dance* (Jefferson, NC: McFarland, 2009), 43–49.
4. Portions of this essay, including part of the title, were developed as part of the educational component of the 2014 Philadelphia Flamenco Festival, held March 1–16, 2014. I am indebted to Elba Hevia y Vaca of Pasión y Arte Flamenco for the opportunity to research, develop, and present this work in progress as the festival's educational curator.
5. Many useful sources with descriptions of nineteenth-century flamenco dancing exist in Spanish, among them Ángel Álvarez Caballero, *El Baile Flamenco* (Madrid: Alianza Editorial, 1998); Manuel Rios Vargas, *Antología del Baile Flamenco* (Sevilla: Signatura Ediciones de Andalucía, 2002); and José Blas Vega and Manuel Rios Ruiz, *Diccionario Encíclopedico Ilustrado de Flamenco* (Madrid: Editorio Cinterco, 1988). Gerhard Steingress ... *y Carmen se fue a Paris un estudio sobre al construcción artística de género flamenco (1833–1865)* (Córdoba: Editorial Almurzara, 2006), offers an indispensible analysis of the emergence of flamenco dance. Other useful sources of descriptions of early flamenco dancing that entered my library by recommendation of my colleague K. Meira Goldberg include Rita de Triana, *Antonio Triana and the Spanish Dance: A Personal Recollection (Choreography and Dance Studies Series)* (London: Routledge, 1994); and Jose Luis Ortiz Nuevo's *Coraje: Del Maestro Otero y su Paso por el Baile* (Sevilla: Tecnographic, S.L., Producciones Editoriales, 2012).
6. An overview of exotic representations of flamenco and Gitano dancers in foreign travel diaries during this period appears in "Desiring Narratives: Flamenco in History and Film" in Hayes, *Flamenco: Conflicting Histories of the Dance*, 38–39.
7. It should be noted that Noel's use of the "picturesque" here is negative and sarcastic. Eugenio Noel, *Señoritos Chulos, Fenómenos, Gitanos y Flamencos* (Madrid: Renacimiento, 1916), 194. My translation. Joan Acocella's "The Critical Reception of Le Tricorne" in this volume explores the concerns among Spaniards regarding national identity in the eyes of other Europeans.
8. For a discussion of the arguments and issues in antiflamenquismo in Spanish, see Félix Grande, *Memoria del flamenco II: De los cafes cantantes a nuestros días* (Madrid: Editorial Espasa-Calpe, S.A. 1979), specifically "Quincalla Meridional: El antiflamenquismo como forma de la sordera," 425–465.
9. Romero, "Pastora: Lo que hay en los bailes de Pastora Galván."
10. For more information about the role of the Concurso de Cante Jondo in flamenco history, see Felix Grande, "¡Don Manuel que nos vamos! Falla. Granada 1922. El concurso de cante jondo," in *El flamenco en la cultura española*, ed. Ángel Álvarez Caballero and Alfonso Carmona González (Murcia: Servicio de Publicaciones, 1999), 27–64.
11. "Volksgeist y Género Español," *Flamenco y Nacionalismo: Aportaciones para una sociologia politica del flamenco*, ed. Gerhard Steingress y Enrique Baltanás (Seville: Fundación Machado, 1998), 201. My translation. Also, John C. Moore discusses the changes in repertory and resulting tensions in opéra flamenca in "Purity and Commercialization: The View from Two Working Artists, Pericón de Cádiz and Chato de la Isla" in this volume.

12. For a sophisticated analysis of *gitanismo*, including the contributions of Antonio Mairena and his followers, see William Washabaugh, "Franquismo, Gitanismo, Andalucismo and the 'Rito' Series," in *Flamenco: Passion, Politics and Popular Culture* (London: Berg, 1996), 79–87.

13. Brook Zern's "Flamenco: The Real Stories" in this volume examines some of the arguments underpinning the rebellions of the flamenco artists of the 1970s.

14. Enrich Folch, "At the Crossroads of Flamenco, New Flamenco and Spanish Pop: The Case of Rumba," in *Made in Spain: Studies in Popular Music* (New York: Routledge, 2013), 23. Folch provides a helpful table (1.1) on page 19 that outlines the stages of flamenco development that closely mirror the intervals I outline here. Folch's analysis is an affirmation that, indeed, these were pivotal moments in flamenco history in terms of stylistic change and ideological conflict.

15. The scope of the contributions of these artists is too vast to explore in this space, but José Manuel Gamboa and Faustino Nuñez, *Camarón Vida y Obra* (Madrid: Iberautor, 2003), and Juan José Tellez, *Paco de Lucía "En Vivo"* (Madrid: ACADAP, 2003) provide biographical information about their lives and careers. Also, the documentary *Tiempo de Leyenda*, directed by José Sánchez Montes (2009), illuminates the critical reception of *La Leyenda del Tiempo* in 1979.

16. I address the coded nature of spontaneity in flamenco improvisation in "The Writing on the Wall: Reading Improvisation in Flamenco and Postmodern Dance" in *Taken By Surprise: A Dance Improvisation Reader*, ed. Ann Cooper Albright and David Gere (Middletown: Wesleyan University Press, 2003), 105–118.

17. Susan Leigh Foster developed the groundbreaking theory for understanding the language and codes for intelligibility in choreography in her *Reading Dancing: Bodies and Subjects in Contemporary American Dance* (Oakland: University of California Press, 1988).

18. Galván is not alone among contemporary choreographers in this deconstruction of flamenco as a language; other artists such as Belén Maya, Rocío Molina, and Juan Carlos Lérida are discussed in Niurca Marquez's "Y Para Rematar: Contemplations on a Movement in Transition" in this volume.

19. Israel Galván, *La Edad de Oro*, https://www.youtube.com/watch?v=BTXf01hRr94 (accessed July 11, 2014).

20. http://elpais.com/diario/2011/01/15/babelia/1295053988_850215.html (accessed July 11, 2014).

21. This is not the first time that Galván has invoked the legacy of Escudero. In his 2002 production *Galvánicas*, he reinterpreted Escudero's *Decálogo de un Buen Bailarín* [Decalogue of a Good Male Dancer] of 1951. Escudero's treatise is a commentary on the role of the male dancer and has implications for the consideration of sexual identity onstage.

22. Escudero was in dialogue with several artists of the early twentieth century who were experimenting with the techniques of primitivism, Cubism, and Modernism in dance and other arts. For a discussion of some of these collaborations, see Ninotchka Devorah Bennahum, *Antonia Mercé, "La Argentina:" Flamenco and the Spanish Avant-Garde* (Hanover, NH: 2000).

23. Assumptions about Escudero's original are based on critic Cristina de Lucas's review of the March 24, 2013, performance of *La Curva* at the London Flamenco Festival: "In the programme notes, Galván explains that the inspiration for this piece came from the testimonials of an avant-garde performance by dancer Vicente Escudero at the theatre La Courbe in Paris in 1924. It seems that the show was an allusive collage with references to the most innovative artists of the time, chiefly those under the banner of cubism. Among the celebrated passages were a number dedicated to football, a tap dance imitating the sound of a pyramid of chairs falling to the ground, and a jazz dance indulging in the hip movements that would bring success to Josephine Baker." Cristina de Lucas, "Israel Galván Presents His Experimental La Curva at the London Flamenco Festival," http://bachtrack.com/review-london-flamenco-festival-2013-la-curva (accessed June 23, 2014).

24. Carmen Amaya's contribution to the world of flamenco extends far beyond her "trouser dances." Two excellent resources about the complexity of Amaya's life and work and their place in flamenco history include K. Meira Goldberg's "Border Trespasses: The Gypsy Mask and Carmen Amaya's Flamenco Dance" (EdD diss., Temple University, 1995); and Montse Madrilejos and David Pérez Merinero, *Carmen Amaya* (Barcelona: Ediciones Bellaterra, 2013).

25. http://www.flamenco-world.com/magazine/about/jerez2014/resenas/linan06032014ing.html (accessed June 23, 2014).

26. Estela Zatania, http://www.deflamenco.com/revista/resenas-actuaciones/manuel-linan-nomada-david-coria-segundo-falcon-1.html (accessed June 23, 2014).

27. http://www.flo6x8.com/content/cuatro-trileros-bbva-sole%C3%A1-por-buler%C3%ADas (accessed July 12, 2014).

28. My translation. Subtitles appear on the video (2:02–2:57): Mas de veinte mil millones/viente mil millones/se fueron pa Bankia… Ni hospitales ni refugio/donde me cobijo yo/si hasta el dia que me muera/a ellos se lo debo to(do).

29. Joshua Brown, "'The Banks are Our Stages': Flo6x8 and Place-Making Through Performance Protest" (PhD diss., University of California, Riverside, 2014), 155–215.

30. For a fuller discussion of *Mujeres*, see Hayes, *Flamenco: Conflicting Histories of the Dance*, 168–171.

31. David Fernandez, "Tres estrellas illuman el Villamarta," in *Diario de Jeréz*, March 1, 2008, 3. Originally published in *Flamenco: Conflicting Histories of the Dance*, 169.
32. Interview with Belén Maya, Jerez, March 1, 2008. My translation. Originally published in Hayes, *Flamenco: Conflicting Histories of the Dance*, 169.
33. Ibid., 170.
34. I am indebted to William Washabaugh for this characterization of Maya's comments and work in a discussion following our presentations on the panel "Flamenco Alive! New Research on the Vital Art of Flamenco," Duke University Dance Program, Durham, NC, February 4, 2012.
35. Hayes, *Flamenco: Conflicting Histories of the Dance*, 171.
36. Interview with Pastora Galván, Seville, March 4, 2008. My translation.
37. Ibid. Casa de Memoria is a cultural center in Seville that features traditional flamenco.
38. Interview with Pastora Galván, Seville, March 4, 2008. My translation.
39. Review of *La Francesa*, Jerez, March 1, 2007, www.flamenco-world.com. Originally published in Hayes, *Flamenco: Conflicting Histories of the Dance*, 175.
40. Ibid. Calado here makes a play on Israel Galvan's *Metamórfosis* of 2000, a breakthrough work that established his experimental aesthetic.
41. Manuel Bohorquez, blog, September 28, 2010. http://blogs.elcorreoweb.es/lagazapera/2010/09/28/sevilla-ya-tiene-a-otra-gran-pastora (accessed June 30, 2014).
42. http://es.mashpedia.com/Escuela_sevillana (accessed August 7, 2014).

Glossary

atracción the principal performer in tablao performances, the "featured attraction," usually a dancer.

bailable "Danceable": works that developed out of short danced theatrical interludes, becoming by the 1820s stand-alone numbers that could be combined flexibly in a variety-show format. For more, see Kiko Mora, "Some Notes Toward a Historiography of the Mid-Nineteenth Century *Bailable Español*," in this volume.

bailaoras, bailaores From *baile* (dance), this is an Andalusian pronunciation of *bailadores, bailadoras*: male and female flamenco dancers.

bailarinas, bailarines Ballerinas, male ballet dancers: dancers in the classical or bolero style.

baile In Spain, the term baile is used separately from the term danza. Baile generally refers to popular forms (and flamenco was or is considered to be one of these), and danza usually indicates classical or concert theatre dance. Thus flamenco dance is referred to as *baile*, rather than *danza*. For more, see Ana Yepes, "From the *Jácara* to the *Sarabande*," in this volume.

bata de cola A dress with a tail, refers to the long train often used by female flamenco dancers.

boleras, boleros Female and male bolero dancers, that is, dancer of the bolero school, the *escuela bolera*.

bulerías From *bulla* (tumult), *burla* (mockery), a festive flamenco form in 6/8 rhythm.

cafés cantantes Establishments catering to working and middle-class audiences, especially in Andalusia, offering both alcohol and performance. Roughly parallel to the French *café chantant* and the English music hall, the Spanish café emerged in the 1850s, and were the stages upon which flamenco was first performed.

cambio In today's flamenco a *cambio* is a hemiola, a duplet rhythm superimposed on a triplet, used as a syntactic element signaling a change of chords in the guitar accompaniment to the song, or, in dance, as a change between quietly marking time while the singer sings to doing a *desplante*.

Cañí Since the 1920s, refers to "Gypsiness" as the essence of pure-blooded, authentic, folkloric Spain. For more, see Montse Madridejos, "Carmen Amaya, 1947: The (Gypsy) Beloved of America Reconquers Europe," in this volume.

cantaor, cantaora From *cante*, this is an Andalusian pronunciation of *cantadores, cantadoras*: male and female flamenco singers.

cante, cante jondo, cante chico *Cante* is flamenco song. *Cante jondo* is "deep song," referring to the more serious flamenco forms, such as *seguiriyas* or *soleá*. *Cante chico*, "little song," refers to festive forms such as *tangos, bulerías*.

cante libre "Free song," refers to flamenco sung without accompaniment of *palmas*, or rhythmic hand-claps, allowing for melismatic extension of the line of song to stretch out and deform the underlying rhythmic structure.

cante p'alante to cante p'atrás Song at the front of the stage, song at the back of the stage, referring to solo song sung in a recital format, as opposed to song that serves as accompaniment to a dancer. For more, see John C. Moore, "Purity and Commercialization: The View from Two Working Artists, Pericón de Cádiz and Chato de la Isla," in this volume.

caseta A caseta is a small, temporary construction used for purposes of entertainment in the popular festivals, such as "ferias," or town fairs. The Feria de Sevilla, the Seville town fair, is considered the largest and most important of Andalusia. To have your own *caseta* in the Feria de Sevilla is expensive and indicates a certain amount of social prestige. For more, see Clara Chinoy, "The First Academy of Flamenco Dance: Frasquillo and the 'Broken Dance' of the Gitanos," in this volume.

chaflán A flamenco dance step, a sounded hop on one foot followed by a stamp on the other, the two sounds very close together as a split single sound.

china poblana A style of women's dress from New Spain of the seventeenth through nineteenth centuries, comprised of a chemise, skirt and shawl. The design of the costume has been attributed by various sources to Catarina de San Juan, a seventeenth-century slave of Indian descent who eventually became a popular saint. For more, see Anthony Shay "Fandangos and Bailes: Dancing and Dance Events in Early California," in this volume.

colmao Establishments, normally urban, where customers eat and drink and there were performances, like a small *tablao*, and also *reservados* (private rooms) where private fiestas could be held. They were generally linked with nightlife, and with minor entertainment. For more, see Cristina Cruces Roldán, "Normative Aesthetics and Cultural Constructions in Flamenco Dance: Female and Gitano Bodies as Legitimizers of Tradition," in this volume.

colocación Placement, alignment, body line.

compás "Measure," refers to flamenco rhythms, as in *compás por bulerías*, and more generally to rhythmic fluency, an indispensable skill in flamenco.

contradanzas The Spanish variant of English country dances taken up by French dancing masters in the late sixteenth and seventeenth centuries and popularized in ballrooms throughout Europe and the Americas.

copla "Verse," refers to the long tradition of Spanish song in both theatrical and popular contexts, upon which flamenco dance is founded.

corral The word "corral," a Spanish word that has been incorporated into English, refers to an enclosure. In Spain, it refers to the architectural legacy of Islamic Spain of buildings incorporating a central open-air patio. In early modern Spain, these were theaters, by the nineteenth century the *corrales de vecinos* (neighborhood corrals) in Andalusia were multi-family dwellings. For more on the *corrales* as theaters, see Rocío Plaza Orellana, "Spanish Dance in Europe: From the Late Eighteenth Century to Its Consolidation on the European Stage"; for more on the *corrales de vecinos*, see K. Meira Goldberg, "*Jaleo de Jerez* and *Tumulte Noir*: Primitivist Modernism and Cakewalk in Flamenco, 1902–1917," both in this volume.

cortijo Ranch, country property.

costumbrismo Interest in local custom, refers to the lauding of a folkloric vision of Spanish culture. For more, see Kiko Mora, "Some Notes Toward a Historiography of the Mid-Nineteenth Century *Bailable Español*," in this volume.

cuadro "Frame" or "painting," refers to the folkloric scene that evolved into a flamenco performing group, with guitarists, singers, and dancers seated in a semi-circle of chairs giving musical accompaniment to a solo dancer.

cuplés, cupletistas From "couplet," refers to the ballads and the singers of those ballads that became popular in Spanish vaudeville in the early-twentieth century.

desplante In bullfighting, a sudden stance of defiance, in flamenco dance, a striking step.

duende A spirit or a goblin, the term in reference to flamenco was made famous in Federico García Lorca's 1933 lecture "Teoría y juego del duende" (Theory and Play of the Duende).

entremés In Spain's Golden-Age theaters, one-act comic pieces, without music, interspersed within a larger work, and protagonized by common folk. For more, see Kiko Mora, "Some Notes Toward a Historiography of the Mid-Nineteenth Century *Bailable Español*," in this volume.

escuela bolera The bolero school was the academic school of Spanish dance that emerged in the nineteenth century out of popular urban dances and became the classical school of Spanish dance. For more, see Marta Carrasco Benítez, "Three

Centuries of Flamenco: Some Brief Historical Notes," in this volume.

falseta   Guitar melody.

festero   Festive forms in flamenco have to do with ritual, with a gathering, with community, with celebration. In flamenco, *festero* has to do with the musical classification of the cantes. Those cantes, tangos and bulerías, mostly, are used within the unfolding of the fiesta (festive) and are called "*festeros*" because of their musical characteristics, in terms of the rhythmic mode of the celebration. For more, see Cristina Cruces Roldán, "Normative Aesthetics and Cultural Constructions in Flamenco Dance: Female and Gitano Bodies as Legitimizers of Tradition," in this volume.

floreo   From *flor* (flower), sometimes used to refer to feminine handwork in flamenco.

golpe   To hit, refers usually to a stamp with the full foot.

gracia   Grace, charm, an essential component of the aesthetics of the Seville School of flamenco dance. For more on the Seville School, see Cristina Cruces Roldán, "Normative Aesthetics and Cultural Constructions in Flamenco Dance: Female and Gitano Bodies as Legitimizers of Tradition," in this volume.

hemiola   "The hemiola is a shifting of rhythmical accentuation in the ratio of 3:2, as when, for example, two groups of three eighth notes (6/8) alternate with three groups of two eighth notes (3/4)." From Ana Yepes, "From the *Járaca* to the *Sarabande*," in this volume.

jarcha (xarchas), zejel (zajal)   In medieval Andalusian music, short ending strophes in Romance, the precursor of Spanish. For more on these musics in relation to flamenco, see Cristina Cruces Roldán, *El flamenco y la música andalusí: Argumentos para un encuentro* (Barcelona: Ediciones Carena, 2003).

juerga   A flamenco party, or jam session. "The term *juerga* is considered archaic and has been largely replaced by the more general *fiesta*, or party." From Clara Chinoy, "The First Academy of Flamenco Dance: Frasquillo and the 'Broken Dance' of the Gitanos," in this volume.

látigo   Whip, refers to a sounded double brush of the ball of the foot out and in, similar to a shuffle in tap dance.

letra   Flamenco verse.

llamada   Call, used in flamenco improvisation to signal a transition from one section to another.

mairenismo   In 1963, flamenco singer Antonio Mairena and poet Ricardo Molina published *Mundo y formas del cante flamenco*, asserting flamenco as an essentially Gitano form born of the pain of social injustice and marginalization, a legacy hidden in the bosom of family and only brought to light by Gitano artists. (*Ricardo Molina and Antonio Mairena, Mundo y formas del cante flamenco* [Madrid: Revista de Occidente, 1963]).

majo/a, majismo   In the late eighteenth century, Spanish aristocrats adopted the fashions, songs, and dances of the urban underclass, as documented in painter Francisco de Goya's luminous tapestry cartoons.

marcaje   Marking step, a step that is usually not noisy, employed while the singer is singing to dance the verse without interrupting the sung improvisation.

mariposa   Butterfly, refers to a type of oil lamp in this famous *Bulería de Cádiz* verse:

Dicen que van a poner
   They say they'll put up
Una fuente iluminosa
   An illuminated fountain
En la Plaza de las Canastas
   In the Plaza de las Canastas
Se alumbran con mariposas
   They light up with oil lamps

For more, see John C. Moore, "Purity and Commercialization: The View from Two Working Artists, Pericón de Cádiz and Chato de la Isla," in this volume.

melisma   Singing many notes to one syllable, a basic technique of flamenco song.

mojiganga   A short burlesque satire, often performed to music, originating in religious carnivals celebrating the beginning of Lent, incorporated as a programmatic element in early modern theatrical performance.

mudanza   A move, a dance step or short sequence of dance steps.

música andalusí (see "jarcha [xarchas] and zejel [zajal] entry)   "Arabic music developed in Al-Andalus, as Andalusia was known during the period of Muslim governance between the ninth and fourteenth centuries. These Andalusian musics expanded throughout North Africa through commercial and cultural exchange, especially following the expulsions that followed the Christian reconquest of the Iberian Peninsula in 1492." From Cristina Cruces-Roldán, "Normative Aesthetics and Cultural Constructions in Flamenco Dance: Female and Gitano Bodies as Legitimizers of Tradition," in this volume.

ópera flamenca *Ópera flamenca* was associated with a particular style of *cante*, which "favored stylized interpretations of *fandangos* and Latin American–inspired forms, often delivered in a falsetto voice (as opposed to the rougher flamenco voice quality associated with *flamenco Gitano*). *Ópera flamenca* was very popular from the early twentieth century until about the 1950s. However, at the time, the term was used to refer to a type of flamenco variety show (regardless of the singing style). The reference to *ópera* was not because of the nature of the singing; rather, it was a designation that producers employed to take advantage of a tax loophole reserved for *bel canto* performances." From John C. Moore, "Purity and Commercialization: The View from Two Working Artists, Pericón de Cádiz and Chato de la Isla," in this volume.

palmas An Andalusian pronunciation of *palmadas*, claps, refers to the sophisticated and intricate use of hand-clapping as a rhythmic accompaniment for flamenco.

palo "Stick," refers to a form of flamenco dance, as defined by rhythm, tonality, and a traditional body of verses. Examples of palos are bulerías, tangos, alegrías, etc.

paseo A stroll. Dating to at least the sixteenth century, this step of approaching and retreating is known in the dance *sevillanas* as the "sevillanas step" (Lynn Matluck Brooks, *The Dances of the Processions of Seville in Spain's Golden Age* [Kassel, Germany: Ed. Reichenberger, 1988], 201). Paseo may also refer to a slow, lyrical section of the alegrías dance, also called the *silencio*.

paso "Step," refers to a dance step, and also to a large and richly decorated float on which the parish Saint or Virgin is carried in a religious procession, especially at Easter.

pitos Finger snaps, used in flamenco to mark the rhythm.

planta "Plant," refers to the sole of the foot and therefore to the stamping sound made with the full foot (a synonym for golpe; *media planta* refers to the sound made with the metatarsal). Also refers to the posture, or visual projection, of the whole body, encompassing body-line, costume, and attitude.

por derecho Straight up, without evasion or adornment, implying knowledge and mastery.

postura Posture (see *planta*).

pregón "Up until the mid-twentieth century, it was common for Spanish street vendors to sell their wares with a *pregón*—a singing advertisement. Some of these became famous and are sung by flamenco artists today—e.g. the candy *pregón* by Cádiz singer Macandé ... or the *mirabrás* verse Venga usted a mi puesto Hermosa ... ('Come to my stand beautiful ...'). From John C. Moore, "Purity and Commercialization: The View from Two Working Artists, Pericón de Cádiz and Chato de la Isla," in this volume.

quiebro/quebrada In seventeenth-century Spanish dance, a small bend of the knees. Today, a bend from the waist to the front, side, or back. In a *vuelta quebrada*, the upper body bends sequentially from side to back to side as the body revolves.

redoble A series of quick stamps.

remate, rematar Finish, refers to the important skill of finishing a phrase with style and expression.

romances Ballads, dating to early Islamic Spain.

sainete Picaresque one-act farces or tidbits. For more, see Kiko Mora, "Some Notes Toward a Historiography of the Mid-Nineteenth Century *Bailable Español*," in this volume.

son "Sound," refers to a style of dance music. For more, see Ana Yepes, "From the *Jácara* to the *Sarabande*," in this volume.

tablao Andalusian pronunciation of *tablado*, or stage, refers to flamenco clubs where patrons can eat, drink, and see a show. John C. Moore, "Purity and Commercialization: The View from Two Working Artists, Pericón de Cádiz and Chato de la Isla, " in this volume.

tocaor/a Andalusian pronunciation of *tocador*, or "player." Refers to a guitarist. For more, see Loren Chuse, "*Las Tocaoras*: Women Guitarists and Their Struggle for Inclusion on the Flamenco Stage," in this volume.

tonadilla Sung theatrical interludes, often satirical in tone, popular in late Enlightenment Spain, ancestors of *zarzuela*.

traje corto Suit with a short jacket and high-waist pants, worn by bullfighters; the typical male dance costume worn through the late twentieth century.

varietées, variedades Variety shows, vaudeville.

venta Situated along the roadside, generally at access points to large cities, they had a similar structure to the *colmaos* and they often had a more-or-less set group of performing artists who would "hang out," informally available for private *fiestas*. For more, see Cristina Cruces Roldán, "Normative Aesthetics and Cultural Constructions in Flamenco Dance: Female and Gitano Bodies as Legitimizers of Tradition," in this volume.

zambra In early Islamic Andalusia, the nighttime festivities involving music and dance, also called *leilas*. Since the nineteenth century, zambras are the Gitano performing groups of the caves of Granada's Sacromonte, catering to tourists.

zapateado, zapateo, escobilla, taconeo From *zapato* (shoe), *escoba* (broom), and *tacón* (heel), refers to footwork percussion.

zarzuela Light opera, operetta.

Bibliography

Acevedo-Muñoz, Ernesto R. *Pedro Almodóvar*. London: British Film Institute, 2007.

Acocella, Joan. "The Critical Reception of *Le Tricorne*." In *Los Ballets Russes de Diaghilev y España*. Edited by Vicente García-Márquez, Yvan Nommick, and Antonio Alvarez Cañibano. Granada: Archivo Manuel de Falla, 2012.

Acocella, Joan. "Reception of Diaghilev's Ballets Russes by Artists and Intellectuals in Paris and London, 1909–1914." PhD Diss. Rutgers, 1984.

Acocella, Joan. "The Refusé: Israel Galvan and the Evolution of Flamenco." *The New Yorker* (March 17, 2014).

Adichie, Chimamande Ngozi. "The Danger of a Single Story." *TED Talks: TED Conferences LLC*. TEDGlobal 2009. http://www.ted.com/talks/chimamanda_adichie_the_danger_of_a_single_story.html (accessed February 15, 2014).

Adorno, Theodor. "On Popular Music." In *On Record. Rock, Pop, and the Written Word*. Edited by Simon Frith and Andrew Goodwin. New York: Pantheon Books, 1990.

Alba y Diéguez, Jerónimo de. *Libro de la gitaneria de Triana de los años 1740 a 1750 que escribió el bachiller revoltoso para que no se imprimiera*. Edited by Antonio Castro Carrasco. Seville: Coria Gráfica, S.L., 1995.

Albi, Mercedes. "Interview with Eloy Pericet." *Danza Eter*. http://www.eter.es/dn/notis/albinoticia.php?id=12550 (accessed May 20, 2014).

Aldington, Richard. "The Russian Ballet." *The Sphere* (August 16, 1919).

Allen, Frederick Lewis. *Only Yesterday: An Informal History of the 1920s*. New York: Harper Perennial, 1931.

Alonso, Celsa. *La canción lírica española en el siglo XIX*. Madrid: ICCMU, 1998.

Al-Rawi, Rosina-Fawzia. *Grandmother's Secrets: The Ancient Rituals and Healing Power of Belly Dancing*. Translated by Monique Arav. New York: Interlink Books, 1999.

Álvarez Caballero, Ángel. *El baile flamenco*. Madrid: Alianza Editorial, 1998.

_____. *Gitanos, payos y flamencos en los orígenes del flamenco*. Madrid: Edición Cinterco, 1998.

_____. *Historia del cante flamenco*. Madrid: Editorial Alianza, 1981.

Amkpa, Awam. "Floating Signification: Carnivals and the Transgressive Performance of Hybridity." In *Performing Hybridity*. Edited by May Joseph and Jennifer Natalya Fink. Minneapolis, London: University of Minnesota Press, 1999.

Andalucía: flamenco. http://www.andalucia.org/es/flamenco/primeras-referencias-escritas/ (accessed September 30, 2014).

Anderson, Benedict. *Imagined Communities: Reflections on the Origins and Spread of Nationalism*. London: Verso, [1983] 2006.

Antonia Mercé, "La Argentina." 1935 souvenir program for Columbia Artists, in the collection of Mariano Parra.

"Antonio Ruiz Soler." Plusesmas.com. http://www.plusesmas.com/biografias/antonio_ruiz_soler/ (accessed February 3, 2010).

Antréas, E. "Le Joyeux Nègre (The Happy Coon): Cake Walk and Two Step, avec théorie par Charles Grégory du Nouveau-Cirque et de Parisiana, Professeur de Cake Walk, Conforme au Cake Walk dansé par Charles Grégory dans la Grande Pantomime Américaine Nautique Joyeux Nègres," 1903.

Aoyama, Yuko. "Artists, Tourists, and the State: Cultural Tourism and the Flamenco Industry in Andalusia, Spain." *International Journal of Urban and Regional Research* 33.1 (2009).

_____. "The Role of Consumption and Globalization in a Cultural Industry: The Case of Flamenco." *Geoforum* 38 (2007).

Arco, Manuel del. "Vd. Dirá." *Diario de Barcelona* (December 18, 1947).

Arco Prieto, Belén del. "Cafés cantantes." *Revista de la Carolina* (June 11, 2008). http://

www.revistadelacarolina.com/news/nuestra-cultura-e-historia-los-cafes-cantantes-y-el-cortijo-real-de-la-carolina/ (accessed April 10, 2010).

"Argentinita Ephemera." Portfolio. 8—MWEZ. 10, 670, Jerome Robbins Dance Division. New York Public Library, Lincoln Center.

Arrébola, Alfredo. *Presencia de la mujer en el cante flamenco*. Málaga: Edición Edinford, 1993.

Asenjo, Antonio. "Crónica—La decadencia del género chico." *Comedias y Comediantes*, vol. 2, no. 15 (May 15, 1910). Madrid.

Aymes, Jean-René, and Serge Salaün. *Le métissage culturel en Espagne*. Paris: Presses de la Sorbonne nouvelle, 2001.

"El baile de moda—el 'cake-walk.'" *Por Esos Mundos* 97 (February 1903).

"Bailes de sociedad—El cake-walk." *Vida Practica—Suplemento mensual de La Última Moda* 789 (February 15, 1903).

Bailey, Derek. *On the Edge: Improvisation in Music, Part 2: Movements in Time*. Produced and directed by Jeremy Marre. Harcourt Films Production, 1991.

Baker, Houston A. *Modernism and the Harlem Renaissance*. Chicago: University of Chicago Press, 1987.

Baldwin, Brooke. "The Cakewalk: A Study in Stereotype and Reality." *Journal of Social History* vol. 15, no. 2 (1981).

Balfour, Sebastian. "The Loss of Empire, Regenerationism, and the Forging of a Myth of National Identity." In *Spanish Cultural Studies: An Introduction*. Edited by Helen Graham and Jo Labanyi. Oxford: Oxford University Press, 1995.

_____ and Alejandro Quiroga. *The Reinvention of Spain: Nation and Identity since Democracy*. Oxford: Oxford University Press, 2007.

Ballet Russe de Monte Carlo (Massine). Clippings. 3 Folders, 1938–1943. MGZR, New York Public Library Performing Arts Research Collection—Dance.

Baltanás, Enrique. "The Fatigue of the Nation: Flamenco as the Basis of Heretical Identities." In *Songs of the Minotaur: Hybridity and Popular Music in the Era of Globalization*. Edited by Gerhard Steingress. Münster: Lit Verlag, 2002.

Bancroft, Hubert. *California Pastoral 1768–1848*. San Francisco: History Co. Pub., 1888.

Baraka, Amiri. *Blues People*. New York: W. Morrow, 1963.

Barceló, Beatriz. "La Escuela Bolera." Portal sobre la cultura escénica en España. http://www.eter.es/dn/artic/artic.php?id=2 (accessed May 20, 2014).

Barthes, Roland. *Mythologies*. Translated by Annette Lavers. New York: Hill & Wang, 1972.

Bartholomay, Paul Bruno. *Die Tanzkunst in Beziehung auf die Lehre und Bildung des wahren Anstandes und des gefälligen Äußeren....* Gießen: beim Autor, 1838.

Batiste, Stephanie Leigh. *Darkening Mirrors: Imperial Representation in Depression-Era African American Performance*. Durham: Duke University Press, 2011.

Baudrillard, Jean. *America*. New York: Verso, 1988.

Beard, George M. *American Nervousness*. New York: Arno Press, [1881] 1972.

Bell, Horace. *Reminiscences of a Ranger*. Los Angeles: Yarnell Press, 1881.

Bennahum, Ninotchka Devorah. *Antonia Mercé, "La Argentina": Flamenco & the Spanish Avant-Garde*. Middletown: Wesleyan University Press, 2000.

_____. *Carmen, a Gypsy Geography*. Middletown, CT: Wesleyan University Press, 2013.

_____ and K. Meira Goldberg. *100 Years of Flamenco in New York City*. New York: The New York Public Library for the Performing Arts, Lincoln Center, 2013.

Beranger. "Courrier des théâtres." *Le Figaro* (January 24, 1920).

Bermúdez, Silvia. *Rocking the Boat: Migration and the Significance of Race in Contemporary Spanish Music*. Toronto: University of Toronto Press, forthcoming.

Blake, Jody. *Le Tumulte Noir: Modernist Art and Popular Entertainment in Jazz-Age Paris, 1900–1930*. University Park: Pennsylvania State University Press, 1999.

Blas Vega, José. "Hacía la historia del baile flamenco, 'cinco preguntas a diez bailaores.'" *La Caña no. 16–17*. http://www.flamenco-world.com/magazine/cana/cana.htm (accessed February 8, 2010).

_____. *La canción española. De La Caramba a Isabel Pantoja*. Madrid: Calambur Editorial, 1996.

_____. *Los cafés cantantes de Madrid: (1846–1936)*. Madrid: Ediciones Guillermo Blázquez, 2006.

_____. *Los cafés cantante de Sevilla*. Madrid: Editorial Cinterco, 1987.

_____. "La escuela bolera." In *Historia del flamenco. vol. II*. Edited by José Luis Navarro and Miguel Ropero Núñez. Sevilla: Tartessos, 2002.

_____, and Manuel Ríos Ruiz. *Diccionario enciclopédico ilustrado del flamenco y maestros del flamenco*. Madrid: Cinterco, 1988.

Blasis, Carlo. *The Code of Terpsichore*. London: James Bullock, 1828.

_____. *Notes upon Dancing, Historical and Practical*. London: M. Delaporte, 1847.

_____ and R. Barton, trans. *The Code of Terpsichore: The Art of Dancing, Comprising its Theory and Practice, and a History of Its Rise and Progress, from the Earliest Times*. London: E. Bull, 1830.

Bohlman, Philip. *World Music: A Very Short Introduction*. London: Oxford University Press, 2002.

Bohórquez, Manuel. "La Campanera o los Brazos de la Giralda." *La Gazapera: El blog de Manuel Bohórquez* (January 26, 2013). http://blogs.elcorreoweb.es/lagazapera/2013/01/26/ (accessed November 13, 2013).

_____. "El Carbonerillo de la Macarena." *La Gazapera: El blog de Manuel Bohórquez* (March 28, 2010). http://blogs.elcorreoweb.es/lagazapera/2010/03/18/el-carbonerillo-de-la-macarena/ (accessed February 19, 2013).

_____. "Manuel Vallejo Gana la Copa Pavón en Madrid." *La Gazapera:El blog de Manuel Bohórquez* (February 24, 2010). http://blogs.elcorreoweb.es/lagazapera/2010/02/24/vallejo-gana-la-copa-pavon-en-madrid/ (accessed February 21, 2010).

_____. "Sevilla ya tiene a otra gran Pastora." *La Gazapera: El blog de Manuel Bohórquez* (September 28, 2010). http://blogs.elcorreoweb.es/lagazapera/2010/09/28/sevilla-ya-tiene-a-otra-gran-pastora (accessed June 30, 2014).

Bohórquez Casado, Manuel. *La Niña de los Peines, en la casa de los Pavón*. Sevilla: Signatura Ediciones, 2000.

Borrow, George. *The Zincali, or, an Account of the Gypsies of Spain with an Original Collection of their Songs and Poetry, and a Copious Dictionary of their Language*. Sevilla: Extramuros Edición, 2007. London and New York: John Lane, [1841] 1902.

Bourdieu, Pierre. *Distinction: A Social Critique of the Judgement of Taste*. London: Routledge, 2010. [Spanish edition: *La distinción. Criterio y bases sociales del gusto*. Madrid: Taurus, 1998.]

_____. *Masculine Domination*. Oxford: Blackwell, 2000. [Spanish edition: *La dominación masculine*. Barcelona: Anagrama, 2002.]

Bowman, Lynn. *Epic of a City*. Berkeley: Howell-North, 1974.

Brandes, Stanley. "The Sardana: Catalan Dance and Catalan National Identity." *Journal of American Folklore* 103 (1990).

Breton, David Le. *Antropología del cuerpo y modernidad*. Buenos Aires: Ediciones Nueva Visión, 2002.

Brickell, Herschel. "A Spanish Poet in New York." *Virginia Quarterly Review* 21 (1945).

Briones, Brigida. "Domestic Life in Monterey in 1827." In *Sketches of Early California*. Compiled by Donald DeNevi. San Francisco: Chronicle Books, 1971.

Brooks, Lynn Matluck. *The Art of Dancing in Seventeenth-Century Spain: Juan de Esquivel Navarro and His World*. Lewisburg, PA: Bucknell University Press, 2003.

Brown, Jayna. *Babylon Girls: Black Women Performers and the Shaping of the Modern*. Durham and London: Duke University Press, 2008.

Brown, Joshua. "Flamenco Capital: Tradition, Revolution and Renewal in Seville, Spain." PhD Diss. University of California, Riverside, 2014.

Browning, Barbara. *Samba: Resistance in Motion*. Bloomington: Indiana University Press, 1995.

Brunelleschi, Elsa. *The Dancing Times* 53, no. 633 (June 1963).

Buckland, Theresa J. *Dancing from Past to Present: Nation, Culture, Identities*. Madison: University of Wisconsin Press, 2006.

Buckle, Richard, ed. *Dancing for Diaghilev*. London: John Murray, 1960.

Bull, Cynthia J. "Looking at Movement as Culture: Contact Improvisation to Disco." In *Moving History/Dancing Cultures: A Dance History Reader*. Edited by Ann Dills and Ann Cooper Albright. Middletown, CT: Wesleyan University Press, 2001.

Burt, Ramsay. *The Male Dancer: Bodies, Spectacle, Sexualities*. 2d ed. London and New York: Routledge, 2007.

_____. "The Performance of Unmarked Masculinity." In *When Men Dance: Choreographing Masculinities Across Borders*. Edited by Jennifer Fisher and Anthony Shay. New York: Oxford University Press, 2009.

Butler, Judith. "Performative Acts and Gender Constitution: An Essay in Phenomenology and Feminist Theory." *Theatre Journal* 40 (1988).

Cabañas, Aaron. "'Blancanieves.'" *Fuera de Campo: El blog de Contrapicado* (February 20, 2013). http://contrapicado.net/2013/02/blancanieves-pablo-berger-2012-cameo-2013/ (accessed January 14, 2014).

Cadalso, Don José de. *Cartas marruecas, por el Colonel Don José de Cadalso, caballero del hábito de Santiago, nueva edición, revista y cuidadosamente corregida*. Paris: J. Smith, [1789] 1827.

Cadenas Muñoz, José Juan. "Escenas Parisienses—Las mañanitas del 'Pre-Catalan.'" *Blanco y Negro* (July 11, 1908). [Reproduced in David Pérez Merinero. "Faíco y La Macarrona en París" (January 30, 2010). http://www.papelesflamencos.com/2010/01/faico-y-la-macarrona-en-paris.html (accessed October 21, 2014).]

Cairón, Antonio. *Compendio de las principales reglas del baile*. Madrid: Impr. de Repullés, 1820.

Calado, Silvia. "An Enlightening Journey." Flamenco-world.com (March 6, 2014). http://www.flamenco-world.com/magazine/about/jerez2014/resenas/linan06032014ing.html (accessed June 23, 2014).

_____. "The Real Thing about 'The Real.'" *Lo Real-Le Reel-The Real* (December 13, 2012). www.flamencoworld.com (accessed January 13, 2014).

Campbell, Neil A., and Jane B. Reece. *Biology*. 8th ed. San Francisco and London: Pearson Benjamin Cummings, 2008.

Campo Tejedor, Alberto del, and Rafael Cáceres Feria. *Historia cultural del flamenco. El barbero y la guitarra*. Sevilla: Ed. Almuzara, 2014.

Campos, Manuel. "Los célebres hermanos de la Barrera no eran si quiera primos." *El cante ... que jondo y profundo* (July 8, 2012). http://elcantejondo.blogspot.com.es/2012/07/los-celebres-boleros-hermanos-de-la.html (accessed November 20, 2014).

Capriccio Espagnol (Argentinita and Massine). Clippings. MGZR, Jerome Robbins Dance Division. New York Public Library, Lincoln Center.

Capriccio Espagnol. Ballet Russe de Monte Carlo. Choreography by Leonide Massine and La Argentinita. Principal roles danced by Leonide Massine, Tamara Toumanova and Alexandra Danilova. 1939. Motion Picture. MGZHB 12–1000, Jerome Robbins Dance Division. New York Public Library, Lincoln Center.

"Carmen Amaya y sus gitanos." *Ritmo* (November 1, 1947).

Carmen Lugo, Don José del. "Life of a Rancher." Translated by T. Savage. *California Historical Society Quarterly* 32 (September 1950).

Caro Baroja, Julio. *Ensayo sobre la literatura de cordel*. Madrid: Istmo, 1990.

Carr, Darrah. "Rhythm Mash-Ups: Percussive Dance Hybrids Send New Sounds Across Globe." *Dance Magazine* (May 2010).

Casero-García, Estrella. "Women, Fascism and Dance in the Coros y Danzas of the Feminine Division Under the Franco Regime (1936–1977)." In *The Society of Dance History Scholars 22nd Annual Conference Proceedings*. Albuquerque, NM: Society of Dance History Scholars, 1999.

Castán Palomar, Fernando. *¿Qué hizo usted ayer? Revista Dígame*. Madrid, November, 25 1947.

Castañeda, Antonia I. "*Presidarias y Pobladoreas*: The Journey North and Life in Frontier California." In *En Aquel Entonces: Readings in Mexican-American History*. Edited by Manuel G. Gonzalez and Cynthia M. Gonzalez. Bloomington: University of Indiana Press, 2000.

Castellano Gutierrez, Ángeles. "Dinastía Galván." *El País* (January 15, 2011). http://elpais.com/diario/2011/01/15/babelia/1295053988_850215.html (accessed July 11, 2014).

Castellanos de Losada, Basilio S. *Glorias de Azara en el siglo XIX. Segunda parte*. Madrid: Imprenta de D. B. González, 1852.

Castillo, José del. "Carmen Amaya, la bailarina española que triunfó en Hollywood." *Solidaridad Nacional* (December 18, 1947).

Castle, Mr. and Mrs. Vernon. *Modern Dancing*. New York: Harper & Brothers Publishers, 1914.

Castro, Antonio. "La Flor de mi secreto, 1995." In *Las películas de Almodóvar*. Edited by Antonio Castro. Madrid: Ediciones J.C., 2010.

Cávia, Mariano de. "Cake-walk." *El Imparcial* (January 22, 1903).

Cervantes Saavedra, Miguel de. "Preciosa La Gitanilla." In *Novelas Ejemplares*. Buenos Aires: Editorial Losada, S.A., [1613] 1938.

_____. "El Rufián dichoso." In *Ocho comedias y ocho entremeses nuevos nunca representados*. Madrid: Por la Vda. de Alonso Martín, a costa de Juan de Villarroel, Mercader de Libros, véndese en su casa en la Plazuela del Angel, 1615.

Chakravorty, Pallabi. *Bells of Change: Kathak Dance, Women and Modernity in India*. Calcutta and London: Seagull Books, 2008.

_____. "Dancing into Modernity: Multiple Narratives of India's Kathak Dance." *Dance Research Journal* 38, no. 1/2 (Summer–Winter, 2006).

Chapman, John V. "The Paris Opéra Ballet School, 1798–1827." *Dance Chronicle* 2 (1989).

Chazin-Bennahum, Judith. *Réné Blum and the Ballets Russes: In Search of a Lost Life*. Oxford: Oxford University Press, 2011.

Cherlin, Michael, Halina Filipowicz, and Richard L. Rudolph. *The Great Tradition and its Legacy: The Evolution of Dramatic and Musical Theater in Austria and Central Europe*. New York: Berghahn Books, 2003.

Chinoy, Clara. "Los Gitanos flamencos, un estudio de caso: los Pinini de Lebrija." Manuscript, Diploma de Estudios Avanzados, Universidad de Sevilla, September 2013.

Chuse, Loren. "Anda Jaleo! Cantaoras in Flamenco Song." In *The Mediterranean in Music: Critical Perspectives, Common Concerns, Cultural Differences*. Edited by Kevin Dawe. Lanham, MD: Scarecrow Press, 2005.

———. "*The Cantaoras*: Music, Gender, and Identity in Flamenco Song." In *Current Research in Ethnomusicology: Outstanding Dissertations*. Volume 7. London and New York: Routledge, 2003.

Clemente, Luis. *Filigranas: Una historia de fusiones flamencas*. Valencia: Editorial La Máscara, 1995.

Cleminson, Richard. "'Beyond Tradition and 'Modernity': The Cultural and Sexual Politics of Spanish Anarchism." In *Spanish Cultural Studies: An Introduction*. Edited by Helen Graham and Jo Labanyi. Oxford: Oxford University Press, 1995.

Collingwood, Robin G. *Outlines of a Philosophy of Art*. Bristol: Thoemme Press, [1925] 1994.

Colmeiro, José F. " Nation of Ghosts? Haunting, Historical Memory and Forgetting in Post-Franco Spain." *452°F: Electronic Journal of Theory of Literature and Comparative Literature*, no. 4 (2011).

———. "Rehispanicizing Carmen: Cultural Reappropriations in Spanish Cinema." In *Carmen: From Silent Films to MTV*. Edited by Chris Perriam and Ann Davies. Amsterdam: Rodopi, 2005.

Colomé, Delfín. "Presentación." In *Los Ballets Russes de Diaghilev y España*. Edited by Vicente García-Márquez, Yvan Nommick, and Antonio Alvarez Cañibano. Granada: Archivo Manuel de Falla, 2012.

Colton, Walter. *Three Years in California*. New York: Barnes, 1850.

Comaroff, John, and Jean Comaroff. *Ethnography and the Historical Imagination (Studies in the Ethnographic Imagination)*. Boulder: Westview Press, 1992.

Combi, Mariella. *Corpo e tecnologie. Simbolismi, rappresentazione e immaginarii*. Roma: Meltemi, 2000.

Cooper Albright, Ann. *Choreographing Difference: The Body and Identity in Contemporary Dance*. Middletown, CT: Wesleyan University Press, 1997.

Corál, Matilde. "Código de la escuela Sevillana de baile." *Pepa Montes*. http://www.pepamontes.com (accessed September 12, 2014).

———. Interviewed in "Conferencia: La escuela sevillana del flamenco a cargo de Marta Carrasco." http://es.mashpedia.com/Escuela_sevillana (accessed August 7, 2014)

———, Angel Álvarez Caballero, Juan Valdés, and Rocío Coral. *Tratado de la bata de cola: Matilde Coral, una vida de arte y magisterio*. Madrid: Alianza, 2003.

Coronel, Antonio. "Things Past." *Touring Topics* (September 1929).

Costa, M. "Carmen Amaya." *Lecturas* (February 1948).

Cotarelo y Mori, Emilio. *Colección de entremeses, loas, bailes, jácaras y mojigangas desde fines del siglo 16 à mediados del 18*, vol. 1. Madrid: Bailly Ballière, 1911.

Covarrubias Horozco, Sebastián de. *Tesoro de la lengva castellana, o española*. Madrid: Por L. Sanchez, impressor del rey n.s., 1611.

Cruces-Roldán, Cristina. *Antropología y flamenco: Más allá de la música (I): Sociabilidad, transmissión y patrominio*. Seville: Signatura Ediciones, 2002.

———. *Antropología y Flamenco: Más allá de la música (II): Identidad, género y trabajo*. Sevilla: Signatura Ediciones de Andalucía, 2003.

———. "El aplauso difícil. Sobre la 'autenticidad,' el 'nuevo flamenco' y la negación del padre jondo." In *Comunicación y música II: Tecnología y audiencias*. Edited by Miguel de Aguilera, Joan E. Adell, and Ana Sedeño. Barcelona: UOC Press, Comunicación 6, 2008.

———. "De cintura para arriba: Hipercorporeidad y sexuacion en le flamenco." *Plataforma independiente de estudios flamencos modernos y contemporáneos*. http://www.pieflamenco.com/investigaciones/de-cintura-para-arriba-hipercorporeidad-y-sexuacion-en-el-flamenco/ (accessed May 27, 2014).

———. *El Flamenco y la música andalusí. Argumentos para un encuentro*. Barcelona: Ediciones Carena, 2003.

———. "Hacia una revisión del concepto 'nuevo flamenco.' La intelectualización del arte." *Interdisciplinary Conference on Flamenco Research—INFLA—and II International Workshop of Folk Music Analysis—FMA*. Universidad de Sevilla, 2012.

———. *La niña de los Peines, el mundo flamenco de Pastora Pavón*. Córdoba: Almuzara, 2009.

———. "Presencias flamencas en los Archivos Gaumont-Pathé. Registros callejeros en la Granada de 1905." *IV Congreso de Investigación INFLA*. Universidad de Sevilla, 2014.

———, ed. *El flamenco: Identidades sociales, ritual y patrimonio cultural*. Jerez de la Frontera: Centro Andaluz de Flamenco, 1996.

Cruzado, Ángeles. "Juana la Macarrona, la estrella de los cafés cantantes." *Flamencas por derecho* (April 5, 2013). http://www.flamencasporderecho.com/juana-la-macarrona-ii/ (accessed May 14, 2014).

———. "La Joselito, el alma de Andalucía en París (III)." *Flamencas por derecho* (March 3, 2014). http://www.flamencasporderecho.com/la-joselito-iii/ (accessed May 14, 2014).

———. "'La Malena, la elegancia de una bailaora de la vieja escuela (1).'" *Flamencas por derecho* (September 13, 2013). http://www.flamencasporderecho.com/la-malena-i/ (accessed May 14, 2014).

———. "Salud Rodriguez la hija del ciego." *Flamencas por derecho* (July 5, 2013). http://www.flamencasporderecho.com/salud-rodriguez-la-hija-del-ciego/ (accessed February 20, 2014).

Csordas, Thomas J. "Somatic Modes of Attention." *Cultural Anthropology* 8, no. 2 (1993).

Cuadro Flamenco. Choreographed by Ted Shawn. Filmed in Santa Barbara, California, 1924. Jacob's Pillow Archives.

"Cuatro Trileros—BBVA (soleá por bulerías)." *FLO6X8* (October 27, 2013). http://www.flo6x8.com/content/cuatro-trileros-bbva-sole%C3%A1-por-buler%C3%ADas (accessed July 12, 2014).

Czarnowski, Lucille. *Dances of Early California Days*. Palo Alto, CA: Pacific Books, 1950.

Daly, Ann. *Done Into Dance: Isadora Duncan in America*. Middletown, CT: Wesleyan University Press, 2002.

Dance Heritage Coalition. "100 Dance Treasures: Sol Hurok." *Dance Heritage Coalition*. http://www.danceheritage.org/hurok.html.

Davies, Ann. "Introduction." In *Carmen: From Silent Films to MTV*. Edited by Chris Perriam and Ann Davies. Amsterdam: Rodopi, 2005.

Davillier, Charles, Gustave Doré, and Édouard Charton. *Le tour de monde: nouveau journal des voyages*. Paris: Hachette, 1864.

Davis, William H. "Indian Insurrection and Treachery." In *Sketches of Early California*. Compiled by Donald DeNevi. San Francisco: Chronicle Books, 1971.

Delgado, Maria. "Flesh and the Devil." *Sight & Sound* 21, no. 9 (September 2011).

Denby, Edwin. *Dance Writings*. New York: Alfred A. Knopf, [1967] 1986.

Dent, Edward. "Manuel de Falla." *The Nation & Athenaeum* (May 28, 1921).

———. "Modern Spanish Music." *The London Mercury* (February 1920).

———. "A Spanish Ballet." *The Athenaeum* (August 1, 1919).

Desmond, Jane C. "Embodying Difference: Issues in Dance and Cultural Studies." In *Meaning in Motion: New Cultural Studies of Dance*. Edited by Jane C. Desmond. Durham, NC, and London: Duke University Press, 1997.

de Torre, Esteban. "Pre-American Monterey." *Touring Topics* (October 1930).

de Triana, Rita. *Antonio Triana and the Spanish Dance: A Personal Recollection (Choreography and Dance Studies Series)*. London: Routledge, 1994.

El Diario de Córdoba (September 3, 1925; September 5, 1925). http://flamencodepapel.blogspot.com/2009_12_01_archive.html (accessed March 24, 2010).

Diezhandino, Ciro. Interview by Clara Chinoy. March 10, 2010.

"Diversiones públicas." *La Época* (February 7, 1903).

D'Lugo, Marvin. *Pedro Almodóvar*. Urbana and Chicago: University of Illinois Press, 2006.

Dolin, Anton. "La Argentinita, a Tribute." *Dance Magazine* (November 1945).

Don Preciso. *Colección de las mejores coplas de seguidillas, tiranas y polos que se han compuesto para cantar a la guitarra*. Jaén: Ediciones Demófilo, 1982.

Doré, Gustave. *Doré's Spain: All 236 Illustrations from Spain*. Mineola, NY: Dover Publications, 2004.

——— and Charles Davillier. *Danzas Españolas. Viaje por España*. Sevilla: Bienal de Arte Flamenco y Fundacion Machado, 1988.

——— and ———. *Voyage en Espagne*. Paris: Hachette, 1862. [English edition: *Spain*. London: Sampson Low, Marston, Low and Searle, 1876.]

Doubleday, Veronica. "Sounds of Power: An Overview of Musical Instruments and Gender." In *Ethnomusicology Forum* 17, no. 1 (2008).

Douglas, Mary. *Natural Symbols: Explorations in Cosmology*. London: Routledge, 1996 [1970].

———. *Pureza y peligro: análisis de los conceptos de contaminación y tabú*. Madrid: Siglo XXI, 1991.

Duncan, Isadora. "I See America Dancing." In *The Art of the Dance*. Edited by Sheldon Cheney. New York: Theatre Arts, 1928.

———. *My Life*. New York: Liveright, 1927.

Ebora, Tony. *Orígenes de la música cubana*. Madrid: Alianza, 1997.

Eco, Umberto. *Travels in Hyperreality*. New York: Harcourt Brace Jovanovich, 1986.

el de Triana, Fernando. *Arte y artistas flamencos*. Madrid: Ediciones Demófilo, [1935] 1978; 1986; 2009.

Elder, Robert K. *The Film that Changed My Life*. Chicago: Chicago Review Press, 2011.

Eliot, T. S. "Dramatis Personae." *The Criterion* (April 1923).

_____. "London Letter." *The Dial* (August 1921).
Elorza, Antonio. "Some Perspectives on the Nation-State and Autonomies in Spain." In *Spanish Cultural Studies: An Introduction*. Edited by Helen Graham and Jo Labanyi. Oxford: Oxford University Press, 1995.
_____. *La modernización política en España (ensayos de historia del pensamiento político)*. Madrid: Endymion, 1990.
"Encarnación Hurtado 'La Malagueñita'" and 'Les Mingorance.'" *Eco Artístico* 3, no. 56 (May 25, 1911).
Encina, Juan de la. "Crítica de arte. 'El sombrero de tres picos.'" *La Voz* (April 6, 1921).
Encyclopaedia Britannica Online. "Fascism." http://www.britannica.com/EBchecked/topic/202210/fascism/219376/The-new-man (accessed December 7, 2013).
E.P. "Cake-walk (danza nueva)." *Actualidades* 6 (February 8, 1903). Madrid.
Erdman, Joan L. "Dance Discourses: Rethinking the History of the 'Oriental Dance.'" In *Moving Words: Re-Writing Dance*. Edited by Gay Morris. London and New York: Routledge, 1996.
_____. "Who Remembers Uday Shankar?" http://www.mukto-mona.com/new_site/mukto-mona/Articles/jaffor/uday_shanka2.htm (accessed August 10, 2014).
Escudero, Vicente. *Arte Flamenco Jondo*. Madrid: Estades Artes Gráficas, 1959.
_____. "Decalogue." Quoted in "'Vicente, esto es'; Vicente Escudero, Greatest Flamenco Dancer of this Century, Returns in Triumph." Alexandra V. Krinkin. *Dance Magazine* (1955).
_____. *Mi baile*. Barcelona: Montaner y Simón, 1947.
Espinós, Victor. "Los Bailes Rusos. 'El sombrero de tres picos.'" *La Epoca* (April 6, 1921).
Esquivel Navarro, Juan de. *Discursos sobre el arte del dançado, y sus excelencias y primer origen, reprobando las acciones deshonestas*. Seville: Iuan Gomez de Blas, 1642.
Esteban, Mari Luz. *Antropología del cuerpo. Género, itinerarios corporales, identidad y cambio*. Barcelona: Bellaterra, 2004.
Estébanez Calderón, Serafín. "Un Baile en Triana," and "Asamblea General de los Caballeros y Damas de Triana y toma el hábito de la órden de cierta rubia bailadora." In *Escenas Andaluzas: bizarrías de la tierra, alardes de toros, rasgos populares, cuadros de costumbres y artículos varios*. Madrid: Baltasar González, 1847.
_____. *Escenas Andaluzas ... el Solitario: Edicion de lujo adornada con 125 dibujos por Lameyer*. Madrid: Balt. Gonzalcz, 1847.
_____. *Escenas Andaluzas*. Edited by Alberto González Troyano. Madrid: Cátedra, 1985.

"Expediente de la Escuela Bolera para su Declaración como Bien de Interés Cultural." http://www.juntadeandalucia.es/culturaydeporte/comunidadprofesional/sites/default/files/expediente_de_la_escuela_bolera_para_su_declaracion_como_bien_de_interes_cultural.pdf (accessed May 20, 2013).
Fanon, Frantz. *Black Skin, White Masks*. New York: Grove Press, 2008.
Faure, Oliver. "La Mirada de los medicos." In *Historia del Cuerpo (II) de la Revolución Francesa a la Gran Guerra*. Edited by Alain Corbin. Madrid: Taurus, 2005.
Fauser, Annegret. *Musical Encounters at the 1889 Paris World's Fair*. Rochester: University of Rochester Press, 2005.
Fear, A.T. "The Dancing Girls of Cádiz." *Greece & Rome*, 2d series, vol. 38, no. 1 (April 1991). Cambridge University Press. http://www.jstor.org/stable/643110 (accessed November 4, 2013).
Feld, Steven. "A Sweet Lullaby for World Music." *Public Culture* 12.1 (2000).
Fellay-Dunbar, Catalina. "Firedance: Sharing a Flame Between Flamenco and Kathak." *Proceeding of the Canadian Dance Studies Conference 2012:* "Collaboration: Intersections, Negotiations, Mediations in the Worlds of Dance." Toronto, Canada: Society for Canadian Dance Studies, April 14, 2013.
Fernandez, David. "Tres estrellas illuman el Villamarta." *Diario de Jeréz* (March 1, 2008). [Originally published in Michelle Heffner Hayes, *Flamenco: Conflicting Histories of the Dance*, Jefferson, NC: McFarland, 2009.]
Fernández Martínez, Lola. "La estética musical del flamenco en *El polo del contrabandista*." *La nueva alboreá* 11 (2009).
Ferriol y Boxeraus, Bartolomé, Joseph Testore, and Santiago Perez Junquera. *Reglas utiles para los aficionados a danzar: provechoso divertimento de los que gustan tocar instrumentos: y polyticas advertencias a todo genero de personas: adornado con varias laminas: dedicado a la S.M. del rey de las Dos Sicilias, &c*. (Capoa: A costa de Joseph Testore, mercador de libros, à la Calle Nueva, 1745).
"Flamencos de antaño." *Papeles Flamencos* (August 29, 2009). http://www.papelesflamencos.com/search/label/1932 (accessed March 26, 2010). Originally appeared in *Revista Estampa* (October 1, 1932).
Flitch, J.E. Crawford. *Modern Dancing and Dancers*. Philadelphia: J.B. Lippincott Company, 1912.
Floyd, Samuel A., Jr. "Ring Shout! Literary Studies, Historical Studies, and Black Music Inquiry." In *Signifyin(g), Sanctifyin' & Slam Dunk-*

ing: A Reader in African American Expressive Culture. Edited by Gena Caponi-Tabery. Amherst: University of Massachusetts Press, 1999.

Folch, Enrich. "At the Crossroads of Flamenco, New Flamenco and Spanish Pop: The Case of Rumba." In *Made in Spain: Studies in Popular Music*. New York: Routledge, 2013.

Ford, Richard. *Gatherings from Spain, Selected from the "Handbook of Spain" with Much New Matter*. London: John Murray Albemarle Street, [1846] 1861. http://www.archive.org/stream/gatheringsfromsp00ford/gatheringsfromsp00ford_djvu.txt (accessed September 12, 2014).

_____. *A Handbook for Travelers in Spain*. 3d ed. London: John Murray, 1855. http://www.books.google.com/books?id=XDcdAAAAIAAJ&printsec=titlepage (accessed July 10–13, 2010).

Foster, Hal. *Compulsive Beauty*. Cambridge: MIT Press, 1995.

Foster, Susan Leigh. *Reading Dancing: Bodies and Subjects in Contemporary American Dance*. Oakland: University of California Press, 1988.

Foucault, Michel. *The History of Sexuality, Vol. I: The Will to Knowledge*. New York: Vintage Books, 1978. [Spanish edition: *Historia de la sexualidad, 1: La voluntad de saber*. Madrid: Siglo XXI, 1978.]

Fra Molinero, Baltasar. *La imagen de los negros en el teatro del Siglo de Oro*. Madrid: Siglo XXI de España, 1995.

Franco, Francisco. "1954 Amendment to *Ley de Vagos y Maleantes*." http://www.boe.es/datos/imagenes/BOE/1954/198/A04862.tif.

Franko, Mark. "Dance and the Political: States of Exception." In *Dance Discourses: Keywords in Dance Research*. Edited by Susanne Franco and Marina Nordera. London and New York: Routledge, 2007.

Frayssinet Savy, Corinne. *Israel Galván: danser le silence*. Arles: ACTES SUD, 2009.

Frenk Alatorre, Margit. *Nuevo Corpus de la antigua lírica popular hispánica: (siglos XV a XVII)*, vol. 1. México: El Colegio de México [u.a.], 2003.

Fuente Ballesteros, Ricardo de la. "Los gitanos en la tonadilla escénica." *Revista de Folklore*, Fundación Joaquín Diaz, vol. 4, no. 40 (1984).

Fundación Antonio Gades, ed. *Antonio Gades*. Madrid: Fundación Antonio Gades, 2005.

Galván, Israel. *La Edad de Oro*. https://www.youtube.com/watch?v=BTXf01hRr94 (accessed July 11, 2014).

Galván, Pastora. Interview with the Michelle Heffner Hayes. Seville, March 4, 2008.

Gamboa, José Manuel. *Una historia del flamenco*. Madrid: Espasa Calpe S.A., 2005.

_____. "'Por qué la denominación ópera flamenca.'" *13 Festival de Flamenco de Ciutat Vella* (May 25, 2006). www.deflamenco.com/revista/noticias/13-festival-flamenco-ciutat-vella-1.html#.Ur8jeMaA1jp (accessed March 12, 2010).

_____, and Faustino Nuñez. *Camarón Vida y Obra*. Madrid: Iberautor, 2003.

Garafola, Lynn. "The Choreography of *Le Tricorne*." In *Los Ballets Russes de Diaghilev y España*. Edited by Vicente García-Márquez, Yvan Nommick, and Antonio Alvarez Cañibano. Granada: Archivo Manuel de Falla, 2012.

_____. *Diaghilev's Ballets Russes*. New York and Oxford: Oxford University Press, 1989.

Garcia Garrido, Luisa ("Luisa Triana"). Interview by Clara Chinoy. December 20, 2013.

García Gómez, Génesis. "Volksgeist y Género Español." In *Flamenco y Nacionalismo: Aportaciones para una sociologia politica del flamenco*. Edited by Gerhard Steingress and Enrique Baltanás. Seville: Fundación Machado, 1998.

García Lorca, Federico. *Deep Song and Other Prose*. New York: A New Directions Book, 1980.

_____. *In Search of Duende*. Edited by Christopher Maurer. New York: A New Directions Book, 1998.

_____. *Line of Light and Shadow*. Exhibition Catalogue. Edited by Christopher Maurer. Durham: Duke University Press, 1991.

_____. *Poet in New York*. Translated by Ben Belitt. New York: Grove Press, 1955.

_____, and Miguel García-Posada. *Obras, VI. Prosa, 1: primeras prosas, conferencias, conferencias-recitales, alocuciones, homenajes, varia, vida*. Barcelona: Akal, 1994.

García-Márquez, Vicente. *Massine: A Biography*. New York: Knopf, 1995.

García Martínez, José María. *Del fox-trot al jazz flamenco: el jazz en España [1919–1996]*. Madrid: Alianza, 1996.

García Navarro, José Luis, and Miguel Ropero Nuñez. *Historia del flamenco*. 6 vols. Sevilla: Ediciones Tartessos, 1996.

García Ulecia, Alberto. *Las confesiones de Antonio Mairena*. Sevilla: Universidad de Sevilla, Colección de bolsillo, núm. 53, 1976.

Gasch, Sebastià. "Presentación de Carmen Amaya." *Destino* (December 27, 1947).

Gautier, Théophile. "Théophile Gautier on Spanish Dancing." Edited and translated by Ivor Guest. *Dance Chronicle* 10, no. 1 (1987).

_____. *Viaje por España*. Prólogo de M. Vázquez Montalbán. Barcelona: Taifa, 1985.

____. *Un Voyage en Espagne*. París, 1843.

____. *Wanderings in Spain*. London: Ingram, Cooke, & Co., 1853. http://www.books.google.com/books?id=JjUBAAAAQAAJ&printsec=frontcover&dq=gautier+spain&lr=#PPR1,M1 (accessed December 2013).

Gell, Alfred. *Art and Agency: An Anthropological Theory*. Oxford: Clarendon, 1998.

George-Graves, Nadine. "'Just Like Being at the Zoo' / Primitivity and Ragtime Dance." In *Ballroom, Boogie, Shimmy Sham, Shake: A Social and Popular Dance Reader*. Edited by Julie Malnig. Urbana: University of Illinois Press, 2009.

Gil. "Embrujo Español." *ABC de Sevilla* (October 24, 1947).

Gilmore, David. "Above and Below: Toward a Social Geometry of Gender." *American Anthropologist* 98, no. 1 (1996).

____. *Honor and Shame and the Unity of the Mediterranean*. Arlington, VA: American Anthropological Association, 1987.

____. "Men and Women in Southern Spain: 'Domestic Power' Revisited." *American Anthropologist* 92, no. 1 (1990).

Goffman, Erving. *Relations in Public: Microstudies of the Public Order*. New York: Basic Books, 1971.

Goldberg, K. Meira. "Border Trespasses: The Gypsy Mask and Carmen Amaya's Flamenco Dance." PhD dissertation, Temple University, Philadelphia, 1995.

____. "Flamenco Fire: Form as Generated by the Performer-Audience Relationship." *100 Years of Gypsy Studies: The Gypsy Lore Society* 5 (1990).

____. "*Jaleo de Jerez* and *Tumulte Noir*: Juana Vargas "La Macarrona" at the Exposition Universelle, Paris, 1889." Oxford: Oxford University Press, forthcoming.

____. "The Latin Craze and the Gypsy Mask: Carmen Amaya and the Flamenco Aesthetic (1913–1963)." In *100 Years of Flamenco in New York City*. Edited by Ninotchka Bennahum and K. Meira Goldberg. New York: New York Public Library for the Performing Arts, 2013.

____. "Sonidos Negros: On the Blackness of Flamenco." *Dance Chronicle* 37, no. 1 (2014).

____. "Tumulte Noir and Jaleo de Jerez: Cakewalk, Tango and Jazz in La Macarrona's Flamenco Dance." Presentation at the joint conference of *Congress on Research in Dance and Society of Dance History Scholars*, Riverside, CA., November 16, 2013; in the panel presentation "Flamenco's Influence on Visual Arts and Popular Culture" at the *Philadelphia Flamenco Festival*, Philadelphia, PA, March 9, 2014; and lecture-demonstration at the *New Perspectives in Flamenco History and Research Symposium*, University of New Mexico, Albuquerque, June 8–9, 2014.

Gómez Tello, José Luis. "Carmen Amaya. Aquella gitana ha vuelto y va a trabajar en el cine español." *Primer Plano* (August 17, 1947).

Gonzalez, Manuel G. and Cynthia M. Gonzalez, eds. *En Aquel Entonces: Readings in Mexican-American History*. Bloomington: University of Indiana Press, 2000.

González del Castillo, Juan Ignacio. *Saynete 7 7*. Isla de Leon: Periu, 1812.

González Jimenez, Pedro. "Lo Tópico de la mujer Andaluza." In *Las mujeres en la historia de Andalucía*. Córdoba: Publicaciónes de la Consejería de Cultura y Medio Ambiente de la Junta de Andalucía y Obra Social y Cultural Cajasur, 1994.

González Troyano, Alberto. *La desventura de Carmen. Una divagación sobre Andalucía*. Madrid: Espasa-Calpe, 1990.

Goodman, Saul. *Dance Magazine*, (September 1965).

Gottschild, Brenda Dixon. *Digging the Africanist Presence in American Performance: Dance and Other Contexts*. Westport, CT: Greenwood Press, 1996.

Graham, Helen, and Jo Labanyi, eds. *Spanish Cultural Studies*. Oxford and New York: Oxford University Press, 1996.

Grande, Félix. "¡Don Manuel que nos vamos! Falla. Granada 1922. El concurso de cante jondo." In *El flamenco en la cultura española*. Edited by Ángel Álvarez Caballero and Alfonso Carmona González. Murcia: Servicio de Publicaciones, 1999.

____. *Memoria del flamenco II: De los cafes cantantes a nuestros días*. Madrid: Editorial Espasa-Calpe, S.A., 1979.

Grau, Andrée. "Dancing Bodies, Spaces/Places and the Senses: A Cross-Cultural Investigation." *Journal of Dance & Somatic Practices* 3 (2011).

Greenberg, Clement. *Art and Culture: Critical Essays*. Boston: Beacon Press, 1961.

____. "Counter-Avant-Garde." Lecture given at Brandeis University, May 13, 1970.

____. "Modernist Painting." In *The New Art: A Critical Anthology*. Edited by Gregory Battcock. New York: E.P. Dutton & Co., 1966.

Greskovic, Robert. *Ballet 101: A Complete Guide to Learning and Loving the Ballet*. New York: Hyperion, 1998.

Grigoriev, S. L. *The Diaghilev Ballet, 1909–1929*. Translated and edited by Vera Bowen. [London, 1953]. New York: Dance Horizons, 1974.

Grooveman, Manu. "Inicios de jazz en España (I): el baile de los negritos." *La música es mi amante* (June 21, 2013). http://lamusicaesmiamante.blogspot.com/2013/07/inicios-del-jazz-en-espana-i-el-baile.html (accessed November 18, 2014).

Grugel, Jean, and Tim Rees. *Franco's Spain*. London: Arnold, 1997.

Grut, Marina. *The Bolero School*. London: Dance Books, 2002.

_____, Alberto Lorca, Ángel Pericet Carmona, Eloy Pericet, and Ivor Forbes Guest. *The Bolero School: An Illustrated History of the Bolero, the Seguidillas and the Escuela Bolera: Syllabus and Dances*. Alton, Hampshire, UK: Dance Books, 2002.

Guest, Ivor. *The Romantic Ballet in England*. London: Phoenix House, 1954.

_____. *The Romantic Ballet in Paris*. Middletown, CT: Wesleyan University Press, 1966.

Gutiérrez, Ramon A., and Richard J. Orsi, eds. *Contested Eden: California Before the Gold Rush*. Berkeley and Los Angeles: University of California Press, 1998.

Hackel, Steven W. "Land, Labor, and Production: The Colonial Economy of Spanish and Mexican California." In *Contested Eden: California Before the Gold Rush*. Edited by Ramon A. Gutiérrez and Richard J. Orsi. Berkeley and Los Angeles: University of California Press, 1998.

Haitzinger, Nicole. *Les Choses Éspagnoles. Research into the Hispanomania of Nineteenth-Century Dance*. München: epodium, 2009.

Haraway, Donna. *Simians, Cyborgs and Women: The Reinvention of Nature*. New York: Routledge, 1991.

Hardt, Michael, and Antonio Negri. *Empire*. Cambridge, MA: Harvard University Press, 2000.

Harlow, Neal. *California Conquered: The Annexation of a Mexican Province, 1846–1850*. Berkeley and Los Angeles: University of California Press, 1982.

Harrold, Robert. *The Dancing Times* 60, no. 651 (December 1964).

Hayes, Michelle Heffner. *Flamenco: Conflicting Histories of the Dance*. Jefferson, NC: McFarland, 2009.

_____. "The Writing on the Wall: Reading Improvisation in Flamenco and Postmodern Dance." In *Taken By Surprise: A Dance Improvisation Reader*. Edited by Ann Cooper Albright and David Gere. Middletown: Wesleyan University Press, 2003.

Hein, Norvin. *The Miracle Plays of Mathura*. New Haven, CT: Yale University Press, 1972.

Hentschke, Theodor. *Allgemeine Tanzkunst. Theorie und Geschichte, antike und moderne (gesellschaftliche und theatralische) Tanzkunst und Schilderung der meisten National und Charaktertänze*. Stralsund: W. Hausschildt, 1836.

El Heraldo de Madrid (December, 5 1934). http://hemerotecadigital.bne.es/issue.vm?id=0001071482&search=&lang=es ed.: 6 (accessed January 12, 2010).

El Heraldo de Madrid (January 28, 1935). http://hemerotecadigital.bne.es/issue.vm?id=0001077037&search=&lang=es ed.: 4 (accessed January 12, 2010).

"Hermanos Gavilan." *Eco artístico* 56 (May 25, 1911).

Heuer, Bronwen Jean. *The Discourse of the Ruffian in Quevedo's "Jácaras."* Doctoral dissertation, State University of New York at Stony Brook, 1991. [ProQuest: UMI Dissertations Publishing, 1991, 9128566].

Highfill, Phillip H. *A Biographical Dictionary of Actors, Actresses, Musicians, Dancers, Managers & Other Stage Personnel in London, 1660–1800*. Carbondale: Southern Illinois University Press, 1991.

Hill, Constance Valis. *Tap Dancing America: A Cultural History*. New York: Oxford University Press, 2010.

Hobsbawm, Eric, and Terence Ranger, eds. *The Invention of Tradition*. Cambridge: Cambridge University Press, 1983.

Horwitz, Dawn Lille. "The Hispanic Influence on Leonide Massine." Proceedings from the Society of Dance History Scholars conference, Miami, 1991.

Hsu, Margarita ("Margarita la China"). Interview by Clara Chinoy. December 19, 2013.

Hughes, Terence M. *Revelations of Spain in 1845*. London: Bradbury and Evans, 1845.

Hurok, Sol. *S. Hurok Presents*. New York: Hermitage House, 1953.

IFFI Daily. 41st International Film Festival of India (November 29, 2010) http://iffi.nic.in/akalpdf/iffidaily29112010.pdf (accessed June 10, 2014).

Inda, Jonathan Xavier, and Renato Rosaldo, eds. *The Anthropology of Globalization: A Reader*. Oxford: Blackwell, 2002.

Infante, Blas. *Orígenes de lo flamenco y secreto del cante jondo: (1929–1933)*. Sevilla: Junta de Antalucia, Consejería de Cultura, 1980.

Instituto Nacional de las Artes Escénicas y la Música. *La escuela bolera*. Madrid, 1992. "Interview with Pedro Almodóvar." *The Flower of My Secret*. Sony Pictures Classics. http://www.sonyclassics.com/flower/.

Iovițță, Radu, and Theodore G. Schurr. "Reconstructing the Origins and Migrations of Diasporic Populations: The Case of the European Gypsies." *American Anthropologist* 106, no. 2 (2004).

Jacara. C. 1680. Biblioteca Nacional de España. MS no. 14059/12.

Jacob, William. *Viajes por el sur. Cartas escritas entre 1809–1810.* Sevilla: Portada Editorial, 2002.

Jaque, Juan Antonio. *Libro de danzar de Don Baltasar de Rojas Pantojah.* 1680.

Jeffery, Brian. *Fernando Sor: Composer and Guitarist.* London: Tecla Editions, 1994.

Jeschke, Claudia, Gabi Vettermann, and Nicole Haitzinger. In *Les Choses Éspagnoles. Research into the Hispanomania of 19th Century Dance.* München: epodium, 2009.

Johnson, Lemuel. *The Devil, the Gargoyle and the Buffoon: The Negro as Metaphor in Western Literature.* Port Washington, NY: Kennikat Press, 1971.

Josephs, Allen. *White Wall of Spain: The Mysteries of Andalusian Culture.* Gainesville: University Press of Florida, 1990.

Jowitt, Deborah. "Squeezing Out All the Good Drops." *The Village Voice* (April 11, 1974).

Junyent, Josep Maria. "Carmen Amaya en Embrujo Español." *El Correo Catalán* (December 20, 1947).

———. *El Correo Cataláan* (December 19, 1947).

Juvenal. *The Satires.* Translation by G.G. Ramsay. http://www.tertullian.org/fathers/juvenal_satires_11.htm (accessed November 4, 2013).

Kagan, Richard, ed. *Spain in America: The Origins of Hispanism in the United States.* Urbana: University of Illinois, 2002.

Kapchan, Deborah. *Gender on the Market: Moroccan Women and the Revoicing of Tradition.* Philadelphia: University of Pennsylvania Press, 1996.

Katrak, Ketu. *Contemporary Indian Dance: New Creative Choreography in India and the Diaspora.* New York: Palgrave Macmillan, 2011.

Kelly, Dorothy. "Selling Spanish 'Otherness' since the 1960s." In *Contemporary Spanish Studies.* Edited by Barry Jordan and Rikki Morgan-Tamosunas. London: Arnold, 2000.

Kinder, Marsha. "Reinventing the Motherland: Almodóvar's Brain-Dead Trilogy." *Film Quarterly* 58, no. 2 (Winter 2004).

Kolodin, Irving. "Ballet Presents Spanish 'Caprice': New Work by Massine has Local Premiere." *New York Sun* (October 28, 1939).

Kraut, Anthea. *Choreographing the Folk.* Baltimore: Johns Hopkins University Press, 2008.

Kurtz, Glenn. *Practicing: A Musicians Return to Music.* New York: Knopf, 2007.

La Argentinita. Clippings. MGZRS, New York Public Library Dance Collection.

La Argentinita. Performed by La Argentinita, Pilar Lopez, and Vicente Argentinita. Mexico, [194?]. Videocassette. MGZIC 9-624, New York Public Library Jerome Robbins Dance Collection.

Labanyi, Jo. "Censorship or the Fear of Mass Culture." In *Spanish Cultural Studies: An Introduction.* Edited by Helen Graham and Jo Labanyi. Oxford: Oxford University Press, 1995.

Lancelot, Francine. *La belle dance: catalogue raisonné fait en l'an 1995.* Paris: Van Dieren, 1996.

Lapidus, Ira M. *A History of Islamic Societies.* Cambridge and New York: Cambridge University Press, [1988] 2002.

Laqueur, Thomas Walter. *Making Sex: Body and Gender from the Greeks to Freud.* Cambridge, MA: Harvard University Press, 1990. [Spanish edition: *La construcción del sexo. Cuerpo y género desde los griegos hasta Freud.* Madrid: Cátedra, 1994.]

Lavaur, Luis. *Teoría romántica del cante flamenco. Raíces flamencas en la coreografía romántica europea.* Sevilla: Signatura Ediciones, [1976] 1999.

Lawler, Lillian B. *The Dance in Ancient Greece.* Middleton, CT: Wesleyan University Press [1964] 1984.

Le Jumel de Barneville d' Aulnoy, Marie Catherine. *The Ingenious and Diverting Letters of the Lady's—Travels into Spain Describing the Devotions, Nunneries, Humours, Customs, Laws, Militia, Trade, Diet, and Recreations of that People.* London: Printed for S. Crouch, 1692.

Leblon, Bernard. *El cante flamenco: entre las músicas Gitanas y las tradiciones Andaluzas.* Madrid: Editorial Cinterco, 1991.

Lebrero Stals, José, Inmaculada Abolafio, and Isabel Garcés. *Prohibido el cante: flamenco y fotografía: 3 abril–30 agosto 2009, Centro Andaluz de Arte Contemporáneo, Sevilla.* Sevilla: Junta de Andalucía, Consejería de Cultura, 2009.

Lema-Hincapié, Andrés. "Carlos Saura's *Carmen*: Hybridity and the Inescapable Cliché." In *Carmen: From Silent Films to MTV.* Edited by Chris Perriam and Ann Davies. Amsterdam: Rodopi, 2005.

Levinson, André. "Grandeur et decadence des 'Ballets Russes.'" In *La Danse d'aujourd'hui: études, notes, portraits.* Paris: Editions Duchartre et Van Buggenhoudt, 1929.

———. "The Spirit of the Spanish Dance." *Theatre Arts Monthly* (May 1925).

Lipovetsky, Gilles. *The Empire of Fashion. Dressing Modern Democracy.* Princeton, NJ: Princeton University Press, [1987] 2002.

Lipschutz, Ilse. "Théophile Gautier et la danse espagnole." *Bulletin de la Société Théophile Gautier* 8 (1986).

Lipsitz, George. *Dangerous Crossroads*. London: Verso, 1994.

London Film Festival Review 2012. http://silentlondon.co.uk/2012/10/16/blancanieves-2012-london-film-festival-review/ (accessed January 14, 2014).

London, John. "The Ideology and Practice of Sport." In *Spanish Cultural Studies: An Introduction.* Edited by Helen Graham and Jo Labanyi. Oxford: Oxford University Press, 1995.

Lucas, Cristina de. "Israel Galván Presents His Experimental La Curva at the London Flamenco Festival." *Bachtrack* (March 26, 2013). http://bachtrack.com/review-london-flamenco-festival-2013-la-curva (accessed July 13, 2014).

Lucientes Rodríguez, Francisco. "El baile flamenco en su preponderancia de ayer y su decadencia de hoy." *Papeles Flamencos* (October 17, 2009). http://www.papelesflamencos.com/search/label/Estampa (accessed February 25, 2010). Originally appeared in *Revista Estampa* (April 2, 1929).

Ludwig, Paul. Henri Justamant (1815–1890). Kommentiertes Bestandsverzeichnis seiner Ballett-Notationen in der Theaterwissenschaftlichen Sammlung Schloß Wahn. Universität zu Köln, 2005.

Luján, Néstor. "El problema del folklore." *Destino* (December 27, 1947).

_____. "El regreso de Carmen Amaya." *Destino* (August 2, 1947).

Lumière, Louis. *Le Cake-Walk au Nouveau Cirque*, 1902. https://www.youtube.com/watch?v=ATEb9RGIBzc (accessed November 1, 2014).

Lyons, Daniel. "The Passion of Pedro: Interview with Pedro Almodóvar." *Interview Magazine* (April 1996).

Machado y Álvarez, Antonio (Demófilo). *Cantes flamencos y cantares*. 1887. Edited by Enrique Baltanás. Madrid: Austral, 1998.

_____. *Colección de Cantes Flamencos recogidos y anotados por Demófilo*.... Madrid: Ediciones Demófilo, [1881] 1975.

Madridejos, Montse, and David Pérez Merinero. *Carmen Amaya*. Barcelona: Edicions Bellaterra, 2013.

Madridejos Mora, Montse. "Carmen Amaya *star* de Hollywood." *Revista de Investigación sobre flamenco. La Madrugá*, no. 6. (June 2012). Murcia: Universidad de Murcia. revistas.um.es/flamenco (accessed September 14, 2014).

Madridejos Mora, Montse, and E. Martín Corrales. *El flamenco en la Barcelona de la Exposición Internacional 1929–1930*. Barcelona: Bellaterra, 2012.

Mairena, Antonio, and Ricardo Molina. *Mundo y formas del cante flamenco*. Madrid: Revista de Occidente, 1963.

Malefyt, Timothy deWaal. "'Inside' and 'Outside' Spanish Flamenco: Gender Constructions in Andalusian Concepts of Flamenco Tradition." *Anthropological Quarterly* 71 (1998).

Mandelik, Gloria. Interview by Clara Chinoy. March 10, 2010; December 12, 2013.

Mann, Vivian B., Thomas F. Glick, Jerrilynn D. Dodds, eds. *Convivencia: Jews, Muslims, and Christians in Medieval Spain*. New York: George Braziller and the Jewish Museum of New York, [1992] 2007.

María y Campos, Armando de. *Un ensayo general sobre el teatro español contemporáneo visto desde México*. Madrid: Ed. Stylo, 1948.

Markessinis, Artemis. *Historia de la danza desde sus orígenes*. Madrid: Libr. Deportivas Esteban Sanz Martier, 1995.

Marnold, Jean. "Musique." *Le Mercure de France* (April 1, 1920).

Marquerie, Alfredo. "Despedida en el Madrid de Carmen Amaya, en function patrocinada por la Asociación de la Prensa." *ABC de Madrid* (October 21, 1947).

_____. "Informaciones y noticias teatrales y cinematográficas." *ABC de Madrid* (August 12, 1947).

Marsh, Steven. "Pedro Almodóvar." *Senses of Cinema* 40 (2006). http://www.sensesofcinema.com/2006/great-directors/almodovar/ (accessed December 2, 2014).

Martial. *Epigrams*. Translation by C. A. Walter. Loeb Classical Library. http://www.archive.org/stream;martialepigramso/martiala (accessed November 4, 2013).

Martin, John. *America Dancing*. New York: Dodge Publishing Co., 1936.

_____. *The Dance*. New York: Tudor Publishing Company, 1946.

_____. "The Dance: A New Spanish Invasion." *The New York Times* (July 28, 1929).

_____. "The Dance: La Argentina. The Memorable Career of the Great Spanish Artist Comes to a Close." *The New York Times* (July 26, 1936).

_____. "The Dance: Summing Up." *The New York Times* (October 30, 1938).

_____. "La Argentina Has Given New Form to Old Spanish Dances." *The New York Times* (November 4, 1928).

_____. "Marvelous Dancer is La Argentina." *The New York Times* (November 10, 1928).

_____. "New York Scrapbook: Ballet Russes Premieres." *The New York Times* (November 5, 1939).

Martín Casares, Aurelia. "Comba y Dominga: la imagen sexualizada de las negroafricanas en la literatura del cordel de la España Moderna." In *La esclavitud negroafricana en la historia de España. Siglos XVI y XVII*. Edited by Martín Casares and Margarita García Barranco. Granada: Comares, 2010.

Martínez, Silvia, and Héctor Fouce, eds. *Made in Spain: Studies in Popular Music*. New York: Routledge, 2013.

Martínez de la Peña, Teresa. "El Baile Flamenco, Arcaico y Renovador, Origen y Trayectoria." *Sevilla Flamenca*, no. 22. http://www.flamenco-world.com/magazine/cana/cana.htm (accessed March 20, 2010).

———. "Treinta años de academias de Madrid." *La Caña*, no. 12. http://www.flamenco-world.com/magazine/cana/cana.htm (accessed February 10, 2010).

Martínez Góngora, Mar. "La invención de la 'blancura': el estereotipo y la mímica en 'Boda de negros' de Francisco de Quevedo." *Modern Language Notes*, vol. 120, no. 2 (2005).

Marx, Karl, and Friedrich Engels. *The Communist Manifesto*. New York: International Publishers Co., [1848] 2014.

Massine, Leonide. *My Life in Ballet*. London: Macmillan, 1968.

Matamoros, Elna, ed. *Carmen/Gades. Veinticinco años. Twenty Five Years, 1983–2008*. Madrid: Fundación Antonio Gades/Ediciones Autor, 2008.

Maurer, Christopher. "Federico García Lorca: His Life in Brief." *Fundación Federico Lorca*. http://garcia-lorca.org/Federico/Biografia.aspx (accessed Oct. 11, 2013).

———. "García Lorca and Spanish Music in New York." *Romance Quarterly* 58 (2011).

——— and Andrés Soria Olmedo. Curatorial statement displayed in *Back Tomorrow: Federico García Lorca / Poet in New York* exhibition. New York Public Library, April 5–July 20, 2013.

Mauss, Marcel. "Techniques of the Body." *Economy and Society* 2, no. 1 (1973).

MC2: Saison 13–14, promotional brochure. Grenoble, France: Season 2013–2014. http://www.mc2grenoble.fr/media/client/saison/13-14-brochure-formulaire_bdef.pdf (accessed January 15, 2014).

Mendelsohn, Daniel. "The Women of Pedro Almodóvar." *The New York Review of Books*, vol. 54, no. 3 (March 1, 2007).

Méndez, Lourdes. *Cuerpos sexuados y ficciones identitarias*. Sevilla: Instituto Andaluz de la Mujer, 2004.

Meri, La (Russell Meriwether Hughes). "La Meri Papers." Mixed material. MGZMD, New York Public Library Dance Collection.

Meri, La (Russell Meriwether Hughes). *Spanish Dancing*. New York: A. S. Barnes, 1948.

Milazzo, Kathy M. "Black Erased: The Tango de Negros in Spain's Romantic Age." In *The Oxford Handbook of Dance and Ethnicity*. Eds. Anthony Shay and Barbara Sellers-Young. Oxford University Press, forthcoming.

———. "The Tango de Negros in Spain's Romantic Age: Lost in Translation." Proceedings from Society of Dance History Scholars conference, Guildford, U.K., July 2010.

Minguet è Irol, Pablo. *Arte de danzar a la francesa, adornado con quarenta figuras, que enseñan el modo de hacer todos los diferentes passos de la danza del minuete, con todas sus reglas, y de conducir los brazos en cada passo: Y en quatro figuras, el modo de danzar los tres passapies. Tambien estàn escritos en solfa, para que qualquier musico los sepa tañer*. Madrid: P. Minguet, en su casa, 1737.

Mitchell, Timothy J. *Flamenco Deep Song*. New Haven, CT: Yale University Press, 1994.

Mitchell, Tony, ed. *Global Noise: Rap and Hip Hop Outside the USA*. Middleton, CT: Wesleyan University Press, 2001.

Molina, Margot. "El 'Tratado de bailes' de 1912 se reedita por suscripción popular." *El País* (August 10, 2012). http://ccaa.elpais.com/ccaa/2012/08/10/andalucia/1344621472_779945.html (accessed May 21, 2013).

Molina, Ricardo, and Antonio Mairena. *Mundo y formas del cante flamenco*. Madrid: Revista de Occidente, 1963.

Moncín, Luis, Antonio Valladares de Sotomayor, Vicente Rodríguez de Arellano y el Arco, José Villaverde Fernández, Juan Pablo Forner, Luis Moncín, et al. *Teatro espanõl del siglo XVIII*. Madrid: Valencia, etc., 1790.

Le Monde Illustré (November 30, 1889).

Monés, Nèlida, Marta Carrasco, Estrella Casero-García, and Delfín Colomé. "Between Tradition and Innovation: Two Ways of Understanding the History of Dance in Spain." In *Europe Dancing: Perspectives on Theatre Dance and Cultural Identity*. Edited by Stephanie Jordan and Andrée Grau. London: Routledge, 2000.

Monroy, Douglas. "The Creation and Re-creation of Californio Society." In *Contested Eden: California Before the Gold Rush*. Edited by Ramón A. Gutiérrez and Richard J. Orsi. Berkeley and Los Angeles: University of California Press, 1998.

Mora, Kiko. "Pepita Soto: una historia del sueño americano (1852–1859)." *Revista de investigación sobre flamenco La Madrugá* 8 (2013).

Mora, Miguel. "Interview with Pilar López." *El País* (January 10, 2006). http://elpais.com/diario/2006/10/01/eps/1159684007_850215.html ed (accessed November 8, 2013).

Mora Contreras, Francisco Javier (Kiko Mora). *Las raíces del duende lo trágico y lo sublime en el cante jondo*. PhD diss., Ohio State University, Columbus, Ohio, 2008. http://rave.ohiolink.edu/etdc/view?acc%5Fnum=osu1196980354 (accessed September 18, 2014).

Moraga, Manuel. "El flamenco me ha dado la posibilidad de ser yo." *Autorretratratos Flamencos*. https://www.artefyl.com/joaquin-ruiz-autorretrato-flamenco.html (accessed February 1, 2011).

Morales Padrón, Francisco. *Los corrales de vecinos de Sevilla (informe para su estudio)*. Sevilla: Universidad de Sevilla, 1974.

Moreau de Saint-Méry, Médéric Louis Élie. *De la danse*. Parma: Bodoni, 1803.

Morrison, Toni. *Playing in the Dark: Whiteness and the Literary Imagination*. Cambridge: Harvard University Press, 1992.

Muñoz, M. "Teatro Real. Los bailes rusos. 'El sombrero de tres picos.'" *El Imparcial* (April 6, 1921).

Murry, J. Middleton. "The Art of the Russian Ballet." *The Nation & Athenaeum* (September 10, 1921).

"Música." *La Acción* (April 6, 1921).

Natavar, Mekhala. "New Dances, New Dancers, New Audiences: Shifting Rhythms in the Evolution of India's Kathak Dance." PhD diss., University of Wisconsin, Madison, 1997.

Nathan, Hans. *Dan Emmett and the Rise of Early Negro Minstrelsy*. Norman: University of Oklahoma Press, 1962.

———. *Semillas de ébano: el elemento negro y afroamericano en el baile flamenco*. Sevilla: Portada Editorial, S.L., 1998.

Navarro, José Luis. "El baile flamenco: tradicion y vanguardia." *Plataforma independiente de estudios flamencos modernos y contemporaneous*. http://www.pieflamenco.com/investigaciones/el-baile-flamenco-tradicion-y-vanguardia/ (accessed March 23, 2014).

——— and Eulalia Pablo Lozano. *El baile flamenco. Una aproximación histórica*. Córdoba: Almuzara, 2005.

———. *Historia del baile flamenco*, vol. 1. Sevilla: Signatura Ediciones, 2008.

———. *Historia del baile flamenco*, vol. 2. Sevilla: Signatura Ediciones, 2008.

———. *Semillas de ébano: el elemento negro y afroamericano en el baile flamenco*. Seville, Portada Editorial, 1998.

———. *De Telethusa á la Macarrona: bailes Andaluces y flamencos*. Sevilla: Portada Editorial, 2002.

——— and Pablo Eulalia. *Figuras, Pasos y Mudanzas, Claves para conocer el baile flamenco*. Editorial Almuzara, S.L, 2007.

Neville, Edgar. "Los cafés de Cante." *La Caña* 11. http://flamenco-world.com/magazine/cana/cana.htm (accessed March 6, 2010).

Newmark, Harris. *Sixty Years in Southern California, 1853–1913*. Los Angeles: Zeitlin & Van Bruge, [1916] 1970.

Ng, Kevin. "Interview: Joaquín Cortés." *Ballet Magazine* (November 2003). http://www.ballet.co.uk/magazines/yr_03/.../interview_joaquin_cortes.htm (accessed October 15, 2011).

Niles, Doris. "El Duende." *Dance Perspectives* 27 (1966).

Nion, Francois de. "Theatre." *Revue Indépendante* (September 1889).

NO-DO, número 242, versión A, AÑO V. http://www.rtve.es/filmoteca/no-do/not-242/1468010/ (accessed February 2014).

Noel, Eugenio. *Señoritos Chulos, Fenómenos, Gitanos y Flamencos*. Madrid: Renacimento, 1916.

Noveli, Rodrigo. *Chorégraphie figurativa y demostrativa del arte de danzar en la forma española*. MS. Madrid, 1708.

Oakley, Ann. *La mujer discriminada: biología y sociedad*. Madrid: Debate, 1977.

The Observer (July 27, 1919). Quoted in Nesta Macdonald. *Diaghilev Observed, by Critics in England and the United States, 1911–1929*. New York: Dance Horizons; London: Dance Books, 1975.

Olivelles, Francesc. *Memòria de las danças que don Joseph Fausto de Potau y de Férran aprèn ab mestre Francesc Olivelles en Barcelona y yuntamén després à ecrits y notats los moviments se fan en ellas segons sa doctrina y ceñansa, avent començat a aprendren lo dia de 8 de abril de 1701*. MS A-30. Barcelona: Unpublished manuscript, Arxiu Històric de la Ciutat (Barcelona), 1701.

Ortiz Nuevo, José Luis. *Alegato contra la pureza*. Barcelona: Ediciones Barataria, 2010.

———. *Añica la Periñaca: Yo tenía muy guena estrella*. Madrid: Libros Hesperion, 1979.

———. *Coraje: Del Maestro Otero y su Paso por el Baile*. Sevilla: Tecnographic, S.L., Producciones Editoriales, 2012.

———. *De las danzas y Andanzas de Enrique el Cojo*. Sevilla: Imprenta Escandón, S.A., 1984.

———. *Se sabe algo? Viaje al Conocimiento del arte flamenco en la prensa Sevillana del XIX*. Sevilla: Ediciones El Carro de la Nieve, 1990.

Otero Aranda, José. *Tratado de bailes de sociedad 1912 (Edición conmemorative del centenario)*. Sevilla: Secretariado de Publicaciones de la Universidad de Sevilla, 2012.

———. *Tratado de bailes de sociedad, regionales*

españoles, especialmente andaluces, con su historia y su modo de ejecutarlos. Sevilla: Tipografía de la Guía Oficial, 1912. [Reedición facsímil Asociación: Sevilla: Manuel Pareja-Obregón, 1987.]

Pablillos de Valladolid. "El conservatorio del flamenquismo—Baila la 'Macarrona.'" *Por Esos Mundos* 15, no. 238 (Nov. 1914).

Pablo Lozano, Eulalia. "Jaleos." In *Historia del flamenco. Vol. II.* Edited by José Luis Navarro and Miguel Ropero Núñez. Sevilla: Tartessos, 2002.

———. *Jaleos y tangos: vengo de mi Extremadura.* Córdoba: Almuzara, 2006.

———. *Mujeres guitarristas.* Sevilla: Signatura Ediciones, 2009.

——— and José Luis Navarro García. *Figuras, pasos y mudanzas: claves para conocer el baile flamenco.* Córdoba: Almuzara, 2007.

Paetzold, Christopher. "'Singing beneath the Alhambra': The North African and Arabic Past and Present in Contemporary Andalusian Music." *Journal of Spanish Cultural Studies* 10.2 (2009).

Pagden, Anthony. *Spanish Imperialism and the Political Imagination.* New Haven, CT: Yale University Press, 1990.

Palacio, Roberto de. "Los flamencos: bailaoras, cantaoras, y cantaores célebres." *Alrededor del mundo* 5 (November 21, 1901).

———. "Transcripción literal de la revista 'Alrededor del mundo' de Madrid" (November 21, 1901). world.com/magazine/about/flamencos1901/eflamenco1901_250808.htm (accessed January 3, 2010).

Pande, Himani. "Delightful Jugalbandi: Kathak and Flamenco." *The Times of India* (December 18, 1987).

Pareles, Jon. "Far Beyond Flamenco, a Zest for Rhythms (and Politics)." *New York Times* (June 30, 2007). http://www.nytimes.com (accessed October 31, 2013).

Payne, Stanley G. *Franco's Spain.* London and Henley: Routledge and Kegan Paul, 1968.

Pedraza Jiménez, Felipe. "De Quevedo a Cervantes: la génesis de la jácara." In *La comedia de caballerías: Actas de las XXVIII jornadas de teatro clásico de Almagro, 12, 13 y 14 de julio de 2005.* Almagro: Ed. de la Univ. de Castilla–La Mancha, 2006.

Pemberton, Ralph. E-mail communication to Nancy G. Heller, September 21, 2011.

Peña Fernández, Pedro. *Los Gitanos flamencos.* Córdoba: Editorial Almuzara, 2013.

Perez de Guillen, Eulalia. "Keeper of the Keys." *Touring Topics* (January 1925).

Pérez, Jorge. "The Soundscapes of Resistance: Notes on the Postmodern Condition of Spanish Pop Music." *Journal of Spanish Cultural Studies* 7.1 (2006).

Pérez Jorba, J. "Cháchara pariense: Baile de última moda." *El Globo* (December 24, 1902).

Perriam, Christopher. "Gay and Lesbian Culture." In *Spanish Cultural Studies: An Introduction.* Edited by Helen Graham and Jo Labanyi. Oxford: Oxford University Press, 1995.

——— and Ann Davies, eds. *Carmen: From Silent Films to MTV.* Amsterdam: Rodopi, 2005.

Phillips, Miriam. "Both Sides of the Veil: A Comparative Analysis of Kathak and Flamenco Dance." Master's thesis, University of California, Los Angeles, 1991.

Phillips, Miriam Sarada. "Becoming the Floor/Breaking the Floor: Experiencing the Kathak-Flamenco Connection." *Ethnomusicology* 57, no. 3 (Fall 2013).

Pineda Novo, Daniel. *Antonio Ramírez, el baile Gitano de Jerez.* Jerez de la Frontera: Centro Andaluz de Flamenco, 2005.

———. *Las folklóricas.* Sevilla: J. Rodríguez Castillejo, 1990.

———. *Juana, "la Macarrona" y el baile en los cafés cantantes.* Cornellà de Llobregat, Barcelona: Aquí + Más Multimedia, 1996.

Plaza Orellana, Rocío. *Bailes de Andalucía en Londres y París (1830–1850).* Madrid: Arambel, 2005.

———. *Los bailes españoles en Europa. El espectáculo de los bailes de España en el siglo XIX.* Córdoba: Almuzara, 2013.

———. *Los caminos de Andalucía: memorias de los viajeros del siglo XVIII.* Sevilla: Universidad de Sevilla, 2008.

———. *El flamenco y los románticos. Un viaje entre el mito y la realidad.* Sevilla: Bienal de Flamenco, 1999.

Pohren, D. E. *The Art of Flamenco.* Shaftesbury: Musical New Services, 1984 [1962].

———. *Lives and Legends of Flamenco: A Biographical History.* Sevilla: Society of Spanish Studies, 1964.

———. *A Way of Life.* Madrid: Society of Spanish Studies, 1980.

Polhemus, Ted. "Dance, Gender and Culture." In *Dance, Gender and Culture.* Edited by Helen Thomas. London: Macmillan Press, 1993.

Pomey, Père François. *Le Dictionnaire Royale.* Reproduced and translated in Patricia M. Ranum, "Audible Rhetoric and Mute Rhetoric: the 17th-century French." In *Early Music: Early Dance Issue* 14, no. 1 (February 1986).

Pound, Ezra. "At the Ballet." *The New Age* (October 16, 1919).

Praetorius, Michael, and Friedrich Blume. *Gesamtausgabe der musikalischen Werke: Terpsichore.* Wolfenbüttel: Möseler, 1612.

Preston-Dunlop, Valerie. *Looking at Dances: Choreological Perspective on Choreography*. Binstead, Hampshire, UK: Noverre Press, 1998.

Prickett, Stacey. "Tradition and Innovation in Cross-Cultural Creativity: Defying Britain's Tick-Box Culture: Kathak in Dialogue with Hip-Hop." *Dance Research Journal* 30, no. 2 (2012).

"Primeros referencias escritas." *Andalucía: flamenco*. http://www.andalucia.org/es/flamenco/primeras-referencias-escritas/ (accessed September 30, 2014).

Pritchard, Jane, and Geoffrey Marsh. *Diaghilev and the Golden Age of the Ballets Russes, 1909–1929*. London: V & A Publishing, 2013.

Propert, W. A. *The Russian Ballet in Western Europe, 1909–1920*. New York: Blom, 1972.

Puig, Alfonso, Flora Albaicín, Sebastià Gasch, Kenneth Lyons, Robert Marrast, Ursula Patzies, and Ramón Vives. *El arte del baile flamenco*. Barcelona: Ed. Poligrafa, 1977.

Quevedo, Francisco de. "Boda de negros, Romance XVIII." In *Obras festivas*. Edited by Pablo Antonio de Tarsia. Madrid: F. de P. Mellado, 1844–45.

Quiñones, Fernando. *What is Flamenco?* Madrid: Editorial Cinterco, 1992.

Quintana, Bertha B., and Lois Gray Floyd. *¡Qué gitano! Gypsies of Southern Spain, Case Studies in Cultural Anthropology*. New York: Holt, 1971.

Quiros, Joaquín. "Aquellos primeros flamencos Madrileños (y los que después les han seguido)." *La Caña, no. 12*. http://www.flamenco-world.com/magazine/cana/cana.htm (accessed April 20, 2010).

"La raíz y la savia nueva." Interviews with Antonia Jiménez and Celia Morales. *La nueva Alboreá* 6 (April–June 2008).

Raya, Andres. "Poniéndole un año a 'Un baile en Triana.'" Flamenco en mi memoria. January 24, 2012. http://memoriaflamenca.blogspot.com/2012/01/poniendole-el-ano-un-baile-en-triana.html (accessed January 5, 2014).

Real Academia Española. *Diccionario de la lengua castellana en que se explica el verdadero sentido de las voces … con las phrases o modos de hablar, los proverbios o refranes y otras cosas convenientes al uso de la lengua*, vol. 1 and vol. 6. Madrid: Francisco del Hierro, 1726.

———. *Diccionario de la lengua española (DRAE)*, 22nd edition. Madrid: Espasa-Calpe, 2011. http://lema.rae.es/drae/?val=cuadro+flamenco (accessed October 6, 2014).

"…Recordarán nuestros lectores…" *Hojas Selectas* 5, no. 1 (January 1906). Barcelona.

Reed, Susan A. "The Politics and Poetics of Dance." *Annual Review of Anthropology* 27 (1998).

Rennert, Hugo Albert. *The Spanish Stage in the Time of Lope de Vega*. New York: Hispanic Society of America, 1909.

Richards, Michael. "'Terror and Progress': Industrialization, Modernity, and the Making of Francoism." In *Spanish Cultural Studies: An Introduction*. Edited by Helen Graham and Jo Labanyi. Oxford: Oxford University Press, 1995.

———. *A Time of Silence: Civil War and the Culture of Repression in Franco's Spain, 1936–1945*. Cambridge: Cambridge University Press, 1998.

Riis, Thomas L. "The Experience and Impact of Black Entertainers in England, 1895–1920." *American Music* 4, no. 1 (1986).

Ríos-Bustamante, Antonnio. "The Barrioization of Nineteenth-Century Mexican Californians: From Landowners to Laborers." In *En Aquel Entonces: Readings in Mexican-American History*. Edited by Manuel G. Gonzales and Cynthia M. Gonzales. Bloomington: University of Indiana Press, 2000.

Rios Vargas, Manuel. *Antología del Baile Flamenco*. Sevilla: Signatura Ediciones de Andalucía, 2002; 2006.

Rivas González, Juan José. *Rojo Vino, historias de una Vida, Esbozos de una generación*. Manuscript, Madrid, 2010.

Rivière, Jacques. "Les Ballets Russes à l'Opéra." *La Nouvelle Revue Française* 78 (1920).

Robinson, Alfred. *Life in California*. New York: Da Capo Press, 1969.

Rodowick, David N. *The Virtual Life of Film*. Cambridge: Harvard University Press, 2007.

Rodríguez, Alberto. "María la Bonita (y II)" (June 12, 2010). http://flamencodepapel.blogspot.com/search?q=macarrona (accessed August 15, 2014). [Reproduced in "París, 13 de Junio." *El Imparcial* (June 15, 1891).]

Rodríguez Mijares, Enrique. "Carmen Amaya." *Diario de Barcelona* (December 19, 1947).

Román, J. Muñoz San. "Transcripción literal de la revista 'Nuevo Mundo' de Madrid" (May 24, 1924). http://www.flamenco-world.com/magazine (accessed January 3, 2010).

Romero, Pedro G. "Pastora: Lo que hay en los bailes de Pastora Galván." http://www.pastoragalvan.com/esp/espectaculos.php?id=3 (accessed July 13, 2014).

Romero Bachiller, Carmen. "El exotismo de los cuerpos y la fetichización de la mirada en la producción de las 'mujeres inmigrantes' como 'otras.'" In *Crítica feminista y comunicación*. Edited by Mª José Sánchez Leyva and Alicia

Reigada Olaizona. Sevilla: Comunicación Social, 2007.

Rondón Rodríguez, Juan. *Recuerdos y confesiones del cantaor Rafael Pareja de Triana*. Córdoba: Ediciones La Posada, 2001.

Rosaldo, Michelle Z. "Woman, Culture and Society: A Theoretical Overview." In *Women, Culture and Society*. Edited by Michelle Rosaldo and Louise Lamphere. Stanford: Stanford University Press, 1974.

Rossy, Hipólito. *Teoria del cante jondo*. Barcelona: CREDSA, 1966.

Rothenstein, John. *Modern English Painters*, vol II. New York: St. Martin's, 1976.

Roxo de Flores, Felipe. *Tratado de recreacion instructiva sobre la danza: su invencion y diferencias*. Madrid: En la Imprenta Real, 1793.

Rubin, Gayle. "The Traffic in Women: Notes on the 'Political Economy' of Sex." In *Toward an Anthropology of Women*. Compiled by Rayana Reiter. New York and London: Monthly Review Press, 1974.

Ruiz, Joaquín. Interview by Clara Chinoy. March 13, 2010; April 21, 2010.

Ruyter, Nancy Lee Chalfa. "La Escuela Bolera." *Dance Chronicle* 16, no. 2 (1993).

Said, Edward. *Orientalism*. New York: Vintage Books, 1979. [Spanish edition: *Orientalismo*. Madrid: Libertarias (1978) 1990].

Salama Benarroch, Rafael. "Rosario: aquella danza española." *El Mundo* (1996). http://www.elmundo.es/larevista/num123/textos/rosario1.html (accessed May 20, 2014).

Salaün, Serge. "La mujer en las tablas. Grandeza y servidumbre de la condición femenina." In *Mujeres de la escena, 1900–1940*. Edited by Mª Luz González Peña, Javier Suárez-Pajares, and Julio Arce Bueno. Madrid: SGAE, 1996.

_____. "Las mujeres en los escenarios españoles (1890–1936). Estrellas, heroínas y víctimas sin saberlo." *Dossiers Feministes* 10 (2007).

Salazar, Adolfo. "Los Bailes Rusos. Estreno de 'El sombrero de tres picos.' Un gran exito en el Real." *El Imparcial* (April 6, 1921).

_____. "Triunfo del arte español. Manuel de Falla y 'El sombrero de tres picos.' Exitos y duelos." *El Sol* (1919). Undated clipping.

Sánchez, Fredrico A. "Rancho Life in Alta California." In *En Aquel Entonces: Readings in Mexican-American History*. Bloomington: University of Indiana Press, 2000.

Saramago, José. *The Double*. Orlando: Harcourt, 2004.

Schreiner, Claus, ed. *Flamenco: Gypsy Dance and Music from Andalusia*. Portland, OR: Amadeus Press, 1990.

Schuchardt, Hugo. *Los cantes flamencos*. 1881. Edited, translated and annotated by Gerhard Steingress, Eva Feenstra, and Michaela Wolf. Sevilla: Fundación Machado, 1991.

Seguin, Jean-Claude. *Pedro Almodóvar: Filmer pour Vivre*. Paris: Éditions Ophrys, 2009.

Sempronio, "Tan gitana como se fue. Carmen Amaya pisa de nuevo la calle barcelonesa." *Destino* (August 23, 1947).

Sentaurens, Jean. "Bailes y entremeses en los escenarios teatrales sevillanos de los siglos XVII y XVIII: ¿géneros menores para un público popular?" In *El Teatro menor en España a partir del siglo XVI*. Madrid: CSIC, 1983.

Shawn, Ted. *The American Ballet*. New York: Henry Holt and Company, 1926.

_____. Letters to Ruth St. Denis, 1923. Jacob's Pillow Archives.

_____. "Ted Shawn Letters to La Meri." Mixed material. Jerome Robbins Dance Division. New York Public Library, Lincoln Center.

Shay, Anthony. "Function of Dance in Human Societies." Master's thesis, California State University, Los Angeles, 1970.

Siegfried, Andre. *America Comes of Age*. New York: Harcourt, Brace & Co., 1927.

Sitwell, Osbert. *Laughter in the Next Room*, vol. IV of *Left, Hand, Right Hand! An Autobiography*. London: Quartet, 1977.

Slopera, L.A. "La Argentina." *The Christian Science Monitor* (November 28, 1929).

Smith, Paul Julian. "Almodóvar and the Tin Can." *Sight & Sound* 6, no. 2 (February 1996).

_____. *Contemporary Spanish Culture: TV, Fashion, Art and Film*. Cambridge, England: Polity Press, 2003.

_____. "Marks of Identification." *Sight & Sound* 21, no. 9 (September 2011).

_____. *The Moderns: Time, Space, and Subjectivity in Contemporary Spanish Culture*. London: Oxford University Press, 2000.

Sneeuw, Arie C. *Flamenco en el Madrid del XIX*. Córdoba: Imprenta San Pablo, 1989.

Sor, Fernando. "Le Bolero." In *Encyclopédie pittoresque de la musique*. Edited by Adolphe Ledhuy and Henri Bertin. Paris: H. Delloye, 1835.

Sotinel, Thomas. *Masters of Cinema: Pedro Almodóvar*. London: Phaidon Press, 2010.

Southern, Eileen. *The Music of Black Americans: A History*. New York, 1971.

"The Spanish Dancer." *The Illustrated American* (October 18, 1890).

"Spanish Dancers Back: 'The Land of Joy.'" *The New York Times* (May 14, 1918).

Spanish Dancing. Film by Ann Barzel. Videocassette. MGZHB 12–2531, Jerome Robbins Dance Division. New York Public Library, Lincoln Center.

Steingress, Gerhard. "La aparición del cante flamenco en el teatro jerezano del siglo XIX." *Dos siglos de flamenco. Actas de la conferencia internacional Jerez 21–25 junio 88.* Jerez de la Frontera: Fundación Andaluza de Flamenco, 1989.

———. "La apropiación de lo extraño: el género andaluz y la escuela de baile agitanado en el París del Romanticismo (1833–1865)." *Cairon. Revista de Ciencias de la Danza.* Universidad de Alcalá, Servicio de Publicaciones, 2004.

———. "La creación del espacio socio-cultural como marco de la *performance* híbrida: el género del canto y baile andaluz en los teatros de Buenos Aires y Montevideo (1832–1864). *Trans-Revista Transcultural de Música/Transcultural Musical Review,* no. 17 (2013).

———. "Flamenco Fusion and New Flamenco as Postmodern Phenomena. An Essay on Creative Ambiguity in Popular Music." In *Songs of the Minotaur—Hybridity and Popular Music in the Era of Globalization.* Edited by Gerhard Steingress. Münster, Germany: Lit Verlag, 2002.

———. *Flamenco postmoderno: entre tradición y heterodoxia: un diagnóstico sociomusicológico (escritos 1989–2006).* Seville: Signatura Ediciones de Andalucia, 2007.

———. "La hibridación transcultural como clave de la formación del Nuevo Flamenco (aspectos histórico, sociológicos, analíticos y comparativos)." *Trans. Revista Transcultural de Música* 8 (2004).

———. "Nietzsche y el caso Carmen." In *ABAO-OLBE 08-09.* Ed. María Carmen, Rodríguez Suso y Willem de Waal. Bilbao: ABAO-OLBE, 2008.

———. *La presencia del género flamenco en la prensa local de Granada y Córdoba desde mitades del siglo XIX hasta el año de publicación de* Los cantes flamencos *de Antonio Machado y Álvarez (1881).* N.p.: 2008. http://www.juntadeandalucia.es/culturaydeporte/comunidadprofesional/sites/default/files/presenciaflamencoprensagranadacordoba.pdf (accessed October 30, 2013).

———. "Social Theory and the Comparative History of Flamenco, Tango, and Rebetika." In *The Passion of Music and Dance: Body, Gender and Sexuality.* Edited by William Washabaugh. Oxford: Berg, 1998.

———. *Sociología del cante flamenco.* Sevilla: Signatura, [1991] 2005.

———. "What Is Hybrid Music? An Epilogue." In *Songs of the Minotaur: Hybridity and Popular Music in the Era of Globalization.* Edited by Gerhard Steingress. Münster: Lit Verlag, 2002.

———. *...y Carmen se fue a París. Un studio sobre la construcción artistic del género flamenco (1833–1865).* Córdoba: Almuzara, 2006.

——— and Enrique Baltánis, eds. *Flamenco y nacionalismo: aportaciones para una sociedad política del flamenco.* Seville: Universidad de Sevilla y Fundación Machado, 1998.

Stemmler, Susanne. "'Sonido ciudadísimo': Black Noise Andalusian Style in Contemporary Spain." In *Sonic Interventions.* Edited by Sylvia Mieszkowski, Joy Smith, and Marijke de Valck. Amsterdam: Rodopi, 2007.

Strauss, Frédéric. *Almodóvar on Almodóvar.* Translated by Yves Baignères. London: Faber and Faber, 1996.

Suárez Ávila, Luis. "Jaleos, gilianas, versus bulerías." *Revista de Flamencología* 10, no. 20 (2° Semestre 2004).

Suárez García, Jose Luis, ed. *Juan de Mariana: tratado contra los juegos públicos.* Granada: Editorial Universidad de Granada, 2004.

Suárez-Pajares, Javier, and Xoán M. Carreira, eds. "The Origins of the Bolero School." In *Studies in Dance History: The Journal of the Society of Dance History Scholars* 4, no.1 (Spring 1993).

Sugarman, Jane. *Engendering Song: Singing and the Social Order at Prespa Albanian Weddings.* Chicago: University of Chicago Press, 1997.

Swinburne, Henry. *Travels through Spain, in the Years 1775 and 1776,* vol. 1. Dublin: S. Price, R. Cross, J. Williams, et al., 1779.

Synnott, Anthony. *The Body Social: Symbolism, Self and Society.* London: Routledge, 1993.

Talvikki Chanfreau, Marie-Catherine. "Les apports étrangers à l'identité culturelle espagnole (XVIIIe–XXe siècles). L'Italianisme de l'école bolera." In *Le Métissage Culturel en Espagne.* Edited by J. R Aymes and S. Salaün. Paris: Sorbonne Nouvelle, 2001.

"La tasa de desempleo cierra 2006 en el 8.3%, el nivel más bajo desde 1979." *El Mundo* (January 27, 2007). http://www.elmundo.es (accessed October 20, 2013).

Tellez, Juan José. *Paco de Lucía "En Vivo."* Madrid: ACADAP, 2003.

Terry, Walter. *The Dance in America.* New York: Harper & Row, 1956.

———. *World Journal Tribune* (September 27, 1966).

Teruel, Isabel. E-mail communication with Nancy G. Heller, September 7, 2011.

Thiel-Cramer, Barbara. *Flamenco: The Art of Flamenco: Its History and Development Until Our Days.* Lidingö, Sweden: Remark AB, 1992.

Thomas, Helen. *The Body, Dance and Cultural*

Theory. London and New York: Palgrave Macmillan, 2003.

Thomas, Katherine. "*Anda Jaleo, Jaleo!* The Flamenco Song and Dance Lineage of Federico García Lorca and La Argentinita." *UCLA Journal of Dance Ethnology* 19 (1995). Los Angeles.

"'The Three-Cornered Hat.' Russian Ballet at the Alhambra." *The Times*. London (July 23, 1919).

Tiempo de Leyenda. Directed by José Sánchez Montes. Ático Siete: Spain. (2009).

TIM. "Carmen Amaya. La bailaora con duendes. 'La novia de América' está reconquistando España." *Diario de Zamora* (February 8, 1948).

Tomlinson, John. *Cultural Imperialism: A Critical Introduction*. Baltimore: Johns Hopkins University Press, 1991.

Torres Cortés, Norberto. *Guitarra flamenca volumen 1: Lo clásico*. Sevilla: Signatura Ediciones, 2004.

_____. *Guitarra flamenca volumen 2: Lo contemporáneo*. Sevilla: Signatura Ediciones, 2005.

Tremlett, Giles. *Ghosts of Spain: Travels Through Spain and Its Silent Past*. New York: Walker & Co., 2006.

Triana-Toribio, Núria. *Spanish National Cinema*. London and New York: Routledge, 2003.

Turner, Bryan. "Avances recientes en la teoría del cuerpo." *Revista Española de Investigaciones Sociológicas*, no. 68 (1994).

Turner, W. J. "Drama." *The London Mercury* (August 1921).

Utrera Macías, Rafael. *Literatura y Cine: Adaptaciones del Teatro al Cine*. Sevilla: Universidad de Sevilla, 2007.

Van de Grift Sanchez, Nellie. *Spanish Arcadia*. San Francisco: Powell, 1929.

Vechten, Carl Van. "The Music of Spain." *The Dance Writings of Carl Van Vechten*. New York: Dance Horizons, 1974.

Vega, José de la. "El baile flamenco en Cataluña a través del esplendor de Carmen Amaya." *Revista Cronopio*, no. 43 (September 9, 2013). http://www.revistacronopio.com/?p=11223 (accessed January 1, 2014).

Vega de Triana, Rita. *Antonio Triana and the Spanish Dance: A Personal Recollection*. Chur, Switzerland: Harwood Academic Publishers, 1993.

Vela-Hidalgo, Vicente. "El Madrid flamenco de los años veinte." *La Caña* 11. http://www.flamenco-world.com/magazine/cana/cana.htm (accessed February 8, 2010).

Véron, Louis. *Mémoires d'un bourgeois de Paris*. París: Gonet, 1854.

Victory, P. "Anoche en el Real. 'El sombrero de tres picos.'" *La Voz* (April 6, 1921).

La Voz (September 8, 1925; September 10, 1925). http://flamencodepapel.blogspot.com/2009/12/copa-de-cordoba-1925.html. September 13, 2009 (accessed March 4, 2010).

Washabaugh, William. "Fashioning Masculinity in Flamenco Dance." In *The Passion of Music and Dance: Body, Gender and Sexuality*. Edited by William Washabaugh. Oxford: Berg, 1998.

_____. *Flamenco: Passion, Politics and Popular Culture*. Washington, D.C., and Oxford: Berg, 1996.

_____. "Flamenco Alive! New Research on the Vital Art of Flamenco." Durham, NC: Duke University Dance Program, February 4, 2012.

_____. *Flamenco Music and National Identity in Spain*. Surrey, UK, and Burlington, VT: Ashgate, 2012.

_____. "Franquismo, Gitanismo, Andalucismo and the 'Rito' Series." In *Flamenco: Passion, Politics and Popular Culture*. London: Berg, 1996.

_____, ed. *The Passion of Music and Dance: Body, Gender and Sexuality*. Oxford and New York: Berg, 1998.

Weber, David J. *The Spanish Frontier in North America*. New Haven and London: Yale University Press, 1992.

Weeks, Jeffrey. *Sexuality and its Discontents: Meanings, Myths, & Modern Sexualities*. London: Routledge & K. Paul, 1985. [Spanish edition: *El malestar de la sexualidad. Significados, mitos y sexualidades modernas*. Madrid: Talasa, 1983.]

White, Julian. "Music and the Limits of Cultural Nationalism." In *Spanish Cultural Studies: An Introduction*. Edited by Helen Graham and Jo Labanyi. Oxford: Oxford University Press, 1995.

Williams, Raymond. *Culture and Society, 1780–1950*. New York: Anchor Books, [1958] 1960.

Woods Peiró, Eva. *White Gypsies: Race and Stardom in Spanish Musicals*. Minneapolis: University of Minnesota Press, 2012.

Wulff, Helena. "Ethereal Expression: Paradoxes of Ballet as a Global Physical Culture." *Ethnography* 9, no. 4 (2008).

Yarza, Alejandro. *Un caníbal en Madrid: la sensibilidad camp y el reciclaje de la historia en el cine de Pedro Almodóvar*. Madrid: Ed. Libertarias, 1999.

Yepes, Ana. "From the *Jácara* to the *Sarabande*," in "All'ungaresca—al espanol: die Vielfalt der europäischen Tanzkultur 1420–1820." Proceedings of the 3d Rothenfels Dance Symposium. June 2012, edited by Uwe Schlottermüller, Maria Richter, and Howard Weiner.

Freiburg: fa-gisis Musik-und Tanzedition, 2012.

Zanger, Anat. *Film Remakes as Ritual and Disguise: From Carmen to Ripley*. Amsterdam: Amsterdam University Press, 2006.

Zatania, Estela. "Manuel Liñán "Nomada" / David Coria / Segundo Falcón." delflamenco.com (March 6, 2014). http://www.deflamenco.com/revista/resenas-actuaciones/manuel-linan-nomada-david-coria-segundo-falcon-1.html (accessed June 23, 2014).

Zavalishin, Dmitry. "California in 1824." Translated from Russian and annotated by James R. Gibson. *Southern California Quarterly* 55 (Winter 1973).

Zoido Naranjo, Antonio. *La ilustración contra los gitanos: antecendentes, historia y consecuencias de la prisión general*. Sevilla: Signatura Ediciones de Andalucía, 2009.

Zuniga León, Mercedes. Interview by Clara Chinoy. 2010; 2013; 2014.

About the Contributors

Joan **Acocella** is a staff writer for *The New Yorker*, where she reviews dance and books. She writes on dance, literature, and other arts for other publications, including the *The New York Review of Books*, *Art in America*, and the *Times Literary Supplement*. She is the author of several books, including *Twenty-Eight Artists and Two Saints* (2007) and *Mark Morris* (1993). She is co-editor of *André Levinson on Dance: Writings from Paris in the Twenties* (1991), and the editor of *The Diary of Vaslav Nijinsky* (1999).

Robert **Atwood** is on the faculty of the Ailey School, through which he teaches for the BFA program at Fordham University, and he is also on the faculty of Marymount Manhattan College (Dance—BFA). He has lectured in the United States and Europe, including before the International Conference of the Congress on Research Topics in Dance, and he served for two years as a contributing editor to *Attitude: The Dancer's Magazine*.

Ninotchka Devorah **Bennahum**, professor of theater and dance at the University of California, Santa Barbara, trained in ballet and music, became a dancer and choreographer and, subsequently, a dance historian and performance theorist. The author of *Antonia Mercé, "La Argentina": Flamenco & the Spanish Avant-Garde* (2000) and *Carmen: A Gypsy Geography* (2013), she co-curated, with K. Meira Goldberg, of *100 Years of Flamenco in New York* at the New York Public Library for the Performing Arts, and co-authored the exhibit's catalog. From 1996 to 2012, she taught dance history and theory for American Ballet Theatre and is now writing a history of the company.

Marta **Carrasco Benítez** is a journalist and dance critic whose publications include *El Maestro Granero* (2000) and *La Escuela Bolera Sevillana: La Familia Pericet* (2013). She is a former member of the National Council on Dance in Spain, and has held leadership positions in the National Forum on Dance, the Strategic Planning Committee for Dance in Spain, the Commission for Dance Development, the Commission on Assessment of Academic Activities of the Andalusian Flamenco Agency, and the Assessment Commission for the Flamenco Bienal of Seville, among others.

Clara **Chinoy** has studied flamenco with El Güito, Concha Vargas, la Farruca, and others and has performed with the companies of Ramón de los Reyes, José Molina, Carlota Santana, Noche Flamenca, and Repompa de Malaga, and well as in the flamenco *tablaos* of Madrid. In private Gitano "fiestas," she has danced to the singing of Fernanda de Utrera, Miguel Funi, and Inés Bacán. She received a grant for "Carmen's Sisters," which explores the life stories of gypsy women, and a Fulbright grant to continue this research as part of her thesis at the Universidad de Sevilla, where she is a doctoral candidate.

Loren **Chuse**'s interests include the role of women and issues of gender in the flamenco tradition, forms of fusion (in particular the collaborations between flamenco and Arabic music), and issues of cultural identity and hybridity in flamenco. Her doctoral dissertation, "The Cantaoras: Music, Gender and Identity in Flamenco Song," was published by Routledge (2003) and in Spain as *Mujer y flamenco* (2007). Her article on *cantaoras* (female flamenco singers) appeared in *The Mediterranean in Music* (2005). She is a member of the Mediterranean Music Studies Group of the International Council for Traditional Music.

Cristina **Cruces-Roldán** is a professor of social anthropology at the Universidad de Sevilla, a member of the Group for the Study of Sociocultural Identities, and she was the first director of the university's multidisciplinary doctoral program in flamenco studies. Her work focuses on issues of identity, gender, labor, and cultural inheritance in flamenco. She has published more than 90 scholarly articles and monographs, including *El flamenco y la música Andalusí: Argumentos para un encuentro* (2003); *Antropología y flamenco (II)* (2003); and *y La Niña de los Peines: El mundo flamenco de Pastora Pavón* (2007).

K. Meira **Goldberg**, "La Meira," is a flamenco performer, teacher, choreographer and historian. From the *tablaos* of Madrid, she became first dancer with several prominent U.S. companies. She curated *100 Years of Flamenco in New York* with Ninotchka Bennahum, and co-authored the exhibition catalog. With Antoni Pizà, she co-edited *Spaniards, Indians, Africans, and Gypsies: The Global Reach of the Fandango in Music, Song, and Dance*, forthcoming in *Música Oral del Sur*, vol. 12 (2015). Her monograph, *Sonidos Negros: On the Blackness of Flamenco*, is forthcoming from Oxford University Press. She teaches at Fashion Institute of Technology.

Michelle Heffner **Hayes** is chair of the Department of Dance at the University of Kansas, where she teaches arts administration, improvisation, choreography, dance history, and flamenco. Her publications include *Flamenco: Conflicting Histories of the Dance* (McFarland, 2009), and chapters in *Dancing Bodies, Living Histories: New Writings on Dance and Culture* (2000), *Taken by Surprise: An Improvisational Reader* (2003) and *The Living Dance: An Anthology of Essays on Movement & Culture* (2012). She was educational curator for the 2014 Philadelphia Flamenco Festival.

Nancy G. **Heller** is a professor of modern and contemporary art history at the University of the Arts in Philadelphia. Her publications include the revised and expanded fourth edition of *Women Artists: An Illustrated History* (2004) and *Why a Painting Is Like a Pizza: A Guide to Understanding and Enjoying Modern Art* (2002), and she is co-editor of *Imaging Dance: Visual Representations of Dancers and Dancing* (2011). She has received awards from the Smithsonian Institution, the American Association of University Women, the Richard C. von Hess Foundation, and the government of Spain.

Claudia **Jeschke** is a dancer, choreographer, historian, and professor of dance studies. She studied Theaterwissenschaft at Munich University and wrote her doctoral dissertation on the history of dance notation systems. Her academic and practical expertise has led her to revive dance history as live stage performance and in academic writing. She has been a full-time, tenured faculty member at the universities of Munich, Leipzig, Cologne, and Salzburg. In addition, she is head of the Derra de Moroda Dance Archives, one of the most important collections on dance in Europe.

Montse **Madridejos** holds a degree in computer engineering from the Polytechnic University of Cataluña and a doctorate in music history from the University of Barcelona, and she has studied flamenco guitar at the Conservatory of Liceu in Barcelona. Her scholarly articles explore the history of flamenco in Barcelona and in Cataluña in general. Her research interests include Carmen Amaya, the Borrull family, Lola Cabello, and flamenco performance in Barcelona. Her publications include *El Flamenco en la Barcelona de la Exposición Internacional (1929–1930)* (2012) and, with David Pérez Merinero, *Carmen Amaya* (2013), and she is editor of www.historiasdeflamenco.com.

Niurca **Márquez** is part of an international cohort that addresses extended forms in flamenco and reclaims the art form's liaisons with political and social discourse. Her work aims to shed light on the female body and stereotypes surrounding traditional flamenco and includes collaborations with visual artists, site-specific works, residencies, and projects that examine the influence of cultural memory on personal and artistic narratives. She is a 2014 recipient of a choreographic commission from the Atlantic Center for the Arts and the only U.S.-based artist featured in platforms of "Flamenco Empírico."

Kathy **Milazzo** is affiliated with the Albuquerque Museum of Art and History and has been a dance studies lecturer at the University of Surrey and the University of New Mexico. Her publications include a chapter on the *tango de negros* for the forthcoming *Oxford Handbook of Dance and Ethnicity* and an essay on the history of jazz and tap dance in Judith Bennahum's revised textbook *The Living Dance*. She holds a PhD in dance studies from the University of Surrey and an MA in dance history from the University of New Mexico.

John C. **Moore** is a professor of linguistics and provost of John Muir College at the University of California, San Diego. Working mainly in the area of theoretical syntax, his publications include *Reduced Constructions in Spanish* (1996; 2013) and *Proto-Properties and Grammatical Encoding: A Correspondence Theory of Argument Selection* (with Farrell Ackerman, 2001). A long-time flamenco aficionado and guitarist, he has extensively studied and performed in Spain and has performed with numerous flamenco companies in the United States for over forty years. In 2008, he released the CD *Cinfución*, a solo guitar performance.

Kiko **Mora** (PhD, the Ohio State University) is a professor of the semiotics of advertising in the Department of Communication and Social Psychology at the University of Alicante and of Spanish cinema for the Council on International Educational Exchange of Alicante. His research explores nineteenth- and early twentieth-century Spanish dancers in the United States, a topic he examines in the articles "Carmencita on the Road: baile español y vaudeville en los Estados Unidos de América (1889–1895)" and "Pepita Soto: una historia del sueño americano (1852–1859)." He is co-editor of *Rock Around Spain: historia, industria, escenas y medios de comunicación* (2013).

Jorge **Pérez** is an associate professor of Spanish at the University of Kansas and the author of *Cultural Roundabouts: Spanish Film and Novel on the Road* (2011). His publications include articles on the Spanish cinema, novel, popular music, and queer culture in journals such as *ALEC, Arizona Journal of Hispanic Cultural Studies, España Contemporánea, Revista de Estudios Hispánicos, Revista Canadiense de Estudios Hispánicos,* and *Studies in Hispanic Cinemas,* as well as chapters in several books. He is also co-editor of a special issue of the *Journal of Spanish Cultural Studies* on the topic of Spanish popular music.

Miriam **Phillips** is an assistant professor in the School of Theater, Dance, and Performance Studies at the University of Maryland. As a dance ethnologist, Laban movement analyst, and dancer, her research centers on notions of dance as embodied culture, specifically, kinesthetic and aesthetic relationships between North Indian kathak and Spanish flamenco dance. She is the author of "Becoming the Floor/Breaking the Floor: Experiencing the Kathak-Flamenco Connection" in *Ethnomusicology* 57 (2013). Known as "La Miri" in flamenco circles, she founded and directed the community-based dance company and school AZAFRÁN Flamenco.

Rocío **Plaza Orellana** is a professor of scenography in the High School for the Dramatic Arts in Seville. She is the author of *El Flamenco y los románticos* (1999), which explores the history of flamenco as an art form in the nineteenth century. She returned to this topic in *Bailes de Andalucía en Londres y París (1830–1850)* (2005). In 2006, she was awarded the Premio Archivo Hispalense for "Los espectáculos escénicos en Sevilla bajo el gobierno de Godoy (1795–1808)." She examines travel diaries of Andalusia in two books and is the author of *Historia de la moda en España* (2009).

Ryan **Rockmore** was awarded a Fulbright research grant and studied in Sevilla, where he explored the various connections between flamenco dance and gender performance. He has studied with Carmen Ledesma, Merché Esmeralda, Alfonso Losa, La Choni, Miguel Vargas, Esperanza Fernández, and Rafaela Carrasco and has performed in New York, London, Madrid, and Sevilla. He completed a master's in dance anthropology at the University of Roehampton, and his thesis focuses on the feminine history of the bata de cola and the contemporary appropriation of the accessory by male flamenco dancers.

Anthony **Shay**, an associate professor of dance and cultural studies in the Theatre and Dance Department of Pomona College, Claremont, California, is the author of six books, including the *The Dangerous Lives of Public Performers: Dancing, Sex, and Entertainment in the Islamic World* (2014). The recipient of James Irvine Foundation, NEH, and NEA fellowships and choreographic awards, he is, with Barbara Sellers-Young, co-editor of the forthcoming *Oxford Handbook of Dance and Ethnicity*. He was founder and co-artistic director of the AMAN Folk Ensemble and the AVAZ International Dance Theatre.

Gerhard **Steingress**' research is on cultural sociology and sociology of the arts and music. For nearly three decades, he has written about Andalusian flamenco and other ethnic music styles, particularly the Greek-Oriental *rebetiko*. His publications include *Sociología del cante flamenco* (1993; 2005); *Flamenco y Nacionalismo* (1998); *Sobre flamenco y flamencología* (1999); *Songs of the Minotaur: Hybridity and Popular Music in the Era of Globalization* (2002); *... y Carmen se fue a París: Un estudio sobre la construcción artística del género flamenco 1833–1865* (2006; 2014), and *Flamenco Postmoderno* (2007).

William **Washabaugh** is a professor emeritus of anthropology at the University of Wisconsin–Milwaukee. He is the author of *Flamenco Music and National Identity in Spain* (2012) and *Flamenco: Passion, Politics, and Popular Culture* (1996), and editor of *The Passion of Music and Dance* (1998). He has authored books on popular culture, linguistic anthropology, and sign language, along with numerous articles and reviews.

Ana **Yepes** is a choreographer who has studied music in Madrid, in The Hague, and with Nadia Boulanger. Among opera productions she has choreographed are *Rinaldo, Orlando, Alceste, Giulio Cesare*, Ginastera's *Beatrix Cenci, King Arthur, Indes Galantes, Hippolyte et Aricie, Carmen*, Massenet's *Manon*, and Lully's *Bourgeois Gentilhomme*. She has collaborated as a dancer and choreographer with Les Arts Florissants, Ris et Danceries, Les Paladins, Elyma Ensemble, and the Yepes Trio, among others. Her company, Ensemble Donaires, presents baroque dance programs and contemporary dance pieces.

Brook **Zern** has written about music for dozens of magazines and newspapers, including the *New York Times*, has contributed to many books and blogs at www.flamencoexperience.com/blog. He has helped in the conservation, restoration, and public unveiling of hundreds of hours of crucial Spanish audio recordings and documentary film. His 3000-page discography is a definitive source on worldwide flamenco recordings. In 2008, King Juan Carlos I of Spain knighted Zern with the Officer's Cross of the Order of Queen Isabella for the dissemination of Spanish culture in the United States.

Index

Numbers in **_bold italics_** indicate pages with illustrations.

Abad, Marina (La Canillas) 255, 257–258
abánico 287
Abhinaya Dance Company 53*n*27
Ablanedo, Enrique C. 7
Abraham Lincoln Brigades 11
Academia Oficial de Baile Teatral (Official Academy of Theatrical Dance) (Madrid) 153*n*6
Académie de Danse, Académie Royale de la Musique et de la Danse 65; *see also* Paris Opéra
Acocella, Joan 11, 15, 18, 128
Adams, Mildred 203
Adichie, Chimamande 52*n*1
Adorno, Theodor 252
Afanador, Ruven ***235***
Africa 9, 10, 14, 46, 98, 129, 136, 226, 255
African American music and dance traditions 195, 196, 199, 202, 211, 212, 256–258; *see also* hip-hop; jazz; rap
Africanist/Africanisms 14, 128, 139*n*2, 194, 196, 199, 200, 201, 208*n*23, 254
Afro-Brazilian dance forms 46
Afro-Caribbean dance forms, music 88, 256
Afro-Iberian 125, 218, 220
agency (historical) 219, 252
Aguado, Alejandro 77
Aguilera, Paco 173
Al 4 por Medio 231
Al-Andalus, Islamic Andalusia, medieval Andalusia 23, 48, 50, 211, 221*n*4
Alba y Diéguez, Jerónimo de (El Bachiller Revoltoso) 4, 24
Albarrán, Lucia ***227***
Albarrán, María ***227***, 228
Albéniz, Eloísa 181
Albéniz, Isaac 160, 163, 183, 199, 207*n*17, 207*n*19, 207*n*20
Aldington, Richard 158
alegrías 64, 66, 127, 128, 143, 149, 151, 169, 170, 183, 189, 213, 268, 288

Alfonso V of Aragon 10
Alfonso XIII 126, 133
Alhambra Palace 117
Alhambra Theatre (London) 127, 200
allemande 74
Almenda, Antonio de 68
Almendro, Carlos 25
Almódovar, Pedro 16, 244–249, 277, 278; *La flor de mi secreto* 244–249; *Habla con ella* 244; *Pepi, Luci, Bom* 244; *Volver* 277; *Women on the Verge of a Nervous Breakdown* 244
Alonso, Pilar ***231***, 232
Alta California (upper California, aka New Spain, 1804–1848) 81–92, 93*n*7
Álvarez, Amparo (La Campanera) 5, 27, ***28***, 71, 144
Álvarez Caballero, Ángel 6, 172
Amaya, Antonia 178, 179, 180
Amaya, Antonio 180
Amaya, Carmen 1, 11, 12, 15, 26, 127–128, 136, 137, 178–186, ***179***, 238, 240, 268, 285
Amaya, Dolores (La Pescaílla) 173
Amaya, Juana (La Faraona) 30, 178, 180
Amaya, Leonor 178, 179, 180
Amaya, Paco 179, 180
American Indians 82–83, 86, 90, 91*n*1, 92*n*25
El Amor Brujo 126, 199, 200, 208*n*28
Amors og Balletmesterens Luner see *The Whims of Cupid and the Ballet Master*
Andalusia 4, 5, 7, 8, 11, 12, 14, 15, 23–27, 33, 38, 77, 78, 82, 103, 105–107, 109–113, 117, 119–123, 124, 125, 130, 133, 163, 169, 170, 176*n*20, 181, 183, 188, 193, 211, 212, 214, 216, 217, 218, 225, 227, 228, 232, 236, 237, 247, 253, 258, 272, 274, 277, 278, 279*n*20, 281, 282
Andalusian scale 211

Andalusization 10, 49, 236, 281
Anderson, Benedict 46, 236
Andújar, Rafael 174
Angelillo 25
Angiolini, Fortunata 75
Anne of Austria (Ana María Mauricia) 62
Antequera, Paco de 174
anti-fascism 204, 266; *see also* fascism; Francoist dictatorship
anti-flamenquismo 13, 17, 26, 281, 289*n*8
anti-guapas 263, 287
Antonio, José 29
Antúnez sisters 29
anxious narratives (concept) 252, 255
Apollinaire, Guillaume 195, 207*n*9
Aquarium (theater, Moscow) 200
Arabic musical influences 6, 23, 24, 38, 50, 190, 211, 218, 221*n*4; *see also* Middle Eastern dance and music
Arbós, Fernando Enrique (conductor) 203, 207*n*19
architecture (corporeal) 194–210
Arco, Manuel del 181–182
Arena (Israel Galván) 285
Argentina 111
La Argentina see Mercé, Antonia
La Argentinita see López Júlvez, Encarnación
Argüelles, Isabel 112
Arias, Imanol 245
Arias Salgado, Gabriel 237, 240
Armani, Giorgio 246
Armory Show (1913) 196
Asafyev, Boris 135
Asenjo Barbieri, Francisco 5, 60
Astarte 34
Atané, Carlos 104, 106–107
Atwood, Robert 3, 14
Aumer, Jean-Louis 73, 74
authenticity 1, 6, 11, 16, 17, 38, 49, 100, 126, 134, 146, 163–164, 166–167, 171–172, 189,

193, 196, 206, 212, 214, 272, 282; *see also* purism; traditional flamenco
auto-exoticization 11
¡Ay jondo! 29
Azagra, Maestro Ruiz de 180
Azaña, Manuel **198**
Aznalcóllar, Pepe 173

Bacán, Inés 285
The Bacchae 248
Bach, Johanne Sebastian 271
El Bachiller Revoltoso *see* de Alba y Diéguez, Jerónimo
Bacon, Francis 266
Bádajoz, Manolo de 168
Badajoz, Porrina de 25
bailable andaluz 112
bailable español, ballet espagnol 14, 103, 106–113, 115*n*31
bailaor 16, 215, 216, 219, 234–242
bailaora 1, 23, 26, 119, 153*n*5, 179, 180, 181, 182, 184, 212, 213, 214, 217, 219, 240, 274
bailaora cañí 178
El Bailarín, Antonio *see* Ruiz Soler, Antonio
bailarines 119, 180
baile 14, 23, 26, 56, 60, 61, 65–67, 119, 120, 130, 210, 212, 282; as formal dance event 85, 87–90; society baile 148; theater baile 60, 64, 145
baile corto 220
baile de hombre, baile masculino 214, 216–217, 240
baile de mujer, baile femenino 214, 216, 240
baile en una loseta 219
baile español 193, 194, 199, 272
baile gaditano 36
baile Gitano 217
baile inglés 130
baile jondo 245, 248, 264
baile largo 220
bailes boleros 144, 148
bailes de candil 212
Bailes de Escuela Andaluza 26
bailes de negros 220
bailes de país 212
bailes de palillos 144; *see also* castanets
bailes nacionales 144
Bailly, Antonio 33
Baker, Josephine 206, 285
Balanchine, George 200; *Apollo* (1928) 200; *Prodigal Son* (1929) 200
Balfour, Sebastian 236
Ball, Edward Hughes 77
Balla, Giacomo 159
ballet 14, 42, 66, 71, 103, 104, 121, 126, 157–164, 213, 215, 216
Ballet Cristina Hoyos 267
Ballet Nacional de España (National Ballet of Spain) 29, 206, 246, 248, 250*n*7, 269*n*4

Ballet Russe de Monte Carlo 205
ballets d'action 72, 105
Les Ballets Espagnols (La Argentina's Company, 1925–1936) 197–210
Les Ballets Russes 15, 126, 127, 135, 157–164, 199, 208*n*27
Baltanás, Enrique 10, 51, 258
la bamba 91–92
Bambino 174*n*5
Bana, Patrick de 30
Bancroft, Hubert 85, 93*n*1
Banderas, Antonio 247
Baraka, Amiri (Leroi Jones) 133
Barbate, Antonio "Cuquito" de 174
Barber, Santiago 266
The Barber of Seville 4, 75
Baretti, Joseph 72
Barón, Sara 30
Baroque period 64, 66
Barrilito **8**
Barry Brothers 203
Barthes, Roland 36–37, 40, 208*n*25
Bartholomay, Paul Bruno 98, 101*n*17
Bartra, Roger 9, 12
bata de cola 127, 152, 184, 216, 220, 262–263, 286, 287
bata de lunares 183
Baudelaire, Charles 195
Baudrillard, Jean 193
Baush, Pina 30
Bayón, Isabel 30
The Beachcomber (venue, New York) 178
Beaumarchais *see* Caron, Pierre Agustín
Behague, Gilbert 94*n*23
Bell, Clive 158
Bell, Horace 90
La Belle de L'Andalusia 112
Benavent, Carlos 7
Benjamin, Walter 19*n*3
Bennahum, Ninotchka Devorah 8, 15, 37, 49, 53*n*15
Berger, Pablo 17, 271–279
Bergman, Ingmar 279*n*15
Bermúdez Cala, Diego (El Tenazas, Tenazas de Morón) 26, 174*n*8
Bibaum, H. 200
bien parado, bienparado, parada 96, 97, 288
Bienal de Flamenco de Sevilla 7, 30
Bilbao, Antonio de *see* Vidal, Antonio
La Bisca 130
Bizet, Georges 5, 117, 119, 272
Blackface minstrelsy 11, 114*n*28, 133, 134, 137; *see also* minstrelsy
blackness (concept of) 14, 17, 124–125, 128–130, 133, 135–136, 137*n*4, 140*n*40

Blake, Jody 128
Blancanieves 17, 271–279
Blanco, Pedro 229
Blanco, Pepe 181
Blas Vega, José 7
Blasis, Carlo 96, 98
Bloomsbury 158
Blum, René 52*n*10
Boabdil *see* Mohammad XII, Abu Abdalla
"Boda de negros" 137*n*4; *see also* Quevedo, Francisco de
Bohlman, Philip 256
Bohórquez, Manuel 113*n*11
Los Bolecos **8**, 29
bolero 27, 72, 73, 74, 76, 77, 78, 81, 95–96, **97**, 98–101, 102*n*11, 104, 106, 110, 111, 112, 121, 122, 144, 148, 153*n*8, 153*n*9, 153*n*16, 212
Bolero (orchestral score) 180, 181, 288; *see also* Ravel, Maurice
El Bolero de la Cachucha 78
El Bolero de la Caleta 78
Bolshevism 200
Bolsi, Teresa **273**
Bonaparte, Napoleon 4–5, 10, 272, 281
Bonet, Manuel 150
Borbolla, Carmelita 155*n*44
Borrow, George 5, 12, 25
botillería 27, 38
Bourdieu, Pierre 12, 214
Le Bourgeois Gentilhomme 63, 64
Bournonville, August 76
La Boutique Fantasque 158, 160, 161
Boyer, Jean 61
Boyle, Danny 271
brazeo 286
brazos 182
Breton, David Le 214
Brooks, Lynn Matluck 6
Brown, Jayna 114*n*28, 126, 129, 135, 136
Las Brujas (tablao) 169, 171–172, 173, 177*n*39
Buckland, Theresa 236
Bueno, Francisca 112
bulerías 64, 66, 116*n*47, 127, 128, 143, 151–152, 167, 169, 189, 219, 220, 288
bulla 124–125
The Bullfighter 78
bullfighting 10, 26, 83, 117, 128, 202, 203, 204, 207*n*9, 226, 236, 271–279, **273**, 279*n*20, 281, 282
Bulos y Tanguerias 266; *see also* Barber, Santiago; Cantizano, Raul
Buñuel, Luis 276, 278
bureo 96
Burt, Ramsay 237
Buti, Francesco 62
Butler, Judith 238

butoh 261
Byzantine chant 23

Cabo de Buena Esperanza (ship) 179
cachucha 27, 73, 76, 77–78, 96, 112, 113n3, 113n5
Cadalso, José 4, 24
Cádiz 23, 24, 27, 33–40, 107, 130, 167–170, 172, 174n2, 192, 228, 272
Cádiz, Beni de 173
Cádiz, Pericón de 15
Cádiz, Ramón de 227
Café de Chinitas (Málaga, Madrid) 154n36, 169, 173
El Café de Chinitas 204–205
Café de la Marina (Madrid) 131, 133
Café el Kursaal 146
Café Novedades (Seville) 146
cafés cantantes 25, 26, 49, 78, 113, 126, 135, 145, 149, 152, 171, 189, 200, 212, 225, 226, 233n3, 240, 281
Cairón, Antonio 6, 96, 97, 99, 100, 102n11
cajón 7, 282
cakewalk 14–15, 125, 128–131, 133–137
Calado, Silvia 286, 288
Calderón, Estébanez 5, 114n17
Calderón de la Barca, Pedro 56, 57, 62
California 14; Mexican colonial period 14, 81–94; Spanish colonial period 14, 81–94
Las Calles de Cádiz 168, 172, 205
Caló 10, 262; *see also* Gitana/o, Roma; Romani
Cámara, Petra 71, 78, **104**, 107, **108**, 109, 110, 112, 121
El Camarón de la Isla *see* Monge Cruz, José
El Camborio, Antonio 174
Camelamos naquerar 29
La Campanera *see* Álvarez, Amparo
Campo, Florencio (Cuqui) 262
Camprubí, Mariano 5, 77, 101n9, 121
Campuzano, Felipe 174
Canales, Antonio 30
cañas 105, 189
Los Canasteros (tablao, Madrid) 169, 172, 174
cancan 103, 121
Candomblé 46
La Cañeta de Málaga 173
cañí 179, 185n1
La Canillas *see* Abad, Marina
Cañizares, José de 56, 57
Canõs del Peral *see* Teatro de los Canõs del Peral
cantaores 24, 26, 212, 215, 227, 266, 274, 282
cante, cante flamenco 23, 25,
128, 166–173, 212, 213, 221n6, 253, 262, 265, 266, 267, 281
cante bonito 190
cante chico 167, 174n4
cante Gitano 153n16, 170, 171, 175n8
cante jondo 7, 152, 167, 174n4, 188, 189; *see also* Concurso de Cante Jondo
cante p'alante 172
cante p'atrás 172
cante puro 252, 282
Cantizano, Raul 266
Capriccio Espagnol 205
Capricho Español (Rimsky-Korsakov) 180
Caracol, Manolo 25, 170, 171, 174n8, 181
El Carbonero, Manolo *see* Serrapí, Manuel (Niño Ricardo)
Carmen 14, 17, 117–121, 188, 227, 271–279, 288
Carmen (film, Carlos Saura, 1985) 276
Carmen 5, 117, 119, 272
Carmen, la de Triana (film) 276
La Carmencita *see* Dausset Moreno, Carmen
Carmona, Jesús 30
Carnegie Hall (concert hall, New York City) 178, 195
The Carnival of Seville 112
Caro Baroja, Julio 107
Caron, Pierre Agustín (Beaumarchais) 4, 75
Carrasco, Manuela 30
Carrasco, Rafaela 30
Carrasco Benítez, Marta 4, 13
Carreira, Joán (Xoán) 7, 96
carrerilla 65, 127, 139n29, 216
Carrese, Giuseppe 112
Carrete 264
Carrión, José 105
Carta de Escarramán a la Méndez 4
Casablanca 277
Casanova, Giacomo 4, 72
Casas, Manuel 104
caseta 150, 155n47
Castañeda, Antonia 81, 82
castanets 13, 27, 33, 61, 65–67, **72**, 75, 77, 81, 85, 92, 97, 107, 109, 144, 199, 200, 216, 250n7, 288; *see also bailes de palillos*
Castellanos de Losada, Basilio 106
Castellón, Augustín (Sabicas) **188**
casticismo 236
Castillo, Elena 232
Castillo, González del 24, 27
Castillo, José del 182
Castle, Irene 135, 203
Castro, Estrellita 181
Catalonia 26, 236–237
Catedra de Flamencología y Estudios Folclóricos Andaluces 7

Catholicism *see* Roman Catholic Church
Cavalli 62
Céleste, Madame Céline 111
Central America 64, 178
Centro Andaluz de Arte Contemporáneo 29
Centro Andaluz de Documentación de Flamenco 7
Cepero, José 25
Cervantes Saavedra, Miguel de 4, 13, 23–24, 56–57, 212; *Don Quixote de la Mancha* 4; *La Gitanilla* 13, 23–24, 212; *El Rufián dichoso* 56–57
Césaire, Aimé 12
Chabrier, Emmanuel 5
Chacón, Antonio 5, 12, 149, 167, 170, 174n8, 190, 222n12
Chacon, Olivia 55n51
chacona (Spanish), chaconne (French) 63, 64, 96
Chakrovorty, Pallabi 48, 51–52
Chambao 17, 254–256; *Con otro aire* 254; *Endorfinas en la mente* 254; *Flamenco Chill* 254; *Pokito a poko* 254
La Chana 264, 269n17
Chandralekha 53n15
La Chaqueta, Adela 174
El Chato de la Isla *see* Llerena Ramos, José
Chavarri, Jaime 52n10
Chazin-Bennahum, Judith 52n10
Cherkaoui, Sidi Larbi 30
chica/Tchéga 98, 99
Children's Tales (ballet) 161
China 98
china poblana **89**
Chinoy, Clara 12, 15
El Chocolate *see* Núñez Montoya, Antonio de la Santísima Trinidad
cholo 94n25
La Choni 30
choreocritic 18
choreography 17, 43–45, 48–50, 56–70, 72, 95, 97, 99–101, 103–107, 109, 112, 126, 159, 161, 162, 180, 183, 212, 238, 245, 261, 262, 280–289
La Chunga 173
La Chunguita 173
Chuse, Loren 16
La Cigarrera de Sevilla 78
ciudad condal 181
civic space 206
Civil War, Spanish *see* Spanish Civil War (1936–1939)
Clapera, Père 182
Cleminson, Richard 235
Cocteau, Jean 1, 26, 126
La Coja, Paca 226
El Cojo, Enrique *see* Jiménez Mendoza, Enrique
El Cojo de Málaga 25
Cole, Jack 203

Colirón 38
Collingswood, Robin 111
colmao 211
colocación 182
Colomé, Delfín 135
colonialism 1, 14, 35, 48, 50, 71, 82, 83, 85, 104, 111, 129, 218, 234, 255, 257–258, 281; *see also* Cuba; Mexico; Peninsular War
Colton, Walter 81
Columbia University 197
comedia de costumbres 106, 110
comique/comic genre (ballet) 14, 74, 103
commercialism 15, 166, 172; *see also* professionalism
compás 171–173, 217, 219, 229, 284, 286, 287
Concha La Carbonera 29
Concurso de Cante Jondo (1922) 10, 13, 25, 26, 126, 148, 167, 282, 289*n*10
"El confort no reconforta" 256–257; *see also* Ojos de Brujo
Congo 98
Congress on Research in Dance 2
La Conja 53*n*11
Les Conscrits espagnoles 95
Consejo Nacional de Deportes 237
Conservatorio Superior de Música, Rafael Orozco 230–231
Constitution of 1812 105
Constitution, Spanish (1978) 7, 10
contradanza 59, 85, 88, 92
Contreras, Antonia 229, 231
Contreras, Lorenzo 180
La Convivencia 49
Copa Pavón 25
copla 122, 236
Las Coquineras 29
Corál, Matilde *8*, 29, 288
Coralli, Jean 76, 77
Córdoba, Antonio de 174
Córdoba, Dolores de 174
Córdova, Rafael de 29
la Coriana, Rosario *147*
corporeality 195, 196, 199, 202, 205, 206, 214, 215, 221*n*10
corps de ballet 78, 105
corral 148, 154*n*37
El Corral de la Morería (tablao) 171, 173
corraleras 77, 131, 141*n*56
corrales de comedias 71
El Corregidor y la molinera 163
corridos gitanos (Gitano ballads) 13, 24
Cortés, Carmen 30
Cortés, Gabriel 174
Cortés, Joaquín 16, 30, 245–249, 250*n*9
Cortés Jiménez, José (Pansequito) 174

cortesía 59, 67
Costa, M. 182
costumbrista 218
costume 3, 38, 73, 75, 77, 78, *89*, 106, 107, 110, 112, 121, 127, 129, *147*, 157–159, 164, 183, *199*, 203, 205–206, 212, 215–217, 219, 233*n*20, 239, 240, 245, 246, 258, 261, 262, 285–287; *see also bata de cola*; cross-dressing
Cotarelo y Mori, Emilio 6, 60
cotillion 88
courante 69*n*31
Courbet, Gustave 106
Le Courrier des États-Unis 109
Courvoisier, Sylvie 285
Covarrubias, Sebastian de 56, 57
Craig, Gordon 159
cross-dressing 181, 219, 237, 244, 249, 262, 285, 286, 290*n*24
Cruces-Roldán, Cristina 8, 10, 16, 125, 240, 253
Cruz, Rafael 150, 155*n*64
Cruz García, Antonio (Antonio Mairena) 6–7, 166, 174*n*2, 184, 189, 191, 252, 282
Csordas, Thomas 220
cuadro, cuadro flamenco, cuadro bolero 144, 146, 149, 171, 172, 212, 213, 214, 221*n*7, 225
Cuatro Trileros—BBVA (Flo6x8) 286–287
cuatropeado 61
Cuba 7, 8, 111, 125, 129, 140*n*49, 141*n*65, 178, 179, 201, 234, 256; *see also* colonialism
cubism 126, 163, 194, 197, 206, 290*n*22
cultural imperialism 129, 252
cuplés, cupletistas 141*n*52, 222*n*12
Currito (El Niño de la Geroma) 154*n*29
La Curva (Israel Galván) 285
Czarnowski, Lucille 94*n*39

Dadaism 202, 206
Dafora, Asadata 203
Dalí, Salvador 197
dancing body 2, 3, 18, 34, 37, 44, 194–210, 234; Spanish 194–210
Dancing with the Stars 43, 246
danse comique *see* comique
danse nègre 98
danse noble 14
Dantas, Rubem 7
danza 64, 66–67, 119, 120
Danza no. 5 (Enrique Granados) 180
Das, Pandit Chitresh 47, 53*n*11
Dauberval, Jean 73
D'Aulnoy, Madame (Marie Catherine le Jumel de Barneville) 4, 61, 62, 64

Dauset Moreno, Carmen (Carmencita) 196, 200
Davies, Ann 274
Davillier, Baron Charles 5, 27, *28*, 38, *39*, 40, 61, 69*n*25, 117, *118*, *273*
Davis, Miles 191, 245
Davis, William 90
Decálogo de un Buen Bailarín (Escudero) 223*n*20, 238, 290*n*21
de la Barrera, Manuel 105
de la Barrera, Miguel 27, 144
de la Encina, Juan 164
de la Vega, José 181
Delgado Esteban, "El Niño de Sanlúcar" *148*
de los Santos, Miguel 105
Delsarte, François 200, 201
demi-caractère 14, 74
Demófilo *see* Machado y Álvarez, Antonio
Denby, Edwin 204
dengue 129
Dent, Edward 128, 160
Depero, Fortunato 159
de Prado, Sebastián 62
de Pradt, Dominique Dufour 21*n*37
Derain, André 128, 158, 161
de Santa Cruz, Antonio 64
el desastre 234; *see also* colonialism
Descan 63
Desmond, Jane 240
DeSouza, Joanna 45, 53*n*11
desplante 180, 217
de Valencia, Lola 78
The Devil's Backbone 277
Un día de feria en Mairena 107
Le Diable boiteux 76, 77–78
Diaghilev, Sergei 1, 29, 126–128, 135, 157–164, 200
Diawara, Manthia 12
Díaz, Rocio 229
Didelot, Charles 76
Di Meola, Al 282
Dionysus 220
La Diosa Blanca 228, 230
Diquela Records 255
divertissement 14
Don Juan Tenorio 248
Don Quixote (Petipa ballet) 76
Don Quixote de la Mancha 4; *see also* Cervantes Saavedra, Miguel de
Doré, Gustave 5, 27, *28*, 38, *39*, 60, 69*n*25, 117, *118*, *119*, *273*
Doubleday, Veronica 225–226, 229
Draper, Paul 203
drunkenness 15, 192
dualism 215
Dubinon, Manuela 5, 77, 101*n*9
duende (concept of) 119, 135–136, 179, 185*n*1, 190, 200, 201, 262
Duff, James (Earl of Fife) 76–77
Dumas, Alexandre (Dumas Davy

de la Pailleteterie) 4, 21*n*37, 117
Duncan, Anna 203
Duquesnay 75, 79*n*17
Durán, Rosita 172
Duvernay, Pauline 71, 78

Echanove, Juan 245
Echeandía, José María 88
El Ecijano, Pepe **147**
Eco, Umberto 279*n*3
The Ed Sullivan Show 247
La Edad de Oro (Israel Galván) 284
educational reform 105, 235, 237
Egypt 98
el de Triana, Fernando (Fernando Rodríguez Gómez) 6, 29, 127, 143, 145, **148**, 150, 222*n*16, 226, 238
Eliot, T.S. 159, 266
Elisabetta Farnese (Queen Consort) 66
Elizabeth of Bourbon 62
Elssler, Fanny 5, 71, 73, 76–78, 111
embodiment (concept of) 101, 193, 199, 206, 220, 238
Embrujo Español 15, 180, 181, 184
Encinias-Sandoval, Eva 8
engachonado 49
Engels, Fredrick 114*n*28
enramada 86, 88
Enriqueta La Macaca 29
entr'acte 103, 110
entr'acte Jácara 56
entremés 56, 59
El Entri 173
Escamilla, Antonio de 56
escobilla 216; *see also* footwork; *zapateado*; *zapateo*
Escudero, Vicente 26, 30, 44, 49, 52*n*10, 133, 134, 223*n*20, 238, 240, 268, 285, 289*n*21; *Decálogo de un Buen Bailarín* 223*n*20, 238, 290*n*21
escuela andaluza 26
escuela bolera (the Bolero School) 4, 14, 27, 66, *72*, 75, 78, 95, 98, 103–104, 109, 112–113, 114*n*24, 119, 120, 121, 127, 144, 145, 146, 152, 153*n*9
Escuela Musical de los Coros y Danzas de Caniles 231
Escuela Sevillana 214, 216, 288
Esmeralda, Merche 29, 287
españolada 180, 276
españoleta 67
españolismo 163
Espert, Rosa 109, 112
Espinós, Victor 163
Esquivel Navarro, Juan de 6, 56–57, 60, 64, 66, 67
El Estampío *see* Sánchez Valencia y Rendón Ávila, Juan
Estatuto de Autonomía (Andalusia) 258

Estébanez Calderón, Serafín (El Solitario) 5, 24, 27, 39–40–40
Estévez/Paños (company) 30
Esto es España 184
Estrella, Ángel 104
estribillo 97
ethnic identity 9, 11, 12, 48, 54*n*29, 126, 157, 164, 188, 210–220, 236, 252, 253, 255, 263
Evans, Gil 245
Eve (Biblical) 37
Excelsior Restaurant **198**
exile (concept of) 193, 204
Exposición Universál (Barcelona, 1929) 149
Exposition Universelle (Paris 1889, 1900) 5, 125, 128, 131

Facebook 286
El Faíco *see* Manzano, Francisco; Mendoza Rios, Francisco
Faiquillo 173
fairytale 17, 40
Falange political party 234–242
Falla, Manuel de 6, 10, 25, 26, 126, 128, 157, 159–164, 167, 189, 207*n*17, 207*n*19, 207*n*20, 282
falsetas 228, 284
fandango, fandanguillo 4, 14, 27, 36, 40, 72, 77, 79, *86*, 91, 95, 98, 99, 113*n*3, 120, 167, 169, 170, 189, 222, 226; as informal dance event 87–90
Fanelli, Rosella 51, 53*n*11
Fanon, Franz 12, 135, 137
Faraona, Juana La *see* Amaya, Juana
Farina, Rafael *see* Salazar Motos, Rafael Antonio
farruca 15, 130–131, 133–135, 145, 147, 149, 161, 162, 183
Farruca del Molinero 29, 127, 128, 140*n*34
El Farruco *see* Montoya Flores, Antonio
La Farruquita 53*n*11
Farruquito *see* Fernández Montoya, Juan Manuel
fascism 6–7, 16, 22*n*52, 207*n*3, 237; *see also* Francoist dictatorship; Nazism
Favier 63
Fear, A.T. 34–35
Fedra 248
Feld, Steven 252
Fellay-Dunbar, Catalina 45
Femina (theater, Paris) 200
femininity 16, 210, 214–217, 220, 222*n*13, 222*n*15, 234–242, 272, 285–287
feminism 49, 81, 137*n*2, 195, 205, 206, 222*n*15
femme fatale 37
Ferdinand and Isabella 48, 124

Féria de Sevilla 78, 155*n*47
Fernández, Antonio (El Planeta) 5, 24
Fernández, David 287
Fernández, Esperanza 228, 262
Fernández García, Félix (El Loco) 29, 126, 127
Fernández Montoya, Juan Manuel (Farruquito) 30
Fernández Vargas, Mercedes (La Serneta) 190, 226, 231
Fernando VII 121
Ferrer y Fontanals 180
Ferriol y Boxeraus, Bartolomé 59
Festival de Jeréz 286, 287
Festival Flamenco Ciutat Vella 263
Festival of Cante Jondo *see* Concurso de Cante Jondo
La Fête Hongroise 75
Feuillet, Raoul 61, 63, 66
fiesta, festero 4, 29, 83, 84, 89, 145, 167–169, 172, 173, 191, 192, 219, 220, 224*n*33, 286
La fille mal gardée 73
El Fillo *see* Ortega Vargas, Francisco
Fischer, Christian August 72
Flamencas en el Cuadro 232
Flamenco (Carlos Saura film) 287
flamenco ballet 14, 120
Flamenco Empírico Festival 261–264, 267
Flamenco Festival Dusseldorf 267
flamenco jondo see baile jondo
flamenco, origin of term 12, 24–25
flamenco puro see puro
flamenquería 217
flamenquismo, nacional flamenquismo 26, 239, 258
flamenquización 45
Flemish (as origin of term flamenco) 12, 25
Flo6x8 1, 265, 267, 283, 286
La flor de mi secreto 16
floreo 284
Flores, José 149
Flores, Lola 181, 182
Flores, Manuel 180
Flores, Marco 228–229
Flores Amaya, Diego (Diego del Gastor) 229
Fokine, Michel 196
Folch, Enrich 282
Les Folies d'Espagne, Les Folies espagnoles, Folías Espagnoles 95, 96
folk songs (Spanish) 61, 82, 94*n*23, 160, 197, 203, 236
folklore, folk art, folk culture 5, 10, 22*n*52, 30, 109, 122, 126, 129, 161–162, 181, 183, 200, 201, 211, 227, 231–232, 236
Font, David 267

Index

Font, Francisco 5, 77, 101n9
footwork 43, 47, 48, 50, 51, 92, 111, 128, 133, 134, 136, 144, 145, 146, 152, 182, 201, 202, 216, 217, 219, 240, 245, 249, 285, 286; *see also escobilla; zapateado; zapateo*
Ford, Richard 33, 37–38, 40, 117, 223n25
Foucault, Michel 11, 12, 214, 216, 220
La Francesa (Galván) 288
Franco, Gen. Francisco 6, 11, 16, 17, 49, 178, 182, 193, 194, 204, 207n3, 227, 233n5, 234–242, 244, 247, 248, 254, 258, 261, 269n4, 276, 282
Franconetti, Silverio 122, 189, 190
Frasquillo *see* León Fernández, Francisco
French Revolution 74
Frenk, Margit 60
Fry, Roger 158
fulanís 140n49
Fuller, Loïe 195, 196, 202, 203, 205, 206
funk 256
fusion 13, 15, 30, 44–45, 48, 112, 131, 190–191, 245, 252–258; *see also* hybridity
Futurism 126, 159

Gades, Antonio 14, 29, 119–123, 238, 239, 269n4
Gala Gada 99
Galeotti, Vincenzo 73
Galician customs 26, 163, 193
The Galician Fête 78
gallarda, galliard 66
El Gallo, Joselito 202
Galván, Israel 13, 30, 44, 45, 190, 261, 264, 265, 268, 281, 283, **284**, 285, 287–288; *Arena* 285; *La Curva* 285; *La Edad de Oro* 284; *La Francesca* 288; *Metamórfosis* 291n40
Galván, José 30, 53n11
Galván, Pastora 283–285
Galvánicas 290n21
El Gambusino 78
Gamelan Sekar Jaya 53n27
Garafola, Lynn 7, 135, 159
García, Félix (nineteenth-century dance maestro) 71, 78
Garcia, Juani 52n11
García, Manuel 106, 114n18
García de León Griego, Antonio 12
García Garrido, Luisa (Luisa Triana) 152
García Gómez, Génesis 282
García Lorca, Federico 1, 6, 7, 10, 15, 16, 25, 124, 128, 136, 167, 180, 184, 189, 195, 197, **198**, 201, 202, 203, 204, 277, 282; *Poet in New York* (1940) 197

García Matos, Antonio (Antonio Triana) 141n75, 146, 152, 205
García Matos, Manuel 25
García Rodríguez, Rafael (Rafael El Negro) **8**
García Vizcaíno, Félix (Félix de Utrera) 173, 191
Gardel, Pierre 74
garrotín 15, 130, 131, 133–134, 145, 213
Garzón, Manolo 173
Gasch, Sebastiá 26, 182, 185n17, 185n20
Gastor, Diego del *see* Flores Amaya, Diego
Gates, Henry Louis 11
Gautier, Théophile 5, 6, 38, 117, 121, 223n24
Gell, Alfred 219
gender 14, 16, 18, 19, 60, 207n9, 210, 212–220, 225–233, 234–242, 262–263, 274, 283, 285–286
gender performativity (concept of) 238, 241
Generation of '27 26, 200
Generation of '98 10, 13, 26, 162, 281
gente de razón 82, 85, 94n25
Gesamtkunstwerk 197
gesto 215
Ghéon, Henri 161
gigue 63
Gil Ojeda, Mario 181
Gilroy, Paul 12
The Girl of Your Dreams (La niña de tus ojos) 276, 278
Gitana/o 4, 5, 6–7, 9–12, 14–16, 23–27, 29, 47–51, 54n29, 109, 110, 112–113, 117, 119, 121, 122, 124–126, 128, 131, 134–136, 145, 146, 148, 149, 152, 153n14, 153n15, 153n16, 170, 174n2, 178–179, 182, 186n20, 187–190, 192, 193, 196, 207n3, 210–220, 227, 229, 233n13, 246, 247, 253, 258, 260, 262, 265, 276, 278, 281, 282
La gitanilla 4; *see also* Cervantes, Miguel de
La Gitanilla de Bronce 174
La gitanilla y el curro 107
Gitanillo de Triana 173
gitanismo 11, 290n12
gitanizado 49
Gitanos *caseros* 218
Goebbels, Joseph 276
Goffman, Erving 222n19
Goldberg, K. Meira 11, 14–15, 18
Golden Ass 36–37
Goldman, Danielle 18–19
golpe de cadera 127, 284
Gómez, Carmen (La Joselito) 149
Gómez, Ramon 180
Gómez Tello, José Luis 179
El Gong (venue) 150, 151
González, Antonio 180

González, Domingo 67
González Martínez, Francisca (La Quica) 143, 146–152, **147**, **148, 149**, 154n32, 154n33
González Toledano, Laura 230–231
González Troyano, Alberto 119
The Good Humored Ladies (ballet) 161
Gottschild, Brenda Dixon 12
Goya y Lucientes, Francisco José de 3
Graham, Martha 195, 196, 197, 201, 202, 203, 245
gran redada 13
Granados, Enrique 160, 180, 183, 200, 201, 207n17; *La danza de los ojos verdes* 201; *Goyescas* 200
Grande, Félix 6
Granier, Jeanne 137n6
Las Grecas 174
Greco, José 29, 49, 204, 205, 209n51, 238, 239
Greece, ancient 34
Greek music 232
Greenberg, Clement 195, 207n9
Gregh, Fernand 161
Gregory, Charles 135, 137
Grigoriev, Serge 158
Grilo, Joaquín 30
Gris, Juan 25, 197
grito 266
grupo de pies 285
Grut, Marina 101n9
Gruzinski, Serbe 12
El Guajiro (tablao) 171
guaracha 77
Guerau, Francisco 64
guerra civíl española *see* Spanish Civil War
Guerrero, Adela 106, 109, 112
Guerrero, Manuel **104**, 112
Guerrero, Patricia 30
guerrilla 286–287
Guest, Ivor 74, 79n6, 79n17
Guillén, José 104
Guillén, Manuel 104
guineo 129
guirilándia 288
guitar as gendered instrument 226, 232
guitarist, female *see* tocaora
El Güito *see* Serrano Iglesias, Eduardo
gunguroos 51
Guymard 75
Guy-Stephan, Marie 5
Gypsy 9–10, 12, 15, 33, 54n29, 112, 137, 150, 153n14, 170, 174n2, 179, 181, 182, 184, 218, 258, 266; *see also* Caló; Gitano; Roma

habanera 105
habitus 214
Halffter, Ernesto 207n17
handkerchief 98

Hardt, Michael 257
Haro, Don Luís de 62
Haskel, Steven 83
Hawkins, Eric 203
Hayes, Michelle Heffner 8, 10, 17, 238, 263
Haymarket Theatre 78
Hazard, Paul 111
Hein, Norvin 54*n*28
Heller, Nancy 16–17
Hemingway, Ernest 11
hemiola 13, 63–64, 65, 185*n*12, 219
Hentschke, Theodor 98, 102*n*17
Her Majesty's Theatre (London) 78, 109
Herder, Johann Gottfried von 5, 126
Heredia, Andrés 173
Heredia, Manolo 174
Heredia, María *147*
Heredia, Maruja (La Marruja) *227*
Heredia, Yolanda 262–263, 264, 269*n*11, 269*n*12
Heredia Maya, José 29
heritage fantasy 93*n*23, 94*n*26
Las Hermanas Pompi 154*n*29
Los Hermanos Reyes 173
Los Hermanos Toronjo 173
hermosa 67
Hernández, Amalia 94*n*29
Hernández, Carlos (Vedrines) 25, 149
hexis, corporeal (concept) 214, 219; see also Bourdieu, Pierre
Hidalgo Paz, Antonio 53*n*11
La hija de Manuel Rayo 107
Hilferding, Franz Anton Christoph 73
Hinduism 479
hip-hop 42, 256–258
hispanidad 236
Hispanism, Hispanist 195, 197, 199, 207*n*9
Hispanomania 95, 101
Hispavox Records 6
historiography 1, 3, 7, 12, 19, 100, 102*n*9, 103–113, 200, 204, 264
Hitler, Adolf 237
Hobsbawm, Eric 39
Hollywood Bowl 178
Hollywood Canteen 18
Hsu, Margarita (Margarita la China) 156*n*65
Huerta, Dolores de la 226
Huertas, Trinidad (La Cuenca) 29, 226, 285
Hughes, Langston 164
Hughes, Russell Meriwether (La Meri) 130, 203
Hughes, Terence McMahon 113*n*3
Hugo, Victor 38
humanism 35–36
Humphrey-Weidman 195, 201, 203

Hurtado, Encarnación (La Malagueñita) *132*, 134, 200, 285
hybridity, hybridization 13, 14, 44–45, 74, 109, 112, 211, 252, 262, 271
hypermasculinity 237
hyperracialized 16, 219
hypersexualized 16, 219

Imperio, Pastora *see* Rojas Monje, Pastora
imposibles 67
improvisation 44, 171, 262, 265, 283
incest 244, 249
Inda, Jonathan Xavier 257
India 48, 50
Indialucia 53*n*11
Indian dance forms, Indian music 42–54, 256
Infante Pérez, Blas 24, 277, 279*n*16
Los Invitados (Belen Maya) 286
Irish dance forms 46–47
Irving, Washington 4
Isabella, Queen 271
Isis 37
Islam, Islamic chant 6, 23, 48, 50, 211, 218
Izquierdo, Paco 173

jácara, Xácara, jaco 4, 6, 13, 56–70; *Jácara entremesada* 56
Jacob, William 76
Jacob's Pillow International Dance Festival 203
Jain, Reetu 55*n*51
jaleo 96, 112, 124, 220*n*1
Jaleo de Jerez 14, 27, 112
Jaleo de la Pandereta 78
jaque 4, 68*n*3, 114*n*24, 138*n*9
El Jaque 107
Jaque, Juan Antonio 56, 57, *58*, 59, 60, 67
jarabe 81, 87, 91–92
jarchas, xarchas 23
Le Jardin de Paris (theater, Paris) 200
jazz 18–19, 125–126, 128, 129, 131, 135–137, 164, 183, 190, 195, 196, 197, 199, 202, 245, 283
jazz hands 128
Jazz Modernism 194, 196, 199
Jerez 188, 192
Jerez, La Paquera de 173
Jerez, Sernita de 173
Jerez, Terromoto de 171
Jerez de la Frontera 23, 218
el Jerezano, Pepillo 154*n*29
Jeschke, Claudia 3, 14
Jewish culture 23, 51, 190
Jhalak Dikhhla Jaa 43
Jiménez, Antonia 228–230, 232
Jiménez Mendoza, Enrique (Enrique el Cojo) 29, 145, 148, 152

Jiménez Peña, Bernarda (La Bernarda de Utrera) 154*n*22
Jiménez Peña, Fernanda (La Fernanda de Utrera) 154*n*22
jitterbug 18–19
joglorio 66
John the Baptist 37
jondo see cante jondo, baile jondo
jondura 29; *see also cante jondo*
Jorba, J. Pérez 129
José, Don 117
José, Juan 180
José Maria, Carmen de *147*
José Matos, María 228, 230
Josephs, Allen 37
jota 81, 99–100, 110, 112; *jota aragonesa* 91, 92
Un jour de Carnival à Seville 111
jóvenes flamencos 282
Jowitt, Deborah 43
Les Joyeux Nègres 129, 131, 135–137
Juan, Juan de 260
Judson Church Movement 263
juerga 24, 27, 145, 150, 155*n*48, 191, 286
juguetes comico-liricos 106
Junquera, Juana *147*
juntar 59,
Justamant, Henri 1, 95, 99–100
Juvenal 35, 40
Juyent, Josep Maria 182

Kafka, Franz 261
Kahan, Akram *see* Khan, Akram
Kahlo, Frida 262
Kant, Immanuel 195
Karsavina, Tamara 158
kathak 13, 42–55
kathakas 47
Kathakbox 54*n*27
kathamenco 45
Katrak, Ketu 44
Keys, Alicia 246
Khan, Akram 30, 44, 45, 53*n*11, 53*n*15
King's Theatre (London) 75–77, 113*n*8
Kisselgoff, Anna 6

Lamparilla 29
Lampreave, Chus 245
Lanfranco, Petra Pilar 88
Lapuerta, Vicente 106
Laquer, Thomas 214
Larkin, Thomas 81
Lasera, Mateo (Loco Mateo) 190
látigo 217
Latina stereotypes 247
Lavaur, Luis 7, 222*n*18
Lawler, Lillian 34
Leboutte, Christine 52*n*10
El Lebrijano *see* Peña Fernández, Juan
Lee, Mary Anne 111
León, Madame 105, 113*n*8

León, Manuel 105, 110, 113*n*8
León Fernández, Francisco (Frasquillo) 15, 133, 143–156, *144*, *147*, *148*, *149*, *141*
León González, Mercedes 133, 143, 148, 150, 152
Le Picq, Charles 75
Le Picq, Margarita *see* Rossi, Margarita
Lérida, Juan Carlos 17, 261–263, *264*, 266–267
lesbian, gay, bisexual, transgender (LGBT) identities/rights 237, 241, 266
letra 286–287; *see also copla*
Lettres sur la danse (Noverre) 75
Levinson, André 6, 162
Lew, Leslie 202
Ley de Vagos y Maleantes 237
La Leyenda del Tiempo 7, 282, 290*n*15; *see also* Monje Cruz, José (El Camarón de la Isla)
Lezana, Sara 174
Liberal Triennium 105
Liñán, Manuel *217*, 283, 286
Linares, Carmen 228
La linda Manola 107
lindy 18–19
Lipovetsky, Gilles 105
Llácer, Pepita 178, 179
llamada 284, 286
Llerena Ramos, José (El Chato de la Isla) 15, 166, 168–172
Llorente family 111
loa 56
Lobato, Chano 173
Lobitos, Bernardo de los 150
Loco Mateo *see* Lasera, Mateo
Logiovine, Pablo 262
La Lola se va a los puertos 277
Lolle, Jens 73
London Flamenco Festival 263, 284, 290*n*23
Loomis, Charles 93*n*1
López, Jennifer 246
López, Pilar 26, 29, 49, 151, 154*n*18, 39
Lopez, Reina 53*n*11
López Clavijo, Antonio (Antonio Ramírez) 127, 133, *147*
López Júlvez, Encarnación (La Argentinita) 16, 26, 49, 175*n*16, 194–210; *El Café de Chinitas* 204–205; *Los calles de Cadíz* 205; *Capriccio Espagnol* 205
Lorca *see* García Lorca, Federico
Loreto, Maleni 173
Losada, Tito 174
Louis XIII 62
Louis XIV 62, 63, 65, 68*n*15
loure 63
Loxa, Juan de 29
Lucia, Paco de *see* Sánchez Gómez, Francisco Gustavo
Luengo, Ladislao 104

Luján, Néstor 182, 183
Lully, Jean-Baptiste 62–63
Lumley, Benjamin 78
Lunar, Perico del 168, 173
La Lupi *see* Lupiáñez Pinto, Susana
Lupiáñez Pinto, Susana (La Lupi) *213*
Luz Esteban, Mari 221*n*10

Macandé 175*n*11
La Macarrona *see* Vargas, Juana and Vargas, María
Macaulay, Alistair 6
Machado, Antonio (son of Demófilo) 26, 266, 281
Machado, Manuel 26, 281
Machado y Álvarez, Antonio (Demófilo) 5, 6, 10, 24, 25, 26, 122, 189, 281
machismo 170
Madridejos, Montse 15
magical realism 15
Maharaj, Birju 43, 50, 52*n*11
Mairena, Antonio *see* Cruz García, Antonio
mairenismo 166, 167, 174*n*2, 252, 282
maître de ballet, maestro de baile, dance master 103
La maja de Sevilla 109, 112
majas/majos 3, 120, 272, 279*n*5
Majestic Theatre (New York City) 203
majismo 104, 107, 120, 272, 279*n*5
malagueña 27, 29, 112, 167, 169, 170, 189
Malagueña (Lecuona) 180
La Malagueñita *see* Hurtado, Encarnación
el Malagueño, Pepe 174
La Malena *see* Seda Loreto, Malena
Mamontov, Savva 162
mandar 219
mandingoy 140*n*49
manola 78, 107, 109, 110, 112, 114*n*24
Manolete 29, 238
mantilla 56, 107
Manuel, Peter 50
Manzano, Francisco (El Faíco) 174
Maquerie, Alfredo 179, 180
marcajes 220, 284, 285, 286
Marchena, Melchor de 174
Marchena, Pepe 25, 168, 169, 170, 175*n*14, 190
Margaret of Austria (1584–1611) 62
Mariá y Campos, Armando de 183
Mariana, Juan de 4
Mariana, Padre 35–36
Marie-Therese of Austria 62
Marín, Andrés 30, *264*
Marín, Rodríguez 24

Marín Delgado, Antonio 156*n*64
mariposas 168, 176*n*19
Marnold, Jean 162
Maroto, Gabriel 203
Márquez, Antonio 30, 112
Márquez, Niurca 17
Marquis of Perales 153*n*6
La Marseillaise 288
Martial *see* Martialis, Marcus Valerius
Martialis, Marcus Valerius (Martial) 27, 34–35, 37
Martin, John 6, 134, 195, 196, 201
Martín, Padre 36
martinet 189
Martínez, Ambrosio 104
Martínez, Antonia 112
Martínez Sierra, Gregorio 127
Martínez Vílchez, Juan (El Pericón de Cádiz) 166–172
Martini, Pura 129
Marx, Karl / Marxism 114*n*28, 252
masculinity 16, 210, 214–217, 220, 234–242, 283, 285–286
Massine, Léonide 29, 126–128, 135, 138*n*13, 138*n*14, 138*n*21, 158, 159, 161, 162, 205
Matisse, Henri 128
Matrona, Pepe de la 116*n*47, 133, 175*n*8
Mauri, Rosita 5
Mauricia, Ana María *see* Anne of Austria
Mauss, Marcel 213
Maxine Elliott Theater (New York City) 195, 202
Maya, Antonio 173
Maya, Belén 13, 30, 262, 263, *264*, 267, 283, 286, 287; *Los Invitados* 286, *Mujeres* 287; *Souvenir* 287
Maya, Juanele 173
Maya, Mario 29, 30, 50, 52*n*11, 238, 239, 269*n*4, 287
Maya, Teresa 180
Maya Fajardo, Mariá (La Pillina) 180
Maywood, Augusta 111
Mazarin, Cardinal 62
mazurka 144
McLaughlin, John 282
McWilliams, Carey 93*n*23
Meckel, Arnold *198*
Medea 248
Mège, F. 112
Mejías, Ignacio Sánchez 202, 203, 204, 208*n*38
melisma 211
Mellizo, Antonio del 169, 170
Mellizo, Enrique 169, 170
Mendes, Cristina 78
Mendoza, Juan Antonio 64
Mendoza Ríos, Francisco (El Faíco) 29, 131, 133, 134, 142, 181, 200; *see also* El Gato;

Manzano, Francisco (El Faíco); Los Pelaos
menuet/minuet 64, 65, 85, 92
Mercandotti, María 71, 75–77
Mercé, José 191
Mercé y Luque, Antonia (La Argentina) 15, 16, 26, 29, 49, 53*n*15, 128, 134, 137, 149, 150, 152, 183, 194–210, *198*; *El Amor Brujo* (1925) 199, 204; *Cordoba* (1923) 199; *La Corrida* (1923) 199; *El Tango Andalou* (1931) 198, 199; *Triana* (1929) 199
La Meri *see* Hughes, Russell Meriwether
Merimée, Prosper 5, 14, 38, 117, 119, 272, 288
Mesopotamia 37
mestizaje 53*n*12
Metamórfosis (Galván) 291*n*40
Metropolitan Opera House (New York City) 195, 201, 204
Metropolitan Theater (New York) 109
Mexican folk dance 92
Mexico 14, 81–94, 178, 181, 204
MGM Studios 202
Middle Eastern dance and music 35, 50, 194, 211
migrants 254, 256–257
Milazzo, Kathy 13
Mills, Florence 135
Milon, Louis Jacques 74
milongas 169
Les Mingorance *132*, 134
Minguet è Irol, Pablo 6, 65
Minstrel 11, 107, 114*n*28, 133, 134, 136, 137, 138*n*7; *see also* blackface minstrelsy
Mir Iskusstva 162
Mira Quién Baila! 43
Miracielos 29
Misra, Anu Arjun 53*n*11
mission system (Alta California) 82
Mitchell, Timothy 166, 167
El Mochuelo 25
modern dance 195, 199, 205, 206, 241
modernism 14, 15, 126, 128, 129, 134, 136, 137, 158–164, 207*n*9, 261, 268; modernist dance theory 196–210, 213; Spanish modernism 193–210; *see also* jazz
Mohammad XII, Abu Abdalla (Boabdil) 48
mojiganga 6, 56, 57, 133
Molière *see* Poquelin, Jean-Baptiste
Molina, Javier *147*
Molina, José 127
Molina, Ricardo 6–7, 166, 174*n*2
Molina, Rocío 30, 190, 262, 264, 287
Molino, Antonia 106
Monchi 173

Monge, Victor (Serranito) 173
Monge Cruz, José (El Camarón de la Isla) 7, 168, 169, 171, 190, 192, 269*n*4, 282
Monge Rivero, Antonio (El Planeta) 24 114*n*17, 190
Monroy, Douglas 94*n*25
Montes, Baltasar 24
Montes (Montez), Lola 5, 71, 78, 111
Montes, Pepa 30
Montoya, Carlos 207*n*17
Montoya, Jarrito 173, 177*n*42
Montoya Flores, Antonio (El Farruco) *8*, 29, 127, 238, 240
Montoya Salazar, Ramón 131, 133, 149, 228, 230
Montserrat, Alberto 25
El Monumental (arena) 274–275, 277
Moor / Moorish 9, 48, 98, 117, 124–125, 136
Moore, John C. 7, 12, 15
Mora, Carmen 287
Mora, Kiko (Francisco Mora Contreras) 14
Moragas, Ricardo 105
Morales, Celia 229–232
el Morcilla, Enrique 169
Moreau de Saint-Méry, Médéric 98
Morell, Carmen 181
Moreno, Antonio 148
Moreno, Félix 71, 78, 105
Morente, Enrique 268, 269*n*4
Moriscos 218
Moroccan music 232
Morrell, Ottoline 158
Moscardó, General 237
Mozarabic song 23
mudanza 56, 59, 60, 65, 67, 68*n*5, 68*n*15, 96, 97, 99, 181; mudanza del amolador 59; mudanza del borracho 60
mueca 215
Mughal Nawabs 47
Mujer Contra Mujer 229
Mujeres (Belén Maya) 287
Muntañola 180
Murcia, Santiago de 64
Murry, J. Middleton 159
música andalusí 211, 220*n*4; *see also* Andulusia; Islam
Muslim 50, 218
Musset, Alfred de 38

nacional flamenquismo see flamenquismo
Najarro, Antonio 30
Napoleonic Wars *see* Peninsular War
napolitana 112
Natavar, Mekhala 54*n*28
National Ballet of Spain *see* Ballet Nacional de España
national dances 3, 11, 14, 27, 73–75, 77, 104–106, 109, 112, 120–121, 144, 152

national identity 1, 12, 14–19, 104, 135–136, 206, 234, 236, 247, 248, 271, 277, 278, 281
nationalism 22*n*52, 37, 46, 103, 104, 120, 162, 218, 236, 237
Navarro García, José Luis 106, 152
Navy War Relief 203
Nazism 203, 237, 276–277
Nebrija, Antonio de 271–272
Negri, Antonio 257
El Negro, Rafael 29; neoclassicism 14, 73
"New" School composers *see* Spanish "New" School composers
New York World's Fair (1964–1965) 247
Newman, Ernest 158
Nijinsky, Vaslav 161
Nin, Joaquín (brother of Anaïs) 207*n*17
La Niña de los Peines 149, 181, 191, 192, 231
La Niña NINJA 17, 265–266
el Niño de Elche 265–266
El Niño Escancena 25
El Niño Gloria 154*n*29
Niño Ricardo *see* Serrapí, Manuel
El Niño Talavera 150
Nion, François de 136
El Nitri, Tomás 5
noble genre (ballet) 74
Noblet, Lise 71
NO-DO (Noticiario y Documentales Cinematográficos) 178
Noel, Eugenio 6, 10, 281
Nómada (Israel Galván) 286
Noverre, Jean-Georges 14, 72, 73, 103
nuevo flamenco, New Flamenco 7, 16, 245–246; *see also jóvenes flamencos*
Nuñez, Faustino 7
Nuñez, José 105
Núñez Montoya, Antonio de la Santísima Trinidad (El Chocolate) 191

Ochs, Robert 200
Odysseus 37
Oedipal complex 245, 248
Ojos de Brujo 17, 255–258
Olé 27, 78, *109*, 112
El Olé 78
¡Olé Catapum! 180
Oliva, Pepita 78, 109, 121
Olivelles, Francesc 56, 57, 60
Olmo, Ruben 30
Olmo Gutierrez, José María 9
Onís, Federico (conductor) 203
Onís, Harriet de 203
Opéra-Comique (theater, Paris) 199, 208*n*28
ópera flamenca 15, 25, 150, 152, 167, 168, 169, 170, 174*n*2, 175*n*13, 239, 240, 281

opera, Italian 103
L'Orgie 77
Orientalism 10, 136, 160, 199, 202, 218, 258, 265–266
Orquesta de Laúdes Españoles "Velasco Villegas" 231
Ortega, Rafaela 149
Ortega, Regla 173
Ortega, Rita 29, *147*
Ortega, Rosarito *147*
Ortega Juárez, Manuel (Manolo Caracol) 26
Ortega Vargas, Francisco (El Fillo) 5, 24
Ortíz Nuevo, José Luis 7, 29, 167, 175n15
Otero Aranda, José (Maestro Otero) 5, 6, 130–131, 133, 136, 144, 145, 148, 152, 155n63
otherness (concept of) 14, 227

pacto de olvido 277
Paetzold, Christopher 253
Pagés, María 30
Les Pages du Duc de Vendôme 75
Palicio, Luisa 30
palmas 5, 171, 216, 219, 220n1, 246, 249, 267, 284, 286
palo 17, 23, 212, 213, 240, 282, 285
panadero 27, 114n24, 127, 139n29, 180
Los panaderos de Cádiz 107
Pan's Labyrinth 277
Pansequito see Cortés Jiménez, José
Pantoja, Diego 173, 174
"Papeles mojados" 254–256; see also Chambao
Parade 159
paradetas 59
Parakilas, James 10, 11
Pardo, Francisco 112
Pardo, José María 173
Paredes, Marisa 244
Pareles, Jon 255
Paris Opéra, Académie Royale de la Musique et de la Danse 5, 73–78, 103, 121
pas de L'Andalousian 111
pas de matelot 111
Pasch, Johann Georg 69n28
paseo 65, 67
pasillos 106, 114n15
paso 59, 61, 65, 96, 97, 114n15, 127, 181
Pasquale, Massimiliano de 53n11
passacaille 64
Passloff, Aileen 133
Pastora (Israel Galván) 284
patá/patada 220
Patrik, Janaka 53n11
Pavana 66
Pavloff, Carlota Mercé de (La Argentina's niece) 198, 199

Pavlova, Anna 48
Pavón, Arturo (father and son) 181
Pavón, Tomás 170
Pavón Cruz, Pastora (La Niña de los Peines) 25
Pawar, Pratap, and Priya 43, 45, 52n11
Pécour, Louis 64
Pedrell, Felipe 6, 162
peina 77
Los Pelaos 173; see also Manzano, Francisco
peña 27, 229, 232, 253, 286
La peña de la gitana 107
Peña Fernández, Juan (El Lebrijano) 191
Peña Flamenca Femenina de Huelva 230
Peña Soto, Fernando (Pinini) 154n22
La Peñaranda, Concha 231
Peninsular War (Napoleonic Wars, War of Independence) 4, 7, 10, 37, 71, 76, 92, 96, 103, 104, 119, 125
Perea, Manuela (La Nena) 71, 78, 107, 109, 112, 121
Pérez, Gertrudis 106
Pérez, Jorge 17
Pérez, Manuel 105
Pérez Dávila, Luis (Luisillo) 29, 180; see also Teresa y Luisillo (dance couple)
Pérez Merinero, David 8
Pérez Padilla, Florencia (Rosario) 148
Pericet, Olga *264*
Pericet, Rafael 154n29
Pericet Carmona, Angel (Maestro Pericet) 144, 145, 148, 153n10, 154n29
El Pericón de Cádiz see Martínez Vílchez, Juan
La Perla de Andalucía 112, 115n31
Perrate, Tomás de 265
Perrot, Jules 74, 76
Persia 48, 50
personas sin papeles 256
perspective, planar 196
La Pescaílla, Dolores see Amaya, Dolores
peteneras 145
Petipa, Marius 5
Petroushka 161
Petschinka, Julia 267
phenomenology 18
Philip III 62
Philip IV 62
Phillips, Miriam 13
Piaf, Edith 288
Picabia, Francis 197–198
Picasso, Pablo 126–128, 157–164, 196, 197, 207n9
picturesque 111
Pilates, Joseph 203
La Pillina see Maya Fajardo, Mariá

Pinilla, Juan 228
Pinney, Christopher 101
Pinto, Pepe 181
el Pipa, Antonio 30
la del Pipa, Tía Juana 29
Piquer, Conchita 168, 175n16, 185n1
Pitingo 191
pitos 284, 286
El Planeta see Fernández, Antonio
planta 59
play party games 91
Plaza Orellana, Rocío 4, 13–14, 105, 113n5
Poet in New York (1940) 197; see also García Lorca, Federico
El poeta calculista 106
Pohren, Donn 7, 166, 167, 169, 239
La Polaca 173
political protest 17, 29, 257, 258, 265–267, 286,
polka 112, 144
polo 24, 95, 105, 114n17
el polo del contrabandista 106–108
Pomey, Père François 61
Ponce, Juan 230
Populism 193–194, 204
Populist Imagination 193, 194
Poquelin, Jean-Baptiste (Molière) (1622–73) 63
por medio 231
pose grotesque 99
postura 284
Potau y de Férran, Joseph de 57
Pound, Ezra 158
Praetorius, Michael 69n28
preflamencos, cantes y bailes 212
pregón 167, 174n11
Preston-Dunlop, Valerie 260
The pretty gipsie and the bullfighter 78
Prieto orchestra 181
primitivism 14, 126, 128, 134, 136, 157, 160–162; see also modernism
Prince Igor 161
Princess Theatre (London) 186n29
Prisión General de los Gitanos (General Imprisonment of Gitanos) 24
Product of Cultural Interest (Bien de Interés Cultural) 11
professionalism 167–173, 247
Progressive 15, 187–192
Propert, W.A. 159
prostitution 119, 213, 214
psalmody 23
public space 226, 286
Pucherete, Antonio 174
puellae Gaditanae 4, 27, 33–40
Puerta Tierra 27
purism, *pureza, puro* 15, 26, 49, 125, 166–173, 187–192, 211,

217, 239, 241, 242, 246, 252, 258, 282

quadrille 81
quebrada, quiebro 60, 65, 216
queer 12, 266; *see also* lesbian, gay, bisexual, transgender identities
quejío 257
Quevedo, Francisco de 4; "Boda de negros" 137n4; *Carta de Escarramán a la Mendez* 4
La Quica *see* González Martínez, Francisca
Quiñones de Benavente, Luis 59
Quiroga, Alejandro 236

race, racism 1, 9, 12, 14, 16, 18, 19, 45, 126, 135, 136, 182, 185n17, 199, 218, 220, 257, 282
Rafael El Negro *see* García Rodríguez, Rafael
Rajasthan 47, 50, 51
Rajmani, Oliver 55n51
Rameau, Pierre 65–66
Ramírez, Antonio *see* López Clavijo, Antonio
Rancapino 173n5
rancho, ranchero 82, 83, 84, 90, 92, 93n1
Ranger, Terence 39
rap 283; *see also* hip-hop
Rastro 56, 59, 68n5
Ravel, Maurice 180, 208n20, 288
Real Academia Española 56–57
Lo Real-Le Reel-The Real 265–266
Real Montosa, Manuel (Maestro Realito) 144, 145, 149, 152, 200
rebozo **89**
Redonda 59
La Redova 29
Reed, Susan 234
reggae 256
Retrato de Mujer 248
revisionist *see* progressive
La Révolte au sérail 77
Rey, Blanca del 172
Rey, Federico 20
Rey, Florián 276
Reyes, Cristóbal 250n11
Ribera y Tarragó, Julián 6
Ricardo, Niño *see* Serrapí, Manuel
Richards, Michael 237
Rimsky-Korsakov, Nikolai 180
Ríos Ruiz, Manuel 7
Ripley, William 21n37
The Rite of Spring (*Le Sacre du printemps*) 161, 208n27
Rivera, Primo de 235
Riverdance 47
Rivière, Jacques 161, 162
Rockmore, Ryan 16
Rodrigo Noveli, Don Nicolas 67
Rodríguez, Alberto 8

Rodríguez, Carlos 30
Rodríguez, José Luis 17, 260, 267, **268**
Rodríguez, Salú (La hija del Ciego) 29
Rodríguez de Villaviciosa, Sebastián 56
Rodríguez Mijares, Enrique 182
Rojas, Amador 30, 262–264
Rojas, Angel 30
Rojas Monje, Pastora (Pastora Imperio) 26, 126, 200, 201, 218, 288
Rojo, José 104–105, 113n5
Roma, Romany, Romani 9–10, 12, 25, 47, 54n29; *see also* Caló; Gitana/o; Gypsy
Roman Catholic Church, Catholicism 4, 13, 16, 34–37, 39–40, 92, 218, 235, 237, 241, 244
Roman dance 13, 27
Roman era 33–40
Romance de la luna (García Lorca) 180
Romantic ballet 14, 74, 106, 112; *see also* ballet
Romanticism 7, 11, 13, 33–34, 37, 39–40, 49, 73, 104, 111, 121, 211, 215, 216, 218, 278; Bohemianism 195; French 195, 199
Romerito 174
Romero, Pedro G. 265, 280, 281, 289
Romero, Rafael 173
romper 59, 61
Ronda, Anilla la de 226
Roosevelt, Franklin Delano 178
Rosa, Antonio de la (El Pichiri) 130
Rosa, María 29
Rosaldo, Renato 257
Rosita 112
Rossi, Margarita (Le Picq) 75, 79n17
Le Rossignol (ballet) 161
Rossy, Hipólito 25
Roteña, Concha la **147**
Roteña, Maria la **147**
Rothenstein, John 158
Roxo de Flores, Felipe 57
Royal Conservatory of Music (Madrid) 105
Rubin, Gayle 222n15
Ruiz, Conchita 112
Ruiz, Joaquín 150
Ruiz, Jovino 150, 151, 152
Ruiz, Mercedes 30
Ruiz de Azagra, Maestro 180
Ruiz de Ribayaz, Lucas 64
Ruiz Soler, Antonio 26, 29, 71, 78, **104**, 105, 107, 148
rumba 167
Russia 157, 160–164

Sabicas 207n17, 230
Le Sacre du printemps see The Rite of Spring

Sacromonte 27
sacudido 65
Sadler's Wells Theatre (London) 30
Said, Edward 218
sainetes 72, 106, 110, 120
St. Denis, Ruth 48
La sal de Andalucía 107
Salamanca, Calderas de 174
Salazar, Adolfo 162–164, 207n20
Salazar, José 173
Salazar Motos, Rafael Antonio (Rafael Farina) 171, 176n33
salida del cante 284
Salomé 37
Salón Variedades 146
Sánchez Gómez, Francisco Gustavo (Paco de Lucía) 7, 191, 192, 230, 250n2, 269n4, 282
Sanchez Valencia y Rendón Ávila, Juan (El Estampío) 29, 149, 150, 152, 155n53
Sancho Rayón, Don José de 60
Sanlúcar, Esteban, El Niño de Sanlúcar *see* Delgado, Esteban
Sanlúcar, Manolo 229, 269n4
Santa Barbara Old Spanish Days 90
Santolio 112
Sanz, Gaspar 64, 226
sarabande 13, 61, 62, 63, 66, 226; *see also* zarabanda
Saramago, José 271, 279n1
Sardana 236
Sargent, John Singer 5
Satie, Eric 126
Saura, Carlos 52n10, 53n11, 276, 278
Saussure, Ferdinand de 208n25, 238
Savigliano, Marta 18
Schéhérazade (ballet) 161
schötish 112
Schuchart, Hugo 6, 25, 122
Sección Femenina 236
Second Spanish Republic 198
Seda Loreto, Malena (La Malena) 29, **147**, 149, 181
Segovia, Andrés 25, 203, 207n17
seguidilla 27, 72, 78, 79, 99, 105, 120, 212
seguidillas manchegas 95, 96, 113n5
Segura, maestro 129
Sejuela, Señorita 24
Sempronio 180
Sen, Saswati 51
señorito 168, 173
La Serneta *see* Fernández Vargas, Mercedes
Serral, Dolores 5, 77, 101n9, 110, 121
serranas 189
Serrano Iglesias, Eduardo (El Güito) 29, 238
Serrapí, Manuel (Niño Ricardo,

Manolo El Carbonero) 154*n*29, 228
sex-gender systems 214
sexual dimorphism 214, 215, 217, 219
sexuality 40, 98, 125, 210, 213, 215, 235, 237, 244, 276
Shankar, Uday 44, 48, 52*n*10, 53*n*15
Shawn, Ted 195, 196, 202, 203
Shay, Anthony 14
siciliana 112
siguiriyas 168, 170, 189, 190, 219, 268
silencio 268
La Silfide 73, 75
Silva, Antonio (El Portugués) 146
Sisón, Manolo 173
Sitwell, Osbert 158
la sivigliana 111
ska 256
Sketches of Spain 245, 250*n*2
slavery 129, 135, 211
Smith, George W. 111, 112, 115*n*40
Smith, Jason Samuels 47
Snow White 17, 271, 272, 274–275, 278
So You Think You Can Dance 43
Society of Dance History Scholars 2
Sokolova, Lydia 158
El sol de Andalucía 107
soleá, soleares, soledades 64, 145, 168, 169, 170, 183, 189, 190, 213, 219, 226, 245, 249, 249, 288
soledad 105
Soler, Manolo 174
El Solitario *see* Estébanez Calderón, Serafín
sombrero cordobés 183
El Sombrero de Tres Picos see *Le Tricorne*
son 56, 61, 81, 86, 87, 91
sonidos negros 137*n*4
Sor, Fernando 96
sostenido 65
Soto, Pepita 5, 109–110, 111
Soto Loreto, Manuel (Manuel Torre) 170, 190
Sousa, John Phillip 128
South America 64, 98
Souvenir (Belén Maya) 287
space, modernist concept of 196
Spanish "New School" composers 200, 201, 205, 207*n*17
Spanish ballet *see bailable Español*
Spanish Civil War (1936–1939) 6–7, 15–16, 49, 136, 150, 168, 176*n*20, 193, 194, 197, 203, 227, 234–235, 281
Spanish divertissement *see bailable Español*
Spanish Inquisition 1, 49, 237
Spanish Modernism *see* modernism

Spanish Wars of Independence *see* Peninsular War
Spanishness (concept of) 99, 100, 107, 180, 183, 193, 194, 195, 196, 197, 199, 202, 205, 235, 237, 241, 271–279
The Star of Andalusia 78
Starkie, Walter 11
Steingress, Gerhard 8, 11, 14, 22*n*52, 45, 49, 53*n*12, 106, 253, 256
Stemmler, Susanne 256, 258
Stéphan, Marie-Guy 71
Stern, Samuel Miklos 6
stock market crash (October 29, 1929) 202
Stravinsky, Igor 160
Sturken, Marita 22*n*60
Suarès, André 161
Suárez-Pájares, Javier 7, 96
Sully, Mariette 129
Sunset Boulevard 275, 277
surrealism 207*n*9
Swinburne, Henry 4, 27, 36, 72
swing 18–19
Sylvain, James 111
symbolist, symbolism(e) 158
Synnott, Anthony 214

tablao 2, 15, 29, 119, 166, 168, 169, 171–173, 240, 253, 266, 286
Taglioni, Filippo 73, 75, 76
Taglioni, Marie 96
Taglioni, Paul 111
Talavera, El Niño 150
Tamiris, Helen 203
tango 15, 18, 105, 116*n*47, 127, 130, 131, 133, 134, 136, 145, 151, 169, 189, 213, 219, 220, 224*n*34, 262; tangos americanos 115*n*47; tangos de las vecindonas 131; tangos de negros 130; tangos de Triana 220; tangos gitanos 130, 131
tañido 57, 61
tap 47, 48, 150, 285
tarantella 74
tarantos 112, 189, 288
Tárraga 56, 68*n*5
La Tati 171
Tax Code of 1926 25, 175*n*13
Teatro Cervantes (Seville) 181
Teatro Colón (Buenos Aires) 200, 208*n*38
Teatro Cómico de Sevilla 104
Teatro de la Cruz (Madrid) 105
Teatro de los Canõs del Peral 106
Teatro de Maestranza of Seville 285
Teatro del Liceo (Barcelona) 106
Teatro Español (Madrid) 114*n*25, 182, **198**
Teatro Fuencarral (Madrid) 184
Teatro Pavón (Madrid) 25, 150
Teatro Real de Madrid 162, 197, 200, 269*n*24
Teatro Tívoli (Barcelona) 181

tecolero 86, 87, 89
Telethusa 34, 40
el Tenazas, Diego 167
Tenazas de Morón *see* Bermúdez Cala, Diego
Tenisheva, Princess Maria 162
Teresa y Luisillo (dancing couple) 180; *see also* Pérez Dávila, Luis
Thamar 161
That Obscure Object of Desire 276
Théâtre de la Ville 30
Théâtre du Chatelet 30
Théâtre La Courbe (Paris) 285
Thiel-Cramér, Barbara 33
Thirty Years' War 62
Thompson, Robert Farris 12
The Three-Cornered Hat see *Le Tricorne*
Tía Marina Habichuela 226
Tiempo de Leyenda 290*n*15; *see also La Leyenda del Tiempo*; Monge Cruz, José
tiple 119
tirana 95, 120
tocaor 26, 215
tocaora 16, 225–233
toná 23
tonadillas, tonadilla escénica 106, 120
toque, anti-toque 212, 267
Los toreros de Chiclana 78, 107
TOROBAKA 45, 53*n*11
torque 18–19
Torre, Manuel *see* Soto Loreto, Manuel
Torre, Néstor de la 91, **199**
Torremolinos 73 (Berger film) 276
Town Hall (New York City) 195, 200, 201
Townsend, Joseph 72
traditional flamenco, traditionalism 239, 247, 260, 262, 264, 280–289; *see also* authenticity; purism
traje corto 152*n*2, 285; *see also* costume
Trajitoma of Granada 231
transsexuality 244
transvestism 237
Tratado contra los juegos públicos (Treatise Against Public Celebrations) 4
Triana 4, 13, 23, 24, 27, 33, 38, **39**, 131, 220
Triana (ballet) **199**
Triana, Agustín 180
Triana, Antonio *see* García Matos, Antonio
Triana, El Chiquito de (Luis Algaba Valdivia) 168, 175*n*15, 180, 184
Triana, Fernando el de *see* el de Triana, Fernando
Triana, Luisa *see* García Garrido, Luisa

Le Tricorne 15, 127, 128, 135, 157–164, 185*n*9
La Trini 231
Trio Los Calaveras 181
El Tripili 107, 114*n*24
trouser dances *see* cross-dressing
Trueba, Fernando 276, 278
Tuareg dialect 254
Tucker, Sherrie 18–19
Tumulte Noir 14, 124–137, 141*n*78
Turina, Joaquín 160, 180, 207*n*17
Turnbull, Julia 111
Turner, W.J. 161
Le tuteur trompé 75, 79*n*17
Twiss, Richard 72

Übermarionette 159
UNESCO 258
Uruguay 111
Utrera, La Bernarda de *see* Jiménez Peña, Bernarda
Utrera, La Fernanda de *see* Jiménez Peña, Fernanda
Utrera, Félix de *see* García Vizcaíno, Félix

vacio 59, 61, 65
Val de Omar, José 267, 270*n*28
Valderrama, Juan (Juanito) 25, 170, 181
Valladolid, Pablillos de 124
Vallejo, Manuel 25, 149, 181
Vallejo, Dr. Platon 85
Van Vechten, Carl 195
Varea, Juanito 174, 177*n*42
Vargas, Carmen 155*n*44
Vargas, Ivan **211**
Vargas, Josefa 71, **109**, 112
Vargas, Juana (La Macarrona) 5, 14, 29, 124, **125**, 127–128, 130, 131, 133, 134–135, 137, 137*n*6, 139*n*23, 139*n*27, **147**, 148, 149, 155*n*38, 181, 214, 222*n*12
Vargas, Manolo 205, 239
Vargas, Manuela 16, 29, 245–249, 250*n*14
Vargas, Marco 30
Vargas, Maria (La Macarrona) 127, 130, 139*n*23, 139*n*27
Vargas, Pepa 106, 107, 121
varietés, variedades, vaudeville 25, 103, 126, 130, 133, 146, 152, 155*n*42, 168, 175*n*13, 200, 212, 222*n*12, 224*n*34, 240
Vedrines *see* Hernández, Carlos
Vega, Alejandro 173
Vega Villar, Manuel (Bencazón) 154*n*22
Vélez, Alberto 174
Velaz de Medrano, Eduardo 22*n*57
Veloso, Caetano 249
el Veneno, Ricardo 173
Venta de Vargas (venue) 169, 192
Verdi, Giuseppe 117
Véron, Louis 76
Vestris, Auguste; Vestris family 75–76
Vichy Government 205
Victoria Eugenia, Queen 133
La Vida Breve 159
Vidal, Antonio (Antonio de Bilbao, Antonio el de Bilbao) 29, 133, 150, 152, 200, 240; *El embrujo de Sevilla* (1905) 200
vidalita 170
Vieira Romero, Teresa 180
Vila, Irma y sus mariachis 181
Villa Rosa (venue) 168
villancico 4
villano 67
Villaviciosa, Sebastian de 56, 57
Villegas, José 112
Viñals 180
Virginia reel 92
el vito 27, 112
"Voces" 255; *see also* Chambao
voladillo 60
Volkgeist 5, 126
Volver (Almódovar) 277
votaries 34–35
vuelta al descuido 65
vuelta de pechos 59, 216
vuelta de tacón 217
vuelta de tornillo 217
vuelta quebrada 216

Walker, Aida Overton 130
Walker, George 130, 134
waltz 81, 88, 92, 144
War of Independence *see* Peninsular War
Washabaugh, William 8, 17
Weber, David 82, 94*n*23, 94*n*26
Weeks, Jeffrey 214
West, Cornell 12
The Whims of Cupid and the Ballet Master (*Amors og Balletmesterens Luner*, 1786) 73
white privilege 129
whiteness 125
Wigman, Mary 195, 196, 200, 201, 202; *Hexantanz* 200
Williams, Bert 130
The Wizard of Oz 274
Woods Peiró, Eva 128, 129
world music 7, 17, 232, 252, 253, 255–256
World War I (1914–1918) 126, 157, 193, 194, 200
World War II (1939–1945) 7, 193, 194, 205

xarcha 6; *see also jarcha*
Xenakis 266
Ximénez, Roberto 239

La Yerbabuena, Eva 30
YouTube 286
Yepes, Ana 13

zambra 23, 218
La Zambra (*tablao*) 168, 171–173, 177*n*42
zapateado 27, 77, 92, 111, 134, 143, 145, 149, 151, 183, 217, 219, 245, 249; *see also escobilla*; footwork; *zapateo*
zapateo 182
zarabanda 4, 13, 35–36, 40, 56–57, 60–63, 65, 66, 129, 218; *see also* sarabande
zarzuela 5, 103, 106, 122, 183, 236
Zatania, Estela 8, 286
zejel, zajal 295
Zern, Brook 15, **188**
zincalí see Caló; Gitana/o; Gypsy; Roma; Romani
The Zincalí (George Borrow) 5, 12
Zizou (soccer player) 288
Zuloaga, Ignacio 164
Zúñiga, Albano de 133, 143, 152
Zúñiga León, Mercedes 143, 145, 150, 152

www.ingramcontent.com/pod-product-compliance
Lightning Source LLC
Chambersburg PA
CBHW081537300426
44116CB00015B/2663